Law and Philosophy Library

Volume 133

The Law and Philosophy Library, which has been in existence since 1985, aims to publish cutting edge works in the philosophy of law, and has a special history of publishing books that focus on legal reasoning and argumentation, including those that may involve somewhat formal methodologies. The series has published numerous important books on law and logic, law and artificial intelligence, law and language, and law and rhetoric. While continuing to stress these areas, the series has more recently expanded to include books on the intersection between law and the Continental philosophical tradition, consistent with the traditional openness of the series to books in the Continental jurisprudential tradition. The series is proud of the geographic diversity of its authors, and many have come from Latin America, Spain, Italy, the Netherlands, Germany, and Eastern Europe, as well, more obviously for an English-language series, from the United Kingdom, the United States, Australia and Canada.

More information about this series at http://www.springer.com/series/6210

David Campbell
Editor

Stewart Macaulay: Selected Works

Springer

Editor
David Campbell
Lancaster University Law School
Lancaster, UK

ISSN 1572-4395 ISSN 2215-0315 (electronic)
Law and Philosophy Library
ISBN 978-3-030-33929-6 ISBN 978-3-030-33930-2 (eBook)
https://doi.org/10.1007/978-3-030-33930-2

This Springer imprint is published by the registered company Springer Nature Switzerland AG.
The registered company address is: Gewerbestrasse 11, 6330 Cham, Switzerland

Preface

The editor of this book would like to claim that it was as a result of his omniscient planning that it has appeared in the year that the *Wisconsin Law Review* celebrates its centenary—for what could be more apt to mark the achievements of one of the leading contributors to the Review, to the Wisconsin Law School, and to the Wisconsin tradition generally? It was, in fact, complete serendipity that led to this nevertheless overwhelmingly fitting coincidence.

This book has two purposes. It was originally conceived as a way of making all of Macaulay's work readily available for the study which it will continue to receive. The preponderant part of Macaulay's work has been published in highly regarded academic journals, principally US law reviews. As such, this part of his work is now available electronically through any library it is proper to call a research library in the common law world, and in leading research libraries elsewhere. But there are a number of works which are not available in this way. One paper appeared in journal which remains relatively difficult to obtain; one paper has not previously been published in English; other papers appeared as informal working papers of research groups, in a magazine or as chapters of books published during the age prior to normal electronic availability; and two are the introductions to textbooks compiled by Macaulay and his collaborators. These works are collected in Part II of this book: *The Uncollected Works of Stewart Macaulay*. It must be said that at least one of these works is slight and its publication is justifiable only because its shortness seemed to make its omission, defeating the goal of completeness, perverse. Others of these works are of considerable or of great interest to researchers in the law of contract or the law in action approach, including, as they do, at least one of the finest things ever written on the law of contract. As this book will itself be available in the normal way and in an electronic edition, I believe that ready access to all of Macaulay's work is now generally possible.

In his capacity as an Editor of the Law and Philosophy Library in which this book will appear, Professor Fred Schauer was good enough to suggest to the publisher that the book might also serve another purpose. The works collected in Part I are, of their nature, a very unrepresentative selection from Macaulay's *oeuvre*. The publisher therefore asked that the book might be expanded to include a representative selection of Macaulay's work, drawing on those articles which were already readily available electronically. I very happily agreed to this suggestion and so Part III contains 'Core Works on Contract' and Part IV contains 'Core Works on Law in Context and New Legal Realism'. With the inclusion of these works, it is now hoped that this book provides a single location for the study of the Macaulay's work, sufficient in itself for almost all teaching and for most research purposes.

So far as is was consistent with achieving a uniform and pleasing presentation of the texts, the originals of those texts have been reproduced. A considerable number of slips have, however, been silently corrected.

It was always intended that this book would include essays on Macaulay's work on contract and on law in action as a guide particularly to those not familiar with his work as a whole. I am very pleased to say that these essays, found in Part I of the book, have been provided by very distinguished commentators: Professor Brian Bix on contract and Professors Elizabeth Mertz and Lawrence Friedman on law in action. I myself declined to write such an essay because what I would say on the subject about which I am competent to write, Macaulay's contract scholarship, I have more or less already said in a chapter of one of the number of publications of the proceedings of symposia held to mark Macaulay's retirement: 'What Do We Mean By the Non-use of Contract?' in J Braucher *et al*, eds, *Revisiting the Contracts Scholarship of Stewart Macaulay: On the Empirical and the Lyrical*, Oxford, Hart, 2013, 159–90.

There remains to me only the very pleasant duty of thanking those who have played a part in this book appearing. First among these is the publisher, for this book is of an unusual sort and undertaking to bring it out reflects very creditably on the publisher's commitment to scholarship. The reflection encompasses the advice Professor Schauer gave to the publisher. I am very grateful to those who granted permission for reproduction of Stewart's writings. The details of original publication are all listed in the complete bibliography of those writings. The Lancaster University Law School gave financial support to work on this book. In addition to those who worked on the book's production on behalf of the publisher, I owe a very considerable debt to Ms Marie Selwood, whose independently engaged, highly professional proofreading and associated work was invaluable. A substantial part of the gathering of Macaulay's works and the permissions necessary for their reproduction was carried out whilst I was a Visiting Professor at the Auckland University of Technology Law School, New Zealand, and I am grateful to the AUT for its hospitality. I am, of course, also very grateful to Professors Bix, Friedman and Mertz for their essays, which greatly enhance the book. I lastly am grateful to Stewart Macaulay, whose constant support for and continuing practical help with this book are but the latest of the kindnesses he has been good enough to extend to me over many years. It is a privilege to be connected, however remotely, with making more readily available the work of this great scholar and wholly admirable man.

Lynesack, County Durham, UK David Campbell
July 2020

Bibliography Stewart Macaulay

1. 'Restitution in Context' (1959) 107 *University of Pennsylvania Law Review* 1133-48
2. 'Justice Traynor and the Law of Contracts' (1961) 13 *Stanford Law Review* 812-64
3. 'Non-Contractual Relations and Business: A Preliminary Study' (1963) 28 *American Sociological Review* 55-69. Reprinted, with introductory essay, in David Kennedy and Willliam W Fisher III, eds, *The Canon of American Legal Thought*, Princeton NJ: Princeton University Press, 2006, 445-79 and in Jean Braucher, John Kidwell and William Whitford, eds, *Revisiting the Contracts Scholarship of Stewart Macaulay: On the Empirical and the Lyrical*, Oxford: Hart 2013, 1-19
4. 'The Use and Non-use of Contracts in the Manufacturing Industry' (1963) 9 (7) *Practical Lawyer* 13-40
5. 'Changing a Continuing Relationship Between a Large Corporation and Those Who Deal With It: Automobile Manufacturers, Their Dealers, and The Legal System', pt 1 [1965] *Wisconsin Law Review* 483-575; pt 2 [1965] *Wisconsin Law Review* 740-858 reprinted as 6)
6. *Law and the Balance of Power: The Automobile Manufacturers and Their Dealers*, New York NY: Russell Sage Foundation 1966
7. (with Ted Finman) 'Freedom to Dissent: The Vietnam Protests and the Words of Public Officials' [1966] *Wisconsin Law Review* 1-92
8. 'Private Legislation and the Duty to Read: Business Run by IBM Machine, the Law of Contracts and Credit Cards' (1966) 19 *Vanderbilt Law Review* 1051-1121. Reprinted in Jean Braucher, John Kidwell and William Whitford, eds, *Revisiting the Contracts Scholarship of Stewart Macaulay: On the Empirical and the Lyrical*, Oxford: Hart, 2013, 20-34
9. (with Lawrence M Friedman) 'Contract Law and Contract Teaching: Past, Present and Future' [1967] *Wisconsin Law Review* 805-821

10. 'Law Schools and the World Outside Their Doors: Notes on the Margins of 'Professional Training in the Public Interest'' (1968) 54 *Virginia Law Review* 617-636
11. (with Lawrence M Friedman) *Law and the Behavioral Sciences*, Indianapolis IN: Bobbs-Merrill 1969 (see also 15, 44 and 61)
12. (with Elaine Walster) 'Legal Structures and Restoring Equity' (1971) 27 (2) *Journal of Social Issues* 173-188
13. 'The Standardized Contracts of United States Automobile Manufacturers' (1974) 7(3) *International Encyclopedia of Comparative Law* 18-34
14. *Access to the Legal Systems of the Americas: Informal Processes*, Working Paper 16, Center for Law and Behavioral Science (now Center for Law, Society and Justice), University of Wisconsin, Madison WI, 1976
15. (with Lawrence M Friedman) *Law and the Behavioral Sciences*, 2nd edn, Indianapolis IN: Bobbs-Merrill 1977
16. 'Elegant Models, Empirical Pictures, and the Complexities of Contract (1977) 11 *Law and Society Review* 507-528
17. (with Jacqueline Macaulay) 'Adoption for Black Children: A Case Study of Expert Discretion' in Rita James Simon, ed, *Research in Law and Sociology: An Annual Compilation of Research*, vol 1, Greenwich CT: JAI Press, 1978, 265-318
18. 'Lawyers and Consumer Protection Laws: An Empirical Study' (1979) 14 *Law and Society Review* 115-71
19. *Professional Competence and the Law*, Dalhousie Continuing Legal Education Series 21, Faculty of Law, Dalhousie University, Halifax, Nova Scotia, Canada, 1981, 48-55
20. 'Review of John H Merryman, David S Clark and Lawrence M Friedman, '*Law and Social Change in Mediterranean Europe and Latin America: A Handbook of Legal And Social Indicators for Comparative Study*' (1981) 29 *American Journal of Comparative Law* 542-47
21. 'Law Schools and the World Outside Their Doors II: Some Notes on Two Recent Studies of the Chicago Bar' (1982) 32 *Journal of Legal Education* 506-42
22. 'Law and the Behavioral Sciences: Is There Any There There?' Working Paper 1983, number 16, Disputes Processing Research Programme, University of Wisconsin-Madison Law School, 1983 (published as 23)
23. 'Law and the Behavioral Sciences: Is There Any There There?' (1984) 6 *Law and Policy* 149-87
24. 'Control, Influence, and Attitudes: A Comment on Nelson' (1985) 37 *Stanford Law Review* 553-64
25. 'An Empirical View of Contract' [1985] *Wisconsin Law Review* 465-82
26. 'The Judge as Mentor: A Personal Memoir' (1986) 36 *Journal of Legal Education* 144-49
27. 'Images of Law in Everyday Life: The Lessons of School, Entertainment, and Spectator Sports', Working Paper, series 2, number 3, Institute for Legal Studies, University of Wisconsin-Madison Law School, 1987 (published as 30)

28. *Lawyer Advertising: Yes But*... Working Paper 1-2, Institute for Legal Studies, University of Wisconsin Law School, Madison WI, 1986 (partially reprinted in 42)
29. 'Private Government', in Leon Lipson and Stanton Wheeler, eds, *Law and the Social Sciences*, New York NY: Russell Sage Foundation, 1986, 445-518.
30. 'Images of Law in Everyday Life: The Lessons of School, Entertainment, and Spectator Sports' (1987) 21 *Law and Society Review* 185-218
31. 'Bambi Meets Godzilla: Contracts Scholarship and Teaching vs. State Unfair and Deceptive Trade Practices and Consumer Protection Statutes' (1989) 26 *Houston Law Review* 575-601
32. 'Popular Legal Culture: An Introduction' (1989) 98 *Yale Law Journal* 1545-1558
33. 'Long-Term Continuing Relations: the American Experience Regulating Dealerships and Franchises', Disputes Processing Research Program, Working Paper, series 10, number 1 (also Institute for Legal Studies, Working Paper, series 4, number 8), Institute for Legal Studies, University of Wisconsin-Madison Law School, 1990
34. 'Long-Term Continuing Relations: the American Experience Regulating Dealerships and Franchises', in Christian Joerges, ed, *Franchising and the Law: Theoretical and Comparative Approaches in Europe and the United States*, Baden-Baden, Germany: Nomos Verlagsgesellschaft, 1991, 179-237
35. 'The Reliance Interest and the World Outside the Law Schools' Doors' [1991] *Wisconsin Law Review* 247-91
36. 'Frank Remington: Defining the Law Professor's Job' [1992] *Wisconsin Law Review* 553-56
37. 'On Rattling Cages: Joel Handler Goes to Philadelphia and Gives a Presidential Address' (1992) 26 *Law and Society Review* 825
38. 'Business Adaptation to Regulation: What Do We Know and What Do We Need to Know?' (1993) 15 *Law and Policy* 259-70
39. 'The Future of American Lawyers' (1993) 2 *Sociologia del Diritto* 51-69
40. 'The Impact of Contract Law on the Economy: Less Than Meets the Eye?' Paper given at a Conference on Law and Modernization, Lima, Peru, July 1994, translated into Spanish and published as 'El Impacto Del Derecho de Contratos en la Economia' (2008) 5 *Revista de Economia y Derecho* 27-40
41. 'Wisconsin's Legal Tradition' (1994) 24 *Gargoyle* (Alumni Magazine of the University of Wisconsin Law School) 6-10
42. 'Lawyer Advertising. Yes But ...' in Deborah Rhode and David Luban, *Legal Ethics*, 2nd edn, Westbury CT: Foundation Press, 1995, 673-82
43. 'Crime and Custom in Business Society' (1995) 22 *Journal of Law and Society* 248-58
44. 'The Last Word' (1995) 22 *Journal of Law and Society* 149-54
45. (with Lawrence M Friedman and John Stookey) *Law and Society: Readings on the Social Study of Law*, New York NY: WW Norton, 1995
46. (with John Kidwell, William Whitford and Marc Galanter) *Contracts: Law in Action*, Charlottesville VA: Michie, 1995. See also 54, 63 and 74

47. 'Organic Transactions: Contract, Frank Lloyd Wright and the Johnson Building' [1996] *Wisconsin Law Review* 75-121
48. (with Lane Kenworthy and Joel Rogers) 'The More Things Change, the More They Stay the Same: Business Litigation and Governance in the American Automobile Industry' (1996) 21 *Law and Social Inquiry* 631-78
49. 'Willard's Law School?' [1997] *Wisconsin Law Review* 1163-1179
50. (with Joel B Grossman and Herbert M Kritzner) 'Do the Haves Still Come Out Ahead?' (1999) 33 *Law and Society Review* 803-10
51. 'Relational Contracts Floating on a Sea of Custom? Thoughts about the Ideas of Ian Macneil and Lisa Bernstein' (2000) 94 *Northwestern University Law Review* 775-804
52. 'Almost Everything That I Did Want to Know About Contract Litigation: A Comment on Galanter' [2001] *Wisconsin Law Review* 629-38
53. 'The Real and the Paper Deal: Empirical Pictures of Relationships, Complexity and the Urge for Transparent Simple Rules' (2003) 66 *Modern Law Review* 44-79 (reprinted in 55 and 69)
54. (with John Kidwell, William Whitford and Marc Galanter) *Contracts: Law in Action*, 2nd edn, Newark NJ: LexisNexis, 2003
55. 'The Real and the Paper Deal: Empirical Pictures of Relationships, Complexity and the Urge for Transparent Simple Rules' in David Campbell, Hugh Collins and John Wightman, eds, *Implicit Dimensions of Contract: Discrete, Relational & Network Contracts*, Oxford: Hart, 2003, 51-102
56. 'Freedom From Contract: Solutions in Search of a Problem?' [2004] *Wisconsin Law Review* 777-820
57. 'Klein and the Contradictions of Corporations Law' (2005) 2 *Berkeley Business Law Journal* 119-133
58. 'The New Versus The Old Legal Realism: "Things Ain't What They Used to Be"' [2005] *Wisconsin Law Review* 365-403
59. 'Contracts, New Legal Realism, and Improving the Navigation of *The Yellow Submarine*' (2006) 80 *Tulane Law Review* 1161-95
60. 'Renegotiations and Settlements: Dr Pangloss' Notes on the Margins of David Campbell's Papers' (2007) 29 *Cardozo Law Review* 261-89
61. (with Lawrence Friedman and Elizabeth Mertz) *Law in Action: A Socio-Legal Reader* New York NY: Foundation Press, 2007
62. 'Stewart Macaulay and "Non-Contractual Relations in Business"' in Simon Halliday and Patrick D Schmidt, *Conducting Law and Society Research: Reflections on Methods and Practices*, Cambridge: Cambridge University Press, 2009, 14-25
63. (with Jean Braucher, John Kidwell and William Whitford) *Contracts: Law in Action*, 3rd edn, New Providence NJ: LexisNexis, 2010
64. (with William Whitford) '*Hoffmann v Red Owl Stores*: The Rest of the Story' (2010) 61 *Hastings Law Journal* 801-57
65. 'The Death of Contract: Dodos and Unicorns or Sleeping Rattlesnakes?' in Robert W Gordon and Morton J Horwitz, eds, *Law, Society and History: Themes in the Legal Sociology and Legal History of Lawrence M. Friedman.* Cambridge: Cambridge University Press, 2011, 193-98

66. 'Notes on the Margins of Lawyering in Three and a Half Minutes' (2011) 40 *Hofstra Law Review* 25-38
67. 'Introduction: Dodging the Worst of the Thorns of the Bramble Bush', in Karl Llewellyn, *The Bramble Bush: On Our Law and Its Study (1930)*, New Orleans: LA, Quid Pro Quo Books, 2012, i-xxi
68. (with Elizabeth Mertz) 'New Legal Realism and the Empirical Turn in Law in Law and Social Theory', in Reza Banakar and Max Travers, eds, *Law and Social Theory*, 2nd edn, Oxford: Hart, 2013, 195-210
69. 'The Real and the Paper Deal: Empirical Pictures of Relationships, Complexity and the Urge for Transparent Simple Rules' in Jean Braucher, John Kidwell and William Whitford, eds, *Revisiting the Contracts Scholarship of Stewart Macaulay: On the Empirical and the Lyrical*, Oxford: Hart 2013, 35-46
70. 'Bill Whitford: A New Legal Realist Seeking to Understand Law Outside the Law School's Doors' (2015) 87 *Temple Law Review* 725-37
71. (with William Whitford) 'The Development of *Contracts: Law in Action*' (2015) 87 *Temple Law Review* 793-806
72. 'I Remember Jean [Braucher]' (2016) 58 *Arizona Law Review* 3-11
73. 'A New Legal Realism: Elegant Models and the Messy Law in Action', in Elizabeth Mertz, Stewart Macaulay and Thomas W Mitchell, eds, *The New Legal Realism vol 1: Translating Law and Society for Today's Legal Practice*, Cambridge: Cambridge University Press, 2016, 29-50
74. (with William Whitford, Kathryn Hendley and Jonathan Lipson) *Contracts: Law in Action*, 4th edn, Durham NC: Carolina Academic Press, 2016
75. 'A New Legal Realism: Unpacking a Proposed Definition' (2016) 6 *University of California-Irvine Law Review* 149-67
76. 'Having a Right But Using it Too Often: The "Oven Bird's Song" about Contracts', in Mary Nell Trautner, ed, *Insiders, Outsiders, Injuries and Law: Revisiting "The Oven Bird's Song"*, New York NY : Cambridge University Press 2018, 113-20

Contents

Part I
Essays on the Work of Stewart Macaulay

Stewart Macaulay and the Law of Contract

Brian H. Bix

Abstract Stewart Macaulay has taken the complicated, almost ironic, position of a prominent contract law theorist who doubts that contract law plays a significant role in contracting practice. And it is his insistence on focusing on how parties actually behave in relation to such transactions that keeps Macaulay's ideas central and influential for many working in contract scholarship.

Macaulay has taught contract law scholars many things: to focus on practice not theory, on relationships not models, and on the power and politics behind everything. Those of us working in this area have learned from Macaulay to be attentive to the way the rules of contract law are used as part of ongoing transactional relationships. At the same time, as he reminded us, we must be conscious that the answer to such inquiries will almost certainly be different for different kinds of transactions. Consumers and employees generally have a different contracting experience than do large corporations, and even in business-to-business transactions, one-shot interactions across industries is likely to be different from transactions that occur within a close-knit business community or as part of a long-term supply arrangement. And we need to pass along these insights to our students, as a necessary if small first step towards improving contract law and practice.

Introduction

Stewart Macaulay has been an important voice in American legal thought for over 50 years.[1] His work has centered on the intersection of contract law and law and society. This chapter will focus on Macaulay's ideas about contract law and contract

I am grateful for the comments and suggestions of Claire Hill and Lisa Bernstein.

[1]A Macaulay bibliography, covering works published up to 2013, appears at Braucher, Kidwell, and Whitford 2013: xix-xii. By one recent account, Macaulay's early article, 'Non-Contractual

B. H. Bix (✉)
School of Law and Department of Philosophy, University of Minnesota, Minneapolis, MN, USA
e-mail: bix@umn.edu

D. Campbell (ed.), *Stewart Macaulay: Selected Works*, Law and Philosophy Library 133, https://doi.org/10.1007/978-3-030-33930-2_1

theory, though there will be inevitable references to the broader theoretical and methodological insights of his scholarship. Macaulay has taken the complicated, almost ironic, position of a prominent contract law theorist who doubts that *contract law* plays a significant role in *contracting practice*. And it is his insistence on focusing on how parties actually behave in relation to such transactions that keeps Macaulay's ideas central and influential for those working in contract scholarship.

In what follows, Section "Macaulay and Contract Theory" offers an overview of Macaulay's views on contract law, contract theory, and contracting practice. Section "Some Elaboration and Criticism" offers a sample of the way in which his approach has been elaborated or criticized by other theorists (with Macaulay's responses noted). Section "Contract Non-Theory?" revisits the question of the extent to which Macaulay's approach should be thought of as a distinctive theory of contract law. Section "Contract and Cultural Theory" re-considers some of the ideas and consequences of Macaulay's approach from a cultural studies perspective, before concluding.

Macaulay and Contract Theory

It is not precise—or at least not especially helpful—to say that Stewart Macaulay has a "theory of contract law," as least not as that label is usually understood. His is not a view that asserts that "contract law is basically X (promise, reliance, civil recourse, etc.)" or that "contract law maximizes Y (efficiency, autonomy, commerce)."[2] Macaulay's work operates orthogonally to all that. An important part of Macaulay's approach is the observation that the rules of contract law play a marginal role in the practice of formation and performance of contracts, and even in parties' responses to breaches of contracts.[3] He argues that doctrine and litigation—the two subjects at which lawyers excel and which most law schools emphasize—in fact play a relatively small role in how contracts are written, performed, and enforced.[4]

The background prescription underlying Macaulay's writings is the same as that present in the works of a number of the American legal realists: that the effect of particular legal rules is something that must be shown, not just assumed, and that it is

Relations in Business' (Macaulay 1963a) is the most cited Contract Law article in American legal academia, and the 15th most cited article of any kind. Shapiro and Pearse 2012: 1489.

[2]For a good overview of (and selection from) different theories of contract law, see Klass, Letsas and Saprai 2014 and Benson 2001.

[3]Macaulay 1963a, 1963b, 1985: 466-467, 477; Llewellyn 1930: 443-460. There is now a large literature on the resolution of disputes using social norms rather than legal norms. Much of this literature derives from Macaulay's work; another large segment of the literature derives from Robert Ellickson's comparable findings in Ellickson 1991.

[4]Macaulay 1985: 482.

such effects, as much as the rules themselves, that should be our focus.[5] Macaulay has been associated with American legal realism—or, what is sometimes today called "New Legal Realism"[6]—in large part because of this emphasis on the actual behavior of citizens, lawyers, and judges ("law in action" rather than "law in books"[7]). For contract law, this means attention to what parties do when negotiating agreements, how disputes are handled while parties are performing the contract, and when and whether litigation is threatened or used when the other party's performance does not meet contractual standards.

Macaulay, in one of his earliest and most influential articles, offered the two questions that have structured his thinking about contract law and practice throughout his career: "(A) How can business successfully operate exchange relationships with relatively little attention to planning or to legal sanctions, and (B) Why does business ever use contract in light of its success without it?"[8]

It is well established that parties rarely read contracts[9]; this is apparently true for many business-to-business deals as well as for nearly all consumer transactions. For business-to-business transactions, one should keep in mind that the lawyers who draft and negotiate the agreements are usually distinct from the employees who created the tentative (sale or service) agreement, who, in turn, are likely different from the parties who will be in charge of the agreement's performance, and each group may be guided by different norms, concerns, and objectives. Even the attorneys who draft the agreement may be unfamiliar with some of the contractual terms, frequently having borrowed them from a form standard in the industry or to that company, with those modifications that are made to tailor the form to the present transaction occasionally done quite clumsily.[10]

Where legal remedies are uncertain, subject to significant delays, and require substantial outlays of time and resources, it is not surprising that social norms of the industry might loom larger in a party's thinking than legal norms, and that reputational sanctions might be more salient than legal sanctions.[11] And, generally, that is

---

[5]Macaulay opined that the original American legal realists focused primarily on the work of appellate court judges, Macaulay 2006: 1161, but a number also focused on the same sort of "law in action" matters that most interest Macaulay: e.g., Llewellyn 1930: 443-460.

[6]Macaulay 2016a, Macaulay 2016b; see generally Mertz, Macaulay and Mitchell 2016.

[7]*E.g.*, Pound 1910, Macaulay, Friedman and Mertz 2007.

[8]Macaulay 1963a: 62.

[9]*E.g.*, Bakos, Marotta-Wurgler and Trossen 2014.

[10]Hill 2009. Some law and economics scholars would say that these failures of drafting are actually just efficient responses to circumstances, where attempting to resolve all issues might take too long or prevent agreement altogether. Posner 2005. And commentators disagree regarding whether the parties' overall costs are more effectively reduced by carefully-drafted contracts than by less carefully drafted contracts. Compare Posner 2005: 1614 with Hill 2009: 215-217. For good general discussions on why American business contracts are as wordy and full of "legalese" as they are, see Hill 2001b, Hill and King 2004.

[11]One commentator has suggested that sophisticated parties might avoid actions and provisions that would make litigation cheaper, *in order to* encourage parties to resolve disputes outside of court. Hill 2009: 207-210.

what Macaulay and other empirical investigators have found.[12] Relating to the litigation option, Macaulay has noted that in predicting who will sue and who will prevail in a lawsuit, it may be more important to know which side has the resources to wait out a long and expensive litigation process than it is to know which party has legal right on its side.[13] Additionally, it is important to note the concern parties will reasonably have that relational and reputational harm may come from suing one's current or former business partners.[14]

While Macaulay has taught us that empirical work on the role and effects of law is central, he also has reminded us that it is also extraordinarily difficult. Interviews with lawyers and other participants in the legal system may create results that are simultaneously unreliable and resistant to replication/confirmation.[15] And what one learns, after much expenditure of effort and time, about one type of transaction in one business community may or may not have much to tell us about the innumerable other communities and transaction types.[16]

Some Elaboration and Criticism

Robert Scott (on his own, and in articles written with Alan Schwartz) argues for the use of more formalistic approaches to legal interpretation when dealing with agreements between two companies; he further asserts that this is consistent with Macaulay's basic lessons regarding empirical work and relational contracts.[17] Scott does not deny that contextual decision-making would lead to more accurate results in many contractual disputes. However, he claims that, at least with business-to-business transactions, the parties will generally favor a more textualist approach because it will usually reduce total costs (which includes drafting, performance, and any litigation costs) relative to a contextual approach, and parties would still have the option to opt into a contextual approach by express agreement.[18] Macaulay has

[12]A different question, posed by other commentators (and experimenters), is the relationship between the two: whether (e.g.) formal enforcement might undermine the use or strength of informal mechanisms. *See, e.g.*, Scott 2013: 111-112, 122-123.

[13]Macaulay 1985.

[14]*E.g.*, Bernstein 2015: 566-572.

[15]Macaulay 2011b: 34-38, Macaulay 2016b: 151, 162-165; see generally Macaulay 1984.

[16]Macaulay 2000: 784-804.

[17]Scott 2013, Schwartz and Scott 2003, 2010.

[18]Even if parties are not empowered to achieve a contextual approach by telling a court (*e.g.*) to choose a different approach to parol evidence, they can reach a similar outcome by incorporating into their agreement references to the objectives of the agreement, providing definitions of terms where the intended meaning varies from "plain meaning," including provisions holding that terms are to be interpreted according to business customs and trade usages, adding detailed specifications governing performance, etc. Scott 2013: 127-128.

raised some doubts about textualist approaches,[19] but has offered a qualified endorsement to the idea of different approaches for different types of contracting parties.[20]

In a series of articles,[21] Lisa Bernstein shows how a wide range of businesses (cotton, grain and feed, diamonds) found ways to opt out of the legal system, and to govern their transactions through a combination of industry-side social norms, privatized adjudicatory and sanctioning bodies, and reputational sanctions. Bernstein uses these studies to raise questions about courts' use of course of performance, course of dealing, and trade usage in their interpretation of agreements.[22] In many ways, these articles follow Macaulay's work, both methodologically, in their grounding on actual contracting behavior, and in the substantive conclusion that informal norms and reputational sanctions are frequently central. Macaulay emphasizes as a basic insight that "(1) law is not free, and (2) people cope with law and often find ways to limit its burden on their endeavors."[23] He has noted his admiration for Bernstein's work, but also some reservations, in particular, in response to Bernstein's criticisms Macaulay reaffirms the value of course of performance, course of dealing, and trade usage in interpretation.[24]

In a recent article,[25] Bernstein investigates some long-term supply agreements, showing how they work simultaneously to offer a detailed structure for ongoing interactions while making the legal system largely irrelevant to those interactions. The lack of need for legal remedies is made possible by the companies' "operat[ing] in a market of highly interconnected firms—a network that itself functions as a contract governance mechanism."[26] Empirical work by Hadfield and Bozovic reaches a similar conclusion, again offering a contrast to Macaulay's earlier work, in which he had argued that contract terms generally were not used to guide and correct contracting behavior.[27] Hadfield and Bozovic argue that Macaulay's analysis

---

19Macaulay's comment about a preference for textualism – "if we are concerned with real expectations, that is, with reasonable reliance and good faith, then we cannot be satisfied with only formal written documents" (Macaulay 2000: 801) – may have its strongest force with agreements involving consumers, but in context it is clear that he means it to apply also to business-to-business agreements.

20Macaulay 2003: 64. Even as regards other sorts of agreements (e.g., consumer, employment, or franchise agreements), Scott expresses a concern that the law and society approach to relational contracts may be too close-minded – "guided more by the strength of . . . a priori beliefs in the efficacy of judicial intervention than by the evidence that generalist courts may lack the tools to address fundamental social problems of which the case at hand is only a symptom." Scott 2013: 119.

21Bernstein 1992, 1996, 2001.

22*See* Uniform Commercial Code §§ 2-202, 2-208.

23Macaulay 2016b: 153 (footnote omitted).

24Macaulay 2000.

25Bernstein 2015.

26Bernstein 2015: 563.

27Hadfield and Bozovic 2016. The authors note that Macaulay had concluded that "parties will resort to formal contracting in complex relationships," Hadfield and Bozovic 2016: 988, citing

works for industries and transactions where there is a background of established standards and expectations that can be used instead of contractual terms.[28] However, where the transactions relate to innovation, there are no established norms to fall back upon. While the authors find results consistent with some of Macaulay's findings (parties did not rely on litigation or the threat of litigation), in other ways the results are different: with contracts for innovation, there is "heavy reliance on formal contracts and legal advice in the initial stages of the relationship and frequent reference to formal agreements and legal interpretations of document to manage behavior during the life of the relationship."[29] The authors emphasize that for these parties, drawing up a formal contract can offer value even if there are no intention to enforce the contract in court.[30]

Contract Non-Theory?

The approach to law in general, and contract law in particular, that one finds from the law and society tradition from which Macaulay comes, might at times be summarized as an unhelpful combination of "it's complicated" and "it depends."[31] This approach, however accurate and (in its own way) useful, hardly counts as a theory of contract law. The challenge to Macaulay as contract theorist has also come from a different direction, deriving from Grant Gilmore's well-known description of Macaulay as "the Lord High Executioner of the Contracts is Dead school."[32] As others have pointed out, this comment (though entertaining) is at least partly misleading. Macaulay may question the life (or at least the accuracy) of "Classical Contract Law Theory," but he is clearly in favor in providing a more accurate picture of actual contract law and practice.[33]

Thus, it is not as ironic as it might at first seem that Macaulay has been the lead author of an influential contract law casebook, now in its fourth edition.[34] After all, Macaulay affirms the importance of asking "who benefits from traditional legal education and its focus on doctrinal systems fashioned by people removed from

---

Macaulay 1963a: 65. However, while Macaulay meant that in such circumstances the parties would rely on court enforcement, Hadley and Bozovic conclude that with contracts relating to innovation "formal contracting is valuable even when formal contract enforcement is not." Hadfield and Bozovic 2016: 988.

[28]Their empirical work with "non-innovative" companies reached conclusions similar to Macaulay's. Hadfield and Bozovic 2016: 991-995.

[29]Hadfield and Bozovic 2016: 987.

[30]And the "drawing up" process can itself bring value, through the various things parties learn (directly and indirectly) about one another through the back and forth of negotiating. Hill 2001b.

[31]Macaulay 2000: 783.

[32]Gilmore 1995: 1 n. 1.

[33]See Campbell 2013; see also Macaulay 2006, 2011a.

[34]Macaulay, Whitford, Hendley & Lipson 2016.

practice"?[35] The criticism of the traditional ways of talking about and teaching contract law entails an invitation to find a better way: the precise point of the casebook Macaulay has helped to write is to teach contract law, not in the usual way of thinking about law, but in a way that better reflects law as actually practiced.[36]

Two of the casebook's authors (Macaulay and William Whitford)[37] have written that the central idea motivating the text was that "you cannot fashion meaningful theories about the role of contract law in society or best train law students without considering context."[38] In particular, the casebook is intended to emphasize "relational contracts – the idea that most contracts occur in the context of many occurrences between the parties,"[39] as well as the "power and politics"[40] that often go into the production of both black-letter law and court opinions. Even if students do not need to know the contextual nature of contracts to pass the bar exam, it is information crucial for practice. Not least, such information helps these future lawyers to understand many aspects of why contracts are drafted the way they are, and why disputes are generally handled the way contracting parties handle them.[41]

In relation with the topic of legal education and the right attitude towards contract law and practice and the legal profession generally, Macaulay commented that

> we want to believe that a lawyer, armed only with reason, can champion the weak and overcome the powerful. This myth drew many of us to law school, and it is hard to give up. A descriptive model reduces many lawyers to little more than captive intellectuals serving those who control significant resources in society.[42]

Similarly: "The formal contract system claims to be neutral and autonomous and to rest on simple rationality. A descriptively accurate model of the process challenges these assumptions."[43] The advantage and disadvantage of empirical

---

[35]Macaulay 2016b: 161.

[36]For example, on the topic of teaching the default contract rules where these rules are generally overridden by standard form (and online) terms, Macaulay writes: "At some point, teaching the default rules becomes misleading because some of them seldom, if ever, go into effect." Macaulay 2016b: 158.

[37]Macaulay and Whitford, along with John Kidwell and Marc Galanter were the editors of the first edition; Galanter was not present for later editions; Jean Braucher appeared on the third edition. For the fourth edition Macaulay and Whitford were joined by Kathryn Hendley and Jonathan Lipson. Macaulay and Whitford 2015: 794 n. 15.

[38]Macaulay and Whitford 2015: 793.

[39]Macaulay and Whitford 2015: 793.

[40]Macaulay and Whitford 2015: 802. "[P]rivate custom and private markets [should not be seen as] the basic fabric of society, with law and the state relegated largely to the (useful and sometimes indispensable) periphery of formal contract enforcement and the (invasive and often inefficient) periphery of state regulation, but as one pattern in the in the weave of a larger tapestry." Gordon 2013: 70; see also Gordon 1985.

[41]Macaulay and Whitford 2015: 800-801.

[42]Macaulay 1985: 479.

[43]Macaulay 1985: 478.

approaches is that they force us to see things as they really are, including hard facts about the way "the haves" generally prevail against the "have-nots",[44] and the way statutes meant to protect consumers rarely do a good job of doing so.[45] In this context, "[t]he challenge," Macaulay notes, perhaps with understatement, is "to avoid cynicism."[46]

One can discern some other messages about contract law from Macaulay's works. As David Campbell points out, Macaulay's works implicitly endorse the same view of contract law advocated by Nathan Oman and others, that commercial exchange is (and should be) central to this area of law.[47] As Campbell points out, this perspective fits in well with the insights that Macaulay has emphasized, regarding the uneven and inconsistent role of contractual language and contract law doctrine in contracting practice. It is how the parties behave—the actual exchange—that is and should be central to our understanding, and contracting behavior frequently involves ignoring much of the contractual language and having recourse to litigation only in rare circumstances.

Contract and Cultural Theory

One question to which Macaulay returns regularly is the following: if the classic view of contract law is seriously inaccurate, why does it persist? In other words, what purpose does it serve?[48] As Arthur Leff once wrote in reviewing an early work by Richard Posner, if the actions of a community are consistently inefficient, it is likely that what the community is trying to maximize is something other than efficiency, and we should try to determine what that "something else" is.[49] This line of inquiry is the sort of question one finds in the cultural study of law (as well as a number of critical approaches to law).[50] For example, if one doubts claims about the rule of law, or the objectivity or neutrality of law, the natural progression (at least

---

[44]Galanter 1974.

[45]Macaulay 1989.

[46]Macaulay 1985: 482. While Macaulay has frequently reaffirmed his view that we generally "overstate the importance of the law of contracts," he adds in one article that the ability of courts occasionally to sanction "outrageous behavior" may make a small contribution "to the trust necessary to make any economic system work." Macaulay 2000: 804; see also Macaulay 2004: 802-820.

[47]*See* Campbell 2013: 165-167; Oman 2016; Encarnacion 2018.

[48]Macaulay 1977: 511-512.

[49]Leff 1974: 462-469.

[50]As a prominent figure in the cultural study of law wrote, whether the object of study is religious belief or law, a "scholarly discipline of the cultural form approaches [propositions internal to the system of belief] not from the perspective of their validity, but from the perspective of the meaning they have for the individual within the community of belief." Kahn 1999: 2-3. On cultural study of law generally, see also Mezey 2015.

in cultural studies) goes to inquiring what role *the ideas of* the rule of law and the objectivity and neutrality of law play in our society.[51] One suggestion, associated with certain critical approaches, is that these and similar ideas work to make inequality look natural or inevitable, and generally to legitimate injustice.[52]

It might be that something similar explains the continued prominence of the classical picture of contract practice in legal education and in media discussions of contracts. The characterization of contracting presented in those settings tends towards a picture of two comparably powerful and sophisticated parties negotiating contractual terms at arm's length. This is in sharp contrast to the contracting experience most people experience, which tends to feature standard forms, on-line contracting, lack of choice regarding terms, waiver of significant procedural and substantive rights, etc. The classical contract theory picture presents contracting as something which clearly values autonomy and generally increases welfare; the extent to which the reality of contracting does so is at least open to serious question. One might reasonably suspect that this rosy presented picture of contract law, which varies so sharply from contracting experience, will have the effect (and perhaps has the purpose) of legitimating questionable practices.[53]

A second line of inquiry: if commercial parties are not governing their transactions and their relationships by their written agreements, why do they go to the great trouble and expense of negotiating and drafting those agreements? Claire Hill argues that the process of negotiating an agreement can itself sometimes educates parties in important ways about the other side.[54] More speculatively, Jeffrey Lipshaw offers that even where contracts do not directly affect how the contracting parties act, the documents can have meaning "as custom, symbol, or ritual."[55] Macaulay offers a similar observation: "Given the costs of litigation, remedies that seldom will achieve protection of the expectation interest, and all the difficulties of enforcing judgments, often contract law will be largely symbolic."[56] He then adds: "Perhaps, a basic question is whether it will symbolize fairness or deference to power."[57]

Conclusion

Macaulay has taught contract law scholars many things: to focus on practice not theory, on relationships not models, and on the power and politics behind everything. In particular, those of us working in this area have learned from Macaulay to

[51]Kahn 1999: 36-40.

[52]*E.g.*, Gramsci 1971; Gordon 1984.

[53]*See, e.g.*, Bix 2012: 128-146; Bix 2013.

[54]Hill 2001a: 46-47.

[55]Lipshaw 2017: 150.

[56]Macaulay 2000: 803.

[57]Macaulay 2000: 803.

be attentive to the way the rules of contract law are used, or not used, as part of ongoing transactional relationships. As he and other commentators have emphasized, we must simultaneously be conscious that the answer to such inquiries will almost certainly be different for different kinds of transactions. Consumers and employees generally have a different contracting experience than do large corporations, and even in business-to-business transactions, one-shot interactions across industries are likely to be different from repeated transactions that occur within a close-knit business community or as part of a long-term supply arrangement. And we need to pass along these insights to our students, as a necessary if small first step towards improving contract law and practice.

Bibliography

Bakos, Y., Marotta-Wurgler, F. and Trossen, D. R. (2014), 'Does Anyone Read the Fine Print? Consumer Attention to Standard-Form Contracts', *Journal of Legal Studies* 43: 1-35.

Benson, P. (ed.) (2001). *The Theory of Contract Law*. Cambridge: Cambridge University Press.

Bernstein, L. (1992). 'Opting Out of the Legal System: Extralegal Contractual Relations in the Diamond Industry', *Journal of Legal Studies*, 21: 115-157.

Bernstein, L. (1996). 'Merchant Law in a Merchant Court: Rethinking the Code's Search for Immanent Business Norms', *University of Pennsylvania Law Review* 144: 1765-1821.

Bernstein, L. (2001). 'Private Commercial Law in the Cotton Industry: Creating Cooperation Through Rules, Norms, and Institutions', *Michigan Law Review* 99: 1724-1790.

Bernstein, L. (2015). 'Beyond Relational Contracts: Social Capital and Network Governance in Procurement Contracts', *Journal of Legal Analysis* 7: 561-621.

Bix, B. (2012). *Contract Law: Rules, Theory, and Context*. Cambridge: Cambridge University Press.

Bix, B. (2013). 'The Role of Contract: Stewart Macaulay's Lessons from Practice', in J. Braucher, J. Kidwell and W. Whitford (eds.), *Revisiting the Contracts Scholarship of Stewart Macaulay: On the Empirical and the Lyrical* (Oxford: Hart Publishing), 241-255.

Braucher, J., Kidwell, J, and Whitford, W. C. (eds.) (2013). *Revisiting the Contracts Scholarship of Stewart Macaulay: On the Empirical and the Lyrical*. Oxford: Hart Publishing.

Campbell, D. (2013). 'What Do We Mean by the Non-Use of Contract', in J. Braucher, J. Kidwell, and W. C. Whitford (eds.), *Revisiting the Contracts Scholarship of Stewart Macaulay: On the Empirical and the Lyrical* (Oxford: Hart Publishing), 159-190.

Ellickson, R. C. (1991). *Order Without Law: How Neighbors Settle Disputes*. Cambridge, Mass.: Harvard University Press.

Encarnacion, E. (2018). 'Contract as Commodified Promise', *Vanderbilt Law Review* 71: 61-119.

Galanter, M. (1974). 'Why the Haves Come Out Ahead: Speculations on the Limits of Legal Change', *Law & Society Review* 9: 95-160.

Gilmore, G. (1995). *The Death of Contract*, 2nd ed. Columbus: Ohio State University Press.

Gordon, R.W. (1984). 'Critical Legal Histories', *Stanford Law Review* 36: 57-125.

Gordon, R.W. (1985). 'Macaulay, Macneil and the Discovery of Solidarity and Power in Contract Law', *Wisconsin Law Review* 1985: 565-579.

Gordon, R. W. (2013). 'Is the World of Contracting Relations One of Spontaneous Order or Pervasive State Action? Stewart Macaulay Scrambles the Public-Private Distinction', in J. Braucher, J. Kidwell, and W. C. Whitford (eds.), Revisiting the Contracts Scholarship of Stewart Macaulay: On the Empirical and the Lyrical (Oxford: Hart Publishing), 49-73.

Gramsci, A. (1971). *Selections from the Prison Notebooks* (Q. Hoare and G. Nowell-Smith, eds.). New York: International Publishers.

Hadfield, G.K. and Bozovic, I. (2016). 'Scaffolding: Using Formal Contracts to Support Informal Relations in Support of Innovation', *Wisconsin Law Review* 2016: 981-1032.
Hill, C. A. (2001a). 'A Comment on Language and Norms in Complex Business Contracting', *Chicago-Kent Law Review* 77: 29-57.
Hill, C. A. (2001b). 'Why Contracts are Written in "Legalese"', *Chicago-Kent Law Review* 77: 59-85.
Hill, C. A. (2009). 'Bargaining in the Shadow of the Lawsuit: A Social Norms Theory of Incomplete Contracts', *Delaware Journal of Corporate Law* 34: 191-220.
Hill, C. A. and King, C. (2004). 'How Do German Contracts Do as Much with Fewer Words?', *Chicago-Kent Law Review* 79: 889-926.
Kahn, P. W. (1999). *The Cultural Study of Law*. Chicago: University of Chicago Press.
Klass, G., Letsas, G. and Saprai, P. (eds.) (2014). *Philosophical Foundations of Contract Law*. Oxford: Oxford University Press.
Leff, A. A. (1974). 'Economic Analysis of Law: Some Realism About Nominalism', *Virginia Law Review* 60: 451-482.
Lipshaw, J. (2017). *Beyond Legal Reasoning: A Critique of Pure Lawyering*. London: Routledge.
Llewellyn, K.N. (1930). 'A Realistic Jurisprudence -- The Next Step', *Columbia Law Review*, vol. 30, pp. 431-465.
Macaulay, S. (1963a). 'Non-Contractual Relations in Business: A Preliminary Study' *American Sociology Review* 28: 55-67.
Macaulay, S. (1963b). '"The Use and Non-Use of Contracts in the Manufacturing Industry," *Practical Lawyer* 9: 13-40.
Macaulay, S. (1977). 'Elegant Models, Empirical Pictures, and the Complexities of Contract' *Law & Society Review* 11: 507-528.
Macaulay, S. (1984). 'Law and the Behavioral Sciences: Is There Any There There?' *Law and Policy* 6: 149-187.
Macaulay, S. (1985). 'An Empirical View of Contract' *Wisconsin Law Review* 1985: 465-482.
Macaulay, S. (1989). 'Bambi Meets Godzilla: Reflections on Contracts Scholarship and Teaching vs. State Unfair and Deceptive Trade Practices and Consumer Protection Statutes', *Houston Law Review* 26: 575-601.
Macaulay, S. (2000). '"Relational Contracts Floating on a Sea of Custom? Thoughts About the Ideas of Ian Macneil and Lisa Bernstein', *Northwestern University Law Review* 94: 775-804.
Macaulay, S. (2003). 'The Real and the Paper Deal: Empirical Pictures of Relationships, Complexity and the Urge for Transparent Simple Rules," *Modern Law Review* 66: 44-79.
Macaulay, S. (2004). 'Freedom from Contract: Solutions in Search of a Problem?," *Wisconsin Law Review* 2004: 777-820.
Macaulay, S. (2006). 'Contracts, New Legal Realism, and Improving the Navigation of The Yellow Submarine', *Tulane Law Review* 80: 1161-1195.
Macaulay, S. (2011a). 'The Death of Contract: Dodos and Unicorns or Sleeping Rattlesnakes,' in R.W. Gordon & M.J. Horwitz (eds.), *Law, Society, and History: Themes in the Legal Sociology and Legal History of Lawrence M. Friedman* (Cambridge: Cambridge University Press), pp. 193-208.
Macaulay, S. (2011b). 'Notes on the Margins of Lawyering, in Three and a Half Minutes', *Hofstra Law Review* 40: 25-38.
Macaulay, S. (2016a), 'A New Legal Realism: Elegant Models and Messy Law in Action', in E. Mertz, S. Macaulay and T. W. Mitchell (eds.), *The New Legal Realism, Volume 1: Translating Law-and-Society for Today's Legal Practice* (Cambridge: Cambridge University Press), 29-50.
Macaulay, S. (2016b). 'New Legal Realism: Unpacking a Proposed Definition', *UC Irvine Law Review* 6: 149-167.
Macaulay, S., Friedman, L. M. and Mertz, E. (2007), *Law in Action: A Socio-Legal Reader*, New York: Foundation Press.

Macaulay, S. and Whitford, W. (2015). 'The Development of Contracts: Law in Action', *Temple Law Review* 87: 101-113.

Macaulay, S., Whitford, W., Hendley, K, and Lipson, J. (2016). *Contracts: Law in Action*, 4th ed. (two volumes), Durham: Carolina Academic Press.

Mertz, E., Macaulay, S. and Mitchell, T. W. (eds.) (2016). *The New Legal Realism: Volume 1 Translating Law-and-Society for Today's Legal Practice*, Cambridge: Cambridge University Press.

Mezey, N. (2015). 'Mapping a Cultural Studies of Law', in A. Sarat and P. Ewick, *The Handbook of Law and Society* (Oxford: Wiley Blackwell), 39-55.

Oman, N. B. (2016). *The Dignity of Commerce*. Chicago: University of Chicago Press.

Posner, R. A. (2005). 'The Law and Economics of Contract Interpretation', *Texas Law Review* 83: 1581-1614.

Pound, R. (1910). 'Law in Books and Law in Action', *American Law Review* 44: 12-36

Schwartz, A. and Scott, R. E. (2003), 'Contract Theory and the Limits of Contract Law', *Yale Law Journal* 113: 541-619.

Schwartz, A. and Scott, R. E. (2010). 'Contract Theory Redux', *Yale Law Journal* 119: 926-964.

Scott, R. E. (2013). 'The Promise and Peril of Relational Contract Theory', in J. Braucher, J. Kidwell and W. C. Whitford (eds.), *Revisiting the Contracts Scholarship of Stewart Macaulay: On the Empirical and the Lyrical* (Oxford: Hart Publishing), 105-139.

Shapiro, F. R. and Pearse, M. (2012). 'The Most-Cited Law Review Articles of All Time', *Michigan Law Review* 110: 1483-1520.

Law in Reality, Law in Context: On the Work and Influence of Stewart Macaulay

Elizabeth Mertz and Lawrence M. Friedman

Abstract In this commentary on Stewart Macaulay's intellectual contributions, Elizabeth Mertz and Lawrence Friedman review just one part of Macaulay's substantial legacy within legal and sociolegal studies. Within legal studies he is well known for his work on contract law, and on the relationship between private and public regulation in institutional settings more generally. However, this essay assesses his influence well beyond the field of contract law, reaching into such areas of sociolegal studies as law in popular culture, the legal profession, and interdisciplinary legal education. A consistent thread draws these interests together: Macaulay's insistent concern with how law actually works out in real life, in other words, in social context. His approach is systematic and disciplined, based on careful engagement with the social sciences whose methods and theories shed particular light on how to study law in action. The chapter's first section gives an overview of Macaulay's early engagement with realist and sociolegal traditions, taking him from how business people actually deal with contract law, through the effects of bureaucracies and international differences on the administration of law on the ground, to struggles with formal law in divorce courts. The second section of the chapter reviews Macaulay's crucial contributions to the study of "popular legal culture," which examines how law is represented to—and understood by—everyday people. This opened the door to studying the effects of law outside of courts and legislatures, and to a broadened empirical lens for examining how social order is maintained—whether through law or in spite of it! Inspired by this broader lens, Macaulay continually pressed for law schools to incorporate a better-informed view of law-in-action within their curricula, arguing that legal educators are failing their students when they don't reach beyond the study of formal doctrine to how law and legal

We thank Dr. Frances Tung for her careful work in helping us prepare this chapter for publication.

E. Mertz (✉)
American Bar Foundation and University of Wisconsin, Chicago, IL, USA
e-mail: emertz@abfn.org

L. M. Friedman
Stanford University School of Law, Stanford, CA, USA
e-mail: lmf@stanford.edu

D. Campbell (ed.), *Stewart Macaulay: Selected Works*, Law and Philosophy Library 133, https://doi.org/10.1007/978-3-030-33930-2_2

careers actually work in real life. This interest in a kind of legal realism brought him, later in his career, to join a younger group of scholars who sought to revive interest surrounding law-in-action within the law schools. Hoping to reacquaint law professors and students with the considerable amount of scholarship that had been conducted within sociolegal studies in intervening decades, Macaulay and his colleagues formed the "New Legal Realism" movement, to which Macaulay again contributed a number of path-charting writings.

This book gathers both the uncollected and the less well-known papers written by one of the most influential scholars of the law and society movement, Stewart Macaulay. Some famous articles also make abbreviated appearances. In the course of his long career, hardly anyone has made a greater contribution than Macaulay; and the aim of this book is to present, in one place, important articles on law and society that he has published over the years, along with some commentaries on his work. He has, of course, also been an important teacher and mentor. All of his teaching has been suffused with the sensibilities of a social scientist as well as the analytic skills of the lawyer. He has also made an effort to supply teaching materials for those who might want to spread the gospel of law and society. Full disclosure: the two authors of this essay have been collaborators with Stewart Macaulay in the latest effort (Macaulay et al. 2007a, b). He is best known, probably, for his landmark article of 1963, on contract law; his empirical investigation of Wisconsin business practice cast doubt on the entire enterprise of doctrinal research on contracts. In this essay we want to pay tribute to some of his other contributions; and to assess as well, the way in which his influence has gone beyond the field of contract law into such areas as law in popular culture, the legal profession, and interdisciplinary legal education. There is, we feel, a consistent thread drawing these apparently disparate interests together: Macaulay's insistent concern with how law actually works out in real life, in other words, in social context. And this concern is just not a vague, general and theoretical position; Macaulay's approach is systematic and disciplined, based on careful engagement with the social sciences whose methods and theories shed particular light on how to study law in action.

1. Law in Context

The idea that we ought to pay attention to law in action, to law as it actually functions in society, might seem totally obvious. And yet, the main body of legal scholarship has somehow always missed this point, and proceeded as if it was irrelevant. From the time that Macaulay entered the legal academy until the present day, law reviews have been filled with articles that diced and sliced and assessed formal legal doctrine with very little attention to how it worked, if it worked, and what influence context had on doctrines and their application. Ironically, Macaulay at one point held a Bigelow Fellowship at the University of Chicago Law School (1956–1957), a school which did have some serious engagement with social science, though even there this kind of engagement arguably remained relatively marginal. During Macaulay's time at the University of Chicago Law School, the faculty included Karl Llewellyn, a Legal Realist who had worked with anthropologist E. Adamson Hoebel to study the on-the-ground "law ways" of the Cheyenne—examining those legal processes in full social context (Llewellyn and Hoebel 1941). Also at that time at Chicago Soia Mentschikoff was running a major research project focused on studying arbitration, an important move away from the over-emphasis on appellate cases that characterized the classic Harvard case method for studying and teaching law (see Mentschikoff 1952, 1961). Chicago was also the school where Kalven and Zeisel (1966) did a major empirical study of the work of the jury. Zeisel himself was trained in both law and social science. From Chicago, Macaulay went on to the University of Wisconsin Law School, where social science and social context were taken seriously as central concerns in both scholarship and teaching. At Wisconsin, Macaulay was at a school dominated in some ways by the towering figure of Willard Hurst. Hurst was, first and foremost, a legal historian. But his brand of history was social and economic history—a sharp break from the aridity of traditional legal history. Hurst was for that reason a powerful stimulus for the law and society movement, which influenced the school, and which provided Stewart Macaulay with an intellectual home (see Macaulay 1994, in this volume).

From the very start of his career, Macaulay rejected the methods and aims of traditional legal scholarship—in particular, their blindness to social context. His earliest publication, called "Restitution in Context," was a book review of John Wade's casebook, *Case and Materials on Restitution*. The editors of the University of Pennsylvania Law Review decided that Macaulay's "stimulating analysis … merits inclusion in the Articles section," and elevated the review to the "Comment" section (Macaulay 1959, p. 1133). Throughout the Comment, Macaulay critiqued Wade's parochial treatment of his subject. Wade isolated restitution from its wider legal, social, and moral contexts, in which it necessarily operated: "Focusing attention on restitution blurs the total picture of the legal system…..Concentration on restitution cases runs the danger of overlooking the relationship of this part of the legal system to certain social institutions and values" (Macaulay 1959, pp. 1138–1139). Macaulay's core themes already appear; he insists that law students and lawyers need to examine openly the "ethical and economic assumptions" underlying legal decisions, citing famed social theorist Max Weber, and the economist, John R. Commons. (Macaulay's fans, especially those who know him personally, will not be surprised to learn that there is a reference to Frank Lloyd Wright in this article.)[1]

[1]This insistence that lawyers and policymakers pay close attention to the methods and validity of studies upon which they rely is a thread found running throughout Macaulay's writings. In 1986, his paper on lawyer advertising performed a painstaking review of available research and concluded that much of the debate missed the point: it was unlikely that lawyer advertising would have either the dramatic benefits or detriments predicted by advocates on either side – and far more research would be needed to come to any definite conclusion (1986). In pointing out the lack of empirical

In the 1960s Macaulay's scholarship took an increasingly sociological turn. His empirical research on business behavior in Wisconsin, published not in a law review but in the prestigious *American Sociological Review*, in 1963, has remained a classic study.[2] It was something of a shock to traditionalists: the business people Macaulay interviewed told him how little formal contracts law meant in the real world of business relationships! So much of what law professors taught and studied turned out either not to matter at all, or to matter only in rare situations, situations in which relationships were shattered or rendered unworkable—in short, when contractual relationships failed. While he continued to expand contracts scholarship in terms of its place in the real world of business, Macaulay also soon branched out into other domains. He co-authored an article with Ted Finman in 1966 that eviscerated a careless "study" issued by the Internal Security Subcommittee of the Senate Committee on the Judiciary (Finman and Macaulay 1966, pp. 76–91). The article considered issues of constitutional law, but in context, in the light of protests against the war in Vietnam, and of the research the government used to claim Communist involvement in the protests. The co-authors pushed their legal audience to critically assess a staff study whose "handling of data and inference can at best be described as eccentric" (1966: 91). Macaulay also spent a year at the Center for Advanced Study in the Behavioral Sciences, where he continued to deepen his study of the sociology of law. He was involved as well, beginning in the 1960s, with the Law & Society Association, which gathered together social scientists as well as legal scholars who shared an interest in the social study of law. Stewart Macaulay has been considered one of the major figures in the movement, from its earliest days. He served as President of the Association from 1985 to 1987, and in 1995 was awarded the Association's prestigious Kalven Prize, which "is given in recognition of a body of scholarly work" that "has contributed most effectively to the advancement of research in law and society."

In the 1970s and 1980s, Macaulay's interest in the social study of law expanded beyond the United States. He spent 2 years as Director of the Chile Law Program of the International Legal Center in Santiago Chile, and he visited a number of foreign universities—Oxford, the University of Western Australia, the University of Toronto, and the Universidade de Coimbra in Portugal. His paper included in this volume on "Access to the Legal Systems of the Americas" at once signals this broadening of scope but also continues to dig into the way law operates in reality, with full consideration of "the complicated process involving discretion, power to command and bargaining that constitutes the very real but informal legal process that operates in most societies" (1976: 1). At this level, waiting in line for benefits becomes a common part of accessing justice across many societies. Access to justice, he notes, cannot really be investigated without attention to the experiences of "less

foundation for claims in this debate, Macaulay could also show how the real questions of quality and access to law were being obscured.

[2]Among articles published in a non-law, peer-reviewed journal, Macaulay's landmark piece became the most highly cited of all time (Shapiro and Pearsen 2012: 1489).

privileged members of a society," which will always "bring us back to questions about the distribution of power in the society" (1976: 3). From this vantage, access to formal legal procedures is important mostly as an unpleasant alternative that can be used to influence the constant bargaining that goes on at the ground level when ordinary people try to access law. And in the end, if everyone knows that you can't possibly win through the formal procedures (i.e., you will lose in court), then the fact that you can file papers and stand in court means little. The impact of the informal—of law in context—undercuts whatever rights you have been formally granted. From this standpoint, the apparent advantage of the U.S. legal system over the situation in Latin America shrinks: "There are too many articles where an idealized picture of law in the United States is compared with informal practices in a Latin American country to the disadvantage of that nation" (1976: 5). By contrast, Macaulay lists some uncomfortable facts about law in action in the U.S., from the criminal behavior of Nixon and Agnew while in office (for which neither served prison time), through the open corruption in many U.S. cities, to the disparate (and unjust) punishments visited on African-Americans, Native Americans, and Japanese-Americans. Building from the work of anthropologists such as Jane Collier, Laura Nader, and Lisa Redfield Peattie, Macaulay draws some important lessons about law in context: one "lesson is that people will attempt to cope with a legal institution as best they can with the means available to them" (1976: 12). If the Mexican state legal apparatus is punitive, indigenous people may rely instead on local or traditional mechanisms of dispute resolution. Or they may turn to someone who can serve as a broker, getting access that they were supposed to be able to get for themselves. Whatever the coping mechanism, it may fall far shy of the ideal envisioned in formal law for those outside the circles of power. At the "street-level," then, navigating bureaucracies in Chicago and Santiago may not be as different as descriptions of law in the United States at that time supposed.

This view from below and from abroad has aspects of the emerging Macaulay trademark: it debunks idealized views of how law works by examining the reality on the ground, it pays attention to differences between disenfranchised and elite users of law, and it looks at a wide social picture to contextualize our assessment of law(s). This is an approach that excavates the "living law" (Ehrlich 2009, 486–503), requiring us to look beneath the façade provided by formal legal procedures. In a 1978 article co-authored by Macaulay and his wife, psychologist Jacqueline Macaulay, we hear a warning about the potential costs of such façades in real life (Macaulay and Macaulay 1978). In an exploration of the way legislators and courts had avoided taking stands on issues surrounding interracial adoption, the Macaulays warned that "legal and political procedures" could serve as "essentially social rituals designed to minimize the costs of conflict" (p. 306). And yet "the price of cheap conflict may indeed be bad problem-solving in terms of the actual consequences of decisions"—a perspective on law as it is on the ground, that makes clear how important it is to engage in this form of analysis (p. 306).

2. Law in Culture and Law in Everyday Life

Indeed, one of the most important and common contexts in which law makes an appearance is everyday life. And yet legal scholars have traditionally largely ignored this context. In his short piece, "Popular Legal Culture: An Introduction" (1989), Stewart Macaulay begins by stating what had by then become a common theme for him: the debate between two groups of scholars concerned with the law. One group consisted of orthodox legal scholars, who arranged rules "in logical patterns;" the other was made up of those who "demand that we look beyond legal scholarship to understand the place of law in society." Most law professors "experience vertigo when they open the doors and look outside appellate courtrooms." This is because the big world, the real world, the outside world, is messy, disorderly—lacking in the "logical patterns" that legal scholarship historically has loved. For this reason, they "slam the door quickly and turn back to rules and great cases decided by elite appellate courts."

"Popular Legal Culture" was the introduction to a symposium on law and popular culture—a field which Stewart Macaulay helped to create. Two years earlier, in 1987, he had published "Images of Law in Everyday Life: The Lessons of School, Entertainment, and Spectator Sports." This was a revision of his presidential address, given at the annual meeting of the Law and Society Association the year before. It would be only a slight exaggeration to say that this seminal article helped make a *field* out of the study of law and popular culture; it also did the same for the related study of law in everyday life.

He begins the piece by addressing his cohort—scholars interested in law in action. They should look "beyond the behavior of judges, lawyers, cops, crooks, and eyewitnesses," and beyond an undue emphasis on litigation and litigation rates. In the piece, he proposes practicing what he preaches: to engage in a "scouting expedition into underexplored territory." For Macaulay, "law" is a system of behavior, together with the ideas that actually animate that behavior. Not the ideas of legal scholars and jurists, but the ideas that rattle around in the heads of the lay public.

His classic article on contract behavior in Wisconsin was revolutionary not only because of what Macaulay found, but also because of the way he found what he found. That is, by actually talking to people—opening the door that legal scholarship was satisfied to keep closed. This is why this study has reverberated so significantly in the years since it was written. And why the approach has been so useful and so seminal in field after field; why it has radiated so far beyond contract law itself. Macaulay has had, or perhaps it would be more accurate to say, should have had, an overwhelming influence on contract law. We say "should have had," because, unless we miss our bet, orthodoxy in the teaching of contract law, in the formation of contracts casebooks, and in contracts scholarship in general, has proved to be far more stubborn than one would like. Nonetheless, in an arena that is very hard to sway, his translation of a sociological perspective for legal scholars is among the most successful such efforts to date—in part through his writings and engagement with other contracts scholars, and in part through his work on the Wisconsin contracts teaching materials, recently published in a fourth edition in 2016 (Macaulay et al. 2016). It is fair to say that the "relational contracts" model he has championed with others has pushed mainstream contracts scholars to consider how contract law works in practice to a far greater extent than would otherwise have happened. A core question here as in his work on law and popular culture is to ask how—and whether—formal law affects people's behavior.

Why do people behave the way they do? No simple answer; but clearly, a lot of behavior is normative behavior—it consists of following rules. Not necessarily formal rules, but rather social norms. That was what inspired Macaulay's study of Wisconsin business people. In the piece on images of law, he takes a further step, by asking not just what the norms are, but where they come from, how people learn them, and what induces them to react to the norms as they do. What, for example, do we really learn in school (besides the three R's)? We learn, he argues, obedience to rules. He might have added: obedience to authority—the authority of the teacher. There is a "hidden curriculum" in school; in this "curriculum," students "learn about coping with multiple authority structures." Some accept these authority structures; but some do not. They "do not internalize the school's values." Rather, they game the system; they manipulate it for their own ends, which are not the classic ends of education. Others learn about breaking the rules: about cheating on exams, about breaking the law. Of course, the school does not explicitly teach these things; but the school cohort—the crowd of young people—may run a kind of seminar in rule-breaking. Hence, paradoxically, students learn in school how to obey, how to disobey, and how to evade.

In this richly suggestive article, Macaulay makes a similar point about what our sports-mad public learns from professional sports. This is, after all, an extremely rule-bound activity: there is no question that, in baseball, if a third strike is called, the batter is out. And there are referees and umpires and officials to enforce the rules, sometimes in an extremely literal way. Nonetheless, there is rule-bending (and sometimes outright rule-breaking); and the philosophy of winning at all costs ("nice guys finish last") so that here too, as in school, the lessons learned are contradictory and paradoxical. In another section of the paper, Macaulay discusses the image of law, lawyers, judges, police officers, prosecutors, and rules in popular culture; and here too the lessons are complex and at times contradictory. And the picture of the legal system is radically oversimplified, when it is not downright wrong. A later literature, building on the foundation laid by articles such as this one, explores the possible impact of cop shows and the like on the official legal system.

3. Order and Law

This approach brings with it a perspective on how social order is maintained that is dramatically different from that commonly conveyed to law students or written about by legal scholars. As we have noted, Macaulay's classic article on contract behavior in Wisconsin was revolutionary in methodology as well as in its findings, and for this reason had broad interdisciplinary impact. Many scholars, who come from a different tradition, but who have managed to keep an open mind (no small achievement), have felt Macaulay's influence. Among these scholars, one notable example has been Robert Ellickson.

In 1991, Robert Ellickson published a study of the legal behavior of ranchers in Shasta County, California, *Order without Law: How Neighbors Settle Disputes* (1991). This is a major and well-known study of living law. It began as an attempt to measure the impact of a famous theorem in law-and-economics, the Coase theorem. Ellickson himself was a devotee of law-and-economics, the tradition in which he had "mostly labored;" and he refers early in his book to the "rational –actor model of human behavior that underlies most work in economics and game theory" (p. 8). That model never quite disappears from the book, and hangs over it like a protective curtain. But Ellickson is not content with the formal model; he wants to test it and, as it happened, Shasta County looked like the place where a natural experiment on the Coase theorem was actually in progress.

That was the starting point. But to explore this natural experiment, Ellickson turned to the research methods of "law-and-society stalwarts such as Stewart Macaulay." Indeed, he explicitly compares his own use of unstructured interviews with the methods used in the Wisconsin study. He makes a confession: he suspects that "law-and-society scholars, because they better understand the importance of informal social controls," would be better positioned to "predict the essentials of what was located in Shasta County." They would, in other words, be better at judging the results of the natural experiment. And indeed, he finds, perhaps to his disappointment, that not only do the methods of Stewart Macaulay fit his study, but the *results* fit as well; what Macaulay found about business people in Wisconsin helps us understand how ranchers in Shasta County behave much more accurately than does economic theory. That said, however, he warns "members of the law-and-society camp not to gloat," because he is not going to abandon his own "camp" of law-and-economics scholars. Rather, he will try to explain what he found in terms that would fit the theories that underlie economic science.

Ellickson, in short, is only a reluctant convert to the Macaulay gospel. Nonetheless, the book is peppered with references to Stewart Macaulay's "path-breaking" work, and the idea that norms of "fair dealing" both constrain and explain how Wisconsin business firms behave. The key to understanding this phenomenon is the close-knit relationships among these business people. Macaulay's work thus illuminates Ellickson's own study of the Shasta County ranchers. The insights are also applicable to other "nonhierarchical groups," and the way in which they "create welfare-maximizing substantive norms" (p. 191). As an example (of some length), he explores the practices of whalers in the days before the steamship. Later there are references to lobstermen in Maine, kibbutzim in Israel, and disciplinary practices of universities—all as part of a general discussion of informal norms, how they develop, and how and when they are enforced.

Even when Stewart Macaulay is not mentioned by name, his work, and the spirit of his work, animate and inform the discussion. But only up to a certain point. Beyond this point, Ellickson is unwilling to go. As the reference to wealth maximizing (above) makes clear, to Ellickson the Macaulay canon, properly understood, does not overturn and undermine his traditional faith in law-and-economics. What Ellickson wants to do, with Macaulay's help, is to assimilate the work; to mine it for refinements and enrichment; to make law-and-economics more realistic, more empirical; but not to abandon it to its rivals.

The recent work of Barak Richman is in this sense strikingly similar. The book in question is *Stateless Commerce: The Diamond Network and the Persistence of Relational Exchange* (2017). It is the latest addition to a rather sizeable literature on "stateless commerce," that is, "pockets of modern commerce" in which "premodern forms of organization remain the norm." Premodern, in that they do not depend on institutions of the modern state (courts, for example). The diamond industry has been exhibit A in the literature. But, Richman says, the credit for the beginnings of a literature on "private governance" must go to, yes, Stewart Macaulay, and his classic study in Wisconsin.[3] Like Ellickson, Richman's background is in economics. And, like Ellickson, it shows. Although he pays homage to Macaulay, he cannot resist translating Macaulay's insights into economics-speak. The "famous study" of Wisconsin, Richman says, "observes that business-people invest in relationships precisely to avoid litigation." The word "invest" is crucial here; and in a later passage, Richman mentions Macaulay again, as one who showed that "much contract enforcement occurs outside courtrooms." This subtly shifts the point of the Wisconsin study; it converts it to a study, not of normative behavior, but of choices, on efficiency grounds, of particular modes of enforcement. Again, like Ellickson, Richman is anxious to analyze the literature on the diamond industry, and similar examples of "stateless commerce," in terms that can be made compatible with economic theory.[4]

There is, of course, nothing wrong with this; and indeed, it is no more illegitimate than doing the reverse, that is, for law-and-society scholars to learn from economic theory. Ideally (as Ellickson himself points out), the two strands of scholarship should work together—should supplement each other. That this does not happen is probably mostly for reasons that have little to do with the actual substance of the fields, but because the two camps on the whole do not particularly like each other, and each stays in its own world of scholarship.

Which brings us to a point worth making: Stewart Macaulay is a contracts professor, who published his most famous piece in a sociological journal. He is an expert on contracts law, and on such related subjects as the Uniform Commercial Code. He has a keen eye and a strong interest in the business world—and he has written about the automobile industry and its franchising system for auto dealers; about credit cards; and about consumer protection laws. In the past, sociologists of

[3]In this regard, Macaulay's 1986 article on private governance had continued the emphasis on non-state informal sources of ordering started in his famous article on non-contractual relations, examining a variety of formal and informal institutions (Macaulay 1986).

[4]See also Lisa Bernstein 1992, which although it does not explicitly build on Macaulay's work, fits with his work on private governance, as well as with his observation that business people did not often see going to court to vindicate rights as worth the high costs (see, e.g., Macaulay 1963).

law tended to stay away from the world of business, and concentrate on deviant behavior, race, class, gender, and other issues. Today, however, a robust sociology has emerged, on issues of business and its interactions with law. At the time Macaulay began writing, there were far fewer resources on which to draw, and a far smaller literature. Here too Macaulay stands out as a scholar who has not been afraid to explore relatively unknown territory.

4. Training Lawyers

The bulk of Stewart Macaulay's work has been about law in action; how law is used, and what impact it has, in the real world. He did this work while he was on the faculty of the University of Wisconsin Law School; and he earned his living as a law professor. It is no surprise, then, that he has been consistently concerned with legal education, with the training of lawyers in law schools. His study of contract *behavior,* first published in a journal of sociology, did not, for obvious reasons, go into issues of legal education. But his work almost begs to be read as an indictment of legal education. Some of his writing makes this indictment explicit. It is implicit also in his work on classroom materials: the three editions of readings on law and society (the two co-authors of this article are co-editors, as we said, of the latest of these); and in his materials for the teaching of contract law.

In the Introduction to the classroom materials on law-and-society, Macaulay and his co-editors stress to law students and lawyers the importance of being able to take an "outside point of view" toward the law (2007: 1). While recognizing the limitations of social science, the Introduction pushes students to engage seriously with the chance to step outside of the internal legal perspective and question some of the assumptions they are being taught, as they go through law school and prepare to enter the legal profession. Where does law come from? What is the impact of law? What is the structure of the legal system and how does it really work? How does law change through history? What do we learn from looking beyond the United States in thinking about law? How do language and culture affect law? These are the kinds of questions the law-and-society reader examines, challenging initiates into the legal profession to think outside the box of legal reasoning as well as inside of it (2007: 16–17).

In other work, too, the indictment of legal education, and suggestions for reform, are quite explicit. Earliest, perhaps, is the article coauthored with Lawrence M. Friedman, that appeared in 1967 (Friedman and Macaulay 1967). This piece was in form mostly about the teaching of contract law; and it was obviously inspired by Macaulay's empirical study of contract *behavior.* The article analyzes the way contract law has been traditionally taught, and what assumptions underlie classical legal education, at least in contract law. The article points out how poorly what is taught reflects the real world of business negotiation and business practice. Teaching is focused almost exclusively on reported appellate cases. But these tell us very little about problems, policies, and practices in the world of business. The current system gives the students a cramped and unrealistic view of contracting behavior. It does not give them the skills they need, which include "negotiation and the architecture of successful transactions" (ibid., at 819). An "empirical basis for teaching and research is essential" (ibid., at 820).[5]

An article in the *Virginia Law Review*, the following year, continued this theme (Macaulay 1968). Law schools must "teach the realities of the legal system." Law has to be taught as an "institution in its full social context." The "many roles" of lawyers should be explored. Anything learned from empirical research "is relevant to training lawyers" (Ibid., at 617). In an article published in the *Journal of Legal Education,* in 1982 (Macaulay 1982), he continued with this general theme. The article begins with a discussion of two prominent studies of the Chicago bar. The studies "reveal a gap between legal education and the practice of many lawyers" (ibid., at 512). Defenders of traditional legal education insist that it teaches students something essential: how to think like a lawyer. But which lawyers, Macaulay asks, are these model thinkers? Not real-world lawyers—not the lawyers he had interviewed in his own studies. Those lawyers "thought tactically rather than what most law professors would call analytically." He suspects that law professors "really are attempting to teach their students to think like *law professors,*" rather than to think like lawyers (Ibid., at 514). Macaulay, explicitly a progressive in politics, also examines the unstated *political* messages of standard legal education. He does not go as far as the members of the critical legal studies movement—he is far too nuanced, far too empirically minded to fit in easily with this movement. But he agrees with Duncan Kennedy that legal education, perhaps unconsciously, spreads political messages: "the first year of law school will be hard on students who question capitalism, liberal pluralism, or the existing distributions of wealth, privilege, and status in the society" (Ibid., at 523). Moreover, what goes on in the classroom teaches a "strong lesson:" that "there is always an argument the other way." This tends to change the role of classroom teaching: it is not a search for truth and justice, but a kind of game; perhaps one might also say (although Macaulay does not put it in this form), that this kind of teaching implies that law is or can be nothing more than a bag of clever tricks. This is in itself a political message, and one that is not helpful to those students whose goal is social justice.

[5]In a similar vein, some years, later, Macaulay urged a Canadian audience to think carefully before applying facile "improvements" to legal education in efforts to improve vaguely conceived "professional competence" (1981). Instead, he suggested, it might be important to use empirical data to aid students in getting "a more accurate picture of what lawyers do" (1981, 55).

5. The New Legal Realism

Decades after he played a key role in starting both the relational contracts and the law-and-society movements, Stewart Macaulay stepped in once again to support a nascent movement aimed at studying—and teaching about—law in the real world. During the late 1990s, a group of law-and-society scholars who were teaching in law schools began to worry about the relative imperviousness of mainstream legal education to core lessons from the social sciences. Many of these scholars held PhDs as well as JDs, a trend that would only grow over the ensuing decades. While the legal academy had to a degree embraced a form of economics, and cognitive psychology, it had yet to open itself to a broader form of interdisciplinary study—one in which various methods were employed depending on the question asked, and one which took advantage of the full range of social science knowledge. Most strikingly, the legal academy had yet to take serious account of social science theories and studies that moved beyond the level of the individual, to consider sophisticated findings about institutional and structural elements of social formation. A group gathered at the 1997 meeting of the Law and Society Association, and then, after taking the name of "New Legal Realism" [NLR] for their effort, in 2004 they moved on to plan an initial conference at the University of Wisconsin Law School, in partnership with the American Bar Foundation (http://www.americanbarfoundation.org/research/summary/34, last visited 8/19/2018). Throughout these founding years, and during succeeding decades, Macaulay remained a key member of the movement. He published a number of important and influential articles in support of this renewed effort to bring social science knowledge of the law in action into the legal academy.

At the initial 2004 conference, Macaulay presented a paper that explored how the new legal realism related to the original or "old" legal realism of the 1920s-1930s (Macaulay 2005). Macaulay's career had begun at a time when he was in contact with one of the original legal realists, Karl Llewellyn; now he was present at the creation of a new form of legal realism. He was thus uniquely positioned to compare the two movements.[6] Macaulay noted that the older realists had a more or less diffuse interest in empirical research on law; and that they insisted on taking "law in action" into account (2005: 369–380).[7] A new legal realism, he goes on to argue,

---

[6]Interestingly, Macaulay's work in contract law was in a sense a continuation and expansion of Llewellyn's approach. Llewellyn had tried to import social context and actual business practices into the doctrine of contracts via concepts like "course of dealing, "course of performance," and common "usage of the trade" (Danzig 1975). All of these concepts push judges to look at the actual relationship in a particular contractual relationship to make their decisions – an idea at the core of the "relational contracts" approach for which Macaulay is famous.

[7]Here Macaulay cited David Nelken's attempt to distinguish between scholarship concerned with the gap between law on books and law as it administered ("law in action") and scholarship that looks beyond those charged with administering law to law in everyday life ("the living law") (Macaulay 2005, pp. 385–387, citing Nelken 1984); however, Macaulay worries that this attempt, while it pushes us to clearer analytical categories, misses the gist of how "law in action" has been

would take these interests further. They would use social science, and generate new research, in a more sophisticated way. They would recognize that informal, non-state, and local forms of ordering intersect with formal legal process (2005: 391–403). With Macaulay's characteristic patience, he reminds readers of seven important features of law in action that have yet to be fully incorporated into legal scholarship or training—but which, with help from a new legal realism, might yet have their day (2005:383–384); these include the fact that law is not free, that it is affected by many extra-legal forces like discretion and limited resources and much more (for the full list, see Macaulay's 1984 article based on his Mitchell Lecture given at SUNY Buffalo Law School, included in this volume). He points NLR toward an expansive program of research that would go beyond the tactics and techniques of the original realists, and examine law in action not only at the "top" in courts and legislatures, but on the street and in the home—and not just in the United States but including the global synapses that connect law in one part of the world with law in the rest of it. He also aims at a middle road that looks far beyond formal law, yet takes that law seriously as part of the system regulating behavior in society. And Macaulay urges an epistemological middle ground: lawyers must be critically aware of the limitations of social science methods and findings, while acknowledging that most well-done social science work is far superior to personal reflection and anecdotes (2005: 390–403). What would characterize the new legal realists—and set them off from the original realists—would be their more sophisticated grasp of these balancing acts, and a more informed use of the social science knowledge their balanced techniques would elicit.

In a number of subsequent talks and articles, Macaulay built further on the foundation that had been laid for a "new legal realism." In 2017, he co-edited the first volume of a two-volume set on NLR published by Cambridge University Press (Mertz et al. 2016); he was the author of the lead-off chapter, explaining the nature of the field (Macaulay 2016a). The chapter mentioned scholars whose realism grew out of the highly quantitative world of "empirical legal studies," as well as the cognitive psychologists who participate in "behavioral law-and-economics" research, and scholars who use a combination of empirical methods to understand why and when people fail to assert their rights as employees. All this work, according to Macaulay, along with other work in the law-and-society movement, demonstrates the benefits to be obtained when we use multiple methods and coordinate within interdisciplinary communities to better understand how law works. Macaulay also warns of the mistakes that can happen when this kind of coordination is missing: law-trained professors can badly misunderstand the limits of social science, while social scientists can make mistakes about legal technicalities or procedures. In either case, attempts to draw legal and policy conclusions from flawed use of empirics can go dangerously astray (as when a law professor mistakenly argued from faulty

used by various of the "realists." He concludes that "'law in action,' as it has developed in the law and society tradition, includes both concern with the gap between written and enforced law, and law in everyday life, viewed from the bottom up" (387, 387-391).

empirical evidence that the death penalty saves lives by deterring crime). At the root of many such errors, Macaulay continues to urge, is our preference for "elegant models" over more accurate but messier interdisciplinary study of the law in action (Macaulay 2016a).

In an article that he has characterized as his last word on NLR, Macaulay joined younger scholars in celebrating the movement's tenth anniversary (Macaulay 2016a).[8] In his typically generous style, he felt it time to step back and let younger scholars chart the future course of the new realism. But as a parting gesture, his article "unpack[ed] a proposed definition" that stressed the importance of a truly integrated form of law-and-social-science in which legal scholars allow social scientists to help them not only in answering questions but in framing the questions in the first place (Macaulay 2016b, pp. 166–167). And if social scientists are to study law on the ground, then they have to grasp and respect the "internal" world of lawyers, who often combine doctrine and strategy in ways that can be missed by too literal a social science approach (Macaulay 2016b, p. 152). Macaulay notes with optimism the growth of joint degree scholars well placed to bridge disciplinary divides, the important contribution of clinicians in law schools, and the growth of fruitful collaborations between law-trained and social-science-trained professors. Casting a broad and welcoming net, he discusses work from a variety of methodological and theoretical traditions, showing how important it is to talk across traditional disciplinary borders, and to do the work of "translation" between different fields. Again stressing the importance of real world considerations like cost and the way people cope with the limits of law in daily life, Macaulay's article tracks threads of research on "real law" from the 1960s through 2016; his footnotes bring a new generation of younger scholars into a seamless conversation with older generations.

***

It is a testament to Macaulay's continuing influence that long after he provided important fuel to two different intellectual movements within the study of law, he again took an important part in founding yet another one, in tune with a new generation that was looking for a way to integrate social science and legal research. Open to new angles on an old problem, he gave younger scholars sturdy support while also at times following their lead ... a balancing act few have been able to maintain over the length of a long and distinguished career. Macaulay is a person of rare humility (a trait not that common among scholars as well-known as he is). This humility has been a significant factor in his high reputation as a mentor and colleague. It contributes, too, to the quality of his scholarship, which is always open and questioning, always pushing for new insights. The articles reprinted in this collection are just a small sampling of his many publications on "real" law, law in action, law as it is lived in our society from bottom to top.

[8]In enviable fashion, Macaulay had by then turned out a series of articles in the field; in addition to the works discussed here, see also Macaulay 2006, 2015, Macaulay and Mertz 2013.

References

Bernstein, L. (1992). 'Opting Out of the Legal System: Contractual Relations in the Diamond Industry', *The Journal of Legal Studies* 21: 115-157.

Danzig, R. (1975). 'A Comment on the Jurisprudence of the Uniform Commercial Code', Stanford Law Review 27:621-635.

Ehrlich, E. (2009[1936]). *Fundamental Principles of the Sociology of Law.* New Brunswick, NJ: Transaction Publishers.

Ellickson, R. (1991). *Order without Law: How Neighbors Settle Disputes.* Cambridge: Harvard University Press.

Finman, T. and Macaulay, S. (1966). 'Freedom to Dissent: The Vietnam Protests and the Words of Public Officials', *Law & Society* 1966: 1-92.

Friedman, L.M., and Macaulay, S. (1967). 'Contract Law and Contract Teaching: Past, Present, and Future', *Wisconsin Law Review* 805-821.

Kalven, H. and Zeisel H. (1966). *The American Jury.* Boston: Little, Brown and Company.

Llewellyn, K. and Hoebel, E.A. (1941). *The Cheyenne Way: Conflict and Case Law in Primitive Jurisprudence.* Norman: University of Oklahoma Press

Macaulay, S. (1959). "Restitution in Context," University of Pennsylvania Law Review 107: 1133-1148.

Macaulay, J., and Macaulay, S. (1978). 'Adoption for Black Children: A Case Study of Expert Discretion,' in R. J. Simon (ed.), *Research in Law and Sociology: An Annual Compilation of Research* (Greenwich, CT: JAI Press), 265-318.

Macaulay, S. (1963). 'Non-Contractual Relations in Business: A Preliminary Study.' *American Sociological Review* 28: 55-67.

Macaulay, S. (1968). 'Law Schools and the World Outside Their Doors: Notes on the Margins of 'Professional Training in the Public Interest," *Virginia L. Review* 54: 617-636.

Macaulay, S. (1976). 'Access to the Legal Systems of the Americas: Informal Processes', Working Paper, Center for Law and Behavioral Science, Madison: University of Wisconsin.

Macaulay, S. (1981). *Professional Competence and the Law*, Dalhousie Continuing Legal Education Series 21, Faculty of Law, Dalhousie University, Halifax, Nova Scotia, Canada.

Macaulay, S. (1982). 'Law Schools and the World Outside Their Doors II: Some Notes on Two Recent Studies of the Chicago Bar', *Journal of Legal Education* 32(4): 506-542.

Macaulay, S. (1984). 'Law and the Behavioral Sciences: Is There Any There There?' *Law and Policy* 6: 149-187.

Macaulay, S. (1986). *Lawyer Advertising: Yes But . . .* Working Paper 1-2, Institute for Legal Studies, University of Wisconsin Law School, Madison WI.(40 pages).

Macaulay, S. (1994). 'Wisconsin's Legal Tradition', *Gargoyle* (Alumni Magazine of the University of Wisconsin Law School) 24: 6-10.

Macaulay, S. (2005). 'The New Versus the Old Legal Realism: "Things Ain't What They Used to Be"', *Wisconsin Law Review* 2005: 365-403.

Macaulay, S. (2006). 'Contracts, New Legal Realism, and Improving the Navigation of the Yellow Submarine', *Tulane Law Review* 80: 1161-1195.

Macaulay S. (2015). 'Bill Whitford: A New Legal Realist Seeking to Understand Law Outside the Law School's Doors', *Temple Law Review* 87: 725-737.

Macaulay, S. (2016a). 'A New Legal Realism: Elegant Models and Messy Law in Action', in E. Mertz, S. Macaulay and T. W. Mitchell (eds.), *The New Legal Realism, Volume 1: Translating Law-and-Society for Today's Legal Practice* (Cambridge: Cambridge University Press), 29-50.

Macaulay, S. (2016b). 'New Legal Realism: Unpacking a Proposed Definition', *UC Irvine Law Review* 6(2): 149-167.

Macaulay, S., Friedman, L., and Mertz, E. (2007a). *Law in Action: A Socio-Legal Reader.* New York: Foundation Press.

Macaulay, S., Friedman, L., and Mertz, E. (2007b). 'Introduction', in *Law in Action: A Socio-Legal Reader.* New York NY: Foundation Press.

Macaulay, S. and Mertz, E. (2013). 'New Legal Realism and the Empirical Turn in Law', in R. Baker and M. Travers (eds.), *Law and Social Theory*, 2nd edition (Oxford: Hart Publishing), 195-210.

Macaulay, S., Whitford, W., Hendley, K., and Lipson, J. (2016). *Contracts: The Introductory Course (4th edition).* Durham, N.C.: Carolina Academic Press.

Mentschikoff, S. (1952). 'The Significance of Arbitration – A Preliminary Inquiry', *Law and Contemporary Problems* 17: 698-710.

Mentschikoff, S. (1961). 'Commercial Arbitration', *Columbia Law Review* 61: 846-869.

Mertz, E., Macaulay, S., and Klug, H. (eds.) (2016). The New Legal Realism, Vol. 1: Translating Law-and-Society for Today's Legal Practice. Cambridge: Cambridge University Press.

Nelken, D. (1984). 'Law in Action or Living Law? Back to the Beginning Sociology of Law', *Legal Studies* 4: 157-174.

Richman, B. (2017). *Stateless Commerce: The Diamond Network and the Persistence of Relational Exchange.* Cambridge: Harvard University Press.

Shapiro, Fred and Michelle Pearse (2012) 'The Most-Cited Law Review Articles of All Time', Michigan Law Review 110: 1483-1520.

Part II
The Uncollected Papers of Stewart Macaulay

The Use and Non-Use of Contracts in the Manufacturing Industry

Stewart Macaulay

Editor's Note: For a number of years the author has been engaged in a study (which is continuing) of the use and nonuse of contracts by business. He has interviewed lawyers and businessmen from at least 75 firms, corresponded with at least 100 other businessmen, collected the form contracts used by about 850 firms, and read the cases involving the 500 largest manufacturing corporations.

On the basis of this study, the author delivered a talk at the Eighth Annual Corporate Lawyers' Institute at the University) of Wisconsin presented by the Corporate Counsel Section of the State Bar of Wisconsin and the University of Wisconsin Extension Law Department. Joseph E. Kerwin, General Patent Attorney, Allis-Chalmers Mfg. Co., was Chairman of the Institute. This talk was the introduction to a panel discussion. Panel members, in addition to Professor Macaulay and Mr. Kerwin, were the following corporate lawyers: Alfred P. Diotte. Secretary. Parker Pen Co.; John H. Lungren. Clark Oil & Refining Corp.; and John B. Baker, Allisk-Chalmers Mfg. Co. P. W. Nelson. Purchasing Agent. Ray-O-Vac Co., also was panel member. Both the talk and the panel discussion are printed here.

This article was original published in Practical Lawyer 9 (1963), 13–40, American Law Institute-American Bar Association Committee on Continuing Professional Education (ALI-ABA), Philadelphia. Reprinted with permission.

S. Macaulay (✉)
University of Wisconsin Law School, Madison, MI, USA
e-mail: smacaula@wisc.edu

D. Campbell (ed.), *Stewart Macaulay: Selected Works*, Law and Philosophy Library 133, https://doi.org/10.1007/978-3-030-33930-2_3

This presentation will first state the business practices concerning the use and nonuse of contracts, the explanations for these practices, and what lawyers do, and can do, about these practices. Then the panel will be asked:

- Whether or not they agree with these observations and explanations;
- How much effort, if any, businessmen and their lawyers should exert to run their affairs on the basis of contracts; and
- What other ideas these comments or the topic bring to mind.

Finally, questions and comments will be invited from members of the audience.

Findings and Explanations as to Business Practices concerning contracts

The Use and Nonuse of Contracts by Manufacturers

Attitudes

First, we must consider some common attitudes of businessmen toward contracts. These attitudes color the answers they give to questions about using or failing to use contracts and are also relevant to any explanation of what goes on.

Most businessmen I have talked to have an attitude toward contracts that can best be described as indifferent or even hostile to the whole idea. They remark, "Contracts are a waste of time. We've never had any trouble, because we know our customers and our suppliers. If we needed a contract with a man, we wouldn't deal with him." "Lawyers are overprotective and just get in the way of buying or selling. If business had to be done by lawyers as buyers and sellers, the economy would stop. No one would buy or sell anything; they'd just negotiate forever."

Yet, some businessmen look at things differently: "We've been sued (or our competitor has been sued), and one ought to be careful. There is no need to skate on thin ice legally. We've learned the hard way." "If you get the intent spelled out, you won't have any trouble. People perform commitments they understand. It's worth a little extra time to make sure everyone is talking about the same thing."

The last statement indicates that people may be thinking of different things when they talk about a "contract." They may be talking about planning a transaction. Whether or not an arrangement is legally enforceable, people may want an understanding about who is to do what and the effect of certain events, such as, what happens if one or the other fails to perform in some respect, or what happens if there is a strike or fire.

On the other hand, people may use the word "contract" to refer to the effect of law, and they may be thinking of several different effects of law:

- They may think of an understanding or a plan for a business exchange that will not run afoul of any of the many regulatory statutes: the Robinson-Patman, Sherman, or Clayton Acts, for example.

- They may think of an understanding that will ward off statutory or common law liability for their conduct: disclaimers or indemnity provisions for patent infringement, products liability, or negligence.
- They may think of a legal sanction that will induce one of the parties to perform his side of the agreement.

All of these ideas about contract are related, but they are sufficiently different to demand separate consideration.

I shall make one final comment about attitudes before reporting on practices. One's job influences his attitudes toward both planning a business exchange and the effect of law in this area:

- The salesman finds contract the work of the devil; it is just one more thing to get in the way of closing a sale. Moreover, suing or threatening to sue a customer who could place orders in the future is insanity.
- The purchasing agent tends to be indifferent. He may carefully plan transactions so that what he is buying and the price are defined, but he feels that provisions on strikes, late deliveries, warranties, etc., are a waste of time. Changed circumstances and disputes can be handled informally. Planning for such things and using, or threatening to use, legal sanctions is simply unnecessary. (Of course, if pressed, he may concede that he deals differently with building contractors on major construction jobs.)
- Financial people tend to be the strongest contract boosters. They want to "get the commitments spelled out."
- Outside counsel also tend to favor planning and the use of legal sanctions to settle disputes.
- The house counsel may have to temper his views favoring contract, because he is part of the organization.

Business Practices

Some businessmen say their firms carefully plan everything and arrange their agreements so they are legally enforceable contracts. But even these firms seldom use their legal rights openly. They are not going to sue anyone or threaten to do so, except in extraordinary situations. The contract remains in the background as a handy club to hold in reserve, in case it is necessary.

However, most firms I've seen do not plan this carefully, except in rare situations, and most are not concerned with legal sanctions. Important agreements often are worked out by the businessmen representing the buyer and the seller. Then an attorney is called in and told to draft something. He is given an hour or an afternoon for what should be several days' careful work. He is told, or he understands without being told, that he is not to "make it complicated." He is not going to be popular if he tries to make the businessmen "work out all the details." Too often the attorney discovers that the businessmen really have not reached agreement on the difficult issues, but have ignored them to avoid argument. If he wakes these sleeping dogs, he may cause his client to lose a bargain that his client thinks is a good one. If he drafts an ambiguous document avoiding hard issues, he exposes his client to serious risks, and his client will hold him responsible if any of the risks should materialize.

Alternatively, an attorney is not consulted at all at the planning stage. One businessman may write a letter with a proposal that is accepted by the other businessman. The letter will cover anything directly and immediately related to money, but little else. Or the businessmen may agree orally, and one may write a confirming letter stating his interpretation of their agreement. Often the one receiving such a letter remains silent, thus manifesting either acceptance of the interpretation in the confirmation, or complete disagreement and a refusal even to continue negotiations. Even when it is clear that the confirmation has been accepted, such letters are often terse and ambiguous.

When we turn to business practices concerning legal sanctions, we note many practices that make the enforceability of many business agreements very doubtful:

- Requirements contracts probably are not legally enforceable in Wisconsin and a few other states. Yet chemicals, containers, and a number of other things are still bought and sold there on the basis of requirements contracts.
- Decisions of the United States Court of Appeals for the Seventh Circuit indicate that a clause calling for "seller's price in effect at time and place of delivery" makes a contract unenforceable. The Wisconsin cases are not clear. Yet steel and steel products usually are sold this way in the area.
- Quotations and offers are often thought to be "firm" by Wisconsin businessmen. Yet orthodox theory says a quotation typically is only a preliminary negotiation and not binding, while an unaccepted offer may be withdrawn at any time before acceptance. Some courts have protected reliance on quotations and offers before acceptance, but the Wisconsin Supreme Court has yet to recognize the principle of section 90 of the Restatement of Contracts (American Law Institute Publishers, St. Paul, Minn., 1932) in any type of case.
- Firms often deal on the basis of "blanket orders subject to releases." Yet, the blanket order, if and when accepted by the seller, is no more than a continuing offer by the seller that the buyer accepts each time he sends the seller a release form. Moreover, these blanket orders frequently contain "agreements to agree in the future," termination-for-convenience clauses calling for cancellation charges to be "equitably adjusted," and change provisions that let the buyer make a completely different offer out of the order.
- Then we have the case contracts teachers like to talk about: the purchase order and acknowledgment forms that have different and inconsistent terms and conditions printed on the back. A great deal of business is done on an offer and counteroffer.
- At times executives write letters "explaining" the company's standard terms and conditions: "We'll never use clause No. 13 in dealing with you." Perhaps, I should call this "explaining away" the terms and conditions.

When disputes occur, there is a hesitancy to use legal sanctions or even to refer to the contract. Businessmen try to "work things out without bringing lawyers into it." Contract lawsuits and appellate cases concerning contract problems are relatively rare.

Why Business Can and Does Ignore Contract

Businessmen can deal without contract for obvious reasons. They have little, if any, trouble, even if they run risks of trouble. It is in the interest of everyone to perform agreements. There are personal relationships between buyers and sellers on all levels of the two corporations. Purchasing agents know salesmen, corporate presidents know corporate presidents, and so forth. This creates an incentive to get along in a continuing relationship. Most importantly, the two businesses want to do business in the future. You don't get repeat orders from unsatisfied customers, and one's reputation can influence future business if word gets around. And word does get around.

Using contract, of course, can have a number of disadvantages. If, in planning a business transaction, one is going to mention all the horrible things that can happen, he may scare off the other side so that the deal is lost. If one does set up a contractual relationship, there is some risk that one will get only performance to the letter of the contract most narrowly construed. Conversely, there is also a risk that one will be held to the letter of the contract and lose "flexibility." Using legal sanctions for breach of contract to settle disputes is costly. Usually it ends the business relationship between the parties. Furthermore, I need not tell you that lawsuits and lawyers cost money.

Of course, there is some use of legal sanctions. Typically, this occurs when someone with power thinks the gains from proceeding this way outweigh the costs. Often this is the lawyer's view, but lawyers do not always get to run their clients' affairs in the way lawyers might wish to run them.

What Are the Lawyers' Responses to the Nonuse of Contracts by Businessmen?

Lawyers respond in many different ways to the businessman's disinterest in, or impatience with, contract. Some would be satisfied to see no more than their clients' being more careful in planning important transactions. Some would be willing to let the common law and statutes fill in the gaps in agreements, but would like to see transactions arranged so they are legally enforceable in all cases. Others want both planning and enforceability.

Attorneys can take a number of steps to handle the situation:

- The lawyer can attempt to educate the businessman, or the businessman can educate the lawyer. That is, the lawyer can try to persuade his clients to plan carefully, with proper attention to legal sanctions, or the clients can convince the lawyer that it is not worth the effort.
- The lawyer may set up systems designed to pull out significant transactions so that they are reviewed. On the one hand, authority of the purchasing agent or sales

manager may be limited to transactions under a certain price or to specific types of transactions. If the transaction is outside this authority, it must be reviewed. On the other hand, one can review all communications from customers, suppliers, or both, when they fall into certain "trouble" categories—a supplier or customer on a "caution list," a government contract, an extreme products liability risk, etc.

- More commonly, lawyers turn to their old friend, draftsmanship. They do not try to bend the businessman's ways, but try to use his procedures in such a way as to plan and provide protection and legal sanctions. For example, it is decidedly unfashionable for any business to send out documents to customers or suppliers that do not have fine print on them. What is the effect of putting fine print on business forms? Practically, perhaps, you can get on the telephone and tell a customer or supplier, "Turn it over and read the seventh paragraph." One doesn't care whether or not the seventh paragraph actually is legally enforceable; it merely gives one a needed argument. But what is the legal effect of fine print? Could one use it if the other side had legal advice? This will depend on how the business documents have been used on previous occasions.

Some Common "Battle-of-the-Forms" Patterns:

The facts in time sequence	*Probable legal classification*
Our Client as Seller:	
[Case #1]	
(1) Catalog or quotation with our terms and conditions [t & c's] to buyer.	Offer (unlikely, but possible).
(2) Purchase order without additional or different t & c's to us.	Acceptance, and a contract on our terms.
[Case #2]	
(1) Catalog or quotation with our t & c's.	Preliminary negotiation.
(2) Purchase order without additional or different t & c's, but clearly in response to our catalog or quotation.	Offer, probably incorporating our t & c's by implication.
(3) Our acknowledgment with our t & c's.	Acceptance; contract on our terms.
[Case #3]	
(1) Catalog or quotation with our t & c's.	Preliminary negotiation.
(2) Purchase order with buyer's t & c's, which are additional to, or different from, ours.	Offer on buyer's terms.
(3) Our acknowledgment with our t & c's clearly stated.	Counteroffer. No contract yet.
(4) We ship goods quickly, and buyer accepts them.	Probably, acceptance of our counteroffer (if not lapsed), and a contract on our terms.
[Case #4]	
(1) Catalog or quotation with our t & c's.	Preliminary negotiation.
(2) Purchase order with buyer's t & c's and an acknowledgment drafted by buyer, which we are asked to sign and return.	Offer on buyer's terms.
(3) We sign and return buyer's form.	Acceptance, and a contract on the buyer's terms.

(continued)

The facts in time sequence	*Probable legal classification*
or	
(3a) We sign and return buyer's form and our own acknowledgment form as well.	? (Probably no acceptance.)
Our Client as Buyer:	
[Case #5]	
(1) Catalog or quotation with or without seller's t & c's.	Preliminary negotiation.
(2) Purchase order with our t & c's.	Offer on our terms.
(3) Seller acknowledges on a form without t & c's without reference to his catalog or quotation, or on our acknowledgment form that states seller accepts our terms and conditions.	Acceptance, and a contract on our terms.
or	
(3a) Seller ships the goods without sending any acknowledgment.	Acceptance, and a contract on our terms.
[Case #6] Same as Seller's case #3.	
[Case #7]	
(1) Oral quotation.	Preliminary negotiation.
(2) Purchase order with our t & c's.	Offer.
(3) Seller ships goods.	Acceptance, and a contract on our terms.
or	
(3a) A long lapse of time.	Buyer's offer lapses.
(3b) Seller ships goods.	An offer with t & c's supplied by the Sales Act or the UCC.
(3c) Buyer accepts the goods.	Acceptance and a contract. The buyer's original t & c's do not apply.

Seller as the Client

We begin by assuming our client is the seller. Obviously, we will be happy with Case #1 and Case #2. In both, our terms and conditions will govern, for the buyer has said, in effect, "I order on the seller's terms and conditions." If most of our client's customers use a purchase order without fine print on it, there is no problem.

Yet, problems arise when we get to Case #3, where the customer's purchase order has a set of terms and conditions on it. Assume we send out a quotation. This, typically, is not an offer. The buyer sends us his offer on his purchase order, which is loaded with demands that we give warranties and with statements that things will be rough if we are one-half hour late in making delivery. We, the seller, respond with our acknowledgment-of-order form that disclaims all warranties and names an approximate delivery date. We have made a counteroffer, and there is no contract at this point. Yet, in most instances, the difference in terms will not be noticed by either the buyer or the seller. The buyer will assume his order will be filled, and the seller will make the items and ship them. When the goods arrive at the buyer's plant, its personnel will accept them and pay the invoice sent by the seller, unless there are obvious defects. Now we can bring the "last-shot" principle into the game. The seller can argue that his acknowledgment form with his terms and conditions was an outstanding counteroffer that the buyer accepted when he accepted the goods and paid for them. By sending the last communication, the seller becomes the offeror, so that his clauses govern if the buyer takes the goods.

I would not place complete reliance on the "last-shot" solution to protect the seller. There are a number of arguments the buyer can make. The buyer's best one will be present when a long time passes between the sending of the seller's acknowledgment and the delivery of the goods. (See Case #7.) Offers lapse after a reasonable time for acceptance passes, and the acknowledgment may no longer have any legal effect. Thus, the sending of the goods could be taken as a new offer unencumbered by any terms and conditions; the seller would have made a contract under the gap-filling provisions of the Uniform Sales Act, with all of its warranties. A seller may not be too pleased to discover he is bound to such a contract.

Case #4 is a simple one. The seller merely surrenders, and agrees to use the buyer's provisions. At times, this may be a sensible business judgment. However, if the seller's sales department signs the buyer's acknowledgment without considering what it has swallowed, the seller's attorney may have some justifiable concern. Some sales departments always sign buyer's forms as a matter of course for "customer relations." Such good will may be purchased at a high price if anything goes wrong.

I have added an alternative third step to Case #4 to reflect a common practice. Sales people often are required to acknowledge on their firm's form; they also want to please the customer who asks that its acknowledgment form (which inevitably has clauses that conflict with the seller's provisions on its form) be used. So the sales people simply sign and return both acknowledgment forms. Everyone is happy—except a lawyer who is asked which, if either, set of provisions governs. Obviously, there is no satisfactory answer to this question.

Buyer as the Client

Now let's consider a different point of view. Let's review the position of our client when it is the buyer. To a great extent, all we need to do is reverse everything we've said so far. Thus, Case #5 is the same as Case #4, except that now we are pleased with the result, because the other party is the seller who surrenders.

Case #6 is the same as Case #3—the "last-shot" principle. However, when we are representing the buyer, we may not like the result, because the buyer's terms and conditions do not prevail. I have found that Case #3 is exceedingly common in manufacturing industry. From a legal standpoint, the seller is not bound to deliver, but if the buyer accepts the goods, he has accepted the seller's provisions, which are likely to disclaim responsibility for almost everything that might go wrong. Does it matter?

Some Attempted Drafting Solutions

Draftsmanship tends to breed more draftsmanship. Some attorneys are not satisfied with just putting terms and conditions on the back of all their clients' business forms. These attorneys draft "battle-of-the-forms" clauses that provide, in effect, whatever happens, "my terms and conditions govern, and yours do not." How do these clauses, printed on the back of purchase orders and acknowledgments, modify the analysis we have just worked through? Usually, they do not modify that analysis at all.

Many of the clauses used by business lawyers do no more than restate the result the law would reach in the absence of such provisions. This may be useful if one can read the provision to a customer or supplier and save a bit of argument. A few draftsmen attempt to do much more in clauses designed to solve some of the problems we've already discussed. One corporation, which we shall call "Sponsor," uses the following clause on the acknowledgment-of-order form it sends to its customers:

> The Buyer's receipt of this acknowledgment without prompt written objection thereto shall constitute an acceptance by the Buyer of all the terms and conditions set forth herein.

Apparently, this clause is supposed to deal with Case #3 we were talking about previously. You will recall that there the purchase order and acknowledgment have different provisions, so that no contract is formed, at least until the buyer accepts the goods. The quoted provision attempts to close the contract sooner on Sponsor's terms and conditions. However, silence cannot be made an acceptance this way. Sponsor's customer has a right to remain silent without binding itself to a contract on Sponsor's provisions, unless the customer and Sponsor agree, expressly or impliedly, otherwise. Of course. Sponsor might be able to use the clause in a telephone conversation with a customer who lacked legal advice, but if one is concerned with legal rights, this clause is ineffective.

At times, buyers attempt to use an equally ineffective device to deal with Case #3. You will remember that sellers usually get the "last shot" with their acknowledgment form, which will be accepted, and, thus, be effective, if the buyer accepts the goods. Another corporation, which we shall call "Modomoc," has on its purchase order:

> 28. The terms and conditions herein stated shall govern notwithstanding any terms and conditions stated on the acceptance of this order by Seller.

How can Modomoc take away the right to make counteroffers from the firms that sell to it? How can one say, "I will deem your counteroffer an acceptance on my terms"?

An interesting and amusing variation on this approach is used by two other corporations on their purchase orders. Somewhat regally they proclaim:

> The buyer recognizes that the Seller may for operating convenience desire to utilize its own form of acknowledgment, contract or other document in connection with this transaction. Therefore, it is agreed that any provisions in the form of acceptance used, which modify,

conflict with, or contradict any provision of this contract or order, shall be deemed to be waived.

One can imagine the reaction of a seller's attorney to this provision. Why did he waste all that time drafting terms and conditions for the firm's selling forms, if they were to be used only for internal "operating convenience"? Moreover, how can the buyer waive the seller's provisions without the consent of the seller?

The Overriding Agreement

As long as we are talking about the conduct of one party without the consent of the other, I do not think there is a solution to the "battle-of-the-forms" problems we've considered. Of course, the buyer and seller together can solve all of them, if they are willing to take the time to do so.

One device that should save a great deal of time is the overriding agreement. The buyer and seller work out an agreement that will govern all of their future dealings and will override the terms and conditions that may be printed on the purchase orders and acknowledgments used in these dealings.

One overriding agreement proposal in use has these provisions:

Gentlemen,

In order to expedite the handling of your purchase orders we propose that a general agreement be entered into between us as outlined herein to cover the conditions of sale which will be considered applicable to purchase orders which you may now have outstanding or which you may hereafter place with the Apparatus Sales Division of our Company.

* * *

5. OVERRIDING CHARACTER OF THIS AGREEMENT

This agreement shall replace any provisions, other than those provided for in Paragraphs 1, 2 and 4 above, set forth either on the face or on the reverse of your purchase order or on any attachment thereto or any document referred to therein, and provisions so replaced shall not be applicable to your purchases from us. This instrument contains the entire and only agreement between the parties respecting the purchase and sale of equipment, and supersedes all pre-existing agreements or arrangements between the parties.

6. MODIFICATION OR TERMINATION

To the extent that there is a subsequent mutual agreement in writing, one or more of the provisions of this agreement may be made inapplicable to or be modified in connection with particular purchases. However, no such change, modification, extension, renewal, ratification, rescission, discharge, abandonment or waiver of this agreement or any of the provisions hereof, or any representation, promise or condition relating to this agreement shall be binding upon the Company unless made in writing and signed on its behalf by a Vice President, Department General Manager, or a Manager—Sales District, Apparatus Sales Division. This agreement may be terminated by either party on written notice at any time with respect to any subsequent purchase orders.

An overriding agreement ought to solve most of the problems related to the "battle of the forms." However, one must negotiate such an agreement, and one may have to make concessions in the process of negotiation. Clearly, this solution makes sense only when one is going to make many repeated sales to a particular source or many repeated purchases from a particular source.

The Uniform Commercial Code

Finally, an attorney can respond to the "battle-of-the-forms" problems by doing nothing and relying on the Uniform Commercial Code to protect his client in those states where it has been enacted. Section 2-207 of the Code provides:

> (1) A definite and seasonable expression of acceptance or a written confirmation which is sent within a reasonable time operates as an acceptance even though it states terms additional to or different from those offered or agreed upon, unless acceptance is expressly made conditional on assent to the additional or different terms.
>
> (2) The additional terms are to be construed as proposals for addition to the contract. Between merchants such terms become part of the contract unless:
>
> (a) the offer expressly limits acceptance to the terms of the offer;
> (b) they materially alter it; or
> (c) notification of objection to them has already been given or is given within a reasonable time after notice of them is received.
>
> (3) Conduct by both parties which recognizes the existence of a contract is sufficient to establish a contract for sale although the writings of the parties do not otherwise establish a contract. In such case the terms of the particular contract consist of those terms on which the writings of the parties agree, together with any supplementary terms incorporated under any other provisions of this Act.

The Code poses two questions:

- Is a contract formed when a purchase order and acknowledgment have inconsistent or different terms?
- If so, what are the terms of that contract?

Subsection (1) changes the common law counteroffer rule when the purchase order and acknowledgment have additional or different terms and conditions. Under this subsection, there is a contract created if:

- There is "a definite . . . expression of acceptance. . ." and
- The ". . . acceptance is [not] expressly made conditional on assent to . . ." the new terms.

Suppose the seller's acknowledgment form with its additional and different provisions states, "If these terms are not acceptable, Buyer must so notify Seller at once." In *Roto-Lith, Ltd. v. F. P. Bartlett & Co.*, 297 F.2d 497 (1st Cir. 1962), the Court found this language made the acknowledgment "expressly . . . conditional on assent to" the seller's terms.

What would a court do with the almost universal phrase on acknowledgment forms, "We acknowledge your order subject to the terms and conditions on the reverse side hereof?" Would this be "a definite . . . expression of acceptance . . . [not] expressly made conditional on assent to . . ." the seller's terms?

Assuming we get past subsection (1), we have a contract, although the purchase order and acknowledgment have additional or different terms. What are the terms of this contract? Subsection (2) deals with this question:

- All of the terms of the purchase order are part of the contract.
- The additional terms on the acceptance:
  - Are not part of the contract if the transaction is not between merchants,
  - Are part of the contract if it is between merchants, unless any of the qualifications in subsections (2) (a), (b), or (c) are applicable.
- Terms on the acceptance that differ from the purchase order are not part of the contract.

Therefore, when the purchase order is the offer, as it is in most cases, all of the buyer's terms prevail, and only a very few of the seller's become part of the contract. The seller's advantages, under the "last-shot" principle are gone, as his acknowledgment, if it qualifies under subsection (1), is no longer a counteroffer that will be accepted by the buyer's acceptance of the goods.

However, many acknowledgments probably will not come under subsection (1), for they will fail to meet its requirements. What happens then? We must turn to subsection (3), which has been overlooked by many people.

It provides that, although the writings exchanged do not create a contract, there is a contract if the parties recognize the existence of one by their conduct. I would argue they would do this by exchanging a purchase order and acknowledgment that do not fall under subsection (1) of section 2-207, and then shipping the goods and accepting them.

If this is conduct that recognizes the existence of a contract, what are the terms of that contract? Subsection (3) says the terms will be:

- All those on which the purchase order and acknowledgment agree—typically, price, description of the goods, and, perhaps, the delivery date—and
- The additional terms needed for a contract that are found in the Uniform Commercial Code — for example, all of the implied warranties imposed by the Code in the absence of an agreement otherwise.

Many sellers will not be pleased by this result. Here, too, the seller loses the "last-shot" advantage; under the Code the advantage swings to the buyer insofar as warranties are concerned. Of course, there are provisions in the Code that are favorable to sellers that would be part of a subsection (3) contract.

You can live with section 2-207 of the Code. Drafting can control subsections (1) and (2). An overriding agreement would avoid subsection (3). But is it worth that effort?

Let's turn to the panel now. I hope I've raised a number of things that will interest them.

Panel Discussion

Mr. Kerwin: Mr. Macaulay, is this a sad commentary on contract law or a compliment to business?

Mr. Macaulay: I suppose both. Business can get along, I'm sure, running on this kind of pattern. I'm not so sure that contract law ought to try to catch up with business every time it twists and turns. I think contract law has some functions of its own, because it is used, after all, in transactions where you don't have a close personal relationship. And it may well be that in those transactions—I'm thinking about the door-to-door salesman of home siding, and so on—we want to have some rather strict and rigorous tests.

Problem of Case #3

Mr. Baker: I would like to ask, just to start the ball rolling, whether or not you have ever come across a court decision faced with this problem of Case #3 and how the court resolved the problem. I have never seen any court decision on that question.

Mr. Macaulay: There are two important cases on it. The first is *Poel v. Brunswick-Balke-Collender Co.,* 216 N.Y. 310, 110 N.E. 619 (1915), where the acknowledgment said, "This acknowledgment, which in any event you must confirm . . ." This was the only different clause; everything else was the same. The Court said that made it a counteroffer, and so no contract was created.

And then there is *Fire Ass'n of Phila. v. Allis-Chalmers Mfg. Co.,* 129 F. Supp. 335 (N.D. Iowa 1955), which upholds the "last-shot" principle, that is, when the goods go out and the buyer accepts them, he is accepting the seller's counteroffer. Those are leading cases on the subject; they are about what we have to go on.

This problem doesn't get litigated, and that fact, in itself, is interesting. I have run through the reported decisions involving the 500 largest corporations from 1946 to 1960, and looked to see when and why they get into appellate litigation. You just don't find many contracts cases. Most that you find involve terminating franchises. Of course, there are cases involving products liability, if you want to call that a contract situation. But as for the "battle of the forms," there are not many cases at all. Again, it may be the success of business or the failure of contract law.

Use and Nonuse of Formal Contracts

Mr. Kerwin: Do you know why your purchasing agents don't get into legal problems on these?

Mr. Nelson: I was thinking of this as you went along. You certainly described our organization with this outline of the way business operates. I would say that we started off with zero contracts and legalities, and we have gradually brought up our thinking along those lines. I would think that, right now, the biggest stimulant to our checking the legality of our contracts or our dealings probably stems from government rules and regulations. This has been a stimulus, at least, if not the end result. We are looking more and more at the legal aspects of our dealings.

I think possibly other reasons why we are going more toward this is the size of the companies, the mergers that are taking place nowadays, and the removing of personalities from some of the business dealings.

You certainly described our company very accurately, because we do some of the things that you have mentioned. We do not actually have a pattern. We have contracts on all of the large items we buy, and we also have some contracts on small items. In the middle, however, there is quite a lack of contracts. I can't actually say that we have a pattern that we're following, although I think we're tending and leaning more and more toward more formal contracts in all areas. There was a time when we would accept a contract and look at it, generally speaking, from the standpoint of the prices, sign it, and return it.

Presently, every contract, even if it's a repeat of a contract we have had, is sent through our legal department. There was a time not too long ago when we didn't have house counsel, although we have always had counsel on retainer fees. I think we are tending increasingly towards the more formal method of doing business in all of our dealings.

Mr. Macaulay: Do you think bringing house counsel in would tend to push people towards more formal contracts?

Mr. Nelson: I think so.

Mr. Kerwin: Al Diotte is in management position. He sits on the board, and I wonder if, from the management point of view, there is a tendency to direct this one way or the other.

Mr. Diotte: Joe, that might be considered a loaded question to have to answer before a group of lawyers. I think, as Stewart mentioned earlier, there is a continuous educational process that goes on between businessmen and their attorneys, whether they be outside or house counsel. Some lawyers make a serious mistake, I feel, when they overlook the fact that they are retained to provide a service to business. The primary purpose remains the conduct of a business. Time is often of the essence, and under these circumstances, I feel, lawyers provide their greatest service in guiding relationships around the major obstacles and pitfalls on a timely basis.

It is extremely difficult and dangerous to generalize in this area. The answer really depends upon the type of business relationship being considered at the moment.

For example, in our merchandising area, our legal division maintains strict surveillance. Not only do our attorneys play an important role in developing our various programs, but they also monitor the actual operation of the programs very closely.

In the supply-purchasing area, we tend to be somewhat more relaxed in our day-to-day operation. A close working relationship exists between our purchasing and legal personnel, and, over the years, purchasing has developed a "feel" as to what should be cleared with the legal division before proceeding. This is not, by far, a perfect solution to the problem. It does result in our operating in the Case #3 area we have been discussing. I will say, however, that to the best of my knowledge, we have never had a problem arise in this area that was not settled on a friendly basis.

Our tendency is to develop continuing purchaser-supplier relationships. This undoubtedly has some bearing on our attitude and the results achieved in this area. Many of our suppliers are small operators. On occasion, we provided working capital or the capital required to install some piece of equipment needed to furnish the parts we ordered. These situations are recognized as exceptions by our purchasing department, and the legal division is brought in from the very beginning.

Sales, acquisitions, mergers, and other matters of that nature require an answer substantially different from that pertaining to our day-today purchasing activities.

Credit Transactions

Mr. Macaulay: I would like to direct a question to John Lungren. He is with an oil company, and, once in a while, I buy gasoline on credit. I wonder how often they have trouble with that kind of contract relationship.

Mr. Lungren: Very often. With credit cards, the credit transaction, the company more or less runs under what you might call basic common law. On the back of your credit card—and every oil company does this—you put three or four basic rules of handling of the credit cards. The customer undoubtedly does not read these rules, but the customer is pretty well stuck with them.

For example, we have found several cases in various jurisdictions holding that if the customer loses the credit card, the customer is responsible for the credit card until he notifies the company in writing. There is a recent case in New York where a man lost his air travel card, and it was found by some vagrant on the streets of Manhattan. He promptly went to Hong Kong, believe it or not, on the air travel card. The Court held that the executive had lost his air travel card and was responsible for this rather substantial bill.

In the oil industry, and in our company particularly, we have tried our best to formalize contract procedure. However, in the area that Professor Macaulay is talking about, which is the purchase contract for supplies and for things that are needed to conduct business, there is not much that you can do. We go to U. S. Steel and ask for certain supplies; if we don't accept their terms, then we do not purchase their supplies.

Influence of the Government

However, when it gets to the area of the many contracts to run an integrated business—I am referring particularly to franchise agreements—we are most careful to draft each contract, or at least have our forms used, for two reasons:

- Usually, the people we are dealing with are not financially substantial.
- We have found that the Government is sitting in as a silent member on our board of directors every time we make a move. In the oil industry, which is constantly being investigated, the franchise contracts we have must be absolutely in order. If they are not, then we face a friendly visit from the office of the attorney general of some state or the federal Government.

I'd like to ask Mr. Baker to comment on this government approach to contracts. Is the Government sitting at your right hand?

Mr. Baker: I have never looked at it in that way, but I believe that is a fair statement, really, when you consider it from the antitrust angle. I don't know that they are sitting at your right hand when you are discussing terms and conditions of your dealer agreements generally. In the automobile business, of course, they are, because they have a federal law. Automobile sales to dealers are covered by a statute called the "Dealer's Day in Court Act."

Mr. Lungren: I think we are feeling more and more the influence of the Government in our business.

Mr. Baker: Yes, because the Government does so much purchasing. When you have a prime contract with the Government, and you start procuring from suppliers, the prime contract requires your suppliers to agree to certain things, too. To that extent, they are dictating the terms that are contained in your purchase order.

Mr. Macaulay: It seems to me, as I look at the backs of purchase orders, acknowledgments, and other business documents, there are a number of termination and change clauses that seem to be modifications of the standard government provisions. I don't know if companies are making use of them, but they are printing these clauses on the back of their forms more and more for use in their nongovernment business. There seems to have been some development in that direction.

Mr. Baker: There has been. I can cover several of your points in commenting on that. We were dealing with a company some years ago, and we were unhappy with their standard terms and conditions. We finally were able to negotiate one of these overriding agreements, and, in the process of negotiation, the purchasing agent said, "Well, I'd like to see in this overriding agreement a termination clause such as is found in government contracts." I said, "Nuts to that." I spoke out of turn, I'm afraid. "Why should we start letting the Government start writing our contracts for us?" "Well," he said, "I like that kind of provision. It seems to me to be a perfectly fair one." On that basis we took it. So I think there is a tendency to recognize some of those contract provisions as acceptable.

Overriding Agreements

On the question of whether or not the overriding agreements are worth the trouble, I rather think they are. It takes quite a time to negotiate them. When I first joined Allis-Chalmers in 1939, I had been there about three months when in came a volume of terms and conditions from a company to which the lawyers commented at great length, pointing out how unfair and unreasonable we thought they were. Finally, in about 1954, we negotiated one of these overriding contracts. The battle went back and forth for 15 years. We did business with them in the meantime. I don't know what the products actually were, or what contracts we took in the interim. However, we finally negotiated an overriding agreement, and now everybody is very happy. We don't worry about the fine print any more. You see, the basic contract controls the sale.

Mr. Macaulay: But has it been your experience that an overriding agreement takes a great deal of effort?

Mr. Baker: Yes, and one reason is that the bigger the company the less likely they are to want to modify their terms for just anybody who comes along.

You asked if contract law matters. I certainly think it does.

Mr. Macaulay: That's reassurring.

Mr. Baker: Contract law, I think, matters not only to the lawyers but also to the commercial people. The first time we get called in on almost any contract of the Company is when there is some dispute between the Company and the customer. The Company requests an opinion from us as to the Company's position. I sometimes feel that all they are hoping for is that we will tell them that they have

> nothing to worry about, that they are in the right. Because then they can go to the customer and say, "We have consulted our legal department, and they tell us that you are all wet."

Basically, the problem here is one of time. If every contract were negotiated between lawyers, you just would not get any business done.

Difficulties with Formal Procedures

Mr. Macaulay: What about setting up formal procedures to pull out particular cases? There are two ways of doing this: you wait until someone comes to you when they spot something, or you set up some organized way of handling this. I'm wondering if a dollar limit might be practicable.

Mr. Baker: The difficulty with that, as far as I am concerned, is that, technically speaking, the $500 contract can cause you just as much grief or more than a $5 million one. You get into products liability, breach of warranty, and have just as heavy damages in one as the other, so that your procedure is not going to do much good.

Another thing, in connection with sales of our products—particularly the heavy line goods, condensers, turbines, transformers, switch gear that we manufacture—of course, these are sold mostly to utilities and municipalities. The municipality, in contracting, sends its request for a bid, stating the terms and conditions that will apply. Then you either bid in accordance with those terms and conditions, or you take what exceptions you want, but usually, if you take an exception, you are thrown out as irregular. In that area, the products department frequently send us the contract papers with a request for our comments on them. We do comment, and I sometimes wonder whether, after the sales people get the comments, they don't just throw them in the wastebasket, because they want the job.

Another factor is controlling here, and that is whether it is a buyer's market or a seller's market. If it is a seller's market, you can pretty well tell your customer, "You're going to buy on these conditions or not at all," and he will take them. Unfortunately, most of the time it is a buyer's market, and you just have to take your chances.

I can see no solution to this problem. I haven't let it bother me, however, because I have always said—and this is my own opinion and not necessarily that of the legal department—there are two ways to draft a contract. One is to draft it so clearly that there is no possibility of any argument. The other is to make it so confused that nobody knows what it means, and then you could probably settle the thing if you get into an argument.

I can't help feeling that the problem here is basically the outgrowth of the second approach, namely, that we're going to muddy up the water, so that we don't know who is going to come out ahead, but at least we have a practical method of dealing.

Mr. Kerwin: Do you like lawyers who talk along those lines? Is that the kind of thinking that pleases the purchasing agent?

Mr. Nelson: Fairly recently we were trying to buy a piece of equipment for about $3500. The company manufacturing this piece of equipment had a standard contract, which they sent along. We disagreed with some of the terms. In attempting to rewrite them, it took several exchanges finally to come to terms, when, actually, right from the outset, I think we were both in agreement as to what we were going to do. It just got involved in terminology. This is disturbing, at least, to purchasing, and this is when we tend to make some uncomplimentary remarks about our lawyer friends.

Our approach to disregarding the contract, if it doesn't actually do what we want it to do, is to say, "It won't be enforced." Our approach to wording of contracts has been pretty much this: "Let's put down what we both want. Let's not put a term in there that one of us doesn't like or neither one of us likes. If we don't like it and don't intend to use it, let's not have it in there. Let's spell it out as clearly and concisely as possible."

I do think that Uncle Sam and the various other levels of Government are sitting at the right hand on a lot of these dealings.

The Role of Lawyers

Mr. Macaulay: One of the things I'm trying to do is to get together a supplement to a casebook on business practices, as related to contracts materials. Should lawyers give strictly legal advice, or should they take a practical business-bargaining approach? Should they give you advice on the law and let you do the bargaining, or should they say, "We should do this tactically, and then that tactically, and so on"?

Mr. Nelson: I think we have to do a little of both. I think we have to become more legal-minded and they more business-minded. I appreciate this is a poor answer to the question, but actually I think what we need is to have some sort of a meeting ground, where everybody gives a little and everybody understands a little bit more of the other fellow's problem.

Mr. Diotte: I was very much interested in an article that Mr. Brown of Allis-Chalmers wrote some time ago on separating the corporate counsel from the business management of the corporation. I personally feel there is a lot of merit in keeping house counsel as lawyers. As such, our primary responsibility is to advise our clients as to their legal rights, requirements, and liabilities.

When you try to wear two hats, one concerned with the legal aspects and the other with the commercial aspects of a situation, there is at least a tendency to become confused. I think it is very difficult to wear both hats. What do you think?

Mr. Baker: I agree with you. I don't feel the lawyer should make the commercial decisions. The difficulty, of course, is that many times the people who make those decisions don't consider the things they should and don't comprehend the many pitfalls. The lawyer, therefore, has to know what to look for and be able to explain the problem areas to the businessman.

I have always told our people that the problem is not so much, in this area of guarantees and warranties, what the wording actually is as what you are selling. If you are selling a standard commodity for a standard application, the theoretical risks still are there, but the practical risks are minimal, it seems to me. I think the lawyer many times has to get it across somehow to the businessman just where his risks are. It would be nice if the lawyer and the businessman could sit down a few times and negotiate contracts, because then the two of them would get educated very fast.

Mr. Macaulay: What about my description of business practices? I am sure I was making a slight overstatement in saying that the lawyer does not get called into the discussion when an important contract is negotiated, or gets called in only at the very last minute and is told to whip out something. Does this happen?

Mr. Baker: Oh, sure. Then, of course, they wonder why the lawyer can't turn a crank and get their contract done for them.

Mr. Kerwin: I think sometimes they often use the expression, "You've heard what we have said; you can put that in simple terms, can't you?"

Do we have some comments from the audience on some of these problems or questions? How about experience in particular areas?

Section 2-207 of the Uniform Commercial Code

Question: I want to ask to have something repeated that was said earlier about the two documents with inconsistent terms and conditions. Are you saying that the advantage under the Commercial Code is the buyer's? Will the Code enforce the buyer's terms so far as there are conflicts, because the seller has assented to the buyer's terms with a counteroffer?

Mr. Macaulay: Yes, if the acknowledgment comes under the first two subsections, the buyer's terms will tend to prevail. If the seller says simply,

> "We hereby acknowledge your order. See terms and conditions on reverse side," I think—I'm guessing, because we don't have cases enough to know—you have a contract. All of the buyer's terms will apply. The seller's conflicting terms are out. He only gets the additional terms that do not materially modify the transaction, if the buyer hasn't objected to them. That will swing the advantage to the buyer.

The seller also loses his present advantage in the so-called subsection-(3) situation, that is, when the acknowledgment comes in stating, "Here are our terms, and only our terms apply, and we mean it." There is no contract under the first two subsections, but assume that the goods are shipped and accepted. Then there is a contract with the terms on which the purchase order and acknowledgment agree. Basically, I suppose, that will be description, price, maybe delivery date, although sellers hedge a lot: "We might get it there on time." Then the Commercial Code applies all of its provisions for anything that is not agreed on.

I think that would be to the seller's disadvantage, because most sellers I have talked with attempt to limit their warranty liability to less than that provided by the Commercial Code. The Commercial Code provides for consequential damages, and I haven't found a seller yet who is going to take consequential damages, if he can get out of it. I think that Section 2-207 of the Commercial Code takes a lot away from sellers.

Question: If both documents contain this language: "Only our terms govern," then what would you say?

Mr. Macaulay: I think you have a subsection-(3) situation. You don't have a contract until the goods are shipped.

Question: Then the worst the buyer can do is what the Code says?

Mr. Macaulay: Yes.

Question: He is not stuck with the seller's terms?

Mr. Macaulay: I think that is right. I think the Code helps buyers here much more than sellers. It doesn't necessarily have to, because you can get more documents going back and forth making seller the offeror. You get some nice variations if you have a blanket order with a release procedure. Then the buyer may have the "last shot." Under the Code, the buyer may be sending the acceptance, and then sellers are favored. Perhaps, I should say offerors are favored, and buyers usually turn out to be the offerors.

I think the basic notion of Section 2-207 of the Code may not be a realistic one. The draftsmen seem to have thought that the one thing that shouldn't happen is to have inconsistent forms just tossed into the files. There is one question we could ask: Does it put too much of a burden on a purchasing or sales department to demand that it really check these things over? The Code puts quite a premium on looking at all business forms.

Mr. Nelson: We have done very little looking. I think, possibly, it is indicated we should do more, and our purchasing department, along with other purchasing departments, should do more. How much more I am not prepared to say.

Attitudes of Purchasing Agents

Mr. Macaulay: Of course, there are a lot of purchasing agents who have said just about the opposite. A lot of them have the attitude that reviewing fine print is all nonsense. One called it "legalistic propaganda."

Mr. Nelson: I think you probably get that feeling from some purchasing people, although their attitudes, I feel, are changing.

Mr. Kerwin: Is this something that the purchasing agents talk about at conferences that they go to?

Mr. Nelson: I would say they are beginning to talk about it more than they have. It is a fairly recent thing in purchasing discussions.

Until the last two or three years, purchasing people were not interested in legal affairs or contracts. They wanted their way, and if they got into trouble, they expected counsel to bail them out. They did very little to keep themselves from getting into trouble. I suppose primarily on the basis that there are very few cases of actual litigation along these lines, as Professor Macaulay pointed out, you have trouble citing cases to study.

The purchasing agent has been in the position where, fortunately or unfortunately, depending on how you look at it, he could jam about anything down a buyer's throat and make him like it. This is probably one of the reasons why purchasing hasn't been too interested in the legal aspects of some of these things. It's pretty easy for a large account to go back to the supplier and, directly or indirectly, threaten him with a loss of business and get him to forget most of the legal aspects of a particular small incident.

We don't like to do it. As a matter of fact, we don't tell the rest of our people, particularly quality control, how easy it is to do some of these things. We are afraid they might give us more opportunity to do it.

Mr. Macaulay: I have noticed that businessmen seem to feel that they can cancel orders any time, until some significant form of reliance has taken place. Apparently, they feel they are not really committed to anything until, as some people put it, "the metal is cut." The signing of a document, therefore, is not as important practically as we tend to assume it is in contracts classes.

Mr. Nelson: I think that is the general impression that purchasing people have and the attitude they take and the approach they take. I think that, generally speaking, sellers will accept cancellations until they have actually incurred some expense.

Mr. Kerwin: What about engineering expense, Phil?

Mr. Nelson: I think you would probably have to tie that into a specific case each time. Let me pin this down to a specific. A box company designed a machine for us that sets boxes up. They were not in the machine business; this was a gimmick for selling boxes to save us some money. I went to them and said, "Now, don't you think we had better sign a contract for the boxes that go over this thing, because what is to prevent me from taking your machine and buying new boxes?" The salesman said, "Thank goodness you said that. I was trying to find a way to say it."

We feel that we have some responsibility along those lines, and we have tried to live up to it. In this case, finally, we did not sign the contract, but we have done business with that same outfit for something like 10 years. The reason why I thought we ought to sign a contract was that the salesman and I made the deal, but what happens if he or I or neither of us is here tomorrow? I think that is one of the reasons from a purchasing angle that we should give more thought to contracts. Personnel changes on both sides, or one side, of the fence can affect these things drastically.

But we feel that we do carry or incur responsibility for engineering, creativity, and the like. We have turned down the uses of things. People have offered things to us that possibly were too expensive or something like that. We might have been able to revamp them and use them and knock the price down, but rather than pirate the ideas or the engineering, we have done one of two things. We have either asked to buy it outright, or we have foregone the use of it, rather than pirate the idea.

Franchise Contracts

Mr. Macaulay: Are franchises contracts? Most of the franchises I have seen tend to say that, "As long as we like you, we'll be nice, and you'll be nice, but we're not promising to do anything, and you can't hold us to anything." Now, is that what a franchise is, or is a franchise a contract?

Mr. Diotte: We do not consider the Parker Pen Company franchise to be merely a piece of paper stating that the two parties will be nice to each other. We consider it to be a contract, with each party making definite commitments to the other. Parker's commitment is to continue to sell to the dealer so long as his credit standing is satisfactory, and the dealer's commitment is to give adequate promotional support to Parker products. It does contain a mutual cancellation clause, however.

Where legal, our franchise also operates as a fair trade agreement. Of course, many of the rights provided are dependent upon whether or not the dealer is located in a fair trade state.

Mr. Baker: I suppose legally they are executory contracts, but they are still contracts.

Mr. Macaulay: They are still contracts, but are they much more than a charter that says, "We'll be nice fellows as long as you're nice fellows." Do they bind anyone to anything?

Mr. Baker: As you complete a transaction, yes. Isn't it true of almost any contract that once it's completed, the obligations arise?

Mr. Lungren: That is why I made that comment about Government. All my corporate law life, which has been some 10 years in the oil industry, the state and federal Governments have had a big hand in the so-called franchise contracts of all the oil companies of the United States. For example, Congressman Roosevelt, from Los Angeles, heads a congressional committee that has been investigating the oil industry dealer situation and their merchandising for some years.

The District Court for the Northern District of California handed down a decision that was turned into a consent decree with all the oil companies of that area, stating specifically what had to be in a franchise contract for the oil industry to retail outlets, dealers, lessees, whatever you would call them. If the contract did not contain these items, the man was an employee, and the company had all the duties and obligations toward him that it would have toward any other employee.

In this franchise business, the District Court said that a lease with a service station operator shall be for a period of not less than two years and noncancellable on the part of the company, but cancellable on the part of the dealer. This is something that I think each one of you will get more and more into in your industry and your company, as time goes on. Don't you think there is a trend towards government intervention in these various fields?

Mr. Macaulay: Yes. You have a statute covering automobile dealers, and you also have the situation you are describing in the oil industry. We are beginning to get a line of cases from a number of states that say you cannot cancel a franchise that is terminable at will, unless you cancel in good faith. And the court in all its wisdom will tell you what good faith means on a case-to-case basis, which means that it isn't terminable at will. Of course, some states have rejected this doctrine. In Wisconsin, you can terminate at will.

Mr. Lungren: For example, a recent North Carolina decision held that an oil company could not sell in the same area at a different price to two independent purchasers of its product. If you take that along the logical route, then you're going to get to the point where Mr. Baker can't sell a tractor to Mr. Diotte for less than he sells one to me, if we both live in Milwaukee, Wisconsin.

Dual Standards

Question: I want to ask the panel whether or not they use a dual set of contracts standards in doing business with big business or small business. From a practical standpoint, will a company do things for a large business it would not do for a small business?

Mr. Kerwin: Does anyone want to offer an answer to that?

Mr. Baker: I think it would primarily be for the purchasing agent to answer that. Legally, I would say that we have never knowingly treated any large customer differently from a small one.

Mr. Nelson: It makes a difference, I think. We treat each case individually, or attempt to treat it individually. I think that we would tend to feel more obligated to a smaller company for extra services than to a large company. The larger companies, generally speaking, have engineering and creative departments, while the smaller companies, quite often, have to go outside to procure some of the special services. However, big companies will shove you around, and sometimes you have to take what they offer.

I would say that it is more than a double standard. It is a problem that has to be answered almost every time that it arises and the individual circumstances considered.

Conclusion

Mr. Kerwin: Stewart, would you like to conclude?

Mr. Macaulay: One purpose of my project is to turn up information that may be useful to house counsel and attorneys with a business practice. I hope that reporting on the practices I have found and analyzing their legal effect has been useful to business lawyers. My project will be going on for a long time, and if something comes up that you think I should hear about, I would appreciate a letter.

The end to be attained in the development of the law of contract is the supremacy, not of some hypothetical, imaginary will, apart from external manifestations, but of will outwardly revealed in the spoken or the written word. The loss to business would in the long run be greater than the gain if judges were clothed with power to revise as well as to interpret. Perhaps, with a higher conception of business and its needs, . . . the time will come when even revision will be permitted if it is revision in consonance with established standards of fair dealing, but the time is not yet. In this department of activity, the current axiology still places stability and certainty in the forefront of the virtues.

Benjamin Nathan Cardozo, Selected Writings 235-236
(Fallon Publications, New York, 1947).

The Standardized Contracts of United States Automobile Manufacturers

Stewart Macaulay

Introduction

21 The automobile industry in the United States is large, very complex and has great economic power. The major manufacturers are run as bureaucratic structures designed to operate efficiently at all levels. Those people and organizations that deal with the manufacturers have patterned their conduct to accommodate this model of economic efficiency. However, new models of automobiles must be designed several years before they are offered to the public and the demand for new automobiles fluctuates significantly. Bureaucratic operation in the service of economic efficiency, time-span and fluctuating demand are all critical factors which are reflected in many different kinds of exchange transactions found in this industry. In this paper we will consider some of the exchange relationships between the manufacturers, and their suppliers, their dealers and their customers in order to generalize about contract as it is found in this kind of large scale industry. This discussion will be limited to practices within the

This article was original published in International Encyclopedia of Comparative Law 7 (1974), 18–34. Reprinted with permission.
Professor, Faculty of Law, University of Wisconsin, Madison (USA).
This paper is based on *Macaulay,* Law and the Balance of Power (New York 1966); *Whitford,* Strict Products Liability and the Automobile Industry – Much Ado About Nothing: 1968 Wis.L. Rev. 83, cited Strict Products Liability; *idem,* Law and the Consumer Transaction – A Case Study of the Automobile Warranty: 1968 Wis.L.Rev. 1006, cited Law; and an unpublished study of the "blanket order" system by the author. I would like to thank Professors *William C. Whitford* and *Robert Gordon,* Dr. *Jacqueline R. Macaulay* and Mrs. *Ruth Wright* for suggestions about this paper.

S. Macaulay (✉)
University of Wisconsin Law School, Madison, WI, USA
e-mail: smacaula@wisc.edu

D. Campbell (ed.), *Stewart Macaulay: Selected Works*, Law and Philosophy Library 133, https://doi.org/10.1007/978-3-030-33930-2_4

United States and the consequences of those practices under its legal system. We lack data for a full comparative analysis. Nonetheless what is said here is likely to have relevance in other nations. The automobile manufacturers are important transnational corporations and their practices are models for other large corporations. While the precise legal techniques used will differ, it is likely that the goal of risk avoidance and minimization will be pursued in all nations in which such organizations operate.[1]

A. Contracts to Build and Sell Cars

i. The Manufacturers and Their Suppliers[2]

a. Description of the Relationship

22 Although the manufacturers can and do make in their own plants some of almost all of the parts which go into an assembled automobile, they also buy many of these parts from suppliers. There are a number of reasons why they purchase from outside suppliers. First, the manufacturer gets a product without investing additional capital in buildings, machines and a trained work force. Second, the manufacturer gets a yardstick which can be used to measure the efficiency of its own division making the same item. If a division making grease seals can produce them at 2 cents each, but an outside supplier can make them for 1½ cents each, the manufacturer knows he must reexamine the efficiency of his internal operation. Third, the manufacturer increases the chance that he may benefit from technological innovation. The supplier's designers and engineers may be able to suggest a different design or an improved manufacturing process. On the other side, most businesses, but not all, that can produce parts for automobiles want to sell their output to the automobile manufacturers because of the possibilities for extremely high volume production which, in an efficiently managed firm, can be highly profitable.

There are three additional factors influencing the course a manufacturer-supplier relationship takes: First, the mass production techniques of American automobile manufacturing require that the assembly line not be stopped. When, for example, a particular Ford sedan arrives at a certain point on the assembly line four hubcaps must be there ready to be installed. It would be extremely costly to the manufacturer if the line had to be stopped because the supplier's machines that stamp out hubcaps broke down, because a suppliers' inventory was not great enough to meet the demand or because the parts were lost in shipment. However, demand for automobiles and even for particular types of automobiles fluctuates. To a great extent, this

---

[1]For a comparative analysis of contract law and contract provisions used in relationships between automobile manufacturers and dealers in the United States, Denmark, Sweden, Great Britain, Germany, Switzerland and Austria see *Foighel and Gammeltoft–Hansen,* The Law of Automobile Dealer Contracts (Copenhagen 1970).

[2]The discussion about the manufacturer-supplier relationship is based on information supplied by and interviews with representatives of automobile manufacturers and suppliers. The information was supplied on condition that it not be used in such a way as to identify its source.

second factor offsets the first. The easiest way to avoid stopping assembly lines would be to produce large quantities of parts far in advance of need. Yet this approach increases costs because of the possibility of waste and the loss of the use of funds thus devoted to inventories. If, for example, the demand for station wagons declines during the year, exhaust pipes that fit only station wagons that will never be produced are mere scrap metal. Third, component parts can be defective, the defect can cause injury to property or person, and in United States law the injured party in such cases has increasingly been gaining rights against manufacturers. Not surprisingly, one finds that manufacturers wish to hold suppliers responsible for such claims, and the suppliers must defend themselves against the costly results of seemingly minor defects in the parts they make.

b. The Blanket Order System

aa. The System Described

23 The *manufacturers* have accommodated all of these economic and legal factors in an imaginative piece of transaction architecture which is usually called a "blanket order."[3] Coupled with the suppliers' great desire to do business with the automobile manufacturers, the blanket order system almost always insures that parts will arrive at the assembly plants at the right time, that the suppliers will take the risk of scrapped parts caused by fluctuations in demand, and that the suppliers will be responsible for claims caused by defects. Moreover, the system gives the manufacturers great leverage to ward off price increases caused by the suppliers' increased costs.

This is how it works: Some time before the beginning of the model year, the manufacturer will issue a blanket order to a supplier of, for example, tail pipes designed specifically for one of the manufacturer's station wagons. The blanket order states a number of "agreements." One of the most important is the price per unit. This price is computed on the basis of an estimated number of units to be ordered, and it will not be increased if fewer are actually ordered. Thus, the manufacturer has made the supplier run the risk that he will not even recover his cost of producing the items actually shipped to the manufacturer in the event that the manufacturer uses substantially fewer than the estimated number. And the blanket order does not oblige the manufacturer to take and pay for *any* of the parts described in it. That obligation comes only when the manufacturer sends the supplier

[3]Many divisions of the General Motors Corporation use what are called requirements contracts rather than blanket orders. However, because of the way the General Motors' requirements contracts are written and administered, the two systems are essentially the same in operation. The General Motors' standard agreement form for production requirements calls for it to "purchase ... approximately the percentage shown on the attached exhibit (of) the Buyer's requirements ..." Legally, the key word would be "approximately" since it might be interpreted to undercut any commitment to buy.

documents called "releases." The idea seems to be that the blanket order creates a force which is held back until released little by little.

Each month, sometimes more often, the manufacturer sends the supplier a release, ordering him to manufacture and ship a specified number of the parts each week. On the release form, the manufacturer also will estimate the number of parts he will require for the next two or three months, but this estimate, to quote one manufacturer's form, "is for planning purposes only and does not constitute a commitment." Typically, manufacturers do not send releases calling for more parts than they will need in a month since their monthly estimates of sales are fairly accurate. However, sometimes they do order too few or too many parts. If there is an increase in public demand for a particular model, the blanket order allows the manufacturer to send another release form to the supplier calling for increased deliveries. Such sudden increases may be a great strain on the supplier if he does not have unused capacity for production. Moreover, a supplier must always guard against a break-down of his machinery, which temporarily destroys his ability to meet the manufacturer's demands. As a result, the supplier usually makes more than the number of parts ordered by the manufacturer so that the supplier will have an inventory to cover anticipated future demands. He builds this inventory at his own risk since the blanket order clearly provides that "Seller shall not fabricate any articles covered by this order, or procure materials required there-for, or ship any articles to Purchaser, except to the extent authorized by ... written releases ... Purchaser will make no payments for finished work, work in process or raw material fabricated or produced by Seller in excess of Purchaser's written releases."

If a manufacturer has "released" too many parts in light of a sudden decrease in demand, the blanket order gives it the right to cancel the amount ordered in whole or in part. It then is obligated to pay the contract price for each part finished and "the cost to Seller (excluding profit or losses) of work in process and raw material, based on any audit Purchaser may conduct and generally accepted accounting principles ..."[4]

bb. Blanket Orders and American Contract Law

(1) Legal Enforceability

24 American contract law would likely support the manufacturer's plan for the transaction so that, when the law is combined with the market situation, the manufacturer's interests would be favored. Under that law there must be an exchange of promises or of performances to create a legally enforceable contract. In a blanket order the manufacturer makes no promise until it sends a "release," and so until then

[4]General Motors' requirements contract reserves no such right. Interviews, however, indicate that General Motors occasionally does cancel these contracts and pays what it deems reasonable cancellation charges. These charges would be no more than those stated in the text.

there has been no exchange and contract rights have not been created.[5] In effect, at the manufacturer's request, the supplier makes an offer—a promise to supply certain goods if they are ordered—which the manufacturer accepts every time it sends a release. The continuing offer and the many acceptances create a series of contracts. It is possible that two developing doctrines in the Common Law of the United States might be applied in the future to offer remedies despite the absence of a contract. Reliance by the manufacturer on the supplier's promise to fill all orders might receive legal protection, in the unlikely event it were needed, by the growing "firm offer" doctrine.[6] Reliance by the supplier on any assurances (most likely implied ones) of the manufacturer that it would order a reasonable quantity might be protected by the development of rules requiring fairness in negotiations.[7]

---

[5]*American Law Institute,* Restatement of the Law of Contracts § 19, 75 (St. Paul, Minn. 1932).

[6]In *Drennan v. Star Paving Co.,* 51 Cal.2d 409, 333 P.2d 757 (1958), the Supreme Court of California found that reliance by a general contractor on a sub-contractor's oral bid made the bid irrevocable. There was no express promise not to revoke the offer, but the Court found such a promise by implication and applied Restatement of Contracts § 90 which provides: "A promise which the promisor should reasonably expect to induce action or forbearance of a definite and substantial character on the part of the promisee and which does induce such action or forbearance is binding if injustice can be avoided only by enforcement of the promise." The UCC § 2-205, provides that one can make an irrevocable offer without consideration in a signed writing which "by its terms gives assurance that it will be held open . . ." It is not clear whether the UCC overrules the *Drennan* decision insofar as it might be applied to transactions in goods. That decision did give protection to an oral bid which by its terms made no mention of irrevocability. The statute may be held to overrule the earlier case or it may be taken as merely providing another way to make a legally binding firm offer: One can do it by reliance under the circumstances involved in *Drennan* or one can execute the writing called for in UCC § 2-205. It is not clear, moreover, whether a supplier's response to a blanket order would be interpreted as an offer which by its terms gives the requisite assurance. A final clause in UCC § 2-205, might offer another difficulty. It provides "but any such term of assurance on a form supplied by the offeree must be separately signed by the offeror." The manufacturer supplies the blanket order form and the supplier only signs the entire document once at the end. Of course, if a manufacturer wanted a legal right to a supplier's continued performance, it would be easy enough to plan the transaction to achieve this under the Common Law. Most simply, it could give the supplier consideration in exchange for an Option to buy parts.

[7]In *Hoffman v. Red Owl,* 26 Wis.2d 683,133 N.W. 2d 267 (1965), *Red Owl's* agent repeatedly assured *Hoffman* that he would become the operator of a franchised *Red Owl* grocery store if certain conditions were met. As *Hoffman* met one set of conditions, *Red Owl* repeatedly made new demands which *Hoffman* also met. Finally, *Red Owl* refused to award *Hoffman* the contract. The Court found that *Hoffman's* reliance on the agent's assurances should be protected under Restatement of Contracts § 90. However, it awarded very limited damages. The decision may mark the beginning of the development of a new doctrine of fairness in negotiations or it may be only a relatively isolated instance. The precise contours of such a doctrine will be difficult to mark out. For similar earlier decisions, see *Goodman v. Dicker,* 169 F.2d 684 (D.C. Cir. 1948); *Kearns v. Andree,* 107 Conn. 181, 139 A. 695 (1928). However, in *Monte Carlo Motors, Inc. v. Volkswagenwerk,* 1 Cal.Rptr. 920 (1960), the Court refused to adopt such a doctrine. It stressed that the plaintiff knew it had yet to conclude a contract and so it was taking its chances when it relied. It seems likely that today most automobile parts suppliers are well aware of the risks they are taking under a blanket order system if this is to be the decisive factor. See, generally, *Henderson,* Promissory Estoppel and Traditional Contract Doctrine: 78 Yale L.J. 343 (1969).

25 One can only speculate about the legal situation in light of general principles of contract law and the Uniform Commercial Code, since litigation testing these conclusions is unlikely.[8] The large automobile manufacturers try to avoid placing total reliance on any one supplier, and other suppliers usually can increase production so that a manufacturer's assembly line is not stopped for lack of an item. Thus manufacturers tend to avoid injury rather than litigate for compensation. On the other hand, no automobile parts supplier is likely to bring a case against a manufacturer; the loss on any one order is very unlikely to be large enough to justify jeopardizing future business. Of course, the trustee of a bankrupt supplier would be free of this constraint. However, in light of the uncertainty of the supplier's legal position, many trustees would think it unwise to risk the cost of legal action against a manufacturer.

26 What are the consequences of the legal situation? If we assume that the developing reliance and fairness doctrines would not apply, the parties get legal rights only after the manufacturer has issued a release and only as to the goods ordered in that release. This means that there can be a great deal of reliance by the supplier which is unprotected by contract rights. On the other hand, legally the supplier would be free to refuse to continue the relationship by revoking his outstanding offer to supply the parts as ordered by the release forms. As we have said previously, few suppliers who were not going out of business could afford to exercise such a right; very few situations short of bankruptcy would justify losing the good will of General Motors, Ford, Chrysler or American Motors. Most importantly for the manufacturer, it does get legal rights once a release is issued. As a result, it manages to avoid any question that the supplier will bear liability for injuries caused by defective parts which it ships. Once the parts are ordered by a release there is a contract which the manufacturer has written, and the disclaimers and limitations of remedy so typically found in documents drafted by sellers are thus avoided.[9] As between Chrysler and its

---

[8]Only one case involving a manufacturer-supplier dispute has been found. This case arose shortly after General Motors started using the blanket order system, and the supplier claimed he was misled. The court was very critical of the General Motors' blanket order system. See *Streich v. General Motors Corp.*, 5 Ill.App. 2d 485, 126 N.E.2d 389 (1955). Perhaps General Motors now uses the form of a requirements contract in response to this criticism.

[9]For example, the Chrysler clause reads: "Seller warrants that the supplies or services covered by this order will comply with the specifications, drawings, descriptions or samples furnished or specified by Purchaser (Chrysler) and that the same will be merchantable, of good material and workmanship and free from defects. Seller warrants that any supplies furnished under this order that are designed by Seller will be fit and sufficient for the purposes intended. Seller specifically agrees to defend, indemnify and hold harmless Purchaser from and against any and all claims, losses, damages and settlement expenses resulting from or arising out of a breach of Seller's warranties and of which Purchaser notifies Seller at any time." Most sellers would give a purchaser no more warranty than replacement or repair of defective goods if the purchaser gives notice within a limited time. It is interesting to contrast what large corporations demand as warranties in the form contracts they use in the role of buyers of goods with what they offer in the forms they use in the role of sellers. See the discussion of the warranties offered by Chrysler and the other manufacturers *supra* s. 40-43 of this article.

suppliers, the responsibility for compliance with federal safety and air pollution regulations is also clearly placed on the supplier.[10]

(2) Remedies

27 The standard blanket order documents drastically limit the remedies to which a supplier would otherwise be entitled under American contract law once a legally binding contract is created by the issuance of a release. Typically, the manufacturer reserves a right to cancel the goods ordered by its release, either in whole or in part. Under American contract law such a cancellation would be a breach if not authorized by the agreement, and, absent a contract provision to the contrary, the seller would be entitled to recover what he had spent in performance before the buyer's notice of cancellation plus the profit he would have made had he been allowed to complete his performance.[11] Most blanket order cancellation clauses, however, exclude a right to profit except as to those parts which have been completed before cancellation. Thus even when a contract is formed by a release, the supplier's rights in most situations will be minimal. The manufacturer gains a practical commitment from the supplier to meet the demands of its assembly line. It retains maximum flexibility by making no commitment to buy any parts until a release is given and making only a very limited payment if it wishes to cancel after one is sent.

c. The Absence of a Reform Movement

28 There are no statutes attempting to regulate this relationship, and no movement seeking such legislation has been discovered. Insofar as statutes in the United States are the result of pluralistic struggle and compromise, one essential element of pluralism seems lacking. It would be hard to form a group of suppliers to seek legislation. Supplying the manufacturers is very profitable for a firm that can accept all of the risks allocated to it by the blanket order system. Such successful firms would hesitate to jeopardize their standing with the manufacturers by supporting an organization taking a stand antagonistic to the manufacturers' interests. Without the most successful firms, such a group would lack political power. Firms that do not wish to assume the risks of the blanket order system can easily seek other customers since their facilities are not limited to producing original-equipment automobile parts. "Exit" is a relatively cheap remedy for dissatisfaction in this case.[12] The facilities devoted to producing original-equipment parts can be converted readily

---

[10]"Parts furnished under this order, being SAFETY/FED items, call for special attention to quality control procedures during their manufacture and/or assembly."

"Supplier's attention is drawn to the application of Chrysler's SAFETY/FED Performance Standard (Form 200-3 5-A) to these parts and the possible effect upon them of Federal Health and Safety Standards."

[11]UCC § 2-704 (2); 2-708 (2).

[12]See the analysis in *Hirschman,* Exit, Voice and Loyalty (Cambridge, Mass. 1970).

to producing parts for repairing automobiles—the so-called "after market"—or to supplying related industries such as truck or industrial engine manufacturers which, generally, do not have the bargaining power to use the blanket order system. "Voice"—using private or legal power to change the allocation of risks—would entail high costs and the chances of success would not be great in light of the many resources of the manufacturers.

Moreover, insofar as statutes flow from the efforts of those with access to the communications media attempting to enhance their status and power by acting as champions of the deserving underprivileged, this seems an unpromising area. The auto parts suppliers typically are not small businessmen but only smaller organizations than the giant auto manufacturers. The image of the suppliers is that of junior partners who are well-paid for taking large but acceptable risks: it would be hard for an ambitious United States Senator to champion them as the exploited victims of the corporate system.

Finally, insofar as one explains United States legislation as an instrument of the powerful to further their interests, no statutory action is needed in this area. The Common Law of contracts serves to legitimate and support the manufacturers' procedures by minimizing or denying rights to the suppliers.

29 In summary, the manufacturers have tailored a relationship whereby they get most of the advantages of producing parts in a division of their own firms while preserving most of the advantages of dealing with an outside organization. The suppliers are offered a chance to make high profits in exchange for assuming great risks. Most suppliers are eager for the chance to play the blanket order game.[13] The

[13]The blanket Order system may not be very different from the pattern of expectations which would exist if the manufacturers made contracts for fixed quantities of parts with their suppliers. Study of the contract documents typically used in other industries and interviews with businessman and their lawyers disclose that in many situations purchasers assume they may "cancel" their orders when a change in demand causes them to no longer need the items ordered; suppliers usually accept this as one of the risks of business, particularly if the item in question is not being made specially for the buyer but is what the seller offers in the normal course of his business. At times the contract documents contain cancellation clauses, but even where they do not, the right to cancel is widely but not always assumed to exist. After cancellation, the key question is what the buyer must pay to the seller to use this privilege. The obligation is not always clear. Many purchasers think that the supplier is not entitled to his full anticipated profit on the transaction. Many would limit cancellation charges to payment at the contract rate for items completed before cancellation and payment for the raw materials which cannot be salvaged in partially completed items. Thus, the conventional measure of contract damages in the UNITED STATES contract law awards an aggrieved party more than many businessmen think appropriate. Of course, the possibility of a breach of contract action with its damage measure defined as the net profit on the entire transaction had it been performed plus expenditures in part performance, may serve indirectly as one factor in inducing industrial buyers to cancel only when suppliers would accept as legitimate the reasons for not wanting the goods. It may be that it is legitimate to cancel an order for steel when there is no demand for the product which the buyer planned to manufacture with the steel; it would not be legitimate to cancel because another supplier of steel offered a lower price. Another way of viewing the matter is that businessmen recognize far broader impossibility and commercial frustration excuses for non-performance than does the law. In summary, the pattern of risk allocation found in the blanket

public may get better automobiles at a lower price as a result of the system, but one cannot be sure. There are important parallels to the contract system used by the United States government to procure military equipment such as tanks and aircraft. Since experience may change the need for a weapon or call for a modification in its design, the government retains great power to change or terminate its orders to private industry while paying less than the damages specified in general contract law (see *infra* ch. 4). It is thought that the risks in dealing with the United States government are reflected in higher prices paid to the weapons industry on government contracts. The automobile manufacturers may also pay for the flexibility in the blanket order system. However, unlike the United States government, the manufacturers make some of their own needs of each type of part. They can turn to their own divisions if prices are too high, and they can negotiate about prices with suppliers in the light of detailed knowledge about what it costs to make the item. Moreover, unlike the government's, the manufacturers' decisions and negotiations are not directly subject to a political process.

ii. The Manufacturers and Their Dealers

a. Description of the Relationship

30 The automobile manufacturers sell most of their cars through networks of "franchised" dealers. The dealers are independent businessmen. The franchise system offers, or at one time offered, a number of advantages to manufacturers as compared to operation of their own stores at the retail level. Instead of having its capital tied up in show-rooms and garages, the manufacturer can pass this burden on to a dealer. Moreover, a dealer who has invested his own money in the business has incentives which would not work as forcefully on an employee managing a factory-owned sales branch. The dealer will want to maximize his own return by his sales success. Selling cars is also a trading business since most potential customers have an older machine to trade in on a new one. A dealer will have more incentive to keep a trade-in allowance at a reasonable level than would an employee. As to the public interest, independent dealerships offer advantages of decentralization in decisionmaking. The dealer should be able to treat the customer as an individual rather than merely apply rules developed by a home office for governing branch office operations. These are the reasons usually offered to explain the franchise system. Today, however, the manufacturers may not need the contribution of capital from their dealers, and they may have adequate incentives and controls as bureaucratic techniques have developed. Nonetheless, the manufacturers would face

---

order system may deviate far more from the contract lawyer's model of business than from the actual expectations of those managing the relationships between large business corporations. See *Macaulay,* Non-Contractual Relations in Business. A Preliminary Study: 28 Am. Soc. Rev. 55 (1963).

significant political opposition if they attempted to end the franchise system suddenly and openly. American society has been concerned about the size and power of the automobile industry for a number of years, and such a display of power and the resulting injury to small businessmen would likely prompt some governmental response.

The franchise contracts impose certain controls which are designed, primarily, to serve the *manufacturers*' goals. A dealer might want to sell fewer units at a high profit on each one; the manufacturer wants to sell more units and wants dealers to take a smaller profit on each to maximize volume. It is easier to coordinate a network of dealers across the United States if there is a certain amount of standardization. A manufacturer wants its trade name used so as to exploit its advertising, but some actions of a dealer can injure that trade name. For example, customers may identify poor service with the manufacturer when the local dealer's performance is poor. All in all, the manufacturer wants to gain the advantages of having a network of independent businessmen handling problems at the retail level while still enjoying the advantages of the control it would have if it ran its own retailing entirely.

The dealer sees the franchise as a way to run a very profitable business, trading on the good name of the manufacturer. And most dealers are among the most successful retailers in their communities. But dealers tend to want independence from factory control; they want freedom to run "their" business as they see fit. From a standpoint of bargaining power, the relationship is one of dependence of the dealers on the manufacturer. A dealer's building, organization and skills cannot readily be shifted into another type of business, and there are few alternative franchises available. Rarely, will a manufacturer ever need the services of a specific dealer.

b. The Original Dealer Franchise: A Contract at Will

31 Sometime in the mid-1950s, the manufacturers changed the relationships they had with their dealers because of the impact of the legal system. Before this time, the relationship with the dealers was very similar to the one they have with the parts suppliers. The franchise document typically was relatively short; it required, in effect, that the dealer keep the company satisfied with his sales, service, facilities, and personality; carefully said that the manufacturer was not promising to fill any of the dealer's orders for cars or parts and that the dealer was not an agent for the company; and allowed either party to terminate the relationship at will. The dealer had no contract rights that could be enforced in court, third parties would have had trouble holding the company responsible for the dealer's actions, and the company could press for greater sales by being hard to satisfy and using its right to terminate at will as a sanction. Upon cancellation a dealer lost any going-business value and found himself with a sales and service building which could not easily be put to any other use. And manufacturers did threaten to cancel franchises and in fact did so. Moreover, dealers were coerced to purchase hard-to-sell types of cars and accessories from the manufacturers. During the depression of the 1930s, manufacturers pushed dealers relentlessly for more sales, sales which were extremely difficult to make. During the early 1950s, General Motors and Ford competed for dominance in the market, and both used great pressure on their dealers to outsell the competition.

c. Reform Through the Legal System

aa. The Law of Contracts

32 Increasingly during this period, cancelled automobile dealers turned to the legal system to try to offset the manufacturers' power under the franchise system. Some sued for breach of contract, attempting to convince courts to construe the franchises as imposing a duty of good faith on the manufacturers.[14] Most of these suits were unsuccessful as the courts stressed that the dealers had assumed the risks of the franchise system voluntarily when they entered into such one-sided relationships. The standard of free contract served to justify the use of the manufacturers' economic power.

bb. The State Legislation

33 In 1937, an automobile dealers' trade association successfully lobbied for legislation in Wisconsin which was to become the model for legislation in 20 other states.[15] The most successful of these statutes required manufacturers and their representatives who contacted dealers to obtain state licenses. Licenses could be revoked if a manufacturer or his representative: (1) induced or coerced a dealer to accept delivery of cars or other things that he did not order, or attempted to do this; (2) induced or coerced a dealer to enter any agreement with the manufacturer or "to do any other act unfair to said dealer"[16] by threatening to cancel the dealer's franchise, or attempting to do this; (3) "(u)nfairly, without due regard to the equities of said dealer and without just provocation . . ." cancelled the franchise of a dealer. As a result of these statutes, in many states informal mediation procedures have evolved. Dealers with complaints meet representatives of the manufacturers in informal hearings before the agencies which administer these statutes and bargain out their differences. Typically, it is unnecessary to hold formal hearings for license revocation or to go to court for enforcement of private rights granted by the statutes, steps which are expensive for both parties and used only as a last resort for recouping losses or for vengeance when all else fails. The statutes create and maintain

---

[14] See, *e.g.*, *Bushwick-Decatur Motors, Inc. v. Ford Motor* Co., 116 F.2d 675 (2 Cir. 1940).

[15] Wis.Stat. § 218.01 (1971). A table of state legislation introduced, passed and defeated appears in *Macaulay* 35-37.

[16] Wis.Stat. § 218.01 (1971).

bargaining power for the dealers to offset, to some degree, the manufacturers' natural advantages.

While many of these state statutes were highly effective, some were not. In a few cases, state supreme courts declared them unconstitutional.[17] In other states, the statutes assigned enforcement responsibilities to agencies which had neither the desire nor the resources to enforce them. Finally, the automobile manufacturers successfully lobbied to prevent passage of such statutes in many states. All of this prompted an appeal to the federal government.

cc. The Federal Legislation

(1) The Impact of Hearings

34 The National Association of Automobile Dealers sought help before the Federal Congress in 1954. Full dress hearings were held before two Senate Committees and received wide press and television coverage. As a result of, and in defense against these hearings, the manufacturers rewrote their franchise agreements. Most significantly, they set up standards of performance. In order to justify cancellation, a dealer would have to fail to meet one of these standards; no longer did the manufacturers reserve the power to cancel at will. For example, now a Ford dealer's sales performance is measured by first comparing the dealer's sales to (1) the total registration of all cars in his locality, (2) the sales objectives established by Ford for his locality, and (3) the sales of Chevrolet, Plymouth and American Motors in his locality. Secondly, the dealer's sales are compared to (1) those of three other Ford dealers of comparable size in the nearest comparable areas, and (2) the average of all Ford dealers in his zone, district, region, and nationally. In making these comparisons Ford will also consider (1) the history of the dealer's sales performance, (2) the availability of cars to the dealer, and (3) "special local conditions that might affect the dealer's sales performance." While this is a more limited right to cancel than the old requirement that a dealer sell "to the satisfaction" of Ford, the factory still retains broad discretion to increase the sales objectives for an area as it conducts new surveys, to select the areas for comparison purposes, and to judge both whether cars were available and whether there were local conditions which adversely affected sales. In addition to rewriting the franchise documents, the manufacturers created internal review systems to which dealers could appeal if they were unhappy with the administration of the relationship. General Motors has an umpire, who acts as a judge within their private legal system.[18]

---

[17]See, *e.g., Rehsamen Motor Co. v. Phillips,* 226 Ark. 146, 289 S.W.2d 170 (1956).

[18]See *Whittaker,* The General Motors Dealer Relations Umpire Plan: 29 Bus. Law. 623 (1973).

(2) The "Dealers Day in Court" Act

35 In addition to these manufacturer-initiated changes, the hearings before Congress in the mid-1950s produced legislation. The federal "Dealers Day in Court" Act[19] giving dealers the right to sue manufacturers who failed to act in "good faith" was passed. "Good faith" was defined as: "the duty of each party to any franchise . . . to act in a fair and equitable manner toward each other so as to guarantee the one party freedom from coercion, intimidation, or threat of coercion or intimidation from the other party: *Provided,* that recommendation, endorsement, exposition, persuasion, urging or argument shall not be deemed to constitute a lack of good faith."[20]

The *proviso* was drafted by the Ford Motor Company and accepted by a House of Representatives Committee. Many dealers have sought relief under the Act, but only a handful have won judgments which have not been reversed by the appellate courts.[21] The *proviso* and the Committee Report on the statute have been used to construe the statute so that it does not apply to any conduct likely to occur within the manufacturer-dealer relationship. Although it is possible that judicial construction may open a new avenue leading to change, so far the statute cannot be shown to have been an important influence on transactions between manufacturers and their dealers.

dd. New Problems: New Attempts at Reform

36 In the mid-1960s, a new problem became significant. Manufacturers, particularly the Chrysler Corporation, turned to creating very large dealerships located in the fastest growing areas in large cities. The factories either put up buildings and ran the dealerships themselves or financed a man to begin such a dealership. The older established dealers were angered—and often financially hurt—by the new competition. They turned to suits under the Dealers Day in Court Act, to lobbying for more state statutes to license manufacturers and to a new round of hearings before the United States Senate.[22] This battle continues.

---

[19] 15 U.S.C. § 1221-1225 (1964).

[20] *Ibidem* § 1221 (e).

[21] The dealers' lack of success is reflected in a table in *Macaulay* 94.

[22] See, *e.g., U.S. Senate, Subcommittee on Antitrust and Monopoly of Committee on the Judiciary,* Hearings on Franchise Legislation (90th Cong., 1st Sess.) (Washington, D.C. 1967).

iii The Manufacturers and Their Customers

a. Description of the Relationship

37 The manufacturers' goals concerning their customers are simple: they want to sell all of the new cars they possibly can. The products are heavily advertised, and people are urged to buy new cars while their old ones still have useful life as machines. Models generally are changed in appearance each year to create a demand for something new. The manufacturer strives to build an image for its products of quality, safety and reliability. Since a manufacturer's ideal customer will buy a new car to replace his old one every year or every other year, manufacturers are concerned about the continuing good-will and continuing loyalty of car buyers. The context in which the manufacturers have pursued their goals has changed over time. Since the Second World War, the United States has become more and more a nation of people who live great distances from their places of employment and shopping areas. At the same time there has been a decrease in the amount and quality of public transportation. Great amounts of government funds have gone into a network of roads to support this pattern of living. The private passenger car has become a "necessity." Judged by the way they used automobiles in the post Second World War period, most Americans formerly believed that their cars were safe and reliable. However, more recently complaints about unreliability and poor repairs have become more frequent and more loud.

b. The Changing Legal Context: The Statutes and Cases

aa. Introduction

38 When an automobile is sold, what obligations concerning safety and reliability are assumed by or imposed on the manufacturer? To what extent are American automobile manufacturers selling safety and reliability in their advertising, and to what extent do they pass through the terms of sales contracts the risk of danger and unreliability on to the people who buy their cars? To what extent have the courts and legislatures influenced the allocation of these risks? At the outset, one must observe that under the law of the various states it is still possible for an individual to sell his used car to another "as is," so that the buyer assumes the risk of any defects (UCC § 2-316 (3) (a)). An uncharitable observer might describe the practices of the American automobile manufacturers as an attempt to create strong expectations of safety and quality but to limit legal liability at the same time to an "as is" sale. There has been a change in the law in many states over the past 20 years; the trend has been to limit the manufacturers' power to avoid liability for unsafe automobiles although its responsibility for unreliability not likely to cause accidents is less clear. Moreover, when one takes into account the practices of the manufacturers, the situation is even more complex.

Suppose an owner of a new automobile is injured in an accident involving his car; suppose his car is damaged in an accident; or suppose his car will not function reliably. The owner believes that his physical or economic injury was caused by a defect in the automobile. What legal remedies might he seek? He could attempt to recover for the manufacturer's negligence in designing or building the car; he could attempt to hold the manufacturer responsible for promising that the car would be safe and reliable; and, since the mid-1960s in many states, he could seek to recover for his physical injuries under a developing liability without fault theory.

bb. The Tort of Negligence

39 At least theoretically, the owner's negligence suit would face two great problems. First, it is very difficult to prove that a manufacturer failed to act reasonably in making any particular automobile since it is almost impossible to recreate the events surrounding the building of any one of the hundreds of automobiles produced daily on an assembly line. Second, it is often impossible to show that damage to the car or to a person was caused by a defective part rather than by some intervening factor completely out of the control of the manufacturer. For example, suppose a car leaves the road and crashes. After the event, we can find broken parts. Did they break causing the accident or did the driver's inattention cause the accident that caused the parts to break? While one cannot be sure of the explanation, before the 1960s, negligence suits were not a major problem for the manufacturers.

cc. Warranty, Disclaimers and Absolute Liability

(1) Before 1960: Liability Limited by Contract

40 The law of the United States has long offered another theory of liability which avoids the problem of proving fault. Typically, a purchaser of goods can sue for breach of contract—a breach of warranty—on the theory of an express or implied obligation that goods supplied under a contract will be suited for their normal functions and will have at least the quality typical of such items. While the origins of this liability rest on implied contract, it is now codified into statute in almost all states (UCC § 2-313–2-315). However, historically, this obligation ran only to a party to the sales contract, one in "privity" with the buyer. The manufacturers once attempted to avoid liability by using this doctrine. They sold their products to their dealers who, in turn, sold them to consumers. Thus the consumers were not in privity with the manufacturer-dealer contract, and the manufacturer was not in privity with the dealer-consumer contract. The privity doctrine has been slowly dying, but any consumer seeking to sue a manufacturer had to be prepared to argue that his case came within one of its many exceptions. Moreover, sellers and buyers could disclaim the warranty obligation by contract (Uniform Sales Act § 71). Before 1960, all American manufacturers used a uniform warranty clause prepared by the

Automobile Manufacturers Association. Most of the clause talked about a guarantee which was being given to the customer by the manufacturer. In essence, the manufacturer promised to repair the car until a specified period of time had elapsed or until the car had been driven a stated distance. The customer did receive a remedy not imposed by the law—repair of defects. However, in 23 words buried in a 154 word sentence, the uniform clause stated that "this warranty ... (is) expressly in lieu of all other warranties expressed or implied and of all other obligations or liabilities on its part ..." Thus, while the customer got a limited right to repairs, he paid a high price in exchange. He lost a right to damages for personal injury or injury to the car caused by its defects and a right to return an unreliable car and recover what he paid for it—all remedies which he would have had if the contract had said nothing. In the words which emphasized what the customer was given, a great deal was being taken away.

(2) After 1960: New Warranty Disclaimers and Liability Imposed by Government

41 During the early 1960s, two developments prompted the manufacturers to cease using the Automobile Manufacturers Association clause and to write their own warranties in a slightly different way. First, during the late 1950s and early 1960s, almost all American states adopted the Uniform Commercial Code. The Code raises questions about the ability of a manufacturer of an advertised consumer product to disclaim all warranties or to limit the remedies available for breach of warranty. Under one plausible reading of the Code, a manufacturer cannot create reasonable expectations of quality and reliability by advertising or representations at the point of sale while warding off legal responsibility by disclaimers or limitations of remedy that are written and presented so as to minimize the chance that the consumer will understand the risks that are being imposed upon him.[23] For example, under this

[23]Put as briefly as possible, the argument would be that statements about quality and reliability are "affirmations of fact" "which relate to the goods and become part of the basis of the bargain" and, therefore, create an express warranty (UCC § 2-313 (1) (a)). Even if a buyer could not point to specific statements, unless effectively disclaimed, there is also an implied warranty of merchantability (UCC § 2-314 (1)), which would require that a new automobile be of such quality and reliability as to "pass without objection in the trade under the contract description ..." (UCC § 2-314 (2) (a)). Exclusion or modification of warranties is covered in UCC § 2-316. Express warranties and disclaimers are to be construed when possible as consistent but where such a construction is "unreasonable," "negation or limitation is inoperative." To "exclude or modify the implied warranty of merchantability or any part of it, the language must mention merchantability and in case of a writing must be conspicuous." "A term or clause is conspicuous when it is so written that a reasonable person against whom it is to operate ought to have noticed it ... Language in the body of a form is 'conspicuous' if it is in larger or other contrasting type or color ..." (UCC § 1-201 (10)). The Official Comment to UCC § 2-316 explains that the section "seeks to protect a buyer from unexpected and unbargained language of disclaimer by ... permitting the exclusion of implied warranties only by conspicuous language or other circumstances which protect the buyer from surprise (no. 1)." One could argue that language of disclaimer should be deemed to be "conspicuous" only if as a matter of fact it does protect a buyer from surprise. Thus, a clause reading, "There is no implied warranty of merchantability" would not necessarily serve as an effective disclaimer

view, Ford could not advertise the high quality of its vehicles and, then, by language hidden in the fine print of a form contract which was understandable only to some lawyers, so disclaim and limit its liability that it was selling its cars "as is" and "with all faults." However, a contrary reading is also possible. Under this interpretation of the Code, the question is a matter of form. If certain keywords are used and the provisions are not too outrageously hidden, warranties may be disclaimed and remedies sharply limited.[24] The meaning of the UCC will remain open until the

---

even though it were printed in slightly larger type or a contrasting color. This might be the case where a reasonable person could have failed to notice the clause as, for example, where the clause was part of a lengthy and complex document customarily used in a manner to discourage reading before signing. Moreover, even if a consumer-buyer ought to have noticed such a clause, it seems likely that a high percentage of consumers would have no idea of the meaning of the statement: "There is no implied warranty of merchantability", particularly when presented as part of a clause purporting to grant consumers valuable rights in the context of the purchase of a product widely advertized to be of high quality and reliability. See *Whitford,* The Functions of Disclosure Regulation in Consumer Transactions: 1973 Wis.L.Rev. 400, 420, 425, 449. Such a taking away of rights in the guise of granting something when done by a national advertiser could well be deemed by a court to be "unconscionable" under UCC § 2-302. The Official Comment to that section states that its principle is "the prevention of oppression and unfair surprise (no. 1)."

Attempts to grant a warranty but to limit the remedy for breach are governed by UCC § 2-719. Generally, one can warrant his goods but limit the remedy to replacement or repair of any that are defective. However, the statute does provide: "Consequential damages may be limited or excluded unless the limitation or exclusion is unconscionable. Limitation of consequential damages for injury to the person in the case of consumer goods is prima facie unconscionable but limitation of damages where the loss is commercial is not" (UCC § 2-719 (3)). Automobile warranties are worded as if only a limited warranty is being given. However, a court might well find that actually a full warranty is being given but that an attempt is being made to limit the remedy to replacement or repair at the option of the manufacturer. Despite the words used by the automobile companies, there is no such thing as a warranty of replacement or repair. Rather there is a warranty of *quality* (either an express one or an implied one of merchantability or fitness for a particular purpose) and *remedies* of replacement or repair. The manufacturers' purported disclaimers are, in substance, remedy limitations subject to UCC § 2-719 (3). If the manufacturer's clause were read as involving a limitation, it would be *prima facie* unconscionable where a defect in the car had caused injury to the person. See *Matthews v. Ford Motor Co.,* 479 F.2d 399 (4 Cir. 1973).

[24]This argument would first emphasize that the manufacturers are careful to create no express warranties. UCC § 2-313 (2) says that "a statement purporting to be merely the seller's opinion or commendation of the goods does not create a warranty." Advertising which commends the goods should not be deemed part of the basis of the bargain; the bargain is reflected solely by the written contract of sale. Second, implied warranties of merchantability are effectively disclaimed by conspicuous language which mentions merchantability (UCC § 2-316 (2)). Section 1-201 (10) says: "Language in the body of a form is 'conspicuous' if it is in larger or other contrasting type or color ..." Automobile manufacturers almost always print a statement that "there is no implied warranty of merchantability" in larger type face, and thus they effectively disclaim the warranty. A court should not find such a disclaimer unconscionable under § 2-302 because the Code itself specifically authorizes such a limitation of risk in the words quoted from § 1-201 (10). Moreover, the language of the disclaimer is just that – a disclaimer. There is no reason to construe it as a limitation of remedy subject to § 2-719. In sum, the Code authorizes a certain form of achieving a purpose, and the legislatures which passed the Code have found that the use of the form of language mentioning merchantability in larger or contrasting type adequately balances the interests of manufacturers and consumers.

highest courts in at least several states address the question. The manufacturers' lawyers took the second interpretation of the UCC, and they were prompted to do what they could to protect the manufacturers by redrafting the form contracts which their dealers used in sales of automobiles.

42 The second development that prompted changes in automobile warranties has received a great deal of attention in legal journals. Appellate courts in several states expressed disapproval of the manufacturers' uniform warranty clause. The highest court of Massachusetts commented that this "is not the kind of agreement which commends itself to the sense of justice of the court."[25]

Then, in *Henningsen v. Bloomfield Motors* (and *Chrysler Corporation*),[26] the Supreme Court of New Jersey found the manufacturers' warranty practices to be against the public policy of that state. The court objected to the fact that all American manufacturers used a single clause, that the clause was hidden from all but the most cautious who had the ability to translate legal language, and that the clause disclaimed a liability which the court implied ought to be assumed by the producers. In sum, the opinion implicitly charged the automobile manufacturers with dealing dishonestly with the public in order to be free to put dangerous vehicles on the road.

43 In order to deal with the set-back of the *Henningsen* case, to meet the challenge of an increase in the coverage offered by the Ford Motor Company warranty, and to gain some competitive advantage in marketing its cars, Chrysler Corporation then announced a greatly expanded warranty on all of its cars. The warranty offered customers a guarantee of some parts up to five years, but still, in terms, disclaimed any liability beyond repair or replacement of defective parts. The other manufacturers followed this lead. The new warranties of the four manufacturers differed in wording and in detail, but there are some common elements. All gave a warranty from the manufacturer to the consumer; they no longer attempted to use privity as a defense. All continued to disclaim liability for personal injuries and consequential damages such as lost profits caused by not being able to use the car. For example, Chrysler's warranty stated that this "warranty is the only warranty applicable to passenger cars manufactured by Chrysler Corporation and is expressly in lieu of any warranties otherwise implied by law (including, but not limited to, implied warranties of merchantability or fitness for a particular purpose). The remedies under this warranty shall be the only remedies available to any owner thereof or other person . . ." This statement still could be overlooked by consumers who were not alerted to look for it, and one can question whether most consumers would have understood its legal effect even if they did read the warranty carefully enough to find it.[27] The legal effect of all this effort at redrafting was limited in about one-third of the states during the mid- and late-1960's, when the highest courts in those jurisdictions adopted a rule

[25] *Hall v. Everett Motors, Inc.*, 340 Mass. 430, 165 N.E.2d 107 (1960).

[26] 32 N.J. 358, 161 A.2d 69 (1960).

[27] For evidence that consumers would not understand the disclaimer, see *Whitford*, Strict Products Liability 143-150.

of liability without fault covering defective consumer products which caused physical harm.[28] In these states the disclaimers apply only to purely economic harm such as damage to the vehicle.

c. Manufacturers' Practices: The Law in Action

44 A study of the litigation involving those injured by automobiles who sought to recover from the manufacturers and of the settlement practices of the manufacturers concluded that in the typical case the manufacturer did not assert its rights under the disclaimer as a defense.[29] The only question really in issue was whether or not a defect in the automobile caused the injury. If there was evidence that it had, the manufacturer was willing to settle despite its legal right to assert the assumption of risk defense or to assert that there was no proof of negligence in making the car. Litigation centered around the causation issue, too. Even in the landmark *Henningsen* case, Chrysler had not raised the disclaimer as a defense; the appellate court raised it on its own motion. At the trial, Chrysler relied on a hospital record on which it was stated that *Mrs. Henningsen* had said that she had lost control of the car because her hand slipped on the steering wheel.[30] Apparently, the manufacturers are moved by public relations considerations to deny that their cars are defective, and they are constrained by these same considerations not to be put in a public posture of saying that even though our car was defective and hurt a buyer, we will hide behind an obscure and technically worded clause to evade liability. The clause has been used when there was a claim of consequential damages. It always could be asserted where public relations considerations were outweighed by some other factor, and it might have an impact on settlement negotiations.

45 A study of the administration of the expanded warranties shows that consumers have had difficulty in many instances in getting the repairs which are promised to them.[31] The warranties were advertised widely in the mid-1960's and may have created expectations in the minds of new-car buyers far beyond the literal words used by the manufacturers. Dealers have reason to make repairs without charge in order to gain customer good-will which might aid the dealer when a customer next was in the market for a new car. While such good-will could also aid the manufacturer, it could be very costly. Moreover, some dealers who did not have enough service business to keep their mechanics busy might solve this problem by making unnecessary repairs if they could freely bill the manufacturer for them. The manufacturers control this process by a complex system governing payment of dealers for claimed warranty repairs. Most questions are covered in a detailed book of regulations given to the

---

[28]See *Titus,* Restatement (Second) of Torts Section 402A and the Uniform Commercial Code: 22 Stan.L.Rev. 713, 714 (1970).

[29]See *Whitford,* Strict Products Liability 160-163.

[30]See Appendix to Appellants' Brief in *Henningsen v. Bloomfield Motors, Inc.* (*supra* n. 26) 401a.

[31]See *Whitford,* Law 1094-1096.

dealer—if the claim is not authorized by regulation, the manufacturer will not reimburse the dealer for the work, and, as a result, dealers usually are careful not to make repairs unless they are clearly authorized. In the case of some expensive repairs, the dealer must notify the manufacturer before the work is begun and a manufacturer's representative must inspect the car and authorize the work. Moreover, many dealers claim that the manufacturer reimburses them for warranty work at a rate lower than that usually charged customers. This, too, provides an incentive to refuse to do warranty work, to do it quickly and not too carefully, or to delay doing it as long as non-warranty work is available to occupy a dealer's staff of mechanics.

46 How far can the legal system aid a consumer in getting repairs? At the outset, one must note that the expectations of many consumers are based on advertising which creates the impression that far more responsibility is being assumed by the manufacturer than the literal words of the warranty do assume. Often, the warranty coverage is not clearly presented to the customer when he is negotiating for the purchase of the car (although some manufacturers and some dealers do make great efforts to make the obligation clear). Secondly, the document which, as a practical matter, controls the extent of warranty coverage is the book of regulations sent by the manufacturer to the dealer, a book which the customer almost never sees. It is likely that the automobile-buyer does have a legally enforceable contract right to the guarantee made by the warranty for replacement or repair of defective parts. Moreover, it is likely that the coverage of that warranty obligation would be construed by a court in light of a customer's reasonable expectations based on the language of the warranty as read in the light of the manufacturer's advertising rather than its regulations sent to dealers. Nonetheless, the new-car buyer faces real difficulty in asserting these rights. Most warranty repairs, although involving significant amounts to the purchaser, still involve too little to make litigation worthwhile in view of the costs of suing a manufacturer. The one clearly effective remedy would be a right to rescind, return the car and obtain a refund of the purchase price. However, the express terms of the warranty bar this remedy and this limitation has yet to be overturned as unconscionable, if, indeed, it is.

d. Safety and Reliability as a Public Issue

47 All of this concerns individual complaints about particular vehicles. On another level, automobile safety became a general public issue in the United States and thus the government became interested in regulation of automobile safety and reliability. Hearings were held before the United States Senate to look into charges that automobiles were generally unsafe.[32] These hearings received wide publicity. The manufacturers made a number of modifications in their designs to better their positions as they appeared before Congress. But these efforts did not succeed.

[32]See, *e.g.*, Hearings on § 3005 before the Committee of Commerce on Safety Standards of Motor Vehicles (89th Cong., 2d Sess.) (Washington, D.C. 1966).

Legislation was passed creating an administrative agency and setting a procedure for framing safety standards for all automobiles sold in the United States.[33] Although controversy continues about whether or not these standards are adequate and about the nature of the enforcement tactics pursued by the agency, there is no doubt that the manufacturers are far more concerned about safety and reliability than in the past. From an era where injured buyers had few if any rights against the automobile manufacturers, we have come to a time when not only are private rights being expanded, but the very design of the automobile has become a matter in which the government has come to assume a responsibility to protect the buyer.[34]

B. Conclusions

i. The Balance of Power and Risk

a. The Manufacturers' Power

48 One can see some common elements in all of these relationships between manufacturers and others. Generally, the automobile manufacturer has great power and the market does not prevent him from writing a contract to serve his own interests, whether the other party is a supplier, dealer or new car buyer. For example, the manufacturer offers both suppliers and dealers the chance to earn unusually great returns on their investments which for most suppliers and dealers makes the power of the manufacturers easy to accept. Buyers of automobiles have relatively few manufacturers to choose from, and there is little competitive advantage in assuming a liability for injuries caused by defects in cars since a manufacturer could not advertise that he had assumed such a responsibility without, at the same time, drawing to the attention of potential buyers the fact that cars are sometimes defective and hurt people. Also buyers often are concerned with the appearance of a car and its price far more than with its safety and reliability—qualities which they just take for granted. Even in the rare instances where the other party—a supplier, for example, writes the contract, the automobile manufacturer's economic power serves to deter any attempt to use rights formally reserved. For example, Ford and Reynolds Aluminum Corporation had a contract drafted by Reynolds whereby it received a legal right to supply up to 30 per cent of the dollar volume of Ford's annual

[33]See 15 U.S.C. § 1381-1410 (Supp. IV 1969).

[34]The Federal Trade Commission in February 1970 proposed a statute to the Congress which "would create a meaningful mandatory, statutory warranty instead of the meaningless involuntary, unilateral warranty now issued by the manufacturers . . ." The quotation is from an F.T.C. Report summarized in the Anti-Trust and Trade Regulation Reporter 24 Feb. 1970, p. A-18, A-19. The *Nixon* Administration gave support to the Bill. See New York Times of 12 March 1970, p. 1 col. 2, p. 18 col. 6-8. The Bill was not enacted.

purchases of aluminum products.[35] A Reynolds executive responded to a question from a Congressional Committee by saying:

> I don't think I agree with you that the contract requires Ford to buy 30 per cent from us ... Maybe that is the final legal commitment but we are not in position to require Ford to do much of anything at the time we try to sell it.[36]

A Ford executive stressed that Ford viewed the contract, despite its express terms, as merely giving Reynolds "an opportunity to quote" prices.[37]

b. Dependent Relationships

49 What kinds of relationships do manufacturers create when they exercise their power? They create contracts of adhesion with all the characteristics of standardization to serve the ends of coordinating large scale enterprise. These contracts can be viewed profitably as a type of private legislation—the Ford dealer franchise document even looks like a statute; it has a preamble, an elaborate organization with cross references and definitions, and a detailed index. Much first class legal and business talent has been applied to planning and drafting these "contracts." These men have produced elaborate systems for dealing with complicated situations in uniform ways. Transaction plans have been mass produced so that lower status personnel have relatively few important decisions to make. Moreover, economic power and standardization have been used to ward off risks by transferring them to others. If demand for automobiles falls, suppliers must assume some of the loss. If the factory wants to replace a dealer, he takes the risk of a loss of going business value. If there is an accident, the consumer takes the risk of injury. Of course, as a matter of administering these relationships the manufacturers can grant favors to suppliers, dealers or buyers,[38] but these are favors and not legal rights except in the instances where legal regulation has interfered.

50 These standardized contracts are carefully worded to avoid contractual liability in most instances. No major commitments are made under blanket orders which could justify a suit for breach of contract. Originally, a dealer franchise was terminable at will. Now it can only be terminated for failure to comply with a complex standard which, however, gives the manufacturer the power to make a series of judgments as to the adequacy of a dealer's sales. While the courts might find that these judgments must be made in good faith, it is unlikely that this would be a serious limitation on the manufacturer's power to behave so as to maximize its economic interests. To a great extent, in these areas freedom of contract is the freedom to have no contract—as far as having a legally enforceable agreement is

---

[35] *Peck,* Competition in the Aluminum Industry 1945-1958 (Cambridge, Mass. 1961) 141-142.

[36] Ibid.

[37] Ibid.

[38] See *Fuller and Braucher,* Basic Contract Law (St. Paul, Minn. 1964) 308.

concerned.[39] The new car warranty granted to buyers, on the other hand, is designed as a legally enforceable contract, but the main reason it is designed to be legally enforceable is to disclaim a liability which would be imposed if no contract were made concerning it. It, too, is an attempt to avoid legal control over private power.

ii. Evaluation: Benefits at What Price?

a. The Balance of Gains and Costs

51 Undoubtedly, this kind of rationalized planning has advantages. It is not an insignificant part of a system which has produced great wealth for executives of automobile manufacturers, stockholders in these companies, automobile dealers, parts suppliers, and even, to some extent, for workers employed by this industry and its satellites. The high demand for automobiles produces opportunities for profit and jobs in many related industries and has a major impact on the total American economy. The system may have produced less expensive automobiles than could be made by any other, since one can assume that if the manufacturers had had to assume all of the risks they avoid by these contracts, they would have passed on these costs to buyers in the form of higher prices for new cars.

52 However, these benefits have not come without important economic and social costs. Perhaps the most significant cost is the contribution that this rationalization has made to a system of private transportation based on replacing private machines before the end of their useful lives. One can point to the waste of scarce resources and the misallocation of public funds that this society has used for super-highways and car storage at the price of the decline of the mass transportation system and the neglect of the needs of those who cannot and do not wish to drive their own automobiles.

There are also costs even if one assumes that the United States' system of transportation based largely on the private automobile is, on balance, a good thing.

---

[39]In one important situation the manufacturers were and are careful to safeguard their formal legal rights against dealers. Many dealers need credit to finance the inventory of new vehicles they must have on hand in order to do business. Usually, the manufacturer sells vehicles to its dealers for cash and not on credit. In order to pay the manufacturer, dealers must borrow money. In a financing arrangement called "floor planning," dealers can use their inventory of new vehicles as security for loans to pay manufacturers. Frequently, the lender will be an organization with no connection with the automobile industry. However, most United States automobile manufacturers have a relationship with a lending institution which offers floor planning to its dealers – the General Motors Acceptance Corporation, for example, is a subsidiary of General Motors. GMAC is very concerned about the legal structure which supports the security arrangements involved in financing the inventory of its dealers. Commercial law makes a difference where security interests are involved. For a study of the law and business practices relating to floor planning, see *Skilton,* Cars for Sale – Some Comments on the Wholesale Financing of Automobiles: 1957 Wis.L.Rev. 352.

The planning structures which have been described here maximize economic rationality at the cost of other values, most of which we can categorize as personal concerns. Parts suppliers and automobile dealers must operate under great emotional pressure, constantly facing economic tests that are hard to pass. The blanket order and the dealer franchise are designed to minimize the pull of considerations such as sympathy and forgiveness of mistakes. These mechanisms call for people to devote major portions of their lives to a kind of competitive "sport"—can Jones Corporation make a grease seal more cheaply than Ford's own division can? Can the Ford dealer in a particular city overtake the Chevrolet dealer and sell more cars? Moreover, in order for rationalized economic plans to work, parts suppliers, dealers and automobile buyers must surrender important amounts of control of their own destinies and enter relationships of dependency on large and relatively impersonal organizations.[40] For example, an executive for a major supplier to the automobile industry has described to me the frustration of trying to talk about changes in the blanket order system or in its administration with a representative of the manufacturer. The representatives with whom the executive could talk have no authority to make changes in procedures. The executive tried to get an appointment with officials who had this power, but these men refused to see him. Automobile dealers make similar complaints. They must use advertising designed by the manufacturer, install the manufacturer's bookkeeping and accounting system, and rely on the manufacturer to offer and make available to the dealers the kinds of cars that they can sell without having any voice themselves in these matters. This dependency and control stands in sharp contrast with the usual invocation of the advantages of being an "independent businessman" in the American "free enterprise" system. The new car buyer similarly cannot negotiate with those who have power to bind the manufacturer; the buyer must deal with a dealer who lacks this authority. The buyer usually gets an automobile of a certain degree of reliability and safety. However, a buyer's ability to purchase cars produced by competitors is only one of many influences on that degree of reliability and safety since most cars offered to the public are about equally safe and reliable. Also, there are few channels of information about the matter so that most buyers will lack knowledge. Manufacturers do warrant their cars against certain defects for a given period of time, but automobile buyers have complained that often they have real difficulty in getting a dealer even to make the warranted repairs. In order to control dealers who might too liberally make repairs for good-will purposes at the manufacturer's expense, the manufacturers have set up great economic disincentives that discourage dealers from performing warranty repairs except in clear cases. If a dealer refuses a claimed warranty repair, there is little a buyer can do. If the buyer writes to the manufacturer, he will be referred back to the dealer. Such a letter and reference will serve to insure that the dealer is applying the manufacturer's standards for repairs which should be made under the

---

[40]One can see interesting parallels to the argument developed in *Cockcraft, Gunder, Frank and Johnson,* Dependence and Underdevelopment. Latin America's Political Economy (New York 1972).

warranty. However, the buyer is subject to the manufacturer's interpretation of its warranty, an interpretation not necessarily consonant with the buyer's expectations based on the manufacturer's advertising. Private lawsuits are too expensive to offer a remedy in any but a few cases. Few buyers have the resources or courage to follow the successful tactics adopted by one man who was very dissatisfied with his new Chevrolet and the dealer's and manufacturer's attempts to fix it. This buyer continually telephoned the home of the man who was then the head of the Chevrolet Division of General Motors and asked for action. Finally, in exchange for an agreement not to harass the Chevrolet executive, General Motors gave its dissatisfied customer a new car.

53 One could point to a mitigating factor, perhaps. One could argue that in each instance an individual made a choice to enter the relationship with the automobile manufacturer. To some extent this is true. The parts supplier is, perhaps, the most free. Exit is a real option for him. There are alternative uses for the supplier's enterprise, most suppliers know the implications of the system, and blanket orders are written anew each year in most cases. If a supplier is willing to sacrifice the chance for a high return offered by the automobile industry, he can turn to other kinds of business. Dealers, too, are probably aware of the implications of the franchise system, but they are locked in with few alternatives. There are few, if any, other uses for their skills, capital investment and going business value. Buyers of new cars neither know the system nor have realistic alternatives. Essentially the same disclaimer is used by all four American manufacturers of automobiles;[41] practically, one cannot bargain for a different contract to buy a new car if one wanted to do so since a consumer must negotiate with a dealer who lacks authority to increase the obligations assumed by the manufacturer; and the disclaimer is, as a practical matter, effectively hidden from the consumer—at the time of the sale, it is not easy to find the disclaimer clause and if one does notice it, its wording would carry meaning only to a lawyer.

Of course, if a manufacturer were to acquire a reputation for producing unreliable or unsafe cars, consumers could deal with its competitors. Whatever the problems with the legal response to disclaimers and poor service, the possibility of this kind of exit could minimize the number of unsafe or unreliable cars produced. Undoubtedly, this is an important sanction influencing manufacturers to build safer and more reliable automobiles or to use public relations techniques to avoid a bad reputation.[42] It has been suggested, however, that dissatisfied customers may tend to cancel each other out thereby lessening the impact of this sanction—unhappy buyers of Fords purchase new Chevrolets only to be replaced as Ford customers by unhappy buyers of Chevrolets. Insofar as cost pressures mean that all automobiles selling for a

[41]Foreign cars sold in the United States offer, generally, no better warranties and use about the same disclaimers as do the American manufacturers. At best, they offer about the same limited remedies for a longer period of time.

[42]See *Hirschmann* (*supra* n. 12) 26-29.

comparable price will be of about equal quality, exit will produce no signal to the managements of manufacturers that there is real dissatisfaction.[43]

b. Legal Ideology and Reality

54 The law of any country tends to support its prevailing economic structures. The United States is no exception. However, bureaucratic rationality is a principle which often clashes with older individualistic values also found in Western culture and in its law. Recently, the accommodations between these competing values made in the late nineteenth and early twentieth centuries have been giving way. English and American contract law have long been based on an ideology of free choice or manifested free choice. Yet economic rationality has been furthered by standardization that disregards individual differences. Large organizations have controlled risks and set patterns with form contracts that minimize the element of even manifested choice. On one hand, these documents originally were drafted to give the party dealing with the organization few or no rights. Until recently, courts were willing to accept this, and they reconciled such economic planning with their individualistic doctrines by speaking of assuming the risk of what might be written in a standard form contract if one did not read and understand it. Where it was obvious that the individual in no way had led the large organization's representatives to understand that he was assuming a particular risk assigned to him by the organizations forms, courts responded by talking of the duty to read and what the individual ought to have known. On the other hand, where the documents purported to create legally enforceable obligations, the courts were willing to enforce them although the individual had very little opportunity to discover particular provisions or to understand them. For example, disclaimers are often buried in small type on the backs of forms. Before 1960, most buyers of new cars could discover the disclaimer of liability for injuries caused by defects in the car only after they took delivery of the automobile and long after they signed the contract to buy it. Courts did not give serious consideration to the question of whether the disclaimer ever had made its way into the contract between the parties. In a real sense, courts were willing to distort the legitimating ideals of contract law—that is, choice or manifest choice—in the service of economic development through facilitating large scale private corporate economic power. To be sure, liability for what one "should have" known can be made to appear consistent with manifested choice, but the appearance is a matter of form rather than substance in light of the announced purposes of the manifest choice doctrine. Perhaps, such a cover for facilitating rational bureaucratic operations of

[43]See the testimony quoted in *Comstock v. General Motors Corp.*, 358 Mich. 163, 99 N.W.2d 627 (1959), that a defect in the power brakes on 1953 Buicks was to be corrected whenever the cars came to dealers for any kind of service but that the defect was not to be communicated to owners of the cars. "It was a hush thing. They didn't want the public to know the brakes were bad and they were alarmed."

private corporations was once socially useful; perhaps, in certain industries, such a policy could be defended openly today.

55 But recently there has been a trend toward recognition of the fictitious quality of the individual choice assumed in the application of contract doctrine and toward substitution of rules imposed by government for those imposed by one party and adhered to by the other. The *Henningsen* decision that overturned the manufacturers' uniform disclaimer is but one manifestation of this. Moreover, government has begun to move in other, perhaps more effective, ways. Publicity techniques of a congressional committee may be the most effective control of a powerful industry-such as automobiles. The operations of the automobile industry are now of great concern to a number of United States Senators, and this concern is publicized in the news media. Charges of unsafe cars, unfair treatment of dealers and customers and atmospheric pollution by the internal combustion engine get attention in the newspapers and on television. Restrictive legislation is introduced. Some is passed. Even that which does not pass is a threat to the industry. Perhaps at one time automobile manufacturing was an infant industry in the United States to be fostered by all means available, including the legal. Today, many would have it face an accounting measured by values other than economic efficiency—most goods for least cost – and bureaucratic rationality. In fact, the success of this view in the past 10–20 years has prompted some to worry about the costs of imposing these new standards. Concern for suppliers, dealers and purchasers of new cars could increase the price of new automobiles and decrease job opportunities in making, selling and repairing the vehicles insofar as increased cost causes decreased demand. To the extent that this is the case, the middle class part supplier, the automobile dealer and the consumer of more costly cars will be benefited at the expense of workers who will lose jobs and the less well off who no longer will be able to afford a car in a society where a car is often both a symbol of success and an economic necessity.

(Completed in April 1973)[44]

---

[44]List of Principal Works: See *supra∗* note on p. 18.

Access to the Legal Systems of the Americas: Informal Processes

Stewart Macaulay

> *"Secretary: Fill in these papers, this is how to begin. Your name is a number, your story is a case, your need a request, your hopes will be filed. Come back next week."*
> Gian-Carlo Menotti, *The Consul,* Act I, Scene 2

I. Introduction

A. Access to What Legal System?

The arguments justifying most legal systems assume that citizens will have access to agencies and courts to seek services or to have wrongs righted. It is almost an axiom that one who has a right must have a remedy. A system in which some people or some groups were formally denied access would violate widely professed norms of equality. To be denied access openly is to be declared a nonperson or an enemy of the state. Whatever the accepted theory, the situation is different in the daily operation of all legal systems. Theories of justice that presume access almost never consider the complicated process involving discretion, power to command and bargaining that constitutes the very real but informal legal process that operates in most societies. Access to this side of the legal system probably is rationed everywhere, and one's share of justice is related to one's status, wealth or both in repressive totalitarian, revolutionary socialist and liberal democratic societies alike.

This article was original published in Working Paper, Center for Law and Behavioral Science, University of Wisconsin, Madison WI, 1976. Reprinted with permission.

S. Macaulay (✉)
University of Wisconsin Law School, Madison, WI, USA
e-mail: smacaula@wisc.edu

D. Campbell (ed.), *Stewart Macaulay: Selected Works*, Law and Philosophy Library 133, https://doi.org/10.1007/978-3-030-33930-2_5

Some nations do a better job of distributing benefits than others, but people will have to wait in line in Santiago, Asunción, Havana, Chicago or Toronto.

The distinction between formal and informal legal processes is not entirely satisfactory because one shades into the other. However, in most societies, if not all, most problems are solved by some kind of a bargain in which the formal legal process as it is described in statutes and constitutions plays but an indirect role. Two or more citizens or groups of citizens will reach an agreement to resolve their dispute without involving the legal system; legal officials will *negotiate* with those they are supposed to control for some measure of compliance with the law or for some benefit to the official. Of course, the latter transaction may take the form of a "gift," but usually we do not have to look far to find the implicit obligation to reciprocate. A critical element in anyone's bargaining power is the view held by the person being bargained with of the alternatives to reaching agreement. You cannot ignore my interests if the failure to satisfy me will prompt a response that you will find more distasteful than meeting my terms for a settlement. One of those distasteful actions might be the use of the formal legal process.

If we survey what I (say, as a private citizen with a business problem) might be able to do to punish you (say, an elected official) for not reaching an agreement with me, we may see better some of the roles of law and access. Borrowing Hirschman's terms,[1] we can say that I can exercise either "exit" or "voice" if I am unhappy with your behavior. I may be able to leave and no longer be in a relationship with you. My influence on you is significantly limited if I cannot leave without a high cost to myself (my threat is not credible), or if you do not care if I leave (I have no threat to make). For example, if we do not reach an agreement, I may withdraw my political support and no longer vote for you. But this assumes that there are elections, or some functional equivalent, and that my vote matters to you. If I am the head of a residents' committee of a large community and I can deliver the votes of my followers to your political party, my "vote" may matter more than that of any isolated individual. Rather than exit, I may attempt to harm you or your family physically or I may yell insults at you. However, usually the powerful are well protected from individual aggression by police and high fences. I am more likely to complain to some authority that purports to be your superior and ask that he, she or it punish you or order you to act. I may call on supernatural forces, but this will influence your judgments in the bargaining process only if you believe that there is a real risk that God or the gods will intervene. I may turn to your superior if I can find one. If you are a local official, I may appeal to a minister or the president. Or I may appeal to the courts which, in most nations, claim to exercise power over all citizens by an equal application of the rules of law. If, in fact, I am unable to present my case to your superior, or if your nominal superior has no real power over you, I lack access and bargaining power. You are then free to ignore me or to put me at a disadvantage.

---

[1]Hirschman, *Exit, Voice and Loyalty: Responses to Decline in Firms, Organizations and States* (Harvard University Press, 2d. ed., 1972); Hirschman, "Exit, Voice and Loyalty: Further Reflections and a Survey of Recent Contributions," 13 *Social Science Information* 7 (1974).

These observations about bargaining are fairly simple if one begins by looking at people with problems and then asks what they can do about them. Some might object that such a focus on individuals obscures the vital importance of the social and economic systems and relationships of dominance and dependence. The choices open to an individual may be severely restricted, but few people in any society lack any choice as to how they will attempt to solve their problems. Moreover, a careful examination of the real options open to the less privileged members of a society ought to prompt an examination of who might oppose reforms to widen those choices. This, of course, would bring us back to questions about the distribution of power in the society.

These observations about bargaining power are also important for the study of access to the legal system. If the formal legal system plays its greatest role indirectly as an unpleasant alternative to avoiding disputes or resolving them by compromise—as seems likely in most societies—people who lack access to the formal process will be at a great disadvantage unless they can find some other unpleasant alternative with which to threaten those with whom they deal. And we must not forget that there are other unpleasant alternatives that can form the foundation of bargaining power. Moreover, if potential access to a legal remedy is to be a factor in bargaining, clearly it is not enough merely to be allowed in the government office or courtroom. There has to be some chance of winning in the official forum—in the language of nuclear politics, the deterrent must be credible. We can underscore the importance of the nature of the access necessary to be meaningful by considering a situation in a hypothetical country where, let us say, the formal rules of law state that certain valuable rights are to be given to anyone applying for them who meets certain fairly objective requirements. Suppose further that the administrative officers charged with providing these rights give them only to members of a privileged elite. The courts engage in legalistic rationalization of their refusal to order the rights given to others. Both the administrators and judges are controlled by the elite. Assume also that all those seeking these rights who are not members of the elite, can afford to pay able lawyers who are available and willing to make impassioned and brilliant legal arguments. These arguments are, however, doomed to fail since the elite controls the formal process. In this situation, we could say that those who sought the rights but lacked the approval of the powerful, had complete access to the formal legal system and no access whatsoever to the informal (and real) legal process as it operated. Put another way, if the reality of a legal system is bribery and influence, one will not reform it by providing more lawyers to make technical arguments.[2]

[2]One need not pose such an extreme situation to indicate one of the real problems with the concept of "access." The less powerful person may be able to get inside the courthouse door, but the structure of the process and the rules of the game may give great advantages to the more powerful. See Galanter, "Why the 'Haves' Come out Ahead: Speculations on the Limits of Legal Change," 9 *Law & Society Review* 95 (1974). In short, access may be a minimum condition for the realization of the ideals of many legal systems, but it is not necessarily a sufficient condition.

B. Of Gringos and the Home of Watergate as a Banana Republic

It is necessary to digress at this point. We must deal openly with a major problem that arises when a North American writer deals with certain features of Latin American societies. There are too many articles where an idealized picture of law in the United States is compared with informal practices in a Latin American country to the disadvantage of that nation.[3] While some parts of what we have called the informal process are unobjectionable, others include bribery, corruption, favoritism and other unsavory elements. Few would be proud of such things; most would want to stress the ways in which their legal system carried out its high ideals. Unfortunately, a student of access cannot afford this luxury.

Only a North American who had not read the newspaper for the last 5 or 10 years could look down on Latin American legal systems as inferior to his own. Although most people in the United States are adept at repressing the memory, President Nixon assured his countrymen that he was not a crook and had to resign to avoid impeachment when it became clear that he was just that. His top aides accepted illegal campaign contributions from the largest corporations, all of which were subject to government regulation or held government contracts to supply weapons or other items to the government. Vice President Spiro Agnew apparently sold the State of Maryland to the highest bidder while he was its Governor. Moreover, Nixon and Agnew escaped prison for their crimes while a poor black who robs a gasoline station is likely to be sent to a horrible prison for 5 or 10 years. Many large cities in the United States are, and long have been, hopelessly corrupt.[4] Those who control gambling, prostitution and drugs are all but immune from prosecution. In many states, public works contracts are awarded to contractors who will "kick back" part of their profit to the official who represents the state. Moreover, the dark side of United States history includes the political bosses who controlled the big city machines and the spoils system whereby government offices (including judgeships) were rewards for faithful service. The treatment of Blacks and Native Americans (Indians), and, indeed, the "relocation" of Japanese-Americans in World War II, are as much a part of our history as the Declaration of Independence or the Bill of Rights.

It is futile to try to classify the legal system of one nation as "clean" and that of another as "corrupt." Corruption, discrimination on the basis of social class, and the

[3]See van Velsen, "Procedural Informality, Reconciliation, and False Comparisons," in *Ideas and Procedures in African Customary Law*, at 137 (M. Gluckman ed., Oxford Press, 1969).

[4]"I have argued, and I think the data demonstrate quite convincingly, that the people who run the organizations which supply the vices in American cities are members of the business, political, and law enforcement communities—not simply members of a criminal society." Chambliss, "Vice, Corruption, Bureaucracy, and Power," 1971 *Wisconsin Law Review* 1150, 1172.

burdens of mindless bureaucracy—the unsavory parts of informal legal processes—are problems that plague governments in all societies to some degree. The privileged classes in the Soviet Union command far more of the benefits offered by their government than do workers and peasants who are left to cope with an infamous bureaucracy; the Chinese stage great "cultural revolutions" to attack bureaucracy and status differences; Fidel Castro finds it necessary to drive through Cuba in a jeep, often arriving without warning, responding to complaints and giving orders that break through channels to get something done. Of course, one society may deal with these problems more effectively than another. However, an attempt to explain the unpleasant side of informal process in terms of Spanish or Portuguese culture is likely to be successful only if we are to assume that China, the Soviet Union and the United States were all settled primarily by the Spanish and the Portuguese.

In summary, what we learn by studying problems of access to the real day-to-day legal process of, say, Brazil is likely to teach us something about the informal but real legal process in Chicago—it should, at the very least, provide important questions to be asked. These informal legal processes probably serve functions common to all legal systems.

C. The Plan of the Article

There is relatively little written in English, Spanish or Portuguese about the day-to-day operation of governmental agencies, including the courts, in Latin America or in the United States. In this paper, I will review three bodies of literature, seeking some of the building blocks for a theory about access to the actual legal process in operation. First, I will consider studies of dispute resolution process in Indian communities done by anthropologists. Next I will review some of the studies of the informal legal processes that have emerged from squatter settlements in large Latin American cities. Finally, I will turn to a few studies that discuss informal processes in some Latin American legal systems. At the end, not surprisingly, I will offer some conclusions.

II. Anthropologists and Law in Indian Communities of Latin America that Exist on the Margins of the National Legal System

Anthropologists who are interested in law have written primarily about people living in non-industrial societies that survive in Africa and Asia rather than in Latin America. The notable exceptions—Laura Nader,[5] Jane Collier[6] and the Hunts[7] have turned their attention to Indian communities existing in one general area in southern Mexico. We must, therefore, be cautious in transporting generalizations from their work to Indians in Brazil, Bolivia, Peru, the United States or other nations in the Americas. Yet, as we shall see, much of what they report raises interesting questions about how the national law of any country relates to groups within that society that do not share all of the dominant culture. While most legal systems claim ultimate authority over all those living within their territory, anthropologists insist that there are multiple legal systems in any society that compete for influence and control. In a federal system, such as is found in several of the Americas, the problem is that much more complicated. This pluralism of formal and informal, official and unofficial, and legitimate and illegitimate legal systems raises opportunities for forum-shopping and manipulation.

Both Laura Nader's Zapotec community and Jane Collier's Zinacantecos resolve disputes among members of their own groups through relatively informal legal systems largely resting on the pressures and sanctions of continuing relationships. The Zapotec *presidente* "makes the balance" after allowing the parties wide range to express their feelings and to air all of their grievances. He draws on his knowledge of the parties and does not confine himself to an issue before the court. He uses the opportunity to reaffirm the shared values of the Zapotec about such things as the proper roles of husband and wife, father and son, neighbors, and the like. Nader describes the process as "compromise arrived at by adjudication or, in some cases, adjudication based on compromise."[8] She says that the "*presidente*'s role is that of mediator, adjudicator, group therapist. His principal function seems to be to listen—often asking questions to clear up contradictions."[9] The Zinacanteco *presidente* may be less directive, but he works toward a compromise settlement such that no anger will remain in the hearts of the parties to the dispute. His court, too, talks out the problem with the parties at great length.

---

[5]Nader, "Styles of Court Procedure: To Make the Balance," in *Law in Culture and Society*, at 69 (L. Nader ed., Aldine Press, 1969).

[6]Collier, *Law and Social Change in Zanacantan* (Stanford Press 1973).

[7]Hunt and Hunt, "The Role of Courts in Rural Mexico," in *Peasants in the Modern World*, at 109 (P. Bock ed., New Mexico Paperbacks, 1969).

[8]Nader, *supra* note 5, at 69.

[9]Nader, *supra* note 5, at 85.

There is much to admire in both systems. Laura Nader, for example, has said.

> ... [T]he single most important difference between the Zapotec legal system of southern Mexico and the American legal system (from the point of view of a middle-class consumer) is that Zapotecs have access to, know how to use access to, the legal system. In the United States, most citizens do not have access to the legal system, either because they are ignorant of the workings of the system or because they cannot afford the professional (lawyer) who would have knowledge of the workings of the system.[10]

Indeed, some law professors in the United States have proposed creating systems of this general type in communities and neighborhoods in this country.[11] Others, however, have questioned whether such systems could be built absent many of the other features in Zapotec or Zinacanteco society.[12] Zapotecs and Zinacantecos have few disputes with the General Motors Acceptance Corporation or similar modern bureaucracies. They live in relatively self-contained communities which are isolated but economically viable. They seem to want relatively little from the Mexican national or state governments. Most importantly these people know each other and value their reputations since they are unlikely to leave.

Nader and Collier's studies suggest that some people do not need access to the formal legal system to solve some problems because they have something better. Perhaps the important thing is to avoid damaging such informal systems in misguided efforts at modernization. Indeed, what lawyers in more industrialized societies can learn from these community-based courts says much about the disadvantages of procedures run by officials removed from the parties, governed by rules that are not understood, proceeding in terms of normative categories that ill fit the real strains on the relationships between the parties, and awarding remedies that do little but prompt further grievances. Clearly, it would not hurt either common law or civil law trained lawyers to think about why anyone would want access to a system that might be exceedingly rational but almost irrelevant to his or her purposes.

While both the Zapotecs and Zinacantecos are relatively self-contained communities, they do live in Mexico. Sometimes the authorities in the state or national capitals act in ways that injure the Indians' interests. Jane Collier notes that the Pan American Highway was put through the Zinacanteco's area without consultation, and it serves their interests poorly. The Zinacantecos do have "foreign relations" with the institutions of the Mexican national and state governments—formally, of course, the Zinacantecos are technically Mexican citizens but in many ways really

---

[10]Nader, "Up the Anthropologist—Perspectives Gained from Studying Up," in *Reinventing Anthropology*, at 284, 300 (D. Hymes ed., Random House, 1969).

[11]See Danzig, "Toward the Creation of a Complementary Decentralized System of Criminal Justice," 26 *Stanford Law Review* 1 (1973).

[12]See Felstiner, "Influences of Social Organization on Dispute Processing," 9 *Law & Society Review* 63 (1974). Professors Danzig and Felstiner have debated the matter further. See Danzig and Lowy, "Everyday Disputes and Mediation in the United States: A Reply to Professor Felstiner," 9 *Law & Society Review* 675 (1975); Felstiner, "Avoidance as Dispute Processing: An Elaboration," *id.* at 695.

they are not. Mexican law is alien to them and mainly serves as a tool for manipulation in their political fights. One faction can strive to have the leaders of another faction arrested at a critical moment, for example. Zinacanteco leaders have learned to make skillfully phrased arguments that appeal both to the values of conservative or liberal Mexicans, and these leaders are, at times, able to prompt action from the state and national governments. Collier points out that a Zinacanteco can choose to take a problem to a village elder, to the *presidente*, or to the Mexican officials. Each level offers very different remedies. The more one moves toward the nationally prescribed patterns of dispute resolution, the more likely one is to leave the realm of conciliation and mediation and to seek awards where one wins what the other loses. Nader has reported some of Forman's unpublished work in an Ecuadorian village:

> She separates into categories cases involving people who have multiplex, ongoing relationships and who are disputing specific kinds of issues. She argues that different issues generate the strategies employed by the disputants regardless of type of relationship, and that the apparently desired outcomes were also different. The non-compromise set of cases involved land and other important property, and prestige and access to power and influence within the community. All were cases dealing with scarce resources. Forman points out that there is no reason to believe that people involved in these zero-sum strategies fail to recognize the potential, or actual, damage of their strategies to their relationships with their adversaries ... In situations in which the object of the dispute is most highly valued, the social relationship will be sacrificed.[13]

We can speculate that the threat of using these higher zero-sum levels of the available legal systems has an important influence on dispute avoidance.

Eva and Robert Hunt did field work in roughly the same general area of southern Mexico as did Nader and Collier. They, however, focused their research not on one community but on "the interlocking of units in the local regional system."[14] What happens when the Indians (those who do not speak Spanish as their first language) come into contact with the Mexican legal system staffed by Ladinos or Mestizos (those who speak Spanish as a first language)? There are problems of translation of both language and culture" Indians and officials tend to stereotype each other with negative characteristics. For example, the Mexican legal official sees the Indians as having no respect for the truth and as always trying to manipulate him. The Indian sees the Mexican as foolishly refusing to hear the truth since he says he does not believe in witchcraft. The Hunts report that the Mexican courts tend to apply their norms strictly and in a mechanical fashion to the Indians, while these courts generally are far more flexible in cases involving Mestizos. The Indians see these legal agencies as expensive since they are located in the cities far from where the Indians live, and the agencies are open only during the hours when the Indians normally would be working. The norms are alien. The Mexican courts tend to overpunish by levying heavy fines when all the plaintiffs expect is public censure. The Mexican courts demand that fines be paid in cash and they will laugh at offers of

---

[13]Nader, "Forums for Justice: A Cross-Cultural Perspective," 31 *Journal of Social Issues* 151, 159 (1975).

[14]Hunt and Hunt, *supra* note 7, at 109.

sacks of corn or labor. As a result, the Indians tend to stay away from these courts. The Hunts call the Mexican courts a "conservative interface institution"[15] because they tend to support the Indians' traditional means of dispute resolution by offering a much less attractive alternative. Collier says that Zinacanteco officials change their norms just enough so that the likely outcomes in the Mexican courts remain less attractive than the outcomes in the traditional settlement process.

Indians living as members of an internal colony within their own country may be an extreme case, but they are not a unique one. To some extent their situation serves to highlight what we might expect to find elsewhere. For example, I would expect to discover common elements in these reports by anthropologists and what I might find if I studied the attempts of Spanish-speaking migrant farm laborers to deal with legal institutions in the State of Wisconsin or the attempts of poor people with but a primary school education to deal with social workers in a government agency in Columbus, Ohio or Santiago, Chile. One lesson of these studies is the difficulty of translation between cultures. Another lesson is that people will attempt to cope with a legal institution as best they can with the means available to them. Jane Collier argues that to understand what is going on, we must view law both as a language and as a procedure that people manipulate in order to try to control their environment. Obviously, it will be more difficult when it is a completely foreign language. The Mexican judge may be seeking what he sees as the truth, but the Indian in his court is seeking a result he wants badly enough to suffer all the costs of appearing before an alien legal institution.

There are some other, more specific lessons for a student of access in these "foreign affairs" problems of Indians in Mexico. The structure of the legal system itself tends to discourage these citizens from using it. Factors of distance and convenience are important. Some agencies are found only in the large towns in a region, and others are located in the capital of the country. The time and cost of transportation becomes a barrier because the citizen must go to the agency in most instances; few agencies come to the citizen. Even office hours are important. High status people can leave their employment at a relatively low cost, but lower status people may lose a day's wages or even their job if they go to a government office or courtroom. There may be problems of translation. Legal systems are worlds of the written word, and this rewards literacy in the language in which the proceedings are conducted. Cultural difference may increase the apparent unreality and abstractness of much legal action. Abstractness is not usually prized by anyone other than a lawyer. Yet legal personnel may be incapable of dealing with a case presented by a poor Indian except by an impersonal application of high abstractions. The officials cannot mediate between parties anyway since they would not trust the officials to understand the situation involved. Legal personnel are unlikely to be able to educate the parties to see their own self-interest because the officials themselves can seldom take the time necessary to fully understand an entire transaction that spreads over the years. Legal personnel cannot appeal to common values because they hold few

---

[15] *Id.* at 137.

values in common with the people before them. Moreover, the application of formal norms usually disposes of the case quickly, and, as far as the official is concerned, the job is done. Finally, problems of status and pride may be critical as well. The Indian who deals with the Mexican official may have to come as a supplicant begging for favors. We might expect that a person with a problem would try to avoid such encounters or would take great glee in trying to manipulate the official with pretensions to superiority.

III. Studies of Squatter Settlements in Large Latin American Cities

There is a vast literature on the *favelas*, *barrios*, *campamentos*, and other settlements of squatters in or near the many large Latin American cities. Only a small number of these studies are relevant to our concern with access to the legal process.[16] Most are single case studies of a settlement selected because of its interesting systems for internal dispute settlement and "foreign affairs" rather than for representativeness. We must be aware that the "pictures described may be accurate, subtle and insightful, but the cases involved may represent atypical rather than typical situations. There is always the possibility that the most highly visible, vivid, poignant or arresting examples . . . are exceptions rather than the rule."[17]

The people living in the settlements studied solve internal disputes much as did the Indian communities described by the anthropologists—family, neighborhood and property disputes are handled by some mixture of therapy, mediation and the imposition of shared norms. Among the reasons for creation of such arrangements

[16]See, *e.g.*, Cheetham, Quevedo, Rojas, Sader and Vanderschueren, *Pobladores: Del Legalismo a la Justicia Popular* (CIDU, Universidad Catolica de Chile, Oct. 1972); Equipo de Estudios Poblacionales del "CIDU," "Pobladores y Administracion de Justicia," 3 *Eure* 134 (Julio 1972); Fiori, "Campamento Nueva Habana: Estudio de una Experiencia de Autoadministracion de Justicia," 3 *Eure* 83 (April 1963); Karst, Schwartz and Schwartz, *The Evolution of Law in the Barrios of Caracas* (UCLA Latin American Center 1973); Means, Book Review, 72 *Michigan Law Review* 1481 (1974); Langton and Rapoport, "Social Structure, Social Context, and Partisan Mobilization: Urban Workers in Chile, 8 *Comparative Political Studies* 318 (1975); Pearse, "Some Characteristics of Urbanization in the City of Rio de Janeiro," in *Urbanization in Latin America*, at 191 (P. Hauser, ed., Columbia Univ. Press, 1961); Perlman, "Rio's Favelas and the Myth of Marginality," 5 *Politics and Society* 131 (1975); Boaventura de Sousa Santos, *The Law of the Oppressed: The Construction and Reproduction of Legality in Pasargada Law* (unpublished paper, 1974); Vanderschueren, "Political Significance of Neighborhood Committees in the Settlements of Santiago," in *The Chilean Road to Socialism*, at 256 (D. Johnson ed., Anchor Books, 1973). See also, Greenfield, *The Cabo Eleitoral and the Articulation of Local Community and National Society in Pre-1968 Brazil* (Univ. of Wisconsin-Milwaukee Center for Latin America Discussion Paper, No. 54, Aug. 1, 1975).

[17]J. Macaulay, *A Skeptic's Guide to the Literature of Poverty* 5-6 (Institute for Research on Poverty, University of Wisconsin, Dec. 1974). See also Campbell, "'Degrees of Freedom' and the Case Study," 8 *Comparative Political* Studies 178 (1975).

are the following: There is little privacy and security behind the thin walls, and disputes may have a tendency to spill over and involve others. There is a need to maintain the ability to live together for it is hard to solve problems by leaving, since for most residents there is nowhere else to go. The formal legal process is too distant and expensive to use for these problems. The group had to work together to survive when it first invaded the land. They had to build houses and find some way to provide essential community services in the face of a formal legal system that saw them as trespassers with no right to exist as a community. Such an outside threat may promote internal unity.

One of the key differences between these settlements and the Indian communities is the impact of the larger society. The *barrio* is not nearly as self-contained as Zapotec or Zinacanteco society. Since the *barrio* is built on another's land, the national legal system could at any time attempt to evict the settlers and to destroy what they have built. Internal disputes and violence could call attention to their existence and provide a pretext for turning a bulldozer on their efforts. Moreover, the residents must look outside for work and for some essential services needed to live in a modern industrial society. Thus, the problem of foreign affairs is vital to these settlers.

The settlement is likely to form a residents' association—there are likely to be leaders available among those who organized the original invasion that created the settlement. The leaders, in turn, must deal with important problems. They must ward off attempts to destroy the settlement, as I have said, and they may turn to a political leader or a party for protection, offering in exchange their votes or support. One can draw important parallels to the role of the political boss and the machine in aiding the immigrant communities in the large cities of the United States fifty to a hundred years ago.[18] On the other hand, the settlement may survive because no one notices it at first, or those responsible for evictions have other things to do. If enough people are involved in the invasion or the settlement has lasted long enough for roots to be put down, the government runs the risk of having to use real force to move the residents. If some are killed or seriously injured, left wing political parties or groups may gain an issue with which to harass the government.

If the settlement survives, one of the first problems is likely to be delinquency within the area. The residents may feel vulnerable to attacks on person and property. The vigilance committee or resident's patrol is a common solution. Another is a kind of bargain with residents who are wanted by the police for crimes committed elsewhere: These people are told to practice their trade elsewhere or their neighbors will lead the police to them. As the settlement acquires some permanence, it is in the interest of the police to patrol the area and provide some protection to the residents. The police often are concerned that vigilance committees will spark violence. The police will not want the area to provide a safe haven from which criminals could go forth to steal elsewhere; they have an interest in knowing who lives there and what

[18]See Merton, *Social Theory and Social Structure* 71-82 (2d ed., Free Press, 1957); Gottfried, "Political Machines" in 12 *International Encyclopedia of the Social Sciences* 248-52 (1968).

they do. Moreover, the police may be able to offer their services in a bargain for information.

Other critical problems for residents' associations are the provision of goods and services such as building materials and tools, water and sewer, electricity and transportation. The government may supply some of these. Even the upper classes in a society have an interest in the health of the poor; viruses and bacteria do not respect class lines. Often the residents' problem is to gain some of what is available to some but not all settlements, and here some political leader may be able to do the necessary favors. Janice Perlman says:

> Local favela groups ... have strong ties to the outside. It is these ties that allow the Residents' Association to bargain for benefits for their community. ... Even sports clubs and social organizations are closely linked to, and often funded by *patrons* interested in building up a political constituency in the favela.
>
> It is not only the funding that is important, but also the contacts to be made with "upper-sector" sponsors. Such contacts are often invaluable for finding a better job or getting medical or educational advantages. And more often than not, relationship is reciprocal: if, for example, the "sponsor" has a friend or relative running for local elective office, he can count on a large ready-made constituency.[19]

Individuals who seek benefits from governmental agencies, often face the problem of documents. For example, they may lack a birth certificate needed to get identification cards and labor permits which unlock jobs paying the minimum wage, health care and disability care. Political leaders and *patrons* may be able to help solve such problems. (On the other hand, identity cards and the benefits they bring may come at a price. One comes to the attention of the police, and a poor resident's economic activity may be at the margins of the law. One may run a higher risk of being drafted into military service. Access by the citizen to the government may also mean access of the government to him.)

Not all squatter settlements have enough access or political connections to solve their problems. In all nations some of the urban poor are left outside the legal and political system. Some settlements never succeed in organizing sufficiently to take more than minimal action; others lack a political protector. An often cited report of a case where a North American professor was able to give help to the small settlement in Venezuela that she was studying will serve to illustrate these problems.[20]

This settlement, La Laja, is a *barrio* in a town included in the planning of a large development by the Corporación Venezolana de Guayana (CVG). It is possible that at the outset of the story the planners did not know that it existed. The CVG ran many activities near La Laja, but the offices that dealt with planning were 350 miles away in Caracas. The political party that was most influential in the national planning agency had but a weak base in the area that included La Laja so there was no patron

[19]See Perlman, *supra* note 16, at 141.

[20]See Lisa Redfield Peattie, "The Sewer Controversy: A Case History" in *The View from the Barrio*, at 71 (University of Michigan Press, 1968).

to offer help. La Laja, itself, had never had a well-functioning organization representing the entire community.

The residents of La Laja did their bathing and laundry in a nearby river. One day construction machinery arrived at the scene to install a large sewer outlet at a point where it would contaminate the beach used by the residents. Representatives of La Laja were told by a local official of the Ministry of Health that he had no control over the project. A delegation went to the public audience of the Governor of the State. Dr. Lisa Redfield Peattie, a North American professor who lived near La Laja, was added to the delegation because of her status as "La Profesora," and because she had a jeep. The delegation was late, but it was seen because of her presence. They were told that the matter would be investigated.

Dr. Peattie sought out the Engineer in Charge of the project, spending a great deal of time and money in the effort to find him. His answer to her complaint was unsatisfactory, and she reported this to residents at La Laja. Some of them then sabotaged the construction machinery by pouring sand into the carburetors of the engines. Dr. Peattie went to a conference of North American economists who were consulting on the development project. The conference was held in Caracas. In response to questions about the sabotage which was being discussed, she told a Director of the American Planning Consultant Group her story" He then used it in a speech, much to the annoyance of the top Venezuelan officials present. After this, another delegation from La Laja called on the Engineer in Charge. It was first received by a junior official who said he would have to investigate. Dr. Peattie then saw the Engineer in Charge and asked him to see the delegation. He ultimately agreed to extend the sewer further into the current in the river so that the sewage would flow away from the beach used by the residents and to monitor the bacteria count. The residents were satisfied.

We must recognize that few settlements have their resident North American scholar to serve as a political intermediary, and we are left to wonder what would have happened to the residents of La Laja had she not been there. Dr. Peattie sees three major barriers to finding a solution had the residents of La Laja not had the help that she alone was able to give. First, the people did not know who to complain to. It took an investigation by someone with some knowledge of organizational structure to find where the decisions were being made. The other agencies simply got the delegations out of their offices by promising to investigate, a standard ploy.

Second, there was the problem of cost:

> The cost of communication in terms of time, distance, effort, and money is something of which I would perhaps not have been so aware if I had been merely an observer of these events; since it was my time, my gasoline, my bus and ferry fares which were involved, I became acutely conscious of it. It was partly as a rich woman that I was useful to La Laja. I had a jeep, I had time, I had money. Other people in the barrio had very limited stocks of any of these commodities.[21]

Third, there was the problem of social class:

[21] *Id.* at 87.

> . . . I was of unique usefulness to La Laja in being a person with some roots in the barrio who was, at the same time, clearly a member of the *gente buena*, a "Doctora," a person of upper-class level. . . . The chief engineer on the site found it . . . intensely difficult to sit down at the same table with a group of delegates from La Laja. . . . At the same time, even though he had already asked that I be fired, when I greeted him and asked him to give us a few minutes, he could not treat me or my request rudely. . . .[22]

Access to the legal system, then, involves finding and getting in the right door. Yet it also involves what one can accomplish once inside, and this turns, as we said at the outset, on bargaining power.

IV. Some Studies of the Informal Side of Latin American Legal Process

The Hunts' study of courts in rural Mexico made a number of points about how they operated when the parties were not Indians but members of the Spanish-speaking middle and upper class. The local elite had the power to control the legal officials sent to their area by the ministries in Mexico City. The local leaders were tied to the national power structure, and they could have a disagreeable official removed. One aware of the risks to his career would not apply abstract rules equally to all no matter what the results. The local elite supplemented the small salaries of these officials by gifts that further tied them to the elite. Many activities of the elite were illegal under Mexican law, but these people had long ago gained an immunity from the law. Legal officials were expected to overlook violations or to manipulate the forms of the law to rationalize this immunity. This can be viewed as a peculiar but valuable variety of access—access to the official.

Laura Nader has remarked that "developing countries send their least qualified law personnel to the hinterlands."[23] Some of these nations send their younger inexperienced people to legal jobs in smaller cities far from the capital. The more talented or better connected ones rise and are moved eventually to the capital, leaving the others behind. Such a policy would leave local officials more vulnerable to the pressures described by the Hunts—one group of officials is anxious to rise and concerned about political influence applied against their chances, while those left behind can only prosper by serving the elite since they have nowhere else to go. It seems likely that a similar allocation takes place in the large cities as well. There may be a tendency to assign the less able or less well connected to contact with lower status people. Whatever the basic competence of officials who lack political connections, we can wonder about their zeal and eagerness to serve the public once they realize that the way upward is blocked. A parallel process may occur in the United States where law-trained people are allocated to government jobs by a system that

[22] *Id.* at 87-8.

[23] See Nader, *supra* note 13, at 168.

reflects the grades the person won as a student and the prestige of his or her law school, which in turn may also reflect the social status or political connections of his or her family. It might be instructive to turn Nader's hypothesis on the United States and then take the conclusions back to the developing world.

Another study relevant to the problem of access is Keith Rosenn's, "The Jeito: Brazil's Institutional Bypass of the Formal Legal System and Its Developmental Implications."[24] He tells us:

> For analytic purposes the *jeito* can be broken down into at least five different kinds of behavior frequently observed in Brazil:
>
> When a public servant deviates from his legal obligations because of private pecuniary or status (friends, family, or clique) gains. *E.g.*, a government contract is awarded to the highest briber.
>
> When private citizens employ subterfuges to circumvent legal obligations which are sensible and just (in an objective sense). *E.g.*, a few essential parts are removed from an illegally imported car which is reported to the authorities as contraband; when the car is sold at public auction, as required by law, the smuggler, who is the only one with the missing parts, is the only bidder, thus enabling him to sell the car with a clear legal title.
>
> When the speed with which a public servant performs his legal obligations depends upon private pecuniary or status gains. *E.g.*, a passport application remains unprocessed for months unless the applicant knows or tips someone in the passport office.
>
> When private citizens employ subterfuges to circumvent legal obligations which are unrealistic, unjust, or wasteful (in an objective sense). *E.g.*, real property is transferred by an agreement of sale rather than by deed to avoid capital gains taxation on nominal profits rendered largely illusory by severe inflation.
>
> When a public servant deviates from his legal obligations because of his conviction that the formal norms are unrealistic, unjust, or wasteful. *E.g.*, a labor inspector condones the failure of a marginal firm in an area of high unemployment to pay the official minimum wage on the theory that strict enforcement would likely throw many employees out of work and perhaps shut down the plant altogether.[25]

Rosenn sees the *jeito* as a response to certain characteristics of the Brazilian legal system, characteristics that to one degree or another would hold for many legal systems. Of course, the use of these techniques will vary widely, even among regions of a single country or among different agencies. Rosenn says the nature of the laws that officials are called on to enforce in Brazil particularly prompts the *jeito*. It is hard to determine just what the law is in Brazil since one must synthesize a large number of decrees and amendments, and it is hard to be sure one has them all. The law is often written without consideration of the reality of the situation, and it is likely to have unintended adverse consequences. Laws are often borrowed from Europe or the United States as a kind of transfer of technology without any effort to adapt them to

---

[24] 19 *American Journal of Comparative Law* 514 (1971).

[25] *Id.* at 515-6.

local conditions. On one hand, laws are often written by legal experts as an exercise in deductive logic with little worry about consequences or the difficulties of enforcement. On the other hand, laws may be written by reformers who are unwilling to bother about logical consistency, technicality or the difficulties of enforcement. As a result, their efforts are often doomed to be largely symbolic while the *jeito* goes on.

The *jeito* is also encouraged by the general nature of law enforcement and law application in Brazil. The structure of authority does not encourage efficiency. Authority to decide a question is often divided among several agencies or divisions of one agency. An applicant must seek approval in several places in a series of steps. Moreover, authority is seldom delegated very far downward from the top. This means that all but the most routine cases must be sent upward in the hierarchy for final resolution. This insures delay. The characteristics of the administrative personnel themselves call for the *jeito* in order to produce results. They are likely to owe their position to someone with power, and they can be removed or transferred to less agreeable jobs if they displease those who influence the agency. They are usually educated people and they view themselves as of a different social class than those they serve. Yet, while educated, they are often poorly trained for the particular job they hold. Generally, they are not well paid, and some hold several full-time jobs in order to cling to the margins of the middle-class.

Something like this kind of system exists in many countries, and features of it exist almost everywhere. What are the likely consequences? The citizen seeking some government service faces delay and what appears to be an utterly unreasonable and irrational process.[26] He or she must get in line and wait, only to be sent to yet another line where he or she is told to come back next week. Any transaction seems to require multiple copies of several documents, and each must bear the documentary tax stamps. One must produce documentary evidence of birth, payment of taxes and entitlement to the service. In Chile, at least, these were part of what was called "*tramites*," a term that often struck an English speaker as far too close to "trauma" in his or her language.

Rosenn also stresses the style of interaction between the citizen and the official, a theme we have already heard sounded by Collier, the Hunts and Peattie. Class difference can lead to paternalism where the official decides what the citizen ought to want, or it can lead to discourtesy designed to signify superiority. Class difference directed to the upper-status applicant usually prompts exaggerated courtesy. Often there are too few officials to handle the number of citizens seeking the service. In such cases, we can expect the harassed decision-maker to resort to easy-to-apply

[26]See Schaffer and Huang Wen-hsien, "Distribution and the Theory of Access," 6 *Development & Change* 13 (1975); Schaffer and Lamb, "Exit, Voice and Access," 13 *Social Science Information* 73 (1974).

rules of thumb whatever their impact on a particular case.[27] Moreover, the system is characterized by a desire on the part of officials to avoid responsibility for mistakes. The official seeks shelter behind technicality or a refusal to decide and a reference to higher authority.

As Schwartz tells us,[28] those with status seldom wait in line. They seldom try to confront the kind of system I have just described. Rosenn stresses the role of the *despachante*, one who stands ready to cope with the system for a fee. At the minimum, the *despachante* knows what lines to stand in and his papers are in order. Those with the right contacts need never stand in line long. Political leaders or parties have long played this role when keeping voters happy matters. For example, this is a major function of representatives at all levels of government in the United States. The network of contacts maintained by high status lawyers in many Latin American countries enables them to call a high official (possibly a cousin or a university classmate) to avoid the entire bureaucratic process. Similarly, in the United States large law firms based in Washington, D.C., have almost immediate access to the top of most administrative agencies or even to the White House when they need it.

Why are these people successful in cutting through bureaucratic systems? The dynamic would seem to be friendship bonds since friends exchange trust and favors. Lawyers with a circle of influential clients often can help a relatively high government official who wants to leave find a very attractive job in the private sector. Professor Sally Falk Moore speaks of "fictive friendships" in referring to attempts to convert adversary or arms-length relationships into situations of mutual obligation.[29] Both the *despachante* and the political leader are likely to operate this way. In some parts of the United States, lawyers often give clerks of court cases of expensive liquor at Christmas. The clerks can reciprocate by speeding the processing of documents or passing along gossip relevant to the lawyer's practice. Sometimes clerks are able to demand tips or gifts for each filing of a motion in court. One violates this custom only at the risk of having his papers lost or placed at the bottom of the pile. And all of this is relatively minor as compared to the sale of major government decisions by high officials. In the United States, apparently, the form the payment took in the recent past was the "campaign contribution," although some key officials have been allowed to invest their personal funds in magnificent business opportunities that, just by chance, end up paying off at an incredible rate.

Those without influence can wait, rebel, or just give up and not seek the service supposedly offered to all by the legal system. Rebellion, usually, can be controlled if it is not organized. Many just stay away, making a calculation, the economists tell us,

[27]See Wright, "The Harassed Decision Maker; Time Pressures, Distractions, and the Use of Evidence," 59 *Journal of Applied Psychology* 555 (1974).

[28]See Schwartz, "Waiting, Exchange, and Power: The Distribution of Time in Social Systems," 79 *American Journal of Sociology* 841 (1974).

[29]See Moore, "Law and Social Change: The Semi-Autonomous Social Field as an Appropriate Subject of Study," 7 *Law & Society Review* 719, 723-9 (1973).

that the value of the service does not outweigh the cost of waiting to get it.[30] Part of those costs may be frustration and a sense of powerlessness in the face of such a process. Others wait, fill out forms (if they are literate), buy tax stamps, go from office to office and finally emerge with the desired documents entitling them to the service. Sometimes it's worth the trouble, sometimes not.

This bureaucratic style of government is functional for some interests and they cannot be ignored in any reform proposal. It provides distance so that clerks, judges and ministers will not have to face human problems that they probably could not solve if they tried. Moreover, the bureaucratic style serves to ration the service actually offered by dampening the demand. Lawrence Friedman has analyzed the use of cost barriers to litigation as a means of rationing judicial services to those who care intensely enough to pay the price. Of course, as Friedman recognizes, this kind of rationing discriminates against the poor.[31] Delay and waiting in line is a kind of cost that may serve the same purpose if it discourages enough people from making application. The poor may, moreover, be better able to pay the cost of waiting than the fees of lawyers. If one were to take down the barriers imposed by the bureaucratic style, the nation would have to provide more services. This often is something that governments are unable or unwilling to do. Thus, access may be related to wealth redistribution or transfers from capital formation to consumption. To the degree that it is, one can predict that tearing down the barriers imposed by the bureaucratic style would result in the erection of new barriers very soon, absent a revolution.

V. Conclusion

When we look at access to the informal and formal legal system from the perspective of the consumer of government services—dispute settlement, documents or benefits—we can make a number of observations. The Indian and the resident of the squatter settlement frequently manipulate the situation with remarkable intelligence given the constraints on their choices. If they can, they seek a *patron* to intervene in their behalf. This is an attempt to duplicate the technique of those who are richer and can hire a *despanchante* or a lawyer with good contacts. Sometimes one cannot find a *patron* and yet one cannot just walk away. Then, to be successful, he or she must cross a number of barriers. Peattie stressed that one must find the government agency that can decide the matter, and often this is not easy. One must have documents and be prepared to create more documents. One must be willing to pay the price of getting to the agency and once there to wait. It is easy to see why the poor choose to avoid contact with governmental agencies when they have a choice.

---

[30]See, *e.g.*, Barzel, "A Theory of Rationing by Waiting," 17 *Journal of Law and Economics* 73 (1974).

[31]See Friedman, "Legal Rules and the Process of Social Change," 19 *Stanford Law Review* 786 (1967).

We can ask whether providing legal services for the poor would confront any of these problems. Lawyers may know where the agency is, but often discovering which official will decide requires investigation or knowledge prompted by experience and contacts. Lawyers should know what documents are needed, and they should be able to help the citizen fill them out. Yet it seems clear that real access for all citizens would require more than just legal aid offered on a one-by-one basis. It might require reform in the very style of government itself. As I have said, if this style serves to ration services to those who can wait while denying them to the discouraged, funds would have to be found to provide services for everyone or another rationing system would have to be devised. In sum, access is not a minor technical problem if we mean access to the legal process as it really operates.

If real reform is to come so that all have access in any meaningful sense of the term, far-reaching changes will have to be made in the bureaucratic structure, the important rewards to be gained by bureaucratic personnel, and, perhaps, even in our socially accepted view of what constitutes equity in a supposedly egalitarian society.

Professional Competence and the Law

Stewart Macaulay

I have been asked to speak about "Professional Competence and the law—What's at Stake: The Educator's Perspective." In the interest of truth in advertising and full disclosure, I must make a few things clear at the outset. Much of my knowledge about the topic comes from a study of 106 lawyers in Wisconsin. I am aware that a study of American lawyers does not necessarily tell us anything about the bar in Canada. However, you are invited to take my remarks as reflecting the quaint native customs of a colorful but primitive people which might be suggestive to a Canadian audience. Moreover, while I am paid to meet classes at a law school, I could hardly claim to be representative of American law professors. This talk will be "an" educator's perspective rather than "the" view of all of my colleagues.

Our topic is professional competence. Let me make clear that I am for it, and I do not intend to advocate greater incompetence. However, my view is that the nature of the problem often is poorly defined and the proposed cures—usually some form of educational change—are likely to be far more symbolic than instrumental. I will first explore the idea of professional competence; I will then consider some of the limits of legal education as a solution to those problems we are able to identify; and, finally, I will talk about a few things which can be done inside law schools which might help.

This article was original published in Dalhousie Continuing Legal Education Series 21 (1981), 48–55. Reprinted with permission.

S. Macaulay (✉)
University of Wisconsin Law School, Madison, WI, USA
e-mail: smacaula@wisc.edu

D. Campbell (ed.), *Stewart Macaulay: Selected Works*, Law and Philosophy Library 133, https://doi.org/10.1007/978-3-030-33930-2_6

Recalling Pirandello, Are We 70 Conferees in Search of a Problem?

In much of the current writing about professional competence, we can find a long list of sins. The more common include the charge that lawyers do not know the law, particularly the newly developing statutory fields where keeping up with developments can be a real burden. Lawyers are said to handle trials poorly in various ways. Some of the criticisms centre on poor public speaking techniques; others on trial strategy; others on the art of direct and cross examination. Lawyers are found to write poorly and lack skill in drafting legal documents of all kinds. Lawyers are seen as sloppy and careless, juggling the demands of their profession and constantly begging for continuances of proceedings.

Insofar as we find such sinners, what have we found? There are a number of possible alternative explanations: The lawyers in question may be stupid or the victims of an inadequate education, before, during and after law school. On the other hand, we may be looking at people coping with structural problems as best they can. Geoffrey Hazard has written that people go into corporate law practice because they can "give their technical best to the problems they work on." He continues, saying that the "rest of the bar ordinarily has to slop through with quickie work or, as one lawyer put it, makes good guesses as to the level of malpractice at which they should operate in any given situation." If competence means Rolls Royce lawyering, then the same people who can afford a Rolls will be able to afford a competent lawyer. A lawyer for a person with limited means may have to "wing it." Such an attorney may not be able to do much legal research, fully investigate his or her case and plan direct and cross examination so as to meet an idealized model of practice. Given the amount at issue and the client's ability to pay, there are real limits on what can be done. The lawyer may have no practical alternative to filling in blanks on a form will, contract or pleading, whatever its literary quality. S/he may be able to do little more than follow the steps in a "cookbook" published by a continuing legal education program. Perhaps such second class legal service is worse than no legal service at all, but this question does not seem to be captured by labelling conduct as competent or incompetent.

Even a lawyer who could bill a client for more time invested in a case, sometimes will be ill advised to do so. Lawyers may be part of a local legal culture which rewards a "common sense" approach and penalizes "legal technicality." Judges may not be pleased with lawyers who push them into ruling on difficult legal issues such as the outer reaches of the hearsay rule or whether the federal Magnuson Moss Warranty Act authorizes particular Federal Trade Commission regulations which can or must control in a state action brought by an individual against a merchant. One younger Wisconsin lawyer told me of his experience in one of the trial courts in a smaller city in the state. The lawyer was something of an expert on Wisconsin's consumer protection laws. He based his case on several provisions of the Wisconsin Administrative Code. It seemed clear that the retailer defendant had violated the regulations and the consumer was entitled to a remedy under a literal reading of their words. Neither the opposing lawyer nor the judge had ever seen the regulations before the trial. The judge ruled for the retailer, remarking that the Wisconsin Administrative Code lacked a good index; the lawyer for the consumer had not played fairly when he raised a law which the bar in the community and the judge were unaware of.

From a client's perspective, competence may have to be defined much more broadly than is common in the literature. We, perhaps, should add several items to our list of lawyer sins, although we might debate whether we were talking about competence or ethics—a distinction unlikely to interest a client. For example, there are lawyers who litigate cases which should have been settled. Sometimes these are lawyers who lack the ability to value their case properly so that their bargaining is realistic. Lawyers who have few clients may let hope cloud their judgment or think that a trial will gain them valuable publicity. Some lawyers resemble surgeons who operate in an attempt to cure the common cold. I have been told stories of some who relish combat and disdain non-adversary more-cooperative means of problem solving. Such a litigator, while ostensibly maximizing the interests of his/her clients, may instead maximize only personal satisfaction in participating in courtroom battle.

Interestingly, a number of large corporations are beginning to attempt to control legal costs by supervising the work of elite law firms. Many of these firms long have had a standard approach to any case which features exhaustive legal research, endless pretrial procedures and large teams of expensive lawyers. The work will be a model of professional craftsmanship, but it may serve a client's interest poorly when the case does not warrant the best legal service money can buy. A policy of spending whatever is needed to deal with a law suit allows a large law firm to bill many hours and so help cover its overhead and produce profits. A policy of quick settlement may not be as advantageous to a corporation's lawyers but it may be a better resolution of the question of costs and benefits for the corporation.

Also there are lawyers who fight to defend their clients' legal rights while doing great damage to valuable relationships. One can produce a technically marvelous estate plan which minimizes the taxes due at the cost of family harmony. One can point out all of the things that might go wrong in a partnership or under a property settlement suggested by divorcing spouses and provoke warfare among the parties. One can insist on precise definitions and terms to cover all imaginable contingencies and thus make it impossible for a buyer and seller to agree to a contract. One can raise endless but perfectly valid objections to testimony during a trial and antagonize jurors who do not appreciate the finer points of legal craft. In short, at least on occasion, the highest levels of technical competence may serve a client's goals so poorly as to be incompetent practice. A client seldom needs technique itself—lawyering is not like competitive figure skating or gymnastics where judges award points for form and may even count off points for routines which impress the audience. Lawyers are hired to produce results.

We must also note the opposite sin: there are lawyers who settle cases which should have been tried or settled more advantageously for the client. These lawyers often are pursuing their own self-interest rather than that of the client—a lawyer who accepts the other side's initial offer or who only goes through the motions of bargaining does not have to invest much in research, investigation or trying the case. If such a lawyer can mass process enough cases, s/he can earn a living or even do better. This lawyer needs few skills other than the ability to persuade clients that a valuable service has been rendered. Blumberg, in a famous article, called this "The Practice of Law as a Confidence Game." While we might be tempted to see selling out a client and persuading him/her to accept the settlement by misrepresentation as a problem of ethics, at least some of the time lawyers who practice this way do so because they lack the skills needed to practice differently. If a lawyer does not know how to try a case (or knows that s/he is not very good at it), it is in his/her interest to settle on whatever terms are offered or are prompted by a bluff.

Of course, even lawyers of ability may pursue the average interest of their clients as a group or their own interest rather than the desires of any one client. For example, one executive of a large corporation has complained that

> many attorneys' practice ... practice before ... administrative bodies consumes much more of their time than the time spent in litigation before the courts. It has therefore become very important to an attorney to maintain strong and close relationships with these respective agencies so that he can get informal rulings, hints as to the agencies' attitudes and other "favors". These are necessary, he believes, if he is to adequately advise his many clients. However, if I want to take a position that is very unpopular with the particular agency and which will almost certainly lead to litigation, I will have difficulty in getting my counsel to go along. If I am unaware that such a position can be taken, he may not suggest it to me. He fears that by serving as an aggressive advocate for my position, he may estrange himself to some extent with the members of the agency and thereby reduce his ability to serve his many other clients who also deal with that same agency.

However we define competence, we lack any sense of the dimensions of the problem. How many of what kind of lawyers lack what kinds of competence? It is not easy to get any idea of a rate. A few "atrocity stories" may be vivid and shocking, but they may be very atypical. We can wonder whether judges are in the best position to observe and evaluate the performance of the bar. They can see what is going on before them, but they seldom know much about what is occurring back-stage. Indeed, my colleague Marc Galanter suggests that we might need something like the "tissue committee" that evaluates operations in hospitals if we were serious about appraising the performance of the bar. One would have to sample each lawyer's cases from the first to last contact with clients, appraising decisions and non-decisions both from the point of view of the degree of legal skill displayed and the degree of service to the interests of the clients. Of course, just stating the proposal should suggest all of the problems of access, privilege and privacy one would face as well as the difficult judgments about settlement offers made, accepted and rejected, decisions about how much to invest in a case and tactics to pursue.

Moreover, we cannot assume that lawyers who do not seem very competent in one area are not serving their clients well in others. A second or third class trial lawyer may handle divorces with sympathy and understanding while the model technician may lack such qualities. One whose legal research and analysis leaves something to be desired may be just the person a client should see to help arrange a zoning variance because of the lawyer's excellent contacts at City Hall. On the other hand, an elite law firm may be almost totally incompetent when faced with an ordinary criminal case—the competent response of such a firm may well be to subcontract the job to a lawyer who knows who to see and how to plea bargain.

In at least some of the writing about competence, there is both an attack on university legal education and a proposal for new kinds of courses or teaching to cure the problems of the profession. Unaccustomed as I am to play the role of an apologist for legal education, let me raise a number of quarrelsome points related to the limits of the effectiveness of this remedy. Much of this literature seems to be symbolic rhetoric rather than careful diagnosis and prescription of a remedy. Often it seems as if we law teachers are being asked to produce 25 year old superlawyers with but a wave of a magic wand. Unfortunately, the magical powers of the law schools are not very great.

A law teacher is likely to notice that proposals to change legal education in law schools avoids inconveniencing those now in the profession. These proposals contain tacit "grandfather clauses", exempting those now in practice. Yet those now in practice are those ones who have so displeased the distinguished judges and lawyers who write about competence. Moreover, lawyers and judges do not pay for training the newcomers eager to join the profession. At least some of these proposals are pleas for a larger subsidy from taxpayers and private donors who fund law schools.

We must recognize that almost all of the lawyer-competence proposals which have been suggested or which might plausibly serve to meet any of the problems identified would be expensive. Classical legal education, for better or for worse, involves one professor facing 100 or more students in a large classroom. The professor leads the class through a casebook produced at an elite university and promoted by an eager publisher. There are no teaching assistants. There is little individual contact, and there is no need for computers, chemistry laboratories, a hospital or the other costly stage props of most graduate education. Compared to a medical school, or even a graduate department of linguistics, legal education may be flawed but it is cheap—it may even make money for the university.

Trial tactics, estate planning, contract drafting, negotiation and client counselling are not going to be taught very well in a large class with little individual attention. To do these things, we must come a good way toward the graduate or medical school model. Yet university administrators have reason to like schools as they are. Great lawyers have gone through a classical legal education, it is cheap, and so why change? In 1981, American universities are looking for programs to eliminate. Indeed, the Chancellor of the University of Wisconsin-Madison recently held a press conference. He discounted suggestions of some legislators that he could simply eliminate "low priority programs." He said,

> Assume we decided to close the Law School—God knows we wouldn't do it—we have students in the pipeline; we have faculty; we have internal planning and regent planning; and we'd have to declare a fiscal emergency. . . .

Despite his disclaimer, some of my colleagues were unhappy with what first came to his mind as an example of a "low priority program". One wonders about his eagerness to revamp the law school budget so that it would approximate that of the medical school or the eagerness of the legislature to support such a proposal.

Occasionally it is suggested that law schools could offer truly practical education if they would only cut out the frills such as jurisprudence, legal history, sociology of law, comparative law and some of the more exotic seminars. You will not be surpised to discover that I think little of the platform of the Know-Nothing Party. I might be willing to consider it if lawyers could find a way to promise me (subject to a right to a decree of specific performance) that they would limit themselves to technical roles of the sort often given today to a legal secretary or a paraprofessional and would never serve in policy-making positions affecting society—former students of mine can or could be found in legislatures, school boards, city councils and all kinds of administrative positions. However, even if this unlikely promise could be extracted and enforced, it is doubtful that law schools would be able to shift enough resources to do many of the things implicitly proposed.

Ending on a Positive Note: Thinking Small About Legal Education and the Competence of the Profession

Keeping in mind all of these considerations, there are some undramatic changes that individual professors of law could make which might contribute something toward increased professional competence. Interestingly, I think that many of these changes would at the same time help us do a better job of carrying out the intellectual analysis of law which law schools have long defined as their mission. My suggestions are minor and certainly not revolutionary; they will not transform the level of practice noticeably. Yet revolutions are far easier to talk about than to carry out. Here I want to consider what we are doing now at Wisconsin rather than what might be done if only the world were different. I use Wisconsin examples primarily because I am familiar with them, recognizing that others undoubtedly are doing important things as well.

Wisconsin, as is true at many law schools, offers practice skills courses taught by lawyers, it has several clinical programs where students offer legal service to various groups, and it makes efforts to improve writing skills. Moreover, our school has an important hidden curriculum. We are located at the state capital. Units of local and state government and the private bar hire many of our students for paralegal work. Of course, the polite fiction is that all of this work is done under the supervision of a lawyer. However, there are days when it seems that the state of Wisconsin is being run by second and third year law students, and legal research in our town seems to consist of law students telephoning professors who teach in certain areas, with pleas for help. Obviously, important practical skills are being mastered. Our students are dealing with real rather than hypothetical problems.

Several of us on the law faculty have been trying to draw on these experiences in aid of our educational efforts. In several seminars and courses we ask students who have these jobs to draw on their experiences at work as a source of data and to analyze their experiences in light of the theories current in various fields. As is true of most jobs, students seldom find the time or inclination to reflect on what they are doing. We hope they will learn something from the papers they write. At the same time, they are able to teach those of us on the faculty about practices which would be hard to discover in any other way, short of a major research project. In turn, what we learn about some of these practices influences our teaching in the classic traditional curriculum.

A group of us teach the contracts course together, and we have worked to develop our own materials. Based on research and experience, we have tried to emphasize alive and important problems rather than the usual offer, acceptance and consideration. We have attempted to place those problems we select in context. We try to discover why the matter was litigated in the first place in light of all of the pressures to avoid problems, settle disputes harmoniously and minimize costs. We look at the facts as disclosed by the record on appeal, noting how they were transformed in appellate opinions. We look at how cases were argued, both stressing questions of advocacy and plausible contentions ignored or downplayed by counsel and the court. We try to discover, where we can, what happened after the appellate opinion. Often we find that the actual outcome is not what might have been expected—orders for a new trial usually lead to settlements rather than trials; affirmances of judgments for money damages yield discharges in bankruptcy or partial settlements because of a lack of assets; court orders are evaded, particularly when it would cost a great deal to attempt enforcement. Moreover, we try to see whether particular cases are part of a larger pattern. Often the same situation yields opinions resting on different doctrines or prompts movement from a common law to a statutory or administrative solution.

We think that these moves at least set the stage for acquiring professional skills. Expanding the context brings into focus the interactions between the total legal process and people and groups seeking their ends. Obviously, there is far more to law than just appellate opinions and doctrines; lawyers are hired to produce results and this task requires legal rules to be viewed as tools. We stress bargaining and settlements which, after all, are what most lawyers do. Our approach stresses costs. Too much legal scholarship and reform proceeds as if law were free. Getting the perfect result is stressed rather than the best result which real people might be able to afford. Finally, our approach raises problems of inequality. Some people can make better use of the legal system as it actually operates than others. If one must pay to enforce his/her rights, then some will be able to buy more justice than others. Some will be able to use legal process, vague standards, the need for expert testimony and the like to run up the costs their opponents must pay to litigate; large law firms often win a war of attrition rather than prevail in a rational search for truth. Of course, we both honor and teach technical skill, but we also try to teach something about when it is worth investing in research, investigation and trial planning. Moreover, our approach offers the beginnings of an answer to a question which bothers many law students. Again and again law teachers demonstrate that a case could be argued either way—whatever a student says, the professor will leap to the other side and challenge the student. Yet if almost any case could go either way, how does a lawyer counsel a client? Once we move from the perspective of the Olympian appellate judge to that of the lawyer and begin to talk of predicting the likelihood, as well as the outcome, of possible litigation as a factor in settlement negotiations or decisions about whether to take action, we begin to deal with one of the most important elements of professional competence—good judgment.

Conclusion

In thinking about professional competence, we must define the problem more precisely. We can offer all kinds of atrocity stories, and we can agree that they should never happen. Nonetheless, we need some sense of how often what kind of lawyer can be said to be incompetent. We need to broaden our view of competence. Most of the practice of law takes place outside court, and we need to worry about mistakes in counselling and settling cases as well as flaws in trial techniques. We must be concerned with the economics of practice as well. What appears as less competent practice may be all that can be done in light of what a client can pay. Blaming the lawyers may be little more than a way of avoiding the costs of changing the way legal services are provided.

At least in the short run, legal education is unlikely to solve such an ill-defined problem as professional competence. Unfortunately, the time for grand experimental programs seems to have passed. Law schools, as all university departments, probably will have to fight to hold as much ground as possible. Individuals acting alone or in small groups seldom can foment revolutionary change. Yet individual law professors could take small steps which might have some impact. Most simply they could give equal time to both a judge's and a lawyer's perspective. They could take seriously the old claim of legal education that it teaches about the legal process or the legal system. If this were done, students would see a picture taken with a wide-angle lense rather than the small part of the total scene now highlighted by the telephoto lense aimed at the analysis of legal doctrine. Perhaps the first step toward professional competence which a law school could offer its students would be a more accurate picture of what it is lawyers do.

Lawyer Advertising: "Yes, But ..."

Stewart Macaulay

Contents

Abstract Recently, in both the United States and great Britain lawyers have been permitted to advertise. Reactions are mixed. Some see the change as an assault on professionalism and opening the door to misleading consumers of legal services. Others hail the change as opening the door to lower prices, efficiency and increased

---

This article was original published in Institute for Legal Studies Working Paper 2, University of Wisconsin, Law School, Madison WI, 1986. Reprinted with permission.
This paper was given on May 23, 1985, at the European Workshop on Consumer Law held in Brussels. I want to thank Thierry Bourgoignie and Monigue Goyens of the Centre de Droit de la Consommation, Universite Catholique de Louvain, for inviting me and for their kindness while I was in Belgium. My colleagues Stuart Gullickson, Neil Komesar, Jack Ladinsky, Theodore Schneyer, David Trubek, and Elizabeth Warren offered helpful comments on earlier drafts of the paper. Dr. Jacqueline Macaulay, PhD., J.D., read the manuscript critically and, as always, made it much better. Among her many qualifications for reworking this manuscript, she is a practicing lawyer who advertises in the Madison, Wisconsin telephone directory yellow pages. Anne Reilly edited the final draft and improved it. Kathy Kolstad compiled and Bill Ebbott edited *Lawyer Advertising: A Bibliography of Articles about its Effects on Business for Attorneys, Consumer Costs for Legal Services, and Public Opinion of the Legal Profession* (University of Wisconsin Law School Library, March 1985). This document made my task much easier. Marc Galanter gave me his file of clippings and articles on lawyer advertising which I merged with my own. Of course, even after all this help, mistakes are mine.

S. Macaulay (✉)
University of Wisconsin Law School, Madison, WI, USA
e-mail: smacaula@wisc.edu

D. Campbell (ed.), *Stewart Macaulay: Selected Works*, Law and Philosophy Library 133, https://doi.org/10.1007/978-3-030-33930-2_7

access to legal services. This article reviews the available data. While they are suggestive, they do not begin to chart the likely impact of lawyer advertising. Some studies are seriously misleading. The issues are complex and raise questions that are difficult to answer. More seriously, the whole debate about lawyer advertising may divert attention from more important issues concerning access to the legal system. Cases that should be resolved by other-than-legal means may be channelled to lawyers. Cases involving complex issues rather than procedures that can be standardized still may require expensive services beyond the reach of much of the population. Advertising may cost lawyers and the public some of the virtues of professionalism. It may, on the other hand, help make some services at reasonable prices available. However, we can wonder whether it will make much difference in the long run. In other words, our conclusion is likely to be, "yes, but . . ."

Until recently, most lawyers everywhere assumed that advertising and the practice of law were incompatible. Over the past decade the rules in the United States changed, and lawyers began to advertise.[1] Many bought discrete notices in the yellow pages of the telephone directory, but a few hired sports stars to endorse them on television. Large corporate law firms hired public relations experts to fashion marketing strategies. Views about these changes differ sharply. United States Supreme Court Chief Justice Burger objected to lawyers "using the same modes of advertising as other commodities, from mustard, cosmetics and laxatives to used cars."[2] He said that his advice to the public was "never, never, never, under any circumstances, engage the services of a lawyer who advertises."[3] The Chief Justice's statements reflect the views of many lawyers. On the other hand, members of the staff of the Federal Trade Commission, writers associated with a law and economics approach, and many consumer advocates see the new freedom for lawyer advertising as a great reform.

[1]In both the United States and the United Kingdom, the rules concerning lawyer advertising have been changed to allow greater freedom. In the United States, *Bates and O'Steen v. State Bar of Arizona*, 433 U.S. 350 (1977), found absolute prohibitions on lawyer advertising unconstitutional in 1977. In the UK, efforts to free solicitors to advertise began in 1976, and after reports favoring advertising by the Monopolies and Mergers Commission and the Royal Commission on Legal Services, the Law Society adopted rules allowing lawyer advertising in October 1984. See Attanasio, "Lawyer Advertising in England and the United States," 32 Am. J. of Comp. L. 493 (1984); Merricks, "Individual Advertising—At Last," 133 New L.J., Nov. 25, 1983, at 1028; Editorial, "Unrestricted Advertising," 134 New L. J., May 18, 1984, at 465; Merricks, "Publicity and Public Relations," 134 New L.J., May 18, 1984, at 467-8. For experience in Victoria, Australia, under changes that went into effect in September of 1982, see Law Report, "Few Solicitors Advertise, and Those Who Do Don't Spend Much on It," 58 Law Inst. J. 178-9 (1984). See, also, New South Wales, Law Reform Commission, *Third Report on the Legal Profession: Advertising and Specialisation* (1982). I will focus on the American experience since the change in the UK is so recent that it is too soon for anyone to study its full impact. I lack information about the nature and impact of the Australian change.

[2]*Chi. Daily L.Bull.*, Dec. 7, 1984, at 1, col. 4.

[3]*Wash. Post*, July 8, 1985, at 1, col. 3.

I will consider lawyer advertising, and what we know about its likely impact. I will review the literature and suggest that we need to learn a good deal more. Also, lawyer advertising is but a means to achieve various ends. While lawyer advertising is significant, advocates and opponents claim far more for its impact than seems likely. We must understand its impact, but, at the same time, we must ask whether attention is being diverted from more important questions. In short, the response to claims for and against lawyer advertising must be "yes, but . . ."

I. The Changes in Rule and Practice

At the outset, we must recognize that it is impossible to state an American law of lawyer advertising. The Supreme Court's *Bates* decision said that a state could not ban all lawyer advertising. *In re R.M.J.*[4] involved a challenge to rules adopted by the Supreme Court of Missouri after the *Bates* case. These rules permitted lawyers only to publish in newspapers, periodicals and the telephone directory yellow pages. Their advertisements could contain only specified information such as areas of practice, schools attended, office hours, credit arrangements, and fixed fees for certain routine legal services. A lawyer tested the rule by advertising in a neighborhood newspaper in a form not approved by the rules and by sending announcements of the opening of his office to potential clients. The United States Supreme Court reversed a decision subjecting the lawyer to professional discipline. It emphasized that a state could regulate where the purpose was to curb false, deceptive or misleading advertising. However, there was no evidence that any of the lawyer's material was misleading.

In *Zauderer v. Office of Disciplinary Counsel*[5] the Supreme Court struck down Ohio's ban on solicitation of clients through advertisements containing advice and information about specific legal problems. The parties stipulated that the advertisement did not contain false, fraudulent, misleading or deceptive statements. The attorney had stated that his firm represented women injured by the Dalkon Shield contraceptive on a contingent fee basis. The advertisement invited women to call for "free information." The lawyer received over 200 inquiries, and he initiated suits on behalf of 106 of those who contacted him. The state's interest in preventing lawyers from "stirring up litigation" did not justify the ban on such ads. "The State is not entitled to interfere with . . . access [to civil courts] by denying its citizens accurate information about their legal rights."[6] Obviously, many questions are left open by the *Bates*, *In re R.J.M.*, and *Zauderer* decisions.[7]

---

[4]455 U.S. 191 (1982).

[5]__U.S.__, 105 S. Ct. 2265 (1985).

[6]*Id.*, 105 S. Ct. at 2278.

[7]For discussion of the *Bates*, and *In re R.J.M.* cases, see Stoltenberg and Whitman, "Direct Mail Advertising by Lawyers," 45 *U. Pitt. L. Rev.* 381 (1984); Note, "Attorney Advertising Over the

There are other reasons why we cannot fashion an American rule on lawyer advertising. The United States is a federal system, and so potentially we could have fifty different rules as long as they pass constitutional review by the Supreme Court. Some states have allowed lawyers to advertise subject only to very few restrictions; others have attempted to limit lawyer advertising as much as they can in the face of the Supreme Court's opinions. On the other hand, the activities of the American Bar Association promote some degree of uniformity. Regulation of lawyers is one of the areas in which distinctions between public and private sectors are blurred. In many states regulation of lawyers is under the control of the state supreme court, but the state bar association, and often bar associations in the larger cities are influential in shaping and administering state rules. The American Bar Association is a private organization representing only those lawyers who join it. Nevertheless, it has long issued model rules about legal ethics and many states have adopted them in whole or in part. At the very least, these proposals influence the agenda for debate in the various states.

The ABA drafted proposals in response to the Supreme Court's *Bates* decision which are likely to be influential. However, the Antitrust Division of the Department of Justice called the ABA's proposed rules "anticompetitive," and said that they would "restrict the flow of useful information from attorneys to consumers."[8] The staff of the Federal Trade Commission has drafted another model code far less restrictive than the ABA's proposals.[9] These comments and proposals, in light of the Supreme Court's opinions, might also influence the rules finally adopted in the various states.

Furthermore, whatever standards are enacted, the rules as applied could vary greatly in different sections of any one state—what is acceptable in New York City would not necessarily go unchallenged in Buffalo. On one hand, almost any set of rules creates a range within which judgments about what is permissible and prohibited can vary. On the other hand, someone must complain to trigger law enforcement, and lawyers in one part of a state might be far more offended by advertising practices of their colleagues than those in other areas. Finally, we must note informal social sanctions also play a part in reinforcing customary norms about proper professional conduct. Many lawyers would not consider advertising because they think it is just not done by true professionals, and they care what other lawyers think of them.

We have seen a great increase in lawyer advertising in the United States since the *Bates* decision in 1977. Most discussions of the subject highlight again and again a

---

Broadcast Media," 32 *Vand. L. Rev.* 755 (1979); Student Project, "Attorney Advertising: Bates: Impact on Regulation," 29 *S.C.L. Rev.* 457 (1978).

[8] *N.Y. Times*, Sept. 25, 1984, at 34, cols. 2–6.

[9] Staff of Federal Trade Commission, *Improving Consumer Access to Legal Services: The Case for Removing Restrictions On Truthful Advertising* (November 1984).

few colorful examples which at least some lawyers see as atrocity stories.[10] For example, Ken Hur advertised his legal clinic in Madison, Wisconsin in several now classic television ads that have become known in professional circles throughout the United States.[11] In one, Hur emerges from a pool wearing a diver's mask and gear and asks whether the viewer is "in over your head" and needs help in dealing with debts. In another, Hur promised to give clients ten-speed bikes if they lost their driver's license after hiring his legal clinic to represent them in drunk driving cases. Most writers are unaware that both ads were parodies of others run by Madison merchants. While neither added to the dignity of the legal profession, most Madison television viewers probably understood the implicit references and appreciated Hur's sense of humor.

Other classic television advertisements for lawyers involve endorsements by famous athletes.[12] In one shown in the Washington, D.C. area, John Riggins, a star of the Washington Redskins football team who is noted for his aggressive play, says,

> I don't like to get hurt. And I don't like to lose. I don't imagine you do, either. But if you have been hurt on the job or by someone's carelessness or negligence . . . call the law firm of Ashcraft & Gerel.

Other advertisements on television are far more dignified. Milwaukee personal injury specialist Robert Habush created a successful campaign and then sold it to other lawyers.[13] He created 54 different 60 second question-and-answer commentaries about various legal issues, most of them related to personal injury law, contingent fees, types of accidents that are actionable and the like. He reportedly spent $150,000 to start the campaign and $10,000 a month to maintain it.[14] However, it increased his case filings and referrals by more than 30 percent.

Instead of making price transparent to consumers, lawyers' advertising tends to offer an image of competent and dignified professionalism. As the *National Law Journal*[15] reported in 1984,

> Bar leaders who once thought legal advertising would bring out the hucksters now admit that most of it is professionally and responsibly done. Thomas S. Johnson of the Rockford, Ill.,

---

[10]For the functions of "atrocity stories," see Dingwall, "Atrocity Stories and Professional Relationships," 4 *Soc. Work & Occupations* 371 (1977). A key point is that atrocity stories are not typical and often are misleading.

[11]See Barker, "Ads: A Case of Contention," *Advertising Age*, April 23, 1984, at 3, col. 3, p. 119, cols. 1–3; *N.Y. Times*, July 8, 1979, at 28, cols. 1–2.

[12]See Middleton, "Ads Pay Off—In Image and Income," *Nat'l L.J.*, Mar. 5, 1984, at 1, col. 4, p. 22, cols. 1–4, p. 24, cols. 1–4.

[13]See Clarendon, "Advice from Some Who Have Tried Advertising," *Fla. B.J.* 19 (Feb. 1985).

[14]Much of the business in an office such as that run by Habush comes from referrals from other lawyers who pass on cases beyond their abilities. Firms specializing in major personal injury litigation want clients to be aware of their firms so that they will welcome having their own lawyers refer their cases to a particular personal injury firm and think well of their own lawyer for arranging such representation.

[15]Nat'l L.J., Mar. 5, 1984, at 1, col. 4, p. 22, cols. 2–3.

firm of Williams & McCarthy, P.C., who serves on an ABA committee on the delivery of legal services, admits that *Bates* threw him into an "apoplectic rage," and that he feared its consequences. But most of today's advertising, he says, "is dignified, non-misleading, effectively produced and high quality."

A large percentage of lawyer advertising tells the reader little or nothing about specific fees for services. Those advertisements that do quote prices deal with only a few routine matters. It is difficult to name a flat fee for all legal services needed in a complex matter where a lawyer must respond to hard-to-predict actions and reactions by an attorney on the other side. Lawyers could advertise that they would handle, for example, any divorce for a specified sum and hope that those cases where the matter was easy would balance out those which were unexpectedly difficult and time consuming. So far, few lawyers have seen any need to accept these kinds of risks.

The Television Bureau of Advertising reported in March of 1984 that 414 lawyers and legal clinics spent more than $28 million on TV advertising. This sum was slightly below the amount spent by stockbrokers and investment firms. It was far less than the $577.5 million paid by restaurants and fast-food establishments, the group that spent the most on television in 1983. Hyatt Legal Services is a chain of 157 low-cost legal clinics in 24 television markets. It spent the most on legal advertising in 1984 of any law practice, some $4,475,000, which was an increase of 45% over its spending the previous year. However, Hyatt reported that its television ads attract 18,000 new clients a month.[16]

Lawyers who invest such sums advertising on television are hardly typical. In 1979, about two years after the *Bates* decision, a public opinion research firm polled a random sample of members of the American Bar Association. Only 7% had advertised; 91% had not. 64% of those who had advertised used the telephone directory yellow pages or newspapers while no one in the sample used television.[17] Linenberger & Murdock[18] studied a sample of Wyoming lawyers. 29% had advertised, 41.5% of these lawyers advertised in a law directory and the telephone directory yellow pages, but none spent money on television. In a similar poll of ABA members published in June of 1984, only 13% had tried advertising. This was the same percentage as in 1983, and bar officials speculated that the number of lawyers advertising was leveling off. About 60% of those who advertised were satisfied, but about 30% were not. 71% indicated that advertising brought in additional business, and two-thirds felt that it led to better recognition among the general public.[19]

How should we interpret these numbers? Peter Levin, a lawyer who chairs the ABA's committee on marketing legal services, said that he was not surprised that

[16] *Nat'l L.J.*, Mar. 25, 1985, at 3, col. 1, p. 32, col. 4.

[17] 65 *A.B.A.J.* 1014 (1979).

[18] Linenberger & Murdock, "Legal Service Advertising: Wyoming Attorney Attitudes Compared with Consumer Attitudes," 17 *Land &Water L. Rev.* 209 (1982).

[19] Reskin, "Lawyer Advertising Levels off; P.R. Use Growing," 70 *A.B.A.J.* 48, 49 (1984).

advertising had leveled off. Newspapers and telephone directories become cluttered with many small advertisements. Television campaigns appearing repeatedly over time may be effective, but only a very few lawyers can afford them. Levin thinks that in the future there will be "more television ads, but less lawyers doing it."[20]

Also, we must remember that the bar in larger cities in the United States is highly stratified, and different types of lawyers serve distinct kinds of clients. Lawyers who are graduates of elite law schools usually work in large firms that handle complex problems of larger corporations and wealthy individuals. Those from less prestigious schools often practice alone or with one or two others and deal with the problems of individuals and their smaller businesses.[21] Most of their work is easier to reduce to routine and to standardize.

Hazard, Pearce and Stempel[22] argue that every law practice combines individualized and standardized production, and this combination determines the approach taken to advertising. For example, lawyers who handle approaches to problems of corporations and the wealthy will not take a shotgun approach to advertising. They must attract clients who need and can pay for time consuming professional activities. Mass media advertising would not target their potential clients. Firms that offer services to corporations and wealthy individuals have begun to engage in what is called marketing as distinguished from advertising.[23] For example, expensive brochures are produced and distributed to likely clients and other lawyers who might refer business. Politically prominent lawyers with contacts in government join firms that deal with government regulation.[24] Members of the firm write articles about technical legal problems that are published in prestigious law reviews, and copies are distributed to lawyers who work for large corporations and hire outside law firms to provide particular services. Some of these larger firms have contributed to public

---

[20]L.A. *Daily J.*, June 20, 1984, at 5, col. 1.

[21]John P. Heinz and Edward O. Laumann, *Chicago Lawyers*; *The Social Structure of the Bar* (New York, Basic Books, 1982).

[22]Hazard, Pearce and Stempel, "Why Lawyers Should Be Allowed to Advertise: A Market Analysis of Legal Services," 58 *N.Y.U.L. Rev.* 1084 (1983).

[23]See, *e.g.*, King, "What Works, What Doesn't in Advertising," 71 *A.B.A.J.* 54 (1985); Curtis & Akins, "Effective Marketing: How Firms Can Improve Their Image," 20 *Trial* 54 (Dec. 1984); Smock & Heintz, "Attracting Clients with Marketing, 69 *A.B.A.J.* 1432 (1983); Taylor, "Law Firms Squirm, Then Turn to Public Relations," *N.Y.Times*, July 27, 1983, at 10, cols. 3–6; "The Blue-chip Lawyers Discover Marketing," *Bus. Week*, April 25, 1983, pp. 89, 93–4; Goldstein, "Marketing Lawyers' Services into the 1980's," 54 *N. Y. St. B. J.* 202 (1982).

[24]For example, Howard H. Baker, Jr. is the former Majority Leader in the United States Senate and a possible presidential candidate in 1988. When he retired from the Senate in January of 1985, he became the head of the Washington, D.C., office of a large law firm with an estimated salary of $750,000 a year. One lawyer explained that "[b]ecause of his name, the people he knows, good judgment, high respect, corporate clients would look at him and think he could give them access in the highest places." The *New York Times* notes that "Mr. Baker will not have to peddle his influence for it to be felt . . . When his partners make their rounds in the Administration and Congress, their powers of persuasion will be enhanced by association with a Republican powerhouse who could be the next President." *N.Y. Times*, Dec. 11, 1984, at 8, cols. 3–6.

television stations in return for credit on the air or supported programs of classical music on public broadcasting stations or FM stations that play this kind of music. Presumably this approach reaches an audience that might use their legal services.

In contrast, lawyers in large cities offering services such as simple wills, uncontested divorces, and routine personal injury negotiation depend on a high volume of work to make money. These firms attempt to attract a broad array of clients. All lawyers willing to handle problems for individuals and small businesses may find some sort of advertisement in the telephone directory yellow pages useful. However, only those who can standardize certain services needed by many people and organize their practice so they can mass process clients are likely to find that the extremely high price of an advertising campaign on television will pay.[25]

II. The Impact of the Changes

A. *Rhetoric and Politics*

What has been the impact of lawyer advertising, and what will the impact be in the future? On one hand, some leaders of the bar and judges offer a morality play, a simple but plausible story teaching that advertising leads to disaster. On the other hand, reformers, both in and outside the academy, counter with a picture of advertising leading us to the promised land. As we might expect, the rules governing lawyer advertising were not established and changed in a vacuum. As always, we must attend to the political context of these positions and predictions. Advocates of lawyer advertising come from both the consumer movement and the champions of deregulation who celebrate the virtues of the market. Motivations and positions are not always clear.

Opponents of lawyer advertising paint a gloomy but easy to recognize picture. Lawyers will advertise, and the relationship between lawyers and clients will be transformed from a professional to a commercial one. Instead of an ethic of service, lawyers will march to the drum of the market and self interest. Advertising will stress low prices for basic legal needs. Lawyers can offer these prices only by standardization. This prompts the growth of large organizations that can afford the staff and equipment necessary to process large numbers of routine cases. Once they lose opportunities for creativity and responsibility, bored lawyers[26] will only put in their hours. The quality of the work will then decline to a mediocre level.

[25]See Mitchell, "The Impact, Regulation and Efficacy of Lawyer Advertising," 20 *Osgoode Hall L. J.* 119 (1982).

[26]Routine and boredom already are part of practice. A survey of ABA members in 1983 showed that only 59% said they would choose law again if given a second chance. "Fourteen percent, including many lawyers 30 or younger, indicated they would like to be doing work that was less routine in nature." See Smith, "A Profile of Lawyer Lifestyles," 70 *A.B.A.J.* 50, 54 (1984). The mass processing involved in highly advertised legal clinics may make practice even more boring.

Advertising legal services, in this gloomy picture, also leads to misrepresentation. It is hard to evaluate legal services. There is no thing called a will or a divorce that is always the same. Low prices will be quoted for basic services, and lawyers will have to meet the competition. In order to offer services at prices driven down by competitive advertising, lawyers will cut the quality of the work they deliver. Clients will be fooled into thinking that they need only a standardized product when actually they need work that takes account of their special situation. Other lawyers may engage in "bait and switch" tactics, luring clients to their offices by advertising low prices but persuading them to buy costly but unneeded personalized services once they are there. In all of this, good ethical lawyers will be driven out by the bad who can successfully win over a gullible public responding to advertising tricks.[27]

Those advocating broad freedom for lawyers to advertise tell a very different story.[28] Informed consumers will compare prices and make judgments about the likely quality of services offered by various attorneys. This will spark competition among lawyers who will lower prices and increase quality. Lawyers will lower costs by increasing efficiency, turning to new technology, and substituting less skilled for more skilled workers wherever possible. Competition will drive untalented and inefficient lawyers from the practice or they will change their ways. Firms will strive to establish valuable trade names as part of advertising their reputations, and this will induce them to avoid doing anything to harm their image. The market will thus police itself against misrepresentation and bait and switch tactics. In addition, advertising will expand the market by attracting new clients who have never used lawyers in the past. Advertising opens access to the legal system. Greater access itself will allow efficient lawyers to exploit economies of scale and further reduce costs.

These morality plays, of course, are rhetorical ploys in a political battle among partisans. Both stories seem plausible, reflecting simple common sense. However, both contain elements of truth well mixed with overstatement. Neither side is much troubled by data and complexity. Claims about lawyer advertising are not put forward as part of a neutral exercise, and much is at stake. If we are to appraise the positions, we need to understand the context of the battle.

Lawyer advertising once was accepted in the United States. Advocates note an advertisement placed in a newspaper in 1853 by Abraham Lincoln promising "all business . . . will be attended to with promptness and fidelity."[29] The ABA's 1908 Canons of Ethics, a model code which was adopted by many but not all states, introduced strong limitations on advertising. These Canons were part of an attempt

---

[27]Attanasio notes that Mr. Justice Powell's dissenting opinion in the *Bates* case states most of the arguments against advertising, 433 U.S. at 389–404, and this opinion is relied on by the Royal Commission on Legal Services in the United Kingdom. See Attanasio, *supra* n. 1, at 507–8.

[28]This morality play can be found in a number of places. For relatively pure versions, uncluttered with qualifications, see Staff of Federal Trade Commission, *supra* n. 9; Greene, "Lawyers versus the Marketplace," *Forbes*, Jan. 16, 1984, at 73.

[29]See Staff of Federal Trade Commission, *supra*, n. 9, at 20, where a copy of the advertisement is reproduced.

to defend the "better element" in the bar from the inroads of a commercial spirit and the practices of those who were not gentlemen. Some writers have stressed that the elite of the bar were anti-Semitic.[30] They see past campaigns against commercialization and for professionalism in part as attempts to limit the upward mobility of Jews and other children of immigrants. Whatever the explanation, Gordon notes that the American bar has lamented a loss of professionalism and the rise of commercialism since the 19th century.[31] Pressure for tougher anticommercialism came in the depression of the 1930s when lawyers found "cut-throat competition" as distasteful as did many other business people in that era. The ABA in 1937 responded by tightening its model rules so that lawyers could only insert notices in approved law lists circulated to other lawyers and not to the public.[32]

Several social movements came together to advocate allowing lawyers to advertise. One was 1960s activism. Reformers saw access to law for those of modest means as a great cause. Minimum fee schedules and the ban on solicitation and advertising priced legal services and justice beyond the reach of many. Furthermore, advertising bans and similar restrictions were seen as control by the upper strata of the bar. Claims of dignity and professionalism were unpopular with the generation coming of age in the 1960s and 1970s, A body of academic writing exposing regulation by the regulated or the capture of administrative agencies by special interests set the stage for this reaction. The claims of the organized bar appeared as but special interest pleading.[33]

Another social movement served the cause of lawyer advertising. By the mid-1970s, many writers and political leaders called for deregulation of the economy to achieve efficiency. Big government and the welfare state could claim less and less legitimacy. This law and economics analysis was easily adapted to decry restraints on competition in professional services. The leaders of bar associations found themselves advocating regulation of their own profession but advocating deregulation elsewhere to benefit many of their corporate clients. However, they saw law as special and different—more than just a business.

At the same time these groups were arguing for deregulation of lawyers in the name of access for those of limited means, others were attempting to limit the

[30]See Auerbach, *Unequal Justice: Lawyers and Social Change* in *Modern America* (1976).

[31]Gordon, "The Devil and Daniel Webster), 94 *Yale L.J.* 445 (1984); Gordon, "'The Ideal and the Actual in the Law': Fantasies and Practices of New York City Lawyers, 1870–1910," in Gerard W. Gawait ed., *The New High Priests: Lawyers in Post-Civil War America*, pp. 53–74 (Greenwood Press 1984). See also Schudson, "Public, Private, and Professional Lives: The Correspondence of David Dudley Field and Samuel Bowles," 21 *Am.J. Legal History* 191 (1977). For a recent example written by a prominent lawyer, see Belin, "The Law Business," 82 *Mich. L.Rev.* 953, 954–5 (1984) ("Indeed, one of the tragedies of our times is that law practice is becoming more and more of a business and less and less of a profession in the traditional sense of the word.").

[32]See Taylor, "For Advertising by Lawyers, A Verdict is at Hand," *Advertising Age*, July 18, 1983, at M. 26–7.

[33]See, *e.g.*, Comment, "Advertising, Solicitation and the Profession's Duty to Make Legal Counsel Available," 81 *Yale L.J.* 1181 (1972).

assertion of legal rights in the name of efficiency or social harmony. These critics attacked contingent fees in personal injury and products liability cases involving claims for large sums as damages.[34] Contingent fees are a triumph of the free market in legal services and have provided a great deal of access to the courts for people of modest means.[35] However, images of greedy lawyers making fortunes from the misery of others were widely circulated. Doctors and their malpractice insurers were joined by manufacturers of consumer products. They all championed less representation of the injured as a means of cutting the costs of doing business.

Still other critics attacked what they saw as a litigation explosion.[36] From the mid-1950s to the mid-1970s, American courts and legislatures created many legal rights for those dissatisfied with traditional practices. In the beginning reformers tried to supply subsidized lawyers to vindicate these rights, conservatives have attacked this kind of public interest lawyering vigorously and successfully. The editors of the *Yale Law Journal* assert

> one suspects that an unvoiced reason for the animus against stirring up litigation is the fear that some of the litigation stirred up will involve socially unpopular causes—such as suits attacking segregation or those brought by tenants against landlords or consumers against corporations.[37]

Silberman, reflecting a very different political viewpoint, supports the Yale editors' suspicion, saying:

> [A]ttacks on legal profession entry limitations and advertising restrictions may be misguided. The economy as a whole may be better off if we considerably toughened bar examinations and thereby reduce the number of practicing lawyers, as well as tightened, rather than loosened, advertising restrictions ... Disdain for capitalism and capitalists, elitism couched in Naderite concern for consumers and the poor, impatience with the democratic process as an inadequate engine for social change—all follow from the power afforded those who join the ministers of the legal process. They respond to the prospect not of the rule of law, but of the rule of lawyers .. . .
>
> Unless our political institutions mount a virtual counterrevolution against the legal process, our only hope of preserving the vigor of democratic capitalism may be for the legal process to become so unwieldy that private and political decision-making gain a comparative advantage. But then the legal process would be less available for those matters for which it is truly needed.[38]

---

[34]See, *e.g.*, Case, "Lawyers Often Are Grossly Overpaid," *N.Y. Times*, Dec. 2, 1984, §3, at 2, cols. 3–6.

[35]See, *e.g.*, Baldwin, "The Sure Way to Protect the Little Guy," *N.Y. Times*, Dec. 2, 1984, §3, at 2, cols. 3–6.

[36]For a very critical review of the alleged litigation explosion, see Galanter, "Reading the Landscape of Disputes: What We Know and Don't Know (and Think We Know) About Our Allegedly Contentious and Litigious Society, 31 *U.C.L.A. L. Rev.* 1 (1983).

[37]Comment, *supra* n. 33, at 1189.

[38]Silberman, "Will Lawyering Strangle Democratic Capitalism?" *Regulation*, at 20, n. 5, 44 (March/April 1978).

Hazard, Pearce & Stempel[39] argue that the opposition to advertising is both instrumental and symbolic. Those lawyers whose practices are undercut by legal clinics and other firms that advertise play important roles in local, state and national bar associations. In addition, advertising suggests that legal assistance is a commodity clients buy and lawyers sell. Opposition is, in part, "a consequence of the inconsistency between providing legal services through the free market and realizing equal justice before the law." The legal profession does not want to acknowledge this tension between ideal and reality.[40]

B. What Do We Know About the Impact of Lawyer Advertising?

Scholars from various fields have written about lawyer advertising. We can distinguish three kinds of studies: (1) surveys of attitudes of potential clients and lawyers toward attorney advertising; (2) applications of economic analysis; and (3) the Federal Trade Commission's staff's research about the impact of various kinds of regulation of advertising on prices and quality. We have some data and analysis, although far less than we need to resolve the issues these writers raise. We will in turn consider these types of studies critically.

A number of articles report research concerning attitudes about lawyer advertising.[41] Questionnaires administered to more or less random samples of lawyers and consumers can tell us who likes and who dislikes advertising. However, they cannot tell us how much weight to give such things as a lawyer's judgment that it will confuse and mislead consumers. These attitude studies reach predictable conclusions, suggesting that consumers favor lawyer advertising while lawyers do not.

[39] Hazard, Pearce & Stempel, "Why Lawyers Should Be Allowed to Advertise: A Market Analysis of Legal Services," 58 *N.Y.U.L. Rev.* 1084, 1113 (1983).

[40] Others championed informal alternatives to litigation where lawyers play little if any role. Rather than have lawyers compete to represent certain kinds of clients, people would settle matters by compromise and the establishment of harmony. Often the compromises and harmony seem produced by a kind of magic in the informalism rhetoric. Santos, "Law and Community: The Changing Nature of State Power in Late Capitalism," 8 *Int'l J. Soc. L.* 379 (1980), argues that informalism without lawyers is only a way to deflect the potential vindication of the new rights created in the reforms of the 1960s and 1970s and coopt social fields that might rival the state. Whether or not Santos' explanation covers everything that has happened, it fits much of the recent history in the fields of civil rights.

[41] See, *e.g.*, Kallis & Vanier, "Consumer Perceptions of Attorney and Legal Service Advertising: A Managerial Approach to the Delivery of Legal Services," 14 *Akron Bus. & Econ. Rev.* 42 (1983); Linenberger & Murdock, "Legal Service Advertising: Wyoming Attorney Attitudes Compared with Consumer Attitudes," 17 *Land & Water L. Rev.* 209 (1982); Smith & Meyer, "Attorney Advertising: A Consumer Perspective," 44 *J. Marketing* 56 (1980); Dyer & Shimp, "Reactions to Legal Advertising, 20 *J. Ad. Research* 43 (1980); Shimp & Dyer, How the Legal Profession Views Legal Service Advertising, 42 *J. Marketing* 74 (1978); Shimp, Ohio Lawyers' Attitudes Toward Legal Service Advertising," 4 *Ohio N.L. Rev.* 576 (1977).

Kallis and Vanier report that 75% of those in a quota sample of 361 adults in Southern California thought lawyers should be free to advertise; 62% did not think that lawyers who advertised did inferior work; and 76% wanted advertisements containing information about specific fees. However, 40% said that advertising would not influence their choice of a lawyer. Only 26% thought that advertising would give them an opportunity to make a better selection of one.

Shimp and Dyer said that the majority of the lawyers in two states answering a questionnaire survey in 1976 before the *Bates* decision believed that advertising would erode public confidence in the legal profession. These lawyers thought it would become deceptive and confuse rather than enlighten potential clients. Dyer and Shimp ran another study after the *Bates* case, questioning both lawyers and consumers. They asked both groups to react to sample advertisements. They found

> both lawyers' and consumers' evaluations improve as more information is contained in the ads, but lawyers are particularly skeptical of including fee information in their ads. The dilemma is that this is probably the kind of information that consumers most desire, but the least likely they will receive. Lawyers feel that fee information in ads is deceptive since many legal services are nonstandard.[42]

Linenberger and Murdock surveyed samples of Wyoming consumers and lawyers in 1981. They tell us that 56% of the lawyers agreed that advertising created a bad public image for the profession while nearly 80% of the consumers disagreed. 70% of the consumers thought that advertising would improve the quality of legal services while 67% of the lawyers disagreed. 57% of the lawyers thought existing sources of information about attorneys were adequate while 69% of the consumers thought they were inadequate.

Most of these surveys were conducted in the late 1970s or early 1980s, before the *Bates* decision had much impact. We cannot be sure of the continued validity of these earlier studies. Research conducted today or in the future could tap reactions based on actual experience.

A second type of study attempts to predict the impact of permitting lawyer advertising by applying economic theory and drawing analogies to what that body of work tells us about advertising in general.[43] Most simply, this theory tells us that if firm A offers to draft a will for $100 and firm B offers to draft *the same will* for $75, an informed consumer will become a client of firm B. Furthermore, we can expect firm A to learn of the situation and seek to find ways to cope. It can lower its price to $75, but, to do this, it must deal with the situation. Firm A can cut costs. Firm A may seek greater efficiency in managing its business. On the other hand, it might seek to differentiate its product and offer a better will for $100 than firm B produces for $75. The consumer then could decide whether the added quality was worth the extra $25.

---

[42]Dyer & Shimp, *supra* n. 41, at 50.

[43]See Attanasio, *supra* n. 1; Mitchell, *supra* n. 25; Hudec & Trebilcock, "Lawyer Advertising and the Supply of Information in the Market for Legal Services," 20 *U.W.Ont. L. Rev.* 53 (1982); Hazard, Pearce & Stempel, *supra* n. 22; Muris & McChesney, "Advertising and the Price and Quality of Legal Services: The Case for Legal Clinics," 1979 *A.B.Found. Research* J. 179.

Mitchell points out that this model is too simple. Advertising works best when relatively little is at stake and buyers are not uncertain about the product. If we respond to an advertisement for a can of peaches and are disappointed, we lose little. Most of us feel fairly comfortable judging the quality of peaches. Our experience tells us there is little quality difference among brands of the same grade of canned fruit. If we are considering purchasing an expensive automobile, advertising will likely only supplement other sources of Information. Often we rely on a trade name as a surrogate for our own quality judgment. For example, Sears stores in the United States sell products ranging from hardware to clothing. Sears advertises its trade name frequently. In particular situations, Sears' price may not be the lowest and its quality may not be the highest. However, consumers can be fairly sure that they will pay a reasonable price and receive reasonable quality. Their purchase may not be the best possible, but it will not be a bad one. In a sense, they hire Sears to serve as their purchasing agent to avoid making major mistakes.

How would lawyers' services fit into this picture? Mitchell argues that some legal services fit better than others. Usually the stakes are high when people go to lawyers. However, few potential clients are in a good position to judge either a lawyer's reputation or the services provided. For example, a lawyer may handle a divorce matter successfully in that husband and wife legally are free to marry again. However, the lawyer may quickly negotiate issues of property division and child custody to get a settlement. He may leave his client far short of what lawyers could have arranged if more time had been put into planning and negotiating. The client may be satisfied but never recognize that the lawyer could have done better.[44] Other clients may worry that they cannot judge what they are getting, and they may go to the lawyer they think has the best reputation. They may be willing to pay large fees, assuming that you get only what you pay for. Indeed, if legal services are advertised at a low fee, some potential clients may assume that the services cannot be of high quality. Clients may be more willing to shop for legal services on the basis of price when they think they are buying something standardized such as a will or a simple divorce.

Mitchell suggests that extensive mass media advertising should be effective in densely populated markets for frequently required services which can be supplied by low cost, high volume production methods. Lawyers can advertise other kinds of services in relatively inexpensive telephone directory yellow pages or newspaper classified sections. This approach is likely to have a limited, but perhaps important, impact on practice. Some lawyers may be able to gain clients they otherwise would not have seen. Consumers who notice lawyer advertising will have some additional information. A potential client can discover, for example, that a particular lawyer is willing to take bankruptcy or divorce cases.

---

[44]The opposite often is true as well. The lawyer may have done as well as possible in light of what the client could invest in the case. However, the outcome may leave the client unhappy and unfairly blaming the lawyer for a poor job. Clients do scapegoat lawyers; often they need to blame someone for their situation and lawyers are handy.

However, once lawyers begin to advertise in the telephone directory or newspapers, others are likely to match their efforts. Consumers often face page after page of lawyer advertisements that say almost the same thing. There are no meaningful statistics such as a won and lost record, and critics do not publish reviews of lawyers as they review restaurants and films.[45] Those who can pay large fees often have better sources of information about lawyers than advertising. Hazard, Pearce and Stempel point out that advertising is relatively ineffective compared with personal knowledge and reputation. Advertising must be brief, and it comes from an impersonal source. Often readers or viewers pay little attention to it.

Hudec and Trebilcock note that some law firms have tried to establish national trade names. They hope these names will attract potential clients who rely on the firm's reputation as a way of getting quality service. If the trade name were promoted by advertising, it might enable the firm to market complex and costly services. People could rely on getting reasonable quality and price from a firm concerned with its reputation. However, this reputational sanction may work better in long-term continuing relationships than in one-shot deals. A seller of goods and services always values repeat customers. Those who need a lawyer but once in their life may learn from the transaction that a firm that advertises offers poor service. Nevertheless, this information cannot affect their future behavior. They may talk to friends, but most of us can broadcast our opinions only to a limited number of people.

On the other hand, Hudec and Trebilcock speculate that highly advertised second-class lawyering may drive out good lawyering where clients cannot tell what they are getting. "[C]lients will not be able to verify advertised quality claims and lawyers providing better quality will be unable to recoup the high cost of providing higher quality service since clients will not be willing to pay a higher price for a feature of the service which they cannot be sure that they are indeed receiving."[46] Attanasio suggests that the case for advertising usually assumes efforts at standardization so that a given product can be sold for a named price. He argues that the aggregate quality may increase, but standardization also "increases the potential to shortchange individuals whose problems stray far from the norm."[47]

These writers also theorize about the impact of advertising on the legal profession, an impact that ultimately could affect society as well. Hudec and Trebilcock think that the situation may be a zero sum game. Advertising "will principally have

---

[45]Law directories rate lawyers, but the rating systems can offer only rough indicators of quality such as time in practice, representative clients, and some suggestion of general reputation in the local legal community. Sophisticated users of these directories often use the ratings to exclude some attorneys. Then they consider those left after seeking recommendations from people who know the local bar. Existing directories would be little help to individuals seeking legal assistance for personal matters. Consumer advocates could produce directories that would be helpful to individuals, but it is not clear that individuals would pay to get this information. Group legal services plans, such as those sponsored by unions and cooperatives, may serve to rate lawyers for members.

[46]Hudek & Trebilcock, *supra* n. 43, at 74.

[47]Attanasio, *supra* n. 1, at 527.

the effect of shifting around market shares amongst existing law firms."[48] Hazard, Pearce and Stempel disagree. They state that advertising will increase the total market for legal services by stimulating latent demand.[49] People will learn that they can afford a lawyer and that they need one in situations where they would not now use one. These people will talk about problems, lawyers and the quality of services they received in their social networks. Conversations at taverns or places of employment may pass along a new legal consciousness as well as suggestions about which lawyers to see.

Advertising appears to have helped the development of high volume, low cost modes of delivering relatively standardized services. This could affect existing modes of practice. Hazard, Pearce and Strempel argue that law practices deliver: (1) primarily individualized services; (2) primarily standardized services; or (3) a mixture of individualized and standardized ones. Mixed practices, they say, cannot maximize profits. They are less efficient on individualized cases because they cannot invest the necessary time. They cannot charge as much as the true individualized law firm. They are less efficient on standardized cases because they do not gain the economies of scale that come from devotion to mass processing. Thus these firms cannot afford to invest in television advertising campaigns. These mixed practices today profit by charging inflated fees for standardized services or, alternatively, by using standardized services as loss leaders to attract individualized service business. Advertising will lead to large well known firms offering standardized services at low prices. Today's mixed service firms, these writers predict, will not be able to compete.

Advertising and commercialization may limit devoting time to cases that will not pay and recapturing the cost by charging other clients more. Hudec and Trebilcock say there "may be a legitimate concern that price discrimination is necessary to sustain viable practices in small communities, but this is not a situation in which advertising is likely to occur in any event."[50] Abel[51] points out that activist lawyers representing progressive causes may finance their activities by covering their expenses through conventional work. Advertising may threaten to channel delivery of inexpensive legal services to middle class clients to legal clinics that advertise and merchandise services. Insofar as it does this, there may be less of a base on which to build legal service to various social causes or support engaging in politics. Price discrimination may be a form of progressive taxation necessary for lawyers to offer low or no fee services to those who cannot pay.

Mitchell, on the other hand, doubts whether advertising by legal clinics will drive many of the present firms from the market or force them to offer low cost standardized products. He points out that in choosing a lawyer, clients consider many factors

---

[48]Hudec & Trebilcock, *supra* n. 43, at 99.

[49]See Besharov & Hartle, "Here Come the Mediocre Lawyers," *Wall St.J.*, Feb. 22, 1985, at 26, cols. 3–5.

[50]Hudec & Trebilcock, *supra* n. 43, at 78.

[51]Abel, "Lawyers and the Power to Change," 7 *Law & Pol'y* 5, 8–9 (1985).

other than price such as competency, honesty, special expertise and general reputation. Not everyone enjoys the clinic style of offering professional services; too often a major event in one's life is slotted into a category by a professional or a paraprofessional who will not listen and who tries to get through the encounter as quickly as possible.[52] Some clients seeking the kinds of legal services offered by clinics prefer to go to lawyers they know, even if they pay more. They value continuing relationships with professionals they know. As they build experience they can judge the intangibles such as empathy and really taking time to understand problems. They use recommendations from friends who have special relationships with lawyers. They hope the connection will distinguish their problem from the rest of the lawyer's cases and prompt understanding and action. This kind of service is worth something beyond the cost of the cheapest lawyer available.

When we consider the writing about lawyer advertising based on theories of information and competition, we must remember that not all stores in a community selling the same or similar products charge the same price. Often there is room in a city both for a discount retailer and a supplier who offers advice, service and convenience. People often invest little effort in shopping and investigation. They may decide that a product offered for less really is not as good as that offered by the retailer in the convenient location who gives advice and is willing to replace or repair troublesome products without question. There probably will be room for legal services sold in discount houses, boutiques, and stores for discriminating customers.

Most of the writing based on theories about economics, advertising and the practice of law is quite speculative. The authors predict the future impact of changing the rules concerning lawyer advertising by drawing on theoretical ideas. They are not describing what has happened in any systematic way. Often their analysis is based heavily on personal experiences with law practice, the newer legal clinics or stories about lawyers who advertised and increased their caseload by incredible amounts. Their analyses are plausible and often insightful. However, they may be wrong. They may have labelled as typical what is rare and unusual. They may have underestimated consumers' problems in gaining the information about lawyers' services and fees needed to make judgments. We must look for any better evidence we can find.

---

[52]Muris & McChesney, *supra* n. 43, at 186–87, discuss using paralegals within a systems approach in a divorce case as an illustration of the possibilities of reducing costs. Essentially, a paralegal fills in the blanks on a form originally drafted by a lawyer, and contact with the lawyer is minimized or absent until the proceeding in court. In footnote 25, the authors concede "if lawyers or clients prefer, some client contacts will involve lawyer time and thus not be delegated. Assuming that the lawyer could productively spend time elsewhere, the more time the lawyer spends with the client, the higher the fee will have to be to meet expenses." At least some people would judge the process described as service of very low quality. See, *e.g.*, Feiner, Primavera, Farber & Bishop, "Attorneys as Caregivers During Divorce," 52 *Am.J. Orthopsychiatry* 323 (1982); Redmount, "Marriage Problems, Intervention and the Legal Professional," 50 *Conn.B.J.* 11 (1976); Redmount, "Attorney Personalities and Some Psychological Aspects of Legal Consultation," 109 *U.Pa.L. Rev.* 972 (1961). Of course, paralegal workers could listen to the clients' stories and offer support and counselling, but this does not seem to be what Muris & McChesney are suggesting.

Instead of theorizing about the impact of lawyer advertising or relying on personal experience, we could hope for a systematic collection and analysis of data. As so often is true, little exists. The major empirical study of the impact of regulations limiting lawyer advertising was conducted by staff members of the Cleveland Regional Office and the Bureau of Economics of the Federal Trade Commission[53] They measured the impact of restrictions on lawyer advertising imposed by different state laws on the prices charged for five routine legal services. The services were (1) a simple will, (2) a simple will with a trust provision, (3) a non-business bankruptcy, (4) an uncontested divorce, and (5) a personal injury where the driver of the other car admits responsibility and there is no permanent pain, disability or lost earning capacity. Lawyers in seventeen cities in different states were asked what they would charge for each service. The fees asked were transformed to reflect differences in the cost of living in each of the cities. The laws concerning lawyer advertising were classified for restrictiveness, and multiple linear regression analyses were applied to the data. The basic finding of the study was

> [g]enerally, ... restrictions on advertising raise prices. Attorneys in the more restrictive states, *on the average*, charged higher prices for most simple legal services than those in the less restrictive states. The fact that stronger restrictions on advertising are associated with higher prices suggests that, in this type of market, the dominant effect of advertising is to enhance price competition by lowering consumer search costs. [Emphasis added.][54]

What are we to make of the FTC study? We should read it carefully because it is likely to play a role in debates about lawyer advertising. Its very title—"The Case For Removing Restrictions on Truthful Advertising"—suggests that it is a partisan brief in the form of a scientific study about the impact of restrictions on lawyer advertising on the price of basic legal services.[55] The study does offer evidence of the expected relationship between restriction and price. However, the case is not as clear as the study's conclusions and the press reports about them claim.[56] At the

---

[53]Staff of Federal Trade Commission, *supra* n. 9.

[54]*Id.* at 79.

[55]We cannot treat the staff report as a scientific study in a refereed journal. We must read it carefully, remembering that its authors are not neutrals. The American Bar Association has tried to gain legislation or judicial decisions which would stop the FTC from regulating lawyers. The FTC, in turn, is very critical of what its staff sees as the ABA's attempt to ward off competition in the delivery of legal services. Nevertheless, while the report is a partisan document, some or all of it may be right.

[56]Linda Greenhouse reported in the *N.Y. Times*, Dec. 25, 1984, at 22, col. 1, "[a] Federal Trade Commission staff report issued earlier this month was only the latest of numerous studies to conclude that advertising by lawyers brings increased competition and lower prices for legal services. . . . The researchers found that legal fees for the same services were lower, by 5 to 13 percent, in states with the fewest restrictions on advertising." As we will see, this misreports what the study actually found and ignores many important qualifications. James J. Kilpatrick, the conservative columnist said that the "significant evidence turned up by the FTC study is that prices for five familiar legal services are lower in the less-restrictive states." Kilpatrick, "Lawyer Advertising Drives Prices Down," *Wis. St. J.*, Jan. 16, 1985, §1, at 9, col. 5. Data reported in the tables of the FTC study do not show this. Kilpatrick was misled by the text of the report.

outset, the sample of cities studied seems strange. The largest cities in the country are omitted. The study does not deal with New York, Los Angeles, Chicago, Philadelphia, Dallas-Ft. Worth or Atlanta. The investigators wanted to match states with different kinds of restrictions on lawyer advertising. However, California is represented by Fresno and not San Francisco, Los Angeles or San Diego. Missouri is represented by Springfield and not St. Louis or Kansas City. A defender of the study could argue that we might expect freedom to advertise to have greater impact in the larger cities where there would be mass markets that could be reached. A critic could object that the study's sample is so far from ideal that its statistical results are suspect.[57]

With one exception,[58] less than a quarter of the lawyers in any city studied advertised at all.[59] Almost none of those who advertised used television or radio. Most used the yellow pages of the telephone directory, a means that is cheap but unlikely to have a powerful effect on fees. Very few of those who did advertise anything stated specific fees that would be charged for particular services. This casts doubt on whether, as the FTC Report asserts, the "dominant effect of advertising is to enhance price competition by lowering consumer search costs."[60] Indeed, we can ask how the nature of the state's rules on advertising caused differences in the cost of the five types of legal services studied if so few of the lawyers exercised their freedom to advertise.

Most of the results stressed in the text of the FTC report were based on averages. However, averages can be misleading and difficult to interpret. We often think of an average as typical, but extreme cases can make an average misleading. When we read the FTC study's tables carefully, we see that the presence or absence of advertising restrictions often does not produce the effect predicted by the investigators' theory. At the very least, we must recognize that limiting advertising is not always associated with higher prices for all kinds of work. For example, Table D of the study shows there is a statistically significant relationship between barring direct mail advertising and a *lower* price for a simple will but *higher* prices for divorces and personal injury work. There is also a statistically significant relationship between limiting the content of advertisements in any way and a *lower* price on simple wills but *higher* prices on personal injury work. Connecticut has very restrictive rules on lawyer advertising. However, the fees of Hartford lawyers for four out of the five services studied are lower than average while the fee for the fifth service is just average.

Furthermore, the lack of restrictions on advertising did not necessarily mean lower prices for all the legal services studied. This was true even where a relatively

[57]See Berk and Ray, "Selection Biases in Sociological Data," 11 *Soc.Sci. Research* 352 (1982).

[58]37% of the lawyers in Albuquerque advertised.

[59]In all but five of the seventeen cities, less than 20% of the lawyers advertised. In the five cities where more lawyers advertised the percentages were Milwaukee 20%, Baltimore 20%, Columbus 21%, Fresno 23% and Albuquerque 37%.

[60]Staff of the Federal Trade Commission, *supra* n. 9, at 79.

high percentage of the lawyers advertised. California, Michigan and Wisconsin were classified by the FTC staff as the three least restrictive states. Fresno is the only California city included in the study. 23% of the lawyers surveyed in Fresno advertised, and this is the second highest percentage in the 17 cities surveyed, Nonetheless, Fresno has *higher* than average rates for each of the five routine legal services except personal injury. Also, in Detroit, Michigan, the average rates for wills with trusts, bankruptcy and divorces were lower than the average fees of the 17 cities in the study; however, the average fees for simple wills and personal injury were higher. Milwaukee, Wisconsin has above average fees for simple wills and divorces but lower than average fees for a will with a trust and bankruptcy. The percentage of the award taken under contingent fees in personal injury was 1% lower than average.

The study also compared fees of attorneys in all 17 cities who advertised and fees of those who did not. Those who advertised a specific service provided it at a lower price than both those lawyers who did not advertise at all and those who advertised but did not mention that particular area of practice. However, personal injury was the exception. "In the three cities with statistically significant results for personal injury service, attorneys who advertised personal injury services appeared to charge about a 3 percent higher contingent fee if the case [was] settled before trial than those who did not advertise personal injury services."[61] In a footnote, the report says

> we have been told by some legal clinics that they expect their other routine services to give them a client base for the more lucrative personal injury case. This would be consistent with advertising firms charging less for the other services to attract clients with personal injury cases.[62]

This statement, submerged below the text, undercuts much of the argument made in the body of the FTC report. Perhaps loss leaders do serve consumer interests, but this is a very different argument than that made in the report.

The FTC report argues that advertising allows informed consumers to compare prices and that this tends to push prices downward. However, exceptions to this axiom, found in the study's tables but not stressed in its text, show that it does not always work this way. The causal mechanism is not simple and direct. Competition and somewhat informed consumers may affect the behavior of those marketing any product or service, but suppliers have many options. For example, Americans came to believe that Japanese cars were of higher quality than American ones. American manufacturers could have responded by improving the quality of their cars or advertising so that the public would think that their quality was better. Of course, they did both, and some of us think they did more advertising than engineering. Lawyers, too, will be able to cope with more, but not fully, informed consumers in a number of ways. Lower prices for higher quality work is not necessarily the only option open to them. Indeed, it may be easier for lawyers to create the false

[61] Staff of the Federal Trade Commission, *supra* n. 9, at 125.

[62] *Id.* at 125, n. 267.

impression of quality than it is for automobile manufacturers. Legal services are harder to judge than automobiles that will not operate.

The FTC study attempted to deal with the concern that lower prices would also lower the quality of service. The authors point out that quality is difficult to define since clients may be satisfied with poor service or unhappy with excellent technical lawyering. They speculate that advertising may compensate for any corner-cutting by pressing for new efficient techniques of delivering legal service. Then they rely on Muris and McChesney's[63] study of the Jacoby & Meyers Legal Clinic in Los Angeles.[64] The clinic advertised extensively, and took steps to control costs. The first part of the Muris and McChesney study compared clients' subjective reactions to Jacoby & Meyers' handling of several types of cases with the reactions of others who had used traditional firms for similar cases. Jacoby & Meyers did better than traditional firms on all seven ratings of lawyer quality used. Clients saw it as "more prompt, interested, and honest; as better at explaining matters, keeping clients informed, and paying attention to customers; and, finally, as more fair and reasonable in its charges."[65] However, Muris and McChesney sent out 650 questionnaires but only 74 (52 from the traditional firms and 22 from Jacoby & Meyers) were returned in a form that was usable. The authors tell us nothing about the 576 clients who did not respond. While Muris and McChesney's results support their position, clearly we must be cautious about using this part of their study.

The second part of Muris and McChesney's study involved comparing the results obtained by Jacoby & Meyers and by traditional firms in cases where monthly child support payments were at issue. They used multiple regression analysis to estimate the degree to which representation by the clinic influenced the amount of the award as compared with other factors. They thought this was an objective measure of the quality of service. "'Better service' for the husband would be defined as a lower award of child support, all else being equal, and for the wife as a higher award of child support."[66] They found that clinic representation of the wife increased the per child award, a result significant at the .025 level. "Clinic representation of the husband reduced the monthly payment, though this figure is not significant at a level that statisticians would consider sufficient to conclude that the clinic provides better quality."[67]

The FTC staff recognized the limitations of Muris and McChesney's article. They point to the size of the data base, and they acknowledge that it is a case study of one clinic that had been in existence seven years. We cannot be sure that the positive outcomes were caused by the clinic form and its high volume approach based on advertising. Perhaps those who ran the clinic would have run a traditional law

[63]Muris & McChesney, *supra*, n. 43.

[64]See Sullivan, "The Upstart Lawyers who Market the Law," *N.Y.Times*, Aug. 26, 1979, §3 at 1, cols. 1–2.

[65]*Id.* at 198.

[66]*Id.* at 202–203.

[67]*Id.* at 205.

practice in such a way as to produce equally positive results. We do not know that Jacoby & Meyers continued what Muris and McChesney argue was its superior service when they conducted the study. We do not know whether other clinics or other lawyers who advertise but do not organize their practice in the clinic form would do as well. Some might want to debate the measures of quality. For example, we might want to appraise an entire divorce proceeding and not just child support. Child support often is but part of a total solution to the divorcing parties' and children's problems. Nonetheless, the FTC staff insist that the study shows at least that low prices and an elaborate advertising campaign do not necessarily reduce quality. They conclude "there are no other empirical studies of the legal services market which contradict these results."[68] However, since when the Report was written there were no other empirical studies at all, the absence of contradiction does not seem like overwhelming evidence of anything.

The search for better evidence about the impact of lawyer advertising yielded some suggestions. There still are many unanswered questions about what is taking place and what will take place in the future. Even if the FTC study clearly had established that advertising lowered the price of the five fairly simple services studied, we could not be sure that advertising would affect more complex legal practice. My review of the literature revealed a great deal of speculation and advocacy of partisan positions. Indeed, as I argue in the next sections, we may not even be asking all of the right questions

[68]Staff of the Federal Trade Commission, *supra* n. 9, at 141. In a study published after the FTC Report, Murdock and White dispute the argument that advertising has no impact on quality. They correlated the ratings of lawyers in the Martindale-Hubbell Directory with advertising in the yellow pages. They found that lower quality lawyers are more likely to place such advertisements. Murdock & White, "Does Legal Service Advertising Serve the Public's Interest? A Study of Lawyer Ratings and Advertising Practices," 8 *J. Consumer Pol'y* 153 (1985). However, Thomas points out that the study does not truly say much about the quality of service. The correlation may be spurious. "It does, however, tend to confirm the unsurprising view that successful, older, well established lawyers, who are respected and admired by their colleagues, are less likely to advertise. They do not need to advertise. The type of services which they provide — and presumably their ability to charge premium fees — are not particularly likely to be directed at the general public." Thomas, "Legal Service Advertising — A Comment on the Paper by Murdock and White," *Id.* at 165, 166. Indeed, it is possible, if not likely, that many of the highly rated lawyers in the Martindale-Hubbel Directory would be incompetent to handle the legal problems of individuals. High ratings may reflect the high status practice involved in representing businesses and wealthy individuals. These lawyers are unlikely to have much experience in family or criminal law or representing individual debtors or plantiffs in personal injury work. This is not to say that reputation among the members of the bar is unrelated to quality of work, but, at best, it is only a surrogate for a hard-to-define concept.

III. Consumer Interest and Lawyer Advertising

The leaders of the bar who resist advertising and the reformers who champion it agree about broad goals. People should have access to legal services. Consumers gain when quality services are available at reasonable prices. Consumers benefit from accurate and relevant information so they can make informed choices whether to seek a lawyer and which one to contact. On the other hand, consumers lose if advertising deceives them. They lose if the costs of advertising lower the quality of services. They also might lose if the cluster of ideals and attitudes associated with professionalism and fiduciary obligations were replaced by lawyer self-interest or by bureaucratic constraints in a standardized system geared for efficiency.[69]

Substantively, we must evaluate a difficult set of uncertain trade-offs to appraise lawyer advertising. For example, Sandy DeMent, Executive Director of the National Resource Center for Consumers of Legal Services, saw the balance this way:

> We all know the abuses (that plague advertising in other fields) are going to appear. It will be a miserable species of communication, but it will bring competition and it will harden consumers in a way they haven't been hardened before.[70]

Moreover, we have to compare lawyer advertising with the way lawyers established reputations before the restrictions on advertising were relaxed. We have to weigh the costs of lawyer advertising against the problems faced by consumers finding lawyers when they have little reliable information. Potential clients rely on recommendations by friends, neighbors and relatives. Choice often is influenced by reputation or notoriety. Writing about the early 19th century, Gordon notes

> if public life was no longer an attractive financial alternative to private practice, it remained an almost indispensable supplement. Despite the stingy salaries of public officers, even lawyers with no taste for politics were driven to seek office to advance their careers. To rise in practice, a lawyer needed clients and was one of the few ways for a lawyer to get public exposure. It produced occasions for oratory—campaign speeches, Fourth of July orations, legislative debates—that might capture the attention of potential clients, those merchants, bankers, and corporate directors who sought to cultivate young politicians for their own purposes.[71]

Recently the number of lawyers in American state legislatures has declined. One explanation is that lawyers no longer need to run and campaign to gain publicity now

---

[69]Many lawyers put more time into cases than they can bill clients for. They want to do the job right, they think the client ought to win or they hope the work will pay off in the distant future. As law offices become more efficient and emphasize commercial rather than professional values, it may be harder to give away services in this manner. The decision may be moved from the lawyer handling the case to a manager. On the other hand, lawyers now may bill other clients more to compensate for putting too much into cases that do not pay. We may differ about whether this kind of progressive income tax is justified.

[70]Falk, "Lawyers Are Facing Surge in Competition as Courts Drop Curbs," *Wall St.J.*, Oct. 18, 1978, at 1, col. 1, p. 15, cols. 1–2.

[71]Gordon, *supra* n. 31, at 453.

that they can advertise.[72] Some of this decline began to occur before the *Bates* decision, and so advertising is not a complete explanation for it. Nonetheless, whether we see a gain or loss from this change, we must consider it in thinking about the possible impact of relaxing the rules against advertising. We also can ask whether fewer or different kinds of lawyers are willing to run for the office of prosecutor or to be judges since these kinds of campaigns may be less necessary to build a reputation than when lawyers cannot advertise directly.

Two writers further sharpen the issues by adding institutional or structural dimensions to the problem of regulating lawyer advertising. Komesar[73] suggests comparative institutional analysis. He says that legal decisions involve a choice among imperfect alternative decision-making institutions. Consider the most obvious possibilities in the case of lawyer advertising. It could be: (1) left to be policed by "the market"; (2) regulated by state supreme courts together with bar associations; (3) regulated by the Federal Trade Commission and state regulatory agencies that deal with trade and consumer protection; or (4) regulated by courts and juries using doctrines of misrepresentation, fiduciary duty, undue influence, unconscionability, warranty and malpractice. Of course, combinations of these four approaches are possible. We could rely, for example, on the market backed up with varying degrees of court and jury determinations of misrepresentation, malpractice and the like. The amount of regulation, and its costs, would turn on the nature of the substantive rules adopted, the defenses recognized, and the procedural and evidentiary rules imposed.

The impact of legal regulation of advertising is further complicated. Friedman [74] suggests that in fashioning an approach to any problem the nature of the rules themselves is important. He argues that a vital part of the legal system depends on "well settled" rules that are actually free of doubt as a matter of ordinary, patterned human behavior. Discretionary rules "are tolerable as operational realities only in those areas of law where the social order or the economy can afford the luxury of slow, individuated justice. If there is a social interest in mass handling of transactions, a clear-cut framework of nondiscretionary rules is vital."[75] Of course, lawmakers can state formal rules in discretionary form, but the rules actually may be nondiscretionary at the point of application. For example, the stated rules concerning sentencing of those convicted of a crime may call for a qualitative weighing and balancing of factors. The working rules of prosecutors, defense lawyers, social workers doing pre-sentence investigations and judges are likely to be quantitative so that all involved will know the price for certain offenses given the number of prior convictions.

---

[72]Barlas, "Where Have All the Lawyers Gone?" *Nat'l L.J.*, Jan. 19, 1981, at 13, cols. 1–4.

[73]Komesar, "In Search of a General Approach to Legal Analysis: A Comparative Institutional Alternative," 79 *Mich. L. Rev.* 1350 (1981); Komesar, "Taking Institutions Seriously: Introduction to a Strategy for Constitutional Analysis," 51 *U.Chi. L. Rev.* 366 (1984).

[74]Friedman, "Legal Rules and the Process of Social Change," 19 *Stan. L. Rev.* 786 (1967).

[75]*Id.* at 792.

We can sketch an application of these ideas in the area of lawyer advertising that suggests the nature of the decisions that lawmakers must make. State supreme courts in the United States make decisions about lawyer advertising. However, in fashioning and applying rules the justices of these courts are influenced by state bar associations. These state associations, in turn, are influenced by standards written by the American Bar Association. A lawmaker must worry that people working in this structure will fashion a cartel favoring lawyers' interests while talking of protecting the public. Organized groups of lawyers will be concentrated. Potential and actual clients, however, are a diffuse group, almost impossible to organize. Other institutions must champion consumer interests. For example, all of this activity is evaluated by the Supreme Court of the United States as it applies the constitution. It is further influenced by the Antitrust Division of the Department of Justice and by the Federal Trade Commission. Both agencies challenge regulation of the profession. Both champion the ideal of competition as the universal solvent for social problems.

Many state bar associations have followed the ABA's lead and proposed strict regulations specifying where lawyers can advertise and what they may and may not say. These rules, whatever their defects, have the virtue of telling lawyers what they can and cannot do. The rules are justified in terms of avoiding misrepresentation or bait and switch tactics, and so speak to this consumer interest. However, certainty and avoiding misleading statements may cost consumers the benefits of competition. The Antitrust Division and the FTC raised this challenge, and the Supreme Court of the United States ultimately will draw the lines by applying the constitution. An antagonistic thrust and parry among these institutions might produce the best compromise we can hope for.

However, it is not clear that any flat rule dealing with where and how lawyers advertise could pass constitutional challenge. Perhaps only a qualitative standard—such as lawyers may advertise as long as the advertising does not contain material misrepresentations—will be upheld. If this is the case, we must ask who could challenge particular advertisements and what body would decide the matter. In many states, a formally independent agency makes recommendations to the state supreme court in a proceeding concerning the suspension or revocation of a lawyer's license to practice. However, state and local bar associations play important roles in the process. They may bring complaints against particular lawyers, and they may be able to influence appointments to the agency and appropriations by the state legislature to support it. Given the organized bar's general hostility to price competition, advertising and new forms of practice, this institutional setting might severely limit advertising. Of course, a lawyer disciplined always could appeal on constitutional grounds. However, the burden of defending particular advertisements itself might be enough to discourage many from advertising in ways that bar officials might question. On the other hand, threats of constitutional challenge and antitrust prosecutions might curb the established bar's eagerness to battle advertising.

Alternatively, we could rely on market sanctions—the risk of losing reputation and custom—backed by the same legal regulation faced by any advertiser of goods or services. Perhaps most lawyers care enough about their reputation with actual and potential clients and with judges and other lawyers as well, to curb advertising excesses. Perhaps clients want a lawyer who fits the conventional image of a professional rather than that of a used car dealer. We might expect only a very few to engage in deceptive advertising or to lower the quality of the service they offer to recover the costs of advertising and mass marketing.[76] As to those few who were not deterred by other-than-legal sanctions, we could ask why conventional legal responses would be inadequate.

Even if there were no special restrictions imposed on lawyers, all sellers of services are subject to some regulation.[77] On one hand, federal and state agencies regulate deceptive trade practices. On the other hand, injured individuals can sue for misrepresentation, undue influence, breach of fiduciary duty and the like.

Consumer protection agencies are unlikely to have the interest or the resources to take on a new area and give it adequate attention, particularly in a time when government expenditures are being cut. Individuals will face difficulty financing private law suits complaining about lawyer advertising. If it were clear that lawyer advertising brought about significant problems of misrepresentation and poor quality work, courts might make suits easy to win so that lawyers would be deterred from unprofessional conduct. For example, the fiduciary duty doctrine could be expanded to hold lawyers to a high standard of honest disclosure in making representations to potential as well as actual clients.[78] A field of lawyer malpractice might develop, following the treatment of the medical profession. If courts allowed emotional distress or punitive damages, the sums involved could make it worth litigating claims for misleading advertising.[79] All of this likely would lead to the formal

[76]My colleague, Neil Komesar, points out that we can question the bar groups' case against advertising insofar as it claims that ads lead to a lowering of quality. Lawyers who do not advertise also face pressures to cut costs by lowering quality so they can pay their bills and make more money. Perhaps some lawyers' professionalism would crumble under the added cost of an advertising campaign. However, the financial burden of an advertisement in the telephone directory yellow pages and a major campaign on television must be distinguished. It is unlikely that the cost of an advertisement in print would change the way any lawyer practiced. Moreover, a wealthy firm with an expanding business might find the added cost of a television campaign to offer little additional incentive for cutting quality than exists without advertising. The bar's argument rests on an image of advertising expense being the straw placed on a scale that tips the balance toward cutting the quality of services. There are many other straws being placed on that scale as well. We should suspect that advertising tips the balance, if at all, in a few limited situations.

[77]In our society, total deregulation is rare. Usually, the real choice is leaving matters to the market supported by general regulation or turning to special regulation. Lawyers' advertising is subject to contract and tort limitations as well as consumer protection legislation. See, *e.g.*, Blumenthal, "Wide Abuses Reported In Ads by Professionals," *N.Y. Times*, Feb. 12, 1979, at B–l, cols. 1–2. The question is whether more is needed.

[78]Compare Frankel, "Fiduciary Law," 71 *Calif. L. Rev.* 795 (1983).

[79]If an expanded liability for misrepresentation or malpractice developed, the price of lawyer's insurance probably would rise, the costs would have to be passed along, and the lower prices produced by competition might be pushed back up again. For a skeptical reaction to what he calls "the landlord will raise the rent and evict the grandmother" argument, see Kennedy, "Distributive and Paternalist Motives in Contract and Tort Law, with Special Reference to Compulsory Terms

statement of highly qualitative rules—fiduciary duties and the standards for emotional distress and punitive damages are hard to reduce to simple and clear rules. We might want lawyers to be unsure as to how close to the line of misrepresentation, breach of fiduciary duty or malpractice they could come. Rules of thumb might develop as to what was safe, but they would require advertising that no one could question. On the other hand, even if such doctrinal developments took place, lawyers might not be eager to represent clients suing other lawyers who practiced in the same area. Perhaps enough deterrence would be produced if only a few marginal but competent lawyers were willing to represent such clients and accept whatever social sanctions other lawyers might use against them.

This sketch of a comparative institutional analysis applied to lawyer advertising is not complete. In Komesar's words, we are "choosing the best, or least imperfect, institution to implement a given social goal."[80] However, it is not easy to decide which institution is the least imperfect, and it will require a great deal of knowledge about interdependent systems in operation. It also will require some normative judgments. For example, serious problems of misrepresentation could slip past reputational sanctions backed up by administrative regulation or individual litigation. How could clients know they had received poor legal service? Perhaps it is enough if unaware clients are happy with what they received, but at least some consumer advocates are unlikely to accept this solution as adequate.

However, conceding that some cases of deceptive advertising might not be remedied still leaves the question of what to do about it. If we thought that such cases were likely to be rare or trivial, we might accept the lack of remedy, recognizing that no realistic choice can be perfect. We might not be so complacent if we thought that such cases were common or serious. We face the difficulty of predicting how often clients will be fooled and of evaluating the seriousness of the likely injury. Comparative institutional analysis poses issues, but it does not guarantee that choices among flawed institutions will be easy.

IV. Lawyer Advertising and Problems of Access and Equality Before the Law

Up to this point, I have accepted the way leaders of the bar opposed to lawyer advertising and reformers who advocate it have framed the issues. However, their debate might divert our attention from important problems. Even if advertising leads

---

and Unequal Bargaining Power," 41 *Md. L.Rev.* 563, 604 (1982). Kennedy says "it is not possible to predict a priori what consequences will follow when the decision maker imposes a nondisclaimable duty. It all depends on the particular conditions of the market for the commodity in question, and its relation to other related markets." *Ibid.*

[80]Komesar, "In Search of a General Approach to Legal Analysis," *supra* n. 73, at 1350.

to delivering conventional legal services that can be standardized to more clients at a reasonable price, major questions of access and equality before the law will remain.

Insofar as it is successful, lawyer advertising may bring the wrong people to attorneys. Some clients might better solve their problems in other ways. The studies talk about the simple will, the consent divorce where there are no children and no issues of property division, and routine personal injury work. But why should lawyers handle these problems in most instances? Advertising legal clinics or cut-rate lawyers may hinder the development of even cheaper kinds of solutions to standardized problems. Today one can buy do-it-yourself books and forms to handle wills and divorces.[81] In a community where adjusters and lawyers settle automobile accidents on a routine basis, many victims could handle the negotiations themselves if information about the rules of the game were available.[82]

If self-help is not appropriate, counselling from non-lawyers might be all that most literate people need. In many nations a person can buy help in filling out forms and taking them to the right place from people lacking the formal training of lawyers.[83] These people charge far less. Legal advertising may work to keep simple matters in the hands of the bar rather than fostering the development of less highly trained people who could handle routine work more cheaply. Law firms and legal clinics delegate more and more work to paralegal workers. This suggests that they are cutting costs by moving problems out of the hands of lawyers and into those of people paid less. But even in these instances, clients probably are paying more than if lawyers were involved only minimally or not at all. Some of the "law store" approaches that have developed in the United States involve kits for such things as divorces or changes of names plus the chance to get advice from lawyers about how to fill out the papers and where to file them.[84]

Lawyers have responded in different ways to proposals calling for limiting or ending their role. Often the bar fights deprofessionalization unsupervised by an attorney.[85] Usually, lawyers argue that qualified professionals should see that the

---

[81]See, *e.g.* , Mack, "For $59, a New Yorker Wins a Divorce Without Lawyers," *N.Y. Times*, Jan. 6, 1977, at 22, cols. 1–6; Hash, "Do-It-Yourself Bankruptcy," *N.Y. Times*, June 27, 1976, §111, at 9, cols. 1–4.

[82]People regularly settle many of these cases without lawyers now. See Ross, *Settled Out of Court: The Social Process of Insurance Claims Adjustments* (1970). Generally, plaintiffs get better settlements when they have a lawyer. The text suggests that individuals might be able to do better than they do now with something less expensive than legal services. Insurance adjusters typically are not lawyers. Injured plaintiffs also might be able to play the game with less expensive help as long as the threat of bringing in a personal injury specialist was in the background.

[83]In the United States, we can buy help in filling out our income tax forms from firms staffed with non-lawyers. Real estate brokers and bankers regularly help fill out the forms needed to transfer property interests although lawyers often are used in this area.

[84]See *N.Y. Times*, July 25, 1978, at B2, col. 2; *N.Y. Times*, Sept. 21, 1979, at D4, cols. 1–3; *Wall St. J.*, Oct. 16, 1979, at 40, cols. 1–3; *Nat'l L. J.*, May 14, 1979, at 7, cols. 1-2; ; "Legal Services Offered in N.Y. Department Store," 65 *A.B.A.J.* 548 (1979).

[85]Compare the effort to stop a legal secretary from selling and filling out legal forms. See "Challenge Facing the Legal System," *N.Y. Times*, Aug. 12, 1984, at A16, col. 1. See also Rothman,

standardized product fits the situation. They offer images of "do-it-yourself brain surgery." Lawyers, unlike others, are licensed and responsible for the advice they give.

On the other hand, some lawyers welcome and promote do-it-yourself approaches. Well designed books, check-lists and forms could minimize the risks by telling lay people "if X, Y or Z is the case, do not use this form but see a lawyer." Good self-help forms please lawyers because they can offer something to those who cannot pay large enough fees to justify a lawyer's time. Others see delegalization of routine transactions as necessary to protect the image of the bar. The President of the Florida Bar Association, for example, stated

> The Bar must "delegalize" matters that really do not require the services of a trained professional. In effect, routine and simple legal procedures that do not require the most important attribute of a professional, *judgment*, should be made available without the intervention of an attorney.
>
> Lawyers can ... be employed for more important tasks where their services are truly needed and can be freed from mundane and repetitious tasks. The public as a whole would then have greater practical access to the legal system.[86]

Assuming clients understand that a routine service comes from someone who is not a lawyer, why should they be prohibited from making this choice? Undoubtedly, it is a good idea to have a professional check to see that a simple solution is appropriate. However, when we cannot afford to pay a professional, the choice often is between no help at all and help from someone without full professional training. It is not obvious that no help at all is always the best solution.

We also can ask what advertising standardized legal services does for people whose problems do not fit into routine patterns. How can we better deliver high quality legal services for the complex will, divorces where child custody and property settlement are in issue, personal injury or products liability cases involving large sums and the like? The legal problems of the poor and the lower middle class often can be exceedingly difficult. They can involve problems of proof, jurisdiction and procedure. Clients find these cases hard to deal with themselves, and the problems call for someone who knows how people usually resolve them. Discussions of lawyer advertising risk diverting attention from this issue, but advertising may have some indirect influence on its solution. For example, through advertising lawyers may be able to recruit clients who have suffered similar injuries for which there is a chance of gaining compensation.[87] In this way, the costs of legal work may be spread over many cases and minimize what any one client must pay.

"Deprofessionalization: The Case of Law in America," 11 *Work & Occupations* 183 (1984); Iramel, "Crossing the Bar: Attorneys Try to Stop Do-It-Yourself Trend in Some Areas of Law," *Wall St.J.*, Sept. 3, 1976, at 1, col. 1.

[86]Richman, "Consumerism and the Law: The Crisis in Communication and Understanding," 58 *Fla. B.J.* 5, 6 (1985).

[87]See, *e.g.*, Moskowitz, "Lawyers Learn the Hard Sell—and Companies Shudder," *Bus. Week*, June 10, 1985, at 70–71.

Advertising may have some impact on access to justice. People may learn just enough to tip the balance and send them to a lawyer. Potential clients can gain at least a little additional information about the kind of person they might hire from advertisements in the telephone directory yellow pages and a little more from television commercials. Sometimes they will sense that they should avoid the lawyer in question. They may learn that lawyers have different personalities and not all are stiff upper-class members of the elite. Advertising also may make the issue of legal advice salient and remind people there are many kinds of legal services available. Furthermore, if a simple divorce is widely advertised as available for $250, this may affect expectations and allow potential clients to make a rough estimate of what their more complex situation might cost. It could limit the fee for a complex divorce. At least, a lawyer who would charge a great deal more might have to convince a client that the increased price is justified by an added degree of complexity.

Given that advertising may have some effect, nonetheless we must recognize its limitations. Many of the studies jump quickly from the idea that lawyer advertising offers information to the conclusion that advertising will produce fully informed consumers able to shop for the best services at the lowest price. Ladinsky[88] points out that even rational consumers who know they need a lawyer face three problems: "(1) finding the right kind of lawyer (that is, one who will do divorce or criminal or real estate work); (2) finding one at the 'right' price; and (3) finding one who is 'good.'" Advertising conveys more useful information about the first, less about the second, and only almost nothing about the third.

It is hard to advertise effectively that one is a good lawyer. Claiming "I am the greatest," may help a professional boxer, but a lawyer who used the technique would risk offending many clients. It is difficult in a limited space or time to convey the kinds of things on which clients can make quality judgments. A lawyer could advertise that she was a graduate of a well known law school and had been in practice for ten years. However, this would be, at best, only a rough surrogate for information directly relating to quality. Even defining "good legal service" is not easy.[89] It is far easier to agree about what are poor legal services than what are acceptable or high quality ones.

What role can advertising play in access to justice and attempts to gain some measure of substantive equality in society? To answer this question we must

[88]Ladinsky, "The Traffic in Legal Services: Lawyer-Seeking Behavior and the Channeling of Clients," 11 *Law & Soc'y Rev*. 207, 216 (1976).

[89]Bryant Garth notes that pressures for increased quality do not always serve the consumer interest. "A collective upgrading effort built on a uniform, high standard of performance will raise the cost of legal services, thus preventing access, and also will reduce the consumer's right to determine the appropriate level of investment in legal services. Individuals gain little when the exaltation of quality prevents the purchase of varying levels of services." Garth, "Rethinking the Legal Profession's Approach to Collective Self-Improvements Competence and the Consumer Perspective," 1983 *Wis. L. Rev*. 639, 686.

consider how advertising fits into the process by which people turn to lawyers. People will not pay much attention to advertising for legal services that they do not think they need now or in the future. Potential clients have a very limited understanding of what lawyers do and when a lawyer could help them. They know little about the price of legal services. Rick Abel argues

> clients tend to bring the kinds of cases that lawyers have taught them are justiciable—which generally means those involving enough property to warrant a substantial fee. If lawyers want to embark on a new era, they must educate their clientele to view the problem as susceptible to legal remediation.[90]

Insofar as lawyers teach what is justiciable,[91] we have to ask what part lawyer advertising plays in this education. We can guess that advertising plays only a limited role.

Felstiner, Abel, and Sarat[92] see three transformations they call "naming, blaming and claiming." One must perceive an experience as an injury, decide that he or she has a grievance against another, and then make a claim against the one blamed. Legal needs are not things that exist in society; rather they are social constructs. Mayhew[93] points out "we have a vast array of disputes, disorders, vulnerabilities, and wrongs which contain an enormous potential for generation of legal actions. But it is only a potential. Ideology and structure affect whether people define their situation as a problem and whether they see it as a problem for lawyers." Or, as Sally Lloyd-Bostock puts it,

> In a situation that is unfamiliar, . . . [a victim] . . . lacks specific norms of his own and does not feel competent to generate them for himself from more general principles because there is a range of possibilities. What he *feels* is, therefore, often largely the results of what his lawyer, trades union, the police, friends and others have suggested to him since his accident.[94]

A person may not name, blame and claim because there are cultural norms and social sanctions against asserting rights through lawyers and courts, and these norms and sanctions may limit the impact of lawyer advertising. Merry and Silbey, for example, tell us

> [a] reluctance to take personal disputes to court is an important ingredient of respectability for working class and middle class families, but not for some segments of the poor. It may be

---

[90]Abel, *supra* n. 51, at 9.

[91]Lawyers may not be the most important teachers. We know little about where people learn what lawyers do.

[92]Felstiner, Abel & Sarat, "The Emergence and Transformation of Disputes: Naming, Blaming, Claiming . . ." 15 *Law & Soc'y Rev.* 631 (1980–81).

[93]Mayhew, "Institutions of Representation: Civil Justice and the Public," 9 *Law & Soc'y Rev.* 401, 404 (1975).

[94]Lloyd-Bostock, *Fault and Liability for Accidents: The Accident Victim's Perspective* 24 (1980).

> that for those families already involved with welfare and other public agencies, the social meaning of turning to a public remedy agent is quite different.[95]

Engel[96] studied a small, predominantly rural county in Illinois undergoing social and economic change. He found

> [t]hose who sought to enforce personal injury claims in Sander County were characterized by their fellow residents as "very greedy," as "quick to sue," as "people looking for the easy buck," and as those who just "naturally sue and try to get something [for] ... life's little accidents."[97]

Attitudes toward debt collection by merchants through legal action were different. In this culture "promises should be kept and people should be held responsible when they broke their word."[98]

Advertising might in the long run contribute to overcoming norms against asserting rights, but the process likely would be subtle and indirect. Perhaps a dignified educational approach would be more effective in doing this than a high pressure effort at salesmanship based on price cutting. The more advertising sells law the same way as used cars, the more the public may view seeking benefits as greedy. Perhaps all lawyer advertising taken together will make the idea of consulting lawyers more commonplace and less remarkable and in this way offset some of these norms prescribing asserting rights. Nonetheless, members of groups that honor self-help, keeping personal affairs out of the public view, and similar ideas will not necessarily be swayed by lawyer advertising. Sending out a message is one thing; its impact is something else.

There are a number of studies of how people recognize they need a lawyer and how they find the one they see. While these articles have yielded useful information, there are still many unanswered questions. Mayhew and Reiss[99] surveyed residents of Detroit, Michigan. They found an association between ownership of property and seeing lawyers because, they argue, the legal profession serves business and property. "The poor have fewer legal problems only in the narrow sense that they have fewer problems that the legal profession habitually serves."[100] They could use help in confronting various bureaucracies, but the effort seldom produces a fund of money from which a client could pay substantial fees. Ladinsky[101] obtained unpublished data from Mayhew and Reiss about the chain of intermediaries that

---

[95]Merry & Silbey, "What Do Plaintiffs Want? Reexamining the Concept of Dispute," 9 *Just.Sys. J.* 151, 176 (1984).

[96]Engel, "The Oven Bird's Song: Insiders, Outsiders, and Personal Injuries in an American Community," 18 *Law & Soc'y Rev.* 549 (1984).

[97]*Id.* at 553.

[98]*Id.* at 575.

[99]Mayhew & Reiss, "The Social Organization of Legal Contacts," 34 *Am.Soc. Rev.* 309 (1969).

[100]*Id.* at 317.

[101]Ladinsky, *supra* n. 88.

channel clients to lawyers. They showed that a substantial number of people, "especially those at the top of the socioeconomic system, were informed about legal services through relatively close personal contacts with lawyers."[102] People were asked how they would find legal help if they needed it. 73% said they would contact a relative, friend or neighbor who was a lawyer or they would seek a referral from a relative, friend or neighbor who knew a lawyer.

Curran reported the American Bar Foundation study of legal needs. The sample represented the adult population of the United States.[103] Her findings paralleled those of Reiss and Mayhew in Detroit. Wills, purchase of real property and divorce were the problems most frequently taken to lawyers. People most often (45%) find lawyers through friends, relatives and neighbors, but about 15% found lawyers by reading the telephone directory yellow pages. 35% had never had any contact with a lawyer, and 28% have had but one contact.

The staff of the *Yale Law Journal*[104] reanalyzed the ABF data, using regression analysis to measure the strength of seven common explanations for lawyer use in personal matters. Income, perceptions about lawyers' fees, awareness of the usefulness of lawyers to handle certain problems and attitudes towards lawyers all failed to account for much of the variance in actual use of lawyers. Experience with legal problems, property ownership and contact with lawyers were much more powerful factors. A cumulative regression equation indicated that experience with legal problems explained 20% of the variation in lawyer use as compared to only 1.8% for ownership of property, and 1.5% for contacts with lawyers. In short, people become accustomed to using lawyers for various things and their use increases.

Campbell and Talarico[105] measured attitudes about hiring lawyers by drawing samples in Atlanta, Macon and Americus, Georgia. They conducted 1,200 interviews. On the basis of their data, they report that the decision to hire a lawyer is a two stage process: first, people must recognize they need a lawyer or one would be helpful; second, having decided a lawyer might be useful, one must decide to contact one. They found that those who are poor, black, and poorly educated often think that lawyers do not offer solutions to their problems.[106] Once people decide they need a lawyer, socio-demographic factors are not as relevant to the decision to seek one. However, 94 people out of the sample of 1,200 saw the need for a lawyer but failed to take the next step. Even when they saw a possible need for a lawyer, blacks in this group wanted to handle matters for themselves. Poor whites and those with little education may use lawyers less because they know less about free or low fee services that are available. They also lack the social skills necessary to contact a lawyer. The

---

[102] *Id.* at 219.

[103] Curran, *The Legal Needs of the Public; The Final Report of a National Survey* (1977).

[104] Project, "An Assessment of Alternative Strategies for Increasing Access to Legal Services," 90 *Yale L.J.* 122 (1980).

[105] Campbell & Talarico, "Access to Legal Services: Examining Common Assumptions," 66 *Judicature* 313 (1983).

[106] Those who are poor, black, and poorly educated may be right.

authors concluded that psychological, rather than racial or economic, factors govern what Felstiner, Abel, and Sarat called "naming, blaming, and claiming."

How does lawyer advertising fit into this picture? Insofar as we accept the suggestions of these studies, advertising may affect naming, blaming and claiming in a limited way. Ladinsky points to the chain of relationships connecting potential clients with lawyers and says "surely we would not expect many of the 73 percent who used relatives, friends, or neighbors to prefer advertising media ..."[107] He argues that lawyer-seeking behavior seems to involve communication networks where "influential intermediaries reinforce media messages."[108] This suggests "if mass media information about lawyers—type of work, fees, quality—is to have personal meaning as a basis for action, it must be grounded in a network of interpersonal relationships."[109] Writing in 1976 just before the *Bates* decision, he predicted that relaxation of the ban on advertising would do "very little to 'open up' information channels."[110]

However, at least some advertising might work together with these other communication networks and prompt people to think about contacting associates for recommendations. Some advertising might remind people of lawyers they know in other contexts. Mayhew and Reiss suggest that law practice is structured to deal with property transactions or the kinds of disputes that those who own substantial amounts of property are likely to face. Following the *Yale Law Journal* reanalysis of the ABF data, we could conclude that those who own property may be more likely to encounter what they see as legal problems. They have "their lawyer," just as they have "their accountant," "their doctor," and "their dentist." Perhaps the institutional or educational kinds of advertising—sponsoring public radio or classical music or running commercials that discuss points of law—are the most likely to reach people who are accustomed to continuing relationships with a group of professionals. They may be willing to accept a broad definition of lawyers' work.

Perhaps advertising standardized services might affect lower income people similarly, bringing them to legal clinics or lawyers who deal with individual problems. If these people were pleased with the experience, they too might establish a relationship with a lawyer. They might return when they encountered other problems. However, we still would face Abel's point—"clients tend to bring the kinds of cases that lawyers have taught them are justiciable—which generally means those involving enough property to warrant a substantial fee."[111] Or, again in Mayhew and Reiss' words, "[t]he poor have fewer legal problems only in the narrow sense that they have fewer problems that the legal profession habitually serves."[112]

---

[107]Ladinsky, *supra* n. 88, at 219.

[108]*Id.* at 221.

[109]*Ibid.*

[110]*Ibid.*

[111]Abel, *supra* n. 51 at 9.

[112]Mayhew & Reiss, *supra* n. 99, at 317.

Advertising and other sources of information might help lower income people learn that lawyers can do many kinds of things for rich or poor clients. Many people think lawyers only draft wills, handle the papers needed to transfer real estate or battle in court before juries. School, television and experience fail to communicate a picture of what most lawyers do. For example, some translate clients' wishes into legal forms such as wills or applications for licenses or government benefits. Some litigate cases and fight appeals to higher courts. Some help plan conduct to ward off or minimize problems. Others work out solutions to problems by knowing who to call and what to say or by drawing on contacts and relationships. Still others help in political action or test cases to change the rules.

A lawyer who knew the system in a particular community could offer a great deal of help dealing with the welfare bureaucracy, seeking unemployment compensation, or coping with a housing authority. Supervisors often treat employees poorly, hoping they will quit. A telephone call from a lawyer representing the employee may be enough to stop the mistreatment. The lawyer may be able to help a client collect evidence enough to support threatening to file a complaint for discrimination. A credible threat may be enough to prompt redress. However, these legal services are not the neatly standardized ones discussed in the articles advocating lawyer advertising. It might be hard to get across in a 30 second television commercial or a small notice in the yellow pages that a lawyer knows the local political system and how to negotiate, bluff and threaten those who participate in it.

However, perhaps the real problem is less making lower income people aware that such lawyers exist as finding a way to finance the provision of these kinds of legal services. On one hand, lawyers can do only a limited amount for those who cannot pay adequately for legal services. Lawyer advertising might create expectations in lower-income people which would be frustrated when they respond and seek legal services. On the other hand, sometimes lawyers are available with skill in coping with the problems of lower-income people, and there are ways to purchase their services for an affordable price. When this is true, it is not that difficult to spread the word through various social networks. An advertisement might reinforce a favorable folk tale being circulated through the social networks of the people who could use such a lawyer. On the other hand, if there are cultural norms and social sanctions against asserting rights, advertisements and folk tales might be less effective against folk wisdom such as "you cannot fight city hall."

All of this is highly speculative because we do not know that much about naming, blaming and claiming and how advertising might affect the process. The dynamics of the process probably are subtle, and questionnaires and correlations are unlikely to capture them. Mather and Yngvesson[113] point out that disputants, supporters, third parties, and relevant publics may seek to narrow disputes by rephrasing and transforming them through imposing established categories for classifying events and relationships. They may, on the other hand, seek to expand them by adding new

[113]Mather & Yngvesson, "Language, Audience, and the Transformation of Disputes," 15 *Law & Soc'y Rev*. 775 (1980–81).

issues, by enlarging the arena of discussion, or by increasing the number and type of active participants. We still have a great deal to learn about where lawyers, or even threats to call in lawyers, fit into this process. And it is clear that while lawyer advertising sometimes may be important, it can play only a limited part in the social rituals leading to these transformations.

We should not exaggerate what lawyers could offer if the poor and members of the lower middle class brought more of their problems to them. Silberman reminds us "the characteristic lawyers' response to the legal problems of the poor is not to attack those problems directly, but rather to provide lawyers at public expense."[114] Abel, reflecting a very different political stance, warns "the continuing emphasis on redistributing lawyers, or on other legal institutional reforms, contains the profound danger that by strengthening the liberal myth that substantive justice can be attained under capitalism we will be simultaneously lulled into a false optimism and discouraged from seeking alternatives [such as different social systems]."[115] These warnings have force. However, again in Abel's words, "*any* redistribution of lawyers has the potential to promote incremental gains in both formal and substantive justice."[116] We must look for real solutions to the problems of the poor and the lower middle class, and we cannot be content with merely providing lawyers. Nonetheless, lawyers can help these people, the problem of access is important, and lawyer advertising, even accepting its advocates' case, can solve only a very small part of this problem.

Indeed, the debate about lawyer advertising may draw our attention from the larger question of access and vindication of rights. Advocates for unrestricted lawyer advertising claim it will lower the prices for lawyers' services in the market. This will solve the problems of access without requiring public subsidy. However, the services made available by increased demand created by advertising will not be the time-consuming counselling and "bargaining in the shadow of the law" that lower-income clients need to cope with public and private bureaucracies. Assuming that lawyer advertising succeeds in delivering low cost wills, uncontested divorces and name changes, we can also ask its advocates to show us what it will do for vindicating the rights found in constitutions and reform legislation.

Some may be content to have the rights promised by the liberal welfare state remain unenforced and merely symbolic. Lawyer advertising may stir up litigation and trouble.[117] Silberman argued for limiting the number of lawyers and

---

[114]Silberman, *supra* n. 38, at 15, 19.

[115]Abel, "Socializing the Legal Profession: Can Redistributing Lawyers' Services Achieve Social Justice?" 1 *Law & Pol'y Q.* 5, 41 (1979). Compare Bachmann, "Lawyers, Law, and Social Change," 13 *N.Y.U. Rev. L. & Soc. Change* 1 (1984–1985); Gabel and Harris, "Building Power and Breaking Images," 11 *N. Y. U. Rev. L. & Soc. Change* 369 (1983).

[116]*Id.* at 39.

[117]Compare Epstein, "Settlement and Litigation: Of Vices Individual and Institutional," 30 [*U.Chi.*] *Law Sch. Rec.* 2, 7 (Spring 1984) ("[A]s the costs of litigation are in themselves deadweight social losses, the improvement they make in the human condition must be very large to justify their expense."); Lee, "The American Courts as Public Goods: Who Should Pay the Costs of Litigation?"

maintaining rules against advertising to control the adverse impact of litigation on capitalism. Galanter,[118] however, contends that contemporary litigation is not "an eruption of pathological contentiousness or a dangerous and unprecedented loosening of needed restraints or the breakdown either of a common ethos or of community regulation." Rather it is a conservative response to learning that we could prevent harms and to a situation "where more of the interactions in the lives of many are with remote entities over which there are few direct controls."[119] "If some litigation challenges accepted practice, it is an instrument for testing the quality of present consensus. It provides a forum for moving issues from the realm of unilateral power into a realm of public accountability."[120] In any event, in a society based on individual rights, it is hard to justify responding to social problems by keeping people unaware of their rights or blocking access to lawyers to prevent those rights from being vindicated.

V. Conclusion

Lawyer advertising has generated controversy. Some, such as Chief Justice Burger, worry that true professionalism based on fiduciary duties towards clients will be lost as hucksters sell legal services in tasteless and deceptive ways. On the contrary, reformers tell us, advertising will inform consumers so that they can shop for services. This will promote efficiency and quality while expanding access to those who could not afford representation before. Both positions are overstated and reflect symbolic stances by those who seek to defend professional ideology or champion the simplifications of deregulation as the cure for all problems.

Lawyer advertising may play some part in enlarging access to legal services. This may provoke more substantive equality in our society. We cannot be sure because we know so little about the transformations involved in processing disputes. We do not know how people decide they need a lawyer and which one to call. We are just beginning to study what happens between lawyer and client when they meet. Advertising may push lawyers to work cheaply rather than doing the job right. However, it is hard to see why advertising will add much to the pressures to cut

34 *Cath.U. L.Rev.* 267 (1985); Editorial, "Settling Out of Court," *Wall St. J.*, Aug. 22, 1985, at 20, col. 1 ("Why should the taxpayers have to support a civil court system? . . . Private disputes, unlike criminal proceedings, often have no social consequences. The full costs should fall on the litigants themselves.").

[118] Galanter, *supra* n. 36, at 67–68.

[119] *Ibid.*

[120] *Ibid.*

corners that have long existed. Advertising alone is not likely to push the bar into crass commercialism or produce a nation of rational informed clients seeking to maximize utility. Recognizing this, we must be concerned that largely symbolic debates about lawyer advertising may divert us from concern with more pressing issues of access and equality.

Private Government

Stewart Macaulay

Much of what we could call governing is done by groups that are not part of the institutions established by federal and state constitutions. If governing involves making rules, interpreting them, applying them to specific cases, and sanctioning violations, some of all of this is done by such different clusters of people as the Mafia, the National Collegiate Athletic Association, the American Arbitration Association, those who run large shopping centers, neighborhood associations, and even the regulars at Smokey's tavern. It may be necessary to draw a sharp line between public and private governments such as these in order to think about law, but in reality there is no such division. To the contrary, one finds instead interpenetration, overlapping jurisdictions, and opportunities[1] for both harmony and conflict among

This article was original published in Leon Lipson and Stanton Wheeler (eds) Law and the Social Sciences, New York NY: Russell Sage Foundation, 1986, 445–518. Reprinted with Permission.

[1]NOTE: Much of this paper has been shaped by the contributions and critical editing of Dr. Jacqueline R. Macaulay. Other demands on her time made it impossible for her to do any of the writing, and so, at her request, she is not listed as a co-author. My colleague David Trubek read the manuscript critically and offered extensive suggestions. Professors William H. Clune, Marc Galanter, Robert W. Gordon, Willard Hurst, Ellen R. Jordan, Leonard V. Kaplan, Marygold S. Melli, Sally Falk Moore, Theodore Schneyer, and Diane Vaughan read some or part of the drafts of the manuscript and made very helpful comments. A draft was written while I was a visitor at the Centre for Socio-Legal Studies, Wolfson College, Oxford, in 1979, and I benefited greatly from discussions with many people there. I presented part of the text in a paper called "Private Government and Functionalist and Marxist Theories of Law" at Osgoode Hall Law School, York University, Toronto, Ontario, in 1980. Again I benefited from the reactions of those who attended the lecture. The last section was presented at the Conference on Reflexive Law and the Regulatory Crisis, held at the University of Wisconsin–Madison, July 18–21, 1983. I learned a great deal from

S. Macaulay (✉)
University of Wisconsin Law School, Madison, WI, USA
e-mail: smacaula@wisc.edu

D. Campbell (ed.), *Stewart Macaulay: Selected Works*, Law and Philosophy Library 133, https://doi.org/10.1007/978-3-030-33930-2_8

public and private governments. Formal legal process typically plays a part only indirectly and as a last resort. We are likely to be seriously misled if we assume that there are sharp distinctions between public and private governments and between formal and informal processes. We must recognize that these concepts are only rough generalizations useful for emphasizing aspects of reality rather than accurate descriptions of things existing in the world.

These are not new observations. The concept of private government goes back at least to Ehrlich's theory (1913) of the "living law." However, despite this distinguished lineage, scholars often have failed to see the importance of private social control as it interacts with and affects the formal legal system. Fitzpatrick (1984) points out that even legal realism narrows its focus to formal legal process and doctrine.

> Academic legal knowledge is generated by applying a certain idea of law to the world. This approach cannot extend to social forms which do not find expression in terms of legal process or doctrine. The integrity of "law" is thus obliquely but potently affirmed in areas of scholarship that claim to be fundamentally skeptical of it. [p. 135]

At the same time, far too often, work in law and the behavioral sciences implicitly accepts the distinction between public and private spheres and assumes that one can study the roles played by law in a society by considering only the actors who play official parts. What is needed is a "private government perspective" which both recognizes private associations that affect government and also treats distinctions between public and private spheres as doubtful rather than as given. (Cf. Spitzer 1984.)

At the outset, I will try to give some shape to the amorphous term "private government." While any formal definition would be arbitrary, we need some idea about what we are and are not discussing. Once this is done, we can turn to specific topics in legal studies and consider possible contributions of a private government perspective which emphasizes private rule-making, interpretation, application, and sanctioning as well as the artificiality of drawing any hard line between public and private governing.

Private Governments and Their Relationships with the Public Legal, System

What Is a Private Government?

The term "private government" draws an analogy intended to highlight certain features of something that is not a public government. As we shall see, if we put aside for a moment our skepticism about the public/private distinction, we could call many actions of individuals and groups "government" (see Evan 1976, pp. 171–85). The test of any analogy is its usefulness as balanced against the risks of overlooking ways the things being compared differ. Probably those engaged in the social study of law should consider first those private governments that bear some close relationships to public ones.

---

the responses of the European and North and South American participants. Yet after all of this help, of course, I am still responsible for all errors.

When might we draw a plausible analogy between private social control and public government? It is easiest to label as a private government a formally defined organization which makes rules, interprets them in the context of specific cases, and imposes sanctions for their violation. The analogy might seem more apt if the organization attempted to mimic the public legal system. For example, at least in the past, "company towns" often sought to govern by using the forms of legal rules, courts, and police—all controlled, however, by a business corporation rather than the citizens.

More typically, however, organizations attempt to take over only some of the functions of public government and mimic only part of the public legal system. Trade associations "legislate" rules of practice and suggest standard forms of agreement (see Leblebici and Salancik 1982); a number of groups "adjudicate" disputes by offering arbitration to their members; corporations establish their own private police to guard against (or engage in) industrial espionage. These groups may borrow some structures and symbols from the public government—for example, private police wear uniforms, badges, and guns; arbitrators may run their hearings by procedures approaching a trial; trade association rule-making may involve established procedures that suggest a legislature and often bring forth political tactics. Even a duel can be viewed as a kind of legal procedure with highly technical rules (cf. Schwartz, Baxter, and Ryan 1984).

Yet we can go beyond these fairly obvious analogies. Any group of people who more or less regularly interact tend to adopt rules, interpret them in light of specific situations, and sanction their violation (see Ford 1983; Schau 1983). If the group has some permanence, and if the actors within it tend to be the same people who value participation, we have what Moore (1978) calls a semi-autonomous social field. These social fields affect the operation of the legal system in many ways. For example, those involved in organized crime have rules that govern buying and selling of illegal goods and services as well as competitive practices and a range of sanctions to support them (see Reuter 1984; Adler and Adler 1983; cf. Cressey 1973). Many of these rules and sanctions serve to make enforcing the law against the group more difficult.

We could call even less formal and temporary relationships private governments if it served any purpose to do so. For example, people are linked in loosely coordinated social networks which may not be as structured, permanent, or valued as a social field (see Hammer 1980; Lee 1980; Nauta 1974). People learn norms and anticipate sanctioning for their violation appropriate to situations such as attending a dinner party with strangers or riding as a passenger on an airplane. We could talk of the legal system of the elevator. There are norms about looking at, talking to, and touching others in such temporary encounters (cf. Taylor and Brooks 1980; Baxter 1984). Sanctions include being ignored, ridiculed, and even threatened with physical violence. Probably these rules and sanctions contribute a great deal to our judgments about the safety of public places; it may be that our greatest demand for the physical embodiment of the criminal law—the uniformed police officer—comes when we see the private government of public places as inadequate. Black (1983) asserts that a "great deal of the conduct labeled and processed as a crime in modern societies . . . is intended as a punishment or other expression of disapproval, whether applied reflectively or impulsively, with coolness or in the heat of passion." He continues.

> most intentional homicide in modern society may be classified as social control, specifically as self-help, even if it is handled by legal officials as crime. From this standpoint, it is apparent that capital punishment is quite common in modern America . . . though it is nearly always a private rather than a public affair. [pp. 35–36]

However, at some point the analogy becomes strained and unsatisfying. There are widely accepted norms about when one should give relatives and friends birthday and Christmas gifts, and there are sanctions for violating those norms. Nonetheless, most of us probably would be uneasy with the idea of the private government of a friendship or an "illegal" failure to give a Christmas gift (see Caplow 1982).

Another way to define a term is to ask how people have used it. The term "private government" has been used even where there was not a close approximation of public governmental procedures and structures. The most common use of "private government" has been as a rhetorical device in aid of arguing that large corporations ought to be accountable for their actions, somewhat as nations and states are held accountable. Employees, customers, suppliers, and those living in cities who are dependent upon corporate decisions, in this view, ought not be subject to arbitrary action by public or private government; the "citizens" of a corporation ought to have a right to free speech and the like. Whatever the merit of these positions, the argument focuses on amount of power and its impact rather than on the presence or absence of such things as judges in robes, doctrines speaking to the use of power, procedures, and the symbols of legal action.

A number of writers, drawing on anthropological tradition, see us living in a world of legal pluralism, subject to the jurisdictions of overlapping and partially conflicting legal systems (see, for example, Galanter 1981; Fitzpatrick 1984; Nader 1984). In this view, the legal system studied in law schools is but one of many. Here the concept of a legal system is expanded, often implicitly, to cover such things as the norms of the Jewish community living in an area, those of the neighborhood and tenant associations there, those of a particular apartment building and of a particular landlord-tenant relationship, as well as those found in the city's building code and the state laws governing landlord and tenant, property and contract as they are enforced. In this kind of analysis, a great deal of private rule-making and sanctioning is analogized to processes in the formal public legal system; again, usage seems not to demand a particularly close approximation to public government.

The major research on relatively institutionalized social fields is part of a yet unpublished project, "Legal Regulation and Self-Regulation in American Social Settings," by Marc Galanter, a law professor well known for his work in the field of dispute resolution. As part of his study, Galanter collected newspaper articles, accounts from the trade press, magazine stories, and reports of academic research dealing in a wide variety of contexts with what most of us would call governing. Galanter stresses that the relatively institutionalized social fields he has been studying show a much wider range of activities than simple dispute resolution (see, for example, *Harvard Law Review* 1949; Ellickson 1982).

One of the organizations studied by Galanter is the American Institute of Architects (AIA), which has drafted, and continues to revise, an elaborate set of terms and conditions for the construction of buildings. These rules have, effectively, become the law of this industry. While parties could negotiate contracts on some other basis, they seldom do so because it is much easier to use the well-understood and accepted AIA forms, perhaps amending them in one particular or another to cover special situations. For practical purposes, the AIA operates as the legislature in the area of building construction (Havighurst 1961, p. 97); its legislative activity features lobbying and logrolling by various interests, just as we would find at state capitals (Sweet 1978, 1983; cf. Johnstone and Hopson 1967, pp. 329–54). The relationship structured by the AIA standard form contracts is one in which the architect, who is the owner's representative for most purposes, is also the arbitrator of disputes about the meaning of the plans and the quality of work performed. While such a mixed role neglects classical ideas about autonomy as a guarantee of impartiality, it allows a quick and inexpensive way to solve common problems that arise during construction (see Johnstone and Hopson 1967, pp. 315–28). Architects who abuse their role in one contract face problems in future transactions; builders have a number of ways to retaliate for unreasonable decisions; and an architect's reputation is likely to be known within the social field composed of those builders, architects, officials of financial institutions, and others who work together in a particular area. Many other trade associations enforce decisions and impose social control through their power over entry into a field and privileges members would dislike losing (see *Yale Law Journal* 1954). For example, in the international diamond trade, one must be accepted into the group in order to do business at all, and reputations must be carefully guarded in order to continue in the trade *(New York Times* 1984).

The legal pluralism approach shows that in American society the processes of rule-making, dispute avoidance, and resolution take place in a variety of settings apart from public governmental institutions. Even public government itself often participates in semi-autonomous social fields as it attends to its affairs—the Civil Aeronautics Board and the President of the United States interact with an association of airlines operated by private corporations and by national governments in setting international airline fares, for example (see Hannigan 1982; Cain 1983).

Many kinds of groups exercise governmental functions. Some are fairly structured entities which sometimes go to great lengths to mimic the procedures and symbols of public government, while others exhibit only a few of these features. What Galanter calls "mini-governments" vary widely in terms of the formality or informality of their operations, rules, and sanctions; their connection with one or more aspects of social life—some deal with a narrow part of the economy, others with living arrangements, with the family, or with multiple aspects—and their power over their members and their autonomy as against outsiders.

We could plausibly analogize many of these private legal systems to public government if it proved useful to do so. However, we are concerned with studies of the place of law in society and not with writing a dictionary. Thus, we should limit our analogizing to legal-like systems which are relevant to understanding the operations and functions of public government. What, then, are some of the relationships between the public government and these other governments? Which of these relationships seem worthy of attention in the social study of law?

The Relationships and Merging of Public and Private Governments

Often it is important to trace the relationships between public government and groups that carry out functions which are thought to be governmental or which deflect the impact of legal action. However, conceiving the problem this way assumes a distinct entity which we call public government and other distinct entities which operate in its shadow. As we shall see, a private government perspective requires that we both see the amount and nature of private governing and recognize at the same time that public and private governments are interpenetrated rather than distinct entities. First, I will consider some of the relationships, and then I will discuss how distinctions between what is public and what is private are questionable.

There are a number of relationships between public and private governments. Social fields govern in areas where we might expect public government to exercise control. Sills (1968) notes that

> [it] is difficult to overstate . . . the part played by voluntary associations in the actual business of governing the United States, in the sense of making decisions on policy and of providing services to citizens. . . . In large cities, voluntary associations seem to serve largely as important pressure groups; in medium-sized cities they virtually run the municipal government. . . . In small towns the decision-making role is filled by families and cliques, leaving to voluntary associations such service tasks as raising funds for the library, decorating the plaza, and maintaining the cemeteries, [p. 375]

Professional groups, for example, practice "self-regulation" in order to ward off public regulation. At times this is done totally apart from public government. At other times, however, a profession or an occupational group "captures" a public agency and exercises self-regulation in the guise of public regulation. Many state statutes, for example, facilitate self-government by organized occupational groups. Often members of state boards that license occupations or professions must be members of these groups.

Large corporations may assume functions usually thought of as governmental when they want control and little accountability. Many organizations have their own private police forces which offer everything from crowd control to protection of executives in foreign countries (see Livingstone 1981). O'Toole (1978) reports that

> General Motors has a force of 4200 plant guards, which makes its corporate police force larger than the municipal police departments of all but five American cities. And the Ford Motor Company has twenty-four ex-FBI agents on its payroll to counter threats ranging from dishonest employees to industrial spies. The business world seems to believe that law enforcement is too important a matter to be left to the police. [p. 42]

(See also Ghezzi 1983; Kakalik and Wildhorn 1977; Shearing and Stenning 1983; Stenning and Shearing 1979). Spitzer and Scull (1977) note that private police can seek to deter or gain restitution rather than gather evidence for criminal trials, and they can use more sophisticated, scientifically advanced, technical equipment than most law enforcement agencies could afford or would be allowed to use under rules specifying constitutionally acceptable evidence.

Large corporations often handle theft, embezzlement, and appropriation of trade secrets by employees by what has been called the "second criminal law system" (Cole 1978). Employees suspected of criminal activity are demoted or fired, and sometimes they are forced to make restitution. Procedures and standards of evidence differ sharply from those found in the public criminal law system in its formal operations; the mere appearance of wrongdoing may be enough to cost an employee his or her job or prompt a transfer to a less desirable position; the employer does not worry about proof beyond a reasonable doubt or the hearsay rule. Indeed, in this process the "facts" may never be established. The employer may have only strong suspicions. The employee may admit nothing or the employee may never be confronted with a charge of wrongdoing and may never be sure why he or she was transferred, demoted, or fired.

In the 1970s, failure to prosecute white-collar crime became a political issue in the United States. However, few who took stands against soft treatment for such criminals recognized the existence and operation of the second criminal justice system. It may be that both "defendants" and "prosecutors" in this system are better off than had cases been tried before courts. Employees accept this resolution of the situation in exchange for a promise not to initiate prosecution in the public criminal process or to make public their wrongdoing. The corporation, by using the second criminal justice system, may avoid damage to its reputation since a public prosecution might bring into question the adequacy of its supervision of its employees, and an accused employee might make countercharges of wrongdoing directed at other corporate officers. On the other hand, the second criminal justice system has costs as well as benefits. Those wrongly suspected may have no opportunity to establish their innocence. Those rightfully suspected may be free to move elsewhere and embezzle or steal company secrets again, unless the story is passed on by a gossip network.

Unionized employees who appear in a grievance procedure before a labor arbitrator could, perhaps, be said to participate in a third criminal justice system. Arbitrators may consider past alleged misconduct such as pilferage on the job, illegally obtained evidence, and information gained by wiretapping (see Fleming 1961, 1962), none of which could be used in a public criminal proceeding on the question of guilt or innocence. Again, this means that some of the values entailed in the public criminal justice system will not be implemented in this private proceeding.

Public government can attempt to facilitate the growth and operation of particular social fields in order to serve some public end. For example, during the Carter Administration, many saw the legal system as failing to cope with disputes within the family; in neighborhoods, workplaces, and retail markets; and in the landlord-tenant relationship. Accordingly, in the 1970s, a number of neighborhood justice centers were established with support from the Law Enforcement Assistance

Administration of the Department of Justice and from some private foundations. Members of a community were to bring their disputes before trained mediators for help in resolving them. Evaluation studies indicate that the programs had only modest success (see, for example, Felstiner and Williams 1978, 1979; Snyder 1978; Tomasic and Feeley 1982). Generally, people did not voluntarily bring cases to these centers. Many of the cases handled came to the centers when prosecutors, clerks of court, or judges diverted criminal charges to mediation. For example, a husband might be charged with beating his wife. When faced with the choice of a neighborhood justice center or a criminal trial, both husband and wife often preferred the less formal setting. However, when there was no outside coercive force pushing everyone inside the doors, those with power to settle scores on their own terms had little reason to play. Landlords, creditors, and retailers, for example, tended to be satisfied with existing structures for the exercise of their power.

Often where delegalized dispute settlement has been successful in the United States, it has been tied to groups viewed as culturally distinct from mainstream American society and subject to discrimination because of bias. Chinese-American, Native-American, and Jewish groups all have mediation systems. It is difficult to leave these communities without paying a high price in lost relationships. Thus, the groups are able to induce their members to participate and accept decisions. In short, one cannot create a community by creating a court. Public government can foster existing social fields and institutions, but if new ones are to be created, there must be incentives to participate in them.

Relationships between public and private governments also may involve partial or total conflict, more or less openly recognized. At one extreme stands the crusading prosecutor heading a strike force attempting to battle organized crime or the British government seeking to control the "Provisional Wing of the Irish Republican Army" (see Burton 1976). Colonial powers long imposed a version of the common law or a civil code on top of "native law." While, in theory, there were principles to coordinate the two systems, often the reality was legal pluralism and competition. In many countries today there are internal colonies wherein national and indigenous governments exist in a variable relationship of conflict and cooperation.

Religious groups, too, may have practices that violate the law of the state, with varying outcomes. The state tried to stamp out polygamy among the Mormons, but special exemptions to formal laws have been carved out to relieve the Amish from the requirements of compulsory education. Sometimes the official law is stated as applicable to everyone, but it is not enforced against members of particular religious groups or is enforced only in response to a complaint from an outsider with power.

Another mixed relationship can be seen between public government and trade associations. While self-regulation by professionals long has been accepted as offering certain values (see Barber 1978), those championing the interests of consumers complain that self-regularion often discourages competition by erecting barriers to entry and fixing prices for services. During the 1970s, various units of the United States government challenged a number of trade associations in the name of competition. One such challenge won lawyers the right to advertise, although the risk of losing professional reputation keeps many from engaging in this kind of competition for clients (see Macaulay 1985).

In addition to these areas of conflict, there are others in which private organizations act counter to official policy (see Biersteker 1980). When American labor unions refuse to unload ships carrying cargo from Communist countries, it makes it difficult for the State Department to implement a policy of increasing trade with eastern European nations in order to lessen the dependence of those nations on the Soviet Union (see Bilder 1970; Friedmann 1957; Miller 1960). This kind of conflict occurs also in less recognizable forms. For example, in the late 1960s, when official United States policy imposed a boycott on Cuba, the Ford Foundation sent a number of Third World scholars and government officials to visit Havana. The foundation could do "privately" what the United States government did not wish to do publicly. However, such action may have furthered United States interests (see Arnove 1970), and so the conflict may have been more apparent than real.

Another kind of conflict between public and private governments may be prompted when members of an organization turn to the legal system seeking to change the balance of power which works to their disadvantage. On the one hand, there are battles before courts and legislatures for rules which, it is hoped, will benefit the less powerful. On the other hand, rules are not self-implementing, and often a battle to vindicate any rights gained is waged before courts and administrative agencies. For example, a faction of a religious group may seek to oust those in control; courts have been asked to arbitrate conflicting versions of the true faith in disputes about control of church property.

While it is important for many purposes to chart relationships between public and private governments, this schematic statement of the task can be misleading. Implicit in the idea of "relationships" between public and private sectors is the idea that they are separate and distinct. Sometimes this is the case, but often it is not. The American legal system has relatively open borders even in its formal description: jurors drawn from the community act as triers of fact; judges and prosecutors often are elected; critically important roles are played by lawyers who typically are thought of as private professionals serving as officers of the courts (see Schmidhauser 1979). The rules of law themselves often are justified as the will of the people or as the product of a pluralistic bargaining process.

"Backstage" one finds even greater penetration of the public sector by the private. "Power elite" theories seek to establish links between private centers of economic power and governmental officeholders and activities (see, for example, Mills 1956; Dye 1978; Hopkins 1978; Kerbo and Della Fave 1983; Milward and Francisco 1983; Useem 1983). Effectiveness of reform legislation often turns on the existence of face-to-face sanctions in a social field that encompasses both governmental officials and private leaders of various kinds. (Cf. the work of Lindblom 1977; see Tilman 1983 on reactions to Lindblom's work.) The effective boundaries of social fields are unsettled and often are the focus of struggle and change (Weyrauch 1969, 1971). Some people are leading actors in a social field, while others are bit players. Yet this relationship can change gradually or rapidly.

Semi-autonomous social fields are likely to be found at the margins of public government itself. For example, American courts are faced with many cases involving personal injuries caused by automobiles. Litigation has grown since the early days of motoring, and there has been the parallel development of insurance to cover liability. This has prompted the growth of professional insurance adjusters who determine what the company is willing to offer in settlement, plaintiffs' lawyers who work for contingent fees and bargain or litigate to increase the amount paid, specialized insurance defense lawyers who come forward when litigation threatens, and experts of many kinds who sell their opinions about the condition of products and patients. All of these actors find themselves in a continuing relationship mediated by judges and clerks of court, governed by a loose system of rules and sanctions (see Ross 1970), and so they are "repeat players," interested in the impact of what they do in today's case on next year's transactions (Galanter 1974). As a result, the vast majority of cases are settled out of court by these specialists, whose moves are governed both by rules enforced through powerful though informal sanctions and by explicit or tacit threats to file a complaint and litigate in court.

Within the criminal justice system, a similar field involves those who regularly prosecute and defend criminal cases. Assistant prosecuting attorneys and defense counsel play leading roles. Other important actors include trial judges, clerks of court, police officers and officials of the department, the public defender's office, and even newspaper reporters and editors (see Carter 1974; Pritchard 1985). In a corrupt city, one might also include the leaders of organized crime and key political officials (see Block and Thomas 1984). Any of these people can look forward to sanctions from some of the others if they make work in the social field more difficult. All find their tasks easier to carry out if they can count on cooperation and favors from the others. Mileski (1971) comments:

> One attorney . . . noted that whenever he obtained an "unreasonable" acquittal, the prosecutor penalized him by not calling his cases until the end of the day's session. This "penalty" would last about a week after the disapproved disposition. Not only the lawyer but also his client, then, must sometimes sit all day in court for reasons irrelevant to the substance of the cases at hand. Ordinarily, clients with attorneys have their cases scheduled for very early or very late in the day's session. The court thus allows the attorneys to salvage most of each day for out-of-court matters. Defendants without attorneys are told the day, but not the time, of their court appearances. This favor may add to the court's leverage in coaxing attorneys toward routine cooperation. [p. 489]

Generally, those who interact repeatedly over time will find themselves in a semi-autonomous social field with rules and sanctions which reflect some balance of the long-term interests of all the actors in that field. Often this balance is not totally congruent with the official definition of roles (see Mechanic 1962). Many studies have shown that agencies charged with enforcing a law may try to mediate, educate, or persuade the targets of the regulation to comply with some part of the law or with its spirit, rather than going to court to seek sanctions for violations. Wherever this kind of "soft" law enforcement exists, there is reason to look for a social field with rules and sanctions of its own that apply both to the targets of regulation and to the regulators.

Anyone familiar with the social study of law will see the relevance of many of these examples of nongovernmental governing to concerns in the field. This review of the relationships between the legal system and various kinds of organizations and social fields which are formally outside the boundaries of government suggests that we must be concerned not only with private associations which mimic the structures and symbols of public government but also with those social fields closely related to the legal system which affect its operations. Ultimately, however, judgments about what the label "private government" requires turn on the usefulness of the analogy. This calls for the consideration of several problems in the field, asking what would be gained by a focus on various kinds of associations that do some of the work of the formal legal system or affect its operations.

Private Government and Topics in the Social Study of Law

A private government perspective could improve work in a number of areas of law and the behavioral sciences. I will consider three major examples: (a) private government and the limits of effective legal action; (b) social fields, the legal system, and stability and change in society; and (c) the autonomy and accountability of private associations.

Private Government and the Limits of Effective Legal Action

At least since Pound's essay in 1917, "the limits of effective legal action" has been a classic problem, but one lacking classic answers. Much of the writing assumes a state issuing commands to individuals who, acting alone, choose to comply or evade in view of the benefits of crime and the costs of punishment considered in light of the risks of being caught. However, Moore (1978, p. 58) suggests that the limited success and unintended and unwanted side effects of innovative social legislation can be explained partly because "new laws are thrust upon going social arrangements in which there are complexes of binding obligations already in existence. Legislation is often passed with the intention of altering the going social arrangements in specified ways. The social arrangements are often effectively stronger than the new laws."

Developing this suggestion, I shall consider the functions of informal, relatively unstructured social networks, more permanent social fields, and then structured private governments of some complexity. Finally, I will examine implementation of regulations calling for affirmative action to hire and tenure women in universities as an example showing how structure and social fields involving both regulators and regulated interact to blunt the impact of laws seen as of questionable legitimacy by many of those affected.

The Impact of Increasing Degrees of Structure Relatively unstructured *informal networks* can serve as gatekeepers, rationing access both to illegal goods and services and to government services and benefits. In both instances, such networks affect the impact of law. Those who sell illegal goods and services seldom can operate at a fixed address with a sign over the door inviting the public to trade nor can they advertise in the newspapers or in the Yellow Pages. Loosely structured social networks of people channel customers to those who can supply what is wanted, filter out unwanted individuals such as police officers pretending to be customers, and serve to insulate most levels of criminal organization from detection and punishment. For example, a visitor to a city can ask a hotel employee, a cab driver, or a bartender for aid in finding prohibited drugs, gambling, or a prostitute. If the visitor has selected the right person, he or she will be sent to one or more people guarding access to the illegal goods or services. Those experienced in finding illegal items will be able to read hints, body language, and situations to minimize difficulty in making links with suppliers. Each person in the network usually can screen out unwanted customers and possible police officers. Those participants at street level are easiest to find, but they know only what they need to know in order to minimize the risks to others in the criminal network. There is a system of rewards and punishments to hold the system together. Those who channel wanted customers can make money; those who tell police too much can be injured or killed.

Such networks sometimes can be used by law enforcement officials, with more or less success, as leverage points for applying the law against major entrepreneurs as well as the street-level sales force. Officers posing as potential customers buy the illegal goods or services and arrest those involved. Prosecutors then sometimes are able to trade a favorable plea bargain for information or testimony against those higher up in the chain of distribution. This works, of course, only when the value of the plea bargain outweighs the danger of retaliation from those who control the criminal network.

Similar networks can ration access to government services. Elected public officials at all levels do "casework" for their constituents (see Lineberry and Watson 1980; Abney and Lauth 1982). Sometimes this involves sending people to the right official with the necessary information. In a close case, at least, it is easier for an administrator to say yes than to reject a claim and explain the denial to a mayor, a representative, or a senator. Union shop stewards, religious leaders, and community leaders also perform such brokerage roles, sending people to the right place and exerting what influence they have on the decision that is made. Friends at school, at the workplace, or at the playground or laundry also can offer more or less accurate information on how to cope with government systems—where to go, whom to see, and what to say to gain access (see Nelson 1980). (Cf. the situation in the Soviet Union. See Simis 1982; Di Franceisco and Gitelman 1984.)

This rationing of access to public services often has impact on the effectiveness of reform law. Those who lack information and endorsements may be at a disadvantage: they fail to ask for services to which they are entitled or their claims may get lost in bureaucratic procedures, prompting them to give up. Moreover, there is reason to expect that the well-connected who can use endorsements from various kinds of leaders to affect administrative decisions will come from some groups in the society rather than others. Some officials are bribed to produce favorable decisions, but bribery costs money. Some will have more opportunity than others to influence action this way (see Deysine 1980). Thus, laws that purport to apply equally to those entitled to their benefits will serve some and not others. Furthermore, some benefits are granted only if certain conditions are met; this is done to influence behavior. Insofar as lawmakers attempt to regulate in this manner, they will be only partially effective to the extent that gatekeepers channel services to some people and keep them from others. Those left out will have little incentive to modify their behavior in the desired direction.

Finally, those who serve as brokers of information and access may tell their clients how to comply with the form and not the substance of the law or how to hide the fact that they are not entitled to licenses or benefits. Here, too, brokerage systems may influence the impact of law. For example, a particular office of a state motor vehicle department may have an informal policy of failing teenage males unless they pass three "rule-of-thumb" tests which the inspectors think demonstrate respect for traffic laws. A group of friends at school may tell X, who is reckless and has great contempt for traffic laws, about these tests. X carefully complies and passes the three tests when he seeks his driver's license. X may pass and be licensed, but his recklessness and contempt may even be encouraged since he has beaten the system.

Lawyers sometimes serve the same function, telling clients how to comply in form but not in substance. Even if few lawyers show clients how to avoid having crimes detected, there is at least anecdotal evidence that many clients think lawyers will provide such service. Lawyers, then, may be hired to serve as substitutes for the gatekeepers involved in informal social networks, offering information about the operation of government agencies and, in some cases, influence over the content of decisions (see *Vanderbilt Law Review* 1984).

The kind of *social field* discussed by Moore as "often effectively stronger than the new laws" usually is more structured and permanent than the informal networks considered so far. Social fields can serve most of the functions of informal networks but their structure and permanence allow them additional means of warding off the influence of legal commands. There are a number of examples of social fields playing this part: Moore's own work considers an elite in an African nation attempting to implement a socialist program in the face of resistance from village and tribal units. In our country the closest analogy to the situation described by Moore might be a religious group that withdraws from ordinary society in order to continue a religious practice deemed illegal by state or federal law. Governments and religious groups have battled, with mixed results, over sending children to secular schools, polygamy, and the use of drugs in ceremonies.

Social fields need not be as structured, permanent, or distinct as a settled community to succeed in warding off regulation by the state. For example, those who work together or who are regulars at a bar may deal in stolen goods. Employees of a lumber yard may offer good bargains on stolen building materials to the group (see Henry 1981). Those who work in restaurants may help each other minimize their income tax burden by devising and sharing strategies for reporting as little income as possible on tax returns. It might look suspicious for a waitress to report no tips, but she may welcome help in determining how little she can report safely. Those who identify themselves as professional criminals may form a fairly structured network to aid their activities. One of the functions of a prison is that of a center for developing and reinforcing criminal networks. For example, safecrackers can share techniques and information about good places to rob, and those in the business are identified so that they may be contacted when ex-inmates resume their criminal careers and need help.

Social fields serve to undercut the impact of law in a variety of ways. A group can delegitimate compliance and make violation seem ordinary and acceptable. Those who would comply or even suggest doing so may be the subject of ridicule, ostracism, or even violence. In such a case, if membership in the group is valued, one has to consider risking loss of his or her position before complying openly. Alternatively, evasion can be legitimated in a number of ways. The definition of a situation can be transformed so that members can deny that they are violating a legal norm. For example, those who take goods from their employer can argue that it is not really stealing but a customary right and part of their compensation (see Tersine and Russell 1981). Or if members of the group have to acknowledge they are violating the law, violation can be rationalized, and this rationalization can be repeated so that it becomes part of the common sense of the field. For example, those who work in restaurants and receive tips justify not reporting all of them on their tax return because of all of the loopholes in the tax system benefiting the rich, the general unfairness of the tax system, or the senseless way in which governments spend money.

Members of the group also can teach techniques of evasion which minimize the risk of detection. Those interested in stealing by subverting the computers that control so much of modern business can share the latest techniques and ways to counter safeguards against tampering. If members of a social field regularly meet for legitimate purposes, this serves to cover their discussions of plans for breaking the law. For example, parents who attend the same church may plan on how to initiate prayers in their local school despite rulings of the Supreme Court. If they are all tied to the community, those who might object and try to blow the whistle could be subject to many powerful sanctions. Their children might be subject to ridicule and ostracism, their businesses might be boycotted, or their homes vandalized. In a small city, no one might be free to object to prayers in the local schools.

Moore's position stresses the power of social fields to resist unwanted regulation. Nonetheless, one wonders how far these groups can ward off the larger society when those who hold power are offended by or fear the social field. The Federal Bureau of Investigation had great success in undermining the Communist party during the 1950s; it had less success in similar attempts against groups in the civil rights and antiwar movements of the 1960s and 1970s. The Brazilian and Uruguayan governments seem to have defeated urban guerrilla movements which were well organized private governments seeking to overthrow public authority, but the British government has not been able to overcome the Provisional Wing of the Irish Republican Army. It seems unlikely that an adequate explanation of these differences can be found in the structures or processes of the revolutionary groups in the various countries—indeed, the processes and structures of most contemporary revolutionary groups draw on a common literature, including, importantly, the writings of the Brazilian Carlos Marighela (1971). At least part of the explanation for the different degrees of success in repressing guerrilla movements might involve the unwillingness of the British to use all of the tactics that the military regimes found acceptable. Probably public governments can overcome most, if not all, social fields if it is worth the price. However, undercover work attempting to infiltrate the group, harassment, and manipulation of public opinion to turn the group into a pariah require skill and money. They also cost valued privacy and freedom of association. More repressive measures carry a higher price.

Social fields also may act in ways apparently serving to implement the operation of the legal process. Groups can support those seeking to enforce their rights under existing laws or to change the rules. A group may supply money and access to lawyers and others who know how to litigate, negotiate, and lobby. It also may serve as an audience, applauding appropriate behavior. If, as often is the case, lawmaking and law enforcement must be triggered by complaints, a group can provide not only resources but a shield against retaliation. In fact, one who speaks out may find it hard to back down and settle or drop the matter if the group defines this as selling out. Of course, all these valuable functions will be supplied only for a price. Groups will not support those they oppose, they will not campaign for legal action against their interests, and they may focus retaliation against the one seeking legal action that offends other members. As a result, individuals may be given powerful incentives to transform their desires and translate them into a vocabulary approved by whatever groups are available. In this way, for example, labor unions can limit the effectiveness of laws designed to give rights to individual union members against union leaders; an American Association of University Professors chapter on a campus can help insulate the administration from challenges by faculty members denied tenure or contract renewal and frustrate laws designed to affect such decisions.

When we turn from informal networks and social fields to what we more comfortably can call *private governments*—formally structured complex organizations such as business corporations, universities, and major charitable foundations—we find still additional barriers to effective legal action. Organizational structure and process itself is an important variable in attempts to control behavior, as a number of writers are beginning to recognize. I will begin by viewing the deviance of business corporations from a private government perspective, generalize this analysis by applying it to universities, and then attempt to show that complex organizations such as corporations and universities cannot always be viewed as something distinct from public government. Social fields often cut across organizational boundaries with important consequences for the impact of law.

Corporations are subject to a wide variety of direct legal controls in all Western societies. However, in the past few decades many have become concerned about the limited effectiveness of rules designed to protect the market, the environment, consumers, or the political system. Apparently, business organizations have a good deal of power to deflect what reformers think is or ought to be the law.

Public government also attempts to induce large organizations to implement certain policies less directly. An enforcement agency may pursue a policy of "soft" law enforcement, seeking to persuade large organizations to comply with agency directives. The threat of legal action may serve as part of the agencies' negotiating power, but this threat is often limited by obvious difficulties in applying sanctions. Also, if an agency can succeed in getting a large business corporation to agree to change practices, it, in effect, gains the use of the private organization's internal communication and sanction system to change the way things are done in local offices and places of business throughout the country. Governments also deal with private organizations by using contracts. By using the benefits of holding a government contract as an incentive, an agency can often gain agreement to carry out social policies more or less related to the transaction. For example, federal contractors must pay certain minimum wages and offer their workers certain conditions of employment. Despite these techniques, however, reformers worry that corporate deviance or mere token compliance is unacceptably high (*New York Times* 1985).

Several authors have stressed the effects of structure and process in studies seeking to understand unlawful organizational behavior and to fashion innovative and more effective sanctions. Coffee (1981) and Vaughan (1982, 1983) draw on sociological theories about the functioning of organizations, while Braithwaite (1982), Fisse (1981), and Fisse and Braithwaite (1984) base their analyses on an empirical research project in which over 200 senior executives of 50 transnational corporations, as well as many government officials, have been interviewed. I will first describe this group of studies, and then I will offer some additional considerations.

Vaughan argues that the environment in which organizations operate and their own processes generate incentives for individuals working within them to engage in deviant activity. Following Merton (1957a, 1957b), she argues that the goal of organizational success is so highly valued that the importance of attaining it outweighs concern about the means used. Businesses seek economic success measured in ways such as market share or the price of the corporate stock. Great efforts have been made in modern business corporations to create decentralized structures and sophisticated accounting systems so that those responsible for profit and loss can be rewarded or punished. At the same time, normative support for succeeding only through legal means has been progressively lessened.

For example, the definition of deviance usually is doubtful. Reforms will not be perceived as sensible and right if they make it harder for managers to gain rewards and avoid punishments within the organization. While reformers may see programs that minimize environmental pollution as highly beneficial, a manager may see only that they increase the costs of operation making it harder to reach the target for return on investment. Also, since it is costly and difficult to prosecute a large corporation quite able to defend itself, government agencies frequently resort to negotiations and informal proceedings. Those who violate the law are seldom sanctioned severely, and, as a result, only a few examples of wrongdoing are publicized. The fact that deals are made may suggest that the subject is not an important issue of right and wrong. Coffee points out that a sanction severe enough to outweigh the benefits of violation would have to be so great as to threaten the existence of the corporation. As a result, sanctions tend to be mere tokens; they are more like fines for overtime parking than punishment for truly wrongful behavior. Since government so often cannot enforce the law, managers evade and achieve success. Thus, illegal action becomes accepted within an organization as just the way things are done. Managers who attempted to comply with the law would face a serious handicap when compared with those who cut corners to get results.

Vaughan recognizes that her structural incentive argument fails to explain the behavior of all corporate actors. Many, if not most, business people do not violate the law. Others violate it but are not aware they are doing so because they do not know the rule or they misunderstand what it commands. She cites with approval Coffee's explanation for illegal behavior which rests on an interaction between psychological and structural factors. Coffee notes that modern corporations tend to be multidivisional and decentralized. Top management allocates funds to managers of profitable divisions and disciplines those who fail to meet targeted goals for return on investment. Thus, the manager responsible for operational decisions is increasingly separated by organizational structure, language, goals, and experience from the financial managers who plan for the future and decide on rewards and punishments. Coffee argues that this means that "the locus of corporate crime is predominantly at the lower to middle management level" (p. 397). He explains that

> [t]he middle manager is acutely aware that he can be easily replaced; he knows that if he cannot achieve a quick fix, another manager is in the wings, eager to assume operational control over a division. The results of such a structure are predictable: When pressure is intensified, illegal or irresponsible means become attractive to a desperate middle manager who has no recourse against a stern but myopic notion of accountability that looks only to the bottom line of the income statement. [p. 398]

Vaughan recognizes that incentives to violate laws are not a sufficient explanation for corporate crime; there must be opportunities for unlawful conduct as well. In large complex organizations unlawful behavior may be both encouraged and hidden from insiders at other levels as well as from outsiders. Officials of subunits are likely to defend their domain whatever the claims of other units or outsiders. Control over subunits largely rests on accounting systems which disclose the consequences of various practices but obscure other things. In Coffee's terms, this allows senior managers to "piously express shock at their subordinates' actions while still demanding strict 'accountability' on the part of such managers for short-term operating results" (p. 410).

The analysis in these articles could be carried further. Vaughan notes that corporate managers may have ties outside the corporation that provide incentives to comply with the law or not to get caught violating it. She says that "[a]lternative skills, alternative sources of income, and alternative validating social roles reduce financial and social dependence on the firm. Consequently, external rewards and punishments may reduce the organization's ability to mobilize individual efforts in its behalf, despite processes that produce a normative environment supporting unlawful conduct" (p. 1392). Obviously, corporate managers, like the rest of us, have acquired complex attitudes about following rules from family, neighborhood groups, schools, mass media, and experience. On the one hand, there are general messages indicating that we should obey the law. On the other hand, we often learn in school, and particularly from competitive athletics, that we may cheat for a good cause. From newspapers and television we learn that respected figures break rules in all kinds of social games. Corporate life can be seen as a game where winning is the only goal.

At the same time, social fields and organizations such as business corporations may reward compliance with the law. In at least some corporations there are ways to avoid the kinds of pressures described by Vaughan and Coffee. For example, one may be able to use members of the legal staff as a way to support compliance rather than violation. Lawyers can be blamed for increasing costs by fashioning procedures in response to new regulations, and a manager may be able to bring his or her department's activities to the attention of the general counsel's office so that he or she will appear to be forced to comply. The legal staff may welcome a chance to symbolize respect for the law since the techniques of compliance are within its domain, and the need to respond to regulation enhances its power within the organization, A manager may be able to dress an ethical stance in prudential garb: complying with the law can be justified in terms of the negative consequences of the likely bad publicity if the firm was caught violating a regulation.

This is not to say that Vaughan and Coffee are wrong in stressing the pressures to evade the law, but more emphasis on possible offsetting pressures supporting compliance would seem warranted. We know little about when the balance falls one way or the other. Furthermore, corporations that have suffered serious blows to their reputations as the result of publicity surrounding getting caught violating the law may modify their incentive systems to ease the pressures for deviance—at least temporarily. Of course, as Coffee stresses, while the formal message from a corporate president's office may call for compliance, the real message communicated may be, rather, "don't get caught."

Coffee's argument that the locus of corporate crime is middle management seems only partially true. Undoubtedly, in many cases the pressures he describes are real. Nonetheless, some kinds of corporate crime must involve the participation of top management. For example, decisions to sponsor a military coup to overthrow the government of a nation which has threatened corporate interests, to bribe high governmental officials, to continue participation in international cartels during wartime with corporations based in enemy nations, and the like are not usually within the power of middle management to make or implement. Certain multinational corporations, moreover, interact with governments, pursuing what could be viewed as their own foreign policies. Lowenthal (1978) observes that

> [in] a curious sense, it is much easier for the [United States] government to manage its relations with the Soviet Union or China than with Chile or Peru. Latin American and Caribbean countries are very strongly influenced by decisions taken by Exxon, the American Smelting and Refining Co. (ASARCO), United Brands, Citibank, Manufacturers' Hanover Trust, or Chase Manhattan, to name just a few examples. And some of the main problems in inter-American relations—especially access to capital and technology—are issues over

> which the U.S. government has considerably less influence than non-governmental actors. [p. 122]

For example, during the Carter Administration, it was United States foreign policy, reinforced by legislation, not to supply arms to nations that repressed the human rights of their citizens. However, American corporations could evade government policy by channeling sales through their foreign subsidiaries. It seems likely that the decisions to make such sales were made at the upper levels of management.

A Case Study: Affirmative Action for Women in Universities Finally, the discussion in these articles draws a rather sharp distinction between public and private spheres and fails to cover social fields that include both the regulators and regulated. We will turn to an extended example—affirmative action for women at universities—to stress that the structure of a large private government and the existence of social networks cutting across formal boundaries can work together to blunt the effectiveness of regulation. In other words, we will use a private government perspective to analyze the limited impact of a legal reform. We will stress both the relationships between public and private spheres and the interpenetrations of the two areas. The example also will make clear that much of the analysis in the articles just considered is not limited to business corporations but applies to other complex organizations as well.

Women have faced barriers to becoming and remaining university professors throughout the history of higher education in this country because of conscious policy or circumstance (Bernard 1964). By 1972, there were three bodies of law designed to eliminate discrimination against women and members of minority groups by large academic institutions. First, Title VII of the Civil Rights Act of 1964 was extended to universities and colleges, allowing academic women who saw themselves as victims of discrimination in hiring, promotion, or tenure to sue for court orders directing that they be granted the position to which they were entitled, damages, or both. Groups of women also could form a class and sue on behalf of themselves and others, seeking judgments placing a university under judicial supervision to ensure the abolition of discrimination. While there were some notable victories, courts have been hesitant to substitute their judgment for those of professionals about the quality of teaching and scholarship. Second, under the Equal Pay Act academic institutions may not pay different salaries to men and women with substantially equal qualifications who occupy substantially equal positions.

Finally, under Executive Order 11375 universities which receive large federal contracts must submit a plan to take affirmative action to overcome the effects of past discrimination against women (see, generally, Prager 1982). Employers must analyze their work force and the pool of qualified potential employees and establish goals so that the composition of a work force eventually will reflect the percentages of women in the pool. This is not a quota system nor a requirement that women less qualified than available men be hired. Rather, the federal contractor must show some progress as a result of good faith efforts in meeting goals when required reports are made.

Generally, this regulation of academic hiring received mixed reviews from the regulated. University professors and administrators did not object to the Equal Pay Act, and few had difficulty with the idea that a woman who had suffered discrimination ought to have a remedy. However, most of them expected almost no valid claims because they believed that universities, with but few exceptions, hire, promote, and grant tenure on the basis of merit. Some were concerned with the potential burden of defending a discrimination claim even when it lacked merit. Most senior professors and administrators saw affirmative action as unsuited to a university.

In the 1970s, women's organizations, along with minority and handicapped groups, sued the federal agencies charged with enforcing the requirement of affirmative action and negotiated promises that the law would be enforced. Nonetheless after more than a decade, members of these organizations remain dissatisfied with the amount of compliance with affirmative action laws by universities while federal grants and contracts continue to flow to them (see, for example, Abramson 1977; Homig 1980; McKenna and Denmark 1975; Page 1978; Vladeck and Young 1978).

A sketch of the process involved in attempts at enforcement over a decade at a major campus of a state university—called State University at Fillmore for purposes of this study—will illustrate the complex and multileveled interactions when a private government is reluctant to carry out the demands of public government (see J. Macaulay 1980). In 1970, after complaints of nonenforcement of the law were made by national women's groups, representatives of the Office of Civil Rights (OCR) of the Department of Health, Education and Welfare visited State University at Fillmore. They told university administrators that they saw a pattern of underutilization of women and of salary discrimination. The 1970 campus affirmative action plan was found to be inadequate, and campus officials signed an agreement to produce an acceptable one, update it annually, and submit the plan and the reports to OCR. The OCR staff announced that it planned a follow-up visit to the campus in January 1971.

The president of State University then issued a directive to all campuses in the system, including the one at Fillmore, to appoint an affirmative action officer (AAO) and a Committee on the Status of Women. This was done at Fillmore, and the AAO and the committee gained a measure of power from the threat to federal contracts and grants posed by the OCR visit and planned return. Salaries were investigated, and a number of extreme cases of discrimination were uncovered. Deans and department chairpersons were told to grant raises to remedy these inequities. A number of women were discovered teaching a major course load without permanent positions and at low pay. Many of these women were promoted to tenure track positions or given tenure in recognition of their long service and the unfairness of their past treatment by the university. A utilization analysis was done, and it revealed a pattern of underrepresentation of women in the majority of departments at the campus.

Once these steps were taken, however, a pattern developed which was to be repeated throughout the decade. The AAO would work on an affirmative action plan and write reports with data on the hiring, promotion, and tenuring of women. Field personnel of the various federal agencies which successively were given enforcement responsibility over universities would write or visit the campus. Members of a social field composed of women with some connection to the university who were dissatisfied with progress on affirmative action would meet with the federal personnel and point out defects in the plan and statistics. The field personnel would recommend that the Fillmore campus be required to take certain steps or have contracts and grants disapproved. But then the threatening clouds would blow away and officials in Washington would pronounce the Fillmore campus still approved to receive contracts and grants although it never produced the kind of plan or data which would seem to be required in order to comply with the letter or purposes of the law.

Moreover, although the number of women hired increased, the proportion of those with permanent tenured positions rose very little. Women's promotion chances remained low, and departments that never employed women in proportion to their availability continued always to fall short of their goals. One year a state civil rights agency found probable cause to believe that a university department had discriminated against a woman when it refused to grant her tenure; another year a state commission on women found the university's efforts in affirmative action to be inadequate. Women, and members of minority groups, continued to point to figures showing that the university was falling far short of its announced goals. Still the university kept saying that it was fully complying with all laws and regulations, and federal agencies took no action against it.

Four explanations stand out for the success of State University at Fillmore in warding off the impact of these laws: affirmative action lacked legitimacy; the structure and process of the university diffused responsibility and made it hard to find reliable data; social networks that included both regulators and the regulated had the power to deflect enforcement; and the consequences of cutting off contracts and grants to a great research university were unacceptable. They will be examined in turn.

Affirmative action for women at universities progressively lost legitimacy in the eyes of those with the power to make decisions. The academic community can be viewed as a loosely coordinated social field, and its culture operated to undercut the legitimacy of this program. Affirmative action was sharply attacked in a number of books and articles written by professors (see, for example, Lester 1974; Posner 1979; Sowell 1976). This literature tended to paint an idealized picture of university life, glorifying an unselfish pursuit of truth, devotion to students, and decision based on merit—the academy was pictured as something like a religious community, fundamentally different from factories and business offices where affirmative action might make some sense. Affirmative action regulations were labeled "reverse discrimination," as the title of one book put it (Glazer 1975). Whatever the merits of the arguments presented, these books and articles helped professors and administrators justify evading or minimally complying with the letter of the law (cf. Lipset 1982).

In addition to questionable legitimacy in the eyes of those making hiring, promotion, and tenure decisions, government officials charged with enforcing affirmative action regulations faced problems of structure and process. Most prestigious universities have a complex structure characterized by a tension between the powers of those who administer and those who teach and do research. Formally, usually a university is run by a governing board which delegates power to a chief executive officer. This administrator, in turn, appoints deans to administer various subunits. Within these divisions, there are departments charged with teaching and research in their own area. In theory, deans and chairpersons administer while the faculty makes policy within boundaries set by statutes or a charter and the decisions of the governing board. In practice, however, professors are "street level bureaucrats" (cf. Prottas 1978; Carter 1974) who operate relatively autonomously with little direct supervision. The faculty claims, and often has, power to decide who is to be hired, promoted, and given tenure. Those higher up the chain of command have veto power, but custom demands that it be used only sparingly. Obviously, there is great opportunity for negotiation and politics within the formal decision-making process.

Just as Vaughan and Coffee suggest, this decentralization of power had important consequences for the enforcement of affirmative action requirements. It was hard to detect violations and noncompliance as long as those in the departments making the hiring and tenuring decisions knew enough not to post signs saying "no women need apply" and to make gestures such as advertising positions and interviewing at least a few women along with the men being considered in the usual course of recruiting.

Government officials exerted pressure for affirmative action at higher administrative levels. Professors usually learn about affirmative action regulations not by reading the law but from directives coming down from above. Those who wrote the directives at Fillmore tended to simplify and pass on interpretations which would not upset traditional practices very much. Professors also learned about the rules from atrocity stories passed along by deans and chairpersons that told of the costs and burdens of red tape and bureaucratic procedures. These stories may well have undercut any impulse to make significant changes in departmental recruiting and decision-making.

Since most important hiring and tenure decisions take place in the departments, administrators were able to close their eyes to evasion as long as they could find some apparent or symbolic compliance. The day-to-day burden of dealing with affirmative action usually is placed on an assistant to the university head. Such assistants have had relatively little power unless the president or chancellor wanted to push for compliance. Assistants who want to keep their jobs are likely to negotiate for gestures and proceed cautiously (see Liss 1977). They have little incentive, from the standpoint of their careers, to make available information that might embarrass the university. Rather, all the incentives are to interpret the data as showing progress in hiring women. (Cf. Weiss and Gruber 1984.) If this proved difficult, assistants could at least make a case for good faith effort to comply in the face of adverse economic conditions, budget constraints, and less hiring and tenuring.

In addition to the questionable legitimacy of affirmative action and structural characteristics of the university, there is also a social field comprising those who are supposed to enforce these laws and those university professors and administrators who are the targets of regulation. For example, State University at Fillmore had acquired a reputation as a leader in affirmative action for women because of its early efforts to correct clear-cut examples of discrimination. As a result, in 1974 its AAO became a consultant to the Department of Health, Education and Welfare. Her role was reflected in a memorandum written in February of that year. She reported that she was "spending almost half of every week in Washington, D.C., trying to win a modification or deletion" of rules such as those requiring the compilation of data about employees. Without these data complete statistical analyses for evidence of underutilization of or discrimination against women could never be done. Moreover, she described her plan to go only so far in complying with the letter of the affirmative action regulations as to be able to comply fully within ninety days if and when the federal government ever insisted that the Fillmore campus meet them; her constant contact with officials in Washington apparently enabled her to judge when it would be necessary to begin to compile a precise plan and detailed and accurate statistics.

The AAO was a member of the faculty of a department at Fillmore, an officer of the campus administration, and a consultant to the federal government's enforcement agency. Her role crossed formal organizational boundaries. The consequences for the impact of the law were shown by events in November and December of 1974. In November, an assistant to the president of State University wrote HEW's director of the Higher Education Division, asking how the affirmative action plans of various campuses of State University should be submitted for approval by HEW. The director and the AAO of the Fillmore campus were well acquainted as a result of all the consulting and lobbying in Washington. On December 3, the director telephoned the AAO at home in the evening after working hours. The AAO's memorandum concerning the conversation states:

> [The director] indicated to me that the agency did not wish to engage in general institution-wide compliance reviews while the standards and procedures . . . [then in effect] are still extant. She further indicated that to the best of her knowledge and belief no major university could be today found in compliance if . . . [these] standards are applied. Consequently, she stated she believed that an on-site review at this time, as required by Revised Order 14 for approval of an affirmative action plan, would find many or all . . . system schools out of compliance, without regard to any excellence or lack of it in real progress in affirmative action. She expressed the further belief that the target of such reviews would automatically become the . . . [State University at Fillmore] . . . and that we were very likely therefore to go to fund cut-off.
>
> She indicated that she felt such compliance reviews in the present circumstances would be very destructive, supportive neither of affirmative action nor of educational goals. But, she noted, in view of the currently pending suit in which NOW, WEAL and others have charged HEW with nonenforcement, she was not at liberty to instruct . . . [the assistant to the President of the University] . . . in writing not to submit the plans.
>
> In view of all these circumstances she asked me if I could insure that the plans were not submitted.

The AAO's solution to this problem was to "draft a tentative letter" for the HEW director to send to the assistant to the president "indicating that the plans *could* be submitted but that the agency maintained a reviewing schedule to which, absent some pressing necessity, it preferred to adhere." The letter was written, the Fillmore campus plan was not submitted, and this threat to the flow of federal money passed.

This was not the only instance of informal contacts designed to blunt compliance with the letter of the regulations. Whenever the threat looked serious, administrators of the Fillmore campus and influential professors were able to go over the head of the field investigators and the regional offices and take their case to top officials in Washington. Those at the top of the chain of command in the agencies charged with enforcing affirmative action regulations are part of the higher education social field. Whatever formal organization charts might indicate, these cabinet officers, top level administrators, and their staffs often were former university professors, foundation executives, or others who held graduate degrees and were sympathetic to the traditions of higher education and who were often linked by friendship or long association with officials in national educational associations if not directly with those who ran the Fillmore campus. These federal officials were not "captured" by the university administrators; they just understood one another and shared similar attitudes and values. Often, during the 1970s, those ultimately responsible were former academics temporarily serving as cabinet officers or administrators. As the Fillmore campus chancellor's lawyer told a group of law students, when a contract or grant was held up because of questions about affirmative action at this campus, administrators, professors, and representatives of higher education organizations in Washington "have been able to find the people who are ultimately responsible for whatever the regional office is off on and help to get them back on the track."

Finally, we have to look to the consequences of enforcing the affirmative action regulations to the letter. If the federal government had cut off all grants and contracts to State University at Fillmore, it would have crippled a major research and teaching center. Both public and private universities are dependent on federal funds. Moreover, if administrators and professors at Fillmore had been forced to comply with the federal regulations as they were written, traditional hiring practices would have been overturned and many members of the faculty would have been antagonized. Yet this price did not have to be paid because affirmative action for women did not have great public support, and those who ran State University at Fillmore had friends with important positions in the legislative and executive branches of the federal government. In short, it was far easier to have symbolic but unenforced regulations than to pay the price for implementing them.

Social Fields, the Legal System, and Stability and Change in Society

Those writing broad social theories often see a need to account for law and legal institutions. One interested in the social study of law frequently finds these accounts unsatisfying because the theorist posits a formal picture of law. When one adds private governments, social fields, and networks to a sociological view of law, much found in these broader social theories seems inadequate if not wrong. Of course, turning from normative claims or theoretical statements about the functions of legal systems to a description of law in operation makes neat theories messy and complex, but oversimplification seldom is a virtue.

While this is not the place to describe and distinguish the variety of existing social theories and their accounts of the role of law, I will consider elements common to many of them and then discuss how concern with private governments, social fields, and networks might add to or question these theories. I am not offering a worked-out picture of society that accounts for the parts played by law and the legal system, but rather examples that suggest some of the things that any theory must deal with if it is to be useful to those concerned with the place of law.

The Roles Played by Law in Various Social Theories Before one can question the treatment of law in a social theory, it is necessary to sketch the way in which it deals with it. Here I will describe briefly and generally the account of law in structural-functional, conflict, and Marxist-derived theories. In the next section, I will consider how elements in these theories might be questioned if a broader view of the place of law were taken.

Many social theorists have offered what are called *structural-functional theories*. Here the focus is on social structure—the more or less enduring patterns of the ways people interact. Social phenomena are seen as interdependent as in a biological system. Action taken in one social unit affects the functioning of others. For example, economic and legal systems affect each other: an impoverished society cannot afford complex legal institutions, but modern industrialized nations have developed legal institutions where police, judges, lawyers, and regulatory agencies importantly affect the way business is conducted.

In most social theories, a major problem is the explanation of social order and the operation and continuation of societies. Most structural-functionalists see law as an important factor in such an explanation (see, for example, Bredemeier 1962; Grace and Wilkinson 1978; Koch 1980; Lamo de Espinosa 1980; Mishra 1982; Parsons 1962; Wilkinson 1981). They draw pictures of a relatively harmonious and stable society with the legal system playing a key role at its margin. People have expectations about the behavior of others and how others expect them to behave. Thus, one can rely on what others will do and pattern one's own conduct in order to fit in. People learn how to act in particular situations, and the norms governing social behavior become part of their psychological make-up. Most obligations are fulfilled naturally, and external sanctions play only a secondary, and often indirect, role. While there is much normative regulation, law is only an objective and visible part of a pyramid of habits, customs, norms, rules, and law.

Compliance with social norms may be enforced by sanctions inherent in reciprocal relationships, which exist in great numbers in any society. One has friends, interacts in groups for recreation, and repeatedly engages in business dealings with the same people. One who complies with the expectations of others in these relationships will continue to receive whatever benefits are involved, which may range from love or esteem to profitable business opportunities. One who disappoints the expectations of those in continuing relationships risks being subject to a range of sanctions: one's partners may frown, use sarcasm or ridicule, discontinue the relationship, or retaliate by using violence. (Cf. Griffiths' 1984 comments on gossip systems.) Only in extreme situations will one's partners call the police or file a lawsuit.

Those disputes that occur despite internalized norms and relational sanctions will be the product of ambiguity in the application of generally held values to particular situations. This creates a need for arbiters who can impose, or threaten to impose, sanctions so that their decisions about the proper interpretation of the norms will be carried out. In this way, legal activity serves the function of social integration by aiding the coordination or unification of various parts of the society.

Adjudication clarifies values in light of changing situations. In most instances, the decision of a court or arbiter will be accepted and does not have to be imposed. However, the legal system must be related to the state so that its monopoly of the legitimate use of force ensures that legal norms override any inconsistent social norms. In a few rare cases, a display of force may be needed to assert the priority of legal norms over all others by sanctioning those deviants who are not contained by other means of social control. Sanctions can be imposed only when permitted by the rule of law: one may be arrested, tried, convicted, and imprisoned for robbery only when the elements of the crime are present. If sanctions could be imposed apart from the rules, they would lose some or all of their normative force.

Some particularly important social values will be institutionalized as special legal agencies are created to protect them (Mayhew 1968). Certain kinds of equality are at least symbolized when a government creates an Equal Employment Opportunities Commission; certain patterns of coping with labor disputes are institutionalized by the creation of a National Labor Relations Board. These agencies must then have access to the people who violate the norms being protected. This means that those aggrieved must have incentives to participate in bringing problems to them.

When important disputes do come to the legal system as complaints, causes of action, or pleas for services, the system can then serve other functions which also carry out social integration. Disputes signal policy-makers and the interpreters of norms that there is need for an adjustment so that similar disputes or claims do not arise in the future.

Many theorists also see actual decisions as serving to legitimate society, the legal system, and the particular judgment in a case in a number of ways. The norms selected for application are seen as appropriate, and their application is consistent with the expectations of those observing the legal process. The legal system itself may have enough prestige so that members of the public will see any norms applied or interpreted by it as just, simply because they are crystallized in legal doctrine. Acceptance flows from at least two sources. First, the legal system is viewed as autonomous and not dependent on other centers of power. It can make and enforce its decisions impartially. Second, legal officials are selected in ways that most members of the society see as appropriate—they are experts who are selected in recognition of their skill, they have long practical experience, they are elected by the people, or they are appointed by those who symbolize the society. Finally, legal action promotes legitimacy because the legal system is perceived as having enough effectiveness to implement the norms it serves; it is more than idle rhetoric and pious preaching in the face of reality.

Conflict theories attack structural-functionalism, but, generally, this perspective tends to criticize ideas about the functions of law in society rather than offer a complete theory of its own (see, for example, Chambliss and Seidman 1971; Chambliss 1973, 1979; Quinney 1975). Conflict theorists see society not as harmonious and stable but held together by the use or threats of force. Law legitimates police violence and other uses of power to undercut attacks on the system. The reality of law is a police officer with a club or a SWAT team with automatic weapons attacking any group that threatens the stability of the existing order. Law supports the structures of property and exploitation. Under a system of division of labor, people are not self-sufficient, and they need cash to buy their needs. This means that they must have jobs and keep them. However, one's claim to a job under the law is always questionable. Those who challenge their employers risk being fired and gaining a reputation as troublemakers so that substitute employment will be difficult to find. These threats, rather than a general normative consensus, dampen open dissent and explain the persistence of societies in which few of the people share most of the benefits.

Conflict theorists turn structural-functionalism on its head. Instead of normative consensus, they say there is a great deal of dissensus and cynical knowledge. Instead of seeing the society, its legal system, and particular decisions as legitimate, they see cheating, manipulation, or simple resignation as the ways to cope with an unjust system which cannot be confronted directly. People at the bottom of the distribution of wealth and status do not accept their place as part of the natural order of things or as their just reward for lack of effort or skill. They see people at the top of the society as having gained their position illegitimately or as descendants of such people. Business executives cheat on their taxes, bribe American and foreign government officials, and foist shoddy products on the public. Elaborate rationalizations are fabricated by those at all levels for violating official norms.

Conflict theory tells us that, contrary to the claim of the structural-functionalists, the legal system and particular decisions seldom yield legitimacy. People do not see law as salient to their lives; at best, it is a background factor with limited impact. While the daily operation of law possibly might reflect common sense, people hear only about extraordinary cases. The acquittal of the man who attempted to assassinate President Reagan did not create legitimacy for either the criminal justice system or the insanity defense (see Hans and Slater 1983). Indeed, those decisions which are publicized are likely to provoke anger and dissensus. One need mention only the opinions of the Supreme Court concerning school prayers, abortion, and racial integration of the public schools as examples. People suspect that legal decisions often turn on wealth and connections rather than on apolitical, rational norms applied by an autonomous body of experts. Awareness of institutions such as plea bargaining and the settlement of personal injury cases would seem to reinforce such a view. Legal procedures do not reassure most people that the game is fair. Rather, they appear to be ploys in a game benefiting the economic interests of the legal profession and those who can pay the best lawyers to play for their side.

Austin Turk (1976) points out that, even when it is not corrupt, the legal system may promote conflict rather than social integration. Control of the system, for example, is a prize about which groups can fight—the power to appoint judges and administrators is one of the things gained by winning elections. Moreover, the chance to mobilize whatever power courts possess can be an incentive to abandon acceptance of the status quo. *Brown* v. *Board of Education* (the school desegregation case) was one of many factors provoking the civil rights movement and conflict in an effort to change traditional ways in the South (see Harding 1975). The chance of victories before courts and legislatures may undercut compromise, generating more conflict rather than stabilizing the society.

Marxist-derived theories show a different view of the functions of the law in postcapitalist societies. (For reviews of this literature, see Greenberg and Anderson 1981; Jessop 1980.) Most of these theorists, rather like the structural-functionalists, see society as composed of a number of subsystems and structures. While in a Marxist-inspired theory, the economic system and class relations will be central, the state and law are seen as necessary or useful in attempting to cope with contradictions, inconsistencies, and imperfections in the interest of the dominant class. Koch (1980, p. 6), in an essay highly critical of Marxist-derived theories, finds that they typically see the state and law fulfilling functions such as "the guarantee of legal relations, especially the relations of private property, the provision of general material conditions for production activity (the 'infrastructure'), the regulation of the conflict between wage-labour and capital and the defence and expansion of total national capital on the capitalist world market."

Many of these theorists see traditional bourgeois law as undercutting the possibility of effective class struggle, as working toward the acceptance of exploitation through mystification. In liberal states, individuals are formally equal before the law and are bearers of rights. Balbus (1977), in an often-cited article, argues that capitalist legal systems make people into citizens, abstracted from their personality and actual social situation. In this way they can be made to appear equal, despite all the real differences in status and power between the dominant and dominated classes. This militates against the formation of class consciousness. "[T]he 'community' produced by the legal form contributes decisively to the reproduction of the very capitalist mode of production which makes genuine community impossible" (p. 580).

Related theories see law as part of the battle for common sense (see Femia 1983). Except in times of stress, all classes accept a world view in which the existing order is seen as natural and proper. However, this view advances the interests of only the dominant class. Traditional intellectuals rationalize concepts of social order as the material basis of the dominant class's power change. Law and legal intellectuals are but part of this larger picture. For example, as economic crisis during the depression of the 1930s began to prompt greater governmental regulation of the economy, economists and law professors in sympathy with the New Deal fashioned a rationalization for action which previously had been thought unconstitutional. Simplified versions of the new ideology were passed along and ultimately became part of the vocabulary of both major American political parties. When economic conditions changed and New Deal regulation inconvenienced business, another generation of economists and law professors appeared ready to champion efficiency, free markets, and other symbols of a capitalist world view.

Adding Private Governments, Social Fields, and Networks to Social Theory None of these theoretical pictures adequately incorporates the roles played by private governments, social fields, and networks and their complex relationships with the formal legal system. In particular settings some writers recognize that theories must be expanded to cover individuals acting in groups (cf. Zimring 1981; Gottlieb 1983; Nader 1984). However, this has been the exception rather than the rule. I will consider a number of instances where the theories seem to assume a state or legal system on one side confronting an isolated individual on the other. I will note where social groups have been added to the analysis. Finally, I will suggest what might be added to these theories if a broader perspective were used consistently.

"Legal" Functions Are Played by Private Systems. At the outset, recall that the state and the legal systems often face competition from private governments which perform some or almost all of their functions. In talking about the effectiveness of law, I noted that corporations may be able to socialize employees to internalize norms different from those of the larger society, and they may be able to sanction noncompliance with corporate norms. If the public law calls for measures to protect the environment, but the cost of these measures threatens the economic health of the corporation, officials must cope with this conflicting set of signals. On the one hand, these officials can comply with the law but seek to influence elections so that new legislators, governors, and presidents will change the rules or enforcement practices. On the other hand, they can try to evade the command of the law, and often do so with great skill.

Other forms of competition with public government were noted earlier. Private governments such as corporations, churches, and labor unions can pursue their own foreign policies, in concert with or in opposition to official policy (see, for example, Kowalewski and Leitko 1983; Teulings 1982). Nations may form alliances with large multinational corporations or such corporations may seek to overthrow governments. Churches may battle nations about human rights, seeking to affect what is called world public opinion. Labor unions may boycott goods from certain nations. Private governments often take over what we think of as state functions. Corporations often provide their own police when the public police seem inadequate to serve their interests, and I have already noted how white-collar crime is often handled privately. Trade associations often make rules governing members, devise standard forms to facilitate making contracts, and arbitrate or mediate disputes.

In short, a social theory cannot assume that public government has a monopoly on those functions the theory assigns to "the legal system" (see Greenberg 1976). Of course, a theorist can escape this problem by expanding the term "legal system" to include whatever agency, public or private, performs what the theorist wishes to call legal functions. However, such a move glosses over whether it makes a difference if a particular function is performed publicly or privately. It seems likely that the more private and decentralized the structures for performing a social function with broad impact, the greater the problems of coordination and integration.

Channeling and Filtering Matters In and Out of the Legal System. Not all problems, disputes, claims, and the like existing in society come before legal officials, and many of those that do are not handled in ways that these theorists assume. Thus, functions assigned to the legal system by many of these theories become questionable. Here I will consider the consequences for these theories of two aspects of social fields and networks: the filtering and channeling done by gatekeepers to the legal system and the coping with recurrent legal problems that takes place on the margins of law.

There has been extensive study of dispute processing during the past decade. Relying on some of this work, Luhmann (1981) expands structural-functional theory to show that whether or how the legal system will play an integrative role is uncertain. He offers a theory of "thematization thresholds" as a barrier to transforming problems into legal questions. While law can stabilize people's expectations in interaction as these theories assume, for this to happen legal norms must be made into the theme of discussion between the parties—concrete situations must be "thematized" as legal questions: a buyer's dissatisfaction with the quality of a new car, for example, could be discussed with the dealer in terms of warranty and the remedy limitation in their form contract rather than in terms of other kinds of norms. However, in many situations there are good reasons to avoid invoking legal norms. By openly confronting another with the question of whether she is acting legally, one shatters the comfortable consensus that is normally assumed in a social relationship. Legal themes introduce the possibility of disagreement about interpretation of norms or the history of the situation and tend to force discussion into a dichotomy of right and wrong. Assertion of legal right is an attempt at coercion, and it may be a challenge to fight to defend one's honor. Interaction is moved from the domain of family life, a continuing economic relationship involving trust, and the like. In these domains what is given up now is likely to be rewarded by benefits that come later. It is difficult to threaten divorce and still keep a marriage alive; it is hard to contest issues in a divorce proceeding and continue to interact afterward.

Whether or not one will cross this thematization threshold is determined, Luhmann says, in large part by the prospects of social support in case conflict should arise. Turning to law usually means withdrawing from the relationship in question, and often one needs support to replace the benefits of the situation rejected. A legal discussion may initiate a chain of events with an unpredictable outcome, and the more uncertain the future, the more support is needed.

Fitzgerald, Hickman, and Dickins (1980) see members of relevant social fields and networks serving not only as supporters but also as audiences, reality-testers, and defusers when disputes arise. For example, the group at the bar separates likely combatants; networks of friends and relatives repair defective products so the buyer does not have to confront a seller and demand a remedy; the women watching over small children at a playground work out potential neighborhood disputes. People in social fields can suppress disputes by making fun of one who voices a complaint or by reacting in such a way as to communicate that an asserted claim of right shows weakness and a lack of self-reliance (see Engel 1984). Baumgartner (1985) suggests that middle-class people may be less willing to use the legal system than those lower on the social scale. The threat of disapproval by one's peers may serve a gatekeeping function. At times those in a social field can act as champions or mediators, offering ways to communicate with the other party in the dispute, suggesting solutions, or adding their own power to press for resolution (see Eisenstadt and Roniger 1980). Significant others, on the other hand, can pour gasoline on the fire and raise consciousness—one can be told to fight and how to do it. Such an audience, moreover, may make it difficult to back down and compromise or withdraw without a loss of face.

Who plays these roles? Members of social fields or networks centered in the workplace or neighborhood may be called on. Ethnic or religious communities may be invoked when members do not view themselves as autonomous. However, Ladinsky and Susmilch (1983) find that in consumer disputes people tend not to contact third parties but to act alone. It may be that people have a repertoire of disputing techniques in certain areas but not others (see Sharp 1980). It may be that Americans, at least, face a complex of norms about "not airing dirty linen in public" and "what will the neighbors think."

Rather than ignoring a problem, acting alone, or consulting acquaintances, some Americans go, or are sent, to lawyers. Social fields and networks may still play a part in dealing with the dispute. Usually, the client is buying access to the social field in which the lawyer acts. The lawyer has contacts and can get things done; the lawyer can act as mediator or go-between; the lawyer can suppress a dispute, encourage the client to fight, or attempt to work out a settlement (see Macaulay 1979).

Most social theories ignore the activities of lawyers and officials and deal with law in its most formal aspect. Law tends to be seen as adjudication or a supreme court giving meaning to guarantees of equal protection. Yet adjudication and the interpretation of norms are only part of a larger process involving negotiation, bargaining, and the assertion of power. Probably the key finding of nearly three decades of the social study of law is that a descriptive model of the legal process in the criminal area involves plea bargaining with trials and appeals operating at the margin as factors to consider during negotiations. On the civil side, insurance adjusters meet injured victims or their lawyers and work out settlements in which the chance of trials and appeals affects what is offered and accepted. This kind of patterned dispute processing frequently is carried on by private governments, social fields, and networks where there are identifiable roles, rules, and sanctions. In some bargaining arenas recurrent problems are dealt with by a relatively fixed cast of characters. For example, those who prosecute and defend criminal cases play defined roles but so do police officers, social workers, and others who are regularly involved. In these arenas the problems of individuals tend to be channeled into limited repertoires of solutions which have been developed by specialists who are influenced as much by their own goals and those of the institution as by the needs of disputants. In such arenas facts are not established beyond a reasonable doubt and rights are not vindicated. Rather, rights and facts are only factors in reaching a deal in which the interests and power of all participants will be reflected.

Even when we find adjudication in its more formal dress, we cannot assume that particular decisions solve the problems and define the rights once and for all (cf. Lindgren 1983). A particular appellate opinion may be but a battle in a larger war. For example, retail gasoline dealers battled the large oil companies for about forty years, seeking to enlarge and redefine their rights. The relationships were structured by lawyers for the large companies so that the dealers would have few, if any, rights. Individual dealers first sued, offering novel legal theories backed by atrocity stories to justify a change in the balance of power. Generally they lost. Eventually their trade associations mobilized and directed resources into a long battle. They also sought relief from administrative agencies. While they often failed to gain a change in the rules, they did gain the services of agency staffs as coercive mediators. Finally, the organized dealers turned to both state and federal legislatures. Here they won what appeared to be major victories. Under some of the statutes that were passed dealers could not be canceled except for cause; under others a requirement of good faith was imposed. However, the war was not over. The large oil companies went to court seeking interpretations of the statutes and challenging them on constitutional grounds.

During the whole course of this legal warfare, the oil companies used their economic power to shape relationships with their dealers. The chance that dealers might win rights from courts and legislatures may have affected the companies' actions, but neither this chance nor the rights ultimately won put dealers in control. The cases and statutes were battles in a war rather than authoritative interpretations of ambiguities in values. Social theories that neglect the impact of legal decisions on bargaining position or fail to see that bargaining power rests on far more than legal rights explain almost nothing.

These social theories tend to identify law's role with conflict. However, much of law in any social system is facilitative. Do we drive on the right-hand or the left-hand side of the street? Can people act in groups with limited liability? Is there a way to notify others about my claims to your property? Can my less tangible claims serve as security for loans? Can we drink the water and milk and eat the lettuce with reasonable assurance that we will not be ill tomorrow? Will there be roads and bridges, and will the snow be cleared from them so we can transport our products to market? Will the conditions exist for a workable system of insurance? Will there be schools, hospitals, libraries, and parks? Private governments, social fields, and networks all draw upon these facilitative resources provided by the public legal system, and often legal regulation provides a focus for the formation or continuation of a relatively private group. In short, social theories must deal with interactions between and interpenetrations of public and private units.

Legitimacy and Mystification as Mediated by Social Groups. Social fields and networks also qualify in other ways some of the social theories we have considered. For example, both structural-functional and Marxist-derived theories tend to assume that societies are held together, at least in part, by a consensus about values. Of course, in one theory the writer talks of legitimacy while in the other the consensus is the product of false consciousness. Law is supposed to serve social integration by *clarifying* values so that disputes will be avoided and expectations realized.

However, it is possible that *ambiguity* in the interpretation of generally accepted social norms and inconsistency in their application may in fact aid in holding societies together (Mills 1983). As Galanter (1979, p. 17) points out, modern society is "a world of loosely overlapping partial or fragmentary communities." Americans, at least, tend to be spatially and ideologically segregated. Certain ethnic and religious groups maintain a separate identity, more or less willingly. Those who live in upper-income suburbs see themselves as distinct from factory workers, who distinguish themselves from the poor who inhabit inner cities. People also form distinct but partial communities based on lifestyle. One way all of these communities can coexist in relative harmony is by the overestimation of consensus on values as well as by a fair amount of physical and cultural isolation.

Sometimes members of a society share allegiances to values at a high level of abstraction, but differ about interpretations. Sometimes our values may have contradictory implications so that people are free to draw their own conclusions without renouncing the value. For example, all Americans might agree that they favor equality, free speech, and constitutional government. However, members of one group may stress equality of opportunity while those belonging to another group advocate affirmative action to offset past discrimination. Some will tolerate freedom for the thought they hate while others distinguish free speech from treason or from pornography that incites violence against women. Some stress the rights of the accused while others remind us of the rights of victims and potential victims.

When matters can be left ambiguous, the members of each social field can support the general norm and be comforted by an interpretation favoring their interests or point of view. As the conflict theorists remind us, an authoritative interpretation through the process of adjudication and appeal may only provoke anger and division rather than integration. Sometimes some of the strain may be reduced by discretionary enforcement. In theory, an authoritative interpretation by a court of last resort settles matters. In practice, those who must enforce the law may hesitate to force groups whose members feel intensely about the matter to comply with a law that affronts them (see Macaulay and Macaulay 1978). Moreover, normative ambiguity allows regulators and the regulated to evade the authoritative interpretation and rationalize their action in terms of fundamental values. They do not have to see themselves as outlaws. Those advocating the official interpretation may be dismayed by what they see as hypocrisy, but those responsible may be unwilling to pay the price of coercing a sizable minority into compliance (cf. Hagen, Silva, and Simpson 1977).

Some writers have turned to social fields to explain deviance. If, following structural-functional theories, one sees social order as resting on internalized norms, perhaps reinforced by sanctions based in reciprocal relationships, how then can crime be explained? Many have found the explanation in deviant subcultures which promote norms counter to the official ones. For example, one can point to adolescent gangs in large cities where one proves courage and gains status by a willingness to engage in violent conduct and to risk arrest. For these people, law provides an official norm to violate, and the police and the rest of the criminal justice system provide the opportunity to display skill in evading, manipulating, or coping with the demands of authority.

There are a number of distinct subcultural theories. Some writers see younger people as surrounded by those who transmit conventional social norms and others who transmit procriminal norms. The ratio of these associations determines whether younger people learn one or the other pattern (Sutherland and Cressey 1978). Other writers stress social learning in interactions with those who can reinforce or punish and offer models of conventional or criminal behavior (see, for example, Burgess and Akers 1966; Akers 1977). Many theorists emphasize more material factors, such as accepting conventional goals of success and material rewards but rejecting conventional limitations on the means of attaining such ends. When people find their access to legitimate opportunities blocked by discrimination or class barriers, they are likely to discover illegitimate opportunities (see, for example, Cloward and Ohlin 1960; Cohen 1955). Instead of gaining a Cadillac by business success in conventional terms, one becomes, for example, a narcotics dealer.

Other scholars have objected to these explanations for deviance as oversimplified. On the one hand, while gangs of poor youths do exist, there is a political dimension to emphasizing deviant subcultures. These theories stress threats to the social order from the poor and invite segregation and various types of social control measures, ranging from crackdowns on gang activity to being drafted into the armed forces. The theories tend to overlook crime committed by members of the middle and upper classes who, presumably, are part of the dominant majority culture. Many of their crimes are committed secretly and not as a group activity—one seldom embezzles, for example, as a way to show off one's courage to other corporate officers or one's associates at the country club.

On the other hand, available empirical evidence does not support the existence of delinquent subcultures standing apart from the main body of society. Delinquents and criminals say they do not approve of their own illegal conduct, such subcultures as one can find do not contain a coherent set of inverse values, and delinquents tend to affirm much of conventional morality (Elliot and Voss 1974; Kornhauser 1978; Regoli and Poole 1978). Some suggest that it may be more profitable to abandon subcultural explanations and turn to theories stressing weakness of social control and increasing opportunity to commit crimes in modern society (see, for example, Cohen and Felson 1979).

Nonetheless, any complete theory of criminal behavior must note that social fields may facilitate if not cause some kinds of violations of the law (see Ekland-Olson 1982). Even if they do not constitute true rival cultures to mainstream society, those who use cocaine often are part of a social field which can help rationalize violating the law. One may be motivated to steal for any number of reasons which may or may not include exposure to a deviant subculture. However, if one who steals is part of a gang of those who also steal, he or she may be provided with a vocabulary with which to derogate the victim and justify the act. Moreover, those who use illegal drugs or crack safes also can pass along information on how to gain access to drugs or offset the latest countermeasures of safe manufacturers. Beginners may learn from professionals techniques of minimizing the chances of arrest, conviction, or a harsh sentence. Group communications may serve to magnify both the amount and success of criminal activity on the part of those who were insiders. In other words, the advantages of considering social fields when theorizing still exist even when the role played by groups fails to provide a complete explanation for behavior.

Many of the social theories we considered see law as playing a part in establishing legitimacy, symbolic satisfactions, or a false consciousness through mystification. These ideas are plausible and undoubtedly contain more than a little truth, but they are unclear about how the process of communication and persuasion is supposed to take place. There is reason to think that any messages broadcast by the legal system are mediated through social fields and networks which may transform and distort them. Moreover, any complete theory must deal with the countermessages which rivals of the state and the public legal system attempt to transmit with varying effect. It is useful to distinguish, and discuss separately, two versions of the impact of law on attitudes which seem to be implicit in these social theories: law and things legal are said to legitimate or mystify the nature of the legal system and liberal society in the eyes of *citizens in general*. Whatever the merits of that assertion, law and things legal may have an impact on the perceptions of *those who seek to enter the legal arena* and must play by its rules.

Many theorists have posited that legality serves to legitimate liberal societies, or some part of their processes, but they are unclear about how this occurs. The public is supposed to have faith because of the relative autonomy of legal officials, formal procedures, and the rule of law. For example, some drew the lesson from the Watergate scandal that "the system works," because the Supreme Court held that President Nixon was bound by the law and could not hide behind a vague "executive privilege."

There are several difficulties with these claims. Schools teach the conventional view of the legal system and mass media communicate a great deal about certain features of it, but people still know little about the legal process in operation and what they know is often distorted (Albrecht and Green 1977; Casey 1976; Cortese 1966; Hearst Corp. 1983; *Michigan Law Review* 1973; National Center for State Courts 1978; Williams and Hall 1972). Perhaps it is enough to sense in some vague and imprecise way that a good legal system is out there. Indeed, there is evidence that those who have the least contact with the American legal system are the most satisfied with it (National Center for State Courts 1978). Nonetheless, vague and distorted pictures of lawyers, judges, police, and administrators would not seem enough to foster a reliable faith or sense of legitimacy. We might suspect that dissonance between the normative claims of American law and an introduction to the realities of plea bargaining, personal injury settlement, and bureaucratic routine would disenchant those who had to confront reality.

Moreover, social fields and networks are not defenseless against messages sent by the legal system. The *Dred Scott* decision, overturning the Missouri Compromise and denying standing to former slaves who had fled to the North, did not change the view of abolitionists about the morality of slavery. The decisions of the Supreme Court of the past few decades dealing with desegregation, school prayers, abortion, and contraception have not legitimated the positions taken by the Court in the eyes of many citizens. Instead, in such instances law has provoked counterreactions and has served as the focus for rallying opposition. Fundamentalist religious leaders and conservative politicians have formed an uneasy alliance to decry the loss of morality symbolized by these decisions. A loose social network has arisen around these issues (Watts 1983). Such groups have targeted elected officials whom they saw as holding the wrong views on one or more of these issues and swung elections against them. Members of the Congress who respond to such views have sought to overturn or undercut many of these Supreme Court decisions with varying success, through withdrawing jurisdiction of the Supreme Court over school prayers, cutting off federal funds to states which provide abortions to welfare recipients, and influencing judicial and administrative appointments. Perhaps in the long run the Supreme Court decisions that prompted all this conflict will become the conventional wisdom of most citizens. However, at least in the short run, instead of enhancing legitimacy they have provoked some measure of conflict and disintegration.

If we recognize that few people in any society ever read legal opinions, legislative committee reports, or statutes in the full original text, we should be prompted to turn to another social field important in the process of promoting legitimacy or provoking outrage—the mass media. Messages about legal action are conveyed to the public by journalists, television reporters, script writers, and novelists. Perhaps some of these people are influenced by law professors and others who can claim expert standing to comment on legal action in light of conventional theories of law. These communicators, however, tend to be at least skeptical if not cynical about the normative claims of legal actors because they see too much of what goes on backstage. Their task, moreover, is to capture public attention and so they are attracted to what is provocative rather than the typical. Accounts of the legal system operating by the book which might reassure readers or viewers seldom are front-page news. On the other hand, for many reasons, news tends to be muckraking rather than revolutionary; bad people rather than the system tend to be blamed.

The chains through which messages about the legal system pass undoubtedly are complex, distorting, and not well understood. Moreover, while it is fairly easy to study what is sent out by the mass media, films, or novels, it is much harder to learn just what different kinds of people receive from such messages. Individuals may reinterpret a report of a distinguished law professor's views about a Supreme Court decision to suit their own world view, and perhaps this is more likely to happen when they are part of a social network with a stake in another view. Some honor civil libertarians but others call them friends of criminals and enemies of the nation. Supreme Court opinions may be seen as upholding basic values or as idealistic but unrealistic. The rule that a defendant is presumed innocent until proved guilty, for example, is seen by members of many groups as an unwarranted attack on the competence of the police.

Perhaps, over time, subtle messages which are repeated on news broadcasts and entertainment programs affect attitudes despite the conservative efforts of fundamentalist churches, organized interest groups, or the regulars at the tavern. However, we must remember the great skill members of many groups possess to reinterpret or reject ideas that offend them. In short, it is clear that if a social theory tells us that law affects attitudes and no more, the theory is, at best, incomplete. To be meaningful, the theory also must describe in a plausible fashion the process by which those whose attitudes are reinforced or changed learn about legal action and what they make of what they learn.

Similar objections can be raised to Marxist-derived theories of law that talk of false consciousness and mystification. Hunt's statement (1976) is typical:

> Legal norms . . . have the role of moulding and inducing acceptance of the power differentials that are encapsulated within them. . . . The concept of citizenship, formal equality of participation in the public affairs of society, is transposed in the field of law through the "rule of law" and associated concepts. Thus the assertion of the legitimacy of law is a celebration of social unity facilitated by the formal universalism of its symbolic content. [pp. 40–41]

The criteria for judging such assertions are a matter of dispute. On the one hand, some Marxist theorists would deny that their writing can be judged by non-Marxist social science. If correct theory tells a scholar that bourgeois law mystifies and helps produce false consciousness, all that is necessary is to find examples. "Data are important in terms of how well they describe the 'actualization of the objective role' played by events and concepts, and they are irrelevant otherwise" (Marenin 1981, p. 10). On the other hand, analyses such as that by Balbus (1977) in the *Law & Society Review,* apparently rest on observation of capitalist legal systems. Therefore, it seems appropriate to ask how much such theories would be altered if the roles played by social fields and networks were considered. As will be seen, such a move both challenges and supports parts of Marxist-derived analyses.

Balbus says that citizenship is a "substitute gratification which compensates for the misery of reality," and the "absence of communal relationships within . . . everyday existence" (p. 580). Without a good deal of qualification, it seems implausible that abstract citizenship is a substitute for community in the minds of many people in capitalist society. Citizenship has meaning only through those partial communities that exist in such nations. One usually votes as part of an undifferentiated mass, and, except in the rare case of an extremely close election, it would not matter if one stayed home and neglected to participate. However, one discusses politics with the regulars at the tavern, the lunch group at the office, neighbors, and the like, and it is here in these partial communities that one's views, vote, and being a citizen gain meaning. At least in the past, some have felt obligations of citizenship called for volunteering to join the armed forces. During World Wars I and II, this won approval from one's social network. One's family members shared in the display of citizenship by putting a banner with a blue star in the window of their home, an act designed to gain approval from an audience of those whose opinions mattered. Finally, we can point out that those for whom reality is the most miserable are least likely to vote and most likely to view political activity with cynicism.

Theorists of the left often see capitalist society as characterized by what they see as a lack of "genuine" community. However, people acting in social fields and networks often feel some sense of community, and, at times, the legal system provides a focus for that sense. For example, a study of older black and white women who had incomes below the government's definition of poverty found that

> Black women made greater use of alternative medical systems, had larger networks of family and friends, participated at greater rates in institutional support systems, and rated themselves higher with respect to health and happiness than did White women. These differences were attributed to the closely cooperative life styles of Black women. These patterns of mutual support were thought to be a highly sophisticated cultural adaptation to historic and economic circumstances. [Curran 1978, p. 39]

The legal system was a focus for cooperative activity within these networks of black women; they had to help each other cope with systems providing government benefits, and, particularly because of their membership in churches, they were organized to do so. We can debate whether this was a *genuine* community, but it is clear that while one should not romanticize their situation, picturing these women as alienated and isolated would be a distortion of their strength. Moreover, it seems unlikely that the lack of a cooperative lifestyle of the older white women studied by Curran is a result of their status as abstract citizens with rights, or their false consciousness about the nature of society and its legal system. At the least, to be convincing Marxist-derived theories must trace the linkages between an ideological picture of legal persons developed by theorists and such matters as the apparent alienation of these older white women.

Another theme related to law as mystification concerns the impact of capitalist ideology on family relationships. The "bourgeois family of liberal capitalism," it has been said, "was privatized and offered a refuge, an emotional haven, from the cold harshness and impersonal competition of the outside reality" (Hearn 1980, p. 131), However, the family in postcapitalist society is losing "its capacity to provide its members with a private space" and is turning into an association which focuses "more on output than on warmth and shared concern." Perhaps theorists such as Balbus have this in mind when they tell us that "the 'community' produced by the legal form contributes *decisively* to the reproduction of the very capitalist mode of production which makes genuine community impossible" (p. 580).

Whatever the problems of the modern family, it is unclear how legal ideology affects the sense of community in family-living arrangements. Furthermore, other social networks—the fellows at the club or tavern, the members of the bowling league, or the women who gather regularly to talk and drink coffee—also may offer some refuge from "the cold harshness and impersonal competition of the outside reality" (see Bissonette 1977; Genovese 1980; Schoenberg 1980). Such social fields and networks often carry some norms of altruism and community, whatever their success in implementing them.

There is little evidence, nor even much of a plausible theory, connecting the attitudes and values of the worker standing with his friends at the bar in a tavern with the logic of the legal system at the doctrinal level. Indeed, there is evidence that people think it wrong to invoke the law within one's social fields. One keeps one's word, for example, rather than finding loopholes in the language of contracts with family and friends (see Engel 1984). Moreover, any theory of mystification by legal concepts must take into account many workers' sophistication and cynical knowledge about power and privilege in their society (see Stack 1978).

People in social fields regularly help each other cope with legal norms. They help each other comply. However, they may legitimate evasions of the law and teach each other how to evade successfully, often redefining legal norms to their own advantage. Port workers, for example, accept the idea that one should not steal, but they do not see taking damaged cargo as stealing (Hoekema 1975). Networks of employees often take, as of right, reasonable amounts of supplies from their employer, viewing this as just part of their compensation. Breaking what are deemed as foolish laws can become a game: even as loosely structured a group as Japanese commuters share their schemes to cheat the national railways by riding without paying the full fare (Noguchi 1979). In short, "[s]ocial relations in capitalism often deceive in appearance, but their observers are not always deceived because 'they have minds of their own,' minds which sometimes accurately reflect contradictory class interests" (Sumner 1979, p. 265).

Another problem with assertions about the legal system's contributions to legitimacy or mystification is that legality may more effectively shape attitudes and conduct of members of some groups than among others. It has been argued that "it is typically the case that subordinate classes do *not* believe (share, accept) the dominant ideology which has far more significance for the integration and control of the dominant class itself." This is true because "the apparatuses of transmission of belief are not very efficient in reaching the subordinate classes" (Abercrombie and Turner 1978, pp. 153, 159). Similarly, Ray (1978, p. 155) asserts that "it is not entirely clear that the market and the economic subsystem perform legitimation functions for the *whole* of liberal capitalist society, rather, this is restricted to the bourgeois class, which must convince *itself* that it no longer rules—hence its development of universal ethics and natural law."

Some support for this idea can be found in a study of the Massachusetts Commission Against Discrimination, which found that compromises and settlements involving small amounts of money were much more common than vindications of rights. Working-class complainants tended to be satisfied with what they received because they did not expect to gain much from a legal agency. In contrast, middle-class complainants, who had the highest percentage of favorable outcomes, tended to be the least satisfied because they thought they had rights and expected the system to vindicate them. "For many, a major cost of filing is the discovery that the legal system does not operate the way it is supposed to" (Crowe 1978, p. 234; cf. Baumgartner 1985). This was not news to the poor and working-class complainants; their social networks and experiences carry that message loudly and clearly.

Of course, it is not clear that even all of the most privileged groups in society believe in the rule of law, the autonomy of the legal system, and the like. Those who seek to capture regulatory agencies, influence the course of legislation, and affect appointments to judicial and administrative posts by making campaign contributions, bribes, and similar exercises of influence seem unlikely to be innocent believers in official rhetoric. Perhaps the few at the top and the many at the bottom, then, share cynical knowledge about how things are done.

Having said all this, it is still possible that legal forms do contribute something to legitimacy or mystification. People often act as if they did believe in the power of law. Legal symbols and rhetoric are appropriated selectively by those in social fields on many occasions to rationalize action. Members of these social fields may also attempt to introduce legal ideas as a limitation on the power of those who dominate the field. For example, private police look like the public police—they wear uniforms with badges, carry guns, and use what we think of as police equipment. Given the multiple and overlapping police forces in the United States, it is easy to confuse private with public officers. Private arbitration panels often meet in courtrooms or other public places which have the architecture of authority, and at least some of their discourse uses the language of legal rights. Employees of private universities and business corporations have increasingly claimed that administration and management must give reasons for decisions, and in American culture such justifications tend to have legal or constitutional overtones. Those who want to curb the power of those in charge often speak of due process and free speech; those who hold power often talk of property and contract rights. Private groups often select leaders and take positions by holding elections. One does not have to sit through too many meetings of governing boards of private organizations to gain a healthy respect for the mystificatory power of Robert's Rules of Order in the hands of a master at the game.

Law also can be a cultural resource, selectively drawn upon to aid in the operation of social fields. Santos (1977) studied a squatter settlement in Rio de Janeiro which he called Pasargada. Under Brazilian law, the entire settlement was illegal because it was built without authorization on land belonging to the government. Yet, the settlers of Pasargada held what they saw as property interests in their houses. They established a private government—the Residents' Association—to deal with disputes and to create a structure under which their homes could be leased, bought, and sold. The Residents' Association borrowed and adapted Brazilian legal concepts and procedures to carry out these transactions. Much of the procedure carried out the evidentiary, channeling, and cautionary functions of legal formality (see Fuller 1941). To effect a transfer, the parties came before the *Presidente* of the Residents' Association. He questioned them to determine whether they understood the transaction, much as a notary does in many civil-law systems. A typed contract or lease was produced which was a powerful formality in a community where typewritten documents are not an everyday matter and literacy cannot be assumed. The signed or marked leases and conveyances were filed at the office of the Residents' Association, and filing itself was an important ceremony, giving the transaction legitimacy much as the recording of a legal document might in public legal systems.

Such legal ritual probably lessened conflict by offering symbols of the transfer of property and increasing the awareness of the parties about the nature of their transaction. It also probably served to assert the authority of the Residents' Association and to clothe it with some legitimacy. Squatter law must be appropriate since it is "just like" the law used by the rich in those parts of Brazil where the streets are paved (which the residents of Pasargada called "the law of the asphalt"). It also was hoped that the legal concepts and procedures used would help defend the autonomy of the settlement against the Brazilian government. Transfers purported to deal only with interests in the houses and made no claim to the land on which they stood. The Residents' Association mediated disputes between residents. Santos observes that "[b]y providing Pasargadians with peaceful means of dispute prevention and settlement Pasargada law neutralizes potential violence, enhances the possibility of orderly life, and thus instills a respect for law and order that may carry out when Pasargadians go into town and interact with official society" (p. 90). This, too, may have protected the settlement. There was always a risk that public authority would send in bulldozers and destroy the settlement, but there was hope that the more self-contained and trouble-free the settlement, the less likely it would be to attract the unwanted attention of governmental authorities.

Santos shows that the legitimating or mystifying power of legal form and rhetoric is a weapon which can be appropriated by both the dominant and the dominated under certain conditions. Of course, groups with wealth can make better use of this weapon and use it in more situations. Moreover, the success of the Residents' Association in Pasargada probably turned on many factors in addition to its adaptation of the forms and vocabulary of Brazilian law. If the land on which the settlement was built was needed for a project which the Brazilian government saw as critically important for the development of the country, we can wonder whether legality would stop the bulldozers.

Whatever the impact of the ideological structure of liberal legal systems on general public opinion, those who use these systems for their own purposes, or who find that they must cope with them, face the necessity of transforming their position into the language of tort, contract, property, due process, free speech, or the like. To what extent, if at all, do such transformations mystify those who want to or must use the legal system?

Groups seeking some degree of social change, or the alteration of the balance of power within a social field or network, seldom are thwarted in seeking favorable readings of basic norms because of the law's emphasis on formal equality, individual rights, and fair procedures. Many of the theorists appear to know little of the reality of modern legal doctrine. Often they credit it with far too much coherence. There are counterprinciples that call for protection of people because of the disadvantaged position of their group. Even where the legal process requires claims to be stated in terms of legal rights, groups can be mobilized around what, in form, is stated as an individual claim. On its face, *Brown* v. *Board of Education* (the school desegregation case) appeared to be a dispute between Linda Brown and the school system in Topeka, Kansas. It is safe to say that few were misled and failed to see that any decision would speak broadly to the position of blacks in American society.

However, Trubek (1980–81) points out that the law itself is one of the filters that determine what disputes will emerge and what forms conflicts will take. He suggests that the entire behavioral system relating to processing particular types of disputes—including the relevant legal doctrine—"not only transforms the various individual conflicts: in so doing it 'transforms,' so to speak, a raw conflict of interest into a social process with limited possibilities. The disputes that do emerge are those in which basic economic relationships are not challenged: all other possibilities are filtered out" (p. 743). For example, I have mentioned the long-term struggle between retail gasoline dealers and the major oil companies about the nature of their relationship. The arguments of the dealers' lawyers were framed in terms consistent with one strain of classical notions of property and contract. One could imagine claims for much broader protections for the dealers which their lawyers would have been foolish to assert in an American court—for example, the dealers might benefit if a court were to appoint a receiver to supervise the relationships between, say, Mobil Oil and all its dealers; few lawyers would ask for anything so broad for fear of prejudicing their chance of getting anything at all.

One might view this kind of transformation and judgment about what kinds of claims are likely to sell before American judges as mystification. On the other hand, it is possible that no one involved in the gasoline dealers' battles was fooled in the slightest. Everyone may have accurately appraised the amount of power dealers could bring to bear and decided that a slight extension of contract and property ideas was the most that could be hoped for at the moment in question. Either way, Trubek's point holds—American judges and legislators are unlikely to redistribute wealth and power other than incrementally. Few with any experience in the system would expect them to. Indeed, many who have never considered the matter, if asked, might prefer a legal system whose output was incremental to revolutionary change. Those who are, or would be, suspicious of revolutionary change might be wrong, but they are not necessarily mystified.

If we focus on legislation rather than adjudication, we can find an area in which some mystification may take place as Marxist-derived theories suggest. The rhetoric heard in the legislative process is similar to that heard before the courts, but it is not the same. Those claiming to represent farmers, organized labor, small businesses, consumers, the unemployed, and the like typically try to relate the claims of their groups to the interests of the nation as a whole. They claim the need for regulation to alter the balance of power in certain relationships in the society. The lawmaking process usually involves a degree of pluralistic bargaining among certain interests. Seldom will claims be made in the name of the working class in a Marxist sense; seldom will legislation be passed which purports to redistribute wealth more than marginally. More often groups win legislation creating rights for individuals who, for example, have been the victims of discrimination or bad faith.

However, such legislative victories may be more symbolic than real. If rights are to be more than words in a statute book, lawyers usually are needed to represent those who think they have been wronged. Sometimes statutes give complainants a reasonable chance of winning a considerable amount of money, but more often these new rights can be protected only by injunctions that courts hesitate to grant, the damages that can be proved are likely to be low, and establishing a cause of action requires difficult and costly legal research and expert testimony.

It is difficult to mobilize groups to raise funds necessary to bring successful cases to vindicate individual rights. After the statute is passed, sympathetic groups may turn their attention elsewhere or just fade away, believing that the war is won. Private lawyers may donate services, but the supply of those able and willing to do this is low. Given these problems, a reform law may at best create a weak bargaining entitlement, setting the stage for negotiation rather than vindication. It would be fair to say that members of groups that win the passage of statutes creating individual rights without providing an adequate means of vindication have been mystified into thinking they had won a war when they had only won an initial battle. Of course, the failure of a particular statute to affect behavior can be the focus for another legislative battle, but fashions in reform change and it may be difficult to argue for the creation of an administrative agency when deregulation is the cause of the moment or for government-paid legal services when those programs displease powerful interests.

When we consider various social theories and their accounts of the roles played by the legal system, and then add private governments, social fields, and networks, we see that whether law plays the parts assigned is unproved. Many social theorists seem to have accepted the view of the centrality of law championed by legal scholars, but an expanded perspective shows that in many, or most, instances law and the legal system may be irrelevant or appear briefly in a walk-on part. While, on occasion, law may be in the spotlight center stage, the task is to account for when law and legal actors play major parts and when these roles are played by others.

Of course, it is possible—but difficult to establish—that legal norms and legal practices play an important background role so that social interaction would be very different if they were not present. People act on the basis of many tacit assumptions about the present and future and things legal may be one of the factors providing the reassurance necessary for social interaction. We assume, in most instances, that we are safe walking the streets during the day, that criminals will be arrested, and that contracts will be performed. When we lose this faith, as in time of civil war or a repressive takeover by a military government, our behavior changes. It would be difficult to show the part played by law in our tacit assumptions as compared with customs, experiences, and the like. Yet it seems plausible that it is there. Moreover, legal norms and procedures are a potential resource which always might be mobilized by one group or another, and the chance that this could happen may affect official behavior, perhaps in subtle ways. Police, mayors, governors, regulatory agency personnel, and legislators know that if they affront the beliefs and interests of groups of people, they might mobilize and retaliate by voting the rascals out or by bringing a suit in the courts.

If law fails to play the roles it is assigned in various social theories, there may be costs unless its parts are well played by other associations and groups. Luhmann (1981) sees the filtering done by social fields and networks as potentially harmful.

> As a conflict-regulating system that is always belatedly set in motion, i.e. only when called upon, the legal system very seldom takes the initiative. . . . Excessive inhibition of the thematization of law may, therefore, lead to a kind of drying up of the legal system, and so leave the regulation of conflict to other mechanisms—e.g. morality, ignorance, class structure, or the use of force outside the law—whose social structural compatibility may be problematic, [p. 247]

Luhmann, thus, seems to believe that there is a function best performed by the public legal system. If disputes, claims, and the like are the basis for the perception of problems by legal institutions, the filtering and channeling done by social fields and networks are likely to offer a distorted view to lawmakers. Cases before agencies and the courts and bills being lobbied before legislatures are a biased sample of problems in the society (cf. Galanter 1983, p. 70).

If we were to look closely at the roles played by private governments, social fields, and networks, we might see an important problem of legitimacy, undeveloped in the theories we have considered. Hurst (1960, pp. 518–19) tells us that throughout American legal history, "we sought to make all secular power responsible to power outside itself, for ends which it alone did not define." Unger (1976) sees the recognition of the power of private associations as bringing into question the legitimacy of the liberal state. He asserts that

> the increasing recognition of the power these organizations exercise, in a quasi-public manner, over the lives of their members makes it even harder to maintain the distinction between state action and private conduct. Finally, the social law of institutions is a law compounded of state-authored rules and of privately sponsored regulations or practices; its two elements are less and less capable of being separated. All these movements, which tend to destroy the public character of law, carry forward a process that begins in the failure of liberal society to keep its promise of concentrating all significant power in government. [pp. 201–2]

The parts played in society by private governments, social fields, and networks are far more diverse and complex than the roles envisioned in the social theories discussed. Individuals are subject to a web of norms and sanctions, only some of which are imposed by the state. If, in Hurst's words, "secular power [is not] responsible to power outside itself, for ends which it alone did not define," we can expect those subject to the jurisdiction of such private governments and more structured social fields to challenge their autonomy. Moreover, some response from public government may be needed to preserve its own legitimacy. I will now turn to such questions.

The Autonomy and Accountability of Private Associations

In the United States, relationships between government and various kinds of associations are complex and uncertain. While much of our earlier disquiet about regulation has been overcome, private associations ranging from the family to multinational corporations still have large claims to autonomy. Advocates of greater accountability tend to find the threat to individual liberty, efficiency, or other values coming from powerful private associations as well as the state. Tocqueville (1835) saw equality in the new democracies leading to control by the bureaucratic state. However, he thought that voluntary associations would serve to restrain the power of the state and, indeed, the power of other associations. Durkheim (1958), on the other hand, saw individual liberty as threatened both by private associations and by the state. Liberty required the balancing of both the power of secondary groups which surround the individual on all sides and that of the nation-state so that "collective particularism" is held in check. "And it is out of this conflict of social forces that individual liberties are born" (p. 63).

There is a sprawling normative and descriptive literature about regulation (see Tomasic 1984). It deals with such things as its justification in terms of market failure, capture of regulatory agencies by those supposedly regulated, the new regulation gained by the reforms in the 1960s and 1970s, and the deregulation movement of the 1970s and 1980s. In order to make the discussion in this section more manageable, I will narrow my focus to attempts by individuals or groups *within* a private association to gain action by the legal system to affect the balance of power inside the group. I will take as an example the claims of employees and those who hold franchises against employers and franchisors. The area is important and provides good examples, and much of what is said would apply also to factional struggles in churches, political parties, athletic organizations, and similar associations.

Much of this discussion also will be relevant to the adequacy of structural-functionalist conflict, and Marxist-derived theories considered in the last section. However, in addition I have had an opportunity to consider neo-evolutionary theory in the sociology of law. Teubner (1983, 1984a, 1984b), in a synthesis of several theoretical works, sees legal systems in Western societies moving from what Weber called a formally rational style to a substantively rational one with the rise of the welfare state. However, recent crises may prompt what Teubner calls "reflexive rationality," as the public legal system more and more seeks to gain substantive goals by working through private associations. However, when we look at concrete examples of the process about which Teubner writes, we will see that reflexive rationality may produce consequences that some would challenge. First, I will sketch the claims for autonomy and for accountability of private associations and will consider their applications to the employment relationship. Second, I will consider Teubner's synthesis of a number of major evolutionary theories and his description of reflexive rationality. Finally, I will consider challenges to the corporatism implicit in reflexive rationality.

Accountability and Autonomy in the Employment Relationship. When we look at the legal response to claims by members of groups against those in control, usually we find plausible theories calling for accountability being matched against norms justifying autonomy from outside authority. This may reflect, to a large degree, the decay of older views which drew a sharp line between public and private spheres of life. Public action was seen as constrained by the rule of law, private interaction within groups was simply a matter of free contract and choice. By the 1980s, if not long before, the purity of such distinctions had been lost. To use Unger's words (1976, p. 193), in postliberal society there is only a "general approximation of state and society, of public and private sphere."

The original theory, which still has a good deal of rhetorical power, saw public governments as holding a monopoly on the legitimate use of force. However, this power to constrain liberty had to be limited. Public officials thus acted only under the rule of law. Citizens were protected from governmental action by a Bill of Rights. Government control rested on elections, and power was constrained by checks and balances, federalism, or both. Private activity, including a right of association, was left free of restraint, subject only to the boundaries set by the law of property, contract, tort, crimes and similar legal categories. Counterbalancing associations offset the power of any particular group. One dissatisfied with a particular club, church, or business organization could go elsewhere, and this threat of exit and competition supplied all the regulation needed. Indeed, an important part of American history involves accounts of groups breaking away from religious organizations and forming new sects to pursue the true faith. This threat of exit constrains leaders to temper their actions.

Of course, the limitations of the rule of law, separation of powers, and federalism on public government and the freedom from state regulation enjoyed by private associations probably always have been less effective than claimed. Government officials probably have acted first and hoped to rationalize what was done later; discretion has long been a major part of our legal system. Private associations have always had to cope with some regulatory elements inherent in contract, property, tort, and criminal law. Nonetheless, one who would rationalize discretion of public officials or regulation of private associations has had the burden of persuasion.

Economic crises and social struggles have prompted the growth of the modern welfare state, which increasingly has attempted to regulate private associations. Instead of a sharp line between public and private purposes, governments promise to take whatever measures are needed to promote the success of the economy, to guarantee equality, and to deal with foreign threats of one kind or another. Instead of applying formal rules through classic procedures, modern governments increasingly rely on those who claim expert status and exercise discretion in the pursuit of these substantive goals. Also, instead of regulating conduct, government officials often bargain with various interests. Government may attempt to affect social conditions by trying to influence the action of the private sector in many ways, ranging from controlling the supply of money to setting terms for government contracting. At the same time, private associations have grown in power and significance and assume what are seen as public functions (see Nachmias and Greer 1982). Business corporations may wield critical influence over the future of employees, customers, suppliers, and the communities or regions in which they operate. Those dependent on them cannot exit easily. If a stable or expanding economy is seen as a public function, the operations of these large business organizations seem to many to be more than mere private action. Moreover, many corporations develop and supply transportation, communication, and weaponry viewed as essential to the national interest. When bad judgments, accidents, or world economic conditions threaten large organizations engaged in such important functions, it has been seen as a matter for public concern and government action.

Kennedy (1982) sees six stages in the decline of the public/private distinction. First, there are hard cases with large stakes—we manipulate the distinction and analyze it. Second, intermediate terms develop—we recognize that some situations are neither one thing nor another but share the characteristics of each. Third, the distinction collapses—we realize that however one tries to apply it, one ends up in a situation of hopeless contradiction. Property and contract, for example, can be viewed as examples of delegated state power since they are supported by cops and courts. Fourth, rather than abolish the distinction, we see matters along a continuum from polar cases of public and private action. Institutions in the middle seem to need rules which are a mixture of those appropriate to public and private modes. One balances factors that cut one way or another. Fifth, we see that questions about where an instance fits on the continuum involve manipulation of balanced pro/con policy arguments that come in matched pairs. Finally, at times the ends of the continuum may seem closer together than either end does to the middle. Kennedy calls this "loopification." Parents act more like judges, legislators, and police than officials of very large corporations; yet the family and legal officials would seem to be at opposite poles of the public/private continuum. When this stage is reached, it is hard to take seriously the distinction between what is public and what is private as a justification for treating one situation differently from another.

We can see something of the process Kennedy describes in the attacks on the claim of what, traditionally, were seen as private associations to autonomy from regulation. While some earlier works questioned this autonomy (see, for example, Hale 1920), attention was focused on the issue by Berle and Means (1932), who argued that there had been a separation of ownership from control of the large publicly held business corporation. The majority of shareholders lacked information and ability to mobilize their voting rights in all but extreme situations. Corporate executives, thus, were free to govern in the light of their own interests, subject only to whatever discipline might be found in the various markets in which the corporation dealt. Since corporate democracy was but an empty form and competitive pressures but an uncertain check, public regulation and control were justified.

Then during the early 1950s, a number of writers saw large business corporations as "private governments," exercising powers similar to those of states unchecked by the market, the rule of law, or the Bill of Rights (see, for example, Friedmann 1957; Hanslowe 1961; Schwartz 1960; Wirtz 1952). Eells (1962, p. 278) observed that "private government is no imaginary construct of academic minds, but is now widely accepted wherever men come to grips with the facts of political life. The corporation of the future is certain to be assessed not only as an element in the economy but also as a contributor—or as a deterrent—to freedom and order." Berle (1952, p. 942) found an emerging principle holding that the "corporation, itself a creation of the state, is as subject to constitutional limitations which limit action as is the state itself."

While separation of ownership from control and private government theories can be challenged on a number of grounds, both became part of the American political and legal culture. (For a modern version of the argument, see Ewing 1977.) One finds traces of each one in many battles before courts and legislatures about the autonomy or accountability of private associations. As Hanslowe (1961, p. 104) notes, during the 1940s and 1950s, "in labor relations, at least, quasi-governmental powers . . . [were] . . . being circumscribed by . . . quasi-constitutional restraints." These kinds of arguments seem to fall somewhere in the middle of Kennedy's six stages. Private government, for example, is an analogy. General motors is both like and unlike the state of Wisconsin. As a result, a matched set of predictable arguments fall into place—one calls for GM employees to be protected by guarantees of due process and free speech while the other argument stresses that, unlike a true government, GM's powers over its employees do not extend to the right to imprison or keep them from seeking work elsewhere. Logically, starting from the public/private premise as it has developed, the case is a tie.

By the 1930s, it was difficult to predict when private associations would be seen as autonomous and which form of regulation, if any, would be imposed. Chafee (1930, p. 1021) said that judicial competence to settle disputes within associations rests on a balance of four normative factors which "may be called, for the sake of vividness, the Strangle-hold Policy, the Dismal Swamp Policy, the Hot Potato Policy and the Living Tree Policy. The first favors relief; the last three oppose relief." The strangle-hold policy involves a judgment about the seriousness of the consequences of expulsion or other injury done to a member: "some associations have a strangle-hold upon their members through their control of an occupation or of property which can be ill spared." The dismal swamp policy reflects the difficulty a court would face in learning enough to decide the case. For example, judicial review of "the highest tribunal of the church is really an appeal from a learned body to an unlearned body." Attempts at judicial control of the internal affairs of a powerful association which commands the devoted adherence of its members might cause great resentment and have small chance of success. Courts will hesitate to pick up such a hot potato. Finally, the value of autonomy itself may induce courts to leave associations alone. Chafee argues that

> [t]he health of society will usually be promoted if the groups within it which serve the industrial, mental and spiritual needs of citizens are genuinely alive. Like individuals, they will usually do most for the community if they are free to determine their own lives for the present and the future. A due regard for the corresponding interests of others is desirable, but must be somewhat enforced by public opinion. Legal supervision must often be withheld for fear that it may do more harm than good . . . [for example, freedom] is desirable for schools and colleges. . . . The courts, like the legislatures, can hardly profess to be better qualified to decide how teaching shall be carried on than are the teachers and their administrative associates. [pp. 1027, 1028–29]

Views about this living tree policy may have changed somewhat since Chafee wrote, but the policy still commands respect.

About thirty years later, the editors of the *Harvard Law Review* (1963) recast Chafee's policy considerations as (1) interest in group autonomy, (2) practical limitations on judicial inquiry, (3) harm caused the individual and society by autonomy, (4) alternative methods of control, (5) extent of monopoly power, and (6) determination of whether a governmental grant of rights or powers imposes, by implication, corresponding duties. Of course, whatever its other functions jurisprudential writing that talks of weighing and balancing such factors is only generally descriptive or predictive. There is no scale on which to place these factors one by one and no dial on which to read their weights in grams or pounds. In most cases contrasting but equally plausible cases for autonomy and for accountability could be made. Indeed, after 117 pages of analysis, the *Harvard Law Review* tells us that judicial control of the conduct of private associations is "an area where few legal principles seem to have emerged" (p. 1100). We face all the problems of Kennedy's fourth stage—what he calls "continuumization." (See also, Ellman 1981; Fuller 1969; *Harvard haw Review* 1962; *Yale Law Journal* 1963.)

Klare (1981, p. 465) observed that liberal theory faces a difficult problem in rationalizing regulation of a supposedly private economy. "The core of the problem is to find a justification for public regulation which does not in logic lead to the notion that *all* economic decisions of societal consequence (e.g., all investment decisions by the 'top 500' corporations) should be subject to public control." As we shall see, legal decision-makers often are concerned about this slippery slope.

We can see many of the difficulties with the distinction between public and private by examining the legal treatment of the employment relationship and its close relative, the franchise. These relationships are social fields and sometimes structured private governments. Throughout the twentieth century, employees have sought to alter the balance of power between them and their employers, and they have enjoyed some success. In this section I will first paint, with very broad strokes, a rough history of the legal response to the claims for intervention in employment relationships in the United States in this century. Second, I will look at some of the factors affecting the actual balance of power in that relationship, including all of the legal activity. The discussion suggests an important question yet to be addressed adequately in the social study of law: why and when do people turn to the formal public legal system rather than some form of private government? I will also set the stage for considering evolutionary theories concerning the parts played by legal systems as the role of the state has changed in capitalist societies.

The starting point for considering legal reaction to the employment relationship in this century is the classic position that the matter is simply one of free contract. Regulation is not needed because if a job is, for example, more dangerous, employees will be paid more to take the risks. In theory, those employees who held contracts for specific terms held rights and were subject to duties determined by voluntary agreement. However, courts almost never would grant specific performance of an employment contract and force people into a distasteful close personal relationship. In most instances, an aggrieved party was left to seek damages. If an employer breached the contract, an employee usually would have to be paid the balance of the salary that would have been earned less any income the employee received from a substitute job taken after being fired. If an employee breached by leaving the job, the employer's damages usually were worth so little that a suit would not be brought. As might be expected, if an employee left taking trade secrets or valuable skills to use in direct competition with the employer, courts might enjoin this attack on property.

However, at the turn of the century as today, most employees did not hold contracts for fixed terms but worked under an employment-at-will. In theory, equality is preserved. The employer is free to discharge the employee, and the employee is free to leave for good, bad, or no reason. However, in times of labor surplus, the employee is at a disadvantage. For example, in *Comerford v. International Harvester* (1938), the Supreme Court of Alabama held that a worker who had alleged that he was fired after his wife refused the sexual advances of his boss had failed to state a cause of action. It explained that the employer "could have well decided that it would be in the interest of good management not to have both plaintiff and the guilty assistant sales manager working together under the circumstances. It could have concluded that the services of the sales manager were preferable and retained him without in the least ratifying or condoning his conduct toward the plaintiff." In short, employees-at-will must please the boss or look for work elsewhere.

In the early decades of the century, reformers sought to gain statutes regulating certain aspects of the employment relationship. Legislation was passed in a number of states attempting to govern wages, hours, and working conditions. Of course, this led to the great constitutional battles concerning liberty of contract and substantive due process. Not until the 1930s was it clear that such legislation was constitutional.

The legal response to labor unions and strikes was hostile. Such activity could be attacked as tortious or as criminal conspiracy. Police and sheriffs used force to remove strikers from their employer's property, and union organizers were attacked by law enforcement officers with both legal and illegal means. Moreover, courts would enjoin union activity and strikes and enforce promises by employees not to join unions—"yellow dog contracts."

As part of the reforms of the New Deal, the American legal system took a very different stance. Collective bargaining was symbolically legitimated in terms of union democracy, a collective contract, and private adjudication through arbitration. The government supported and attempted to influence a private legal system. Employees in a bargaining unit could vote to determine whether they wanted to be represented by a union, and, if so, by which one. Once a union was certified by the National Labor Relations Board as the bargaining representative, the employer had a duty to bargain in good faith. The result of this process would be a contract governing wages and conditions of employment for a fixed term, which had to be ratified by the individual workers. The contract typically is interpreted and applied to specific problems through a grievance procedure. There are a number of steps, usually beginning with a complaint to a foreman and ending with arbitration. The courts, particularly since World War II, have supported arbitration in a number of ways and have sharply limited challenges to an arbitrator's power. Unions, in turn, have been subjected increasingly to a duty of fair representation in the grievance procedure. On the other hand, during the life of a collective bargain, employees lose the right to strike and wildcat strikes can be enjoined. All parties, as well as the public, are deemed to have an interest in continuing production. Displeasure with the grievance process can be expressed legitimately only by seeking a new arbitrator for future disputes, by collective bargaining when the current contract expires, or by voting for new union officers or a new union.

Over half of the American labor force continues to work under only an employment-at-will, and there have been a number of developments over the last thirty years indicating an increasing willingness to cut away at the autonomy of the employment relationship. For example, franchisees have battled franchisors before courts, legislatures, and administrative agencies. Their successes influenced attempts of employees-at-will to gain rights.

Before the changes in the law that occurred from the 1950s through the 1970s, those holding franchises to sell nationally advertised products and services were in form independent business people but in substance they resembled employees.

Franchisors create a nationally known product and a trademark. They plan how retailing is to be conducted and often select the location of each place of business. The franchisee contributes capital and management to the particular outlet and will share in the profit or loss generated there. However, a franchise was a highly dependent relationship. The franchisor could cancel at any time without having to show justification. If a franchisee had invested in the business and had built up a local reputation tied to the franchisor's trademark, the franchisee had a great deal to lose. Thus, there were real incentives to please the franchisor's supervisors in charge of the particular location. Franchisees often complained of a contradiction between the symbols used by the franchisors and the reality of the relationship—franchisees were supposed to be independent business people, but the form contracts drafted by Wall Street lawyers gave the franchisees few, if any, rights and reserved all power to a not always benevolent authoritarian ruler. While franchisees often look like small capitalists, before statutes offered some protection, their franchises could be terminated without cause. While franchisees may appear to be "running their own business," they actually occupy a position hard to distinguish from that of an employee-at-will. Franchisees, however, often can afford to organize and lobby for legislation while employees-at-will have been limited to individual appeals for help from the courts.

While there were some victories by franchisees before the courts, generally their decisions favored the large corporations that created the relationships. With some exceptions, the courts protected a property interest in the product or service and the trademark (see Jordan 1978). It was just a matter of free contract. Franchisees were held to have taken the risk when they accepted the standard form contract as the blueprint for the relationship.

Then automobile dealers and retail gasoline dealers gained statutes, both at the state and federal levels (see *Minnesota Law Review* 1975). These statutes were thought to affect the balance of power within the private governments of franchising. The symbols found in this legislation tend to involve due process, the use of a franchisor's power in good faith, or the existence of reasonable cause for its use after an opportunity to cure defaults by the dealer. However, the rights gained by the automobile and gasoline dealers were limited and subject to performance of duties. It seems clear that the legislators accepted the case offered by the lobbyists for the dealers but were concerned, as well, with what they saw as the franchisors' legitimate interests and the rights of the public. The statutes and their legislative histories exhibit great concern that there not be too great an invasion of private decision-making.

Another example of our willingness to whittle down the autonomy of the employment relationship can be found in the results of the civil rights struggles during the 1950s and 1960s. Legal protections against discrimination based on race, sex, and age are now widespread. Such laws may have the greatest impact on employees-at-will who lack union or contract protection against unfair treatment by their employers. Cases such as the *Comerford* decision, involving an employee fired because his wife rejected the sexual advances of his supervisor, likely are no longer the law.

During the 1970s, the employment-at-will doctrine was subject to challenge in many states, with very mixed results. Many states continued to uphold the older view. The Supreme Court of Alabama, for example, refused to find a cause of action when an employee of a hospital alleged she had been fired because she refused to falsify medical records as part of a fraudulent scheme. The court remarked that to rule otherwise would "abrogate the inherent right of contract between employer and employee." Any change had to be left to the legislature.

However, other state courts created causes of action for employees-at-will (see *Harvard Law Review* 1980). Cases have involved discharges for such reasons as refusing to respond to sexual advances, being absent from work to serve on a jury, blowing the whistle on illegal activity within a corporation, and making insurance claims which would affect the rates paid by the employer. The theories used to justify intervening in the employment relationship have varied widely, and, typically, the nature of the cause of action is left extremely uncertain. Some courts found an implied obligation of good faith inherent in any contract, but the requirements of that duty were left to case-by-case definition. Others appraised the reason an employee was fired to see if it violated public policy. The California courts recognize a tort cause of action for wrongful discharge that carries with it the possibility of punitive damages.

However, many courts which recognized some right of action also seemed concerned about making it too hard to discharge incompetent workers and prompting nuisance settlements when there was any doubt about the propriety of a termination. In *Pierce* v. *Ortho Pharmaceutical Corp.,* the Supreme Court of New jersey required a "clear mandate of public policy" to be violated in the discharge before relief would be given. Such policy could be found in "legislation; administrative rules, regulations or decision; and judicial decisions," and in "certain instances, a professional code of ethics." An employee's own ethical objections to an employer's practices were not enough to justify a refusal to work on a project, and so firing the employee did not violate public policy. Employment still remains more private than public; employers still have a claim to autonomy, and accountability, so far, is reserved for cases involving atrocity stories (see Lopatka 1984).

Reflexive Rationality: The Legal System Working Through Private Associations to Achieve Substantive Goals. We have seen that the relationship between the public legal system and private associations is uncertain and there is conflict among normative claims concerning autonomy and accountability. Teubner (1983, 1984a, 1984b) sees legal thought evolving through a number of stages to one where dispute resolution and social integration will be decentralized and handled within various private associations. Law will play a role at the margin, influencing outcomes by demanding procedures and new forms of participation rather than prescribing substantive results. We will consider his evolutionary theory in light of our discussion of the employment and franchise relationships and attempts to influence the balance of power within them. Finally, we will consider Klare's challenge (1981, 1982a) that such reflexive approaches only mask the exercise of power and stand in the way of further development of real decentralization of power and control to the level of individuals and small groups.

Teubner looks at neo-evolutionary theories about the place of law in society fashioned by Nonet and Selznick (1978), Luhmann (1982), and Habermas (1979) and offers a synthesis which predicts the direction development of legal thought is likely to take. All of these writers argue that while law is affected by social change, there are limitations on its adaptability. External needs and demands are selectively filtered into the legal system and adapted in light of the logic of normative development. This process, however, can lead to crisis. Legal structures may not provide the conceptual resources nor the effective regulation needed for maintenance of the overall social system. Moreover, legal action may be seen as illegitimate if legal norms are out of phase with social ones. There was such a crisis when the legal approach appropriate to early capitalism confronted its later development. We may face another today as the legal approach appropriate to the welfare state is under attack in many Western nations.

In the nineteenth and early twentieth centuries, capitalism was facilitated by what Max Weber (1954) called *formal rationality,* Internally, law was rationalized by rule-oriented reasoning, which was manipulated by professionals who shared a legal culture. The justification for this style of law rested on its contributions to individualism and autonomy from government control. Externally, this style of law facilitated private ordering by guaranteeing a framework within which substantive judgments could be made by individuals. In this manner, it contributed to mobilizing and allocating resources, and it appeared neutral and autonomous from political and economic power. With the rise of the regulatory welfare state in the mid-twentieth century, Western legal thought evolved to a style which, in Weberian terms, was *substantively rational.* Law lost most of its formal characteristics. Internally, law was then rationalized in terms of achieving substantive ends—law was an instrument and not an end in itself. It was justified in terms of the perceived need for collective regulation of social life because of the failures of the market. Externally, this style of law is the main instrument by which the state affects market-determined patterns of behavior. It is seen as legitimate when it works to provide full employment, end discrimination, assure consumers that they will get a certain level of quality, and the like. Formal rationality was primarily a judicial style; substantive rationality was a tool of legislatures and administrative agencies, although some courts followed legal realism in this direction.

Increasingly in the 1970s and 1980s, substantive rationality is caught in the crisis of the regulatory welfare state. (Cf. Tomasic 1984.) On the one hand, social processes and economic arrangements seem too complex to be governed by the kinds of regulatory arrangements that can be fashioned within our traditions. On the other hand, the regulatory welfare state has been losing legitimacy. Insofar as it was justified by its claims to gain substantively valued ends, to a great degree it just has not worked. For example, despite the claim that the economic system would be managed, inflation has cut real income and unemployment has become a significant problem in many Western nations. Despite promises to desegregate American society, race, class, sex, and ethnicity still affect one's life chances significantly apart from talent and effort. The substantive style of legal and political rhetoric loses its power to convince those who listen to it, particularly in light of the claims of traditional formal rationality. Substantive rationality does not seem to be "law"; rather, the ends sought and the methods used can be labeled as the preferences of those who have captured power. In short, formal rationality can be turned against substantive rationality to delegitimate it.

One response to this crisis is to call for a return to formal rationality, deregulation, and governmental retreat. The public sector will withdraw and the private sphere will produce efficiency and freedom once again. There is reason to doubt whether such a strategy could succeed. Too many are interested in at least some of the benefits of the welfare state to allow a recreation of the governmental system of 1900—the cry often seems to be, "cut the budget for your programs but not mine." Moreover, even if such a recreation of what we think was the past could work, the transition from governmental systems of, say, the 1960s to a passive and neutral state likely would produce socially unacceptable burdens.

Teubner suggests, rather, that the next stage of legal evolution will be from substantive rationality to what he calls *reflexive rationality.* Here, the legal system would regulate self-regulation. Law would seek to facilitate rather than endanger self-regulatory processes, organizations, and the distribution of rights. Teubner (1984a) notes that the model of social reality found in substantive rationality is

> rather primitive in comparison with the complicated self-referential structure of the various social subsystems. . . . Taking self-reference seriously means that we have to give up conceptions of direct regulatory action. Instead, we have to speak of an external stimulation of internal self-regulating processes which, in principle, cannot be controlled from the outside. [p. 298]

Law would not take responsibility for outcomes, seeing such an effort as often beyond its capabilities. The justification for this style of law would be success in coordinating forms of social cooperation. It would not be a return to formal rationality, merely adapting to or supporting what were seen as "natural" social orders. It would attempt to guide human interaction by redefining and redistributing property rights. Externally, reflexive law would structure and reform semi-autonomous social systems, by shaping both their procedures of internal discourse and their methods of relating to other social systems. The major goal would be neither power-equalization nor participatory democracy. It would be the design of organizational structures which made institutions such as corporations, semi-public associations, mass media, and educational institutions sensitive to the outside effects of their attempts to maximize their own goals.

He offers examples to lend some empirical support to his theory. "Labor law . . . is, with respect to collective bargaining, characterized to some degree by a more abstract control technique in which we can recognize a 'reflexive' potential." Teubner recognizes that a strategy of decentralization will fail if asymmetries of power and information successfully resist attempts at equalization through law. He suggests that the legal system can operate reflexively by imposing standards of good faith and public policy in order to prompt processes of social self-regulation in semi-autonomous social systems. Also private associations could be commanded to develop constitutions which require them to operate in harmony with the requirements of other social institutions. He concedes that the adequacy of such approaches is unclear. However, reflexive rationality is an attempt to gain many of the benefits of both formal and substantive rationality with fewer of the costs of each. Whatever its normative status, one can find examples of this approach in modern law.

Teubner is unclear about how he thinks legal thought influences activity in other subsystems. Other subsystems may incorporate conceptions of legal rights and duties, transformed to meet their requirements, into their expectations and procedures. Legal thought may make issues salient and may affect background assumptions about what is natural or proper. Those acting within other subsystems may respond to the threat of the application of power to implement legal thought. However, there are many kinds of legal power. At one extreme, legal thought can be crystallized in a judgment which various state officials may enforce. People can be put in jail, property can be seized, licenses can be granted or revoked, and these orders may be enforced by agents of the state armed with weapons. At the other extreme, even the suspicion that another might commence legal action may affect behavior. Tacit and explicit threats to sue or seek new legislation or regulation may force the one threatened to examine legal arguments, the costs of defending a position in the process, and the impact on reputation of being challenged. The one threatened may decide to surrender, fight, or attempt to negotiate a settlement. Some legal agencies, such as higher appellate courts, often are relatively autonomous from direct applications of political and economic power. (However, one must recall the great contrast in views between judges appointed to the United States courts of appeal by Presidents Carter and Reagan.) Other legal agencies, such as administrative agencies and legislative committees, are influenced in varying degree by legal, moral, and political ideas as well as power and privilege. This, too, affects decisions about how to respond to actual or potential assertions of legal power.

We can only speculate about how Teubner would fit a description of the way legality is delivered into his theory. As we will see, it is easier to make the case for possible influence on self-regulation than for social integration. Many of the attempts to regulate employment and franchise relationships might be examples of what we could call indirect reflexive rationality. Even the chance that formal or substantive rationality might be exercised within the legal system may affect procedures and the balance of power within private associations. Whether such changes, in fact, serve to integrate the functioning of these associations with that of other social structures is hard to establish, but the possibility is present. I will look at the impact of some of the legislation and other legal activity dealing with, first, franchises, and, second, employment-at-will. Finally, I will turn to collective-bargaining law and the possibility that decentralized activity may prompt social integration at the price of the interests of individual workers.

The threat of lawmaking and negative public relations affected self-regulation in the area of automobile dealer franchises in the United States. The publicity given the hearings before a committee of the United States Senate and the challenging questioning of the top officials of the automobile manufacturers provoked a response that was more beneficial to the dealers than the statute that finally was passed

(Macaulay 1966). After being embarrassed by testimony about the past practices of General Motors, its president sought to take the public relations initiative. During the hearings he announced a revised franchise contract which gave General Motors dealers a number of valuable rights. Moreover, dealers' representatives would meet regularly with the top officials of the company in a setting in which they could raise questions, offer suggestions, and learn of the reasons for future plans. Furthermore, decisions to terminate a dealer could be reviewed through a process ending with a decision by a retired justice of the Supreme Court. Other manufacturers followed suit, defining rights and duties in some detail, and creating different types of systems of review. Ford's revised contract with its dealers even looked like an elaborate statute, with definitional sections and a detailed index.

In several states, the dealers' association or the administrative agency regulating manufacturer-dealer relationships began mediating disputes. One important part of such mediation was bringing new representatives of the manufacturer into the transaction, Instead of a fight between a dealer and a zone or area supervisor who is judged by the rate of sales in the territory, dispute processing now involved the dealer, the zone or area supervisor, a representative of the manufacturer from the home office, and someone from the state agency or trade association. Instead of acting as the final authority, the zone or area supervisor's decision and past actions were now subject to review. It seems likely that the possibility of such review would have a deterrent effect. Before supervisors acted, now there would be a real incentive to get their facts straight and to build a file justifying terminating the dealer or taking other action. Moreover, bias, nepotism, and similar factors that are unrelated to the goals of the manufacturer but often play a role in dependent relationships also were likely to be deterred.

Of course, a number of cases were brought before the courts under the federal and state statutes by dealers against manufacturers. The dealers rarely won. Yet the flow of litigation itself may have had some impact on large bureaucratic organizations such as the automobile manufacturers. Lawyers and executives much more senior than those normally involved in day-to-day contact with dealers had reason to establish policies and see that they were implemented so that the manufacturers could defend themselves in litigation. Again, this was likely to restrain the discretion of area or zone supervisors who were directly responsible for decisions concerning dealers. In order to structure practice so that an automobile manufacturer was ready to cope with a flow of litigation involving its relationship with dealers, it would want evidence that the dealer had had the opportunity to retail the best-selling models and that the dealer had failed to do as well as other similarly situated dealers. Such record-keeping likely added to the objectivity of judgments about terminating dealerships.

> All of these private systems have far more meaning for most dealers than lawsuits for damages under the [federal] Good Faith Act or proceedings under [state] administrative-licensing statutes to revoke licenses of factory representatives. The major significance of these formal legal proceedings is that they support the private other-than-legal ways of dealing with problems. [Macaulay 1966, pp. 204–5]

The various civil rights statutes and the cases creating some remedies for employees-at-will may have a similar impact. There is some risk of legal challenge if an employer passes over for promotion or fires a member of a racial minority, a woman, a handicapped person, or anyone over forty. Drucker (1980) comments that "[i]t's getting harder to dismiss any employee except for 'cause.'" He continues:

> Standards and review will, paradoxically, be forced on employers in the United States by the abandonment of fixed-age retirement. For companies to be able to dismiss even the most senile and decrepit oldster, they will have to develop impersonal standards of performance and systematic personnel procedures for employees of all ages. [p. 18]

Such procedures, of course, will limit the powers of supervisors and constitutionalize more and more employment relationships. As Selznick (1968, 1969) has argued, once reasons must be given to justify action, those reasons are open to examination and challenge. At least in close cases, many supervisors are likely to avoid the burden of persuasion and give an employee a second chance to meet defined standards of performance.

The relatively few cases involving employment-at-will in which employees have gained some measure of victory have prompted a great deal of writing in business publications such as *Fortune*, the *Harvard Business Review*, and the *Wall Street Journal*, as well as the law reviews. A number of major corporations have created some type of internal review system governing discipline, failure to promote, and discharge of such employees. The cases and the writing may have made the matter salient to those in charge of personnel. Seminars and training sessions about coping with the new employee-at-will cases have been sold to personnel managers and corporate lawyers. Many consulting firms offer to create informal dispute resolution processes to deal with the rights and duties of such employees. Part of the reason for the interest in such programs may have been an attempt to show courts that new rights need not be recognized; part may have been an attempt to offset claims of unfairness in case firms were sued by an employee. The informal dispute resolution procedure adopted may be more or less elaborate, but most call for review by people without a personal stake in the case. Whatever the difficulties facing an employee claiming to have been treated unfairly before such an internal body, the chance that a supervisor's decisions might be reviewed by those who could affect the supervisor's career again could serve some deterrent function. Supervisors ought to be prompted to create files on employees which could withstand review. Of course, crafty supervisors could manipulate such files, and those who conducted the review might tend to back up supervisors automatically and distrust employees. Nonetheless, the need to be able to make a case should serve as some limitation on arbitrary power.

These may be examples of reflexive rationality. Certainly, legal action affected procedures of internal discourse, and we could say that property rights had been redefined and redistributed in the franchise and employment cases. However, Teubner stresses that reflexive rationality is neither power-equalization nor participatory democracy. In addition, this kind of rationality must affect the ways semi-autonomous social systems relate to other social systems. On the one hand, it may be that the cumulative effect of all the increases in the rights of employees and franchisees will be to raise costs and make it harder to discipline and discharge the lazy and incompetent. As a result of this factor and others, American products could cost more and become more shoddy. In turn, cheaper and higher quality foreign products could enter American markets, ultimately prompting unemployment and economic crisis. On the other hand, perhaps fair procedures, a measure of job security, and the accountability of supervisors diminish the price paid for the effects of arbitrary action by supervisors. Moreover, the systems described may aid supervisors to better target and deal with the truly incompetent or inefficient since responsibility and performance ought to be better identified and evaluated. Changes in a social institution such as employment probably will affect other institutions such as the family or the economy as a whole.

Teubner sees "reflexive potential" in the "abstract control technique" used in labor law. Here, public government fosters a private legislative and adjudicatory system for the social end of promoting labor peace while redistributing wealth and affording workers some influence over working conditions. Klare (1981, 1982a, 1982b) criticizes what he calls liberal collective-bargaining theory by showing that its inner logic "deflects and demoralizes popular participation and, through cooptation of popular struggle, ultimately reinforces the institutional infrastructure of capitalism" (1981, p. 482). Klare's argument enables us to consider Teubner's reflexive rationality in more detail.

Klare argues that liberal collective-bargaining law theory ultimately rests on a delegation of power to make socially important decisions to corporations and large, bureaucratically run labor unions. This delegation results in management decision-making about what is critically important and gives it the power of command in the workplace. Essentially, of course, this is the private government argument. However, Klare stresses that liberal theory actively promotes workers' rights in certain limited and carefully defined contexts. Our collective-bargaining law has engendered some democratic participation of employees in workplace governance. Unions do protect employees from some unilateral and arbitrary dictates of management. The grievance procedure is the most important source of whatever due process Americans have on the job. Unions can be a context within which workers form and express aspirations and experience the dignity that comes with having some influence on decisions governing one's life. Nonetheless, Klare argues that the accepted theory of collective bargaining defines for workers, for union leaders, and for the public what is possible and desirable in the workplace. It stands in the way of progress toward freedom there and toward gaining for workers a dominant voice respecting the organization and purposes of work and the disposition of the products of labor.

Liberal collective-bargaining theory uses a legislative and private government metaphor to serve a number of key rhetorical purposes. Workers vote for union representatives who negotiate a collective bargain in light of the power to strike. The bargain will concern wages and conditions of employment. However, management will not surrender control over such things as whether to open new plants or close old ones, or whether to adopt new basic manufacturing techniques. Management, for example, designs a new model automobile, plans the organization of the factory and the division of labor among people and machines, and then employs unionized workers who are governed by a bureaucratic chain of command within which decisions of importance often are made far removed from anyone at the local level. Collective bargaining can influence, but not control, this process.

Once a collective bargain, usually published as a small book written in legal language, is ratified by the membership, workers then lose their right to strike during the life of the contract. Workers, management, and the public are deemed to share an interest in continuing production or providing services. In place of a strike, during the life of the contract the exclusive remedy for disputes is the grievance process which leads, ultimately, to arbitration. But unions also become large bureaucracies removed from their membership. They are held responsible for the compliance of their members with the contract. Union officials develop their own interests which are not always congruent with those of the workers at a particular plant or in smaller work groups. Their role becomes political, involving manipulation of both managers and workers. Almost inevitably, some groups of workers will be favored over others.

Liberal collective-bargaining theory presents grievance arbitration as a technical and apolitical matter of contract interpretation. Collective bargains are seen as contracts which, as other contracts, primarily concern the parties. The role of public law is limited to enforcing a bargain, and since the agreement provided an institutionalized, private internal dispute resolution process, arbitration will be enforced. This helps vindicate a limited role of government in supporting the grievance arbitration process while still continuing to recognize a private character of industrial decision-making. The end result is that procedure is separated from substance so that the quality of working life and fairness of compensation turn on bargaining power rather than norms of substantive justice. The workers have only the form of industrial due process rather than democratic self-governance. They must surrender control of their disputes to union officials and ultimately to labor lawyers who transform them into grievances phrased as interpretations of the collective bargain. The process itself involves a multilayered series of stages, hearings, and legal forms which ensure that decisions are delayed. Arbitration may resolve the dispute as so transformed but leave the real problem untouched. Decision-makers, though deemed expert, may understand little of life in a particular plant or the experience of workers in general. Labor lawyers and law professors who serve as arbitrators seldom have experience of life in the workplace or the impact of layoffs and unemployment.

Moreover, workers often face disincentives at many plants to bringing a grievance and pursuing it. Whyte (1956, p. 13) reports that "[w]orkers don't like to be considered 'trouble-makers.' It isn't a case of the worker thinking, if I pass on this grievance, I will be fired; nothing as crude as that, but rather an uneasy feeling that if I put this in the grievance procedure, management will not forget and maybe somewhere along the line I will not get the breaks that I am entitled to." At one time, union officials also filtered out grievances that they thought unwarranted or tactically unwise to push in light of positions to be taken at the next collective-bargaining negotiating session. While the expanding definition of the duty of fair representation may inhibit the more open forms of gatekeeping, union officials cannot be expected to support fully what they see as unwarranted or unwise claims (see Weir 1976).

When workers see a major portion of their lives under the control of management and union officials and see collective-bargaining and grievance procedures as largely meaningless rituals, they may exercise what power they still retain (see Farrell 1983). When economic conditions are such that jobs are not scarce prizes, often they can slow down the pace of the work; do passable but not high-quality work; engage in horseplay and foolishness to confront boredom; take, sometimes as of right, goods and materials from the employer; or engage in an illegal wildcat strike (see Atleson 1973). They can also turn to factional fights within their unions. Such practices can damage the reputation of their company's products, subjecting the firm to competitive pressure. On the one hand, this may provoke new and better forms of work organization, but it may also provoke company demands for concessions from unions or spur decisions to use more industrial robots and high technology to eliminate the need for many workers.

Klare and Teubner differ in their appraisal of reflexive rationality. To a great extent, they are seeking different ends. Klare (1981, p. 456) sees the philosophy of collective-bargaining law as "an important effort to conceptualize, justify and legitimate the modern, regulatory state in the period of advanced industrial capitalism." Unions and large corporations are seen as engaging in *private lawmaking,* "although their *de facto* power rivals or even supersedes that of public agencies and although their actions are of societal consequence." Welfare-state social democracy, acting in support of collective bargaining, loses sight of the ideal that "the highest aspiration of democratic culture should be to generate and nurture in all people the capacity for individual and collective *self*-governance and *self*-realization of their potentials" (1982a, p. 83).

Teubner, on the other hand, does not see the main goal of reflexive rationality as "power-equalization nor an increase of individual participation in the emphatic sense of 'participatory democracy'" (p. 440). He tells us that, rather, "law must act at the subsystem-specific level to install, correct, and redefine democratic self-regulatory mechanisms. Law's role is to decide about decisions, regulate regulations, and establish structural premises for future decisions in terms of organization, procedure, and competencies" (p. 437). The goal is "to create the structural premises for a decentralized integration of society by supporting integrative mechanisms within autonomous social subsystems" (p. 417). Integration requires that corporations, semi-public associations, mass media, and educational institutions be sensitive to the outside effects of their attempts to maximize internal rationality (cf. Cohen 1983). Teubner would like to have both social integration by decentralized means and power equalization in self-regulatory processes. However, he recognizes the danger that reflexive rationality could be "perverted easily into a sheer moralistic appeal" (p. 439).

Whatever our views about social integration and increasing individual control of one's own life, there is a tension between self-regulation and social integration. This suggests that while the law may be evolving toward some version of reflexive rationality, the process may not solve all problems and avoid crises. It may be that the legal system is doomed to make a succession of vain efforts to offset the contradictions of late capitalism and late socialism as it is practiced in the Soviet Union and eastern Europe today (see Bowers 1982; Sabel and Stark 1982; Simis 1982).

Moreover, we can note that both Teubner and Klare seem curiously apolitical. Klare writes as if those who worked to gain the rights for workers to organize and collectively bargain were free to write any program they pleased. Teubner writes about evolution from formal to substantive to reflexive rationality. Evolution in a biological sense implies that things just happen, perhaps by a cumulative series of accidents and a process of natural selection. In social science, evolution seems to connote a systematic and almost inevitable progression following an inner logic. Taken either way, there is some plausibility to the idea of evolution from one legal style to another. However, we may be disquieted by the absence from the picture of those who attempt to plan changes or individuals and groups struggling for advantage and power. (Cf. Ray's criticism [1983] of Luhmann's theory, a theory that serves as part of the foundation for Teubner's position.) In Joerges' words (1983, p. 29), "the Achilles' heel of reflexive rationality . . . is that a requirement [that affected groups] . . . renegotiate does not change the balance of power which determines the outcome of the negotiations." (Cf. Hearn 1984.)

Insofar as we accept the idea of an evolutionary tide as the product of natural forces, however, there is no reason to assume that evolution will stop with reflexive rationality. This is particularly true as long as we continue to have difficulty distinguishing public from private action. Reflexive rationality would seem only to postpone the day of reckoning for a distinction that Kennedy (1982) tells us is hard to take seriously.

Teubner's progression assumes a legal system with sufficient autonomy to control other social systems so that they will be integrated into a total collective unit. However, if an empirical picture of modern societies shows interchanges between and interpenetration among legal and other systems, major questions remain unanswered. It is easy to imagine legal agencies delegating self-regulatory power to various social units; it is harder to see how reflexive law would enable legal officials to coordinate and resolve conflicting claims in light of the powers of private governments and social fields and networks to influence legal outcomes and evade commands.

If Klare clears away the mystifications of liberal collective-bargaining theory, he seems to assume that the way will be open for "democratic self-management of the workplace by workers; [for] . . . giving a dominant voice respecting the organization and purposes of work and the disposition of the products of labor to those who perform work . . ." (1981, p. 451). However, the abandonment of "industrial democracy" might lead to a kind of corporatism or state socialism where workers had less power rather than more. The experience of those who have attacked liberal institutions in the name of lifting false consciousness is not reassuring.

On the other hand, due process, rights, and bureaucratic structures often break down into bargaining in the shadow of the law. Henry (1982) reports that a number of legal measures in Great Britain during the 1970s prompted management to formalize rules and procedures to deal with the disciplining of individual workers for acts such as theft of company property. In a sense, this was another example of reflexive rationality. However, as Klare might have predicted, Henry reported that the procedures functioned to give management a legitimate method of dismissing workers without being subject to question. Henry found, however, that many employers had moved from formal internal procedures to reliance on automatic employee self-discipline, often reinforced by a trade union. This

> was especially apparent where work was structured into small teams or gangs, working for pooled bonuses. Under such circumstances, said one employer, "employees wish to be seen contributing to their working groups and are reluctant to disrupt the normal pattern" since, as another pointed out, "equal effort is required by gang members." Here there can be "pressure from other workers on slackers" or "sanctions on people whom the team don't feel are pulling their weight." This pressure can be informal, "from colleagues to the offending employee" or more formally by "shop stewards who make points cautioning members who break company rules" and whom they "get to toe the line" by either having a "quiet word" or in extreme cases, "advising local district officers of the union." [p. 374]

Henry sees the possibility that, as suggested by Abel (1981) and Santos (1980), "participatory disciplinary technology becomes the ultimate form of capitalist control" (cf. Scraton and South 1984). However, participation of this type may also bring with it some limited autonomy and self-confidence. This could bring about the "penultimate stage of the process whereby the existing relations of production are undermined and replaced." Perhaps this is the road an evolution to reflexive rationality will take, and perhaps it will prompt the next evolution (cf. Derber and Schwartz 1983; Feldberg and Glenn 1983).

I doubt that those capitalists who now benefit by the distinction between public and private spheres and the delegation of power justified by it will be content to sit and watch the "natural" evolution to worker control. Indeed, Blankenburg (1984) points out that instead of an evolution from stage to stage in the style of legal thought, all forms of rationality may exist at once. Substantive rationality did not end the claims of formal rationality, and reflexive rationality is unlikely to erase formal or substantive rationality from the minds of those concerned with legal thought. Distinguished jurists often use inconsistent styles of legal thought. They serve as ideological ploys rationalizing shifting positions about autonomy and accountability of private social control. They reflect the power of those who control associations and those affected by them.

Conclusion

As we have seen, viewing society as involving relationships between only the state and individuals presents major difficulties for the social study of law. Theories about the state or society tend to overlook the remarkable ability of individuals to cope with attempted regulation by evasion, manipulation, conscious ignorance of the law, and bargaining in the light of more or less plausible legal arguments. Yet a picture of law confronting or confronted by isolated individuals also is too simple to capture enough of reality for many purposes. We live in a world of legal pluralism. Private governments, social fields, and networks administer their own rules and apply their own sanctions to those who come under their jurisdiction. Sometimes individuals are insulated from public governmental activity by social fields; sometimes public government officials are members of social fields which cut across formal boundaries of the public and the private.

These complicated interrelationships are important for the social study of law. An article in the *New York Times* (1982), for example, reported that those who supply and those who use cocaine constitute an integrated social field. In return for access to the drug, lawyers provide information on changes in the narcotics law, and on the doctrine of search and seizure, and keep track of arrest warrants. From these lawyers, dealers have learned to use occupied buildings because police need a warrant before they can enter. Often the process of obtaining a warrant will prompt a warning so that drug operations can be moved. Plumbers who use cocaine convert the pipes in a building so that drugs can be sent in tubes to other rooms quickly. Telephone repair people and others with experience in electronics make their contribution by installing sophisticated equipment so that conversations in other rooms can be monitored. Electricians install doors that can be opened only by remote control. Scanners are used to listen to police radio calls, and communications equipment helps alert people on upper floors that unwelcome visitors are entering the building. Of course, police officers, too, can become users of cocaine, and they are in a position to make valuable contributions to the maintenance of the network.

Clearly, this report suggests some of the limits on effectiveness of drug laws. However, it also suggests some of the difficulties with theories that see people as so socialized to comply with law that it is part of their personality. We can question whether the story describes a true deviant subculture or just a social network in which commonly held values other than complying with the law are stressed. Americans are socialized to gratify their desires. They learn to win at games, and clever shading of the rules is a matter for amusement rather than horror. Law enforcement officials commented that many in the middle class no longer thought of cocaine use as against the law.

Many involved in the cocaine trade learn and use entrepreneurial skills which they, because of class or race, could not learn or use in legal occupations. A large part of underemphasized American history involves ill-gotten gains serving as the base for the next generation of a family or a group moving into mainstream society. We can view participation as a form of rebellion and taking control of one's life, or we can see it as exploiting the weaknesses of one's fellows for personal gain. Undoubtedly, the illegality of the cocaine trade has prompted the creation of deviant norms within the group of users and suppliers as well as the use of swift and severe sanctions for even suspected deviation. I wonder whether Teubner would want to find "elements of reflexive rationality" in this decentralized system of private lawmaking. Do networks distributing illegal drugs contribute to social integration or disintegration? All in all, the example is a good one with which to test the kinds of theories about law and society which have been discussed in this paper.

The relationships between the state, individuals, and various human associations ranging from the family to multinational corporations are as poorly described in the law-and-society literature as they are difficult to evaluate. It is often assumed that there has been a great loss of community in modern industrial societies. Novelists and playwrights dramatize these themes. In this view, people are but cogs in an industrial machine who live rootlessly in interchangeable neighborhoods, unencumbered by real ties to family, friends, those who share their job skills or their tastes in recreation, or those who share religious observances. This picture undoubtedly shows some of the reality of modern life, but it is an overstatement, more applicable to some people than others.

Even at the bottom of the economic and status ladder, one often finds strong family ties, a religious-based system of coping with problems, and associations functioning to provide recreation and self-defense. Irving (1977, p. 879), after studying people in urban settings in England and the United States, concluded that social networks "remained close-knit in a surprising variety of urban situations, and they continue, even in this mobile age, to remain substantially rooted in the residential locality." Galanter (1979) reminds us that the

> survival and proliferation of indigenous law in the contemporary United States remains concealed from those who are looking for an inclusive and self-contained *gemeinschaft,* unsullied by formal organization, which enfolds individuals and integrates their whole life experience. What we find instead is a multitude of associations and networks, overlapping and interpenetrating, more fragmentary and less inclusive. . . .
>
> Such partial communities, linked by informal communications and sometimes by formal communications devices as well, provide much of the texture of our lives in family and kinship, at work and in business dealings, in neighborhood, sports, religion, and politics. There are varying degrees of self-conscious regulation and varying degrees of congruity with the official law. This is a realm of interdependence, regulated by tacit norms of reciprocity and sometimes by more explicit codes. The range of shared meanings is limited but the cost of exit is substantial. If we have lost the experience of an all-encompassing, inclusive community, it is not to a world of arm's length dealings with strangers, but in large measure to a world of loosely joined and partly overlapping partial or fragmentary communities. In this sense our exposure to indigenous law has increased at the same time that official regulation has multiplied. [pp. 16–17]

Ferguson (1983, p. 51) says that "[t]he standard anarchist recommendations for post-revolutionary society—workers' collectives, producers' and consumers' cooperatives, neighborhood councils—are all attempts to provide . . . [an open public] . . . space, where the ideas and goals of diverse individuals could come together and form the direction for collective action." She continues to say that "[i]n an open public situation, with full participation by all members, power need not be seen as the ability of some to make others do that which they would not otherwise have done. Instead, power could become the capacity to shape the collective situation—a positive force enabling individuals to do together that which they cannot do separately." However, Ferguson recognizes that anarchism cannot eliminate all coercion and all law. The pressure of one's peers is not the most innocent kind of coercion. In contrast to Kennedy, she concludes that "[t]he members of the collective must continually establish and reestablish the boundary between public and private acts, and not try to either erase the boundary or fix it once and for all."

Those who have been frustrated by the mindless operation of bureaucratic formal rationality can see much to admire in the anarchist vision. Yet there are two matched classic objections. Frug (1980, p. 1070) tells us that "[w]hat makes the concept of popular participation so unrealistic to us is not only its frightening unfamiliarity, but also our conviction that all decision-making requires specialization, expertise, and a chain of command." We can imagine a chaotic attempt to design a new automobile or stereo receiver and produce it by popular participation or an attempt of a major symphony orchestra to produce a work of the stature of a Beethoven concerto by a collective participatory process. Efficiency, our civil religion, seems to demand supporting hierarchies by deeming an area to be private, by leaving matters to the logic of property and contract. Yet the benefits of a division of labor do not establish that present chains of command are natural or inevitable. Ferguson mentions the second concern. All collective action is a threat to the individual who does not agree, who promotes an alternative view, or who just wants to be left alone. One speaking with the authority of the collective may act against such individuals for the good of the group or for the official's own self-interest. Given all the difficulties in asserting rights successfully—the cost barriers to litigation, the contradictory nature of our theories of rights, and the power of those with whom one has long-term relationships to retaliate later—rights are a feeble defense against power. Yet until we think of a way to achieve what now looks to be a Utopia where all power is neatly equalized and balanced, rights may be all we have. As Kennedy (1981, p. 506) observed, "[e]mbedded in the rights notion is a liberating accomplishment of our culture: the affirmation of free human subjectivity against the constraints of group life, along with the paradoxical countervision of a group life that creates and nurtures individuals capable of freedom." These normative contradictions help explain the problematic relationships between the larger public government, private governments, social fields, and networks.

An appreciation of the role of private governments, social fields, and networks, as we have seen, is critical for the development of many of the classic topics of the social study of law. The relationship of public and private normative orderings tells us much about the place of law in society and the fate of attempted reforms. Lurking in all of these concerns are great questions about freedom and control of individuals and their associations, the autonomy of centers of power and their integration into a functioning society, and problems of the interrelationships and interpenetration of public governments and private associations. Our present understanding of more and less institutionalized social fields and their connections with the larger legal system is, to say the least, underdeveloped and in need of attention. Articles surveying fields often end by calling for either more research or more theory. Here, I can safely do both. In addition, we ought not forget what we already know. Private government performs many of the functions commonly associated with public government, and it is likely that the more decentralized the structures for carrying out a social function, the greater the problems of coordination and integration. At the same time, the public/private distinction is suspect. While it may be useful or vital to carve out areas of activity and put them beyond public control, reifying public and private governments and seeing them as distinct entities only obscures reality. In Zimring's words (1981):

> It is sometimes possible both to know something important and to ignore that knowledge. To do this is to generate the phenomenon of the well-known secret, an obvious fact we ignore. When Edgar Allan Poe suggested that the best location to hide something is the most obvious place, he was teaching applied law and social science. [p. 867]

Cases Cited

Brown v. Board of Education, 347 U.S. 483 (1954).
Comerford v. International Harvester, 235 Ala. 376, 178 So. 894 (1938).
Dred Scott v. Sandford, 60 U.S. (19 How.) 393 (1857).
Pierce v. Ortho Pharmaceutical Corp., 84 N.J. 58, 417 A.2d 505 (1980).

Bibliography

Abel, Richard L. 1981 "Conservative Conflict and the Reproduction of Capitalism: The Role of Informal Justice." *International Journal of the Sociology of Law* 9:245–67.

Abercrombie, Nicholas, and Turner, Bryan S. 1978 "The Dominant Ideology Thesis." *British Journal of Sociology* 29:149–67.

Abney, Glenn, and Lauth, Thomas P. 1982 "Councilmanic Intervention in Municipal Administration." *Administration and Society* 13:435–56.

Abramson, Joan 1977 "Measuring Success or, Whatever Happened to Affirmative Action?" *Civil Rights Digest* 9:15–27.

Adler, Patricia A., and Adler, Peter 1983 "Relationships Between Dealers: the Social Organization of Illicit Drug Transactions." *Sociology and Social Research* 67:260–78.

Akers, Ronald L. 1977 *Deviant Behavior: A Social Learning Approach.* Belmont, Calif.: Wadsworth.

Albrecht, Stan L., and Green, Miles 1977 "Cognitive Barriers to Equal Justice Before the Law," *Journal of Research in Crime and Delinquency* 14:206–21.

Arnove, Robert F. 1970 "The Ford Foundation and 'Competence Building' Overseas: Assumptions, Approaches, and Outcomes." *Studies in Comparative International Development* 12:100–126.

Atleson, James B. 1973 "Work Group Behavior and Wildcat Strikes: The Causes and Functions of Industrial Civil Disobedience." *Ohio State Law journal* 34:751–816.

Balbus, Isaac D. 1977 "Commodity Form and Legal Form: An Essay on the 'Relative Autonomy' of the Law." *Law & Society Review* 11:546–88.

Barber, Bernard 1978 "Control and Responsibility in the Powerful Professions." *Political Science Quarterly* 93:599–615.

Baumgartner, M. P. 1985 "Law and the Middle Class: Evidence from a Suburban Town." *Law and Human Behavior* 9:3–24.

Baxter, Leslie A. 1984 "An Investigation of Compliance-Gaining as Politeness." *Human Communication Research* 10:427–56.

Berle, Adolph A., and Means, Gardner C. 1932 *The Modern Corporation and Private Property.* New York: Macmillan.

Berle, Adolph A., Jr. 1952 "Constitutional Limitations on Corporate Activity: Protection of Personal Rights from Invasion Through Economic Power." *University of Pennsylvania Law Review* 100:933–55.

Bernard, Jesse 1964 *Academic Women,* State College: Pennsylvania State University Press.

Biersteker, Thomas J. 1980 "The Illusion of State Power: Transnational Corporations and the Neutralization of Host-Country Legislation." *Journal of Peace Research* 17:207–21.

Bilder, Richard B. 1970 "East-West Trade Boycotts: A Study in Private, Labor Union, State, and Local Interference with Foreign Policy." *University of Pennsylvania Law Review* 118:841–938.

Bissonette, R. 1977 "The Bartender as a Mental Health Service Gatekeeper: A Role Analysis." *Community Mental Health Journal* 13:92–99.

Black, Donald 1976 *The Behavior of Law,* New York: Academic Press.

Black, Donald 1983 "Crime as Social Control." *American Sociological Review* 48:34–45.

Blankenburg, Erhard 1984 "The Poverty of Evolutionism: A Critique of Teubner's Case for 'Reflexive Law.'" *Law & Society Review* 18:273–89.

Block, Alan A., and Thomas, Philip A. 1984 "Beyond the Courtroom Door." *Australian Journal of Law and Society* 2:110–28.

Bowers, Stephen R. 1982 "Law and Lawlessness in a Socialist Society: The Potential Impact of Crime in East Germany." *World Affairs* 145:152–76.

Braithwaite, John 1982 "Enforced Self-Regulation: A New Strategy for Corporate Crime Control." *Michigan Law Review* 80:1466–1502.

Bredemeier, Harry C. 1962 "Law as an Integrative Mechanism." In *Law and Sociology,* edited by William Evan. New York: Free Press.

Burgess, Robert L., and Akers, Ronald L. 1966 "A Differential Association-Reinforcement Theory of Criminal Behavior." *Social Problems* 14:128–47.

Burton, Frank 1976 "The Irish Republican Army and Its Community: A Struggle for Legitimacy." In *The Sociology of Law,* edited by Pat Carlen. Keele: University of Keele.

Cain, Maureen 1983 "Introduction: Towards an Understanding of the International State." *International Journal of the Sociology of Law* 11:1–10.

Caplow, Theodore 1982 "Christmas Gifts and Kin Networks." *American Sociological Review* 47:383–92.

Carter, Lief H. 1974 *The Limits of Order.* Lexington, Mass.: Lexington Books.

Casey, Gregory 1976 "Popular Perceptions of Supreme Court Rulings." *American Politics Quarterly* 4:3–45.

Chafee, Zechariah, Jr. 1930 "The Internal Affairs of Associations Not for Profit." *Harvard Law Review* 43:993–1029.

Chambliss, William J. 1973 "Functional and Conflict Theories of Crime." *MSS Modular Publications* 17:1–23.

Chambliss, William J. 1979 "Contradictions and Conflicts in Law Creation." In *Research in Law and Sociology,* vol. 2, edited by Rita J. Simon and Steven Spitzer. Greenwich, Conn.: JAI Press.

Chambliss, William J., and Seidman, Robert 1971 *Law, Order and Power,* Reading, Mass.: Addison-Wesley.

Cloward, Richard A., and Ohlin, Lloyd E. 1960 *Delinquency and Opportunity.* Glencoe, Ill.: Free Press.

Coffee, John C, Jr. 1981 "'No Soul to Damn: No Body to Kick': An Unscandalized Inquiry into the Problem of Corporate Punishment." *Michigan Law Review* 79:386–459.

Cohen, Albert K. 1955 *Delinquent Boys.* Glencoe, Ill.: Free Press.

Cohen, Lawrence E., and Felson, M. 1979 "Social Change and Crime Rate Trends: A Routine Activity Approach." *American Sociological Review.* 44:588–608.

Cohen, Steven R. 1983 "From Industrial Democracy to Professional Adjustment." *Theory and Society* 12:47–67.

Cole, Richard B. 1978 "The Second Criminal Justice System." *S.A.M. [Society of Advanced Management] Management Journal* 43:17–23.

Cortese, Charles F. 1966 "A Study in Knowledge and Attitudes Toward the Law: The Legal Knowledge Inventory." *Rocky Mountain Social Science Journal* 3:192–204.
Cressey, Donald R. 1973 "Advanced Notice and Government by Law Within Criminal Confederations." *International Journal of Criminology and Penology* 1:55–67.
Crowe, Patricia Ward 1978 "Complainant Reactions to the Massachusetts Commission Against Discrimination." *Law & Society Review* 12:217–35.
Curran, Barbara W. 1978 "Getting By with a Little Help from My Friends: Informal Networks Among Older Black and White Urban Women Below the Poverty Line." *Dissertation Abstracts International* 39(4-A).
Derber, Charles, and Schwartz, William 1983 "Toward a Theory of Worker Participation." *Sociological Inquiry* 53:61–78.
Deysine, Anne 1980 "Political Corruption: A Review of the Literature." *European Journal of Political Research* 8:447–62.
Di Franceisco, Wayne, and Gitelman, Zvi 1984 "Soviet Political Culture and 'Covert Participation' in Policy Implementation." *American Political Science Review* 78:603–20.
Drucker, Peter F. 1980 "The Job as Property Right." *Wall Street Journal* September 25, 1979, p. 20.
Durkheim, Emile 1958 *Professional Ethics and Civic Morals.* Glencoe, Ill.: Free Press.
Dye, Thomas R. 1978 "Oligarchic Tendencies in National Policy-Making: the Role of the Private Policy-Planning Organizations." *Journal of Politics* 40:309–31.
Eells, Richard 1962 *The Government of Corporations.* Glencoe, Ill.: Free Press.
Ehrlich, Eugen 1936 *Fundamental Principles of the Sociology of Law.* Translated by Walter L. Moll with an introduction by Roscoe Pound. Cambridge, Mass.: Harvard University Press.
Eisenstadt, S. N., and Roniger, Louis 1980 "Patron-Client Relations as a Model of Structuring Social Exchange." *Comparative Studies in Society and History* 22:42–77.
Ekland-Olson, Sheldon 1982 "Deviance, Social Control and Social Networks." In *Research in Law, Deviance and Social Control,* vol. 4, edited by Steven Spitzer and Rita J. Simon. Greenwich, Conn.: JAI Press.
Ellickson, Robert C. 1982 "Cities and Homeowners Associations." *University of Pennsylvania Law Review* 130:1519–80.
Elliot, Delbert S., and Voss, Harwin L. 1974 *Delinquency and Dropout.* Lexington, Mass.: Lexington Books.
Ellman, Ira Mark 1981 "Driven from the Tribunal: Judicial Resolution of Internal Church Disputes." *California Law Review* 69:1378–1444.
Engel, David M. 1984 "The Oven Bird's Song: Insiders, Outsiders, and Personal Injuries in an American Community." *Law & Society Review* 18:549–79.
Evan, William 1976 *Organizational Theory: Structures, Systems, and Environments.* New York: Wiley.
Ewing, David W. 1977 *Freedom Inside the Corporation: Bringing Civil Liberties to the Workplace.* New York: Dutton.
Farrell, Dan 1983 "Exit, Voice, Loyalty, and Neglect as Responses to Job Dissatisfaction: A Multidimensional Scaling Study." *Academy of Management Journal* 26:596–607.
Feldberg, Roslyn L., and Glenn, Evelyn Nakano 1983 "Incipient Workplace Democracy among United States Clerical Workers." *Economic and Industrial Democracy* 4:47–67.
Felstiner, William L. F., and Williams, Lynne A. 1978 "Mediation as an Alternative to Criminal Prosecution: Ideology and Limitations." *Law and Human Behavior* 2:223–44.
Felstiner, William L. F., and Williams, Lynne A. 1979 *Community Mediation in Dorchester, Massachusetts: Alternatives to Adjudication. An International Study.* Los Angeles: Program for Dispute Systems Research, University of Southern California.
Femia, Joseph V. 1983 "Review Article: Gramsci's Patrimony." *British Journal of Political Science* 13:327–64.
Ferguson, Kathy E. 1983 "Toward a New Anarchism." *Contemporary Crises* 7:39–57.
Fisse, Brent 1981 "Community Service as a Sanction Against Corporations." *Wisconsin Law Review* 1981: 970–1017.

Fisse, Brent, and Braithwaite, John 1984 "Sanctions Against Corporations: Dissolving the Monopoly of Fines." In *Business Regulation in Australia,* edited by Roman Tomasic. North Ryde, N.S. W.: CCH Australia Limited.

FitzGerald, Jeffrey M., Hickman, David C., and Dickins, Richard L. 1980 "A Preliminary Discussion of the Definitional Phase of the Dispute Process." Paper presented at the Law and Society Association Conference, Madison, Wisconsin, June.

Fitzpatrick, Peter 1984 "Law and Societies." *Osgoode Hall Law Journal* 22:115–38.

Fleming, R. W. 1961 "Some Problems of Due Process and Fair Procedure in Labor Arbitration." *Stanford Law Review* 13:235–51.

Fleming, R. W. 1962 "Some Problems of Evidence Before the Labor Arbitrator." *Michigan Law Review* 60:133–68.

Ford, Frederick R. 1983 "Rules: The Invisible Family." *Family Process* 22:135–45.

Friedmann, Wolfgang G. 1957 "Corporate Power, Government by Private Groups, and the Law." *Columbia Law Review* 57:155–86.

Frug, Gerald 1980 "The City as a Legal Concept." *Harvard Law Review* 93:1057–1154.

Fuller, Lon L. 1941 "Consideration and Form." *Columbia Law Review* 41:799–824.

Fuller, Lon L. 1969 "Two Principles of Human Association." In *Voluntary Associations,* edited by J. Roland Pennock and John W. Chapman. New York: Atherton Press.

Galanter, Marc 1974 "Why the 'Haves' Come Out Ahead: Speculations on the Limits of Legal Change." *Law & Society Review* 9:95–160.

Galanter, Marc 1979 "Beyond Legal Representation: Dispute Processing, Non-judicial Alternatives and the 'Third Wave' in the Access-to-justice Movement." Paper presented at the Colloquium on Access to Justice After the Publication of the Florence Project Series: Prospects for Future Action, Florence, Italy, October 15–18.

Galanter, Marc 1981 "Justice in Many Rooms: Courts, Private Ordering, and Indigenous Law." *Journal of Legal Pluralism* 19:1–47.

Galanter, Marc 1983 "Reading the Landscape of Disputes: What We Know and Don't Know (and Think We Know) About Our Allegedly Contentious and Litigious Society." *UCLA Law* Review 31:4–71.

Genovese, Rosalie G. 1980 "A Women's Self-Help Network as a Response to Service Needs in the Suburbs." *Signs: Journal of Women in Culture and Society* 5: S248–56.

Ghezzi, Susan Guarino 1983 "A Private Network of Social Control: Insurance Investigation Units." *Social Problems* 30:521–31.

Glazer, Nathan 1975 *Affirmative Discrimination: Ethnic Inequality and Public Policy.* New York: Basic Books.

Gottlieb, Gidon 1983 "Relationalism: Legal Theory for a Relational Society." *University of Chicago Law Review* 50:567–612.

Grace, Clive, and Wilkinson, Philip 1978 *Sociological Inquiry and Legal Phenomena.* London: Collier Macmillan.

Greenberg, David F. 1976 "On One-Dimensional Marxist Criminology." *Theory and Society* 3:611–21.

Greenberg, David F., and Anderson, Nancy 1981 "Recent Marxisant Books on Law: A Review Essay." *Contemporary Crises* 5:293–322.

Griffiths, John 1984 "Village Justice in the Netherlands." *Journal of Legal Pluralism* 22:17–42.

Habermas, Jurgen 1979 *Communication and the Evolution of Society.* Boston: Beacon Press.

Hagen, John, Silva, Edward T., and Simpson, John H. 1977 "Conflict and Consensus in the Designation of Deviance." *Social Forces* 56:320–40.

Hale, Robert L. 1920 "Law Making by Unofficial Minorities." *Columbia Law Review* 20:451–56.

Hammer, Muriel 1980 "Social Access and the Clustering of Personal Connections." *Social Networks* 2:305–25.

Hannigan, John A. 1982 "Unfriendly Skies: The Decline of the World Aviation Cartel." *Pacific Sociological Review* 25:107–36.

Hans, Valerie P., and Slater, Dan 1983 "John Hinckley, Jr. and the Insanity Defense: The Public's Verdict." *Public Opinion Quarterly* 47:202–12.
Hanslowe, Kurt L. 1961 "Regulation by Visible Public and Invisible Private Government." *Texas Law Review* 40:88–135.
Harding, Vincent 1975 "The Black Wedge in America: Struggle, Crisis and Hope, 1955–1975." *Black Scholar* 7:28–30, 35–46.
Harvard Law Review 1949 "Private Lawmaking by Trade Associations." *Harvard Law Review* 62:1346–70.
Harvard Law Review 1962 "Judicial Intervention in Disputes over the Use of Church Property." *Harvard Law Review* 75:1142–86.
Harvard Law Review 1963 "Judicial Control of Actions of Private Associations." *Harvard Law Review* 76:983–1100.
Harvard Law Review 1980 "Protecting at Will Employees Against Wrongful Discharge." *Harvard Law Review* 93:1818–44.
Havighurst, Harold C. 1961 *The Nature of Private Contract.* Evanston, Ill.: Northwestern University Press.
Hearn, Frances 1980 "Adaptive Narcissism and the Crisis of Legitimacy." *Contemporary Crises* 4:117–40.
Hearn, Frank 1984 "State Autonomy and Corporatism." *Contemporary Crises* 8:125–45.
Hearst Corporation 1983 *The American Public, the Media and the Judicial System: A National Survey on Public Awareness and Personal Experience.* New York: Hearst Corporation.
Henry, Stuart 1981 "Decentralized Justice: Private v. Democratic Informality." In *Informal Institutions: Alternative Networks in the Corporate State,* edited by Stuart Henry. New York: St. Martin's Press.
Henry, Stuart 1982 "Factory Law: The Changing Disciplinary Technology of Industrial Social Control." *International Journal of the Sociology of Law* 10:365–83.
Hoekema, Andre 1975 "Confidence in Justice and Law Among Port Workers." *Sociologia Neerlandia* 11:128–43.
Hopkins, Raymond F. 1978 "Global Management Networks: The Internationalization of Domestic Bureaucracies." *International Social Science Journal* 30:31–46.
Hornig, Lilli S. 1980 "Untenured and Tenuous: The Status of Women Faculty." *Annals, AAPSS* 448:115–25.
Hunt, Alan 1976 "Perspectives in the Sociology of Law." In *The Sociology of Law,* edited by Pat Carlen. Keele: University of Keele.
Hurst, James Willard 1960 "The Law in United States History." *Proceedings of the American Philosophical Society* 104:518–26.
Irving, Henry W. 1977 "Social Networks in the Modern City." *Social Forces* 55:867–80.
Jaffee, Louis L. 1937 "Law Making by Private Groups." *Harvard Law Review* 51:201–53.
Jessop, Bob 1980 "On Recent Marxist Theories of Law, the State, and Juridico-Political Ideology." *International Journal of the Sociology of Law* 8:339–68.
Joerges, Christian 1983 "Regulatory Law, Private Government and Self-Regulation: A Comment on Stewart Macaulay." Paper presented at the Conference on Reflexive Law and the Regulatory Crisis, Madison, Wisconsin, July 18–21.
Johnstone, Quintin, and Hopson, Dan, Jr. 1967 *Lawyers and Their Work,* Indianapolis, Ind.: Bobbs-Merrill.
Jordan, Ellen R. 1978 "Unconscionability at the Gas Station." *Minnesota Law Review* 62:813–56.
Kakalik, James S., and Wildhorn, Sorrel 1977 *The Private Police: Security and Danger.* New York: Crane, Russak.
Kennedy, Duncan 1981 "Critical Labor Law Theory: A Comment." *Industrial Relations Law Journal* 4:503–6.
Kennedy, Duncan 1982 "The Status of the Decline of the Public/Private Distinction." *University of Pennsylvania Law Review* 130:1349–57.

Kerbo, Harold R., and Della Fave, L. Richard, 1983 "Corporate Linkage and Control of the Corporate Economy: New Evidence and a Reinterpretation." *Sociological Quarterly* 24:201–18.

Klare, Karl E. 1981 "Labor Law as Ideology: Toward a New Historiography of Collective Bargaining Law." *Industrial Relations Law Journal* 4:450–82.

Klare, Karl E. 1982a "Critical Theory and Labor Relations Law." In *The Politics of Law: A Progressive Critique,* edited by David Kairys. New York: Pantheon Books.

Klare, Karl E. 1982b "The Public/Private Distinction in Labor Law." *University of Pennsylvania Law Review* 130:1358–1422.

Koch, Koen 1980 "The New Marxist Theory of the State or the Rediscovery of the Limitations of a Structural-Functionalist Paradigm." *Netherlands Journal of Sociology* 16:1–19.

Kornhauser, Ruth R. 1978 *Social Sources of Delinquency.* Chicago: University of Chicago Press.

Kowalewski, David, and Leitko, Thomas A. 1983 "Transnational Corporations and Intergovernmental Organizations: The Trilateral Commission Case." *Journal of Political and Military Sociology* 11:93–107.

Ladinsky, Jack, and Susmilch, Charles 1983 "Community Factors in the Brokerage of Consumer Product and Service Problems." Working paper no. 14, Disputes Processing Research Program, University of Wisconsin Law School.

Lamo De Espinosa, Emilio 1980 "Social and Legal Order in Sociological Functionalism." *Contemporary Crises* 4:43–76.

Leblebici, Huseyin, and Salancik, Gerald R. 1982 "Stability in Interorganizational Exchanges: Rulemaking Processes of the Chicago Board of Trade." *Administrative Science Quarterly* 27:227–42.

Lee, Trevor R. 1980 "The Resilience of Social Networks to Changes in Mobility and Propinquity." *Social Networks* 2:423–35.

Lester, Richard A. 1974 *Antibias Regulations of Universities: Faculty Problems and Their Solutions.* New York: McGraw-Hill.

Lindblom, Charles 1977 *Politics and Markets.* New York: Basic Books.

Lindgren, Janet S. 1983 "Beyond Cases: Reconsidering Judicial Review." *Wisconsin Law Review* 1983:583–638.

Lineberry, Robert L., and Watson, Sharon M. 1980 "Neighborhoods, Politics, and Public Services: The Case of Chicago." *Urban Interest* 2:11–18.

Lipset, Seymour Martin 1982 "The Academic Mind at the Top: The Political Behavior and Values of Faculty Elites." *Public Opinion Quarterly* 46:143–68.

Liss, Lora J. 1977 "Affirmative Action Officers: Are They Change Agents?" *Educational Record* 58:418–28.

Livingstone, Neil C. 1981 "Fighting Terrorism: The Private Sector." *Conflict* 3:177–219.

Lopatka, Kenneth T. 1984 "The Emerging Law of Wrongful Discharge—A Quadrennial Assessment of the Labor Law Issue of the 80s." *Business Lawyer* 40:1–32.

Lowenthal, Abraham F. 1978 "Latin America: A Not-So-Special Relationship." *Foreign Policy* 32:107–26.

Luhmann, Niklas 1981 "Communication About Law." In *Advances in Social Theory and Methodology,* edited by K. Knorr-Cetina and A. V. Circourel. Boston: Routledge & Kegan Paul.

Luhmann, Niklas 1982 *The Differentiation of Society.* New York: Columbia University Press.

Macaulay, Jacqueline 1980 "The Failure of Affirmative Action: A Case Study." In *Rocking the Boat: Academic Women and the Academic Process,* edited by G. DeSole and L. Hoffman. New York: Modern Language Association.

Macaulay, Jacqueline, and Macaulay, Stewart 1978 "Adoption for Black Children: A Case Study of Expert Discretion." In *Research in Law and Sociology,* vol. 1, edited by Rita J. Simon, Greenwich, Conn.: JAI Press.

Macaulay, Stewart 1963 "Non-Contractual Relations in Business: A Preliminary Study." *American Sociological Review* 28:55–67.

Macaulay, Stewart 1966 *Law and the Balance of Power.* New York: Russell Sage Foundation.

Macaulay, Stewart 1979 "Lawyers and Consumer Protection Laws." *Law & Society Review* 14:115–71.

Macaulay, Stewart 1985 "Lawyer Advertising: 'Yes, but . . .'." Forthcoming. (Louvain, Belgium: European Workshop on Consumer Law.)

McKenna, Wendy B., and Denmark, Florence L. 1975 "Women and the University." *International Journal of Group Tensions* 5:226–34.

Marenin, Otwin 1981 "Essence and Empiricism in African Politics." *Journal of Modern African Studies* 19:1–30.

Marighela, Carlos 1971 *For the Liberation of Brazil.* New York: Penguin Books.

Mayhew, Leon H. 1968 *Law & Equal Opportunity: A Study of the Massachusetts Commission Against Discrimination.* Cambridge, Mass.: Harvard University Press.

Mechanic, David 1962 "Sources of Power of Lower Participants in Complex Organizations." *Administrative Science Quarterly* 7:349–64.

Merton, Robert K. 1957a "Social Structure and Anomie." In *Social Theory and Social Structure.* Rev. ed. Glencoe, Ill.: Free Press.

Merton, Robert K. 1957b "Continuities in the Theory of Social Structure and Anomie." In *Social Theory and Social Structure.* Rev. ed. Glencoe, Ill.: Free Press.

Michigan Law Review 1973 "Legal Knowledge of Michigan Citizens." *Michigan Law Review* 71:1463–86.

Mileski, Maureen 1971 "Courtroom Encounters: An Observational Study of a Lower Criminal Court." *Law & Society Review* 5:473–538.

Miller, Arthur S. 1960 "The Corporation as a Private Government in the World Community." *Virginia Law Review* 46:1539–72.

Mills, C. Wright 1956 *The Power Elite.* Oxford: Oxford University Press.

Mills, Edgar W., Jr. 1983 "Sociological Ambivalence and Social Order: The Constructive Uses of Normative Dissonance." *Sociology and Social Research* 67:279–87.

Milward, H. Brinton, and Francisco, Ronald A. 1983 "Subsystem Politics and Corporatism in the United States." *Policy and Politics* 11:273–93.

Minnesota Law Review 1975 "Regulation of Franchising." *Minnesota Law Review* 59:1027–63.

Mishra, Ramesh 1982 "System Integration, Social Action and Change: Some Problems in Sociological Analysis." *Sociological Review* 30:5–22.

Moore, Sally Falk 1978 *Law as Process: An Anthropological Approach.* London, Henley, and Boston: Routledge & Kegan Paul.

Nachmias, David, and Greer, Ann Lennarson 1982 "Governance Dilemmas in an Age of Ambiguous Authority." *Policy Sciences* 14:105–16.

Nader, Laura 1984 "The Recurrent Dialectic Between Legality and Its Alternatives: The Limitations of Binary Thinking." *Pennsylvania Law Review* 132:621–45.

National Center for State Courts 1978 *State Courts: A Blueprint for the Future.* Williamsburg, Va.: National Center for State Courts.

Nauta, A. P. N. 1974 "Social Control and Norm Restrictiveness: Some Results of an Inquiry into Neighbor Relationships." *Sociologia Neerlandia* 10:233–43.

Nelson, Barbara J. 1980 "Help-Seeking from Public Authorities: Who Arrives at the Agency Door?" *Policy Sciences* 12:175–92.

New York Times 1982 "Cocaine Use by Middle Class Called Widely Accepted in the New York Area." *New York Times,* December 13, p. 15.

New York Times 1984 "A Diamond Maverick's Clash with the Club on 47th Street." *New York Times,* November 13, §iv, p. 5.

New York Times 1985 "White Collar Crime: Booming Again." *New York Times,* June 9, §3, pp. 1, 6.

Noguchi, Paul H. 1979 "Law, Custom, and Morality in Japan: The Culture of Cheating on the Japanese National Railways." *Anthropological Quarterly* 52:165–77.

Nonet, Philippe, and Selznick, Philip 1978 *Law and Society in Transition: Toward Responsive Law.* New York: Harper.

O'Toole, George 1978 *The Private Sector: Rent-a-Cops, Private Spies and the Police-Industrial Complex.* New York: Norton.
Page, Barbara 1978 "The Assault on Affirmative Action." *Politics & Education* 1:31–38.
Parsons, Talcott 1962 "Law and Social Control." In *Law and Sociology,* edited by William Evan. New York: Free Press.
Posner, Richard A. 1979 "The *Bakke* Case and the Future of 'Affirmative Action.'" *California Law Review* 67:171–89.
Pound, Roscoe 1917 "The Limits of Effective Legal Action." *American Bar Association Journal* 3:55–70.
Prager, Jeffrey 1982 "Equal Opportunity and Affirmative Action: The Rise of New Understandings," In *Research in Law, Deviance and Social Control,* vol. 4, edited by Steven Spitzer and Rita J. Simon. Greenwich, Conn.: JAI Press.
Pritchard, David 1985 "Homicide and Consensual Justice: The Agenda-Setting Effect of Crime News on Prosecutors." Unpublished manuscript.
Prottas, Jeffrey Manditch 1978 "The Power of the Street-Level Bureaucrat in Public Service Bureaucracies." *Urban Affairs Quarterly* 13:285–311.
Quinney, Richard 1975 "Crime Control in Capitalist Society: A Critical Philosophy." In *Critical Criminology,* edited by Ian Taylor, Paul Walton, and Jock Young. London: Routledge & Kegan Paul.
Ray, Lawrence J. 1978 "Habermas, Legitimation, and the State." *Journal for the Theory of Social Behaviour* 8:149–63.
Ray, Lawrence J. 1983 "Review Essay: Systematic Functionalism Revisited." *Journal for the Theory of Social Behaviour* 13:231–41.
Regoli, Robert M., and Poole, Eric D. 1978 "The Commitment of Delinquents to Their Misdeeds: A Re-Examination." *Journal of Criminal Justice* 3:3–28.
Reuter, Peter 1984 "Social Control in Illegal Markets." In *Toward a General Theory of Social Control,* edited by Donald Black. New York: Academic Press.
Robbins, James J., and Heckscher, Gunnar 1941 "The Constitutional Theory of Autonomous Groups." *Journal of Politics* 3:3–28.
Ross, H. Laurence 1970 *Settled Out of Court: The Social Process of Insurance Claims Adjustments.* Chicago: Aldine.
Sabel, Charles F., and Stark, David 1982 "Planning, Politics, and Shop-Floor Power: Hidden Forms of Bargaining in Soviet-Imposed State-Socialist Societies." *Politics & Society* 11:439–75.
Santos, Bonaventura de Sousa 1977 "The Law of the Oppressed: The Construction and Reproduction of Legality in Pasargada." *Law & Society Review* 12:5–105.
Santos, Bonaventura de Sousa 1980 "Law and Community: The Changing Nature of State Power in Late Capitalism." *International Journal of the Sociology of Law* 8:379–97.
Schau, Maryan S. 1983 "A Communication-Rules Approach to Organizational Culture." *Administrative Science Quarterly* 28:557–81.
Schmidhauser, John R. 1979 *Judges and Justices: The Federal Appellate Judiciary.* Boston: Little, Brown.
Schoenberg, Sandra Peilman 1980 "Some Trends in Community Participation of Women in Their Neighborhoods." *Signs: Journal of Women in Culture and Society* 5:S261–68.
Schwartz, Louis B. 1960 "Institutional Size and Individual Liberty: Authoritarian Aspects of Big Business." Northwestern *University Law Review* 55:4–53.
Schwartz, Warren F., Baxter, Keith, and Ryan, David 1984 "The Duel: Can These Gentlemen Be Acting Efficiently?" *Journal of Legal Studies* 13:321–55.
Scraton, Phil, and South, Nigel 1984 "The Ideological Construction of the Hidden Economy: Private Justice and Work-Related Crime." *Contemporary* Crises 8:1–18.
Selznick, Philip 1968 "The Sociology of Law." In *International Encyclopedia of Social Sciences,* vol. 9, edited by David L. Sills. New York: Macmillan and Free Press.
Selznick, Philip 1969 *Law, Society, and Industrial Justice.* New York: Russell Sage Foundation.

Sharp, Elaine B. 1980 "Citizen Perceptions of Channels for Urban Service Advocacy." *Public Opinion Quarterly* 44:362–76.

Shearing, Clifford D., and Stenning, Philip C. 1983 "Private Security: Implications for Social Control." *Social Problems* 30:493–506.

Sills, David L. 1968 "Voluntary Associations: Sociological Aspects." In *International Encyclopedia of the Social Sciences,* vol. 16, edited by David L. Sills. New York: Macmillan.

Simis, Konstantin 1982 *USSR: The Corrupt Society—The Secret World of Soviet Capitalism.* New York: Simon and Schuster.

Snyder, Frederick E. 1978 "Crime and Community Mediation—The Boston Experience: A Preliminary Report on the Dorchester Urban Court Program." *Wisconsin Law Review* 1978:737–91.

Sowell, Thomas 1976 "'Affirmative Action' Reconsidered." *Public Interest* 42:47–65.

Spitzer, Steven 1984 "The Embeddedness of Law: Reflections on Lukes and Scull's *Durkheim and the Law." ABF Research Journal* 1984:859–68.

Spitzer, Steven, and Scull, Andrew T. 1977 "Privatization and Capitalist Development: The Case of the Private Police." *Social Problems* 25:18–29.

Stack, Steven 1978 "Ideological Beliefs on the American Distribution of Opportunity, Power, and Rewards." *Sociological Focus* 11:221–33.

Stenning, Philip, and Shearing, Clifford 1979 "Private Security and Private Justice." *British Journal of Law and Society* 6:261–71.

Sumner, Colin 1979 *Reading Ideologies: An Investigation into the Marxist Theory of Ideology and Law.* New York: Academic Press.

Sutherland, Edwin H., and Cressey, Donald R. 1978 *Criminology.* 10th ed. Philadelphia: Lippincott.

Sweet, Justin 1978 "Lawmaking by Standard Forms: A Study of AIA Contract Documents." Unpublished manuscript.

Sweet, Justin 1983 "The Architectural Profession Responds to Construction Management and Design-Build: The Spotlight on AIA Documents." *Law & Contemporary Problems* 46:69–82.

Taylor, Ralph B., and Brooks, Debra Kaye 1980 "Temporary Territories?: Responses to Intrusions in a Public Setting." *Population and Environment* 3:135–45.

Tersine, Richard J., and Russell, Roberta S. 1981 "Internal Theft: The Multi-Billion-Dollar Disappearing Act," *Business Horizons* 24:11–20.

Teubner, Günther 1983 "Substantive and Reflexive Elements in Modern Law." *Law & Society Review* 17:401–46.

Teubner, Günther 1984a "Autopoiesis in Law and Society: A Rejoinder to Blankenburg." *Law & Society Review* 18:291–301.

Teubner, Günther 1984b "After Legal Instrumentalism? Strategic Models of Post-regulatory Law," *International Journal of the Sociology of Law* 12:375–400.

Teulings, Ad 1982 "Interlocking Interests and Collaboration with the Enemy: Corporate Behaviour in the Second World War." *Organizaüonal Studies* 3(2):99–118.

Tilman, Rick 1983 "Social Value Theory, Corporate Power, and Political Elites: Appraisals of Lindblom's *Politics and Markets." Journal of Economic Issues* 17:115–31.

Tocqueville, Alexis de 1945 [1835] *Democracy in America.* 2 vols. Translated by Henry Reeve, revised by Francis Bowen, and edited by Phillips Bradley. New York: Knopf.

Tomasic, Roman 1984 "Business Regulation and the Administrative State." In *Business Regulation in Australia,* edited by Roman Tomasic. North Ryde, N.S.W.: CCH Australia Limited.

Tomasic, Roman, and Feeley, Malcolm M. 1982 *Neighborhood Justice: Assessment of an Emerging Idea.* New York: Longman.

Trubek, David M. 1980–81 "The Construction and Deconstruction of a Disputes-Focused Approach: An Afterword." *Law & Society Review* 15:727–47.

Turk, Austin 1976 "Law as a Weapon in Social Conflict." *Social Problems* 23:276–91.

Unger, Roberto Mangabeira 1976 *Law in Modern Society: Toward a Criticism of Social Theory.* New York: Free Press.

Useem, Michael 1983 "Business and Politics in the United States and United Kingdom: The Origins of Heightened Political Activity of Large Corporations." *Theory and Society* 12:281–308.
Vanderbilt Law Review 1984 "Self-Help: Extrajudicial Rights, Privileges and Remedies in Contemporary American Society." *Vanderbilt Law Review* 37:845–1045.
Vaughan, Diane 1982 "Toward Understanding Unlawful Organizational Behavior." *Michigan Law Review* 80:1377–1402.
Vaughan, Diane 1983 *Controlling Unlawful Organizational Behavior: Social Structure and Corporate Misconduct.* Chicago: University of Chicago Press.
Vladeck, Judith P., and Young, Margaret M. 1978 "Sex Discrimination in Higher Education: It's Not Academic." *Women's Rights Law Reporter* 4:59–78.
Watts, Jerry 1983 "The Socialist as Ostrich: The Unwillingness of the Left to Confront Modernity." *Social Research* 50:3–56.
Weber, Max 1954 *Max Weber on Law in Economy and Society.* Edited, with an introduction and [1922] annotations by Max Rheinstein. Cambridge, Mass.: Harvard University Press.
Weir, Stanley L. 1976 "Book Review of Carl Gersuny, Punishment and Redress in a Modern Factory." *Contemporary Sociology* 5:631–33.
Weiss, Janet A., and Gruber, Judith E. 1984 "Deterring Discrimination with Data." *Policy Sciences* 17:49–66.
Weyrauch, Walter O. 1969 "Governance Within Institutions." *Stanford Law Review* 22:141–53.
Weyrauch, Walter O. 1971 "The 'Basic Law' or 'Constitution' of a Small Group." *Journal of Social Issues* 27:49–63.
Whyte, William F. 1956 "The Grievance Procedure and Plant Society." In *The Grievance Process.* East Lansing: Michigan State University Labor and Industrial Relations Center.
Wilkinson, Philip J. 1981 "The Potential of Functionalism for the Sociological Analysis of Law." In *Sociological Approaches to Law,* edited by Adam Podgorecki and Christopher Whelan. New York: St. Martin's Press.
Williams, Martha, and Hall, Jay 1972 "Knowledge of the Law in Texas: Socioeconomic and Ethnic Differences." *Law & Society Review* 7:99–118.
Wirtz, W. Willard 1952 "Government by Private Groups" *Louisiana Law Review* 13:440–75.
Yale Law Journal 1954 "The American Medical Association: Power, Purpose, and Politics in Organized Medicine." *Yale Law Journal* 63:937–1022.
Yale Law Journal 1963 "Private Government on the Campus—Judicial Review of University Expulsions." *Yale Law Journal* 72:1362–1410.
Zimring, Franklin E. 1981 "Kids, Groups and Crime: Some Implications of a Well-Known Secret." *Journal of Criminal Law & Criminology* 72:867–85.

Long-Term Continuing Relations: The American Experience Regulating Dealerships and Franchises

Stewart Macaulay

Contents

I. Introduction

Problems of distribution must be analyzed in the context of long-term continuing relations. Far too often legal writers, lawyers and judges talk about franchises and dealerships as if they involved discrete transactions. Most American scholars are

This article was original published in Christian Joerges (ed) Franchising and the Law: Theoretical and Comparative Approaches in Europe and the United States, Baden-Baden, Nomos Verlagsgesellschaft, 1991, 179–237. Reprinted with permission.

Malcolm Pitman Sharp Professor, University of Wisconsin-Madison. Dr. Jacqueline Macaulay took time from her law practice to edit this article. My colleague Bill Whitford offered valuable suggestions. They greatly improved my original draft. I did not take all their good advice, however, and, as always, all errors remain mine alone.

S. Macaulay (✉)
University of Wisconsin Law School, Madison, WI, USA
e-mail: smacaula@wisc.edu

D. Campbell (ed.), *Stewart Macaulay: Selected Works*, Law and Philosophy Library 133, https://doi.org/10.1007/978-3-030-33930-2_9

aware of relational ideas about contracts, but, with a few notable exceptions, they reject these ideas by partial incorporation. These neoclassical contract theorists deal with long-term continuing relations in several unsatisfactory ways: they create exceptions and use wild cards such as waiver and the reliance doctrine or they damn judicial and legislative attempts to cope with modern economic transactions. Nonetheless, the tension between neoclassical and relational ideas will not go away. Messy reality keeps intruding on elegant theories.

This essay will survey some of the American literature and doctrine concerning distributional problems. We will also describe an ongoing struggle from the early 1930s to the present day between large business organizations and those who hold their franchises and dealerships. First, we will review the literature concerning relational ideas in contract theory, empirical work about modern contract relationships, and judicial doctrine. Second, we will consider American efforts to change the balance of power in dealership relations. Here we will look at the elaborate federal and state regulation of dealer-manufacturer interaction. Then we will present an account of the struggle between franchisors and franchisees before courts, legislatures and administrative agencies on both the federal and state level. Finally, we will offer some conclusions. Here we will bring together the theoretical literature and the franchise story.

II. A Review of the Theoretical and Empirical Literature

Little of the significant theoretical literature has focused on franchises and dealerships. Nonetheless, we will find no difficulty in applying ideas about private government and long-term continuing relations to distribution arrangements. We begin with private government and then turn to relational theories about contract.

1. A Private Government Perspective and Relational Contract

Over the past thirty years, legal scholars have written much about relational theories and perspectives. American ideology, culture and law focuses on individuals. Often we talk and write as if we believed people act alone or interact with others apart from the context of social relations. When, however, we add long-term relationships, social fields and private governments, our theories and laws become more complex but more accurate. In this section, we will consider aspects of an empirical picture of human action and then turn to the implications for law and legal systems.

We begin with a simple but often overlooked empirical observation: human transactions range from the discrete to the highly relational, and interaction toward one end of the range will differ from that at the other end. For example, suppose a motorist on a long trip drives into a service station located near a major highway and far from a city. The attendant points out that the motorist's tires are dangerously defective, and the motorist recognizes that he can continue safely only by buying new tires. The station attendant understands that the motorist is far from home and unlikely to return to the station. The motorist knows that he will not patronize the station again. The sale of new tires is a discrete transaction.[1]

Suppose, however, another motorist discovers that she needs new tires and she drives to a service station near her home that she regularly patronizes. The dealer values his regular customers, and the motorist recognizes that she may want to claim favors in the future, such as the dealer's help in starting a stalled automobile on a cold morning. The sale of tires is but one of many actual and potential transactions which form a larger relationship.

We can suspect that these two transactions will differ. Of course, the owner and attendants at the freeway service station might believe that they should treat travelers in distress with great compassion. Their consciences and guilt might sanction exploiting the situation. They might assume that a few well-treated travelers would find ways to reward them. Nonetheless, our motorist is vulnerable because he has very limited power to exit without buying tires from this service station. Moreover, the station attendant does not expect that the traveler will ever return, and so the traveler's potential future business provides little incentive affecting this sale of tires. In a more typical case, we expect competition to regulate the transaction. If there were other service stations and tire stores near the one our traveler visited, and if the traveler knew of them and could get to them, market incentives should affect the tire purchase transaction.

The other motorist shopping for tires at her local station faces a different situation. The tire transaction is but part of a stream of transactions extending from the past to the present and possibly into the future. A major sanction is the threat of exit. The motorist always could take her business elsewhere. However, she is unlikely to do this without provocation. She would have to search for another service station as good as her present one. Moreover, she would then have to establish a similar relationship at her new station. If she were to violate the norms of the present relationship, the service station might cease treating her as a special regular customer entitled to advice and favors. Even if market forces would push the service station to continue special treatment despite her violation of the norms of the relationship, she might not feel entitled to ask for treatment above and beyond the call of duty.

Ian Macneil has produced an impressive body of work about relational theory.[2] He notes that bargains almost always take place in a rich context that colors the

---

[1]Even this example may include relational elements. The driver could hold a credit card, and the credit card company may exert influence on the practices of businesses that accept the card. The service station could be a franchised dealership of a major oil company, and the franchisor could exert some influence on the practices of its dealers. Pure discrete transactions in modem society are hard to imagine.

[2]See, e.g., I. R. Macneil, The New Social Contract (New Haven: 1980); Macneil, Relational Contract What We Do and Do Not Know, 1985 Wisconsin Law Review 483; Macneil, Values in Contract: Internal and External, 78 Northwestern University Law Review 340 (1983); Macneil, Contracts: Adjustment of Long-Term Economic Relations Under Classical, Neo-Classical, and Relational Contract Law, 72 Northwestern University Law Review 854 (1978); Macneil, The Many Futures of Contracts, 47 Southern California Law Review 691 (1974).

parties' expectations. He points out that relationships are based on trust and the assumption of mutual advantage over the long-term. Culture and experience in relationships develop expectations which may crystallize into norms.

Relationships involve overarching obligations of good faith, solidarity, role integrity, and mutuality. Solidarity demands that the parties preserve the unique and continuing relationship within which transactions take place. They must maintain some measure of role integrity: highly complex roles govern a transaction, and we assume that others will stay in role. A partner cannot suddenly become a self-interested hard bargainer. There also must be mutuality: the parties must divide the exchange surplus properly so that each gains appropriate but not necessarily equal returns.[3]

Recognizing that much human interaction takes place in a rich and complex relational context affects theories about law and functioning legal systems. For example, writing about legal regulation often assumes that only two entities are involved: the state confronts an individual with a command. The individual then complies because of his conscience, his fear of sanctions or both. However, the state is composed of people working in organizations who are subject to political influence if not control. Furthermore, the targets of regulation usually are not isolated individuals but rather people involved in multiple and overlapping groups. Moore drew our attention to what she called "semi-autonomous social fields".[4] Any group of people who regularly interact tend to adopt rules, interpret them in light of specific situations, and sanction their violation. If the group has some permanence, and if the actors within it value participation, we have a semi-autonomous social field.

Social fields can blunt enforcement of laws and transform their practical meaning. Moore notes "new laws are thrust upon going social arrangements in which there are complexes of binding obligations already in existence. Legislation is often passed with the intention of altering the going social arrangements in specified ways. The social arrangements are often effectively stronger than the new laws".[5]

Macaulay began with Moore's idea and developed what he called a "private government perspective".[6] We can observe many more or less continuing

---

[3]Kaufmann and Stem, Relational Exchange Norms, Perceptions of Unfairness, and Retained Hostility in Commercial litigation, 32 Journal of Conflict Resolution 534 (1988), empirically tested part of Macneil's theory. They studied parties to contract litigation in The United States District Court for the Northern District of Illinois. They found support for Macneil's norms of solidarity and role integrity. They say "[t]entatively, findings indicate the character of an exchange relationship prior to a major dispute erupting between exchange partners, can be linked to the feelings they retain after their dispute has been terminated. Adherence to the norms of the relationship may dampen retained hostility; betrayal of those norms may heighten it. The existence of a relational (as opposed to a discrete) exchange may, in the absence of a sense of willful betrayal, lead to more tolerance of conflict behavior attributed to circumstances beyond the parties' control". Id. at 549.

[4]S. F. Moore, Law as Process: An Anthropological Approach (London: 1978).

[5]Moore, ibid, at 78.

[6]Macaulay, Private Government, in: L. Lipson & S. Wheeler (eds.), Law and Social Science, 445-518 (New York: 1986).

relationships in society which fashion rules, allocate resources, and sanction deviance.[7] We can arrange these relationships in terms of structure and formality of processes. There are customary rules and sanctions that govern actions in places: there is a private law (which we often call custom or social norms) regulating behavior in an elevator or in an airport. Family relationships, friendships, and business relationships also rest on predictable norms and private sanctions. Residential relationships often rest on a more structured private government. Private organizations increasingly take over what most of us think of as public functions. Apartment dwellers', condominium owners', and neighborhood residents' associations may publish formal rules and provide for mediation or arbitration of disputes. Some neighborhood associations, many shopping centers, and many large business corporations run their own private police forces and dispute resolution arrangements.[8] Private governments may organize activity which public government declares illegal. Industry cartels are illegal in the United States, but, nonetheless, they exist. They regulate, or suppress, patterns of competition. Apparently, the illegal drug industry is organized, patterned, and operates as a very strong private government. There are few breaches of contract in this industry. Macaulay advocates a private government perspective. On one hand, thought about law must deal with functioning legal systems, and these systems exist in a world of legal pluralism. Public government is both aided and hindered by social fields and private legal structures. On the other hand, Macaulay stresses that distinctions between public and private break down when we examine functioning legal systems. Public governmental officials may have to strike bargains with private governments in order to provide some measure of effective regulation. Regulators and the targets of regulation may share a culture and speak the same language. Those who work for governmental regulatory agencies may plan for a future where they will work for those they now regulate. Moreover, the process of law making involves complex interactions between judges and legislators and representatives of private interests.

Relational theories and stories of legal pluralism may paint a picture of neat self-regulating social systems and harmony. Often these social fields and private governments do operate to satisfy most of those affected by them. Those who are disaffected leave and find satisfying roles in other groups. However, relationships break down, and some of those involved suffer serious injury. Exit, or being forced out, may impose high costs. Often those aggrieved seek help from the courts, asserting contract or related theories to justify redress.

Macneil argues that classic and neoclassic contract law largely assume a world of discrete transactions. As a result, our legal tradition responds poorly to disruptions of long-term continuing relationships. For example, traditional contract law focuses on

---

[7]See, e.g., Asbury, Social Control in a Local Community: The Role of the Apartment Superintendent, 25 Journal of Research in Crime and Delinquency 411 (1988); Leblebici/Salancik, Stability in Interorganizational Exchanges: Rulemaking Processes of the Chicago Board of Trade, 27 Administrative Science Quarterly 227 (1982).

[8]Private police often adopt the symbols — uniforms, badges, and equipment — of public police, and private arbitration systems increasingly look more and more as do public courts.

a magic moment of formation. Until a contract is formed, a party is free to back out without regard to the other's expectations and reliance. There is no duty of good faith in negotiations. Negotiating a contract involves bringing the future to the present. Risks then are allocated and the entire transaction is planned once and for all. As a result, disputes during the life of a transaction are to be resolved by returning to the planning at the outset, largely ignoring all that has taken place thereafter. Moreover, the terms "contract" and "agreement" can slip subtly from referring to the reasonable expectations of the parties to only the formal text of the document that they signed. Neoclassical contract law accepts this general picture but imposes exceptions designed to bring contract law closer to modem business practices. Unfortunately, it is not clear when the general body of law applies and when the exceptions come into play.

Macneil stresses that relational transactions usually do not involve a magic moment at which all the planning is final. "[R]elations are characterized by extensive post-commencement planning, the fundamental source of which is the ongoing operation of the relations themselves".[9] The parties often write extremely general and vague contract provisions and continue their planning and adjustments throughout the life of the transaction. Even when the parties to a relational contract sign a precise lawyer-drafted document, they may assume that it is just a formality or that its provisions are subject to many tacit understandings and will be modified as circumstances change. As Gordon says, in relational contracts:

> parties treat their contracts more like marriages than like one-night stands. Obligations grow out of the commitment that they have made to one another, and the conventions that the trading community establishes for such commitments; they are not frozen at the initial moment of commitment, but change as circumstances change; the object of contracting is not primarily to allocate risks, but to signify a commitment to cooperate. In bad times parties are expected to lend one another mutual support, rather than standing on their rights; each will treat the others insistence on literal performance as willful obstructionism; if unexpected contingencies occur resulting in severe losses, the parties are to search for equitable ways of dividing the losses; and the sanction for egregiously bad behavior, is always, of course, refusal to deal again.[10]

What does all this mean for the law of contracts? Neoclassical contract law may serve discrete transactions reasonably well,[11] but writing about relational

---

[9]Macneil, The Many Futures of Contracts, 47 Southern California Law Review 691, 774 (1974).

[10]Gordon, Macaulay, Macneil, and the Discovery of Solidarity and Power in Contract Law, 1985 Wisconsin Law Review 565, 569.

[11]Campbell criticizes Macneil for not going far enough in rejecting neoclassical views: "What emerges from this radically relational view is, or should be, the theoretical rejection of the basic *explanatory* adequacy of the neoclassical economic model articulated in the classical law. When contracting is viewed as being constituted of the relations which facilitate it, the assumption of the independent, utility maximising individual must be replaced by that of a cooperative relation. However, Macneil does not press his argument this far". Campbell, The Social Theory of Relational Contract Macneil as the Modern Proudhon, 18 International Journal of the Sociology of Law 75, 81 (1990). He continues, "Macneil actually manages to find a central place for discrete exchange in the

transactions falls short of creating a body of law better suited for their governance. For example, Whitford tells us,

> Macneil believes the legal system needs to take radically different approaches to relational contracts than it traditionally has. In dealing with disputes, he favors greater reliance on procedures oriented toward mediation and less emphasis on adversary processes looking toward adjudication. In regulating contracts, he counsels greater reliance on proactive administrative agencies that can take account of the many third-party interests at stake and less reliance on courts able to apply regulatory rules only when a disadvantaged party initiates a court procedure.[12]

Macneil points to the norms implicit in transactions and says that courts could use them to develop a modern contract law.[13] In some relationships there are elements of coercion and dependence; in others, trust, cooperation, reciprocity and role integrity are essential. But Macneil counsels that the legal system should proceed cautiously. While lawmakers could recognize relational norms, they also must consider the consequences of imposing legal duties on parties. This is not a neutral act. People may resent being coerced to do what they recognize they ought to do. The more powerful may seek to offset or evade the legal norm in order to preserve more control over the relationship. This behavior itself may undermine trust and reciprocity.[14]

My colleague William Whitford has offered several propositions about relational contracts which could be, but have not been, tested empirically.[15] They bring together Macneil's perspectives with Whitford's insights about how these perspectives might affect legal action. Three of these propositions suggest difficulties in fashioning contract law based on relational theories. Whitford says:

- As contracts become more relational, the parties will comply less frequently with formalities (including the parol evidence rule). Hence, a strict enforcement strategy with respect to formalities is more likely to raise issues about protection of reasonable reliance with respect to relational than discrete contracts.
- As contracts become more relational, it becomes more difficult for courts to apply sensibly doctrine that requires courts to make qualitative judgments about a course of conduct. Courts lack the capacity to understand complex relations between all the affected parties.
- As contracts become more relational, there is an increasing tendency of the parties to value nonmaterial aspects of the relation (continuation of the relation,

---

social theory of relational contract ... By virtue of his liberal leanings, Macneil substantially undercuts his attack on neo-classicalism and limits its impact". Ibid, at 83.

[12]Whitford, Ian Macneil's Contribution to Contracts Scholarship, 1985 Wisconsin Law Review 545, 551.

[13]See Feinman, The Significance of Contract Theory, 58 University of Cincinnati Law Review 1283, 1299-1304 (1990).

[14]For a discussion of an exchange relationship model of contract cognate with Macneil's relational theories, see Lightsy, A Critique of the Promissory Model of Contract, 26 William & Mary Law Review 45 (1984).

[15]Whitford, Unpublished Memorandum.

maintenance of harmony and respect, etc.). Courts have no effective way to protect these expectations, and hence they tend to over commodify the relation — that is, they try to compensate in money for that which is really not commensurable this way.

Scott also urges caution. He uses the techniques of decision analysis and game theory to clarify the relationship between the risk distribution and adjustment functions of long-term contracts. He suggests that legal rules could function to ameliorate tensions in efforts to reallocate risks.[16] He accepts much of the picture of relational norms and sanctions that we have drawn up to here, explaining cooperative behavior in terms of decision analysis. He points out that legal enforcement of contracts becomes important "whenever the shadow of the future proved insufficient to prevent evasive behavior".[17]

Scott argues that categorical binary contract rules may complement the more flexible extralegal mechanisms that regulate adjustment of ongoing relationships. Legally imposed adjustments may create perverse incentives that undermine the stability of the cooperate equilibrium of contracting parties.[18] When the stakes are large, the chance that a court may rework the distribution of risk in a contract may be enough to offset possible future rewards for cooperative behavior. Even the threat of going to court to seek relief may affect how the parties readjust matters. Scott concedes that we do not know how judicial activity will affect decisions about cooperation and readjustment. He concludes:

> [T]he relational context is a complex environment of many regulatory systems, including individualized and patterned responses, legal and social norms, and ex ante and ex post bargains. The challenge for contract law is to construct a legal apparatus that complements these forces. As a first step, we must abandon the assumptions of legal centrism and acknowledge our incomplete understanding of contractual relationships and of the linkages between legal rules and social norms.[19]

Even when long-term relationships are functioning, they may reflect marked inequality of power.[20] While the less powerful could exit, often they would prefer to continue the relationship with a change in its power configuration. Their interest groups can bring test cases, seeking rules which will affect functioning relationships, and they can lobby for statutes granting their members rights. American state and

---

[16]Scott, Conflict and Cooperation in Long-Term Contracts, 75 California Law Review 2005 (1987). John Kidwell makes a point similar to Scott's; Kidwell asks whether neoclassical contract law may best support relational exchanges. See Kidwell, A Caveat, 1985 Wisconsin Law Review 615.

[17]Scott, ibid, at 2044.

[18]Ibid, at 2051.

[19]Ibid, at 2053-4.

[20]Joerges criticizes Macneil for neglecting this aspect of relational transactions. See Joerges, Relational Contract Theory in a Comparative Perspective: Tensions Between Contract and Antitrust Principles in the Assessment of Contract Relations Between Automobile Manufacturers and Their Dealers in Germany, 1985 Wisconsin Law Review 581.

federal statute books are filled with provisions reflecting this process. As we shall see, many of these statutes deal with franchise and distribution relationships.

However, the powerful seldom are silent when the weaker appeal to the legal system for modifications of the balance of power. Sometimes the powerful can block passage of a reform statute. When the powerful cannot defeat such proposals, they will work to modify the terms of the legislation so that the new rights burden them as little as possible. At times, the powerful can so influence the definition of rights and remedies that a statute is largely symbolic. If a reform statute has real teeth, the powerful challenge its constitutionality or seek to have courts construe it as narrowly as possible.

The beneficiaries of reform, in most instances, do not assert their new rights directly. Usually we find them bargaining in the shadow of the law and using their rights as bargaining entitlements. For example, Moore[21] points out that actors within social fields often attempt to use law as a resource with which to control their environment. Legal regulation designed to bring about what a legislator thought desirable may be traded for something the beneficiaries want more. Moore's example involves workers, most of them women, in the better dress industry in New York City. The law and union collective bargaining agreements purport to regulate their hours and working conditions. However, demand in this industry is seasonal. Sometimes there is much work which must be done by a deadline; sometimes there is relatively little to do. When work must be done on time, employees do the job and work overtime and skip breaks. This means their employer has violated laws and union contract provisions about the hours and conditions of work. However, now the employer owes the employees something. For example, an employee's friend will register the worker present at work — punching in on a time clock — when there is little to do. Actually she has taken the day off. The employer knows this but accepts it as part of the system.

Gottlieb responds to legal pluralism and this common use of claims in bargaining by advocating a relational perspective based on patterns established in international affairs.[22] He views what he calls "the formal system", "the mediating systems", and "the regime of relational orders" as sources of juridical obligations. A mediating system consists of the techniques used to reconcile the informal system with the requirements of the formal system of rules and institutions. A regime is composed of the rules, procedures, precedents, and practices of particular relationships. It is a combination of the formal, informal and mediating systems.

Gottlieb observes that relationalism does not outline an ideal form of legal relations but rather a necessary one. Relational approaches force us to confront difficult problems, particularly insofar as we recognize legal pluralism: Conflicts may occur between the juridical systems of different relational orders and the State. The rights and interests of third parties may be adversely affected by a course of

[21]Moore, op. cit. (supra note 5).

[22]Gottlieb, Relationism: Legal Theory for a Relational Society, 50 University of Chicago Law Review 567 (1983).

dealing between parties to an ongoing relationship. Moreover, the conduct of the parties may cease to bear any relevance to the underlying juridical order. The resolution of these conflicts poses serious problems which are difficult to solve without high costs. Nonetheless, Gottlieb concludes, any legal theory that emphasizes courts and legally enforceable remedies, and which focuses mainly on individuals, the State, regulation, and discrete transactions in markets, is based on a woefully inadequate model of modern societies.

2. *Empirical Work on Long-Term Continuing Relations: The Wisconsin Research Program*

Macaulay[23] wrote about business practices related to the problems dealt with by contract law in 1963. He found that business contracting typically does not involve complete planning for performance and nonperformance. As Rogowski notes, Macaulay's explanations were largely cultural.[24] Relational norms and sanctions define obligations with needed flexibility as well as offering adequate incentives to perform or negotiate acceptable settlements. Many business people see the costs of planning for trouble as unnecessary. They dislike formal contracts and litigation. Business people also desire flexibility to deal with the future. Lawyers often draft a contract tailored for a transaction or written as standardized planning. Business people, however, often ignore these documents and as a transaction progresses it creates expectations. Any particular transaction may be but part of a larger relationship. As a result, there is often a tension between the real and the paper deal.

Moreover, usually the legal system involves high costs, considering what it offers. Contract law's remedies as delivered through the functioning American legal system offer little to all but a small subset of litigants. Contract law in action is a defective product, promising far more than it can deliver.

In 1985, Macaulay reviewed his earlier article from the perspective of twenty years of experience.[25] He observed that both journalism and appellate reports show that in the 1970s and 1980s there have been many more major contracts cases than his 1963 article suggested that we should expect. He thought that the culture of cooperation he found twenty years early had been strained by major economic changes. Relational sanctions still played a significant role, but economic change had exposed their limits. Nonetheless, these demands on applied contract law have shown its strengths and weaknesses, much as described in the 1963 article. For

---

[23]Macaulay, Non-Contractual Relations and Business: A Preliminary Study, 28 American Sociological Review 55-69 (1963).

[24]Rogowski, West German Business Litigation: Some Preliminary Observations and Research Proposals, paper delivered at the 1989 Annual Meeting of the Law and Society Association, June, 1989.

[25]Macaulay, An Empirical View of Contract, 1985 Wisconsin Law Review 465-482.

example, Pennzoil sued Texaco for interfering with the performance of a contract under which Pennzoil was to buy control of Getty Oil.[26] The parties disputed whether Getty and Pennzoil had gone far enough to create a contract before Texaco offered a higher bid for Getty. After full-scale legal warfare, Pennzoil won a multimillion dollar verdict, defended it on appeal, and collected a judgment. Newspapers, television, and the business press endlessly discussed the case. Most of the comment in the business press and the law reviews was highly critical. Scholars concluded that Pennzoil had won a questionable remedy in light of its actual damages at an extraordinarily high cost to the two companies and to third parties affected by the litigation.[27]

The highly publicized Westinghouse cases were more typical of modem contract litigation. Westinghouse promised to supply uranium oxide at a fixed price so it could sell nuclear power plants to electric utilities. Producers of uranium formed a cartel, and, as a result, the world market price soared. Westinghouse unexpectedly faced extremely burdensome obligations: performing the contracts could have destroyed Westinghouse. It announced that it would not honor its many uranium oxide contracts, asserting that it was excused by the doctrine of commercial impracticability. Westinghouse's customers sued. Ultimately, the entire litigation proved to be an expensive exercise in coercive mediation, orchestrated by a federal trial judge, leading to a multiparty settlement. The judge used the threat of an adverse judgment as an incentive for settlement. Contract litigation here served as an alternative to bankruptcy. However, contract doctrine played a marginal role in this drama. The litigation provided a theater where the drama could be played out.

In 1989, Professors Galanter, Macaulay, Palay and Rogers of the University of Wisconsin Law School began the Wisconsin Business Disputes Group Project.[28] The project was prompted by several observations: there has been a sharp increase in all business disputing over the past two decades.[29] Firms in cooperative relations have contracts (or contract-related) disputes with each other. The number of such cases filed in the federal courts has increased; the use of alternative dispute resolution also has risen rapidly. Firms in competitive relations increasingly sue for patent, copyright and trademark violations as well as various unfair business practices.

Corporate legal practice also has changed substantially over the same period. Large corporations spend more money on legal services, and many have brought

---

[26]See *Texaco, Inc.* v. *Pennzoil, Co.*, 729 S.W.2d 768 (Texas Ct. Ap. 1987).

[27]See Epstein, The Pirates of Pennzoil: A Comic Opera Made Possible by a Grant from the Texaco Corporation, 32 The [University of Chicago] Law School Record 3 (Fall 1986); Weintraub, The Ten Billion Dollar Jury's Standards for Determining Intention to Contract: *Pennzoil* v. *Texaco*, 9 Review of Litigation 371 (1990).

[28]This is a large long-term research project which has been underway for a little over two years; all statements here reflect planning and initial work rather than firm conclusions. See Galanter, Macaulay, Palay and Rogers, The Transformation of American Business Disputing: A Sketch of the Wisconsin Project, Institute for Legal Studies Dispute Processing Research Program Working Paper DPRP 10-6 (March 1991).

[29]This supports Macaulay's 1985 observations which were based on appellate opinions.

legal functions inside their businesses. The size of law firms serving corporate clients also has increased rapidly. Law firms have become national and international organizations with many branch offices. Litigation has become a greater part of large elite corporate law firm practice.

There are several possible explanations for these changes. Macaulay's 1963 article could have been wrong or misleading as to the use of the contract legal system by business. It was essentially an attitude study and established no hard empirical baseline. It does not tell us, for example, even roughly what proportion of disputes were litigated. There are more transactions today than in 1963, and it is possible that the ratios of disputes to transactions and disputes to litigation are exactly the same today as then. Alternatively, there may have been a major change in the rate of disputes and litigation caused by drastic changes in national and world economic conditions. We do not have data that allows us to choose between these explanations. We do have some suggestive correlations.

What the Business Disputes Group sees as the sharp post-1970 increase in business use of law coincides with a period of fundamental change in the environment and strategy of American business firms. Prominent environmental changes include[30]: the rapid internationalization of American product and capital markets; declining rates of growth, profitability, and productivity; a qualitative increase in the importance of the financial sector in the economy and the greater availability of debt in corporate financing; changes in the style and extent of government regulation (from the introduction of "new" generic regulations of firm behavior such as OSHA and employment discrimination to movements to deregulate such sectors as transportation, communication, banking and professional services); and increased instability in the labor market.

Partly in response to these changes, and partly facilitated by them, there are new firm strategies. They include: increasingly specialized products tailored to niche markets; the tighter integration of design, engineering, marketing, and production facilities within and across firms; general efforts to internalize scarcity and externalize risk in an increasingly competitive and uncertain environment, including downsizing and outsourcing of production tasks to affiliates and subcontractors, heavier reliance on contingent workers, and increased use of joint ventures and other mechanisms to spread risk among competitors; firm-led industrial restructuring ("merger mania"); and increased use of financial instruments and opportunities as a supplement to or substitute production.

These factors may affect business disputing and resort to litigation in many ways. Business people are more accountable to third parties. They are not as free to look to the long-run and work out solutions that benefit all concerned. For example, mergers have created larger bureaucracies and less freedom to ignore standard procedures within organizations. The rise of regulation requires business people to refer more things to lawyers to avoid major problems.

[30]This section relies heavily on material written by my colleague on the Business Disputes Project, Professor Joel Rogers.

Important forms of wealth more and more involve intellectual property. It is hard to protect exclusive rights without careful and formal procedures. The economic incentives are to come as close to violating intellectual property rights as possible without crossing the line (e.g., the original IBM-PC was matched by clone machines which could process software written for the PC). Parties frequently debate whether the line has been crossed. Moreover, when a firm buys the product of intellectual property, such as computer software, often the buyer may not receive the benefits it expected. Parties often debate whether the buyer's expectations were justified. Sellers complain that buyers have unreasonable expectations about what computers can do. Buyers think sellers promise more than they know how to deliver. This may lead to disputes involving amounts that make negotiated solutions difficult to achieve.

Many factors have contributed to some erosion of structures of continuing relations and their sanctions. Competition increases firms' attention to short run "bottom-line" concerns. Many executives cannot wait for long-run rewards for cooperative behavior. Product specialization increases the number of disputes because of the lack of readily available substitutes and because the parties do not deal repeatedly. Multiparty transactions make it harder to gain agreement from everyone for readjustments and settlements. Spatial and cultural dispersion of the parties may undercut long-term relationships. Parties may assume they agree and discover that their words taken in context have very different meanings. As transactions get bigger, stakes get higher. The amounts in question may tempt parties to invest in litigation. Rapid economic change increases instability, and thus increases the temptations and opportunities for defection from present commitments.

Legal system variables also may affect litigation rates. Legal costs have increased sufficiently to catch the attention of business people. Many have responded by creating or expanding the role of house counsel. Lawyers, because of their roles and training, tend to call for formality in planning. They also represent the regulatory state within the corporation, and they press business people to attend to regulation that they otherwise might have ignored or evaded. Business lawyers also may try to prove their worth by offering cutting-edge legal theories in response to disputes. Often the theories are creative but because their strength only can be tested by litigation, these theories may not prompt settlements.

Drastic economic changes have caused large losses, and these losses have prompted litigation. Most simply, unlike in the late 1950s and early 1960s, litigation began to be seen in the 1970s as a paying proposition. Some firms broke contracts and ignored conventional understandings when large sums were at stake. Some aggrieved firms responded by going to court. These refusals to honor commitments were well publicized, and this may have further undercut traditional assumptions and trust. Other firms tried to hold buyers to strict performance of contracts despite established customs calling for performance to be excused or stretched out over a long time. Formal written contracts often contain only absolute promises without excuses for changed economic conditions. Other contracts contain traditional but vague *force majeure* clauses. Customary responses to drastic economic changes did not fit within older legal ideas of impossibility or frustration. These customs also may have involved excusing performance when reasonable amounts were at issue; it was not clear that they required excuse when there were huge gains or losses to be had from performance or excuse.

Finally, we must distinguish filing law suits from litigating cases to a final conclusion. Often filing a complaint or pretrial motions is but a way to facilitate or coerce settlement. These steps may focus the issues and clarify facts and bargaining power. Judges attempt to prompt settlement in various ways before they try a case. Pressures from the threat of reversals on appeal and orders for new trial may prompt settlement even after trial has begun or a verdict rendered. Often the parties do not want to invest what would be necessary to start over again. At present, the existence and scope of the business disputes problem is still to be studied. Although the Wisconsin Business Disputes Project is still in its early stages, it is clear that disputes concerning franchises and dealerships are an important part of American federal and state courts dockets. These disputes also may be an important part of the business of federal and state administrative agencies, but the nature of administrative records means that this will be much harder to establish.

III. American Law and Relational Disputes in the Area of Distribution of Goods and Services

Manufacturers can buy the services of dealers and distributors to get their product to consumers. When everything works well, the interests of a manufacturer and a dealer coincide. The dealer sells many products to the public, and both manufacturer and dealer profit. However, friction in the relationship is common. For example, unforeseen events can cause losses which burden manufacturer, dealer or both. Manufacturers and dealers may disagree about how these losses should be allocated. Manufacturers may want more sales effort and investment than dealers offer. Manufacturers may want many dealers competing while dealers may want protected sales territories. Disputes between manufacturers and their distributors or dealers often enter the American legal system. Often, too, these disputes raise the tension between views of business as resting on discrete contracts versus views of long-term continuing relations. Just as often, these disputes raise the tension between reasonable expectations and justifiable reliance on one side and power and authority on the other.

In this section of the report on American developments, we will look first at strains in the way judges apply the Uniform Commercial Code[31] to problems of

[31]Article II of the Uniform Commercial Code was passed by all but one of the American state legislatures between the 1950s and 1970s. Its provisions apply to "transactions in goods". Courts have debated whether a distributorship is a transaction in goods because the relationship involves services and trademarks as well. American state appellate courts seek uniformity in construing the U.C.C., but appellate courts in each state are free to give their own reading to the Code's provisions.

distribution. Then we will turn to a sketch of franchise regulation found at both federal and state levels.

1. Distribution, the Uniform Commercial Code, and Relational and Neoclassical Approaches to Contract

Macneil recognizes that the existing body of contract law contains doctrines which could serve relational purposes. Indeed, he calls the eclectic collection of contract rules which rest on both discrete transaction and relational assumptions, "neoclassical contract". Sometimes our courts recognize that businesses often work together almost as partners over the long term. Sometimes, however, they write as if they assumed the typical business transaction was a swap between strangers who do not expect to meet again. Judicial reaction to "price protection" in asphalt distribution offers an example of neoclassical contract law.

The oil producing nations' cartel (OPEC) raised oil prices in the early 1970s. The Nixon Administration responded by imposing regulation and price controls on petroleum products. However, asphalt was left unregulated, and the major oil companies suddenly raised their prices sharply. Asphalt distributors had bid on paving jobs, using the original prices as the basis for their price calculations. When they were awarded the paving jobs after the oil companies' price increases, the distributors faced obligations to perform at substantial losses.

Documents and practice conflicted. The written distribution contracts were explicit. Buried in the pages of clauses were provisions allowing the oil companies to raise prices at any time before a distributor placed an order. However, before OPEC's actions, oil companies would "price protect" distributors — that is, a distributor awarded a contract could order asphalt at the price in effect at the time it made its bid rather than at the higher price in effect when it received the award. The oil companies ignored the pricing clause in the standardized written contract. Were the major oil companies bound by this customary practice or could they assert their contract clauses which did not recognize it?

Nanakuli v. *Shell Oil*[32] represents one court's answer. We can tell a simplified story about the case: Shell wanted to compete with Standard of California in supplying asphalt to the Hawaiian market. It developed Nanakuli Paving Co. as its Hawaiian distributor. Nanakuli used Shell's trademarks and colors, and the line between the two corporations was blurred in practice. Shell's Hawaiian representative influenced Nanakuli's business decisions, and he was aware of Nanakuli's outstanding bids.

The Shell-Nanakuli printed form distribution contract gave Shell the right to increase prices until Nanakuli placed an order for a specific quantity. However, Shell's Hawaiian representative knew of the price protection practice in the local

[32]664 R2d 772 (9th Cir. 1981).

road paving trade. All suppliers followed the practice. On the only two prior occasions when Shell had raised prices between Nanakuli's bid and an award, Shell had price protected Nanakuli's orders.

Nanakuli bid on a state road paving job, Shell greatly increased the price for asphalt, and then the State of Hawaii awarded Nanakuli the contract. Shell refused to price protect and demanded the new higher price. Shell's asphalt sales had been transferred to a new division, and the old senior managers had retired. The new managers knew nothing of the practices in the field, but they did not ask those who did know.

Nanakuli sued Shell for its failure to price protect. The trial court found for Shell, saying that the parol evidence rule barred evidence which would contradict the Shell-Nanakuli written contract. The appellate court reversed this decision, finding that price protection did not contradict the price term of the written contract. It said that when printed stock forms were used, "if the trade regards an express term and a trade usage as consistent because the usage is not a complete contradiction but only an occasional but definite exception to a written term, the courts should interpret the contract according to the usage". A usage may be used to qualify the agreement, which means to cut down the express terms although not to negate them entirely. Moreover, Shell did not set its new price in good faith. Unlike its competitors, Shell did not give notice before it raised prices, and its new higher prices went into effect immediately.

The case exemplifies the common gap between the real expectations of the parties and the written document drafted by corporate lawyers and imposed on the transaction by the dominant party. Here, the court focused on the actual expectations created by practice during the life of the long-term relationship. By its application of a good faith standard, the court denied Shell the power to control the relationship entirely for its benefit. In short, the court policed the private government which Shell's lawyers had created. It honored the expectations created by the long-term business relationship.[33]

But there was a counterrevolution: Other courts rejected *Nanakuli,* using a narrow interpretation of the U.C.C.'s statute of frauds writing requirements. *W.H. Barber Co.* v. *McNamara-Vivant Contracting Co., Inc.*[34] involved a suit by a contractor-against a supplier of asphalt which had failed to price protect on work not completed in 1973 and carried over into 1974. The jury found that the supplier's representatives orally had agreed to keep the old price in effect. The trial judge then held that the statute of frauds barred the contractor's claim. There was no writing adequate to show the *quantities* of asphalt to be supplied. The court read the U.C.C. as demanding this term be reduced to writing.

[33]See Hadfield, Problematic Relations: Franchising and the Law of Incomplete Contracts, 42 Stanford Law Review 927 (1990), advocating such an approach.

[34]293 N.W.2d 351 (Minn. 1979).

If a proper reading of the statute demanded that courts apply the writing requirement (and this is debatable[35]), courts could have turned to widely recognized exceptions. Many courts have protected reliance on oral statements in situations where they found enforcing the statute of frauds unjust. However, in *Lige Dickson Co.* v. *Union Oil of California*,[36] the Supreme Court of Washington rejected this approach and came to the same conclusion as the *W.H. Barber* case on similar facts. At the trial, a Union Oil official conceded "there was an unwritten custom in the Tacoma area, well known and acted upon by suppliers and users, that any increase in the price of liquid asphalt would not be applicable to ... [outstanding bids]". Nonetheless, the court said that while it appreciated the contractor's dilemma, "we cannot help but foresee increased litigation and confusion as being the necessary result of the eroding of the U.C.C. if promissory estoppel is held to override [the statute's writing requirements]".

These courts, then, are ready to ignore relational considerations in order to facilitate bureaucratic functioning through standardization. In essence, these opinions grant power to corporate lawyers to control relationships through contract drafting. While actual practice may create or reinforce norms honoring a relationship, it is hard for the home office to control agents in the field or even know what they have done. Large organizations cut costs when they standardize transactions; courts support this when they treat the charters for these private governments as if they were the frozen expectations of the parties. The courts appeal to ideology for comfort, talking about distributors' obligations to protect themselves by reading standard form contracts and assuming that expectations to the contrary will not control. Such an approach may run counter to business practice, but it does serve to justify empowering corporate lawyers. Perhaps the *W.H. Barber* and the *Lige Dickson* courts reached the best result. But they did decide to protect authority at the price of defeating reasonable expectations, with little explanation of why they made this choice.

---

[35]Section 2-201 of the Uniform Commercial Code states: "the contract is not enforceable under this paragraph *beyond the quantity* of goods shown in such writing [Emphasis added]". A court could read this as saying that if, and only if, a quantity is stated in writing, then a party cannot claim more than this amount. Most courts have read the provision as requiring a quantity to be stated in writing in order for a contract to be legally enforceable. In other words, if no quantity is stated, the contract is to be read as calling for 0 goods. Any amount, then, is an amount "beyond" 0. For a strong criticism of the common judicial reading of Section 2-201, see Bruckel, The Weed and the Web: Section 2-201's Corruption of the U.C.C.'s Substantive Provisions — The Quantity Problem, 1981 University of Illinois Law Review 911. But see Gibson, Promissory Estoppel, Article 2 of the U.C.C., and the Restatement (Third) of Contracts, 73 Iowa Law Review 659 (1988).

[36]96 Wash.2d 291, 635 P.2d 103 (1981).

2. *Protecting Distributors and Dealers Through Legislation*

For over fifty years, franchisors and franchisees have struggled to pass or defeat proposed legislation which would limit the control of franchisors over franchisees. Various dealers' associations took the lead over the years. Automobile dealers were the first and the most successful. Retail gasoline dealers came next, and while they enjoyed some success, their victories were not as impressive as those of the automobile dealers. More recently, farm implement and heavy equipment dealers, beer and wine distributors, and office equipment dealers have sought legislation and have had some success. About a third of the states have general franchise protection laws, offering some protection to all dealers and distributors. We will consider motor vehicle dealer, retail gasoline dealer and general franchise statutes in turn.[37]

a) Automobile Dealers

Automobile dealers were the pioneers. Reacting to manufacturers' practices during the depression of the 1930s,[38] Wisconsin passed a statute in 1935 and amended it in

---

[37]The farm implement and heavy equipment dealers' and beer and wine distributors' statutes are very similar to the ones we will discuss.

[38]Economics and law writing paints a vision of manufacturer-dealer relations as one of happy harmony based on pure merit. For example, Klein and Saft, in an otherwise interesting article, state:

> Postcontract . . . a franchisor can use the threat of termination to "hold up" a franchisee that has made a specific investment in the marketing arrangement . . . The arrangement creates a potential contracting problem, one that . . . is a necessary part of the efficient scheme of franchisor policing. The franchisor is not likely to terminate franchisees merely to confiscate their sunk investments opportunistically because franchisors must be concerned about their reputations when attempting to sell additional franchise locations.

Klein & Saft, The Law and Economics of Franchise Tying Contracts, 28 Journal of Law & Economics 345, 356 (1985). They continue in a footnote: "Termination of only some franchisees is unlikely to be wealth maximizing because the remaining franchisees will be convinced that they also will be unfairly terminated. Therefore the remaining franchisees will cheat on quality". Id. at n. 38. For a similar argument, see Wiggins, Franchising — A Case of Long-Term Contracts, 144 Journal of Institutional and Theoretical Economics 149, 151 (1988).

Undoubtedly, this is one of many incentives which franchisors must consider. Nonetheless, franchisors have acted opportunistically toward their franchisees when other incentives proved more powerful. See A. Nevins & F. Hill, Ford — Expansion and Challenge: 1915-1933 at 580-583 (New York: 1957); S. Macaulay, Law and the Balance of Power: The Automobile Manufacturers and Their Dealers, 16-21 (New York: 1966). Moreover, it is one thing to deduce what is in the franchisor's long-term interest. It is another to consider what is in the interests of the various people who make up a corporation. Middle and lower level officials who supervise and evaluate franchisees often are evaluated on short-run bottom-line standards. They do not have the luxury of worrying about the impact of their actions on the franchisor's long-run reputation. They assume that they can detect and punish any dealer who might react to coercion by cheating on quality. This may not be wealth maximizing for the franchisor, but it may be wealth maximizing for the franchisor's employees. Indeed, as Henry Ford II conceded at a congressional hearing and Nevins

1937. The Wisconsin act requires all automobile manufacturers, dealers, and the representatives of both to be licensed to do business in the state. The statute is administered by an independent state agency with an advisory board of dealers available for consultation. The act labels as wrongful many kinds of conduct, including the following actions by manufacturers and their representatives: (1) inducing or coercing a dealer to accept delivery of cars or other things the dealer did not order, or attempting to do this[39]; (2) inducing or coercing a dealer to enter any agreement with the manufacturer or "to do any other act unfair to said dealer" by threatening to cancel the dealer's franchise, or attempting to do this[40]; or (3) "[u]nfairly, without due regard to the equities of said dealer and without just provocation ... canceling the franchise of a dealer".[41]

The primary sanction under this statute is the denial, suspension or revocation of a manufacturer's, dealer's, or individual representative's license. The statute also provides for criminal penalties[42] and allows injured dealers to bring civil actions for damages.[43]

After World War II, automobile manufacturers put great pressure on dealers to sell cars by threatening to cancel franchises. In 1953, Oklahoma passed its manufacturer-dealer statute. This statute follows the Wisconsin pattern closely, but with several significant changes. Importandy, the Oklahoma act is administered by a Motor Vehicle Commission composed of seven members appointed by the Governor. "[E]ach shall be of good moral character and each shall have been actually engaged in the manufacture, distribution or sale of motor vehicles in the State of Oklahoma for not less than ten (1) consecutive years ..." Few, if any, automobiles are manufactured in Oklahoma. In effect, rather than an independent state agency as in Wisconsin, a group controlled or influenced by established automobile dealers sits in judgment on other dealers and on manufacturers and their representatives.[44] Many states have followed the Oklahoma pattern and allowed dealers to exercise state powers, thus blurring the line between the public and private governments.[45]

---

and Hill discuss, during the 1930s Ford dealers had to bribe Ford roadmen with lavish personal gifts to retain their franchises.

Macaulay argues that one of the functions of all of the dealer protection legislation is to bring the actions of franchisor "roadmen" to the attention of those at the top of major corporations.

In short, the law and economics approach is not necessary wrong, but it is sadly incomplete and ignores history. Compare Hadfield, Problematic Relations: Franchising and the Law of Incomplete Contracts, 42 Stanford Law Review 927, 978 n. 232 (1990).

[39]Wisconsin Statutes 218.01(3)(15).

[40]Id. at 218.01(3X16).

[41]Id. at 218.01(3X17).

[42]Id. at 218.01(8).

[43]Id. at 218.01(9).

[44]The Oklahoma statute was amended to add two lay members to the Commission in addition to the seven members from the industry. See Oklahoma Statutes Annotated 563A.

[45]Brown, State Motor Vehicle Franchise Legislation: A Survey and Due Process Challenge to Board Composition, 33 Vanderbilt Law Review 385,432-433 (1980), argues "many motor vehicle

By 1956, seventeen states had some form of dealer-manufacturer legislation, and many of them followed the Wisconsin and Oklahoma patterns. Attempts to pass such statutes had been defeated in at least ten states. The National Automobile Dealers Association then turned to the United States Congress. Their original bill would have allowed dealers to recover double damages and attorneys' fees where manufacturers had failed to act in "good faith" in doing business with a dealer or in canceling or failing to renew a dealer's franchise. The bill defined "good faith" as:

> the duty of the automobile manufacturer ... to act in a fair, equitable, and nonarbitrary manner so as to guarantee the dealer freedom from coercion ... or intimidation, and in order to preserve and protect all the equities of the automobile dealer which are inherent in the nature of the relationship between the automobile dealer and automobile manufacturer.

William P. Rogers, then a Deputy Attorney General, announced the Eisenhower Administration's position. While it did not object to protection against coercion, it opposed anything which would deny consumers the benefits of competition. Rogers took aim at the "equities of the dealer" language. He argued that a dealer with a large investment might have an equity in a certain margin of profit, and the manufacturer might have to produce and operate to protect that margin rather than to get as many cars as possible sold to customers at the lowest price. Thus, the language could build "a sanctuary from the rigors of competition".

The sponsors needed votes to get the bill passed, and they worried about a presidential veto. They amended the bill to meet objections. They dropped the right to double damages and offered a new definition of "good faith" which read:

> The term "good faith" shall mean the duty of each party to any franchise ... to act in a fair *and* equitable manner toward each other so as to guarantee the one party freedom from coercion, intimidation, or threat of coercion or intimidation from the other party: Provided, That recommendation, endorsement, exposition, persuasion, urging or argument shall not be deemed to constitute a lack of good faith.

The federal statute stated that it did not preempt state legislation regulating automobile manufacturer-dealer relations. The Department of Justice and the Federal Trade Commission did not object to the bill in this form. Congress passed the "Dealers Day in Court Act of 1956", and President Eisenhower signed it on August 8.

While one could stress the obligation to "act in a fair and equitable manner", the courts have read the statute narrowly and limited its protections to coercion. There are few dealer victories under this statute. However, the manufacturers changed franchise terms and business practices as they tried to block passage of the legislation. These changes may have had more impact than the statute itself. The automobile dealers organizations returned to the state legislatures. Many states passed statutes offering motor vehicle dealers some protection during the early 1970s, and by the mid-1980s almost every state had some type of restriction on terminating or

---

commissions [composed of dealer members] violate due process irrespective of the fact that other commissions regulating other professions are often composed of members of that profession". So far, the courts have not agreed.

failing to renew dealer franchises.[46] The standards vary. Four states follow the Wisconsin phrase: "unfairly, without due regard to the equities, of the dealer". Many use some variant of "due cause", but they differ as to whether they continue and define the term. About half of the states create a cause of action to be enforced through the courts; about half use an administrative-licensing provision. During the 1980s, states began to pass restrictions on manufacturers placing another dealership in a dealer's marketing area without good cause.[47]

It is difficult to assess the impact of motor vehicle dealer protective legislation. In the twenty-eight years from 1959 to 1988, there was an average of about five reported cases a year under the federal Dealers' Day in Court Act. Each of the three major American manufacturers faced about the same number of cases. The cases disclose few notable dealer victories. Close analysis of the text of the federal statute suggests that few dealers will be able to establish the required lack of good faith. Of course, when dealers might win major victories, manufacturers are likely to settle the case or not appeal a defeat before a jury. Thus, the cases which prompted reported decisions may not be good ones for dealers.

It is even harder to assess the impact of the state motor vehicle dealer statutes. Records of proceedings before state administrative agencies are not published regularly. There are few reported appellate cases. When Macaulay interviewed dealer trade association representatives in the early 1960s, they did not see these statutes as very effective.[48] Nonetheless, motor vehicle dealer trade associations worked to get these statutes passed in the 1970s and 1980s. There was a major legislative battle in Florida in 1988. That state had a "sunset law", which automatically repealed many regulatory statutes including the dealer protection act. Manufacturers and officials of Reagan Administration Department of Justice sought to

46Comparative studies of state legislation in the United States are very difficult to carry out. The researcher faces fifty sets of statutes and fifty different indexing schemes. Computer data bases such as LEXIS and WESTLAW make the task much easier. Nonetheless, it is still hard to be sure that one has found every relevant statute. One can miss a provision that uses a synonym for the terms in the search request. Thus, in the discussion that follows, I have avoided offering exact counts of the number of states with particular provisions.

47Anderson, *American Motors Sales Corp.* v. *Peters:* Green Light to Territorial Security for Automobile Dealers, 63 North Carolina Law Review 1081 (1985), argues that provisions in the North Carolina dealer statute protecting dealers' sales territories unfairly burden consumers.

48See S. Macaulay, Law and the Balance of Power: The Automobile Manufacturers and Their Dealers 39 (New York: 1966).

persuade the Florida legislation not to reenact the dealer protection law.[49] They failed, and a revised version of the statute was enacted.[50]

At the very least, these statutes offer dealers some protection against the most arbitrary actions by manufacturers. Unfortunately, it is not in the manufacturers' interest to tell us if there is a significant deterrent effect. The statutes could be taken as a warrant for some degree of relational contract law. However, most courts have construed them too narrowly to serve this purpose.

During the 1950s and 1960s, the Wisconsin statute prompted an informal system. When a manufacturer wanted to cancel a dealer, it would present its case to the Executive Director of the Wisconsin new car dealers trade association. This man had supervised the drafting of the Wisconsin statute, and he could provide dealers with lawyers expert in its provisions. If the Executive Director thought the factory did not have a case, he would tell its representative this. The representative knew that the trade association and its lawyers could stage a costly fight before the Motor Vehicle Department officials who administered the statute. As a result, usually the representative gave the dealer another chance, often setting precise sales targets to be reached by specified dates. If, however, the Executive Director thought that the factory had

---

[49]See, NEXIS, Press Release Newswire, April 13, 1988, Motor Vehicle Manufacturers of America Release. "The Federal Track Commission (FTC) and a report by the staff of the Florida Senate's Economic, Community and Consumer Affairs Committee advocate termination of those provisions of the Florida Motor Vehicle Dealer Franchise and Licensing Law that limit a manufacturer's ability to establish new franchises ... 'Residents of states with similar laws are paying an average $800 more for a new car, according to an FTC study ... The FTC, in a letter to Florida State Sen. Gwen Margolis, said, 'We believe that repeal would likely result in lower automobile prices for consumers'".

The FTC study is Rogers, The Effect of State Entry Regulation on Retail Automobile Markets, Bureau of Economics Staff Report to the FTC (1986). The study was based on data General Motors supplied to the FTC about the prices charged by Chevrolet dealers for each of nine Chevrolet body-types for the year 1978. Rogers said:

> Our results indicate that increasing population growth leads to greater RMA [Relevant Market Area law] effects. In areas where population had increased since the passage of an RMA law, our estimates of the effect of the RMA laws had on the average price of a new Chevrolet range from 3.68 percent for the Sportvan to 16.82 percent for the Corvette. We estimate that the RMA laws caused the average price across all nine models to increase by 7.63 percent.

Rogers at 7. He also says: "the RMA laws appear to have little or no effect in areas where population growth is zero or negative". Id. at 83.

We must notice that Rogers is analyzing an average. Some of his results reflect the great impact RMA laws had on Corvette prices. It may be that interbrand competition has little effect on Corvette buyers. Perhaps these buyers see no other car as a substitute. However, I have difficulty basing a judgment about RMA laws on their impact on Corvette buyers. For example, these buyers might want their cars to cost more because then fewer others would own them. Practical considerations must be far from the mind of anyone considering purchasing a Corvette.

[50]Florida Statutes Annotated Chapter 88-395, 320.27-320.6991 (West's Florida Session Law Service, Aug. 1988.) Section 320.642 deals with "dealer licenses in areas previously served". The amended version runs three and one half printed pages, creating an elaborate procedure to review a proposed new dealership after an objection by a dealer or dealers with standing to protest.

good cause to cancel, he would make sure that the factory would give the dealership a good price for its inventory and treat the dealer fairly as the business was closed. Then the Executive Director would persuade the dealer to accept this solution rather than fight.[51] Moreover, the Motor Vehicle Department tried to avoid formal hearings about franchise terminations. Its officials held prehearing conferences which served as mediation and bargaining sessions.[52] These forms of alternative dispute resolution are rare today. To a large extent, the automobile manufacturers have established internal units such as Ford's Dealer Policy Board which offer dealers second chances, compromise settlements and the like. Moreover, the automobile manufacturers' legal staffs now are experts on state regulation. Manufacturers now act only when they think they have a strong case.

Smith[53] studied the impact of state dealer protection statutes. He compared data from 1954, when most states did not have dealer protection statutes to data from 1972, when many states had such regulation. He found "state regulation has enhanced the ability of dealers to restrict new entry and has protected them from involuntary termination. Over all states, the average impact of regulation from 1954 to 1972 appears to be a 15.3 percent reduction in the number of new-car dealerships". Using data from the Census of Retail Trade on the new-car dealer total revenue per new registration,[54] Smith calculates that the impact of regulation on vehicle prices is an increase of 13.7% in states with low growth rates. The increase in states with high growth rates is 9.9%, but this result is not statistically significant. He argues "the net effect is fewer dealerships and increased market power resulting in higher prices. The impact appears mitigated somewhat by increased scale economies arising from restricted entry".[55] Smith's data suggest that the impact of regulation on dealer revenue per vehicle may be to compel consumers to buy unwanted optional equipment. "This could occur if the scarcity of competing dealerships of the same line-make makes it hard for the consumer to locate the exact set of product attributes he desires".[56] Finally, Smith concludes "[t]he estimated resource loss attributable to

[51] S. Macaulay, Law and the Balance of Power: The Automobile Manufacturers and Their Dealers 152-153 (New York: 1966).

[52] Id. at 153-155.

[53] Smith, Franchise Regulation: An Economic Analysis of State Restrictions on Automobile Distribution, 25 Journal of Law & Economics 125 (1982).

[54] Rogers questions Smith's data:

> Because Smith's quantity data are for total sales of all makes of cars in the given states, he has an aggregation problem. The price differences between various types of automobiles make it difficult to determine whether or not the apparent regulation effects result from the differences across states and over time in the composition of vehicles sold. For dealer costs and other variables, he also uses aggregate state data which might present a similar problem.

Rogers, op. cit (supra note 49), at 28.

[55] Smith, op. cit (supra note 53), at 150.

[56] Id. at 151.

regulation-fostered increases in price packing, based on an average price increase of \$390, was \$3.9 billion for 1979".[57]

Perhaps Smith is right. However, he makes several assumptions which we might question. These concerns about Smith's assumptions may not affect his analysis of the data, but they should prompt us to read his argument carefully. For example, he assumes there is no gap between the law on the books and the law in action. Some of the dealer protection statutes may be enforced in such a way that the dealer always wins. In other states dealers may not be able to prompt the enforcement agency to act except, perhaps, in very clear cases. We can assume that those statutes which are not enforced rigorously will have little impact on prices unless manufacturers lack information about the actual situation.

Smith also tells us that manufacturers use a sales quota system to prevent dealers from gaining an above competitive return available to them when they have territorial security.[58] If dealers failed to sell their quota, then they would risk cancellation of their franchise. He then assumes that under state regulation this means of dealer discipline is lost or so severely restricted as to have little impact.[59] However, even in states with regulatory statutes, manufacturers can and do still use quota systems. Under regulation, the quota must be set in relation to the sales of dealers in comparable situations. In most states, failure to meet such a sales objective, after notice and an opportunity to cure, would be cause for cancellation.[60]

Smith assumes that absent regulation there would be more dealers in a state. If manufacturers were free to do so, he assumes that they would open more dealerships in order to increase competitive pressure on each dealer. However, since the 1960s, manufacturers have wanted to close small dealerships in rural areas and small towns. They find it more efficient to deal with fewer but larger dealers who order both cars and parts in large quantities.

We might agree that, given total freedom, manufacturers would want to cancel more dealers than they can under regulation. Manufacturers will not want to cancel their best dealers, and they can and do cancel their poor performers. Presumably borderline dealers gain the most under regulation. Some of them remain in business only because their manufacturer does not think it worth the cost to try to establish that there is good cause to cancel them. However, bankruptcy and other responses to a poor return on investment probably end franchises in many of these cases. The legislation does not require banks to continue to lend money to dealers who are not performing well.[61]

---

[57]Id. at 154.

[58]Id. at 128-129.

[59]Id. at 136

[60]But see 73 Pennsylvania Statutes 202-3(d)(2), note 63, infra. This statute prohibits use of a sales quota system. It is very unusual and has been preempted by federal regulation.

[61]While regulation may affect opening new dealerships and canceling old ones, it is not clear what the balance will be. It is possible that, absent regulation, manufacturers would have exactly the same number of dealers that they have under regulation. However, absent regulation, they might have

Finally, Smith discounts the effect of interbrand competition. He compares 1954 with 1972, but 1972 is before Japanese car markers were such an important factor in the American car market. Even a Ford dealer with a nicely protected sales territory and a requirement of reasonable cause and a chance to cure before cancellation, faces great competition from the Toyota, Nissan, and Honda dealers. Chevrolet, Pontiac, Oldsmobile and Buick dealers long have sold essentially the same car with only a few differences in trim and the name stamped on the front and back. A state statute might prohibit General Motors from opening another Chevrolet dealership a few blocks away from its existing Chevrolet dealer, but General Motors could establish a Pontiac dealer nearby. For many customers Fords, Chevrolets and Plymouths were more or less interchangeable cars. Even a customer with a not-totally-rational brand loyalty to, say, Chevrolet always could get a price quotation from a Ford dealer to use in negotiating with the Chevrolet dealer. Unless we assume that absolute brand loyalty exists, it is not clear why establishing a second Chevrolet dealer in a city would create enough additional competition to have a substantial effect on car prices.

Having said all this, Smith's general conclusion is plausible. Dealers fight for these statutes because they think such legislation will have impact. At least in the short run, dealer protection statutes should ease some of the pressure from manufacturers to sell the maximum number of cars possible. This may mean that some consumers pay more for new cars.[62]

b) Retail Gasoline Dealers

Retail gasoline dealers tried to follow the precedent set by motor vehicle dealers. After the OPEC cartel raised petroleum prices, the major refiners sought to close many service stations and change the way others did business. Gasoline dealers won major victories in many states. From 1972 to 1978, about twenty states passed statutes regulating terminations and non-renewals of franchises as well as unfair practices of petroleum refiners and distributors. Most of these statutes required "good cause" for termination or non-renewal. Some statutes did not define the term. Others offered elaborate definitions of good cause and stated that certain

---

more larger dealers in big cities and fewer smaller dealers in small towns. This might increase some consumers' costs and lower the prices paid by others.

[62]Even if manufacturers were free to push dealers to sell the maximum number of cars, consumers might not obtain all of the benefits which Smith suggests. There is always the problem of information.

Sales persons can walk the borders of fraud to make customers think they are paying less for a car than they actually are. Dealers can minimize new car preparation and warranty repairs. Dealers can sell cars at what appear to be very low prices, but recapture some or all of the profit lost in the sales price by selling financing with high finance charges. It is possible that regulation penalizes the very-well-informed consumer who is a skilled bargainer but benefits the average consumer who is less well informed and less skilled at bargaining. Compare Ayres, Fair Driving: Gender and Race Discrimination in Retail Car Negotiations, 104 Harvard Law Review 817 (1991).

actions were not good cause.[63] Many statutes required that in most instances a dealer be given a notice of deficient performance and an opportunity to cure its performance.

After lengthy lobbying and negotiation among representatives of oil companies, dealers and others, the United States Congress passed the Petroleum Marketing Practices Act (PMPA) in 1978.[64] This statute provided that franchisors could not terminate or fail to renew franchises except for reasons provided in the act. For example, a franchise could be canceled during its term because of "[a] failure by the franchisee to comply with any provision of the franchise, which provision is both reasonable and of material significance to the franchise relationship . . .".[65]

A franchisor could *refuse to renew* a franchise because of "[t]he failure of the franchisor and the franchisee to agree to changes or additions to the provisions of the franchise, if— (i) such changes or additions are the result of determinations made by the franchisor in good faith and in the normal course of the business; and (ii) such failure is not the result of the franchisor's insistence upon such changes or additions for the purpose of preventing the renewal of the franchise relationship".[66] There are several other reasons justifying non-renewal as well. For example, a franchisor can refuse to renew if "in good faith and in the normal course of business" it determined

---

[63]For example, 73 Pennsylvania Statutes 202-3(b) provides:

(b) It shall be a violation of this act for any lessor supplier to directly or indirectly terminate, cancel or fail to renew an agreement with the lessee dealer unless the termination, cancellation or failure to renew is for one of the following reasons:

   (1) The lessee dealer has abandoned or has given notice of its intention to abandon the leased premises, in which event the requirement of 90 days' notice need not be given.
   (2) The lessee dealer has filed for or has been declared bankrupt or has petitioned for a reorganization, creditor arrangement or insolvency under the applicable statutes . . .
   (3) Failure to pay financial obligations to the lessor supplier when due including, but not limited to, rents or payment for gasoline, petroleum products or accessories supplied to the lessee dealer by the lessor supplier.
   (4) Adulteration, commingling, or mislabeling or misbranding of products supplied by the lessor supplier . . .

(c) Nothing in subsection (b) shall prohibit termination, cancellation or failure to renew: . . .

   (3) where there is such cause for termination as a court of competent jurisdiction might find to be reasonable and just under all of the circumstances.

(d) In determining whether or not an agreement shall be terminated, canceled or not renewed the failure or refusal of the lessee dealer to do any of the following shall not be grounds for such action: . . .

   (2) Failure by the lessee dealer to meet sales quotas suggested by the lessor supplier . . .

[64]15 U.S.C. 2801-2806.

[65]Sec. 2802(a).

[66]Sec. 2802(3)(A).

that "renewal of the franchise relationship is likely to be uneconomical to the franchisor despite any reasonable changes or reasonable additions to the provisions of the franchise which may be acceptable to the franchisee".[67] Oil companies also can terminate or fail to renew when they make a determination "in good faith and in the normal course of business to withdraw from the marketing of motor fuel through retail outlets in the relevant geographic market in which the marketing premises are located ...".[68]

Finally, the PMPA preempted state regulation dealing with franchise termination and non-renewal and the notices required to take these steps.[69] This wiped out the gasoline dealers' victories in over twenty states. It is the most important difference between the federal statute governing automobile dealers and the one governing gasoline dealers.

Again, it is difficult to determine the impact of these statutes on relationships between large international oil companies and their local dealers. From 1978 to 1988, there were 178 cases reported under the PMPA or an average of about 18 a year.[70]

However, Kleeger argues that the federal courts' application of the PMPA "have frustrated congressional intent and have permitted the major oil companies to terminate their franchise relationships arbitrarily".[71] For example, Kleeger comments:

[67]Sec. 2802(D)(i)(IV).

[68]Sec. 2802(E).

[69]Sec. 2806(a) provides: 'To the extent that provisions of this subchapter applies to the termination (or the furnishing of notification with respect thereto) of any franchise, or to the non-renewal (or the furnishing of notification with respect thereto) of any franchise relationship, no State or any political subdivision thereof may adopt, enforce, or continue in effect any provision of any law or regulation (including any remedy or penalty applicable to any violation thereof) of any such franchise or to the non-renewal (or the furnishing of notification with respect thereto) of any such franchise relationship unless such provision of such law or regulation is the same as the applicable provision of this sub-chapter".

[70]Reported cases give only a rough indication of the impact of a law. See Siegelman & Donohue, Studying the Iceberg from Its Tip: A Comparison of Published and Unpublished Employment Discrimination Cases, 24 Law & Society Review 1133 (1990). However, reported cases show that the Petroleum Marketing Practices Act clearly is not a dead letter, there are many published opinions dealing with the statute. There were 78 cases reported from 1978 to 1983. The dealer lost in 68% of them, and the dealer had a positive outcome in 23%. In one case a dealer won a judgment for money. In 13 a dealer was awarded a temporary injunction against termination of the franchise, and summary judgment for the oil company was denied in 4. In 7 of the reported cases the ultimate result was unclear.

[71]Kleeger, Judicial interpretation of the Petroleum Marketing Practices Act: Conflict and Diversity, 32 Emory Law Journal 273 (1983). Compare Greco, Franchise Legislation in the Petroleum Industry: The Petroleum Marketing Practices Act, 25 Mid-Atlantic Journal of Business 59 (1988). Greco examined 92 PMPA cases brought between 1978 and 1984. He found that the statute did not unduly benefit either franchisors or franchisees.

> In *Pabnieri* v. *Mobil Oil Corp.*[72], Mobil proposed to renew the franchise agreement with a 377 percent increase in monthly rent. The rent increase was calculated by using a formula based on Mobil's desired gasoline sales rather than actual gasoline sales by the franchisee. In affirming the lower court's holding that Mobil legally ended the franchise relationship, the Second Circuit stated that the PMPA requires only that a franchisor who institutes rent hikes calculated by formula act without intent to discriminate against selected franchisees. The court held specifically that the Act does not require the franchisor to act in an objectively reasonable manner. This holding is remarkable ... because it apparently condones all uniform rent hikes regardless of their harsh effects.[73]

United States District Courts in Michigan, for example, have emphasized that they are prepared to play only a very limited role in the relationship between oil companies and their dealers. One said that the statutory requirement of reasonableness and materiality of franchise provisions did not permit the court to substitute its judgment for decisions of the franchisor derived from ordinary business experience and knowledge.[74] Another decision stressed that Congress intended to recognize the legitimate needs of the oil companies to terminate franchises or not renew when market conditions and consumer preferences changed.[75] Another court approved non-renewal when the dealer would not agree to convert his station from a full-service gasoline station with repair facilities to a high-volume "pumper" type station. The economic impact on the dealer was irrelevant, as was the fact that the franchisor had encouraged the dealer to operate a repair business in the past. The franchisor acted for a legitimate business reason in the context of changing economic circumstances. The court said that Congress did not intend to destroy a franchisor's flexibility to meet changed economic circumstances or impair its ability to remain competitive.[76]

Chafee might view this as a clash between what he called "the strangle hold policy" and a combination of "the dismal swamp" and the "living tree".[77] The courts

[72]529 F. Supp. 506 (D. Conn.), *aff' d per curiam,* 682 F.2d 295 (2d Cir. 1982).

[73]Kleeger, supra at 313-314. In *Meyer* v. *Amerada Hess Corp.,* 541 F. Supp. 321 (D.N.J. 1982), the court said that an oil company's proposed new franchise agreement did not violate the statute where the rent formula was developed in the ordinary course of business, was not shown to be applied discriminatorily, and called for the dealer to pay a rent significantly below the reasonable rate of return on the value of the land, improvements and equipment made available to him. Although the new rent might make the operation of the station unprofitable, this was not enough to show that there was an improper purpose.

[74]*Gruber* v. *Mobil Oil Corp.,* 570 F. Supp. 1088 (D. Mich. 1983).

[75]*Ames* v. *Texaco, Inc.,* 568 F. Supp. 1317 (D. Mich. 1983).

[76]*Baldauf* v. *Amoco Oil Co.,* 553 F. Supp. 408 (D. Mich 1981). In *Bellmore* v. *Mobil Oil Corp.,* 524 F. Supp. 850 (D. Conn. 1981), the court stressed that the statute directed courts to inquire into a franchisor's intent rather than the effects of its actions.

[77]Chafee, The Internal Affairs of Associations not for Profit, 43 Harvard Law Review 993 (1930). Chafee said that sometimes a relationship is so important to one or both parties that changing or leaving it would have unusually serious consequences. The relationship then has a "strangle-hold" on one or both parties. However, legal agencies may hesitate to get into a "dismal swamp" where they will not be able to sort out conflicting claims in a complex relationship. Moreover, legal agencies may hesitate to intervene when their attempts will cause great resentment and resistance.

have refused to look into the reasonableness of the business judgments made by the oil companies or consider the impact of their decisions on individual dealers. All the many years of effort to produce the state and federal statutes have not brought drastic changes. Whether or not we agree with Kleeger's view that the federal courts "have frustrated congressional intent", it is clear that the gasoline dealers received far less under the federal act than under most of the state statutes which the PMPA preempted.[78]

After their disappointment with the federal statute, the gasoline dealer trade associations returned to the state legislatures. Once again their political power produced success in many states. They could not lobby for statutes which dealt directly with termination or non-renewal because the federal PMPA took away the states' power to regulate these matters. Instead the dealers lobbied for statutes designed to solve specific problems they faced. For example, in 1984 Massachusetts passed a detailed statute which required oil company franchisors to make certain disclosures to those considering becoming dealers, barred franchisors from requiring dealers to participate in sales promotions, required franchisors to repurchase inventory if they did cancel or fail to renew a franchise, provided that franchisors could not insist on the service station being open certain hours, and established an elaborate procedure whereby a dealer could sell the business to another or pass the business to a successor upon his or her death. It also prohibited franchisors from interfering with

---

They will avoid these "hot potatoes". Refusing to intervene may help the "living tree" of relationships grow.

[78]Bloom, Heinzelmann & Alt, An Evaluation of Franchisee-Protection Legislation in the Petroleum Industry, 5 Journal of Policy & Marketing 105 (1986), evaluated the impact of state legislation in the 1970s before it was preempted by the federal statute. Using interrupted time series analysis, they found that the state statutes were somewhat effective at slowing the decline of the number of dealer-operated stations during the 1970s, but they did not significantly affect competition and efficiency in gasoline retailing. They note that having more competitors does not necessarily lead to greater competition and efficiency. Moreover, these laws could not divert the strong trends that were developing in the petroleum industry during the 1970s.

Nevin, Hunt & Ruekert, The Impact of Fair Practice Laws on a Franchise Channel of Distribution, 28 MSU [Michigan State University] Business Topics 27 (1980), conducted in 1978 a mail survey of retail gasoline dealers in two states with state franchise protection statutes and two states without such legislation. Dealers were asked: "Has your franchisor ever threatened to revoke your franchise (terminate your franchise agreement)"? There were no significant differences in the responses between either of the two states that had fair practice legislation and the control states that had no such law. The authors concluded that the statutes had not reduced the use of termination threats. However, they speculated that "oil companies [may] have discontinued using certain unfair practices as a result of recent widespread attention by the press, the Federal Trade Commission, and the courts". Id. at 36. It is also possible that the laws in some states affect practices in other states. Oil companies are national or regional organizations. It may not be worth the effort to have different procedures in New Jersey which had a statute at the time of the Nevin, Hunt and Ruekert study and New York which did not. Indeed, as Nevin and his colleagues speculate, as a result of the New Jersey and other laws, the oil companies might change their practices in New York to help their lobbyists there argue that no law was needed.

dealers' participation in trade associations.[79] California has a similar law,[80] and many other states have enacted some but not all of these provisions.[81]

In 1987, Nevada enacted a number of provisions advocated by its retail gasoline dealer association which were aimed primarily at refusals to renew dealerships.[82] The legislation had to deal with the problem indirectly because the federal PMPA preempts the power of a state to limit the right not to renew. For example, the Nevada legislation requires compensation "at a fair going business value" for a dealer's capital investment if a refiner fails to renew in bad faith.[83] Refiners must give written notice at least thirty days before the end of a term specifying "[a]ll the reasons for any intention of the refiner not to renew".[84] If a refiner fails to give the required notice, the franchisee has an option to renew for one year under the same terms.[85] Finally, and importantly, refiners may not begin to operate any additional service stations themselves with their own employees after July 1, 1987, and they may not "engage in the direct operation of more than 15 service stations in this state . . ."[86] This last provision is designed to inhibit oil companies from pushing out franchised dealers and taking over stations themselves or installing large company owned stations which would compete against franchised dealers.

c) General Franchise Protection Laws

At least ten states have franchise protection laws which apply to all dealers.[87] The Wisconsin Fair Dealership Law[88] provides broad protection to dealers.[89] A

[79]Massachusetts Laws Annotated, Ch. 93E, 1-9 (1985).

[80]California Business & Professions Code, 21140-21150.1 (1986).

[81]See, e.g., 7A Minnesota Statutes Annotated 80C.146(2) (Cumulative Annual Pocket Part 1989), providing "[t]he agreement must provide that if the motor fuel franchisor eliminates one or more service bays during the term of the agreement, the franchisor must first pay to the franchisee in cash an amount that fairly and adequately compensates the franchisee for the loss of the service and repair business".

[82]31 Nevada Revised Statutes 598.660-598.679 (1988). These provisions were enacted after a tremendous battle between the dealers and the oil companies before the Nevada Legislature.

[83]Section 598.660(1).

[84]Section 598.665(l)(b)(l). We can question whether this provision will withstand a federal pre-emption challenge in light of Section 2806(a) of the PMPA.

[85]Section 568.670.

[86]Section 598.677(1), (2).

[87]Some of these states also have laws specifically applicable to motor vehicle, petroleum, farm equipment or other kinds of dealers. Sometimes the general statutes state that they do not apply to such dealers; sometimes the statutes leave open whether a dealer may choose which statute to use or whether a specific statute displaces a general one.

[88]Wisconsin Statutes 135.01-.07 (1988).

[89]Compare similar protection given dealers by the Arkansas Franchise Practices Act, Arkansas Statutes 4-72-201 et seq.; the California Franchise Act, California Business & Professions Code 20000 et seq.; the Delaware Security for Franchised Dealers Act, 3 Delaware Code Annotated 2551

"dealership" covered by the statute requires "a community of interest in the business of offering, selling, or distributing goods or services at wholesale, retail, by lease, agreement or otherwise".[90] A "community of interest" means "a continuing financial interest between the grantor and grantee in either the operation of the dealership business or the marketing of such goods or services".[91] There has been a great deal of litigation testing the meaning of these terms. Lawyers for those engaged in relationships other than traditional franchises and dealerships have tried to bring their clients within the bounds of the act.

A grantor of a franchise in Wisconsin may not cancel, fail to renew or change the competitive circumstances of a dealer without carrying the burden of proving there was good cause.[92] Good cause is defined as:

> (a) Failure by a dealer to comply substantially with essential and reasonable requirements imposed upon him by the grantor, or sought to be imposed by the grantor, which requirements are not discriminatory as compared with requirements imposed on other similarly situated dealers either by their terms or in the manner of their enforcement; or
> (b) Bad faith by the dealer in carrying out the terms of the dealership.[93]

The statute also provides for notice of deficiencies and an opportunity to cure them in all but a few situations.[94] Dealers can sue for damages and injunctive relief, and, if they prevail, they can recover reasonable attorney fees.[95]

From 1976 to 1988, there were 112 reported cases under this statute. While franchisors usually win these cases, dealers have won some important victories.[96] Riteris and Robertson review the Wisconsin litigation and say,

> The past decade has shown that termination litigation abounds. It normally starts with a complaint and a request for a temporary injunction filed by the soon-to-be-terminated dealer. The request is then usually turned into a motion for a preliminary injunction, and an evidentiary hearing is scheduled ... Then there is a rush of needed, as well as superfluous, discovery.[97] After the hearing, the trial court will make every effort to end the controversy at that point ...

---

et seq.; the New Jersey Franchise Practices Act, New Jersey Statutes 56:10-1 — 56:10-15; the Pennsylvania Fair Dealership Law, 73 Pennsylvania Statutes 205-1 et seq.

[90]Wisconsin Statutes 135.02(3).

[91]Sec. 135.02(1).

[92]Sec. 135.03.

[93]Sec. 135.02(4).

[94]Sec. 135.04.

[95]Sec. 135.06.

[96]See *Kealey Pharm. &. Home Care Serv., Inc.* v. *Walgreen Co.,* 761 F.2d 345 (7th Cir. 1985). However, the Supreme Court of Wisconsin took away some of the gains franchisees won in the Kealey case. See *Ziegler Co.v, Inc.* v. *Rexnord, Inc.,* 147 Wis.2d 308,433 N.W.2d 8 (1988).

[97]The lawyer who drafted the Wisconsin statute has said "[t]he non-discrimination clause in the Act is really a kicker. It allows you to go through all the franchisor's records. That doesn't make them too happy but its essential". William F. Nelson, Legislative History, in State Bar of Wisconsin, Advanced Training Seminars — Continuing Legal Education, Magna Carta for Wisconsin Businesses: The Wisconsin Fair Dealership Act (Nov. 1979). Franchisors who do not want franchisees searching their files might be more inclined to settle a case quickly.

> Of course, exceptions exist but experience has shown that much more often than not the fight is at the preliminary injunction stage and over thereafter. Except for jury trials on the issue of damages, there are no reported decisions of jury trials on the issue of good cause.[98]

Again, we have no measure of the indirect or deterrent effects of the statute. Riteris and Robertson conclude: "it is fair to assume that as time goes on grantors will learn to live with the concepts of good cause and cure. It seems that they will not have an alternative".[99]

But perhaps franchisors still have a move or two left in the game. Faruki, a corporate lawyer, wrote an article which offered franchisors advice on how to cope with statutes such as Wisconsin's.[100] He notes:

> The Wisconsin act's standards import into distribution agreements a far more stringent set of requirements than is usually contained in a dealer agreement prepared by a manufacturer. However, the selection of the law of another state, coupled with an arbitration provision, should enable a manufacturer to avoid the applications of the statute.[101]

A franchisor probably cannot avoid Wisconsin law by a clause in a franchise contract stating that it will be governed by the law of another state.[102] However, the arbitration move works. The Supreme Court of the United States declared that the federal arbitration act controls state regulation of franchises.[103] A United States

[98]Riteris & Robertson, The Fair Dealership Law: Good Cause for Review, Wisconsin Bar Bulletin, March, 1986, at 8, 49.

[99]Ibid. At an April 1991 meeting of the American Bar Association's Section on Antitrust Law, several lawyers experienced in advising clients about state franchise protection laws appraised their impact:

> Andrew C. Seiden, of the Minneapolis office of Briggs & Moran, asserted that the practical marketplace effect of state franchise laws, enacted in some states for about 20 years, has been "very slight" outside Wisconsin.
>
> Except under Wisconsin's statute, "very little case law" has developed, he observed. One reason a statute may have little effect is because of "a constitutional problem with applying an anti-termination statute to a preexisting franchise", Seiden explained. By and large, the statutes are "aimed at the wrong target", he lamented. In most cases, even if the franchisee breaches the contract in a material respect, the franchisor's decision to terminate is based on the franchisor's prediction of whether the breaches will continue to occur. [Arthur I.] Cantor, [of Washington, D.C.] suggested that "the real place the state laws may have bite" is with respect to shorter-term relationships where the franchisee has not insisted on protective provisions in the contract. Seiden, concurring, noted that most contracts involve longer-term relationships and that most of those contracts "have due process protections built in".

60 Bureau of National Affairs, Antitrust and Trade Regulation Report, April 18,1991, at 533.

[100]Faruki, The Defense of Terminated Dealer Litigation: A Survey of Legal and Strategic Considerations, 46 Ohio State Law Journal 925 (1985).

[101]Id. at 973-974.

[102]See *Bush* v. *National School Studies, Inc.,* 139 Wis.2d 635,407 N.W.2d 883 (1987).

[103]*Southland, Corp.* v. *Keating,* 465 U.S. 1 (1984). See, also, *Saturn Dist. Corp.* v. *Williams,* 905 F.2d 719 (1990).

District Court, sitting in Wisconsin, has said that the Wisconsin Fair Dealership Act was subject to the Federal Arbitration Act.[104] Lawyers can debate what rules arbitrators must follow in applying franchise contracts to disputes.[105] More importantly, franchisors are likely to hold significant influence over who will serve as arbitrator and where the arbitration will take place.[106]

d) Evaluations of the Statutes

Several writers have argued that all franchise protection legislation unduly curbs the franchisors' power to control dealers and to end relationships with them. Epstein[107] argues that franchisors and good franchisees share an interest in protecting the reputation symbolized by the trade mark. The organization defends itself by ending the relationship with poor performers, and the termination threat serves as an incentive for better performance by all franchisees. Franchise protection legislation, he assumes, destroys these incentives. Moreover, Lockerby[108] objects:

> By requiring case-by-case adjudication to establish a franchisor's right . . . state and federal «good cause» statutes impose a heavy burden in terms of litigation costs. The fact that every franchise termination under a good cause requirement may be the subject of litigation greatly increases monitoring costs in anticipation of litigation. Even clear cases must be carefully documented to survive possible court challenge . . . The litigation process also imposes on the terminating franchisor «error costs», i.e. the possibility that a factfinder may find even valid reasons unpersuasive makes any termination more difficult.

Lockerby asserts that these statutes achieve little more than burdening franchisors with litigation costs. Franchisors, he says, are not going to cancel without cause because franchisor and franchisee are mutually dependent. "A franchisor who terminates an experienced franchisee thus incurs substantial costs himself".

---

[104]See *Good(e) Business Services, Inc.* v. *Raytheon Co.,* 614 F. Supp. 428 (W.D. Wis. 1985).

[105]Wisconsin Statutes, sec. 135.05 states that "[t]his chapter shall not apply to provisions for the binding arbitration of disputes . . . if the criteria for determining whether good cause existed for a termination, cancellation, non-renewal or substantial change of competitive circumstances, and the relief provided is no less than that provided for in this chapter". In the Good(e) Business Services case, supra, the court said "federal law governing the arbitrability of commercial contracts entirely displaces state regulation of the field. States simply lack the power to enact limits on the arbitrability of commercial contracts that go beyond those contained in 9 U.S.C. sec. 2".

[106]See Speidel, Arbitration of Statutory Rights Under the Federal Arbitration Act: The Case for Reform, 4 Ohio State Journal on Dispute Resolution 157 (1989).

[107]Epstein, Unconscionability: A Critical Reappraisal, 18 Journal of Law and Economics 293, 314-315 (1975).

[108]Lockerby, Franchise Termination Restrictions: A Guide for Practitioners and Policy Makers, 30 Antitrust Bulletin 791, 847-848 (1985). Lockerby draws on a classic article dealing with attempts to regulate gasoline franchises by the Uniform Commercial Code's unconscionability provisions. See Jordan, Unconscionability at the Gas Station, 62 Minnesota Law Review 813 (1978). For similar arguments see Mosser, Franchise Regulations: The Good, the Bad, and the Ugly, 29 Cornell Hotel and Restaurant Administration Quarterly, August 1988, at 8-9.

Lockerby then notes that good cause is relatively easy to establish under the various dealer protection statutes. From this he concludes: "the good cause statutes allow a franchisor — after litigation — essentially to do that which he could also do with an unrestricted power of termination — but without litigation".[109]

Undoubtedly, franchisors value skilled and experienced franchisees. Most terminations cost franchisors something. And legal review of business decisions can impose costs. However, we cannot establish deductively whether without these statutes there would be enough arbitrary, bad faith or foolish terminations to justify imposing these costs. Such normative judgments must rest on greater empirical knowledge than we now have.

However, we can offer counterarguments to these attacks which seem just as plausible, based on what we know. Again, it is important to remember that these statutes should have little impact in clear cases. Excellent and terrible franchisees can be treated appropriately. This leaves a middle range of situations where both franchisors and dealers have credible arguments. This range may be broader or narrower depending on whether the law defines cause to cancel or not renew in general or specific terms. Even a statute that does not define cause should become more precise over time as courts give it meaning in specific cases.

When franchisors are not sure whether they have cause to cancel, they can buy a franchisee's business or arrange a sale to another to settle the dispute and avoid the courts. Ford Motor Company, for example, offers termination benefits to dealers unless they are canceled for actions involving bad faith. If a dealer is terminated, it may elect to require Ford to purchase or accept return of vehicles, parts, signs, and special tools and equipment. However, the Ford franchise also provides for a release from all other liability:

> If dealer fails to return the form stating such election within such thirty (30) days, the Dealer shall be deemed to have elected to accept such benefits. Upon the Dealer's election to accept any of such [repurchase or return] benefits, or upon the Dealer's demand of any such benefits upon any termination or non-renewal by the Dealer, the Company shall be released from any and all other liability to the Dealer with respect to all relationships and actions between Dealer and the Company ...[110]

While a good cause statute undoubtedly does increase franchisor costs, it is not clear how great this burden is. Large franchisors will collect much of the data necessary to establish cause as part of the regular process of monitoring dealers. Franchisors regularly measure the sales and profits of one dealer against other comparable dealers, and they keep records of consumer complaints and their resolution. Good dealers are valuable. Few franchisors allow field level supervisors to cancel dealers without preparing a formal reviewable justification.

---

[109]Lockerby, ibid, at 846-847.

[110]This provision was upheld in *DeValk Lincoln Mercury, Inc.* v. *Ford Motor Co.,* 811 F.2d 326 (7th Cir. 1987). Among other things, the court refused to find the clause to be unconscionable: "Ford is entitled to a valid exercise of its corporate power in offering dealers a choice of either electing benefits in exchange for a release of liability or of declining benefits altogether". The court cites five other cases to this effect.

Furthermore, in Galanter's terms[111] franchisors are "repeat players" while dealers usually are "one shotters". Repeat players enjoy economies of scale in handling common disputes and litigation. The costs of preparing a basic legal argument and strategy can be spread over many transactions. Their lawyers become expert in this type of case. Dealers, on the other hand, often have to use lawyers who must research and plan without prior experience.[112]

Dealers who have been canceled also face high cost barriers to litigation. The American practice of the contingent fee may help some dealers overcome these barriers. However, lawyers take cases on contingent fees only when there is some chance of success and where the potential damages are great enough to justify taking the chance of receiving nothing for a large amount of legal work. If franchisors win most of the cases under these statutes, fewer lawyers will be willing to gamble and take dealers' cases.

Moreover, poorly run dealerships are unlikely to be profitable, and banks and other creditors are likely to act to protect their interests. Such actions by creditors themselves may be cause to cancel a franchise. Few dealers are likely to invest large sums to save a failing business by trying to assert rights created by a statute. Some dealers may have personally guaranteed the debts of their corporate dealership to lenders. These individuals have reason to push losses back on franchisors. However, the legal system presents many filters to block such cases from courts and agencies absent a plausible claim. On one hand, lawyers will want to be paid. On the other, it is not easy to survive motions for summary judgment.

As Lockerby says, the statutes may do little more than reinforce a franchisor's interest in preserving dealerships whenever possible. However, inevitably there will be close cases that raise questions of judgment. All the statutes may do is influence choices where there is something to say for the dealer. The chance of legal challenge may prompt superiors to review more carefully recommendations to cancel by field people who supervise dealers. If qualified dealers are an asset, the costs of this careful review may be offset by avoiding a mistaken cancellation.

Furthermore, despite manufacturers' costs in coping with federal and state regulation for over 30 years, automobile distribution has not been frozen in place. As Spinella points out:

> Slow and plodding Darwin-like evolution already has weeded out the weakest [automobile] dealers. In 1950 there were 50,000 dealerships. By 1987 the figure had been halved. And by 1991 it is likely that only 17,500 will remain.
>
> Even more dramatic, the number of dealer principals tumbled from 45,000 to 17,000 between 1950 and 1987, with the prospect of only 14,000 dealership owners by 1991.[113]

[111] See Galanter, Why the "Haves" Come Out Ahead: Speculations on the Limits of Legal Change, 9 Law & Society Review 95 (1974).

[112] If dealers are members of a trade association, they may gain some of the benefits of repeat player status.

[113] Spinella, The Dealer Dimension, 24 Ward's Auto World, May, 1988, at 53.

Finally, dealer protection statutes do not take away from franchisors all means of giving franchisees incentives to perform their duties. Franchisors reward dealers who do well. Some rewards are symbolic, such as ceremonies and plaques to hang on the wall. Others are more tangible. For example, an automobile manufacturer often has easy-to-sell popular cars and hard-to-sell less popular ones. It can allocate more of the popular models to dealers who sell more of the less popular ones. There are also sanctions. Franchises still can cancel for cause, and franchisees cannot be certain how poorly they can run their dealerships without crossing the line and giving the franchisor cause to cancel. General Motors puts dealers who are selling only 65% of their sales target into a Dealer Improvement Program. Such dealers are offered help in improving sales, customer satisfaction, and facilities, but they know that they are being watched and records are being prepared to justify termination. Just being singled out for this unwanted attention is itself a sanction.[114]

IV. The Campaign of the Retail Gasoline Dealers: Law and the Balance of Power

Up to this point, we have reviewed academic theories as well as judicial and legislative attempts to regulate long-term continuing relationships in the distribution of goods. However, judgments about whether and how to regulate in this area are not only disinterested exercises of reason. Power and politics affect whether laws are passed, what form they take and their impact. Or, as Joerges put it in challenging Macneil's relational theories:

> To conceive of . . . [the argument about the legal form of the manufacturer-dealer contractual relation] simply as a discussion on the merits of "neo-classical" or "relational" contract law, of either a hidden or explicit legal response to relational elements in contract law, abstracts the controversies being fought out by the participants on the legal status of "quasi-entrepreneurs" . . . I interpret his [Macneil's] concept as a possibility for overcoming the abstractions from social problems by means of classical and also neo-classical contract law. For exactly this reason, however, I insist that the social problems and conflicts concerned be recognized as such and that the colliding legal claims be taken seriously.[115]

The struggle over franchise laws teaches us much about the reality of regulation in the United States. The process involves battles in a never-ending war, moves in an endless game.[116] Both franchisors and franchisees are well-armed with rhetorical symbols dear to Americans: "the free market" and "efficiency" battle "the virtues of

---

[114]See Krebs, GM Maps Franchise for the '90s, Automotive News, April 3, 1989, at 1. See also Automotive News, March 13, 1989, at 1.

[115]Joerges, Relational Contract Theory in a Comparative Perspective: Tensions Between Contract and Antitrust Law Principles in the Assessment of Contract Relations Between Automobile Manufacturers and Their Dealers in Germany, 1985 Wisconsin Law Review 581, 608-609, 613.

[116]See the discussion of the "typical sequence of stages" in challenging power through legal action in S. Macaulay, Law and the Balance of Power, at 22-23 (New York: 1966).

small business", and the claims of expectations created by practice. While both sides bring experts into the contest, the manufacturers' economists more often are pitted against the dealers' victims of atrocities at the hands of franchisors. Dealers have advantages at the state level while franchisors usually are large corporations, well versed at playing in the national arena in Washington, D.C.

This is a story of the efforts of the retailers of branded gasoline to improve their position against the major oil companies. The tale of prolonged legal warfare will illustrate all the difficulties in such battles as well as the uncertain nature of the outcome. First, we will examine the nature of this "franchise" relationship — the norms and sanctions in this semi-autonomous social field, looking at the strains which prompted the dealers to seek outside help. We will then sketch the endless battles they won and lost, and we will try to indicate something of the impact of all these efforts.

Before the energy crisis in the early 1970s, the major oil refiners sought to maximize the amount of gasoline sold.[117] Much of their profit came from products such as petrochemicals, and often gasoline was a by-product to be disposed at the best price available. It was uneconomic, because of the structure of the tax laws, to keep crude oil in the ground. Refining petrochemicals or heating oil also yielded gasoline which, as a practical matter, could not be stored for long. Even when a refinery run was planned to produce gasoline, the nature of the technology called for production in large quantities.

The major oil companies sold gasoline in many ways. Much, of course, was sold through service stations bearing the trade mark of a major oil company. The company usually owned some of these stations itself, hiring employees to manage them. Most companies, however, contracted with franchised dealers and leased service station premises to them. Until the 1970s, most oil companies worked to increase the number of stations offering their products, and many attempted to build national networks of distribution.[118]

The major oil companies made the franchised dealer the focus of their retailing efforts in the 1930s. For a relatively small investment of capital, the companies told dealers that they could run "their own business". For example, a Shell Oil Company advertisement seeking new dealers said,

Work for a good man-yourself. A Shell Dealership offers:

- Paid training;
- Financing Assistance;
- High Income Potential.

---

[117]See Roche, Major Oil Firms Seek Earnings on Gasoline, Long a "Loss Leader", Wall Street Journal, March 28, 1977, at 1, col. 6, at 11, col. 3.

[118]Gasoline also was available at service stations which did not display the trademark of a major oil company. Typically, this gasoline was sold for a few cents a gallon less than branded fuel. Many consumers distrusted this gasoline although usually it was chemically indistinguishable from branded fuel, and often one of the major oil companies had refined it. These independent stations served to impose competitive pressure on the franchise dealers. If branded gasoline prices went too high, some consumers would put aside their distrust and elect to save money.

When it suited their purposes, the oil companies characterized the dealers as independent business people. However, the companies managed to retain almost the same degree of control over the dealers as they would have had over employees. The companies drafted standard form contracts and leases which guarded their interests. Dealers assumed many obligations under these contracts, including such things as the hours they stayed open, the products they would sell, and responsibility for handling credit card purchases. The franchise usually was for a relatively short term — sometimes as little as 30 days with an optional renewal feature — and franchises could be canceled at will with no need to show cause. Furthermore, some oil companies frequently refused to allow a dealer to have an attorney review their contracts and leases before they were signed because they would allow no changes.

Dealers were well aware that it was good policy to keep the companies' district managers pleased. Dealers knew that their franchise ran for a term, but most assumed that they would be renewed. This view was reinforced the longer they stayed in business and obtained renewals. District managers often told their dealers that there was nothing to worry about, as long as there were no problems. This both reassured dealers and served as a warning of what might happen if there were problems. If a dealer's performance were questionable, the company also could open another station across the street or a block or two away. Finally, the companies offered training for dealers in management skills and business systems. This not only helped dealers become profitable but also served to channel their operations into the companies' patterns.

The dealer was thus given a strong incentive to pour time and effort into managing the station, building good will in the immediate area, and investing in tools, tow trucks and the like. The companies benefited by characterizing their dealers as independent business people rather than as employees. Oil companies could not have devised a better incentive structure which would prompt most employees to work the long hours and take the responsibility assumed by dealers. Also, "independent" dealers were not subject to minimum wage and maximum hour regulations, and they would not unionize and ask to collectively bargain.

Sometimes everyone was happy. Often the oil company and the dealer shared interests. Successful dealers made money and had a degree of independence. Sometimes successful dealers even had some countervailing power. When major oil companies were expanding into new regions of the country, they might seek to entice experienced and capable dealers away from other companies. Companies probably threatened to cancel, both expressly and impliedly, far more than they actually terminated dealers. Oil companies usually renewed even slightly marginal dealers. There were costs in changing dealers by canceling franchises — the replacement, for example, might not do as well.

However, there often were strains in the relationship. These strains were provoked in part by the contradiction between the reality of the situation and the fiction that the dealer was an independent business person. Until the energy crisis of the 1970s, there were recurring price wars in many areas when one refiner wanted to get rid of surplus gasoline or wanted to establish itself. The oil company would order its dealers to cut prices to increase sales. The other major oil companies would respond by telling their dealers to meet the price cuts or to drop the price even lower in order to bring in new customers. The dealer usually had to bear part of the burden of lower prices. Dealers would be given allowances to enable them to survive a price war, but the major oil companies decided how great an allowance to offer and how long to keep it in effect. Truly independent dealers would have had the power to set their own prices based on their own judgment about long term benefits and their own particular situation. This independence was denied to most franchisees in gasoline price wars. Price competition was a tactic which might help a major oil company get rid of gasoline or bring in a few new people to a station once or twice. However, cuts were met quickly by cuts from the station across the street.

Also, dealers often could make more profit selling tires, batteries and accessories (TBA) and even motor oil which they bought from wholesalers than by offering only products supplied by the major oil companies. Refiners controlled the TBA offered by their dealers in many ways, ranging from requirements contracts to what the Federal Trade Commission and the courts later were to label as coercion.

In the late 1960s, many major oil companies decided to deemphasize neighborhood stations and the servicing and repairing of automobiles, and use marketing techniques which would sell more gasoline at fewer stations. Experts began to say that the United States had far too many gasoline stations for efficient distribution. Jordan described the tensions in the relationship as follows:

> The company sees the station as its means of selling petroleum products, with price competition and high volume as keys to profit. The dealer, in contrast, often sees the station primarily as *his* repair and maintenance operation. Since the bulk of his income tends to come from automotive services that he, not the oil company, provides, he is less concerned than the company about increasing sales of the relatively low-profit gasoline. Moreover, though some agreements do specify a maximum rent, rental rates are often based on a percentage of gasoline sales, in effect giving the dealer a *negative* incentive. This disparity between the interests of the company and the operator simply does not exist where both are exclusively interested in selling the same product and splitting the profits.[119]

Dealers were told to close service facilities which had been highly profitable to them and turn to self-service, trading stamps, contests, premiums, and extended hours of operation. Major companies began to withdraw from regions of the country where they did not have a large share of the market, leaving many canceled dealers in their wake. After the Arab Oil Embargo in 1973, many major oil companies worked even harder to close their less profitable stations. Gasoline no longer was merely something to be disposed of. This part of their operation had to maximize profit rather than volume.

The major oil companies rationalized their control of their dealership network by their property, trademark and contract rights. Often they owned the stations which were leased to dealers; they claimed ownership of trademarks such as "Standard",

[119]Jordan, Unconscionability at the Gas Station, 62 Minnesota Law Review 813, 817-818 (1978).

"Shell", and "Texaco" and thus controlled those who displayed them; and they drafted form contracts that gave them the right to cancel dealerships at their discretion. Often the oil companies justified their power and policies in terms of efficiency and benefits to consumers. They pictured canceled dealers as inefficient operators who survived by charging customers high prices and running dirty stations. They argued that consumers expected to find the same high quality of product and service at all stations displaying, for example, the "Shell" trademark. The oil companies also pointed out that they supplied most of the capital involved in the network of gasoline stations, and they said that as conditions changed, any particular dealer had few equities to offset required changes in the entire franchise system.

The dealers, of course, saw matters very differently. They said that they were independent business people who created the value of their service station by their labor and their efforts to build good will. They relied on having their franchise renewed because of representations made to them, expressly and impliedly, by the oil companies. They did not deal with the lawyers and top officials who fashioned the legal paper work. They talked to field representatives who led them to believe that they would keep their stations and their independence as long as they did a good job. The dealers' efforts, in partnership with the oil companies, had created the business at the local level. It was unfair for oil companies to pass back to the dealers a major part of the burdens of economic change brought about by OPEC — which was a response to the conduct of the major oil companies in Third World Countries. Finally, dealers made the classic argument of small business against competition: price competition in gasoline destroyed service and would end with a few near monopolists able to impose whatever prices they wanted, without offering service to customers. Perhaps the dealers' appeal to American ideology was best put by Justice Douglas,[120] in one of the earlier antitrust cases involving gasoline dealer franchises:

> The lessons Brandeis taught on the curse of bigness have largely been forgotten in high places. Size is allowed to become a menace to existing and putative competitors. Price control is allowed to escape the influences of the competitive market and to gravitate into the hands of the few. But beyond all that there is the effect on the community when independents are swallowed up by the trusts and entrepreneurs become employees of absentee owners. Then there is a serious loss in citizenship. Local leadership is diluted. He who was a leader in the village becomes dependent on outsiders for his action and policy. Clerks responsible to a superior in a distant place take the place of resident proprietors beholden to no one. These are the prices which the nation pays for the almost ceaseless growth in bigness on the part of industry.

The tensions in their relationship with the oil companies prompted gasoline dealers to organize. Gasoline dealers, both individually and through their organizations, tried to change the nature of their relationship with the major oil companies for more than thirty years. Trade associations proposed informal dispute resolution panels, but the oil companies were not interested. District managers of the oil companies would not allow a dealers' organization to represent dealers in meetings

[120] *Standard Oil Co. of California* v. *United States,* 337 U.S. 293, 318-319 (1949) (dissenting opinion).

with the company. The managers said that they would only talk with dealers as individuals, and they pointed out a possible conflict of interest — the organizations represented dealers selling competitive products.

When these efforts at informal dispute resolution failed, the organized dealers turned to the legal system. Their basic strategy was to search for a new legal categorization of the relationship, and to collect atrocity stories to provoke a scandal. And dealers hired lobbyists and lawyers with enough experience and skill to counter the representatives of the major oil companies. They appealed to the Federal Trade Commission, state and federal courts, state legislatures, and the United States Congress with varying success over the years. Every legislative representative has retail gasoline dealers doing business in his or her district, and these retailers are "small business", a symbol dear to both major political parties. From World War II through the 1960s, a number of antitrust actions attempted to protect the status of retail gasoline dealers as independent business people by lessening the oil companies' control. Victories were won by and for dealers; a notable line of cases in the Supreme Court of the United States developed. The Federal Trade Commission and private suits attacked the oil companies' control over the prices charged by their dealers and the response to price wars as well as various attempts to induce dealers to stock only the companies' TBA. The FTC won consent decrees limiting the use of short-term leases of service stations, which the Commission said made the dealers more vulnerable to the oil companies' coercion.

The FTC also attempted to solve many conflicts informally. President Nixon's Task Force on Productivity and Competition complained:

> The efforts of the Commission to protect small dealers from allegedly unfair and coercive business practices constitute a dark chapter in the Commission's history. Much of this enforcement activity does not eventuate in formal proceedings. What happens is that a dealer who is terminated, for whatever reason, is likely to complain to the Commission, knowing that the relevant Commission staff is well disposed toward "small business". The staff uses the threat of an FTC proceeding to get the supplier to reinstate the dealer, and if threats fail — usually they succeed — the FTC may file a complaint charging the supplier with having cut off the dealer because he was a price cutter, or for some other nefarious reason. Our impression, in sum, is that the Commission, especially at the informal level, has evolved an effective law of dealer protection that is unrelated and often contrary to the objectives of the anti-trust laws.[121]

While these victories undoubtedly changed day-to-day practices of major oil companies, some companies asserted that they always had honored the status of their dealers as independent business people. Amoco Oil Company's Statement of Dealer Policy said, for example:

> Amoco's commitment to recognizing the dealers' rights as independent business men has been stressed to employees at all levels of our Company. Should dealers at any time receive an indication that our Policy is not receiving strict adherence from all of our personnel, they have the right to bring this fact to the attention of the District Manager. If after a discussion

[121]BNA Antitrust and Trade Regulation Reporter, 1969: X-3.

with the District Manager, disposition of the dispute is not made to their satisfaction, they may contact the Chairman of the Regional Dealer Relations Committee.

Despite such policy statements, some dealers thought that too much pressure to take orders remained. The General Counsel of the National Congress of Petroleum Retailers appeared before a Congressional committee hearing on problems in gasoline retailing. He explained:

> The district manager comes in and sees that another TBA is in your station. That doesn't happen to be the brand they are selling, and he says, "Good heavens. What is this oil doing here"? And the dealer says, "You know, I thought I could sell it, and the *Texaco* case, and the *Simpson* case, and all the others say that I am entitled to sell anything I want to sell".
>
> The district manager says, "You certainly are, Joe Blow; you are a nice family man; you have six kids. Your lease will be over in 4 months, and I will tell you just a little ahead of time so you can be looking around for a new job".
>
> The Pennzoil goes out to the backroom. This is the problem with the antitrust cases. As long as someone is choking you, and they have got their hands around your throat, you can't say "I know my rights". But sometimes, your knowing your rights, and their knowing your rights, isn't enough to stop them from choking you. When the pressure gets hard enough, you go along with them.

The Executive Director of the National Congress thought that the pressure often was more subtle. Dealers would be told that the company expected all aspects of the station to be highly profitable and certain targets would be set. Dealers could not achieve the goal for selling, say, Standard's brand of oil if they sold too much Pennzoil or Quaker State.

Since the 1950s, the retailers sought to limit the power of oil companies to cancel or refuse to renew franchises because this power is the source of much of their leverage over dealers. In 1956, Congress passed the "Dealers Day in Court Act", giving some protection to franchised *automobile* dealers. Franchised dealers selling other products found this statute a legislative precedent for claiming a right to similar protection. Throughout the 1950s and 1960s, both the House and Senate Small Business Committees held hearings where franchised dealers, including those who operated gasoline stations, made the populist appeal against big business again and again. In the mid l960s, Senator Philip Hart of Michigan held hearings and then offered several bills that would have protected *all franchisees* from termination or non-renewal except for cause. The oil companies, particularly Mobil, vigorously attacked these proposals as benefiting only the inefficient. The bills also ran counter to the ideas of the Nixon Administration about efficiency and competition, and even had they passed, they risked a presidential veto. The bills did not pass. However, Senator Hart's effort brought attention to the franchisee's claim that there was a problem, and it may have played a role in changing attitudes when events later made the plight of the gasoline dealers appear more worthy of sympathy.[122]

[122]Scandals may also have played a similar part in influencing attitudes about franchisees. During the 1960s, promoters sold franchises of little value. Prominent entertainers and sports figures sold their names to promoters who announced that "John Smith Fast Food" franchises were available for a price. The promoters represented them as potential gold mines, and people invested their life

After the failure of the Hart bills at the federal level, the legislative battle moved to New York. In 1969, the legislature there passed a statute which would have required all franchisors to act in a fair, equitable and honest manner and in accordance with reasonable standards of fair dealing when granting, modifying, terminating or failing to renew a franchise. However, Governor Rockefeller vetoed the bill because of the "unreasonable injunctive rights it would grant dealers".

Next, individual gasoline dealers who had been canceled or not renewed, went to court. Their lawyers, backed by their trade associations, searched for legal concepts which would override the oil companies' carefully fashioned positions based on property, trademark and contract. Wall Street very successfully warded off Main Street, and the dealers usually lost. For example, two lower New York courts refused to apply the Uniform Commercial Code's provisions concerning "good faith" and "unconscionability" to gasoline dealer franchises.[123] The Code, the courts explained, applies only to transactions in goods, and a franchise involves both goods and a lease of real estate. These courts also refused to consider evidence of a custom to renew station leases absent cause for cancellation. Any such custom would contradict the express terms of the franchise document drafted by the oil company lawyers. Yet even these defeats were to play a role in later developments as indicating the need for legislation.

One of the judges emphasized the vetoed legislation and saw legal change in this area as an appropriate legislative task. He remarked that he was "not unsympathetic to the plaintiff's plight ..." and said he was sending copies of his opinion to the appropriate legislative committees.[124] The other judge made the interesting statement that it is "unconscionable, although legal at present, for the ... [Mobil Oil Company] ... to be allowed, without cause, to terminate this lease after 19 years of annual renewal". He thought Mobil's action "harks back to the early days of our nation's industrial development when corporations were King and the workers were only to be used". He concluded that he "the Legislature and the Governor of this State will see fit to enact, again, legislation which will protect this vast number of our citizens".[125]

Still a third New York lower court judge did not think he had to await legislation. He pointed to representations made by the Mobil Oil Company to a canceled dealer, noted that Mobil had not allowed the dealer to have an attorney present when the lease was signed since it "would not tolerate changes in any of the provisions of the printed agreements", and stressed that Mobil's refusal to renew because the dealer had not followed Mobil's price-setting directions violated the antitrust laws. He

---

savings only to discover that there was little substance in the franchise. While these fraudulent schemes did not involve gasoline retailers, the scandal may have helped some legislators see franchisees as needing protection similar to that given consumers or buyers of corporate securities.

[123] *Mobil Oil Corp.* v. *Rubinfeld,* 357 N.Y.S.2d 589 (Ap.Term, 2d Dept. 1974), reversing 339 N.Y. S.2d 623 (Civ.Ct.N.Y.C. 1972); *Division of Triple T Service, Inc.* v. *Mobil Oil Corp.,* 304 N.Y.S.2d 191 (S.Ct. Westchester Co. 1969), aff'd without opinion, 311 N.Y.S.2d 961 (2d Dept. 1970).

[124] *Division of Triple T Service, Inc. v. Mobil Oil Corp.,* supra note 123.

[125] *Mobil Oil Corp.* v. *Lione,* 322 N.Y.S.2d 82 (3d Dist., Suffolk Co. 1971).

concluded that there was a "fiduciary relationship" which Mobil had violated.[126] Thus, the court refused to grant Mobil's petition to recover possession of its station.[127] However, this innovative exercise was reversed on appeal.[128]

In the early 1970s, state and local gasoline dealers' organizations pressed for legislation in many states. After several failures, a bill offering all franchisees protection was passed in Wisconsin. Both Connecticut and New Jersey passed statutes providing that franchisors could not cancel or fail to renew franchises "without good cause". In addition, the Connecticut law provided that any franchisee could submit the question of "good cause" to arbitration in accordance with the rules of the American Arbitration Association.

In Connecticut, Mobil Oil Company led the attack on the new statute. It told twenty-six of its dealers who ran the most valuable stations in the state that it would not renew their franchises and would take over their stations. It could adopt this strategy because the statute did not apply retroactively to franchisees which had been created before the law became effective. At a legislative hearing, a representative of Mobil said that it could not leave $300,000 stations in the hands of dealers who had tenure granted by the law. Unless the statute were repealed, Mobil would have to take over all of its stations in the state.[129]

Members of the legislature reacted angrily to what they saw as coercion. Some legislators discovered that Mobil's representative was not registered as a lobbyist, and they demanded prosecution. A story appeared in the *New York Times*,[130] which noted that if "Mobil was going to get in trouble for its efforts on behalf of all the oil companies, Mobil's brass would be embarrassed and many of the company's officers live in Connecticut — including the chairman of the board . . ." Mobil's officers may have recognized this. At any rate, they withdrew the heavy attack, apologized, and then joined with the Connecticut Gasoline Retailers Association to offer amendments to the statute. Under these changes, franchisors could cancel or refuse to renew a dealer's lease for failure to perform obligations under a contract or where the franchisor converted its property to a use not covered by the franchise agreement. In

---

[126] *Mobil Oil Co.* v. *Rubinfeld,* 339 N.Y.S.2d 623 (Civ.CtN.Y.C. 1972), aff'd, 357 N.Y.S.2d 589 (Ap. Term 1974).

[127] Fiduciary relationships exist when one purports to act for the benefit of another — lawyers are in such relationships with their clients, for example.

[128] *Mobil Oil Co.* v. *Rubinfeld,* 370 N.Y.S.2d 943 (Ap. Term. 1975).

[129] A member of Mobil's legal staff explained his firm's position in Connecticut:

> Our concern with the 1973 amendments to the Connecticut Franchise Act was that they had the effect of giving a dealer, who had invested approximately $10,000 in inventory and equipment, the same long-term property rights in a service station as an oil company supplier-landlord that had invested $300,000 in acquiring the property and constructing the service station improvements . . .

Letter of November 14, 1974 to Professor Stewart Macaulay.

[130] March 19, 1974, at 47; March 20, 1974, at 53.

addition, the provision for arbitration was deleted as an interference with the franchisor's constitutional right of trial by jury.[131]

In New Jersey, major oil companies canceled or refused to renew franchises in response to that state's franchise law. The Supreme Court of New Jersey, however, decided in *Shell Oil Co.* v. *Marinello*[132] that franchise agreements entered into before the state's law became effective were subject to an implied covenant that the franchisor would renew as long as dealers had substantially complied with their obligations.[133] The New Jersey court was able to rely on the legislation as a declaration of the state's policy warranting the imposition of an implied term in the contract. Imposing an "implied term" is a well-known move in the contract doctrine game, but this was the first time that it was applied to franchises.

Once again action prompted reaction. At the request of oil companies, a federal district court found invalid the decision which implied a covenant to renew as well as the New Jersey statute because they conflicted with the federal Lanham Act governing trademarks.[134] This decision later was reversed on appeal,[135] but for a time it brought all efforts of gasoline dealers in the state legislatures into question.[136]

---

[131]The Mobil lawyer continued:

> While we resumed our leasing practices in the state of Connecticut in response to the 1974 amendments, we are still philosophically opposed to any law that restricts a landlord's right not to renew a lease agreement after it has expired. We believe that this type of legislation unconstitutionally transfers long term property rights from a land owner, who has invested substantial sums of money to acquire property, to a lessee dealer who has put up little or no capital that he can't otherwise get back out of his business.

Letter of November 14, 1974 to Professor Stewart Macaulay, supra note 129.

[132]63 N.J. 402,307 A.2d 598 (1973), *cert, denied,* 415 U.S. 920 (1974).

[133]The trial court found an implied covenant not to terminate based on the parties' course of performance, Shell's own practices, and considerations of public policy. See *Shell Oil Co.* v. *Marinello,* 120 N.J.Super 357, 294 A.2d 253 (Law Div. 1972). The trial court's opinion is very similar to the Nanakuli decision discussed supra.

[134]*Marinello* v. *Shell Oil Co.,* 368 F.Supp. 1401,1407 (D.N.J. 1974).

[135]*Marinello* v. *Shell Oil Co.,* 511 F.2d 853 (3d Cir. 1975).

[136]In *Ashland Oil, Inc.* v. *Donahue,* 223 S.E.2d 433 (W.Va. 1976), the court found that the Uniform Commercial Code applied to a gasoline dealer's franchise and that a ten-day cancellation clause was unconscionable. Other state courts were unwilling to follow New Jersey's implied covenant approach, to apply the Uniform Commercial Code to a gasoline dealership so that an implied condition of "good faith" would be imposed on the relationship, to find fiduciary obligations, or to apply the reliance principles of Restatement of Contracts, Section 90 to terminations of dealer franchises. See, e.g., *Cornitius, Inc.* v. *Wheeler,* 276 Ore. 747, 556 P.2d 666 (1976); *Clark Oil & Refining Corp.* v. *Leistikow,* 69 Wis.2d 226, 230 N.W.2d 736 (1975). In the Clark case, the Supreme Court of Wisconsin said,

> defendants have alleged a promise or representation of occupancy as long as they did well, made by Clark's agents or servants to induce them to enter the agreements. They allege that they left their former employers of long-standing as a result of these promises and entered into the agreements. We think these allegations are not sufficient to raise promissory estoppel. There is no allegation that injustice can only be avoided by enforcing the promise and it is questionable if the leaving of former employments are actions of "a definite and

Despite the dealers' difficulties in getting courts to protect existing franchises, the dealers' organizations did well before many state legislatures. By the mid-1970s, over thirty states had some kind of franchise protection law applicable to retail gasoline dealers whose franchises were created or renewed after the statutes went into effect. Some of these statutes applied only to gasoline dealers; others applied to all franchises including gasoline dealerships.

The dealers' lobbying organizations tried still another approach. They pressed for statutes that would restrict oil companies' operation of retail outlets. If these statutes were passed, oil companies no longer could threaten to take over stations before the effective date of franchise protection statutes as Mobil had done in Connecticut. They also could no longer open company stations to compete with franchised dealers or threaten to do so for leverage. By 1977, twenty eight states had given some consideration to such bills, and laws to this effect had passed in Maryland, Florida, Delaware, Virginia and the District of Columbia. Several bills to this end were introduced in Congress.

Exxon, Shell, Gulf, Phillips, Ashland, Continental and Commonwealth Oil Companies joined to challenge the constitutionality of the Maryland statute. However, the Supreme Court of the United States upheld it.[137] After this decision, the threat of passing these statutes was used to promote a federal legislative solution. The dealers' trade associations continued to struggle in the 1970s to gain federal legislation that would limit termination and non-renewals and protect existing dealers. Senator Claiborne Pell of Rhode Island said "if these small people are put out of business, there isn't going to be the competition or the retail service in the local neighborhoods".[138] He proposed divestiture of retailing under the antitrust laws might be needed if adequate legislation to protect dealers could not be passed.

At the beginning of the decade, the large oil companies were supported by people in the Nixon and Ford administrations who opposed these bills as anticompetitive and promoting inefficiency. In 1974, President Nixon vetoed a comprehensive energy bill which included provisions prohibiting fuel sellers from terminating dealer franchises unless the dealer had failed to comply with reasonable requirements of the franchise. The Senate failed to override the veto, and the dealers suffered still another defeat.

However, the Federal Energy Administration found itself dragged into the question of franchise termination by the Emergency Petroleum Allocation Act, which had been passed after the Arab oil embargo in 1973. This statute prohibited an oil company canceling a dealer and moving its allocation of fuel to a company-run station. FEA Ruling 1974-3, prohibited franchise terminations without a legitimate business purpose, those taken to circumvent the allocation program or those retaliating for dealers exercising rights created by FEA regulations. In 1976, the FEA

substantial character." [When relief has been given] . . . the plaintiff suffered monetary losses in preparing . . . [himself for association with the defendants].

[137] *Exxon Corp.* v. *Governor of Maryland,* 437 U.S. 117 (1978).

[138] Wall Street Journal, June 16, 1977, at 24.

handled between 300 to 400 dealer-company disputes, a job which its officials viewed as a diversion from the agency's major responsibilities. The dealers' lobbyists were undaunted after the veto of the energy bill in 1974, and they began still another major federal campaign. Individual dealers and groups of dealers met with their congressional representatives in district after district. They dramatized their plight by recounting atrocity stories and dwelling on the ideology of small business and traditional American hostility to large multinational corporations. International developments now made the dealers' story even more appealing. As the price of gasoline increased in the early 1970s, many Americans were angered by the major oil companies' extraordinary profits. Many thought that the large oil companies had manufactured the entire "oil crisis" to excuse price increases. Dealers claimed that these companies should not pass on the burdens of disruption in the oil business to their dealers and customers when the companies were making record profits.

During 1977, some of the major oil companies changed their position and supported federal dealer protection legislation. The dealers' lobbyists and the companies' lawyers worked out most of the technical objections to earlier legislative proposals, arriving at a compromise with the help of the staffs of the House and Senate committees considering legislation in this area. Exxon's representative was able to say, "it is a reasonable bill and one with which all marketing segments can live". Chevron, U.S.A. noted that the bill "has wide support throughout the industry because it is a compromise measure".

Perhaps a major reason for this change was that many companies now felt that they needed federal legislation to preempt the many varying state statutes and to ward off the threat of divestiture of all retail operations. The dealers' associations had produced enough state law that the companies valued uniformity itself. Furthermore, there was always a threat that the dealers could get states to pass laws less favorable to oil company interests than the compromise worked out at the federal level. Finally, the major oil companies were concerned about congressional reaction to proposals for such things as gasoline rationing and a windfall profits tax. Some officials of the large corporations thought it was time to withdraw from the public role as the villain who pushed around local small business.

Congress passed the Petroleum Marketing Practices Act (PMPA), which became effective in June of 1978.[139] While this statute limits cancellation of a franchise to specified grounds, it also leaves the major oil companies relatively free to not renew dealer franchises. The franchisor need only negotiate in good faith for a renewal; it need not negotiate reasonably in light of the dealer's interests. The federal courts have read the PMPA's provisions on non-renewal so that a dealer's threat of formal legal action is but a paper tiger. Moreover, the PMPA preempts all state legislation which might otherwise benefit gasoline dealers.

In 1984, The Service Station Dealers of America, Inc. returned to Congress seeking amendments to the PMPA, and it has lobbied for legislation at every session

[139]The statute appears at 15 United States Code, 2801-2806.

since then.[140] Its president painted a picture of problems under PMPA to a United States Senate Committee on Energy and Natural Resources[141]:

> Dealers are being forced to sign take-it-or-leave-it leases with provisions so coercive that signing one can be an agreement to self-destruction. Oil companies can now force a dealer to accept any lease provision if their determinations are made as a result of their interpretation of what constitutes good faith in the normal course of business, as stipulated in the act. The kicker is that under PMPA failure to agree to any provisions proposed by the supplier in "good faith" is grounds for non-renewal.
>
> Unreasonable franchise provisions have resulted in dealers being canceled for not being able to sell unattainable minimum volumes even though their wholesale prices are competitive. They must agree to 24-hour operation and risk employees' lives when there is no business to justify it.
>
> Dealers have been given rent increases of 1,000 percent because an oil company imposes its own appraisal of real estate value . . .
>
> Dealers are now being forced to sign bulldozer clauses which allow a company with thirty days' notice to bulldoze a dealer's location and rebuild it as a convenience store or a pumper without service bays. Thousands of locations are now being converted annually.
>
> A major misinterpretation of the intent of PMPA language by a Federal judge in *Baldauf v. Amoco* in 1981 opened the floodgates for conversions. Many are used to force dealers out by including huge rent increases based on promised new profits which never materialize. The dealer is forced out and the location becomes a company operation.
>
> In other cases, oil companies have used expiration of underlying leases to close dealer-operated stations that would offer competition to new company-operated facilities that appropriate the dealer's goodwill. Dealers and their customers have been forced to pay as much as 20 cents per gallon more for gas when refiners have passed on price reductions to their other customers but not to their own captive dealers.

The dealers and legislators championing their cause proposed a statute which would require changes and additions proposed by a franchisor in renewal negotiations to be "fair and reasonable" in addition to being in good faith.[142]

Chevron's Vice-President of Marketing responded for the American Petroleum Institute: "[u]nder the amendments, the courts would be compelled, on a case-by-case basis, to second guess the business judgment of franchisor decisions. Franchisors would naturally be reluctant to be innovative because of the threat of protracted litigation. For the most part, current contract terms and methods of operation would be frozen in place".[143]

In 1988, the proposed statute amending the PMPA was passed by the House of Representatives but not by the Senate. It was reintroduced in 1989. The Director of Legislative and Political Affairs for the Petroleum Marketers Association of America

---

[140]See 77 National Petroleum News, July, 1985, at 27.

[141]U.S. Senate, Committee on Energy and Natural Resources, Subcommittee on Energy Regulation and Conservation, Hearings on the Petroleum Marketing Practices Act Amendments of 1987, 100th Cong., 2d Sess. 1988, at 13-14.

[142]See Senate Bill S.2179, l00th Cong. 2d Sess. 1988.

[143]Id. at 103,107.

stated that he thought there was a "50:50 chance that President Bush would veto" the PMPA Amendments if they were passed.[144]

The retail gasoline dealers also returned to the state legislatures.[145] During the 1980s, they won victories in Massachusetts, Nevada and other states. However, their lawyers are now defending these statutes against constitutional challenges and charges that they attempt to regulate in an area taken from state power by the PMPA.[146] Once again, move prompts countermove. The Federal Trade Commission began rule-making hearings on proposed franchising rules in 1986. This process continued through 1990.[147] The announced objective is to provide a single uniform law governing disclosures franchisors must make to prospective franchisees. Most states have statutes requiring such disclosures, but a disclosure required by the laws of some states violates those of others. The resulting FTC rules, however, may do more than provide a uniform system for disclosures. The FTC, under the Reagan Administration, opposed state franchisee protections as ill-serving the consumer by limiting competition. The FTC, now under the Bush Administration, may propose rules which preempt state legislation limiting canceling and not renewing franchises.

What has been the impact of all this legal warfare? Certainly the organized gasoline dealers gained a federal law which gives them broad protection against cancellation during the term of a franchise. It is, for example, much more favorable on this score than the 1956 "Dealers Day in Court Act" which applies to automobile dealers' franchises.[148] However, the PMPA offers little protection against

144 67 Platt's Oilgram News, No. 84, May 2, 1989, at 4.

145 The International Franchise Association's treasurer discussed the success of this franchisor organization in blocking proposed state franchise protection legislation. The group works to kill these proposals in committee. This allows legislators to vote against these bills without publicity. He said in 1986, the IFA defeated 27 bills introduced in 18 states. See Bernstein, IFA Faces Franchise Law Fracas, 21 Nation's Restaurant News, Feb. 9, 1987, at 1.

146 Compare, Deutsch, Franchisees Fight Back, N.Y.Times, Dec. 4, 1988, Sec. 3, at 1, col. 4:

> When the Southland Corporation went private last year in a leveraged buyout, franchisees of its chain of 7-Eleven convenience stores stepped up lobbying in several states for legislation that would make it more difficult for franchisors to change or terminate franchise contracts. After the buyout, Southland ... [raised] fears among the 3,000 franchisees that it would slash services and advertising support, would increase royalties as contracts came up for renewal, or would withdraw from some regions.
>
> Terrified of new laws, Southland met with Joe Saraceno, chairman of the franchisees' national organization, and worked out a program to give every franchisee the option of extending existing contracts and terms to the year 2000. «We got rid of uncertainties, so there was no longer a push for stronger laws or a need for lawsuits», said Thomas B. Kanawyer, manager of Southland's franchise department Apparently, the franchisees are satisfied. "We do have some problems to deal with, but if things don't get any worse than they are today, we are in good shape", said Mr. Saraceno.

Experts say such amicable agreements are few and far between these days ...

147 See 54 Federal Register, No. 31, Feb. 16, 1989, at 7041.

148 See, S. Macaulay, Law and the Balance of Power (New York: 1966) for the background of this statute.

non-renewal of a franchise. Moreover, unlike the federal motor vehicle dealers statute, the PMPA preempts state legislation dealing with cancellation and non-renewal.

The number of franchised dealers of gasoline has continued to decline even after the federal legislation went into effect.[149] The price of fuel remains high, and many motorists drive less and buy cars that get high mileage. This limits gasoline sales. Motorists are less willing to pay a few cents a gallon more at their neighborhood stations which do not discount their prices. Automobile manufacturers have decreased the frequency of needed maintenance, and dealers have lost oil change and lubrication business. Automobiles have become more difficult to repair, requiring specialized tools for each make and trained mechanics. This decreases the opportunity to repair cars at service stations. And the federal legislation came in 1978 rather than in 1968. Many of the dealers who might have benefited when the great wave of terminations and non-renewals began, lost out long before the law was passed.

Thus, the long struggle to gain federal legislation may have produced a law with more symbolic significance than instrumental impact. Of course, it may have benefited those who managed to survive until it was passed. Some dealers may have won renewals before the oil companies established the judicial interpretations that are so favorable to them. There might have been even a greater decline in the number of service stations had there been no federal law.

As we noted, the gasoline dealers' efforts in some states produced statutes offering protection to most franchisees rather than just those who sold gasoline. These statutes are preempted by the federal Petroleum Marketing Practices Act only insofar as they apply to gasoline dealers. There is an ironic twist here. The gasoline dealers worked to pass these statutes, and they included other franchisees only to broaden the appeal of the proposed legislation. Those who just went along for the ride are the major beneficiaries of the retail gasoline dealers' lobbying efforts.

V. Conclusion

Dissatisfied participants in several unstable private governments have sought and gained statutes and victories in court. Participants generated many overlapping and contradictory images. When franchisors are recruiting dealers, franchisors use pictures of community and partnership. When everything is going well, the success of one is the success of the other. When problems arise, franchisors use images of competition and efficiency while franchisees call on pictures of David and Goliath.

[149]"Although nobody knows the total number of retail gas outlets — estimates range from 150,000 to 300,000 — Government figures show that the number of service stations is now 112,000, less than half the 1972 peak". Hershey, Fill'er Up and Check the Doughnuts, N.Y.Times, July 1, 1989, at 16, col. 1,3.

Franchisees' power and control of their businesses is ambiguous. They must invest significant resources in the dealership, and they must manage skillfully. They are not employees taking orders, but they are not independent business people either. Franchisor and franchisee define the range of permissible discretion differently. In most successful franchises, the franchisor retains authority to chart the course for the group. Franchisors can insist on uniformity rather than diversity, defending this in terms of the interests of the larger community. It helps all those operating Hilton Hotel franchises if consumers know what to expect when they go to any Hilton.

The interests of franchisor and franchisee may conflict. Then, the franchisor asserts that its interests take priority. The image now is that of free contract and choice; the franchisee signed a document which, when properly translated, gives priority to the franchisor over all others. Franchisors also talk about protecting consumers by retaining the flexibility necessary to adapt to changing consumer tastes.

Franchisees read the situation differently. They argue that there are relational norms such as those described by Macneil. Franchisees claim that neither party should do anything to imperil the relationship and call on the norm of solidarity. They challenge the franchisor's role integrity. The franchisors may talk of pursuing a collective good, and their officials' actions usually match this image. However, when franchisors want to eliminate dealers or revise business strategy, the trusted partner turns into a bargaining adversary playing hardball. This violates the tacit rules of the game.

Finally, franchisees see mutuality as their right. In Macneil's terms, again, the "parties must divide the exchange surplus so that each gains appropriate but not necessarily equal returns". One atrocity story dealers tell judges and legislators pictures a dealer developing good will in a locality and a franchisor who then appropriates it by pushing out the dealer. Another atrocity story involves franchisors who impose new programs which benefit them at great cost but little benefit to franchisees. Macneil's mutuality principle has a contrary implication as well: losses should be divided so that each bears an appropriate but not necessarily equal amount

Even in the best of times, dealers perform differently. Some fail when measured by any standard, and franchisors can cancel these dealerships. Others are clear successes, and their efforts profit both themselves and the franchisor. Even here, difficulties may arise. A franchisor may cancel a highly successful franchisee if that franchisee is located in an area which becomes uneconomic for the franchisor to serve. The franchisor will lack cause to cancel or not renew as measured by the conduct of the franchisee, but its decision will be in perfect good faith. This is a difficult case to resolve to the satisfaction of all concerned.

Problems usually arise when situations are not so clear cut. Some dealers offer barely passing performance; others do well when they might be able to do much better. The solidarity norm calls for notice of deficiencies, a chance to cure and, perhaps, help in doing so. Most franchisors accept this obligation, and many statutes codify it.

Close cases, however, involve judgment. Franchisor representatives and franchisees often construct sharply differing stories about the causes of problems. They may not share the same vocabulary of excuses. Dealers' sales, for example, are compared to those of comparable dealers. The factory representative may see, say, a Ford dealer in one city as comparable to one in another city of similar size. The dealer whose performance is challenged may see that city as having a noncomparable market because of historical dominance by a competitor.

Changes in international markets may strain comfortable patterns of doing business. The success of Toyotas, Datsuns and Hondas in the American market changed the game for Ford, Chevrolet and Plymouth dealers and their franchisors. All parties in a long-term relationship are likely to accept that a relationship must change as the world changes. The problem comes when they cannot agree on the responses needed or on who will bear what share of the costs.

If we accept this general picture of the situation, what are appropriate legal responses? The case for doing little, if anything, is familiar and is not without wisdom: Macneil, for example, is skeptical about legal action to remedy relational problems. People, he reminds us, resent being ordered to do what they do not wish to do. This resentment triggers evasion and coping strategies which threaten norms of cooperation.

Whitford stresses the difficulty of asking legal agencies to make qualitative decisions about good faith, due cause and reasonableness. These agencies may lack capacity to gather enough facts, see all interests, and make necessary judgments. Both Gottlieb and Smith warn about unrepresented third party interests which may be injured by regulation and protection from market forces. Dealers' happiness may come at the expense of higher prices paid by consumers.

Scott and Kidwell remind us that legal doctrines are filtered through bargaining systems and social norms. Rights do not vindicate themselves, and judicial or administrative procedures are costly. When we consider legal reform, we must picture it in the context of the costs of triggering the reform and changing the balance of power. It is possible, if we are not careful, that a reform may give the undeserving too much and the worthy too little.

Jordan argued that many franchisees know that they may lose their business whether the franchisor decides to cancel for good, bad or no reason. Experienced dealers may read franchise documents or they learn of the real risks from contacts with other dealers and officials of their own trade associations. They may assume that they will not be canceled absent cause, but they know that the franchisor claims to be the court of last resort on the question of cause. Indeed, the years of legal battles by dealer trade associations stand as good evidence that many, if not most, dealers are well aware that franchisors can act for their own interests without regard to the interests of franchisees. Many know that the courts, both before and after the passage of franchise protection statutes, have been hesitant to intervene to change the balance of power.

Some dealers may be unaware of the rights reserved by the franchisors and the duties imposed on franchisees.[150] General Motors apparently recognizes this. Speaking about proposals for new franchise documents, Robert H. Ogden, G.M.'s General Director of Sales Operations and Dealer Relations, said: "We don't want something that they [the dealers] stick in the drawer for another five years. It needs to be something that will provide everybody direction and help us all do a better job in selling cars and trucks". Dick Smith, Chairman of the National Automobile Dealers Association's G.M. line group, agreed: "Usually, a dealer only reads the agreement when he's in trouble".[151] However, Jordan notes that demanding that franchisors prove that dealers actually understood the franchise document would involve prohibitively high costs. Governing officials of major corporations control what is written in form contracts. They have much less power over dealers' expectations which are formed by contact with company agents and each dealer's own experiences. It is difficult to imagine any system which could counter these expectations which would not be extremely costly. Holding dealers responsible to read and understand their franchise document eases the burdens on franchisors and courts alike.

In short, although she did not consider the point, Jordan probably would argue that Macneil's relational norms do not describe the actual expectations of many franchisees. Or, perhaps franchisees understand that while they can hope franchisors will honor relational norms, they know that franchisors may not do so. Jordan recognizes that in particular cases trade usage and course of dealing may qualify the provisions of standard form franchise agreements. However, she argues, this is a question of fact in each case.

American legislators have heard all of this, but they continue to enact franchise protection legislation of various types. Perhaps this reflects the power of small business as a symbol in the American public drama, but more may be involved. Part of the power of the image of contract is the idea that we can rely on our reasonable expectations. Most of us think that trust is to be preferred to paranoia. Upsetting expectations and mocking trust produces anger and cynicism, and it endangers useful commitments. We might console ourselves by imagining that franchisors never would use unfettered power against franchisees who deserved better. But this comforting picture rests on the assumption that there are only deserving and undeserving franchisees and that it is easy to tell the difference.

---

[150]Reference to documents signed at the initiation of the relationship may be little more than a magical way of answering the questions raised. This can be true even when those documents purport to deal with major changes in the economic context of the relationship. Neither franchisor nor franchisee may have understood how general provisions in a form contract might apply to a specific situation. Operation of the relationship over time may create expectations not totally congruent with the commands of a form contract. Of course, officials of a large corporate dealership, represented by experienced commercial lawyers, are more likely to understand the formal franchise system than the operator of a gasoline station. Nonetheless, even corporate officials are likely to rely on practice rather than printed contract clauses.

[151]Krebs, GM Maps Franchise for '90s, Automotive News, April 3, 1989, at 1.

This is not true. Cases at the extremes may be clear, but inevitably there will be close questions. Trust and expectations are subjective perceptions based on reactions to situations in context. Legal procedures exist, in part, to guard trust and expectations. At some point, defeating expectations and trust might endanger the patterns of cooperation needed for a working large-scale society. Roberto Unger has commented:

> [A] higher standard of solidarity — the one that gives primacy to the other party's interests — is necessarily exceptional. Any attempt to insist upon it in the generality of dealings would depart so radically from the standards by which people ordinarily deal with each other that it would merely encourage massive circumvention and hypocrisy coupled with a stifling despotism of virtue. It does not follow, however, that ordinary contracts and human encounters should be surrendered to the notion that one may treat other people's interests as if they were nonexistent. In fact, the parties to continuing or recurrent contractual relations, and often even to one-shot transactions, seem generally to adhere to a far stricter standard ... [D]octrine might develop a series of distinguishing criteria to characterize situations suitable for the application of a more limited solidarity constraint requiring each party to give some force to the other party's interests, though perhaps less than to his own.[152]

We can ask how close we may have come to Unger's ideal through the private government of franchises interacting with the various franchise protection acts as they are implemented in practice. None of our statutes freezes distribution systems in place permanently. Under the federal PMPA, oil companies can refuse to renew franchises when they cannot negotiate new arrangements, and the courts will not questions the companies' business judgment. Whatever the text of other statutes, courts seldom will order specific performance, forcing a relationship to continue when it makes no sense to do so. Even a dealer who cannot be canceled except for good cause and who has carried out all of the terms of the franchise, is likely to accept some amount of money to end the business and the dispute.[153] If a dispute went to court, the dealer would have to prove damages with reasonable certainty. The dealer faces delay and some costs, even where a statute awards attorneys' fees to those who win. The American legal system in practice controls most of those who view litigation as an indoor sport. Our judges now take pride in their skill at coercing litigants to settle, and those who refuse to settle may get no further than summary judgment for their opponents.

Several writers have argued that franchise protection legislation unduly burdens franchisors.[154] Franchisors, they say, cannot act without being ready to defend their

[152]The Critical Legal Studies Movement, 96 Harvard Law Review 561, 641-642 (1983).

[153]This situation should be rare except when a franchisor wants to withdraw from business or withdraw from an area entirely.

[154]See, e.g., Lockerby, Franchise Termination Restrictions: A Guide for Practitioners and Policy Makers, 30 Antitrust Bulletin 791 (1985); Pitegoff, Franchise Relationship Laws: A Minefield for Franchisors, 45 The Business Lawyer 289 (1989); Jordan, Unconscionability at the Gas Station, 62 Minnesota Law Review 813 (1978).

Lockerby adopts a relational contract approach. He thinks that we have focused too much on the franchisor's unrestricted right to terminate and not enough on protecting each party's expectations in the event of termination. See Lockerby, at 839. His argument assumes litigation rather than

actions in court or before an administrative agency. I see the situation differently. Franchisors can cancel franchisees when there is no doubt that they have cause, and legal challenges by franchisees are unlikely in those cases. In most other situations franchisors can buy out a franchisee who is having difficulty operating the business or they can help the franchisee arrange a sale to another entrepreneur. Riteris and Bleakley, lawyers who handle franchise cases regularly, spoke to the American Bar Association's 5th Annual Franchising Forum in November of 1982. Riteris said that if it were possible, a buyout or permission to sell the franchise is, in the end, the least expensive and traumatic alternative to litigation. He recommended that litigation be avoided at all costs. Bleakley said, "I haven't seen more than one or two cases that should not have been settled". Bleakley suggested renewing troubled franchises conditionally. A franchisor should clearly state problem areas, and renew subject to the condition that these problems are solved within the next renewal period.[155]

Franchise regulation, in all but a few instances, only changes the bargaining position of the dealer. The major burden that franchise legislation imposes on franchisors may be the cost of keeping records to preserve the power to cancel for cause.[156] Larger corporate franchisors are likely to keep such records for their own purposes whether or not they are burdened by franchise regulation.

Thus, if my assumptions about practice are warranted, the issue is whether our legal structures interacting with the private government of franchise relationships give too much, too little or just enough as the price of ending the relationship through settlement. Of course, we must specify what we mean by enough compensation to serve as a transition payment upon cancellation. Statutes often require the franchisor to repurchase inventory, special tools and the like even when dealers are canceled for cause, as long as the case does not involve bad faith. People may differ about whether this is enough. However, it is hard to make a firm judgment without better evidence about how the various franchise systems work at the negotiation for termination stage. We do not know who gets how much and why. We can suspect that auto dealers do better than gasoline dealers. The Dealers Day in Court Act, unlike the Petroleum Marketing Practices Act, does not preempt state franchise protection statutes, and the state statutes give automobile dealers some important rights. If these suspicions are right, we might wonder about a system that offers the most to automobile dealers, less to service station operations, and the least to ordinary employees working for wages — most of whom in the United States can be fired for good, bad or no reason.

Of course, we can also suspect that dealer protection comes at the consumer's expense, but the actual cost is unclear. Some researchers report a large and precise

---

settlement as the norm; I think this highly unlikely. I would expect litigation or an administrative proceeding only in the close case, and I think that most cases will not be close cases. I suggest that regulation affects bargaining to end franchises and the price for accepting termination often is some protection for a dealer's expectations.

[155]See Bureau of National Affairs, Daily Report for Executives, November 18,1982.

[156]Franchisors also spend a great deal of money lobbying before Congress and state legislatures to ward off increased regulation. It is hard to know how much of this investment is money well spent.

amount of increased cost based on correlational studies. However, their data are not that good. Moreover, we cannot be sure that the researchers have controlled for all other explanations of the correlations they find. Indeed, no study controls for whether a franchise protection statute is enforced aggressively or only passively. We can assume that manufacturers have found ways to cope with unwanted regulation. Factories and refineries can push dealers to compete whatever a regulatory statute may say. Moreover, it is not clear that everyone benefits from extreme forms of price competition. People cope with the market as well as with regulation, and dealers can offer the illusion of competition rather than the costly reality. Seemingly low prices can be combined with high financing charges, and many consumers will not see that they have been duped. Getting warranty service from a dealer who advertises low prices is never easy. Sophisticated self-reliant consumers are likely to do better in competitive markets than most Americans who dislike bargaining and comparative shopping.

Perhaps automobile dealers have more opportunity to cope than gasoline dealers. A consumer seeking information about purchasing an automobile needs to know much about makes and models, warranties and a dealer's reputation for service as well as financing. Many consumers think gasoline is a generic product, and so it may be harder for dealers to exploit imperfect information.

Whatever we may think is an ideal solution, we must recognize that dealer protection law has been fashioned through a political process. Our story has not been one of philosophers debating the good, the true and the beautiful. Rather we have looked at endless battles in a long war. Legal action provokes reaction, and reaction provokes further reaction. Lawyers drafted contracts placing all power in the hands of franchisors. Franchisees organized, litigated and lobbied, and won apparently favorable laws. Franchisors found ways to avoid the thrust of the statutes by changing their procedures and tactics. They challenged the constitutionality of the statutes, they sought restrictive interpretations of key provisions, and they used legal procedures to delay results and increase the costs of seeking remedies. Franchisors were sufficiently successful to provoke franchisees to litigate and lobby again. Additional successes were met with more evasion and more challenges. And we must remember that the number of new car dealers and retail gasoline dealers in the United States has continued to decline at least since 1970.

The American legal system offers almost unlimited opportunities for opposing interests to wage a long-term war, but it is not a neutral battlefield. There is a burden of persuading a legal agency to act. It is easier to block legislation than get favorable statutes enacted. It is easier to persuade legislators to pass statutes that are largely symbolic than to enact laws with real teeth. Judges, too, avoid generating new theories and expanding old ones to cover new situations. Moreover, legal warfare costs money. Almost always, franchisors are better able than franchisees to hire lawyers, lobbyists and expert witnesses as well as make campaign contribution to friendly legislators. Most franchisors are large corporations, some of them are the largest in the Americas if not the world. These corporations buy excellent legal services. A classic role played by the American corporate lawyer is that of saboteur of populist legislation.[157] Yet saboteurs typically only blunt the impact of legislation. Even symbolic legislation can have an indirect impact on behavior. Franchisee organizations are not without resources — all representatives in both state and federal legislatures have automobile dealers and retail gasoline dealers as constituents. If franchisor behavior is too outrageous, franchisees can use this conduct as an atrocity story in legal battles. This possibility alone may affect franchisor behavior and deter some abuses, at least when the gains from outrageous behavior are not too great.

The challenge is to see how all of these battles affect the beginning, the long-term life, and the ending of relationships between manufacturers and dealers. In Gottlieb's terms, we must look to the mediating systems of the relational order. We must see the techniques used to reconcile the informal systems and patterns of conduct with the formal requirements of the system of rules and institutions.

[157]Some have claimed that corporate lawyers help enforce regulatory legislation by drafting documents and devising procedures to bring their clients into compliance with these laws. I have discussed this client control function in Macaulay, Control, Influence and Attitudes: A Comment on Nelson, 37 Stanford Law Review 553 (1985). ("Any theory about the role of the legal profession in serving social integration or any other positive function must be scaled down to fit the facts. Some lawyers play such parts, but others simply serve those who hold power — using legal argument, procedures, delay, and technicality, as tools to defeat legal ideals".) Id. at 562-563. See, also, Arkin, Be a Good Corporate Citizen: Fight the Feds, Wall Street Journal, March 13, 1990, at A18, cols. 3-6. ("Aside from the business benefits that may flow to the company, standing up to authority that is unwisely, arrogantly or selfishly exercised services a higher good"). Ibid.

Wisconsin's Legal Tradition

Stewart Macaulay

Introduction

Speaking for everyone at the Law School, I want to thank Mrs. Mary Virginia Brazeau for the generous gift of the professorship. I also want to thank my colleagues for nominating me for this great honor.

Dean Bernstine has asked me to talk about the Law School, considering issues that might interest both alumni and faculty. The most significant development at the Law School is that the faculty is changing rapidly. In the past five years, seven senior faculty members have retired and one has died. Two more will retire at the end of this year. Six more are in their sixties and could retire within a few years. These are experienced and talented people. In addition, seven extraordinary faculty members have left over the same period to teach at such places as Columbia, Princeton and Yale.

We have appointed many excellent new faculty members, and we will appoint more soon, Alumni who have been practicing for some time will have to look hard to find people at the Law School who taught them during their student years. Sweeping changes in the faculty could make us better, as new people bring new ideas and energy, but drastic change also involves risks. I don't have to tell members of this Law School community that Wisconsin is not just a generic state law school. It long has been something special in American legal education. In a time of great change of the faculty, can Wisconsin continue to be something special?

This article was original published in Gargoyle (Alumni Magazine of the University of Wisconsin Law School) 24 (1994), 6–10. Reprinted with permission.
Theodore W. Brazeau Professor of Law, Speaking to the Benchers Upon Receiving the Brazeau Professorship.

S. Macaulay (✉)
University of Wisconsin Law School, Madison, WI, USA
e-mail: smacaula@wisc.edu

D. Campbell (ed.), *Stewart Macaulay: Selected Works*, Law and Philosophy Library 133, https://doi.org/10.1007/978-3-030-33930-2_10

To keep our tradition alive, we must understand it. Our merit does not rest on those indirect indicators of quality so beloved by U.S. News & World Report. In terms of return on investment, Wisconsin must be one of the world's greatest law schools. As is true of so many things in Wisconsin, dedicated people, working above and beyond the call of duty, have overcome resource constraints. Wisconsin law professors have drafted path-breaking statutes that have become models for other states. They have answered calls for help from legislators and the staff of administrative agencies. They have served on local, state, national and international committees and boards. Many have responded to a steady flow of questions about their areas from practicing lawyers. They have produced innovative teaching materials and done highly original research. As law school enrollment has increased, they have taught students in large classes, small seminars and clinical programs. Many have done a great deal of one-on-one teaching. At a time when professor-bashing is a popular indoor sport, I must call attention to the contributions to the state and the nation of so many of my colleagues.

Another part of the Law School's tradition is our "law in action" approach to issues. This is recognized nationally and internationally, and it is something that we cannot afford to lose. We are one of the few state law schools that want to be more than a version of Harvard or Yale.

I'll try to sketch important elements of this Wisconsin tradition by looking at three great faculty members who served here during the period 1929 to 1981: Nate Feinsinger, Jake Beuscher and Willard Hurst. All three were teaching here when I joined the faculty 37 years ago, so I'll draw on my own memories as well as those of others. In addition, I'll quote excerpts from tributes that appeared in the Wisconsin Law Review.

Three Sketches

Nate Feinsinger served at the Law School from 1929 to 1973. He was one of the inventors of modern labor law. He was the permanent umpire under several important collective bargaining contracts. But we are more likely to remember that he was called many times when major strikes created great social problems. Willard Wirtz said:

> Leaving to less adventurous counsel and judges the arguing and deciding of cases in court, where there were rules to go by, he chose emergency situations that developed so fast that a sometimes rough frontier justice had to be improvised to put out flames that were spreading.[1]

Nate had a photograph on his wall that showed him with President Truman at the White House. Nate said that he had told President Truman that as president he had the power to seize the steel mills that had been closed by a strike during the Korean conflict. The Supreme Court, of course, disagreed much later in a famous case defining the limits of presidential power in wartime. Nevertheless, by the time the decision was announced, the emergency was over. Nate had solved the immediate problem even if he hadn't gotten the doctrine just right.

[1] 1984 Wis.L.Rev. 282.

One way or another, Nate could get contending parties to sign an agreement. Douglas Soutar, a corporate vice president in charge of labor relations, commented:

> Such was his charm, wit, finesse, and genius in difficult situations that even those occasionally on the losing end were not always immediately aware of their condition, accepting the results in good humor and the realization that at least they had been in the hands of a master.[2]

I know just what Mr. Soutar meant. Nate often "mediated faculty meetings," and we'd be back in our offices before we realized what we'd voted for as a result of Nate's maneuvers. Often I was annoyed that we hadn't resolved an issue. However, I must admit that often Nate pushed us to reach an acceptable solution so that we could get on with the business of the Law School rather than debate endlessly.

I once met the chief executive officer of a major Wisconsin corporation at a large family party. This CEO was one of the founding members of the John Birch Society. His firm had faced several very bitter strikes, and Nate had settled them while serving as mediator. The CEO said that he didn't have much use for Nate's "socialistic" views. (Nate, after all, thought that labor unions were not the work of the devil.) However, the CEO then talked at length about what a wonderful human being Nate Feinsinger was.

Nate brought his wide experience to his students in many ways. Corporate lawyer Edward B. Miller recalled:

> It was Nate's excitement about labor and labor law that started so many of us on a career path in the labor relations field. Nate insisted that we probe into the economic, the legal, and the practical foundations of every fundamental labor law concept.[3]

Prof. Stewart Macaulay: "To keep our tradition alive we must understand it."

Nate founded a Center for Teaching and Research on Dispute Resolution where he applied lessons learned in labor disputes to other problems as well. A high spot of his seminars and classes was the parade of important visitors who had made a great deal of American labor law. My office was next to Nate's. One week I'd bump into Jimmy Hoffa, the next Walter Reuther. And if I had known them by sight, I would

[2] 1984 Wis.L.Rev. 290.

[3] 1984 Wis.L.Rev. 295.

have recognized Vice Presidents in Charge of Labor Relations from many of America's major corporations.

In sum, then, Nate Feinsinger was involved with national and local problems, carrying forward the University of Wisconsin's tradition of public service. He was one of the first to focus on dispute resolution. He brought this experience to his students in a vivid way. Also, he often exhibited great courage in the face of hostile public opinion. In 1994, it is hard to remember how controversial labor unions and collective bargaining were during Nate's professional career. Nonetheless, he won over many of his critics, and most people held him in high regard. The State of Hawaii even declared a Nathan P. Feinsinger day in appreciation for his work in settling a bitter prolonged dock workers strike.

• • •

Jake Beuscher served at the Law School from 1934 to 1967. Jake was the country lawyer from Yale. He loved to talk as if he lacked sophistication, but, he was a brilliant and well-educated man. Jake knew the writings of the legal realists, and he never tired of pointing to Eugen Ehrlich's work on "the living law."[4] Ehrlich's living law was:

> . . . in contrast to that which is in force merely in the courts and with the officials. The living law is that law which is not imprisoned in rules of law, but which dominates life itself. The sources of its knowledge are above all the modern documents, and also immediate study of life itself, of commerce, of customs and usage, and of all sorts of organizations, including those which are recognized by the law, and, indeed, those which are disapproved by the law.

Jake, his colleagues and students conducted empirical research on actual practices related to property doctrine. He was the one who labeled this approach "law in action research."[5] Jake transformed property doctrine into areas of law and practice that mattered to people in their daily lives. He developed a course in farm law. The topic might not thrill Jake's former colleagues at Yale, but in Wisconsin it is central to our economy, and it taught Jake and his students much about the law in action. Jake taught land-use planning before it became fashionable. He was concerned about the ability of people to use property as security to gaining financing. He saw threats to the environment before environmental protection became a popular cause, and he taught students about these problems and worked hard for reform in this area.

This University has long boasted that the boundaries of the campus are the boundaries of the state. Jake looked to the nation and the world as well. He was one of the Law School's first internationalists. He started a tradition that has given this school a tremendous reputation abroad.

---

[4]See E. Ehrlich, *Fundamental Principles of the Sociology of Law* (1913, 1936); N.S. Timasheff, Ehrlich, Eugen in 4 Int'l Encyclopedia Soc. Sci. 540, 541 (David L. Sills, ed. 1968). A famous Wisconsin law professor of an earlier day, William Herbert Page, wrote an appreciation of Ehrlich's work and presented it at the Association of American Law School's Annual Meeting in 1914. It is reprinted as W. H. Page, Professor Ehrlich's Czernowitz Seminar of Living Law, in *Readings in Jurisprudence* (Jerome Hall ed. 1938).

[5]The contracts teaching materials being developed at Wisconsin appear under the title: *Contracts: Law in Action.*

Jake Beuscher's career suggests several things: Jake saw theory as vital, but Jake demanded that theory be grounded in experience. Following Eugen Ehrlich, Jake dealt with "the living law." Jake worked with engineers and natural and social scientists comfortably. He wanted to solve problems, and he was impatient with turf wars. Late in his career, he turned to problems of land tenure in third world countries. However, he did not see this project as Americans as experts bringing enlightenment to "backward" nations. Rather he knew that he would learn as much as he taught. As the Land Tenure Center's publications list shows, that is just what happened.

Jake was an institution-builder, interested in developing the careers of younger scholars. He was a remarkable grant-getter. He pushed deans and university presidents to pursue new opportunities. He did not always succeed in gaining the resources and starting the programs that he advocated. Nonetheless, he continued to champion new ideas as long as he served on the faculty.

Finally, Jake worked with the legislature and administrative agencies, drafting and advocating innovative proposals in many fields. Former Governor Gaylord Nelson said:

> Jake Beuscher was one of those rare educators who could perform as brilliantly in the governmental and political area as in the halls of the university. It is difficult to see how a democratic system based upon intelligent decisions involving difficult problems could survive without men like him.[6]

• • •

Willard Hurst served at the Law School from 1937 to 1981. He created a new kind of legal history. Instead of focusing on the origins of legal doctrine, Willard asked what roles law had played in Wisconsin's development. Early settlers used the law for practical ends. It served to "release energy" so the pioneers could exploit the resources found here. Hurst was also one of the first scholars to look seriously at the part lawyers had played in the story. For example, he describes how lawyers "contrived or adapted institutions (the corporation), tools (the railroad equipment trust certificate), and patterns of action (the reorganization of corporate financial structure or the fashioning of a price structure for a national market)."[7] These social inventions made possible the growth of railroads. In turn, this provoked the expansion of markets. Nineteenth-century Americans moved from buying and selling within the reach of a horse and wagon to regional and then national opportunities to market what was produced on farms and in factories. It could not have happened without structures that allowed entrepreneurs to pay to lay track and buy equipment, and these structures were lawyers' inventions.

Hurst saw law as a system of ideas about managing affairs, and he developed some of the first analyses of what today we call the legal culture, those attitudes and assumptions held by Americans about what is acceptable, necessary and just. What we see as common sense colors our statutes and judicial decisions and what they mean in practice. As part of this project, Willard developed a command of history,

---

[6]1967 Wis.L.Rev. 799.

[7]J. Willard Hurst, *The Growth of American Law: The Law Makers* 337 (1950).

social theory, social science and realist legal thought. He also commanded the facts. If there was a small-town newspaper in the state, you could safely bet that Willard had read it. One university press found it appropriate to publish two versions of one of his major works: One had the major text standing almost alone with relatively few references; the other added the vast body of his footnotes reflecting his explorations and excavations in the raw material of this history.

Hurst saw that new courses were needed to train Wisconsin lawyers to play their social roles, and he created them. With several colleagues in the late 1930s, he fashioned a legal process course that focused on the development of worker's compensation. He arrived here in the middle of the New Deal, and he proposed developing a course on legislation. Dean Garrison agreed with the young man's innovative idea, but Willard was still an assistant professor and had to pay a price. The Dean assigned Hurst to teach personal property. I've always wondered what he did with such a course. My guess is that he made a desert bloom.

Willard crusaded throughout his career for the Law School to play its part in the university. Thorstein Veblen said, "The law school belongs in the modern university no more than a school of fencing or dancing."[8] Willard would not accept such a dismissal. He saw the mission of a university law school as more than training lawyers in the dance steps of a narrow received tradition. Rather, a university law school had to develop knowledge about law and society so that it could train lawyers to play their actual social roles.

He saw that our Law School trains those who staff local, state and national executive, legislative and administrative bodies. All of us who have taught here for some time recognize, often with a smile, that we are governed by our former students. The Governor and his opponent in the next election are both loyal alumni of this institution. So is the Mayor of Madison. Our graduates serve as elected officials, on legislative and executive staffs and even on the Board of Regents of this university. Many, if not most of the judges in the state once sat in our classrooms.

Hurst was a highly successful and popular teacher. Lawrence Friedman commented:

> Some rare teachers ... set off explosions in peoples' minds. They break old habits of thought. Anyone who has had contact with Willard Hurst, who has listened to him or discussed things with him, recognizes him as this kind of teacher.[9]

What do we learn from Willard Hurst's career at Wisconsin? He asked fundamental questions about the functions of law, but he tested theories against the detail of everyday experience. Rather than studying the great cases, which by definition are atypical, he preferred to look for general patterns in the flow of ordinary ones. From this commonplace raw material, he fashioned a brilliant description of our legal institutions and their place in our society.

---

[8] T. Veblen, *The Higher Learning in America* 211 (1918).

[9] 1980 Wis.L.Rev. 1121.

He saw that law students need to be trained to play a large role in governing human affairs. Lawyers serve in all branches of government. In private practice, too, lawyers give life to the common law, legislation and regulation by helping clients comply or cope with its commands. Willard sought to train lawyers to play these public and private roles with intelligence. He was impatient with "drift" and "inertia." He wasn't satisfied with "bastard pragmatism"; that is, with short-run solutions that evaded real problems. Margo Melli points to one of his most simple lessons: Lawyers must stay abreast of current affairs, and this means that they must read newspapers. And Willard meant "newspapers," in the plural.

His legal history class was not an attempt just to give tone to an otherwise grubby and technical legal education. It definitely wasn't a fluff course. Willard stressed lawyer-like analysis in coping with policy problems. Among his many gifts, Hurst is an excellent lawyer, quite capable of holding his own with the very best fellow professionals. Any former student who once had to cope with one of his examinations can testify that no law school offered a more rigorous course than Hurst's American Legal History. Hurst did not gift-wrap grades. Students either earned high marks or they didn't get them.

What Should We Say About the Wisconsin Tradition?

Wisconsin professors have done research for many purposes, but they've not played a game just to amuse other professors.

The most simple generalization about the Wisconsin approach is that law must be studied in its full social context. Wisconsin professors have done research for many purposes, but they've not played a game just to amuse other professors. Wisconsin research has been a tool for criticism, seeking to transform the legal culture, the attitudes and assumptions of ordinary citizens and professionals. It has been a tool for reform, seeking to implement values through what we know about the operation of law in our society. It has been a tool for solving particular problems of individuals within existing social structures.

However, we must remember that law in action research also plays a vital part in educating new lawyers. People sometimes criticize university professors for focusing on research and neglecting teaching. It can happen. However, critics often forget that a professor must have something to teach, and each professor must create her course. You can report the work of others, but the greatest teachers work with their own ideas and observations of their subject. Moreover, matters taught in universities seldom are static. A professor constantly must revise and recreate her course. Five-year-old lecture notes probably should be thrown away on principle unless the margins are richly annotated.

Of course, law schools must teach some of the body of received wisdom and lawyer skills and teach this well. Students must learn to read carefully. They must distinguish cases and construe statutes. They must fashion a legal argument and respond to one. They must draft a complaint. But this is not enough. The challenge is to prepare students to deal with the law in action during their legal careers. Rules matter, but we cannot teach our students all the rules they might have to master to practice the day they are admitted to the bar. Three years is a short time, and our graduates enter diverse legal careers. The demands of Wall Street and Main Street differ, and government lawyers deal with different bodies of law than do small-town practitioners. Furthermore, we cannot teach our students what they will need ten to twenty years from now. Even if we could, it would not be enough.

I need not remind practicing lawyers that law is not only rules or appellate opinions. It is structures and practices in courts and administrative agency hearing rooms. It is the attempts by the Governor and the legislators to cope with emerging social problems. It is the quaint native customs of bench and bar in particular cities. It is the lawyer seeking new ways to deal with corporate take-overs or Superfund litigation in her office. It is also the not always consistent collection of ideas about law held by Wisconsin citizens.

At our best, Wisconsin professors have emphasized testing ideas in practice. To paraphrase Frank Remington, the criminal law becomes real in the front seat of a squad car. As a young professor, I borrowed Frank's idea and looked at business practices related to contract. Not surprisingly, I found that contract law becomes real when the machine is not delivered on time or when it doesn't perform exactly as promised and engineers and business executives want to do something about it.

When we focus on the law in action, often we discover important theoretical and policy problems. For example, what are we to say about a society that promises due process and offers only a deal? About a society that claims to follow the rule of law but is characterized by discretion, negotiation and cost barriers to asserting rights? Our research and teaching cannot avoid questions of justice. William G. Tapply writes mysteries featuring his lawyer-detective, Brady Coyne. In the most recent novel, Coyne reflects:

> If law school doesn't make you cynical, the practice of law quickly does.
>
> Lawyers rarely admit they're committed to justice. They never admit that to each other. We talk mostly about billable hours, sometimes about winning. Among ourselves, we call the law a business and ourselves businessmen.
>
> But most of the lawyers I know still nurture the vestige of what got them into law in the first place. The quest for an abstraction. Justice.[10]

The Wisconsin approach at its best seeks justice. However, we know that we must look for it not only in doctrine but in police cars, courtrooms, lawyers' offices and the lives of ordinary people as well.

[10]William G. Tapply, *The Snake Eater* 183–184 (1993).

Conclusions

This Law School faces all the challenges and risks of change. Nevertheless, we have a strong tradition that is the envy of many at other institutions. We must keep this tradition alive. It will take work; it won't just happen.

However, while we must remember our tradition, we cannot assume that it will carry us through the 1990s into the next century. We should recall that Pan American World Airways also had a great tradition, but it is just a memory today. Times changed, but Pan Am didn't change enough. Duke Ellington used to feature Johnny Hodges playing "Things Ain't What They Used to Be." We must keep that melody in mind. The world has changed from the one that Nate, Jake and Willard knew. We no longer live in the Progressive Era, the New Deal, the Fair Deal, the New Frontier or the Great Society. Rather we live in a time of trying to make do with less. And think of the bodies of law faced by lawyers today that didn't exist as recently as when Nate, Jake and Willard were teaching.

Our Wisconsin tradition itself demands that we try to anticipate and understand the new problems and new demands that will face lawyers and the legal system in the future. We cannot hope to meet the highly ranked elite law schools head-on. We've long struggled to run a first-class law school on a third-class budget. When our deans have been faced with a faculty member who has had an offer to move to, say, Yale or Columbia, it is too much like Bud Selig and Sal Bando trying to compete with the Toronto Blue Jays for Paul Molitor's services. Wisconsin law professors are well paid as compared to many practicing lawyers and most citizens of the state. Nonetheless, there is a market for talent that sets the price, and we must scramble to come close to meeting what our best professors can command elsewhere. I remind you that in the 1993 U.S. News & World Report rating, while we ranked 23rd in overall quality, we ranked only 69th in law school resources. Give Dean Bernstine the average of the resources of all Big Ten law schools, and you would watch our national ranking soar. But this is unlikely to happen soon.

As always, this Law School must specialize and look for things that we can do better than others and things that do not demand major investments from the state budget. Thus, we need a strategy. We need to discover where law is going and get there before the traditional schools discover the destination. As we do this, we must remember our tradition: We must look at what lawyers, police officers, taxpayers, drug dealers, gang leaders, insurance adjusters, social workers and all the rest who create and recreate the living law do as well as look at what judges and statutes say.

It is clear that we need our graduates to play a major role as we look to the future. Alumni and friends have contributed much-needed resources such as the building and the Brazeau Professorship. Nevertheless, we also need intellectual contributions from our graduates and friends. If we glory in a lawyer-centered tradition of education and scholarship, we must listen to lawyers who encounter the problems of practice daily because our tradition won't work in an ivory tower. Much of my research is based on interviewing lawyers, many if not most of whom are UW graduates. Their cooperation, interest and, indeed, enthusiasm made my work possible. Our graduates also can teach the faculty about new areas of law and how lawyers are coping with them. Lawyers must face problems long before there is a line of appellate cases to debate, and lawyers must understand the practical consequences of proposed and newly enacted regulation. Lawyers, for example, already are organizing programs to learn about how the North American Free Trade Agreement will affect their clients. Few, if any, law schools have begun to consider how NAFTA will affect teaching in courses ranging from contracts to trade regulation. I'm told that we will face this problem soon.

I'm sure that the law faculty, our students and our graduates share a great deal and can work together to keep this Law School special. One thing we share, I'm sure, is the conviction that this has been and still is a fine law school, and it ought to stay that way.

The Impact of Contract Law on the Economy: Less Than Meets the Eye?

Stewart Macaulay

We assume that contract law plays an important role in a market economy, but we may over-estimate its significance. A study of the Peruvian economy recently has been the focus of scholarly discussion in the United States. An entire symposium in the *Yale Law Journal*,[1] the lead article and a lengthy comment in the *Law & Society Review*,[2] and an article in *Social & Legal Studies*[3] all have focused on norms and sanctions in underground or second economies. All of these articles have considered in some detail Hernando de Soto's *The Other Path*.[4] De Soto's study of Peru has

This paper was original given at a conference on Law and Modernization in Lima (Peru) in July 1994. It was translated into Spanish and published as 'El Impacto Del Derecho de Contratos en la Economia' (2008) 5 Revista de Economia y Derecho 27–40.

Malcolm Pitman Sharp Hilldale Professor and Theodore W. Brazeau Bascom Professor of Law, University of Wisconsin Law School, Madison, WI. USA. This is a revision of a paper originally presented at the Congreso Internacional de Derecho Civil Patrimonial, August 8-12, 1994, of the Facultad de Derecho of the Pontificia Universidad Católica del Perú. Dr. Jacqueline Macaulay took time from her law practice to edit this article. As always, all errors remain mine alone.

[1]See Symposium: The Informal Economy, 103 Yale Law Journal 2119-2436 (1994). See, particularly, Arthur J. Jacobson, The Other Path of the Law, 103 Yale Law Journal 2213 (1994).

[2]See Jane Kaufman Winn, Law and Relational Practices in Taiwan, 28 Law & Society Review 193 (1994); Frank K. Upham, Comment—Speculations on Legal Informality: On Winn's "Relational Practices and the Marginalization of Law," 28 Law & Society Review 233, 236-237 (1994).

[3]See Lauren Benton, Beyond Legal Pluralism: Towards a New Approach to Law in the Informal Sector, 3 Social & Legal Studies 223 (1994).

[4]Hernando De Soto, The Other Path: The Invisible Revolution in the Third World (1989). De Soto's title, of course, suggests a contrast with "The Shining Path," a radical Marxist revolution advocated by other Peruvians. See David Scott Palmer (ed.), Shining Path of Peru (1992).

S. Macaulay (✉)
University of Wisconsin Law School, Madison, WI, USA
e-mail: smacaula@wisc.edu

D. Campbell (ed.), *Stewart Macaulay: Selected Works*, Law and Philosophy Library 133, https://doi.org/10.1007/978-3-030-33930-2_11

come to stand for second economies in all of Latin America, Africa and much of Asia.

The Other Path contains several distinct elements. De Soto describes the practices of Peruvians in housing, retailing and transportation transactions, many of which violate Peruvian law. He explains why such transactions succeed even though they stand apart from the official legal system. Finally, there is a prescription for a "revolution" that would encourage and focus the entrepreneurial energy of the popular classes in Peruvian society toward greater prosperity. In essence, *The Other Path* advocated by de Soto is deregulation and the "rule of law," so beloved by international monetary organizations.[5]

De Soto calls for deregulation to legalize the practices of those who now participate in a second economy. Most significantly for this paper, de Soto calls for the courts to enforce the contracts of those now in the second economy to encourage planning and risk taking. He found that those in the informal sector use inefficient tactics to insure performance of agreements. They create and maintain trust, dealing primarily with family members, and fashioning long-term continuing relationships. De Soto argues that these practices impose unnecessary transaction costs on traders. He advocates legally enforceable contracts so traders can rely on the legal system to increase the likelihood of performance and remedy defaults rather than on family loyalties and friendship. He writes as if legally enforceable contracts, standing alone, would make trust and the sanctions of long-term continuing relationships unnecessary in a modern economy. In other words, only a impersonal market is efficient.[6]

This paper will consider the role of contract law in market economies, particularly that of the United States because I know more about it than others.[7] Much of my research has involved interviewing business people and their lawyers about their practices, collecting standard form contracts, and analyzing the context of contracts cases brought before courts. Thus, I will offer an empirical perspective on contract in modern economies.

[5]Udo Reifner remarks: "While in former times capitalist nations used priests, soldiers and merchants to convince less developed peoples to adhere to their system, we can now rely on the convincing forces of IMF, World Bank, BERD and other financial institutions where nations cue up to be accepted as members." Reifner, The Vikings and the Romans—Contract Law and Social Economy 6 (Paper presented at the Conference on Perspectives of Critical Contract Law, Tuusula, Finland, May 7 to 10, 1992).

[6]Although I am critical of de Soto's claims for contract law, I do not want to be misunderstood as being critical of so much that I admire in *The Other Path.* It is a great book, and I would support many, if not most, of his policy recommendations.

[7]See Stewart Macaulay, Non-Contractual Relations in Business: A Preliminary Study, 28 American Sociological Review 55 (1963); Stewart Macaulay, Elegant Models, Empirical Pictures, and the Complexities of Contract, 11 Law & Society Review 507 (1977); Stewart Macaulay, An Empirical View of Contract, 1985 Wisconsin Law Review 465.

I. The Received Model of the Role of Contract in Market Economies

De Soto's argument about contract law's role is familiar. In Western culture there is a classic model of the functions of legally enforceable contract. This model rests on common but inconsistent assumptions. One version of the story suggests that in a state of nature we are all selfish, and we are forced to cooperate to gain economic rewards. Law supports our needed interdependence by coercing us to honor our agreements with others. Ideally, it should make no difference whether we perform or breach a contract because legal action will redress any harm resulting from breach. We get performance or a judgment, and one is as good as the other in a world where we can transform everything into a monetary equivalent.

The historical story of contract's development is similar. We began by trading within real communities. Capitalism then destroys community, and we became alienated strangers. We might like to act to help others, but we risk becoming exploited fools. The legal system then supplied a synthetic community based on rights and duties enforced by courts. We can risk acting cooperatively because the law will discipline those who act opportunistically.

The classical model also rests on many assumptions about the behavior of bargainers: They plan, perform and resolve disputes guided by their legal rights. Bargainers know that they must state all their rights and duties in a detailed contract because they can expect performance only to the letter of their agreement. Indeed, if parties fail to plan and specify everything, they are at fault. They are responsible for their own injury when they fail to receive what they expected from the bargain. It is assumed that contract law is a body of clear rules that help traders plan and perform contracts. Bargainers know, or can learn, the formal steps necessary to create a legally enforceable contract. A bargainer always knows or can learn what a court would do in case of a dispute, and bargainers make contracts and perform them in light of this knowledge. Contract law also provides default rules to minimize transaction costs. Unless bargainers want other terms, they can rely on the law to fill in standard provisions. This avoids the costs of negotiating about all possible contingencies. Finally, the classic model assumes that, directly or indirectly, contract litigation is a primary means of determining breach, providing remedies and resolving disputes.

This classic model has an illustrious history. We find traces of it in Shakespeare's *The Merchant of Venice*. As you will recall, Antonio has breached a contract, and, under its terms, he owes Shylock a pound of flesh. Several characters look for a way out, but others argue that the economy of Venice depends on the certain and predictable enforcement of contracts. Even Antonio himself rejects a suggestion that the judge should not enforce such a bargain. He says that if the course of the law is denied, it will "impeach the justice of the state." This will harm the "trade and profit of the city." Of course, Shakespeare finds a way out of the dilemma, but remember that it involves at least claiming to enforce the letter of the contract.

We also find traces of the classic model of the role of contract in the writings of the great sociologist Max Weber. Weber argued that capitalism and increasing "formal rationality" go together. David Trubek[8] tells us that Weber thought only a formal system of law can be predictable. Law seeking substantive ends leads to particularistic decisions. Such decisions make it impossible for business people to know in advance the right answers to legal questions. Formal justice, Weber argues, enhances individual opportunities, promotes self-determination and helps assure individual freedom. Trubek notes that Weber also argues, perhaps paradoxically, that formal thought in law may actually defeat the intent of transacting parties, and benefit those with power and wealth. In fact, Weber suggested that completely formal thought may be impossible.

II. An Empirical Appraisal of the Classic Model

How well does this classic model of the role of contract law fit an empirical picture of the law in action? It is not all wrong, but it certainly is an overstatement.[9] Contrary to de Soto's position, and that of others who celebrate contract law, formal law may not be able to reduce transaction costs by placing great reliance on rights and courts.

The North American story is complex. Sometimes something approaching the classic model tracks well with the empirical picture. In certain situations, business people do engage in elaborate planning, performance and dispute resolution in light of contract law. Typically, lawyers control or influence these transactions. They may involve, for example, the sale of a major building, transfers of the control of a corporation or the licensing of intellectual property. The risks and amounts involved warrant elaborate written contracts and formal behavior. The parties' lawyers will take care to dot all the "i"'s and cross all the "t"'s.

---

[8]David M. Trubek, Reconstructing Max Weber's Sociology of Law, 37 Stanford Law Review 919 (1985). See, also, David M. Trubek, Max Weber's Tragic Modernism and the Study of Law in Society, 20 Law & Society Review 573 (1986).

[9]Roberto Mangabeira Unger in Law in Modern Society: Toward a Criticism of Social Theory 12-13 (1976), remarks:

> By tightening or relaxing the strictness of the premises, by making them more or less complex and therefore more or less faithful to the social reality we want to apprehend, we are able to control the balance between simplicity of explanation and descriptive fidelity.
>
> The more we lean toward the former [simplicity], the greater the danger that our inferences will fail to apply to any world in which we are actually interested. The more we tend to the latter [descriptive fidelity], the higher the risk that our conjectures will degenerate into a series of propositions so qualified and complicated that we are just as well off with our commonsense impressions. Whether simplicity or faithfulness to fact is emphasized will depend on the particular purpose for which we choose between them.

Even the most carefully planned transactions may go wrong. When business people face disputes, sometimes they litigate to final judgment. Some losers appeal these decisions. In some of these cases, we get an appellate opinion applying the Uniform Commercial Code or the common law of contract as envisoned in the classical contract model. Often transactions that provoke judicial opinions involve a power imbalance. A franchisee, such as a local Ford dealer, may be suing a franchisor, such as the Ford Motor Company. A small supplier may sue a large corporate buyer. Appellate opinions often reveal a weaker party attempting to gain the power of the law to offset its lack of market power. But as Galanter tells us usually "the haves come out ahead" before the legal system.[10]

Other disputes that go to court may involve attempts to salvage something from a near-disaster. Our Wisconsin Business Disputes Research Project has found that during the last few decades, there has been a marked increase in contract litigation involving the largest corporations in the United States. The great economic dislocations of the recent past have melted the relational glue that held transactions together. Long-term continuing relationships have collapsed. One party may be on verge of declaring or actually in bankruptcy. Moreover, modern economic transactions often involve great sums of money that neither party can afford to lose without a fight.

However, in other situations where transactions have failed, the role of contract law is muted or absent. Instead of relying on contract law alone, business people often turn to legally guaranteed security interests in property. My colleague, the great legal historian Willard Hurst, celebrates the role of lawyers as social inventors in 19th century America. Lawyers, he says, "contrived or adapted institutions (the corporation), tools (the equipment trust certificate), and patterns of action (the reorganization of corporate financial structure or the fashioning of a price structure for a national market)." [11] Hurst views these social inventions as critical for the economic development of the United States. We can analyze these social inventions as contracts, but usually they involve much more than a simple contract. If, for example, an airline fails to pay for a Boeing 747, Boeing can seek damages. However, it also can take back title and possession of the aircraft through legal procedures. Of course, the value of repossessing goods is uncertain. If the used aircraft market is weak, recovering a 747 airplane may benefit Boeing very little. However, reselling the 747 after repossession may not be the most important goal of Boeing. The threat of losing the use of the aircraft may be a powerful incentive for an airline to pay or renegotiate its arrangement with Boeing.

Having said all this, however, very often the classic model is far from the reality of United States business. This is particularly true in transactions involving manufacturing firms. Often business people do not plan transactions in detail. As part of closing a deal, sometimes they fill in blank lines on standardized forms that

---

[10]Marc Galanter, Why the "Haves" Come Out Ahead: Speculations on the Limits of Legal Change, 9 Law & Society Review 95 (1974).

[11]J. Willard Hurst, The Growth of American Law: The Law Makers 337 (1950).

contain numerous printed clauses. However, often signing such forms is only an empty part of a ceremony. No one negotiating the contract has read or understands the standard provisions printed on the form. The parties file the documents away and forget them. They perform to business and engineering standards rather than legal ones captured in contract documents. Sometimes form provisions are important. Often the goal of a large corporation that uses them is to ward off results that otherwise the law would impose. The corporation wants to be sure that those with whom it deals have no legally protected rights and cannot sue the corporation. Freedom of contract becomes freedom to have no legally enforceable contract. For example, in the automobile industry manufacturers often deal with suppliers on documents called blanket orders. They are documents with extremely flexible quantity and price provisions. The manufacturers make no commitment to buy a specified quantity of parts or components or they make a commitment that they can "cancel for convenience." The position of the parties is not that envisioned in the classic model of contract law. The contract document offers guidance rather than a fixed commitment.

Even where the parties are more or less equal, business people usually seek to avoid disputes or settle those that occur without reference to rights and the threat of legal proceedings. Instead of rights, they talk of solving problems and seeing the other's position. They continuously modify contracts during performance to adapt to changes in the market. Buyers may agree to pay more than the contract price when the seller's costs drastically increase. Sellers will accept cancellation or postponement of some or all of an order when buyers cannot use the items they bought. The parties may modify the product itself to cut costs or adapt it to market demand. If a product does not work satisfactorily, both firms work to fix it. Engineers from both seller and buyer may devote a great deal of time to diagnose problems and remedy them. Deadlines for delivery often, if not usually, are target dates rather than absolute requirements. Buyers may accept even long delays as a cost of doing business, particularly if a seller has an excuse recognized by business custom.

Why does business so often operate inconsistently with the classic model of the place of contract law in the economy? Most simply, business seldom needs contract law. Even when informal measures are not enough, the benefits of contract law seldom outweigh its very high costs. Business seldom needs formal contract law because transactions rest on trust, power, the sanctions of long-term continuing relations or some blend of these factors. These are the same factors that de Soto finds important in holding together the informal sector in Peru. He sees them as inefficient transaction costs and prescribes legally enforceable contracts instead. North American business people would disagree. Undoubtedly, there are costs in creating trust or dealing only with those with whom you have long-term continuing relationships. Nonetheless, these may be necessary costs because formal impersonal contract is too weak a reed to support business transactions. It cannot substitute for trust, power and long-term continuing relationships that keep both the first and second economies going.

The relevance of formal contract turns on the nature of the transaction. Arthur Okun speaks of "auction" and "consumer" markets.[12] Economists usually like auction markets where price competition for fungible goods should bring all the benefits promised by their theories. For example, both American and United Airlines fly many times a day from Chicago to New York. Their aircraft are the same or very similar. There is little difference in the food they serve or the way they handle baggage. Both have been in business since the 1930s and have experienced pilots and good safety records. Most people are likely to see all other things as equal, and so their decision about which airline to fly will turn on which offers the lowest price. This competitive pressure also pushes both airlines to avoid disputes with customers and to exert great effort to resolve any that arise. Both value their reputation, and they will avoid litigation with customers in all but unusual situations.

Consumer markets are different. Goods and services are not standardized, and the customer cannot be sure that more than one supplier will offer what it needs. If anything should go wrong, the buyer probably cannot find reasonable substitutes on the market that can be delivered on time. The product may require continuing maintenance and spare parts over time. The buyer's personnel may have to learn how to use the supplier's goods, and they would have to be retrained to use a competitor's product. Often, as well, suppliers know that there are few customers. Sales people will be under great pressure not to lose "their accounts." In such transactions, long-term continuing relations offer a potent sanction—neither party can afford to lose the other. In these situations people do not assert their rights. Rather, they seek to keep the other content with the relationship by resolving problems or offering attractive compromises.

The second reason for the nonuse of contract law is that the costs of litigation outweigh its potential benefits in all but a few situations. One cost is what the German sociologist Niklas Luhmann calls crossing "thematization thresholds."[13] We use distinct vocabularies to talk about transactions with others. If we talk in terms of trust, cooperation and mutual advantage, we invite a response in those terms. Compromise is appropriate; conflict is not. If, however, we talk of legal rights, we are asking for a fight. I am right and you are wrong. I am innocent but you are at fault. You have breached your promise and broken your word. Or, in other words, there is a law of physics that says lawyers attract lawyers, and courts attract lawyers. Luhmann says: "it takes a certain amount of courage to openly confront the other with the question of whether he is in the right. The comfortable consensus that can normally be assumed in living and acting together will be shattered."

The costs of using contract law may be more tangible and economic. Contract litigation in the United States often is an expensive game of chance. When others fail to perform, aggrieved parties cannot be sure that they will win a contract lawsuit.

---

[12]Arthur Okun, Prices and Quantities: A Macroeconomic Analysis (1981). Okun says that consumer markets are often held together by an "invisible handshake."

[13]Niklas Luhmann, Communication About Law in Interaction Systems, in K. Knorr-Cetina and A.V. Circourel, eds., Advances in Social Theory and Methodology (1981).

Many potential litigants must conclude that they cannot afford to roll the dice. First, United States contract law is not predictable and certain. Much of it rests on hard-to-apply qualitative standards. For example, it asks whether there has been "a material failure of performance." It asks whether the other party has "substantially performed." It asks whether the aggrieved party's response to the other's default has "waived" exact performance of the contract. It asks whether the default was excused because it was caused by "the occurrence of a contingency, the nonoccurrence of which was a basic assumption of the contract." Of course, we can image clear cases under any of these rules, but in reality many situations will only produce equally cogent arguments for both sides.

Contract litigation also often turns on hard-to-prove facts. Justifiable expectations may be dashed on the burden of proof, the parol evidence rule and the statute of frauds. Furthermore, clauses commonly buried in form contracts may block legal protection of the actual expectations of the parties. In theory, contract terms are a matter of free choice, but, in practice, many times such provisions enter a contract by subterfuge via a form contract. Business people often sign documents without reading and understanding all the terms and conditions. The lawyers who draft such documents are well aware of this. Sellers' forms usually disclaim all consequential damages, limit buyer's remedies to replacement and repair of defective goods, and excuse or suspend performance when it becomes difficult because of any event listed in a long menu of contingencies. Buyers' forms may allow them to cancel a contract for convenience, paying only the seller's actual out of pocket expenses. Standard forms can contain trick clauses designed to deter successful vindication of the weaker party's rights. For example, a standard form may provide that litigation must take place in a state far from the weaker party's place of business. It may provide for arbitration by an arbitrator certain to favor the stronger party. It may require a buyer to give written notice of all claimed defects within an unreasonably short period after delivery. Such forms may disclaim responsibility for the statements of agents—these are "license to lie" clauses. Sometimes courts will overturn such clauses; other judges will refuse to do so, writing opinions based on a rich fantasy about choice and the responsibility to read, understand and negotiate away such provisions in situations where few people would think to do so.

Moreover, courts in the United States will seldom put aggrieved parties in the position they would have been in had their contracts been performed—even when they win their lawsuit. United States contract law is a misrepresented product. The primary remedy will be damages because courts seldom award specific performance of contracts except in real estate transactions. Various policies limit money damages in United States law. Contract damages, for example, must be foreseeable and proved with reasonable certainty. The monetary equivalent of a performance in the future always will be difficult to prove.

Even more important, a successful plaintiff may get an award of damages, but she must deduct the costs of winning the suit from her net recovery. Absent statutes to the contrary, successful plaintiffs in the United States legal system must pay their own lawyer's fees. Lawyers seldom agree to accept contingent fees in contract litigation. Moreover, the costs awarded to a victorious plaintiff may not include the full fees for the experts necessary to establish damages. Furthermore, collection of the damages awarded in a judgment may be uncertain. An insolvent party often fails to perform its contract. A judgment is not cash; the winner must try to execute it against resources that the losing party may not have. Indeed, filing a law suit may lead the defendant or its other creditors to file bankruptcy. If this happens, usually a party aggrieved by the other's breach can only hope to recover at best some percentage of its total claim, and it risks recovering nothing. The weaker party may use the chance of declaring bankruptcy as a bargaining tool against its creditors as it demands to settle claims for a small fraction of the amounts due.

Our understanding of other market economies suggests that what I found in North America is a broader phenomenon. Studies in Great Britain,[14] France[15] and several Scandinavian countries[16] find similar patterns of the use and nonuse of contract law in planning, performance and dispute resolution. Also, we must remember the highly developed and successful Asian economies when we consider the role of contract law. There is little contract litigation in most Asian societies. In these societies we find a number of features at least analogous to what de Soto found in the Peruvian informal sector.[17] Business contracts rest on trust. People prefer to deal within the long-term continuing relationships of an extended family. Often a written contract is but a starting point for negotiations as the parties perform the arrangement and deal with changed circumstances. Okke Braadbaart, after studying vegetable marketing in Java, points out: "Personal relationships often develop between representatives of firms cooperating closely over a longer period. These ties are of strategic value in recurrent crisis management."[18]

---

[14]See Hugh Beale and Anthony Dugdale, Contracts Between Businessmen, 2 British Journal of Law & Society 45 (1975).

[15]See Edward H. Lorenz, Flexible Production Systems and the Social Construction of Trust, 21 Politics & Society 307 (1993).

[16]See Britt-Mari Blegvad, Commercial Relations, Contract, and Litigation in Denmark: A Discussion of Macaulay's Theories, 24 Law & Society Review 397 (1990).

[17]Compare De Soto, The Other Path 163-165 (1989) where he argues that such relational sanctions and trust are high cost and inadequate for modern development. Perhaps the Peruvian and the, say, Taiwanese situations described by Winn, supra, note 3, differ. Nonetheless, we can point to remarkable economic success that rests on just the mechanisms that de Soto finds inefficient and inadequate.

For studies about squatter settlements in Hong Kong that describe similar practices but offer a very different analysis from that of de Soto, see Alan Smart, The Informal Regulation of Illegal Economic Activities: Comparisons Between the Squatter Property Market and Organized Crime, 16 International Journal of the Sociology of Law 91 (1988); Alan Smart, Invisible Real Estate: Investigations into the Squatter Property Market, 10 International Journal of Urban and Regional Research 29 (1986); Alan Smart, The Squatter Property Market in Hong Kong, 5 Critique of Anthropology 23 (1985).

The classic study of a squatter settlement and its production of other-than-state law is, of course, Boaventura de Sousa Santos, The Law of the Oppressed: The Construction and Reproduction of Legality in Pasargada, 12 Law & Society Review 5 (1977).

[18]Okke Braadbaart, Business Contracts in Javanese Vegetable Marketing, 53 Human Organization 143, 144 (1994).

International trade flourishes despite the lack of formal contract law as such. International contracts can channel disputes to courts in such places as London or to arbitration systems in major centers around the world. However, when it is sufficiently profitable, international trade takes place even where courts and arbitration are absent. Often lawyers and others work to build "self-enforcing" structures that substitute for legal enforcement of contracts. In Erich Schanze's words: "the theory of self-enforcement implies that in the course of the anticipated project life, breach by one party will be prevented by the fact that in any stage of the investment process the ongoing 'working relationship' makes the parties to the agreement better off than breaching."[19] Today, in Russia and the other countries of the former Soviet Union a working formal law of contract is largely absent. Nonetheless, a market economy is developing and many multinational corporations are present. Indeed, in 1992, the New York Times ran an article with the title: "The Art of a Russian Deal: Ad-Libbing Contract Law."[20] It reported that in Russia deals turn on mutual benefit and trust. Besides mutual benefit and trust, transactions in the former Soviet Union often involving paying off what the Russians call their "Mafia"[21] or hiring private guards for protection.[22] If relationships break down, the attitude is "we've made money in the interim, and if the deal stops, O.K." Or as one American lawyer working in Moscow put it: "We'll dance together until the music stops."

We can conclude, then, that a strong functioning system of legally enforceable contracts is not essential to a market economy. Indeed, de Soto's story about the informal and often illegal sectors of the Peruvian economy illustrates that. Minimizing risks, trust and long-term continuing relations will support much business activity.[23] De Soto, however, sees these steps as transaction costs and advocates legally enforceable contracts as a way of reducing them. Business people around the world, nonetheless, seldom rely on contract law alone to support business transactions. Yet what does contract law contribute to a market economy?

---

[19]Erich Schanze, Regulation by Consensus: The Practice of International Investment Agreements, 144 Journal of Institutional and Theoretical Economics (JITE) 152, 166 (1988). See, also, Erich Schanze, Constructive Jurisprudence in Mining Agreements: Institutional Innovation and Practical Drawbacks, in Gunther Jaenicke, Christian Kirchner, Hans-Joachim Mertens, Eckard Rehbinder, and Erich Schanze, eds., International Mining Investment: Legal and Economic Perspectives 161 (1988); Terence Daintith, Mining Agreements as Regulatory Schemes, in the same book; Terence Daintith, The Design and Performance of Long-Term Contracts, in Terence Daintith and Gunther Teubner, eds., Contract and Organisation: Legal Analysis in the Light of Economic and Social Theory 164 (1986); Wolfgang Streek and Philippe G. Schmitter, Community, Market, State—and Associations? The Prospective Contribution of Interest Governance to Social Order, 1 European Sociological Review 119 (1985).

[20]Louis Uchitelle, The Art of a Russian Deal: Ad-Libbing Contract Law, N.Y. Times, Jan. 17, 1992, at A1, cols 3-4.

[21]See Stephen Handelman, The Russian "Mafiya," 73 Foreign Affairs 83 (1994).

[22]Michael Specter, U.S. Business and the Russian Mob: Some Hire Guards: Others Tough It Out, N.Y. Times, July 8, 1994, at C1, cols. 3-5.

[23]cf. Edward H. Lorenz, Flexible Production Systems and the Social Construction of Trust, 21 Politics & Society 307 (1993).

III. The Contribution of Contract Law

The major contributions of contract law may be more symbolic than instrumental. Contract law in most countries with market economies stands for the idea that people should perform their commitments unless they have a very good excuse. It, thus, reinforces norms that are common in all business communities. However, once we accept this, we still must ask how contract law communicates its message to a relevant audience. Lawyers learn contract law in law school, and as they read statutes and judicial opinions, they renew their appreciation of the law's lessons. Business people and the general public seldom read statutes and legal decisions, and so we can suspect that the symbolic contribution of this body of law is at best indirect and subtle. Occasionally, newspapers cover important contracts litigation, and business people gossip about those who sue and are sued. Lawyers may tell clients entertaining "war stories," that also suggest the lawyers' importance in warding off litigation risks.

Perhaps it is enough that business people see contract disputes and litigation as trouble they should avoid whenever possible. Invoking formal contract procedures involves turning control of events over to lawyers. It diverts business people from profitable and enjoyable activities. There is always the risk of unfavorable publicity. Even if a charge of breaching a contract is groundless, others in the business community might wonder about what had happened. Insofar as avoiding trouble exerts influence, it would serve as one of many things pushing for performance of contracts or reaching satisfactory compromises of disputes. Contract law also may exert influence when people ***think*** that they know what a court would do even when their lawyers would see doubts and questions. Udo Reifner suggests: "Law in market societies is a useful lie because the economy needs to reduce complexity to be able to give answers where they are needed."[24]

Contract doctrine also may provide a vocabulary for negotiation. The contract litigation process may function as a bargaining arena. For example, a letter from a lawyer for one party written in terms reflecting the law may open a process for resolving a dispute that the parties could not handle by cooperation and compromise. While talking legal rights may have costs, it usually is better than refusing to perform because of self-interest. At least in the United States, our judges more and more have become involved in settling disputes rather than trying lawsuits. One of our federal judges became known for bringing the top executives of both parties into his chambers and refusing to allow their lawyers to be present. The judge then sought to persuade these business people to resolve the dispute among themselves rather than litigate. In several noted cases he was successful. While his action is atypical, it is far from unique.

---

[24]Udo Reifner, The Vikings and the Romans—Contract Law and Social Economy 5 (Paper presented at the Conference on Perspectives of Critical Contract Law in Tuusula, Finland, May 7 to 10, 1992.

IV. Conclusions

What should we make of my skepticism about de Soto's enthusiasm for legally enforceable contracts? Perhaps we should reform the contract system so it comes closer to fulfilling the functions claimed for it in the classic model. We could refashion the rules to be simple, clear and formal. We would abandon rules that rested on qualitative concepts such as "substantial performance," "unconscionability," and "reasonable notice." We might award specific performance more often or accept estimates of loss as sufficiently certain proof. We could change our rules so the losing party paid a significant amount of the winner's lawyer's fees. The goal would be to make contract law something that more business people would want to use more often. Many countries have attempted this in specific areas. Often law-makers remove transactions from the general area of contract and create special bodies of law when they seek to offset inequalities of market power. For example, in the United States, many states have consumer protection or unfair and deceptive trade practices acts that provide incentives to sue and advantageous remedies.[25] These statutes often provide for lawyers' fees to be paid by a defendant to a successful plaintiff and double or triple damages.

Our economies might be better off, however, if we sought to recognize and legitimate compromise rather than rights vindication as the goal of the legal system. Perhaps we should take what we can call the Dr. Pangloss position: the high cost barriers and uncertain payoffs of our legal system are part of the best of all possible worlds. People will litigate only important cases that involve significant sums of money or issues of principle. Otherwise, the functioning legal system gives people strong incentives to share losses, consider the interests of the other side, and work out solutions by agreeing to deal in the future. Possible breach of contract litigation serves as a vague threat affecting but not controlling behavior in most cases. Undoubtedly, this solution requires parties to build trust and create long-term continuing relations. They will have to take security or create self-enforcing contracts. As de Soto points out, these are transaction costs. However, they may be cheaper or more acceptable as judged by various norms than anything the law can provide.

Indeed, we must remember that market economies exist despite, in Max Weber's terms, substantively rational contract law with uncertain remedies. We can remember that Shakespeare, in *The Merchant of Venice* had Portia find a way to deny Shylock his pound of flesh. In form, she just enforced Antonio's promise. In substance, she denied Shylock legal enforcement of his actual expectations. As a result, *Shylock v. Antonio* may have deterred others from claiming a pound of flesh as their remedy for breach of contract. (Some rational maximizers, of course, might

[25] Lawrence M. Friedman, Contract Law in America (1965), argues that United States legal history teaches that whenever problems become important they are removed from the common law of contract by a statute. Thus, the common law of contract is, largely, law for problems too new or unimportant to have their own statute.

provide in their contract that they could take all necessary blood as well as a pound of flesh). Shakespeare, however, never tells us whether Portia's sophisticated or sophist treatment of Shylock's contract undermined the economy of Venice. Somehow, I suspect that it did not.

Law in Action: Introduction

Stewart Macaulay, Lawrence M. Friedman, and Elizabeth Mertz

This is a book of readings about law, legal systems, and legal institutions. But it is a book with a particular slant. The readings primarily approach that system from an *outside* rather than an *inside* perspective. The *inside* perspective focuses on legal rules and procedures the way that lawyers and judges usually see them—from *within* the legal system, so to speak—and it usually accepts them more or less at face value. This introduction will try to explain what we mean by the outside perspective. It will also give a brief account of the history and present status of outside approaches to law.

I. The Outside Point of View

When we say "the outside point of view," we mean, roughly, looking at legal phenomena from the standpoint of one or more of the social sciences: sociology, anthropology, economics, psychology, political science, and perhaps others. Of course, these are all quite different fields, and each has its own slant, its own special way of looking at human behavior and human thought. An economist might be

This article was original published as chapter 1 in Elizabeth Mertz, Lawrence M. Friedman, and Stewart Macaulay, Law in Action: A Socio-Legal Reader, New York NY: Foundation Press, 2007. Reprinted with permission of West Academic.

S. Macaulay (✉)
University of Wisconsin Law School, Madison, WI, USA
e-mail: smacaula@wisc.edu

L. M. Friedman
Stanford University School of Law, Stanford, CA, USA

E. Mertz
American Bar Foundation and University of Wisconsin, Chicago, IL, USA

D. Campbell (ed.), *Stewart Macaulay: Selected Works*, Law and Philosophy Library 133, https://doi.org/10.1007/978-3-030-33930-2_12

interested, for example, in asking whether it makes more sense to give companies subsidies as an incentive to refrain from dumping toxic wastes rather than using a regime of fines and criminal sanctions. An anthropologist might be interested in how cultures differ in the ways they handle disputes between husband and wife. A psychologist might want to find out how juries actually go about making their decisions. A political scientist might wonder how lobbyists affect the votes of legislators. A sociologist might ask how race and gender affect the behavior of judges and juries. Each field has its own little stock of favorite questions (and answers), and its own pet methods.

But the social sciences do have certain traits in common. Perhaps the most important is a commitment to empirical observation and scientific measurement, as far as this is possible. Related to this is a commitment to objectivity and neutrality, again, as far as possible. Sophisticated social scientists are not naïve about science and its limits. They know that they themselves are only human. They realize that they have prejudices and values, just as everyone else. They know too that these prejudices and values can affect their work. The best of them will try very hard to keep their personal values from prejudicing their work.

There are some critics who think that objectivity and scientific neutrality are delusions; that "value free" social science is a myth, or, worse, a fraud. There is a grain of truth in this accusation. A social scientist does not pick her topics at random; values, attitudes, viewpoints and prejudices inevitably color the way questions get asked and even how data get analyzed. Actually, we owe this insight itself to social science—in particular, to the sociology of knowledge and the sociology of science. The social sciences use many methods, but all of them are flawed or limited. None can promise to produce pure, objective, uncontrovertible truth.

Moreover, our subject matter—law and legal systems—is particularly cantankerous and resistant. It is very hard to study law scientifically. The things that we want to describe and analyze, often enough, are not tangible objects that can be measured with practical yardsticks. They involve morals, ideas, attitudes, personal privacy, economic interests, and other tangled and delicate stuff. Doing research on law and legal behavior is not like studying, say, the muscular structure of rodents. The legal process is, in part, a labeling process—it is a set of social constructs, ideas and concepts. Raw material from the real world—whatever that might mean—gets transformed and twisted and renamed and reconceived when it enters the world of the legal order. It is easier, for example, to study accidents than to study torts. Judgments of judges, jurors or lawyers transform a collision between two autos—an objective event—into a "tort." This is a legal concept. Furthermore, people inside the legal system often manipulate data and ideas. They may produce a picture that is not at all like the picture and the perceptions of the people who actually lived through the collision or were affected by it.

The people who make and run the legal system in any society are not a random cross-section of the public. In our society, for most of our history, these people—the judges, lawyers, legislators and others—have been white males who belonged to the upper middle-class. They made the law more or less in their image. The situation today (2007) is quite different. Almost half of all law students now are women. Women are lawyers, judges, law professors, and deans. Members of racial minorities have also gained more representation. This is one kind of progress for women and minorities—filling the roles that once belonged exclusively to men. But some women and minority group members have gone further. They have challenged core assumptions and concepts that underlie law and legal institutions. Theorists and practitioners have had to confront the experience of subordinated groups. The voices of sexual minorities and other disadvantaged people have also begun to be heard. Much of the scholarship, of course, is deeply controversial. But legal scholarship, and law-and-society scholarship, can only benefit when it is forced to confront underlying assumptions, ruling ideas and habits. Law-and-society scholarship has had to learn, the hard way, how much gender, race, class, and lifestyle colored the way that people, including legal officials and scholars, have looked at the world.

Still, having said all this, we have to reject the deep skepticism about what law-and-society studies show. Felice Levine has expressed a more optimistic view:

> [O]ne learns from the various critiques and . . . these critiques are not necessarily separate and apart from science, but part of the dialogue of doing science in a better way. For those who value the process of learning and the value of understanding without any illusion of absolute certainty of what we know, such critiques are instructive and integral to the activity and integrity of science itself. We must keep in mind that science is a social process and, like all social processes, it is dynamic, even at times erratic, but capable of change. Thus, the critiques are grist for doing science in a more profound way.[1]

After all, despite all the doubting and theorizing, there is a big difference between honest research on law and no research at all; between trying to interpret data fairly and combing through data to find an example or two in support of some political or ideological position. There is a big difference, on the one hand, between measuring litigation rates and trying to interpret the zigs and zags in the data, and, on the other, fulminating about a "litigation explosion." (Or just making up the data out of one's head or offering colorful anecdotes.)

In any specific study or research project, there are bound to be problems and failings. But this is no reason to discard the whole enterprise. One test of fairness is whether the researcher is willing to accept results that are surprising or that contradict the researcher's own desires and expectations. Social science is far from perfect, but it is, after all, a kind of science. In science a "theory" is something testable, a guide to research, an idea that leads the researcher in a particular direction. Or it may be a general concept that sums up and explains a mass of data. Legal scholars often use "theory" in a different way. They describe a philosophical or political position which has not been and cannot be tested.

In any event, the social sciences have over the years developed a toolbox of traditions, methods and credos. (These are, to be sure, sometimes in conflict with each other.) The social scientific study of law borrows from this toolbox. There are also *distinctive* traditions, methods, and credos relating to the social scientific study of law. What they have in common is the "outside" approach to the legal system.

---

[1]Felice J. Levine, "'His' and 'Her' Story; The Life and Future of the Law and Society Movement," 18 *Florida State University Law Review* 69, 86 (1990).

"Insiders," mostly lawyers, law professors and judges, are not usually well-trained in the social sciences. They have practical experience and insights, but the insights are not always entirely accurate.

A researcher, using the tools of social science, can often gain valuable insights into a society, community, or group dynamics that "insiders" overlook or take for granted—although the researcher, who might well be an "outsider," also risks projecting his or her own values or prejudices onto that society, community or group. However, trained anthropologists and other social scientists try hard to put aside cultural prejudices in order to understand other societies in less biased or "ethnocentric" ways. The tools of social science can also be turned back on parts of our own society—the legal system, for example—to acquire new insights and analytic clarity.

Law professors, lawyers and judges (and often the public) are concerned not so much with empirical, measurable reality, with what is going on in the world, as they are with what is on the books, what is right and wrong, what is legally correct or incorrect. To be sure, most legal questions do have—and must have—some sort of answer. A woman who runs a consulting business out of her home asks a tax lawyer whether she can deduct some of her heating bills as business expenses. She expects a professional answer—she wants to be told that she can deduct, she can't or whether it depends on this or that factor. She expects that answer to come from the law, although she may not be clear about where one finds that or what it consists of. She is asking an inside question, and she demands an inside answer.

There also is a very large normative element in discussions of law. People argue and discuss what *should* be legal or illegal and what is morally, politically or otherwise right or wrong. Indeed, lawyers and lay people alike often fudge or confuse legal correctness and ethical rightness. Is it a good thing to put murderers to death? Should we let teachers in public schools offer prayers in class? These are normative or ethical questions about what should be done. But they also happen to be legal issues in this country. It is not easy to keep the two dimensions apart, if we assume that they should be kept apart.

To take one example, the Bill of Rights forbids cruel and unusual punishment. Many opponents of the death penalty say that it is cruel and unusual and therefore forbidden. But in some ways this is a rather odd statement. After all, the justices of the Supreme Court in a number of cases have specifically held that the death penalty is not cruel and unusual punishment. And the Supreme Court has the last word on the official meaning of the Constitution.

However, the person who insists that, despite the Supreme Court's decisions, the death penalty is cruel and unusual is saying: "I think that the death penalty is wrong and should be abolished." But she is also saying something more about law, the role of the Supreme Court, the Constitution, and what the correct reading of the Constitution ought to be. She is making a point about the differences between legal and moral validity. The point may be, and often is, inchoate and confused. However, that people make this point is an important social fact about such things as values, beliefs, ideals and attitudes. These are basic to any legal system.

Of course, the social scientist has no way to suggest an answer to the question of whether the death penalty is constitutional. She can only discuss and describe why people think it is or it is not. She can only tell us which people (or judges) think that it is valid, and which ones do not. She can tell us how opinion varies from men to women, whites to blacks, young to old, and the like. She can compile and analyze data on the actual impact of the death penalty. She can show where movements for and against the death penalty come from, politically or historically speaking, and so on.

These are not trivial contributions to the debate itself, and they are not frivolous or unimportant questions for researchers. Some of us (including the editors of this book) think that understanding the factual and social underpinnings of the legal system is very important indeed. In a society that thinks that it is committed to the rule of law—whatever that may mean—grasping the nature of the legal system, explaining it, observing it in action, is absolutely crucial.

It would seem easier to defend the death penalty if you could prove that it saved lives by deterring murderers. Moreover, people who are in favor of the death penalty would be a lot more comfortable if they could prove that no innocent people had been or were likely to be put to death by mistake. Better yet if we could show that racial discrimination was not involved in the choice of which convicted murderers get the death penalty and which do not.

However, it is possible that we cannot prove or disprove any of these propositions. What do we do if we cannot answer such questions? Is common sense good enough? Do we keep putting people to death unless the opponents can make a stronger case? Who has the burden of proof? Suppose we could show that the death penalty deters, but only somewhat. Moreover, suppose we could show that there is some racial discrimination but not an enormous amount. Who decides how much is too much? Obviously, the social sciences do not and cannot give us answers to such questions. Nonetheless, without data and research, without the perspective of the social sciences, it is easy to ignore these issues and reduce the whole matter to political sloganeering.

Law, however, is not just social engineering. Law is one way of declaring what is morally right and wrong. The death penalty is an important symbol of a society's abhorrence of murder. Capital punishment could be viewed as a factor in reinforcing all of the norms in the culture that keep individuals to some degree safer in their daily lives. Some people may simply feel better if they see that those who commit horrible murders pay the ultimate price. Indeed, for them, putting murderers to death may be part of what the legal system must do to gain and retain legitimacy. (In some cultures, for example, it is legitimate for a victim's family to seek revenge, and, arguably, our culture does not totally condemn a person who takes revenge on a rapist or killer). Many people, however, have a strong moral objection to the death penalty. They see the symbolism and the lesson as all wrong: the death penalty, along with violence in film and television, teaches that killing is an appropriate solution to problems. Other opponents point to instances where people on death row have been shown to be innocent. Still others have shown that the actual process in death penalty cases is frequently flawed. What the death penalty actually symbolizes, how people perceive it, and how it operates—and on whom—are also empirical questions.

In other words, we think that a law-and-society perspective can do much to clarify and improve debates about issues such as the death penalty. However, if we are realistic, we have to ask, who is the audience for this kind of scholarship? The Supreme Court? The President? Legislators? The Supreme Court, at times, seems to ignore or distort social science findings to suit preconceived policy positions. The President, members of Congress, and local legislators are interested in getting elected or reelected. Sometimes it seems that the only social science studies that they care about are public opinion polls. Interest groups look for data and findings that they can use that suit their cause as they battle to get their way in the legislative market-place. Sometimes interest groups even buy the social science findings that they want. These groups ignore or distort data that comes out the "wrong way."

Claims about facts do not *by themselves* automatically change the world. The social study of law *also* includes the study of the way that law gets made and remade. Good empirical studies have an influence, but so do other things such as colorful anecdotes, scandals, conventional wisdom, popular stereotypes, and sometimes outright lies. We should neither claim too much nor too little for the impact on society of our enterprise—of our ongoing attempt to understand how the law actually works.

II. The Riddle of Legal Autonomy

It is one thing to describe a legal system from the outside. It is quite another to say that the outside viewpoint *explains* what makes a legal system tick much better than any inside explanation. Which approach gives you a better handle on how legal systems work hinges on whether or not legal systems are autonomous.

An "autonomous" legal system would be "one that is independent of other sources of power and authority in social life," according to Richard Lempert and Joseph Sanders.[2] A legal action in an autonomous system is "influenced only by the preestablished rules of the legal system." It defines events "in its own terms," and is "independent of society's other mechanisms of social control." Lempert and Sanders also insist that an autonomous system is "self-legitimating." Its "rules and rulings are accepted because they are legal" and not because of some other reason. An autonomous legal system is not legitimated by political, social or ethical considerations. And in an autonomous system, such outside factors do not influence what the legal system does. We will not enter into a long discussion of legal autonomy here. Nobody thinks that the legal system is *totally* autonomous and completely independent of the society in which it is imbedded. Nobody really thinks that a legal system goes entirely its own way, deciding everything according to legal criteria with no

[2] *An Invitation to Law and Social Science* 402 (1986).

room for political pressure, ethical considerations, economic consequences and the like. A totally autonomous legal system would be very undesirable. Such a system also is probably impossible, at least in any society that we know about.

However, is our legal system *partially* autonomous? Is there something tough, unyielding and resistant to external influences, something self-contained about law? Does law march to its own drummer at least sometimes? Does it follow its own internal program when it can? Many law professors, and probably many lay people, seem to think so. Yet the real question is *how* autonomous? How much of the system is self-generated, technocratic, traditional, insulated from the outside world, and how much is not?

A judge may say that he decides cases "according to the law," and he does not let any other consideration sway him. The head of an agency like the Food and Drug Administration may say that FDA has decided to ban a "morning after" pill because this is the legally correct thing to do under the agency's rules and procedures. The commissioner can insist that political pressures or public opinion had nothing to do with the decision. The judge and the commissioner are claiming political independence and some sort of autonomy. It is not easy to know whether they are telling the truth or even whether they really *think* that they are telling the truth.

Many of us tend to be cynical about statements such as the ones the judge and the commissioner made. But surely some actors feel (and behave?) this way sometimes. The exact situation makes a difference. Birth control pills are controversial, but routine decisions about food dyes are much less so. The *structure* of the legal system may also make a difference. If the director of an agency is likely to be shot at dawn if she does something that displeases the head of state, she is unlikely to make herself a martyr. However, if a judge has life-tenure as our federal judges do, or if an agency head cannot be removed by the President or governor, it may be a different story.

What does seem fairly clear is that legal systems as a whole cannot be autonomous *in the long run.* Sooner or later their shape will get bent more or less in the direction of their society regardless of any technical, traditional or historical elements. Medieval law looked, smelled, and acted medieval. The law of the Trobriand Islanders or the ancient Egyptians fit with the structure and culture of those societies. The law of modern free-market states is full of rules that support or presuppose free markets. Modern legal systems contain an endless list of prescriptions and institutions concerning clean air and water, toxic waste, gene splicing, computer hacking. All of these are specific to the age in which we live. We cannot label these legal arrangements as autonomous.

How could it be otherwise? Legal systems do not exist to answer abstract questions. They solve (or mis-solve) real problems. Legislators react to demands of their constituents and lobbyists. Judges decide real cases between real people who live in real time and who have real problems. These problems necessarily are problems of the society in which the litigants, constituents, and lobbyists live, and not those of any other society. And the outcomes or solutions to the problems, too, will take on the coloration of the society and the culture that supplies both questions and answers.

Social scientists who study law tend to emphasize the role of the culture, the society, and the world outside the courtroom, legislative hall or police station. In other words, they tend to explain happenings within the system in terms of social forces—political pressures, internalized values, cultural norms, economic interests and so on. They tend to deemphasize "internal" aspects of the system—the technical stuff of the law. Law professors, and others who make their living explaining the law, traditionally have taken an "inside" point of view. Insiders are bound up in their daily work with details of law. They tend to explain what happens in the system in such terms.

Some of the biases of the editors of this book should be obvious by now. We would not have put this book together if we did not believe that an external perspective on the legal system offers important benefits not available to those using an internal point of view. But nobody can prove that the outside approach is a better one or measure the exact degree to which legal systems respond or relate to their specific societies. Nor can we presuppose that each legal system is as autonomous as every other one. It is *possible* that American law is more legalistic than the law of some other country or society. It is also possible that some subfields of law are more autonomous than others. A person who favors an outside approach must still consider the degree to which *internal* legal doctrines influence the output of a legal system. It would be foolish to assume that legal thought never makes a difference. After all, the language of doctrine is an integral part of the culture of law. Similarly, it would be foolish to assume that legal thought explains everything, or even most things, about a legal system.

The problems raised in this introduction will not be solved here or anywhere. They will run through almost every page of the readings that follow.

III. Complexity and Change

Legal systems, we must remember, are incredibly complicated. They also change over time. And they are also culture-bound or at least tied to specific cultures. These are three elementary but crucial facts about legal systems throughout the modern world.

The complexity of any legal system is obvious. The law is an enormous and complicated business. Nobody knows all of American law, even all of American tax law or even all of American law relating to taxes on corporations. There is simply too much of it. Law is conventionally divided into subfields such as personal injury law, divorce law, food and drug law, copyright law, criminal law, tort law, and so on. These subfields, taken together, cover or touch on almost every conceivable aspect of life. This fact—the sheer size and scope of the legal system—is true of every modern society. But there is an added wrinkle to the law of the United States. Americans live in a federal system. The country is blessed (if that is the word) with 50 legal systems, one for each state. In addition, there is the national (federal) system of laws and courts, not to mention various territorial systems, and the system in the

District of Columbia. There is also a system of courts for some of the native American peoples—there is, for example, a Navajo Supreme Court. And there are distinct legal systems in Puerto Rico, Guam, and the Virgin Islands.

To complicate matters further, there are also thousands of cities, towns, townships, counties, and special subdivisions (sewer and school districts, port authorities, and so on) that have the power to make rules and regulations or municipal ordinances. Every state, every city, and above all the federal government has an enormous number of administrative agencies, large and small. For example, on the federal level, we can point to the Securities and Exchange Commission, the Food and Drug Administration, the Social Security Administration and so forth. On the state level, we find medical and dental licensing boards and highway commissions as well as human rights commissions, occupational safety and health boards and the like. On the local level, zoning and school boards are at work. These also churn out rules, regulations, decisions and orders beyond counting.

And of course this vast body of legal material is constantly changing. Each rule and regulation as well as each published court decision is at least a minor change, a footnote, in the immense book of the laws. The pace of social change has increased enormously in our times, and the pace of legal change has increased along with it. So many legal issues are new: in vitro fertilization, copyright problems relating to computer software and others. There is a Department of Homeland Security in Washington, D.C., and a body of law devoted to the "war on terror," most of which didn't exist before 2001.

Finally, law is a remarkably parochial discipline. Chemical engineering or molecular biology is more or less the same subject in China or Honduras as it is in the United States. Even the social sciences tend to transcend national boundaries. Economics can be studied anywhere, and while the emphasis may be different, the core of the discipline will be more or less the same. If you learn any subject in one country, it will at least give you a foothold anywhere else. However, a knowledge of French law does not equip you to practice law, say, in Iran or Japan. Every country has its own official legal system. No two are the same or even approximately the same. They vary according to differences in the culture, traditions, economics, and politics of the particular countries. There is, therefore, an immense number of legal systems all over the world. Even so tiny a country as Andorra or so new a country as East Timor has its own unique system of law.

A "science" of law should in theory have principles or generalizations that go beyond a particular legal system. Do any such principles exist? Can we say anything of value about legal systems in general?[3] Or about some subgroup such as legal systems in Western industrial countries, for example?

---

[3]There have been some attempts to offer such generalizations. For example, Donald Black, *The Behavior of Law* (1976) offers a number of propositions. For a critical analysis of this work, see Gloria T. Lessan and Joseph F. Sheley, "Does Law Behave? A Macrolevel Test of Black's Propositions on Change in Law," 70 *Social Forces* 655 (1992).

Most of these questions have no answers that would command general agreement. It is difficult to compare systems of law or even parts of them in a systematic empirical way. There are theoretical and practical obstacles. But in an age of global communication and global economics, the legal systems of the world are becoming more and more interconnected. This trend is likely to continue. Law, and its study, are likely to become at least a bit less parochial. So, too, the social study of law.

IV. Private Government

Thus far we have spoken mostly about official, formal legal systems. These systems are what law students generally study and what most legal scholars write about. But the formal legal system, as it exists on paper, is not the real living and lived system of law. The social study of law is concerned with the whole system and all its working parts. It looks at the formal and informal, official and unofficial, and legitimate and illegitimate aspects.

The real legal system differs from its official picture in at least two significant ways. First, it contains much behavior that is informal and unofficial and which cannot be deduced from the official texts of the rules. These informal and unofficial elements are everywhere. They surround, supplement, supplant and complement the official and formal elements. In criminal law, this is the world of plea bargaining ("copping a plea") and the dozens of arrangements, shortcuts, rules of thumb and patterns of behavior that people inside the system know about, but that law school courses seldom mention or develop. It is the world in which the police sometimes beat prisoners and in which the police sometimes let other prisoners go free. It is the world in which some police officers even take bribes.

Second, everywhere in society we find law-like systems or institutions that exist side-by-side with or acting as rivals to the official system. There are, for example, what we might call "private governments."

> We live in a world of "legal pluralism" where rules are made and interpreted and sanctions imposed by many public and private governments which are only loosely coordinated. . . . Examples of private governments range from the Mafia to the American Arbitration Association. Trade associations, sports leagues, church groups, neighborhood organizations and many other "private" units such as business corporations exercise what are, effectively, legal powers. They make rules . . . they interpret them in their day-to-day operations; they offer benefits . . . and they may suspend or expel members, associations or employees as a sanction.[4]

Throughout this book, we will see examples of informal patterns of legal behavior, and we will also see examples of pluralism and of "private governments." Some patterns amount to what we might even call legal *subcultures*. No society of any

---

[4]Stewart Macaulay, "Law and the Behavioral Sciences: Is There Any There There?" 6 *Law and Policy* 249 (1984).

size—and the United States is certainly a big and heterogeneous society—has a single general culture. In the United States, for example, ideas and behaviors differ as between men and women, young and old, black and white, Protestant and Catholic, and within communities of Asian Americans or Armenian-Americans. They differ also within communities of auto dealers, jazz musicians, nurses, cab drivers, gang members and heroin addicts—any community or group that can be described at all has its own "dialect" of culture. The same is true of legal culture. Any society will have many legal cultures, and they will not necessarily be consistent with each other. This adds another layer of complexity to our subject, but throughout this book of readings, these subcultures will figure very prominently. The legal system cannot be understood without them.

V. Law-and-Society Scholarship

The study of the relationship between law and society, practically speaking, goes back to the 19th century, when modern social science began to develop. Sir Henry Maine, whose book, *Ancient Law,* appeared in 1861, was one of the pioneers. Maine looked at the law in a broad historical sweep, and he tried to discern relationships between types of legal systems and types of society (or types of social structure). Karl Marx, another seminal if controversial 19th century figure, wrote little explicitly about law. He considered law as a by-product of economic structure and an instrument of repression in the hands of social and economic elites. His general approach has continued to be influential with neo-Marxists and others. Emile Durkheim (1858–1917), another of the founding figures of modern social thought, has had particular influence on the sociology of crime and deviance.[5]

Max Weber (1864–1920) is probably the most important historical figure in the development of the sociology of law. Weber himself was trained as a lawyer. Concepts developed by Weber still are extremely useful in law-and-society scholarship, and we will meet some of them later in these materials.[6]

After the death of Weber, the social study of law seemed to enter a kind of dormancy phase. The work done in the next 30 or so years hardly compares to that done during the golden age of Weber and Durkheim. There were, however, some important contributions from anthropologists who were studying law.[7] But neither

---

[5]See Kai Erikson, *Wayward Puritans* 6–13 (1966).

[6]Another classical figure worth mention is Eugen Ehrlich (1862–1922), whose fame rests on the concept of "living law." Ehrlich was one of the first jurists seriously interested in the rules people followed in their everyday lives as opposed to the rules "in the books."

[7]One notable example was Bronislaw Malinowski's *Crime and Custom in Savage Society* (1926). Another classic of legal anthropology, *The Cheyenne Way: Conflict and Case Law in Primitive Jurisprudence* (1941), deserves special mention because it was a rare collaboration between a law professor (Karl Llewellyn) and a social scientist (E. Adamson Hoebel, was an anthropologist). See

legal academics nor the bulk of social scientists paid much attention to the relationship between legal and social systems—whether in America or in other societies.

Fortunately, the field came into its own in the second half of the 20th century. Social science in general had a boom period after the Second World War. In the United States, such dramatic decisions as *Brown v. Board of Education* (1954) refocused attention on the social importance of law. In addition, private foundations began to invest money in socio-legal research, which provided yet another stimulus.

The last 40 years have been a time of steady and impressive growth in the field. In many ways, law-and-society studies are flourishing. The Law and Society Association, the umbrella group for scholars in the field in the United States, is more than 40 years old. It was founded by a handful of social scientists, aided and abetted by an aberrant law professor or two.[8] Much of the founding energy was generated at the University of Wisconsin, and Professor J. Willard Hurst of the Law School was a potent influence. Hurst himself was a legal historian, but his influential works on that subject pointed the way to the social study of law in American society.[9]

Today, the Law and Society Association (LSA) has well over 1,000 members, holds annual meetings, and publishes a journal, the *Law & Society Review*. Another leading journal in the field is *Law & Social Inquiry*, a publication of the American Bar Foundation. Other journals on the subject published in the United States include *Law & Policy*, as well as the *Journal of Empirical Legal Studies* and the *Annual Review of Law and Social Science*, both of which appeared in the early years of the 21st century. There are also journals on specialized subjects. For example, *Law and Human Behavior* concentrates on articles about psychology and law. The *Journal of Law and Economics* does the same for economists who look at law.

The field shows considerable vitality in many other countries as well. The Japanese counterpart to the Law and Society Association, established long before LSA, has hundreds of members. There are a number of national law-and-society organizations in Europe, and journals on the subject are published in, for example, Australia, Canada, France, Germany, the Netherlands, Italy, Japan and the United Kingdom. There is considerable activity in other countries too—for example, Spain and Mexico. At one time there was an active law-and-society group in Poland, and the fall of Communism has opened the door to further development in that country. There are, however, somewhat distinctive national styles. Many continental scholars who teach and write about law-and-society come from backgrounds in legal philosophy and tend to be more interested in large questions of theory rather than the nitty-

---

John M. Conley & William M. O'Barr, "A Classic in Spite of Itself: *The Cheyenne Way* and the Case Method in Legal Anthropology," 29 *Law & Social Inquiry* 179 (2004).

[8]On the history of the law and society movement and the Association, see Bryant Garth and Joyce Sterling, "From Legal Realism to Law and Society: Reshaping Law for the Last Stages of the Activist State," 32 *Law and Society Review* 409 (1998).

[9]See, e.g., J. Willard Hurst, *The Growth of American Law: The Law Makers* (1950); J. Willard Hurst, *Law and the Conditions of Freedom in the Nineteenth–Century United States* (1956). See, for an assessment of Hurst's work, the collection of essays in 18 *Law and History Review*, No. 1 (Spring 2000).

gritty of empirical research. To be sure, there is also a tradition of empirical research in Europe, but the United States seems to be the leader in research on the law in action. There is in this global world more and more interest in issues that transcend national boundaries. And today scholars of foreign law—those who study Japan, France, Russia or Latin America, for example—are more likely to be using a sociological approach than would have been true in past decades.

Law-and-society studies on the whole have not made as much of a dent in legal education as one might have expected. The Law and Society Association is flourishing, but the majority of its members are not legally trained and not associated with law schools. They are social scientists in political science, sociology, psychology, anthropology and economics departments. There is a scattering of philosophers, historians and others. A fair number of colleges and universities have departments of legal studies or offer courses and programs on criminal justice, business law or the like. In some of these programs, law-and-society studies form an important component. Probably there are over 1,500 people working in all sorts of disciplines. These scholars generate a substantial output of essays, review articles, research projects and monographs every year. There are, in addition, many criminologists, historians and other scholars who write about subjects that have intimate connections with the legal system but who do not identify themselves as law-and-society scholars. Their work is, of course, nonetheless extremely relevant.

With all of this output, it is fair to ask what the field has accomplished. What do we know that we did not know before? What are the insights, the contributions to understanding? A fair number of scholars have tried to come up with a general survey of the field, a synthesis or even some sort of general theory.[10] In the vast body of work, as Stewart Macaulay has put it: "social science and law has washed up a few shining nuggets."[11] He summed up some of the basic insights that the field has contributed, as follows:

1. *Law is not free.* There are barriers to access to the legal system which some people can jump far more easily than others. ... When we turn to social regulation, we find that it involves costs which some can pass along to others. It usually is fruitful to ask who benefits from and who pays for any type of legal action. Often we will find that regulation operates as a kind of regressive taxation, burdening the have-nots far more than the haves.
2. *Law is delivered by actors with limited resources and interests of their own in settings where they have discretion.* "Street-level bureaucrats" such as police, assistant

[10]See, for example, Richard Lempert and Joseph Sanders, *An Invitation to Law and Social Science: Desert, Disputes, and Distribution* (1986); Lawrence M. Friedman, *The Legal System: A Social Science Perspective* (1975); Roger Cotterrell, *The Sociology of Law: An Introduction* (2d ed. 1992); Donald Black, *Sociological Justice* (1989); Reza Banakar, *Merging Law and Sociology: Beyond the Dichotomies in Socio–Legal Research* (2003).

[11]Stewart Macaulay, "Law and the Behavioral Sciences: Is There Any There There?" 6 *Law & Policy* 149, 152–55 (1984). Frank Munger, "Mapping Law and Society," in *Crossing Boundaries: Traditions and Transformations in Law and Society Research* 21, 42–55 (Austin Sarat et al. eds., 1998), looked at Macaulay's seven propositions and reported that fourteen years after he wrote, "our vision of contemporary law and society field are remarkably consistent with the earlier empirical results summarized by Macaulay...."

prosecuting attorneys, caseworkers, clerks of court, those handling intake at administrative agencies and many more, have discretion although no one planned it that way. This is true for a number of reasons. Policies conflict and the rules may be unclear. As a result, those who deal with the public may have a choice of goals to pursue or rationalizations for whatever they want to do to serve the public or their own self interest. Those who do the day-to-day work of a legal agency often are hard to supervise because they control the official version of events by writing reports in the files. Resource constraints often make it impossible to "go by the book" since officials cannot do everything mandated. If those enforcing a law cannot carry out all their duties, they must choose which of them, under what circumstances, they will attempt to implement. Those choices of "street-level bureaucrats" are unlikely to be random or neutral in their impact. They will be affected by folk wisdom or bias, reward and punishment structures, and self-interest.

3. *Many of the functions usually thought of as legal are performed by alternative institutions, and there is a great deal of interpenetration between what we call public and private sectors. . . .*
4. *People, acting alone and in groups, cope with law and cannot be expected to comply passively.* Many people are able to ignore most legal commands, or redefine them to serve self-interest or "commonsense," and live with a vague and often inaccurate sense of the nature of law and legal process—all without encountering serious problems. There is great opportunity for evasion in a society that values privacy, civil liberties, and limited investment in government. Coping with the law can become a game that offsets any sense of obligation. Many participants in social fields and networks pass along techniques of evasion, legitimate breaking the law, honor the crafty, and even sanction those who would comply. The law is frequently uncertain and plausible arguments can be fashioned to rationalize much of what many people want to do. This means that there is great opportunity for bargaining in the shadow of the law or in the shadow of questionable assumptions about the law. Thus, people's view of the likely legal consequences of action at best affect but do not determine their behavior. Sometimes, however, the command of the law rings loud and clear and has direct impact on behavior. In short, the role of law is not something that can be assumed but must be established in every case.
5. *Lawyers play many roles other than adversary in a courtroom.* Lawyers' self-interest, and their view of what is best for a client, often dictates that litigation should be avoided, and lawyers seek other ways to provide service to clients. They tend to know who makes decisions and what kinds of appeals, legal and other types, are likely to be effective. They know how to bargain and how to manipulate situations so that accommodations can be reached. Often they serve as coercive mediators, acting in settings where their profession itself is a tacit threat of trouble if people do not behave reasonably. Instead of pursuing only their client's immediate interest, lawyers often act as what Justice Brandeis called "counsel for the situation," seeking what they see as the best long term solution for all concerned. Other lawyers, with more or less success, seek to transform clients' perceptions about what is just, or at least tolerable. Often they deal with bruised egos and manage public relations far more than they vindicate clients' rights. ... [T]he wide variety of roles played by lawyers is a factor in making the functioning of social institutions far more complex than formal descriptions assume. For example, many lawyers' stock in trade includes their contacts with officials, knowledge of acceptable rhetoric, and awareness of mutually advantageous possibilities. Thus, they are able to cut through formal channels and get things done. When this happens regularly, behavior in a corporation or a public agency no longer follows official procedures. . . .
6. *Our society deals with conflict in many ways, but avoidance and evasion are important ones. . . .* We may pass symbolic laws declaring the good, the true and the beautiful, but we leave enforcement to local option. We find social consensus at a high level of abstraction and so keep our doctrines ambiguous or contradictory. This avoids the

costs of definition and of deciding that some interpretations of values are right while others are wrong. Thus, a simple means-and-ends view of law should be suspect. . . .

7. *While law matters in American society, its influence tends to be indirect, subtle and ambiguous.* It is easy to find gaps between the promise and performance of our law. Americans are selectively law abiding. . . . Nonetheless, law matters in a number of ways. For example, many ideas that are part of our common normative vocabulary are crystallized in law, and they both help rationalize action and affect our expectations about the social world. . . . While the ability of the legal system to prompt social change that is unwanted by a large or powerful minority may be limited, often law can be the focus of a social movement, forcing reformers to define goals and select means to obtain them. Even failed reform efforts may influence the behavior of both proponents and opponents. Moreover, law can restrain power in many situations. For many reasons, those with power hesitate to exercise it too crudely. The effort to cloak an exercise of power with a mantle of right or to cover up abuses are costly exercises which, at times, deter action. Law and lawyers have helped gain accommodations for some of the less powerful by using legal symbols and procedures. In this culture even the counterattacks by the powerful have to be rationalized in legal rhetoric. This effort may affect both the form and substance of the way such battles are fought and resolved.

Stewart Macaulay is one of the editors of this book; naturally, he thinks highly of the field, and is cautiously impressed with its accomplishments. Not everybody agrees.[12] Some scholars think that the field is guilty of repetitiveness, triviality, spinning wheels.[13] Also, in the last generation or so, there are scholars who have raised some fairly fundamental questions about social science in general, and about the value of empirical research. This has spilled over into socio-legal research as well. Some qualitative scholars espouse what they call a more "interpretive," self-conscious style of examining legal phenomena while others do not. Regardless of orientation, qualitative researchers tend to pay more attention to the cultural meanings and ideologies that underlie legal phenomena; their work, though not quantitative, is nonetheless fundamentally empirical in nature. We will return to these issues at various points. After going through the material, readers should be able to judge for themselves whether the law-and-society enterprise has been worthwhile, and whether some or all of the criticisms directed at it are well-taken.

The various social sciences, after all, do not agree on methods, approaches, and points of view. In many ways, the economists stand apart from the other social scientists. In the law school world, "law and economics" refers to a movement which attempts to use the tools of neoclassical economics to critique legal rules in terms of efficiency and wealth-maximization. Some of its practitioners seem to feel that the other social sciences are weaklings, that they lack a solid unitary theory to give them backbone, and that many social sciences are tilted politically to the left.[14] On the other hand, some of the leading figures in law and economics work with theory

[12] See, for example, Austin Sarat and Susan Silbey, "The Pull of the Policy Audience," 10 *Law & Policy* 97 (1988); David M. Trubek, "Where the Action Is: Critical Legal Studies and Empiricism," 36 *Stanford Law Review* 575 (1984).

[13] Richard Abel, "Redirecting Social Studies of Law," 14 *Law & Society Review* 805 (1980).

[14] See Richard A. Posner, "The Sociology of the Sociology of Law: A View from Economics," 2 *European Journal of Law & Economics* 265 (1995).

rather than data. (Politically, too, they tilted to the right). But in recent years, many of the younger economists interested in law have shown much greater interest in grounding their work in a solid empirical basis. They are also reaching increasingly beyond a narrower economic scope in their efforts to understand law.

VI. What Lies Ahead?

In Chapter 2, we will deal with descriptions of the legal system. The general idea is that there are different ways of describing legal systems involving different methods and approaches. These affect the way one actually sees a legal system.

Chapter 3 asks the question: where does law come from? We examine ideas about the social sources of law, and the way different social contexts shape the form (and relative formality) of legal responses. The chapter also asks more particular questions about the emergence of laws, legal doctrines and legal institutions. How do we explain, say, why American courts began to pay attention to gender discrimination, or why Congress passed a law outlawing discrimination on the basis of sex? This chapter will deal with pressure groups, public opinion, and related subjects, all of them touching on the question of where law comes from. It concludes by examining the way that society and law are in an influential ongoing interaction with each other.

Chapter 4, in a way, turns the question of Chapter 3 upside down. It asks about the impact of law. Congress passes a law, the President issues an executive order, or a court comes out with a decision. What happens next? What effect does any one of these have on the way people think or behave? The question of impact is actually quite complex, and it includes a whole range of subquestions. For example, it includes the much debated question of deterrence. Does the death penalty have any effect on the murder rate? How would social scientists go about answering this question? In this chapter, too, we ask how messages from the legal system get communicated to at least some of the public. We also examine the effect that the way these messages get transmitted has on obedience or disobedience to law. Questions of impact draw our attention to the limits of effective legal action. How much can lawmakers change the world by changing the law?

Chapter 5 deals with the structure of the legal system—its organizational shape—and what difference this structure might make. The chapter also introduces readers to the sociology of legal roles. That is, we look at the social organization and impact of the work of the main players and actors inside the system, especially judges and lawyers.

Most of the readings in the book have been written by Americans and are about the American legal system. There were always connections between legal systems, but in this global era the connections are denser and more complex. Chapter 6 invites us to look outside the United States and across history. It considers, first, the question of how different histories impact the development of law. It then turns to examine legal cultures—how they differ, how they are interrelated—including the impact of globalization on the legal order. Chapter 6 concludes by considering the interaction of language and culture in law.

In some ways this book is modeled after the typical law school casebook which provides raw materials and questions, but hesitates to give answers. The student is supposed to work out at least tentative answers for herself. The main points are not neatly summarized at the end of each section and chapter.

And the book also is not a "reader" in the social science tradition. The materials are used to develop certain major themes. There is a strong overall structure reflecting the judgments—perhaps the biases—of the authors. Opposing views are frequently paired. If you work with this book, you will have to deal with controversy and important questions that have no certain, fixed and knowable answers. This reflects, of course, the law school style of teaching. We think that it leads to active class participation and discussion. The many notes and citations after each article are meant to help students see what is at issue as well as making suggestions for those who might want to pursue some of these matters in more detail. (Some of the notes that introduce new topics begin with underlined headings as guideposts for the reader.)

We have taught from these materials as they took shape over time. For us, the book works. Generally, students respond favorably to the course. Some law students are a bit leery of the social science vocabulary and methods at first. Some students trained in the social sciences worry that they are not sure footed enough on the paths of the law. Our experience is that as the course rolls on, the students deal with common problems and distinctions between law students and others tend to blur and disappear.

We are amused that some law professors who are ready, willing and able to master the black arts of the Internal Revenue Code or the tangled web of the Rule Against Perpetuities, seem to turn pale when confronted with simple tables and graphs. And sociologists who think nothing of invading the world of medicine or religion sometimes treat the legal domain as if it were a cave inhabited by fire-eating dragons.

We have tried to avoid the more exotic methods and vocabulary of social science. Sometimes we offer explanations in notes and questions after readings. The law, too, is kept clean and simple. We feel that this book can be taught even by a law professor with little background or experience in the social sciences. Social scientists without legal training can also cope quite nicely. Perhaps the ideal teacher would have training or sophistication in both realms. More and more, law schools are hiring professors with doctorates in social science fields as well as law degrees. (Indeed, this describes one of the editors of this book). Nonetheless, such people are and will be rare enough so that this area is likely to remain open to amateurs in one field or another for a long time to come. That indeed is part of its charm and its potency.

Contracts Law in Action: Introduction

Stewart Macaulay, William Whitford, Kathryn Hendley, and Jonathan Lipson

A. Overview of Law in Action

This book takes a law in action approach to the study of contract law. This approach questions overemphasis on legal rules. Of course law students must learn legal doctrine, but they need to learn much more. Legal reasoning has a tendency to overclaim for the impact of law on human relations. Furthermore, most lawyers are not litigators but rather play an advisory role in the planning and adjusting of relationships. In law practice, contract doctrine is a tool, but it is often less important to a lawyer's work than the ability to understand the business or other context, assess the goals and positions of parties, and find common interests and compromises.

The law in action approach stresses that very few disputes become lawsuits, let alone progress to an appeal that produces the appellate opinions typically studied

This article was original published as chapter 1 in Stewart Macaulay, William Whitford, Kathryn Hendley, Jonathan Lipson, Contracts: Law in Action, Volume 1: The Introductory Course, 4th edn, Durham NC: Carolina Academic Press, 2016. Reprinted with permission.

S. Macaulay (✉)
University of Wisconsin Law School, Madison, WI, USA
e-mail: smacaula@wisc.edu

W. Whitford
Law Emeritus, University of Wisconsin Law School, Madison, WI, USA
e-mail: bill.whitford@wisc.edu

K. Hendley
Law and Political Science, University of Wisconsin Law School, Madison, WI, USA
e-mail: khendley@wisc.edu

J. Lipson
Law, Temple University, Beasley School of Law, Philadelphia, PA, USA
e-mail: jonathan.lipson@temple.edu

D. Campbell (ed.), *Stewart Macaulay: Selected Works*, Law and Philosophy Library 133, https://doi.org/10.1007/978-3-030-33930-2_13
Published by Springer International Publishing AG 2018.

in law schools. In most situations, legal rights serve as but a vague bargaining entitlement in a negotiation process. People settle differences in the shadow of the law. For example, the victim and an insurance adjuster who is not a lawyer settle most auto accident claims in a fairly routine way. Even in the small percentage of disputes where the victim hires a lawyer, that lawyer is likely to negotiate a settlement without bringing a lawsuit. In the tiny fraction of cases where a complaint is filed in court, lawyers usually settle before a trial begins. Of course, legal rules play a part in the outcome, but often a minor one. As a result, the liability rules discussed in law school classes often will not have the impact on behavior assumed in approaches such as legal realism or law and economics, discussed further below.

Moreover, we may err if we assume that appellate decisions are final resolutions of matters. The loser may battle on through administrative agencies or state and national legislatures to change the rules. And sometimes people win victories in these other law-making institutions so slighted in the first year of legal education. Furthermore, even where a plaintiff wins an appellate decision affirming a judgment for a large sum of damages, one must execute the judgment and turn it into money. However, the defendant may have no assets subject to execution in the jurisdiction. The defendant may file for bankruptcy or delay matters through a state creditor-debtor proceeding. One of the lessons of a law in action approach is that while rules and upper-level decisions are important, one has to look at the real options open to the parties. This approach insists that we look at the legal system from the bottom up as well as from the top down. Criminal law, for example, is both a matter of the statutory definitions of crimes as interpreted by appellate courts, and behavior as seen from the front seat of a police squad car.

The law in action approach reminds us of practical issues lawyers face, particularly in contract law. The approach emphasizes the gaps between stated policies of legal rules and their impact and the ways in which business norms and imperatives are often more powerful "law" than formal law on the books.

Use of "law stories," investigations of the background of cases, can help to bring out law in action insights. Your professor may choose to use another book with such material to provide detailed background about cases in this book.[1] Furthermore, the notes in this book often contain background such as excerpts from trial transcripts and briefs and information from interviews of lawyers and parties about their motivations and what happened after the reported decision. While cases often announce elegant abstract principles, implementation is usually partial and messy. Lawsuits do not necessarily reveal truth or produce justice.

---

[1]*See* Richard Danzig & Geoffrey Watson, The Capability Problem in Contract Law (Foundation Press 2004); Contracts Stories (Douglas Baird, ed., Foundation Press 2007). For discussion of the advantages of law stories, see Stewart Macaulay, *Contracts, New Legal Realism, and Improving the Navigation of the Yellow Submarine*, 80 Tul. L. Rev. 1161, 1175–77 (2006).

B. Studying Law: What Am I Here For?

1. Classical Legal Education

Beginning law students often have difficulty understanding what they are supposed to learn. Students may bring expectations with them to law school that cause part of the problem. Some assume that being a law student is a larger version of learning the rules of the road in order to get a motor vehicle driver's license. Law is rules, and the best student is the one who knows the most rules. Some expect to be offered a cookbook approach to such things as how to write and probate a will, how to draft a contract, and how to transfer real estate. Others expect basic training in how to try a lawsuit, including how to trip up a lying witness by vigorous cross-examination. These students' model is learning golf or tennis from a pro — law is a game, and they want to know how to win. Most law schools — certainly those with the highest prestige — will disappoint all of these expectations. Legal education directs primary attention elsewhere. Memorizing rules alone will not get a student very far. Moreover, while students may get some exposure in law school to skills such as legal drafting and cross-examination techniques and questions of tactics and strategy, their skills will be greatly refined in practice once formal legal education is over.

The traditional style of law school teaching causes many law students to misunderstand the game they are called upon to play. In the old-fashioned style, a professor assigns a collection of legal raw materials — appellate opinions and occasionally statutes — for preparation before class. Then the professor questions students about them, pointing out flaws in their answers. If a student takes the plaintiff's side in discussing a case, the professor attacks with challenges supporting the defendant. But if another student offers support for the defendant's arguments, the professor neatly leaps to the other side and attacks the defendant's case. At the very least, students in such a class are supposed to learn to impose structure on what seems to be a jumble of cases, questions, fellow students' attempts at answers, jokes, and perhaps professorial war stories. They are supposed to recognize that plausible arguments can be made by a lawyer for just about any proposition but that some arguments are easier to sell than others. Judicial opinions offer examples of formal legal argument and conventional assumptions of legal culture. Needless to say, students are misguided if they assume that studying involves only memorizing what a professor or textbook author states. Students who have firm, simple ideas of right and wrong may be disturbed by the apparent chaos and relativism of many law school classes.

Law professors often speak of class discussion, but this phrase suggests more equality between professor and student than usually exists. Students cannot remain passive note takers. They can be forced to participate and fear making fools of themselves.[2] Moreover, the professor controls the agenda, grants and withholds

---

[2]*See* Elizabeth Mertz, The Language of Law School: Learning to "Think Like a Lawyer" 51 (Oxford University Press 2007) (noting that forcing students to participate in classroom dialogue is in one sense authoritarian but in another empowering, because students "are pushed to remain in and

permission to speak, and is armed with rhetorical ploys that few in the class will have mastered. Students learn to make cautious statements and recognize that the other side often has a good argument. Beginning law students can find themselves at the end of a limb arguing that a particular result is "just" or "fair." After having the limb sawed off a few times, students learn to say something qualified.

Today, professors often want law students to learn both the classic approach to doctrine and several other ways of looking at cases and legal problems. In classic legal education, one learns the application of legal doctrine to various situations. For example, suppose the tort of X allows a plaintiff to recover damages from a defendant if the plaintiff can prove (1) defendant hit plaintiff, (2) defendant intended to hit plaintiff, and (3) plaintiff did not consent to being hit. A professor expects students to discover "the elements" (that is, factors (1), (2), and (3)) of the tort of X from reading one or more cases. These elements are legal doctrine, but knowing them is only the start of the game.

A classic law professor would push students to unearth many difficult problems of definition lurking within this seemingly simple example. At the outset, what does "hit" mean? Suppose Defendant (hereafter D) tried to hit Plaintiff (hereafter P) but missed. However, as D's fist swung past P's chin, the sleeve of D's jacket brushed the sleeve of P's shirt. Did D "hit" P? And what does "intend" mean? Suppose D tried to hit Mr. A, but hit P instead when P jumped in the way trying to defend Mr. A. Suppose, alternatively, D intended to swing his fist at P but only to scare P, not to hit him. However, P moved into the path of D's punch and took it on the chin. Suppose, to change the case again, D swung his fist at P but was indifferent whether he hit P or came close enough to scare him. Suppose, finally, D testifies at trial that he actually intended only to make a broad gesture while arguing with P, but D's fist came in contact with P's chin by accident. X, Y, and Z, three reasonable people who watched the encounter, testify that D seemed to them to have intended to hit P. Does the definition of "intend" in the tort refer to some subjective inner state? Must actors in the legal system judge it objectively by outward appearances?

The next step would be to ask: what does "consent" mean?[3] Few people who are not masochists would want others to hit them. Nevertheless, many do put themselves

master the dialogue. The law school professor is thus at once giving students no choice and telling them that they are capable of performing this genre."). Mertz's study of legal education in the first-year contracts course is a work of anthropological linguistics. She concludes, at 219, that legal education inculcates "methodological arrogance," in which the main focus is examination of legal textual authority with great rigor, but "when it is time to discuss the assumptions about society and people that underlie the judicial decisions students read, law professors routinely invite speculation and anecdote." The law in action approach attempts to bring more rigor to questions about the impact of legal rules on human relations and reduce reliance on supposition.

[3]The meaning of consent has become the focus of political controversy in the crime of rape. A man has not raped a woman who consented to sexual intercourse. Whatever the formal definition of consent, what is the folk definition of the term as imposed by juries? One study suggests American jurors often rule that if the woman knew the man, if sexual intercourse took place in a social situation, and if no weapon was used, the woman will be deemed to have consented. Many feminists see the social definition of rape as a reflection of the sexism in the society. Apart from the merits of

into situations where it is likely they will be hit. Does this constitute "consent" and thus a defense to the tort of X? Suppose that both P and D are professional football players for rival teams. In the course of a game, D hits P to block him so that a runner can advance the ball. Does P "consent" to D's hitting him just by participating in the game of football? Or does consent require a formal act such as signing a written contract whereby P gives up his protection from being hit by D in exchange for the privilege of playing the game? Suppose that D's block was illegal under the rules of football.[4] Would P's consent to being blocked in the game extend to being blocked illegally under the league rule? Would it matter if the rule were frequently broken or almost never broken? Suppose during a time-out, P took off his helmet, and D then punched P in the face. Does P's consent to being hit during the course of a game extend to this kind of behavior that is not part of the contest?

Suppose, to shift the situation again, P and D are baseball players,. P, a pitcher, threw a ball at D, a batter, that just missed him. D ran to the mound and hit P in the face. P knew that while this is not an everyday occurrence, it is not unheard-of. Did P consent to D's retaliatory blow just by playing the game? Suppose that P is a spectator at a baseball game and a foul ball off D's bat went into the stands, hitting P. Did P consent to being hit in this way just by attending the game? Suppose P is French, and this is the first time he has ever seen a baseball game. On the back of P's ticket of admission to the game a number of sentences appear printed in tiny type. They say that anyone attending the game shall be deemed to have consented to being hit by foul balls coming into the stands. Is P bound by a contract whereby he gave up his rights as a result of accepting such a ticket and entering the stadium?

It is possible to dream up hypothetical situations endlessly that test what seems to be a straightforward rule of law. This illustrates something about the nature of the words so often used to state legal rules such as "hit," "intend," and "consent." Constructing hypotheticals is itself an important lawyer's skill, often useful in argument. Could we avoid all of these problems of classification by drafting rules of law more carefully and using more precise terms? Drafters of legal rules pay a price when they try to anticipate most situations. Think of the Internal Revenue Code and the regulations drafted under it. They are exceedingly complex, and complexity creates work for accountants and tax lawyers.

How do we answer these endless questions? The classic law professor, by questions and body language, would push students toward several possible sources of answers. First, we could search for *authority* — cases, statutes, administrative regulations, and other sources of law dealing with some aspect of the problems we have posed. Suppose we add to one of our hypothetical cases that P played football for the Chicago Bears, and D played for the Green Bay Packers. D hit P in a game

---

their argument, the example suggests that consent is not a simple concept, and its definition often involves controversial normative choices.

[4]Notice the interesting use of the term *illegal*. Can we say that the National Football League has its own "law"? If so, should lawyers, and law students, concern themselves with this kind of "private government"? Is this footnote an example of a digression from the main theme of the discussion? If so, is it unimportant? Can you just ignore these questions without fear of sanction?

played in Green Bay. Thus, we can assume that the case is governed by the law of Wisconsin. Suppose, further, that the Supreme Court of Wisconsin decided in 1960 that professional football players consent, within the meaning of that term in the tort of X, to the common and ordinary hitting involved in the game by their participation in the sport. If we assume that the Wisconsin court would not overrule its 1960 decision (and this might be a large assumption), then we could answer some of the questions about the meaning of consent with a degree of assurance.

We could consider the implications of this decision by using the techniques of common law case analysis. This is the art of generating both broad holdings for cases, so that they may be applied beyond their intuitive scope, and narrow holdings, so that they will not apply where it seems they should. Most narrowly, a court could limit the 1960 decision to professional football and the particular facts of the case. More broadly, a court could read the decision as establishing that a player takes the risk of common and ordinary physical contact in *any* sport. Of course, we still would have to determine whether the particular hitting involved in our case would be deemed common and ordinary within the sport. We might expect that some hitting would clearly be part of football while other hitting clearly would be outside the ordinary risks assumed by anyone who played the game. Even so, we might expect to find a large range of cases in the middle where reasonable people might differ about how common and ordinary the type of hitting involved was. These would be the close and difficult cases where both P and D would have good arguments — the type of case likely to be posed on a law school examination. Even skilled and experienced lawyers would not be able to be certain of the outcome of these cases; at best, they could make informed judgments about the probabilities that P or D would win.

Law students must learn to "spot the issues" — that is, to identify ambiguities in rules, conflicts among rules, and gaps where particular situations fail to fit rules. Clearly, this 1960 decision does not answer all the questions we raised. For example, does it apply to baseball players as well as football players? The classic law professor would push his or her students to reason by *analogy*. One could say, for example, that the key idea in the 1960 decision was that professional athletes — whatever the sport — can be assumed to understand the ordinary risks of the game. As a result, they can be deemed to choose to take those risks when they choose to play. In this sense, baseball is like (analogous to) football, although the precise risks assumed by baseball and football players would differ as the two sports differ. Of course, this judgment based on an analogy would be strengthened if we were to discover that the highest courts in 10 other states had decided just this way on these very grounds. Then we could combine an argument by analogy with an appeal to authority. While the decisions of the courts in other states would not bind the Wisconsin Supreme Court in interpreting its 1960 decision, it is likely that its members would find these other cases *persuasive* since, absent good reason to the contrary, uniformity among the states itself is an important value.

Classic legal thought refers to the ordinary meaning of language as a second major source of answers to the questions we raised earlier. This approach might ask whether most people (which unfortunately might mean most educated people, or most members of the same socioeconomic class as the legal elite) understand "hit," "intend," or "consent" to include or exclude the cases presented. On occasion, judges, lawyers, and law professors look to dictionary definitions, raising the vexing questions whether words have fixed meanings apart from context and whether dictionaries capture meanings accurately. Resort is sometimes made to "common sense," but different people may have different views of easily accepted common norms.

2. Criticism of Classical Legal Thought: Other Perspectives

Legal Realism Beginning just before the First World War, a group of American law professors attacked the kinds of approaches we have just described. Their movement, traceable to the pragmatism of Oliver Wendell Holmes Jr.,[5] was called "legal realism," and its leading figure was Karl Llewellyn, later the chief architect of the Uniform Commercial Code. It is far easier to describe what the legal realists were against than what they were for. One idea common to the group was that judges do not "find" the law in the clouds or by manipulating techniques of distinguishing cases. Rather, judges "make" the law by normative choices. And if this is true, the realists told us that we would get better decisions and more predictable law if judges openly recognized their role and candidly explained how they arrived at their choices. Many realists relied on the teachings that came to be known as general semantics to attack definitional approaches. Words such as "hit," "intend," and "consent" have many meanings in ordinary speech, and definitions serve better to rule out extreme cases than to decide close ones. Since past decisions almost never involve the identical situation now brought before the court, cases almost always can be distinguished if a judge wants to do so. Thus, appeals to authority may affect judgment but they do not compel one result rather than another.

Analogies, too, are suspect. For example, baseball and football are both professional sports, and those who play them are likely to be aware of certain risks of being hit by another player that are just part of the game. But football is supposed to be a contact sport while baseball is not. We could say that a football player has less need of the deterrent of the law of torts than a baseball player because of the nature of his athletic equipment and the opportunity to retaliate. Or one could argue that football needs the support of tort law more than baseball because it is necessary to control the violence inherent in the sport. Whatever the merit of these arguments, they illustrate that the very nature of an analogy is that the things being viewed are both *like* one another in

[5]Oliver Wendell Holmes Jr., The Common Law 1 (1881) ("The life of the law has not been logic; it has been experience. The felt necessities of the time, the prevalent moral and political theories, intuitions of public policy, avowed or unconscious, even the prejudices which judges share with their fellow-men, have had a good deal more to do than the syllogism in determining the rules by which men should be governed.").

some respects and *not like* one another in others. The problem is to decide if the common factors are more important than the uncommon ones. However, this is a judgment that rests on values, facts, and predictions about the consequences of decisions each way. Analogy may be a step in the process of decision, but it does not end the discussion.

A law professor who embraced realism would ask a student to argue in terms of the goals to be served by one decision or another. For example, a student might argue for a consent rule in professional sports that turned on the likely reaction of fans viewing the event. A player should be deemed to consent to the normal risks of the game, even including blows that violate its rules, but those blows that would likely incite fans to violence should be deterred by all means available, including tort liability. This, the student might argue, would aid in crowd control — a worldwide problem at sporting events — and, in the long run, in the continuation of professional sports. Another student might disagree, arguing that the private government of professional sports has enough internal sanctions to control the behavior of competitors so that we need not incur the costs of trying lawsuits between athletes. She might remind us that players in any sport, from golf to boxing, who hit others outside the rules of the game can be suspended or thrown out of the game for good. Those who violate the working norms of competitors are subject to a variety of sanctions ranging from attacks on their reputations in the form of gossip to ostracism and even physical retaliation. We should have evidence that more is needed before we waste the time of over-crowded judicial machinery on such cases.

Whatever the merit of these arguments, they accept that the term "consent" could be interpreted to include or exclude the behavior in question, and they attempt to influence the choice of a meaning in a particular situation on the basis of some impact on behavior that the advocate thinks good or bad. Definitions and analogies only offer a number of possibilities. Choices must be made on the basis of normative evaluation of statements of the rule or predictions about its consequences. This being the case, one must argue policy just as if one were trying to convince a legislator to vote for passage or defeat of a statute.

Realism, of course, relies on wise judges to make policy choices. How, then, does law differ from politics? Republican governors appoint one group of judges while Democratic governors appoint another. These political backgrounds might play important roles in forming attitudes and coming to decisions. In its extreme form, realism might see each judge as having a roving commission to do good as he or she sees fit. Many find this unsatisfactory and in fact an abandonment of the rule of law.

"Neutral Principles," or "Legal Process": By the 1950s, most law professors accepted many of the teachings of realism. Predictably, there was a reaction sometimes known as the "legal process" or "neutral principles" school of thought. This view holds that judges should leave major policy decisions to legislatures because the courts lack the capacity to make such decisions well or to implement them. This approach, which advocates legal craft and procedure to restrain judicial innovation to an incremental, step-by-step approach, is subject to the criticism that it favors the status quo and thus is inherently conservative rather than apolitical. Furthermore, particularly when it comes to common law such as contracts and torts, made by judges without the necessity of legislative intervention, it is the traditional role of the courts to review and adapt the law to current needs and norms.

***Law and Economics*:** An influential school of thought derived from legal realism is the law and economics approach, which has become popular in many American law schools and among some judges. The founding fathers of the movement are identified with the University of Chicago and its tradition in economics. Realism tells judges and other decision-makers to make normative choices openly, but offers little advice about how to choose among possible normative positions. Legal process thinking imposes a requirement of due process on almost every important decision but accepts whatever substantive choices emerge from formally fair procedures. Law and economics, in contrast, generally favors efficient allocation of resources; if one wants to seek some other goal, at least one should be aware of the costs.

For example, we must pay a price if we insist that all decisions be taken only after procedures that comply with due process. Sometimes the cost will be outweighed by the benefits, but sometimes not. The position teaches a powerful lesson overlooked in much of legal realism or legal proceduralism — sometimes the lesson is summarized as "there is no such thing as a free lunch." In the 1960s and 1970s, Congress decided to regulate the safety of automobile design, environmental pollution caused by automotive exhaust, and the fuel consumption of cars. The law and economics approach emphasizes that such regulation is not free, and the cost of these changes in the design of vehicles raises prices for cars. This, in turn, is likely to have many consequences, some of which may be hard to see at first. On the one hand, the regulation reduces externalities — costs imposed on third parties in the form of impact on habitats and on human health from pollution and safety risks. On the other hand, less transportation may be available to the poor if higher prices cause middle-class owners to drive their cars longer so there is less usable life left when they trade in their cars. The total market for automobiles may contract as prices increase, and this limits the number of available jobs connected with automobile manufacturing, servicing, tourism and so on. People may be willing to accept these costs of regulation as the price for what they see as real benefits. Nonetheless, we cannot pretend that there is no cost or that costs just come out of the pocket of wealthy corporations in some magical fashion. This approach reminds us that law is not free.

The law and economics approach also suggests that, absent transaction costs, it makes no difference where legislatures and courts place liability for accidental injuries and deaths.[6] Suppose we have a rule that says car buyers must pay for

[6]*See* Ronald H. Coase, *The Problem of Social Cost*, 3 J.L. & Econ. 1 (1960). It is sometimes lost on those who cite the "Coase theorem" (which refers to the idea that allocation of resources is independent of default legal rules if transaction costs are zero) that Coase was not arguing that transaction costs typically *are* zero. Rather, transaction costs of changing a background rule of law, for example by entering into a contract, are often high, so it very much does matter what the background rule is. *See* Coase, *The Problem of Social Cost: The Citations,* 71 Chi.-Kent L. Rev. 809 (1996) (noting many more citations for the "Coase Theorem" than for the reciprocal point).

repairs to their vehicles whatever the cause of damage. A court or legislature changes the rule to place the burden of certain repairs on car sellers. We then can expect sellers to raise prices or to make contracts shifting the burden of repairs back to buyers. In either event, buyers will still pay for repairs.

Many who advocate the law and economics approach see it as value-neutral. If we care about efficiency, we should try to predict the economic consequences of proposed changes in legal rules. Moreover, we can explain much of what courts have done since the Industrial Revolution in terms of seeking efficiency. Many proponents of law and economics tell us that it does not deal with the justice or fairness of the present distribution of wealth, status, privilege, or power in the society. Law and economics, however, has much to say about the costs of measures designed to change such distributions.

Critics of the approach see it as a highly successful effort to legitimate the position of the well-off in society. Law and economics just ignores law's role in symbolizing values and morals.[7] Often the message of the approach is that reform is impossible or unwise, and if only government would go away, all would be as good as it can be. Some law and economics scholars hold as an article of faith that competition and free markets solve all problems, and they deny that there can be any private power unchecked by the market apart from advantages granted by government.

Critics also point out that the law and economics approach is highly abstract and based on logical deduction from doubtful assumptions. A great deal of law and economics assumes a world without transaction costs, but that is not the world in which we live. Too little attention is given to implementation of rules — writers sometimes treat people as if they were puppets tied by strings to legal rules that control their behavior. That the formal statement of a legal rule can be rationalized in efficiency terms does not necessarily indicate that the rule promotes efficiency in practice. Of course one could take a law and economics approach to the law in action, looking at whether social relations are efficient. It just has not been done often.

In recent decades, behavioral economics has complicated the earlier assumptions of law and economics. Neoclassical economics assumed, with elegant parsimony but some sacrifice in accuracy, that humans act rationally in their own self-interest. Behavioral economics complicates this assumption and emphasizes that humans have bounded rationality and bounded willpower. People sometimes systematically fail to predict accurately their future behavior because they do not fully understand their own desires and risks. People may think they will always pay credit card bills on time and avoid interest charges and thus not pay attention to interest rates. They may underestimate the bad things that could happen to them, such as getting sick or losing their jobs, events that would make it hard or even impossible to pay on time. They may engage in impulse purchases and regret them later. This behavior is more

[7] *See* Lawrence Friedman, *Two Faces of Law*, 1984 Wis. L. Rev. 13.

problematic for big purchases than small ones, where people can learn over time to make better decisions without suffering large losses.

In addition, buyers typically act under limited information, not the perfect information of simple economic models. It is time-consuming to shop for the best deal, and some deals are very complicated, so that looking into competitors' terms on many points is virtually impossible. Cellphone contracts are a good example of consumer contracts with very complex terms. In theory a small number of shoppers might introduce competition in such terms, but the terms of competitors often look the same. Furthermore, sellers may be able to segment the small number of shoppers into better deals, while giving poorer deals to those who do not shop. In other words, markets do not work perfectly for a multitude of reasons. Onerous terms may be suggestive of market failure. Behavioral economics and attention to market failures can lead to very different conclusions about how to design legal rules than a more simple law and economics approach.

***Critical Legal Studies and Its Variants*:** In the 1970s, legal realism developed a more radical branch known as "critical legal studies." From this perspective, the existing distribution of wealth, status, privilege, and power is central, and legal doctrine is mystification, legitimating the status quo. For example, in the 19th century lawyers and judges came to see the business corporation as a legal person with all the rights of real individuals. More generally, there is great inequality in wealth and power between a large business such as Microsoft and an individual. In theory, if Microsoft breaches a contract, an individual consumer could sue and recover damages as compensation. But all of this is ideology that ignores the advantages Microsoft has over any individual who attempts to assert legal rights against it.[8] Lawyers are both necessary and expensive. Wealth has an impact on the outcome of litigation. People and organizations with wealth can better afford the long delays that so characterize our legal system. Moreover, organizations that engage in repeated standardized transactions can plan these relationships to their advantage. Individuals who deal with them sign standard form contracts that serve to ward off most unwanted liability from the large organization. Most individuals are not aware of what they are giving away when they sign. Even if they were aware, one could say they have little *real* choice but to sign away their rights.

Scholars associated with the Conference on Critical Legal Studies (CLS) examined the assumptions hidden within legal doctrine concerning what is necessary, tolerable, and just. What do those who make and work with our law take as "common sense"? Which groups in society benefit from these tacit assumptions in our law and which are disadvantaged by them? Critical scholars see American legal consciousness as favoring wealth and privilege. Some of these scholars find American law characterized by contradictory principles. They hope that by showing underdeveloped but long established counterthemes in our law, they can open the

---

[8]*See* Marc Galanter, *Why the "Haves" Come Out Ahead: Speculations on the Limits of Legal Change*, 9 Law & Soc'y Rev. 95 (1974).

way to a new conception of rights more consistent with a less competitive and more cooperative society.

Critical feminists and critical race theorists have challenged the white male law professors who made up most of CLS. They have charged them with insensitivity to the benefits of a rule of law. While rights may be flawed weapons, women and people of color can use them both as symbols and as instruments to better their position. Moreover, when we look at any body of law, including contracts, from the perspective of gender or race, we recognize easily overlooked and debatable assumptions. For example, the alleged neutrality of contract ideas served well the institution of slavery in the United States until the Civil War — humans bought and sold other people under a law that claims to be one of the foundations of liberty.[9] People of color are almost entirely absent from contracts casebooks, suggesting that this body of law deals with power as much as it deals with questions of free choice. A leading critical feminist wrote an analysis of how a popular contracts casebook treated women either as sex objects or as the subject of paternal care.[10]

Radical lawyers sometimes see all varieties of critical legal thinkers as trying to bring about a revolution from within the academy rather than taking risks and fighting the battle on the front lines. Critical scholars respond that it is better to change ideas about what could be, than to win court victories seeking rights: lawyers championing the "have-nots" can implement rights only marginally in legal institutions controlled by the powerful. When workers, people of color, women, or other less powerful groups threaten to win significant victories through the assertion of rights, the system tends to adjust to support the status quo. Statutes are construed narrowly, procedural rules are put in place to minimize the chances of success, the costs of asserting rights are raised to limit their use, jurors reject valid claims as something they do not wish to believe, and businesses use standard form terms mandating arbitration to prevent their customers from going to court, restricting them to a private forum chosen by the contract drafter.

We could debate most of these assertions. Nonetheless, all varieties of critical legal thought invite students to consider how the legal system works in practice and what kinds of people benefit. Seemingly neutral legal rules may privilege certain positions.[11] Whatever the statement of legal ideals, law on the books may differ from law in action, and the differences may not be random or neutral.

***Law in Action*:** The law in action approach, also known as the law and society approach, can be seen as another branch of legal realism, along with law and economics and critical approaches. Its particular concern is with how human relationships actually play out in the shadow of the law. This approach is not opposed to

[9]Patricia Williams, The Alchemy of Race and Rights 17–21, 216, 224 (1991).

[10]Mary Jo Frug, *Re-reading Contracts: A Feminist Analysis of a Contracts Casebook*, 34 Am. U.L. Rev. 1065 (1985).

[11]Anatole France once wryly noted that "[t]he law in its majestic egalitarianism, forbids the rich as well as the poor to sleep under bridges, to beg in the streets, and to steal bread." Le lys rouge, Ch. 7 (1894).

pursuing policy goals through law, but it is highly skeptical of claims that particular policies will be easily implemented by adopting legal rules. Read again the opening pages of this introduction for an overview of law in action. As for criticism of this approach, its dependence on empirical examination of the impact of law may make it focus on things that are easy to study empirically rather than on bigger justice concerns. Furthermore, law and society research is not always up to the most rigorous standards of the social sciences, although sophisticated empirical study of the impact of law has been gaining favor in the legal academy in recent decades.

3. Law School Examinations

Part of the "what am I here for" topic concerns law school exams and how the skills tested on exams relate to preparing for the practice of law. Once a student masters the blend of approaches demanded by his or her professor, the student still must pass an exam. Typically, a student will be confronted with a story (often called a fact pattern) and asked to play the role of judge or that of a lawyer for plaintiff or defendant. To take a very simple example, suppose the question set out the story of P and D, two professional baseball players employed by rival teams. P, a pitcher, threw a ball that just missed hitting D, who was batting. D ran to the mound and threw a punch at P. However, D hit U, the first base umpire. U had come to the mound to try to prevent a fight. You are U's lawyer. Make the best case you can to justify recovery of a judgment against D.

In an exam, the student's job is often to identify the relevant legal doctrines and the elements of those doctrines that are debatable (debatable elements raise "legal issues," which must be "spotted" and then discussed) and then bring policy considerations to bear to develop opposing arguments. Arguments about legal issues are typically more important than "answers."

Your first task would be to try to fit the facts into some legal category. You recognize that it is worth considering the tort of X. There is no question that D hit U, and so the first element of the tort seems to be present, a point you should mention. However, unless you can persuade a judge and jury to interpret the word "intent" very broadly, you face trouble establishing the second element of the tort. Moreover, you should at least recognize the possibility that D's lawyer is going to argue that just by being an umpire U "consented" to the risks of getting hit in a fight between players. (The process of fitting facts into legal categories is "spotting the issues," the first step in legal analysis. Most of those who get low grades do so because they fail to see that they should discuss the tort of X or that there would be difficulty in establishing that D "intended" to hit U or that U did not consent.)

How would you argue that it was enough that D intended to hit someone and that the tort of X does not, or should not, require that he have intended to hit his actual victim, your client U? You could turn to whatever authority had been discussed in your course. You probably would not have a case directly deciding the question. You would have to draw analogies to those decisions that adopted a broader definition of "intent" in other contexts. You would do what you could with the ordinary understanding of the word "intent." Perhaps you could argue that in common speech we assume that one "intends" the ordinary consequences of one's actions, and one consequence of throwing a punch is missing the intended target and hitting something else. You would make policy arguments that would justify an expanded definition of the term so that the rule would include third parties such as U. You would deal with D's likely arguments that changes in liability rules are properly the task of a legislature and that such broader liability is economically inefficient. You might consider whether all a new rule would do is prompt disclaimer clauses in umpires' contracts. You might consider a distributional argument concerning highly paid players striking lesser paid employees of organized baseball such as umpires.

Then after all of this analysis concerning "intent," you would turn to the consent issue. Do umpires assume the risk of injury in fights between players just by being umpires? Again, you would make all the types of arguments we've catalogued. You would anticipate those arguments your opponent is likely to make and respond to them as best as you could.

Once you had dealt with the tort of X, you would then consider whether D's conduct came within the tort of Y. It applies to unintentional but "negligent" hitting of others. Why not start with tort Y and avoid all the difficult problems with the idea of "intent" in tort X? Because, as you should state in your answer, U might be able to get punitive damages in addition to compensation for his actual injuries if the hitting were deemed intentional. He could recover only actual compensatory damages for negligence. Indeed, this possibility might affect arguments about how a court should define intent for purposes of tort — in essence, you would assert that D's conduct warranted strong punishment so both he and others would be deterred in the future and therefore the word "intent" should be defined broadly to achieve this goal. D's lawyer, of course, would argue that D's conduct did not warrant such punishment. This may seem to be arguing backwards. Logically, one might expect a determination of whether D has committed tort X and then the remedies would just follow if he had. Here, we begin by asking what remedy makes sense in light of D's conduct. You will find that many of your courses reflect this concern with the bottom line. This is another example of the realists' point that deciding cases involves policy choices and not just definitions and deductions.

Yet, you might ask, what am I here for? What does all this have to do with becoming a lawyer? You did not come to law school to become an expert in taking examinations. Examinations are supposed to be a means to the end of becoming a lawyer. The theory is that those who can write good exam answers will be able to evaluate and make persuasive arguments to legal decision-makers. Lawyers who are good at evaluating arguments will know what cases to accept from potential clients and what to do with those they do take. When a lawyer has a strong legal argument — assuming all other things are equal — he or she can demand far more as the price of a settlement than when he or she has a weaker legal position. Furthermore, lawyers who can anticipate legal arguments can also write contracts to address them directly and perhaps create greater predictability for their clients. They will be better planners.

Notice that here we arrive at an explanation for legal education's emphasis on arguments rather than answers. A lawyer who can fashion a plausible argument, even one involving creative new theories, usually is in a better bargaining position in settlement negotiations or when drafting a contract than a lawyer who can do little more than blunder through a cookbook approach to practice. A lawyer who can anticipate arguments can rearrange the relationship at the outset to minimize the risk that those arguments will be successful. All lawyers are equal only in the yellow pages of the telephone directory; savvy, well-prepared, creative lawyers do better than foolish, ill-prepared ones who proceed by rote. Of course, creative theories must fall within the range of arguments acceptable within legal culture. Whatever the merit of Marxist theories about American law, one would be a fool to offer them so labeled to most American judges. There are fashions in ideas acceptable to the courts. Certain views are "in the air" at one time but not another. A wise lawyer would not make the same arguments before the present Supreme Court of the United States as she made when Earl Warren was Chief Justice. Consumer protection was far more popular in the early 1970s than in the early 1980s. Also, some judges delight in technical lawyering while others are annoyed by nice distinctions among cases and clever readings of statutes.

Indeed, the law of nearly every state as applied in its cities, towns, and villages will reflect the state's diversity and is likely to differ substantially around a common core found in the state's statutes, administrative regulations, and appellate cases. Knowing what is likely to sell before the judges who would decide a case is also part of a lawyer's skill. Of course, a sociologist of law would remind us that bargaining power flows from far more than legal arguments and so settlements may turn on other factors. One party may need money now while the other is able to await a final decision after several appeals, and this fact is likely to affect how they settle a case. This, too, is part of our subject matter.

In a sense, good lawyers never cease being law students. The practice of law is far more than knowing a body of formal statements of rules. Of course, learning certain rules and a vocabulary is an essential step in the process of becoming a lawyer. However, it is but one step. Moreover, many of the rules one must learn to practice are not what one normally thinks of as laws. Lawyers who represent those injured in auto accidents and lawyers who represent insurance companies know the going rate for various kinds of accidents. They know how much it will take to settle a rear end collision where the police gave neither driver a traffic ticket and where the plaintiff has suffered damage to his car and personal injuries. While all this is true, a great deal of law practice also involves judgments about probabilities in light of specialized knowledge. Lawyers must cope with the knowledge that they cannot be certain; a court or legislature may change the rule, there are good arguments for alternative interpretations of the rule as applied in the present situation, and what one knows and what one can prove in court are very different things. Legal education aims to provide part of the basis for making such informed judgments in the practice of law.

While legal education could always do a better job in preparing students for practice, it is impossible to mint finished lawyers in only three years at a university. "Lawyer" is a label applied to many distinct professions, and faculty and students cannot predict whether certain students will go to Wall Street or Main Street, work in governmental agencies, or enter politics. Formal legal education is just the beginning of a career-long process of learning. This is why law, like medicine, is known as a "learned profession."

C. Contracts Courses

1. The Goals of the Law-in-Action Approach to the Contracts Course

Almost all law students in what was once the British Empire begin their study with a course called "contracts." Students naturally assume that the course deals with an important part of law practice. However, in recent years many law professors and others have questioned this conventional view. They point out that there are large gaps between the law school law of contract, what happens in courts, and what practicing lawyers do. *Contracts: Law in Action* reflects our doubts about the traditional course.

Professors and students long assumed that contract rules were fundamental to the practice of law. While this may or may not be the case, contract doctrine clearly is only part of what lawyers need to understand to serve their clients. Lawyers are involved in the planning and structuring of business relationships. Producing a successful contract involves, first, an assessment of the goals and positions of the parties. What a lawyer proposes must be acceptable so that the parties can make a deal. Second, success involves planning a relationship so that both sides will be satisfied with the performance of the contract. Thus, the lawyer must understand business and social relationships, the techniques of planning and writing, and many bodies of law so that the arrangement will have desired legal consequences. Clearly, a good deal more is involved than a knowledge of contract doctrine.

Lawyers also perform an important advisory role in managing ongoing contractual relationships. For example, the parties may disagree about their obligations under a contract. One party may come close to performing but not quite make it. Is a miss as good as a mile or must a client accept substantial but not complete performance? Or the seller may fall far short of full performance, but the buyer may need the defective performance so badly that she takes it. Once the need has passed, can the buyer assert the original obligation or has she modified the contract by accepting the defective performance? Or the seller's failure to live up to the letter of the contract may have been caused by an unexpected event such as a fire, a strike, or a flood. To what extent, if at all, do such contingencies constitute excuses from contractual duties? Finally, once relationships are wrecked, lawyers may face questions of salvage. Can one turn to the legal system to force the other party to assume some or all of the losses caused by the breach of the contract? Again, contract doctrine speaks to all these questions, but lawyers and clients often must make difficult business judgments that are more important than legal arguments.

Lawyers do play a part in planning contracts, carrying them out, and clearing away the wreckage of those that fail, but business people are often able to handle these problems themselves without legal advice, and real estate brokers, land developers, investment bankers, sales people, engineers, and accountants all compete with lawyers to offer this kind of advice. Nevertheless, complicated contracts problems do arise in many contexts — not just in business — and their solution may require the services of someone who understands the law of contract. However, lawyers are more likely to face some questions than others. All lawyers must recognize the important contracts issues, but exposing every law student to all the classic contracts puzzles is an inefficient use of law school time and resources.

Contract ideas are indirectly relevant to most lawyers' practices. Contract ideas form part of the ideology[12] of capitalism, and this ideology affects many branches of the law and many lawyers' tasks. The ideology is familiar to us all. Many writers see contract as the solution to the conflict between individualism and community. In a society based on command, rulers order people to perform tasks. In a free society, individuals make choices about what they will and will not do. There are, however, ends that cannot be achieved without social interaction that is only possible by coordinating individual choices. By exchanging some measure of our freedom or property for what we value, our choices serve to allocate resources to desired uses. Contract thus enables people to unlock the value of their labor and the tangible and intangible things they control. I want your money more than I want my Chevrolet. You want a car more than you want your money. By making an exchange we are both better off. Neither of us can take advantage of the other in a perfect market (which involves a lot of assumptions, including perfect information). Others will offer you cars and others will offer me money for my car. These alternative potential contracts serve to limit our bargain so that we exchange the automobile at a price within the range of many similar choices by willing sellers and buyers. Self-interest, in this way, is channeled into a tool for cooperation in collective action.

Many theorists see contract law in capitalist societies as providing needed security of transactions. Any bargain where people exchange goods and money at the same time is almost self-policing. This is not true, however, when the exchange involves complex performances that take place over time. Suppose I am to paint your house and you are to pay me when I finish. Until I complete the job, you risk losing opportunities to hire someone else who might do the job more quickly and better. I risk your willingness and ability to pay me when I finish. Of course, many nonlegal sanctions give both of us incentives to perform. For example, we both may want to be known as people who carry out commitments. We may want to deal again, and I must worry that what I do under this contract will affect your willingness to enter new ones in the future. Members of my family may work for members of yours and

---

[12]We use the term *ideology* rather than *political philosophy* because ideology connotes a system accepted and assumed, rather than a thought-out view.

depend on their good will for their economic success. You might badmouth me to other potential customers if I do not perform. Nonetheless, those who write about law see a need for official sanctions to reinforce nonlegal ones that support the making and performance of contracts.

Contract law tells those who would plan and take risks how to make legally binding commitments. One who follows the accepted formula can know that she has made a contract. Contract law provides standardized interpretations of forms of language — it is a kind of authoritative dictionary. Contract law fills in gaps in agreements so that it is unnecessary to plan everything in each contract. Economists call legal rules that can be changed by contract "default rules." Most gap-filling terms are default rules, but there are some mandatory rules that cannot be changed. Contract law also offers remedies for breach, and these are mostly default rules. While these remedies may provide some salvage of wrecked bargains, perhaps their most important function is to deter breach in the first place. One who would default must consider the threat that contract law will cause trouble. It costs money to defend oneself, even if one is successful. Moreover, contract law symbolizes the importance of commitments. Society spends resources supporting performance of bargains, and this itself is a statement of what is right.

There is a vast literature debating the assumptions we have sketched. If one truly believes in freedom, why say that a person loses it by making a promise? To reject the freedom to change one's mind, one must look to policies other than choice. Suppose, for example, College makes a five-year contract with Coach to guide its football team. Two years later, State University offers Coach twice the salary to coach its team. Why should he not be free to change his mind and take the offer? Suppose Manufacturer Corporation orders parts from Supplier Corporation but then finds that the sales of the product in which it used these parts are very disappointing. Why should it not be free to cancel the order? If we look at customs in the football and manufacturing industries, we find that coaches and industrial buyers do feel free to cancel their commitments, whatever contract law says. Both universities and suppliers often accept cancellations without too much objection. And we should note that the law of contracts seldom, if ever, would tell judges to order either Coach or Manufacturer Corporation to perform or send them to jail for breach. Both could buy their way out by paying damages if either College or Supplier Corporation did not release them. Thus, the law itself suggests there may be reasons to allow people to break promises at not too great a price. Capitalist law does not seem to find absolute security of transactions an overriding value.

Some writers argue that free choice never really exists anyway, except in theorists' ivory towers. Suppose a robber with a gun sticks it in the back of a man walking past and says, 'Your money or your life!" The victim cannot say "None of the above"; he is being given a choice between unpleasant alternatives. In the example about buying a car, your real preference might have been a better car for a lower price, but people are always constrained by their circumstances. The line between a choice we deem free and one we call coerced usually is difficult to draw. It is a normative evaluation rather than a description. The distribution of advantages in society affects freedom of choice in important ways. Perhaps seeing all but a few choices as free and not the product of coercion is a useful working assumption, but it cannot be confused with an empirical description.

Furthermore, the theorists' model is that of a negotiated deal, in which the parties give and take and are aware of the terms or accept the risks of incomplete knowledge. While this may describe some transactions involving expert buyers and sellers, it is a poor representation of many bargains. It is hard for most consumers to appraise products before they buy them. Few consumers understand that the form contracts they sign drastically limit their ability to do anything about unsatisfactory purchases. Of course, other-than-legal sanctions operate in this area, and many consumers' complaints will prompt real efforts by sellers to produce a remedy. However, the power of these sanctions is not equally distributed across society. Mercedes-Benz buyers are likely to have more attention paid to their complaints than Chevrolet buyers, and buyers of new Chevrolets will do better than buyers of used ones.

When you examine contract law closely, you will discover that it reflects competing tendencies. Scholars have fashioned an abstract system of rules that appear relatively clear and suitable for use for almost any purpose by anyone. Courts have used some parts of this system at various times and places. Nonetheless, if we look carefully in area after area within the body of contract doctrine, we find counterrules and approaches that seek substantive justice at the expense of predictable abstraction. While skilled lawyers can predict the results of cases with some degree of accuracy, they must draw on information outside the rules of law to do this.

It is a mistake, then, to assume that your professors are going to hand you a beautifully worked out, consistent, and coherent system called "contract law." We doubt that such a system could exist without great changes in American society. Instead, we hope to show you the contradictions within contract law and how to use this imperfect language to accomplish your clients' goals. This is what the good contracts lawyer must take from a law school class, rather than details of doctrinal refinements.[13] First, you should understand the rhetoric of contract with all of its ambiguities and inconsistencies. Whatever the doctrinal area, you will find that certain basic but inconsistent themes appear again and again. Lawyers have to learn to speak contract rhetoric because it will be the accepted vocabulary in negotiation as well as before trial and appellate courts.

Second, you must understand that contract law is a tool that you can use to try to solve your client's problems, rather than a set of answers to all your questions. Instead of offering certainty and predictability, it often offers good arguments for all concerned. Lawyers are people who know how things work and how to get things done. They spend a good deal of their time coping with uncertainty and risk. They

[13] Details of doctrinal refinements might prove important sometime in your practice. However, there is not time to teach everything in three years of law school. Furthermore, contracts doctrine, as all law, has a short shelf life; details learned today may be out of date tomorrow. Fortunately, there is an impressive literature in contract law to help you exhaust the refinements of any nice point of doctrine. This course certainly should acquaint you with enough of the conventional wisdom in the field so that you will recognize a problem and understand what you read in treatises and journal articles.

may turn to drafting contract provisions that define what the law has left unclear. They may use uncertainty about the meaning of rules or about proving facts as bargaining tools and not as legal arguments before decision makers — for example, a client's uncertain chance of winning at trial is something you can sell to the other side for a price; that's called a settlement.

Lawyers often turn out to be policy makers. The actual jobs of lawyers often surprise law students. Rather than spending all their time in trial or appellate courtrooms, many lawyers act politically, both directly and indirectly. They are in the business of making deals with both public officials and representatives of private organizations. Contract often provides a vocabulary for negotiations in all kinds of settings. Furthermore, lawyers are elected to legislatures at all levels of government and even more often serve on legislative staffs. Much legislation of the past century has involved withdrawing areas from the domain of contract and creating specialized bodies of law. However, when we shift to these new areas, we do not leave contract assumptions behind. They continue to color thought, particularly in labor law, real estate transactions, business organizations, commercial law, family law, trusts and estates, and regulation of specific areas. For example, since the 1960s, consumer advocates have made effective use of phrases such as "inequality of bargaining power" and "unconscionability" that have long been a countertheme in contract. In the 1980s, ideas about consumers' needs for protection began to change. Once again there was talk of self-reliance, efficiency, and the power of the market to impose all the discipline needed. In the 1970s through the 1990s, the debate was about where we should draw the boundaries of free contract and social control, and much of it was carried on in contract rhetoric. In the wake of the worldwide financial crisis that began in 2007, reregulation became an important theme. Of course, we must be sensitive to the possibility that the terms of debate can get in the way of seeing what really is at stake, but that, too, is on our agenda.

2. The Law-in-Action Course in Historical Perspective

The classic course from about 1900 until World War II followed a life history of contract. Materials were considered in what seemed a simple, logical order: (1) the parties formed a contract by indicating agreement or by doing certain things that courts deemed to constitute concluding a bargain; (2) the contract was interpreted so that the obligations of each party could be established; (3) the performances of the parties were appraised, both as to whether one had fallen short of what had been promised and the importance of the degree of nonperformance involved; and (4) appropriate remedies for breach would be given. In short, a lawyer did not think about performance or remedies until she established that the parties had made a contract in the first place.

The course followed a blend of several scholarly positions. Samuel Williston, Harvard's great authority on the subject, developed in the first decades of the last century a system of contract based on relatively few principles.[14] Professor Williston saw contract law as largely formal and abstract. One system of concepts, with but few exceptions, should govern formation, performance, and remedies for insurance, employment, sales of goods, building construction, and all other kinds of contracts. The law was the same even if one party was rich and the other poor, or skilled lawyers advised one while the other was uneducated and lacked legal advice, or one party had behaved according to usual expectations but had failed to comply with all the rules. Contract law was objective. It depended on outward appearances rather than subjective intentions and hopes. One applied the rules and accepted the result. One did not ask whether the outcome was fair as judged by some standard apart from contract law.

Professor Lon Fuller, in a 1939 essay criticizing Williston, comments:[15]

> Turning to Professor Williston's legal method, if we ask at what point he gives up the attempt to shape the law by direct reference to social interests, I think the answer will have to be, at the very outset. What may be called the bases of contract liability, notions like consideration, the necessity for offer and acceptance, and the like, are nowhere in his work critically examined in the light of the social interests they serve. These things are accepted on faith. This neglect to refer to underlying social desiderata cannot properly be called "logic." It is simply an acceptance of what is conceived to be received legal tradition....
>
> It seems reasonably clear that our American law has been going through a positivistic phase during the last seventy-five years, and that it is this positivistic philosophy which has been the predominant influence in shaping Professor Williston's legal method. He believes that there exists in the cases "a law of contract," and that it must be sufficiently simple and consistent with itself to be capable of intelligible statement. Believing this, he fears the intrusion of vague ethical and philosophical considerations, even in the interpretation of existing law, because their corruptive and dissolving influence threatens to make impossible the very task which the positivist sets for himself, that of stating what "the law" is.

Arthur Corbin, who lived from 1874 to 1967, was Yale's great contracts scholar. He published an influential casebook in 1921, and revised it in 1933 and 1947. His eight-volume treatise on the subject appeared in 1950. While later writers often use the two men as symbols of opposing approaches to the subject, Williston and Corbin were good friends. Corbin wrote that he viewed Williston as "an older brother." He said that Williston was his chief teacher in contracts. "As a beginning instructor in

---

[14]Samuel Williston, a famous professor at Harvard Law School, lived from 1861 to 1963. He taught contracts to several generations of American law teachers, influential lawyers, and judges, and wrote the classic American treatises on contracts (published in 1920 and in 1936) and sales of goods. He edited leading casebooks in contracts, sales, and bankruptcy and drafted several uniform commercial statutes passed by many states. Justice Felix Frankfurter of the Supreme Court of the United States, a former student of Williston's, said, "While Williston enchanted by his charm and wit, he elevated and stimulated by these moral qualities which were ingrained in the man.... And upon each of us he left not only the happy memory of having seen the greatest artist in teaching, but the indelible impress of having had aroused in us the ambition to approach and reflect his moral qualities." Felix Frankfurter, *Samuel Williston: An Inadequate Tribute to a Beloved Teacher,* 76 Harv. L. Rev. 1321, 1323 (1963).

[15]Lon L. Fuller, *Williston on Contracts*, 18 N.C. L. Rev. 1 (1939).

that subject at Yale, sixty years ago, it was to his articles and his edition of Pollock that I had to go for instruction."[16]

However, Williston's and Corbin's approaches to the subject differed. Corbin edited an edition of *Anson on Contracts* in 1919. In the preface he said that students

> ... should be warned that the law does not consist of a series of unchangeable rules or principles.... Every system of justice and of right is of human development, and the necessary corollary is that no known system is eternal. In the long history of the law can be observed the birth and death of legal principles.... The law is merely a part of our changing civilization. The history of law is the history of man and society. Legal principles represent the prevailing *mores* of the time, and with the *mores* they must necessarily be born, survive for the appointed season, and perish.

Corbin called his great treatise "a Comprehensive Treatise on the Working Rules of Contract Law." He explained that "*all* rules of law and human society are no more than tentative working rules, based on human experience, necessarily changing in form and substance as human experience varies in the evolutionary process of life." Compared to Williston, Corbin makes a more direct use of the purposes and policies behind specific legal rules in order to analyze how they are likely to be applied to specific instances.

American legal realists saw Professor Williston's work as a symbol of what was wrong with traditional legal thought.[17] Arthur Corbin was an inspiration to the realists. Karl Llewellyn and Harold Havighurst developed a very different view of contract in the 1920s and 1930s. They argued that no one simple set of rules could govern transactions as distinct as dealings among family members, sales of goods in business, real estate transfers, and employment relations. Moreover, they pointed out that Professor Williston's system failed to take into account large bodies of both American and British contract law inconsistent with Williston's assumptions. They called for a contract law that sought substantive rather than formal justice. Everything was to depend upon the particulars of each case. Rules were to be based on general standards such as "good faith," "reasonableness," and "risk assumption" that called for judges to make choices. The realists dealt in a new way with what Williston had seen as the important problems in the field. However, they did not challenge his view about what the important problems were. Moreover, with a few exceptions, they accepted the traditional assumption that appellate cases were the only appropriate subject for analysis.

In the decade following World War II, two contracts casebooks appeared that changed the very definition of the field. The first, Professor Lon Fuller's *Basic Contract Law,* was published in 1947. The most obvious innovation was that the course began with contract remedies. Students considered most of the other topics in

[16]Arthur Corbin, *Samuel Williston*, 76 Harv. L. Rev. 1321 (1963).

[17]For a famous critical treatment of Williston's treatise on contracts, see Walter Wheeler Cook, *Williston on Contracts,* 33 Ill. L. Rev. 497 (1939). Williston replied to both Fuller and Cook, although he did not mention them by name. *See* Samuel Williston, *Fashions in Law With Illustrations From the Law of Contracts*, 21 Tex. L. Rev. 119 (1942).

light of Fuller's concern with remedial theory. By now, this part of Fuller's revolution is a recognized way to begin a course.

There are several justifications for beginning a contracts course with remedies. Fuller argued that decisions in the chain of reasoning about formation and performance of contracts were affected by their remedial consequences. One cannot understand judicial decisions about contract formation or performance without understanding what difference they make. Fuller insisted that courts did not decide abstract questions of whether there had been an offer and an acceptance so that a legally enforceable contract had been formed. He suggested that the real problem was whether the parties' conduct justified awarding a remedy to one of them or whether the court should just leave both parties where they were after their transaction had failed.

There are other good reasons to start with remedies. The subject is a good introduction to the conflicting goals of this body of law. There is a large gap between announced policy and the likely impact of the rules. Moreover, the material is difficult to learn on your own. If we put it at the end of the course, we will teach it hurriedly if at all. Indeed, if we begin at the beginning of a relationship — asking whether a contract has been formed — we are likely to spend most of our time on problems of least practical and theoretical importance.

Fuller also included excerpts from classics in political philosophy and jurisprudence relevant to issues of individualism and altruism, freedom and regulation, and the nature of the process of judging. He offered materials that compared American and British approaches to those found in continental legal systems. He also introduced a few selections dealing with the way American businesses used contract. For example, he included provisions of the Worth Street Rules. These are the practical law of the cotton grey goods industry, a form of private government that codified norms and resolved disputes by arbitration apart from the public legal system.

In spite of Fuller's then-radical innovations, his work was recognizable as a contracts casebook and enjoyed great success from the start. The classic Willistonian problems were all there plus many of the familiar cases. Also, during the preceding decade Fuller had written two great articles. They enabled law teachers to see what he was trying to get across by the arrangement of materials in his book. One of those articles — *The Reliance Interest in Contracts Damages*[18] — is by now part of the conventional wisdom of any contracts course — though it has recently come under attack.[19]

The second post–World War II book that broke out of the classic mold was by Friedrich Kessler and Malcolm Sharp. The influence of their innovative contract

[18]Lon L. Fuller & William R. Perdue, *The Reliance Interest in Contracts Damages* (pts. 1 & 2), 46 Yale L.J. 52, 373 (1936–1937). Professor Fuller became one of the great figures in American legal scholarship. He taught contracts, jurisprudence, and sociology of law at Harvard Law School.

[19]Richard Craswell, *Against Fuller and Perdue*, 67 U. Chi. L. Rev. 99 (2000); *see also* Symposium: *W(h)ither the Reliance Interest?*, 38 San Diego L. Rev. 1–230 (2001).

materials was more subtle and indirect. Relatively few teachers used this book because it looked too hard and too different. The book's message spread more widely when Grant Gilmore became Kessler's co-author for the second edition after Sharp declined to participate further.[20] Kessler and Sharp, and later Kessler and Gilmore, saw contracts as an expression of the political philosophy and ideological struggles of this nation. On one hand, there was an ideal of free contract and a minimal limited state. This was rationalized in the name of freedom and unleashing creative energies. On the other hand, there was always a countertheme calling for regulation in various forms seeking substantive justice. Kessler and Sharp saw American contract law as expressing theme and countertheme, overgeneralizations and overcorrections. In short, they saw it as contradictory. Contract doctrine reflected deeper, more basic, but inconsistent themes in the national consciousness. Furthermore, these themes could be traced back to classic views about law, government, markets, and justice.[21]

Although Kessler and Sharp devoted most of their attention to the traditional problems of law school contracts, the first cases in their book were an overview of the underlying policy themes running throughout the course. Then a last section looked at modern commercial problems expressing the tension between free contract and regulation. For example, they described the struggle between automobile manufacturers and dealers over the balance of power in their relationship. Kessler and

[20]A third edition was revised by Professors Kessler and Anthony Kronman of Yale Law School.

[21]Karl Klare, after praising the book's innovations, offers the following criticism of Kessler and Sharp:

> The book does not suggest a theory to explain *why* an advanced capitalist society must continually reproduce the conflict between private autonomy and state regulation. The resulting impression, perhaps contrary to Kessler and Sharp's intentions, is that the dichotomy of individualism and social control is a necessary and unresolvable conflict in all modes of social organization. Autonomy and community ultimately become reified "first principles" or "fundamental values" to be, as though by some inevitable process, "balanced." The possibility that personal autonomy and communal need are not, in principle, in conflict and that, indeed, autonomy and community might support and enhance each other in a different, noncapitalist mode of social organization is not explored. One of the central ideological missions of law in advanced capitalism is to legitimate state regulation of private economic activity while upholding private enterprise as the proper system of ownership and control. Kessler and Sharp, perhaps unwittingly, contribute to this ideological mission. No matter how vital Kessler and Sharp's historical, antiformalist emphasis, in the end key categories such as individual autonomy and social control become for them abstractions cut off from their historical roots. Kessler and Sharp thereby not only revitalize conceptualism, but, ironically, by suggesting that freedom of contract and state regulation of private behavior can be comfortably balanced within our institutional framework, they obscure the fundamental contradictions of our mode of social organization which they must have intended to illuminate.

Klare, *Contracts Jurisprudence and the First-Year Casebook*, 54 N.Y.U. L. Rev. 876, 886–87 (1979).

Consider the degree to which Klare's criticism of Kessler and Sharp applies to these contracts materials. Insofar as it does, in what "different, noncapitalist mode of social organization" would "autonomy and community support and enhance each other"? In terms of the schools of thought discussed above, Klare's criticism is an example of what approach to legal scholarship?

Sharp saw contract law as but one of many tools for coping with these larger social problems. In this section, their focus was on important problems, rather than the logic of doctrine. They saw law in the mid-20th century as involving statutes and administrative regulations rather than common law cases. Although it was not emphasized in their book, both Kessler and Sharp were interested in the relationship of business practice to contract law, and such issues were raised easily at many places in their course.

In the late 1960s, Ian Macneil published his contracts materials. He began with contract remedies, and he also saw contracts as expressing fundamental philosophical conflicts. His distinct contribution was a relational approach. Macneil argued that underlying contract law was the assumption of a single discrete transaction between strangers. However, Macneil pointed out that the reality of most modern business is the long-term continuing relationship.[22] Sometimes lawyers formally structure business relationships in a requirements contract (in which the buyer commits to buy all its requirements from a particular seller) or a blanket order system (in which any order is subject to agreed terms). Often, however, X Corporation just views Y Corporation as a valued long-term customer. While no formal contract may exist, officials of both organizations feel there are rights against and duties to one another, although they may be imprecisely defined. Obviously, such relationships have their own norms and sanctions. Do contract law and the legal system offer anything to the management of these relationships? Or is the law necessarily limited to performing a salvage function at the time of a divorce?

Macneil's large body of writing on the subject and his casebook seek to develop the implications of a relational contract law. Some of these issues relate to contract law's call for careful and specific definition of obligations. This call conflicts with custom in many business relationships. People leave things to be worked out as a long-term transaction progresses. They want flexibility to deal with changed circumstances. Some issues relate to whether the parties have overriding duties requiring them to attempt to keep the relationship alive and beneficial to both in the long run. He emphasizes that parties in relational contracts frequently temper wealth maximization goals with other objectives:

> Macneil believes the legal system needs to take radically different approaches to relational contracts than it traditionally has. In dealing with disputes, he favors greater reliance on procedures oriented towards mediation and less emphasis on adversary processes looking towards adjudication. In regulating contracts, he counsels greater reliance on proactive administrative agencies that can take account of the many third-party interests at stake and less reliance on courts able to apply regulatory rules only when a disadvantaged party initiates a court procedure.[23]

Professor Jay Feinman describes Macneil's approach to deciding contracts cases. First, a court must decide whether a transaction involves a discrete or a relational

---

[22]*See* Robert Gordon, *Macaulay, Macneil, and the Discovery of Solidarity and Power in Contract Law*, 1985 Wis. L. Rev. 565.

[23]William C. Whitford, *Ian Macneil's Contribution to Contracts Scholarship*, 1985 Wis. L. Rev. 545, 551.

contract. Discrete transactions call for enforcing the agreement struck by the parties when they entered the deal. However, in a relational contract,

> the court would consider how ... [norms of flexibility and contractual solidarity] are manifest in the parties' action, the community's actions and understanding, the broader society's values, and the legal system's principles. That inquiry suggests the choices to be made: not what would the parties have done, but what kind of relationship is most desirable in this setting. What the parties would have done is but one element that goes into that assessment. Finally, the effect of legal intervention in support of these norms must be considered.... [T]he resort to law may upset the operation of several of the most important values of the relation; imposing a norm of flexibility may cause parties to be more precise in specifying the terms of their contracts and therefore less flexible.[24]

So much for a brief history of American contracts scholarship as it has been translated into teaching materials. When you read works by legal scholars, opinions by judges, and statutes passed by legislatures you must recall that they were written by people who were influenced by the kinds of people they were and the times in which they lived. To make matters more complicated, legal writers of a later generation often construct their own picture of a scholar who wrote at an earlier time, the meaning of an earlier ease, or the purposes of a statute passed in response to a particular now-forgotten crisis. Often these later understandings are little better than caricature or parody. For examples, the names Williston and Corbin today have each come to stand for ideas and assumptions that seem oversimplified in light of what they actually wrote.[25]

3. *Law in Action—Building on This History*

These materials, *Contracts: Law in Action*, offer a blend of all these approaches plus their own features. Following Fuller, we begin with remedies. Following Kessler and Sharp, we look at issues of freedom and regulation, and we highlight the contradictions and inconsistencies found in contract doctrine. Following Macneil, we emphasize long-term continuing relationships. We adopt a law and society perspective. We

---

[24]Jay Feinman, *The Significance of Contract Theory*, 58 U. Cin. L. Rev. 1283 (1990).

[25]Williston had a formalist streak (note, for example, his use of the phrase "correct results" in the quote below), but he was also a progressive, as indicated in this excerpt from his treatise:

> When it is now said that courts "will neither make nor modify contracts, nor dispense with their performance," if it is meant that such power will not be exercised except in accordance with legal principles, the statement is sound; but if the meaning is that parties to contracts are always liable in accordance with their terms, it is far too narrow a limitation of the functions of the common law, and a court which insists upon such a statement obliges itself in various situations to use the confusing language of fiction in order to achieve correct results. Under the name of implied contracts (quasi-contracts) courts have wisely imposed obligations on parties to contracts which they never agreed to assume; and because of fraud, mistake, duress, impossibility, and illegality, have modified contracts or dispensed with their performance, simply because justice required it.

Samuel Williston, 3 The Law of Contracts 3281–82 (1920) (footnotes omitted).

examine the gap between the law on the books and the law in action. We emphasize both the virtues and vices of symbolic law that declares ideals but hides a reality that is less pleasing. We stress the functions of contract law as delivered to its ultimate consumers. We see contract doctrine as but one of many tools with which lawyers and others attempt to cope with individual and larger social problems.

We try to put contract law into its full context. We stress such things as the costs of using courts and bringing appeals. We see lawyers playing active roles reflecting both their clients' and their own interests. We see litigation and appeals as only part of a much larger social process. The chance that one might sue plays an important part in negotiation. Processes such as mediation and arbitration are supported by tacit threats of what might happen if one party declines to participate. Lawyers themselves often judge the merits of both sides' claims and attempt to work out problems in acceptable ways. We also try to keep students well aware that modern law involves legislation and administrative regulation. We see our course as helping beginning law students learn to be lawyers rather than just masters of the fine points of legal doctrine. At the same time, legal craft demands that lawyers recognize the conflicting goals of the field. Good lawyers understand the ways things work whether or not they work as they should.

Students have mixed reactions to the course. Some find to their surprise that our contracts course is not as dull as they feared the subject would be. It is, after all, about very real problems. Other students, however, sometimes find it hard to understand what we are driving at and may think we are "hiding the ball." Doctrinal structure can be comforting, as Elizabeth Mensch notes:[26]

> Viewed in retrospect, Williston's majestic doctrinal structure may have been silly, but...appeals to reasonableness and justice appear sloppy and formless by comparison. Williston's structure was, at least, a real structure, however misguided. Perhaps much Willistonian dogma survives simply because it provides a challenging intellectual game to learn and teach in law school — more fun than the close attention to commercial detail required by thorough-going realism.

This demand for structure reminds us of a statement printed on a bookbag carried by one of our former students. It said, "I have given up the search for truth. Now all I want is a good fantasy." We understand our students' desire for simple answers and structure. Students, particularly beginners, assume there are clear rules and seek to master them. Commercial publishers play to that demand and offer outlines and books aimed at students. They may assist some students in their struggle with the basic issues of a topic. However, professors hope to encourage students to go beyond the comforting half-truths of doctrinal knowledge.

In addition, the approach taken in these materials questions many things some students want to hold dear. Macaulay suggests:[27]

---

[26]Elizabeth Mensch, *Freedom of Contract as Ideology*, 33 Stan. L. Rev. 753, 769 (1981).

[27]Stewart Macaulay, *Elegant Models, Empirical Pictures, and the Complexities of Contract*, 11 Law & Soc'y Rev. 507, 521–22 (1977).

> The classical model of contract . . . appeals to many legal professionals [and law students] because it seems to offer those without political or economic power the possibility of overturning the structures of the powerful in the society. Judges are supposed to respond to reasoned argument, and if their decisions importantly affect behavior, then a single skilled advocate or author of a law review article, armed only with reason, could right wrongs by persuading judges. Not only would the powerless win, but the legal professional who championed their cause would need to do only honorable and enjoyable things in order to help them. The champion works through appeals to reason and intelligence, and talks of economic and social norms, the "findings of science," efficiency, or some other highly valued body of thought. Problems of politics, interest, power, and dominance need not be faced because they do not appear to be relevant in the world of doctrine, where it is assumed that right ideas will be crystallized into rules that are self-enforcing. . . . But many of those who examine the legal process in operation today find it difficult to retain their faith that the key to the good society resides in appellate judges, administrative agencies exercising discretion, pluralism, the morality of adjudication, or economic theory. Instead of justice, the empiricists describe a system of bargaining where "the haves come out ahead."[28]

One major theme of the course is that things are not as they seem. But debunking can be upsetting. It can lead to a resigned cynicism that undercuts any effort toward bettering the world. It is true that naive idealism may seriously mislead those whose goal is to effect change. However, legal rules do often matter. Lawyers for various causes have won remarkable victories, and reform efforts have affected life in the United States over the past half-century or more. We think good lawyers are skeptical idealists, aware of how the system works but unwilling to retreat into an easy cynicism.

The authors of these materials organized them to emphasize what they see as important problems. In many places this calls for something other than a doctrinal arrangement. Indeed, often a doctrinal arrangement would distort our thinking. For example, Professor David Trubek argues that the behavioral system related to processing particular types of disputes — including the relevant doctrine — "not only transforms the various individual conflicts: in so doing it 'transforms,' so to speak, a raw conflict of interest into a social process with limited possibilities. The disputes that do emerge are those in which basic economic relationships are not challenged: all other possibilities are filtered out."[29] We want to avoid these limitations on what we can see. Nonetheless, we make a major effort to explain the ins and outs of the doctrines and traditional approaches. We accept the point that as silly as some may be, they influence the vocabulary and expectations of lawyers. We have struggled to explain the logical structure of, say, the consideration doctrine without allowing it to set boundaries around our thought.

In sum, these materials are challenging, but they only reflect the difficulty in both the claims of contract law and its actual role in social life in this country. Those who find the materials disorganized are looking for something other than the organization that is there. We have signaled where we are going and why.

---

[28] *See* Galanter, *supra* note 8.

[29] David Trubek, *The Construction and Deconstruction of a Disputes-Focused Approach*, 15 Law & Soc'y Rev. 727, 743 (1980–81).

These materials, divided into two volumes, were designed for two courses: Contracts I, a required course that meets four hours a week for the first semester, and Contracts II, an elective that meets three hours a week in the second semester. Contracts I deals with a background we think useful to everyone. Contracts II is a course designed for those with particular interest in the field. Contracts I introduces ideas that Contracts II develops in much greater detail. However, the more basic notions found in Contracts I also find expression in many other law school courses and areas of practice.

We divide Contracts I into three parts. First, we consider contracts remedies, looking at many of the difficulties involved in announced goals and means to implement them. Then, in the second part, we turn to the long-term continuing relationship. Here we look at problems in applying the contracts remedies system to these common and important situations. We also look at alternatives to the formal legal system, considering both their merits and flaws when applied to various kinds of relationships. In the course of this second part, we also address the rudiments of the law of contract formation. Finally, in the third part, we look at attempts to regulate the bargaining process in various ways. On the one hand, this material raises all of the tensions between freedom and regulation and the conflicting principles found in American contract law. On the other hand, it stresses the limits of various kinds of legal action.

This structure emphasizes what we see as important problems. Examination of the materials reveals we do cover most of the important contract doctrines associated with traditional courses. Offer, acceptance, consideration, the parol evidence rule, and conditions all appear on stage as do the expectation, reliance, and restitution interests. Wise students will master the rules as they would have if they attended law school in 1935. However, this knowledge is necessary but not sufficient. We show these doctrines playing their parts in dealing with real problems. Abstract rules of contract could govern any kind of relationship, but each of these rules is likely to come into play only in particular situations. We see doctrine as a means and not as an end. We seek not only to understand the internal logic and political or philosophical positions the statement of these rules reflect but also their likely impact on different kinds of people.

Contracts II is a more technical course building on Contracts I. Here we try to select some of the issues of offer, acceptance, mistake, and interpretation that are very much alive in modern business transactions. We give major emphasis, however, to issues of performance and excuse both at common law and under the Uniform Commercial Code, issues that seem to matter most to modern business. Moreover, we do what we can to put those cases into context so that students can understand the real disputes that brought the parties into the legal process rather than turning to some other means of resolution. Just as in Contracts I, there is great emphasis on cost barriers to use of the legal process and on the roles played by lawyers.

These materials accept that messy reality provokes messy answers to difficult questions. The discussion in class flowing from the materials may push you to the boundaries of your Republican, Democratic, independent, reactionary, or radical beliefs. You should expect this, for most of the fights about the good, the true, and the beautiful lurk just beneath the surface of the law of contracts. Contract law mirrors the conflicting visions that many of us accept as just common sense. Whether you find satisfying answers will depend in large part on your vision of the society in which you live and your definition of social justice. In good liberal fashion, we have not written the materials to indoctrinate students with any political point of view. During the late 1960s and early 1970s, those teaching from the earliest versions questioned students from somewhat to the right of the accepted wisdom of the vocal members of the class. In the 1990s, many students had moved toward the right, and our challenges seemed to come from the left. It may be that another shift in student perspective has occurred too recently to accurately identify it. Whatever your perspective, we strive to test ideas and assumptions and see this as a valuable experience for those learning to be lawyers.

After many years of exploring the area, those who have contributed to these materials still find the subject fascinating and find something new each trip through them. The process of learning anything worth learning probably must involve a degree of frustration. Everything is related to everything else, and it seems impossible to understand anything without understanding everything. Moreover, many Americans, including entering law students, expect law to be clear and consistent with simple ideas of right and wrong. Whatever the merit of that idea, students learn that the law embraces complexity and reflects a view that concepts of right and wrong are anything but simple. We hope that you will share our interest in contracts as a way of learning about life in this country and considering possibilities for stability and change.

Part III
Core Works on Contract

Non-contractual Relations in Business: A Preliminary Study

Stewart Macaulay

Abstract Preliminary findings indicate that businessmen often fail to plan exchange relationships completely, and seldom use legal sanctions to adjust these relationships or to settle disputes. Planning and legal sanctions are often unnecessary and may have undesirable consequences. Transactions are planned and legal sanctions are used when the gains are thought to outweigh the costs. The power to decide whether the gains from using contract outweigh the costs will be held by individuals having different occupational roles. The occupational role influences the decision that is made.

What good is contract law? who uses it? when and how? Complete answers would require an investigation of almost every type of transaction between individuals and oganizations. In this report, research has been confined to exchanges between businesses, and primarily to manufacturers.[1] Futhermore, this report will be limited

---

This article was original published in American Sociological Review 28 (1963), 55–69. Reprinted with permission.
Revision of a paper read at the annual meeting of the Americal Sociological Association, August, 1962. An earlier version of the paper was read at the annual meeting of the Midwest Sociological Society, April, 1962. The research has been supported by a Law and Policy Research Grant to the University of Wisconsin Law School from the Ford Foundation. I am grateful for the help generously given by a number of sociologists including Robert K. Merton, Harry V. Ball, Jerome Carlin and William Evan.

---

[1]The reasons for this limitation are that (a) these transactions are important from an economic standpoint, (b) they are frequently said in theoretical discussions to represent a high degree of rational planning, and (c) manufacturing personnel are sufficiently public-relations-minded to cooperate with a law professor who wants to ask a seemingly endless number of questions. Future research will deal with the building construction industry and other areas.

S. Macaulay (✉)
University of Wisconsin Law School, Madison, WI, USA
e-mail: smacaula@wisc.edu

D. Campbell (ed.), *Stewart Macaulay: Selected Works*, Law and Philosophy Library 133, https://doi.org/10.1007/978-3-030-33930-2_14

to a presentation of the findings concerning when contract is and is not used and to a tentative explanation of these findings.[2]

This research is only the first phase in a scientific study.[3] The primary research technique involved interviewing 68 businessmen and lawyers representing 43 companies and six law firms. The interviews ranged from a 30-minute brush-off where not all questions could be asked of a busy and uninterested sales manager to a six-hour discussion with the general counsel of a large corporation. Detailed notes of the interviews were taken and a complete report of each interview was dictated, usually no later than the evening after the interview. All but two of the companies had plants in Wisconsin; 17 were manufacturers of machinery but none made such items as food products, scientific instruments, textiles or petroleum products. Thus the likelihood of error because of sampling bias may be considerable.[4] However, to a great extent, existing knowledge has been inadequate to permit more rigorous procedures—as yet one cannot formulate many precise questions to be asked a systematically selected sample of "right people." Much time has been spent fishing for relevant questions or answers, or both.

Reciprocity, exchange or contract has long been of interest to sociologists, economists and lawyers. Yet each discipline has an incomplete view of this kind of conduct. This study represents the effort of a law teacher to draw on sociological ideas and empirical investigation. It stresses, among other things, the functions and dysfunctions of using contract to solve exchange problems and the influence of occupational roles on how one assesses whether the benefits of using contract outweigh the costs.

---

[2]For the present purposes, the what-difference-does-it-make issue is important primarily as it makes a case for an empirical study by a law teacher of the use and nonuse of contract by businessmen. First, law teachers have a professional concern with what the law ought to be. This involves evaluation of the consequences of the existing situation and of the possible alternatives. Thus, it is most relevant to examine business practices concerning contract if one is interested in what commercial law ought to be. Second, law teachers are supposed to teach law students something relevant to becoming lawyers. These business practices are facts that are relevant to the skills which law students will need when, as lawyers, they are called upon to create exchange relationships and to solve problems arising out of these relationships.

[3]The following things have been done. The literature in law, business, economics, psychology, and sociology has been surveyed. The formal systems related to exchange transactions have been examined. Standard form contracts and the standard terms and conditions that are found on such business documents as catalogues, quotation forms, purchase orders, and acknowledgment-of-order forms from 850 firms that are based in or do business in Wisconsin have been collected. The citations of all reported court cases during a period of 15 years involving the largest 500 manufacturing corporations in the United States have been obtained and are being analyzed to determine why the use of contract legal sanctions was thought necessary and whether or not any patterns of "problem situations" can be delineated. In addition, the informal systems related to exchange transactions have been examined. Letters of inquiry concerning practices in certain situations have been answered by approximately 125 businessmen. Interviews, as described in the text, have been conducted. Moreover, six of my students have interviewed 21 other businessmen, bankers and lawyers. Their findings are consistent with those reported in the text.

[4]However, the cases have not been selected because they *did* use contract. There is as much interest in, and effort to obtain, cases of nonuse as of use of contract. Thus, one variety of bias has been minimized.

To discuss when contract is and is not used, the term "contract" must be specified. This term will be used here to refer to devices for conducting exchanges. Contract is not treated as synonymous with an exchange itself, which may or may not be characterized as contractual. Nor is contract used to refer to a writing recording an agreement. Contract, as I use the term here, involves two distinct elements: (a) Rational planning of the transaction with careful provision for as many future contingencies as can be foreseen, and (b) the existence or use of actual or potential legal sanctions to induce performance of the exchange or to compensate for non-performance.

These devices for conducting exchanges may be used or may exist in greater or lesser degree, so that transactions can be described relatively as involving a more contractual or a less contractual manner (a) of creating an exchange relationship or (b) of solving problems arising during the course of such a relationship. For example, General Motors might agree to buy all of the Buick Division's requirements of aluminum for ten years from Reynolds Aluminum. Here the two large corporations probably would plan their relationship carefully. The plan probably would include a complex pricing formula designed to meet market fluctuations, an agreement on what would happen if either party suffered a strike or a fire, a definition of Reynolds' responsibility for quality control and for losses caused by defective quality, and many other provisions. As the term contract is used here, this is a more contractual method of creating an exchange relationship than is a home-owner's casual agreement with a real estate broker giving the broker the exclusive right to sell the owner's house which fails to include provisions for the consequences of many easily foreseeable (and perhaps even highly probable) contingencies. In both instances, legally enforceable contracts may or may not have been created, but it must be recognized that the existence of a legal sanction has no necessary relationship to the degree of rational planning by the parties, beyond certain minimal legal requirements of certainty of obligation. General Motors and Reynolds might never sue or even refer to the written record of their agreement to answer questions which come up during their ten-year relationship, while the real estate broker might sue, or at least threaten to sue, the owner of the house. The broker's method of *dispute settlement* then would be more contractual than that of General Motors and Reynolds, thus reversing the relationship that existed in regard to the "contractualness" of the *creation* of the exchange relationships.

Tentative Findings

It is difficult to generalize about the use and nonuse of contract by manufacturing industry. However, a number of observations can be made with reasonable accuracy at this time. The use and nonuse of contract in creating exchange relations and in dispute settling will be taken up in turn.

The Creation of Exchange Relationships In creating exchange relationships, businessmen may plan to a greater or lesser degree in relation to several types of issues. Before reporting the findings as to practices in creating such relationships, it is necessary to describe what one can plan about in a bargain and the degrees of planning which are possible.

People negotiating a contract can make plans concerning several types of issues: (1) They can plan what each is to do or refrain from doing; e.g., S might agree to deliver ten 1963 Studebaker four-door sedan automobiles to B on a certain date in exchange for a specified amount of money. (2) They can plan what effect certain contingencies are to have on their duties; e.g., what is to happen to S and B's obligations if S cannot deliver the cars because of a strike at the Studebaker factory? (3) They can plan what is to happen if either of them fails to perform; e.g., what is to happen if S delivers nine of the cars two weeks late? (4) They can plan their agreement so that it is a legally enforceable contract—that is, so that a legal sanction would be available to provide compensation for injury suffered by B as a result of S's failure to deliver the cars on time.

As to each of these issues, there may be a different degree of planning by the parties. (1) They may carefully and explicitly plan; e.g., S may agree to deliver ten 1963 Studebaker four-door sedans which have six cylinder engines, automatic transmissions and other specified items of optional equipment and which will perform to a specified standard for a certain time. (2) They may have a mutual but tacit understanding about an issue; e.g., although the subject was never mentioned in their negotiations, both S and B may assume that B may cancel his order for the cars before they are delivered if B's taxi-cab business is so curtailed that B can no longer use ten additional cabs. (3) They may have two inconsistent unexpressed assumptions about an issue; e.g., S may assume that if any of the cabs fails to perform to the specified standard for a certain time, all S must do is repair or replace it. B may assume S must also compensate B for the profits B would have made if the cab had been in operation. (4) They may never have thought of the issue; e.g., neither S nor B planned their agreement so that it would be a legally enforceable contract. Of course, the first and fourth degrees of planning listed are the extreme cases and the second and third are intermediate points. Clearly other intermediate points are possible; e.g., S and B neglect to specify whether the cabs should have automatic or conventional transmissions. Their planning is not as careful and explicit as that in the example previously given.

The following diagram represents the dimensions of creating an exchange relationship just discussed with "X's" representing the example of S and B's contract for ten taxi-cabs.

	Definition of Performances	Effect of Contingencies	Effect of Defective Performances	Legal Sanctions
Explicit and careful	X			
Tacit agreement		X		
Unilateral assumptions			X	
Unawareness of the issue				X

Most larger companies, and many smaller ones, attempt to plan carefully and completely. Important transactions not in the ordinary course of business are handled by a detailed contract. For example, recently the Empire State Building was sold for $65 million. More than 100 attorneys, representing 34 parties, produced a 400 page contract. Another example is found in the agreement of a major rubber company in the United States to give technical assistance to a Japanese firm. Several million dollars were involved and the contract consisted of 88 provisions on 17 pages. The 12 house counsel—lawyers who work for one corporation rather than many clients—interviewed said that all but the smallest businesses carefully planned most transactions of any significance. Corporations have procedures so that particular types of exchanges will be reviewed by their legal and financial departments.

More routine transactions commonly are handled by what can be called standardized planning. A firm will have a set of terms and conditions for purchases, sales, or both printed on the business documents used in these exchanges. Thus the things to be sold and the price may be planned particularly for each transaction, but standard provisions will further elaborate the performances and cover the other subjects of planning. Typically, these terms and conditions are lengthy and printed in small type on the back of the forms. For example, 24 paragraphs in eight point type are printed on the back of the purchase order form used by the Allis Chalmers Manufacturing Company. The provisions: (1) describe, in part, the performance required, e.g., "DO NOT WELD CASTINGS WITHOUT OUR CONSENT"; (2) plan for the effect of contingencies, e.g., ". . . in the event the Seller suffers delay in performance due to an act of God, war, act of the Government, priorities or allocations, act of the Buyer, fire, flood, strike, sabotage, or other causes beyond Seller's control, the time of completion shall be extended a period of time equal to the period of such delay if the Seller gives the Buyer notice in writing of the cause of any such delay within a reasonable time after the beginning thereof"; (3) plan for the effect of defective performances, e.g., "The buyer, without waiving any other legal rights, reserves the right to cancel without charge or to postpone deliveries of any of the articles covered by this order which are not shipped in time reasonably to meet said agreed dates"; (4) plan for a legal sanction, e.g., the clause "without waiving any other legal rights," in the example just given.

In larger firms such "boiler plate" provisions are drafted by the house counsel or the firm's outside lawyer. In smaller firms such provisions may be drafted by the industry trade association, may be copied from a competitor, or may be found on forms purchased from a printer. In any event, salesmen and purchasing agents, the operating personnel, typically are unaware of what is said in the fine print on the back of the forms they use. Yet often the normal business patterns will give effect to this standardized planning. For example, purchasing agents may have to use a purchase order form so that all transactions receive a number under the firm's accounting system. Thus, the required accounting record will carry the necessary planning of the exchange relationship printed on its reverse side. If the seller does not object to this planning and accepts the order, the buyer's "fine print" will control. If the seller does object, differences can be settled by negotiation.

This type of standardized planning is very common. Requests for copies of the business documents used in buying and selling were sent to approximately 6,000 manufacturing firms which do business in Wisconsin. Approximately 1,200 replies were received and 850 companies used some type of standardized planning. With only a few exceptions, the firms that did not reply and the 350 that indicated they did not use standardized planning were very small manufacturers such as local bakeries, soft drink bottlers and sausage makers.

While businessmen can and often do carefully and completely plan, it is clear that not all exchanges are neatly rationalized. Although most businessmen think that a clear description of both the seller's and buyer's performances is obvious common sense, they do not always live up to this ideal. The house counsel and the purchasing agent of a medium size manufacturer of automobile parts reported that several times their engineers had committed the company to buy expensive machines without adequate specifications. The engineers had drawn careful specifications as to the type of machine and how it was to be made but had neglected to require that the machine produce specified results. An attorney and an auditor both stated that most contract disputes arise because of ambiguity in the specifications.

Businessmen often prefer to rely on "a man's word" in a brief letter, a handshake, or "common honesty and decency"—even when the transaction involves exposure to serious risks. Seven lawyers from law firms with business practices were interviewed. Five thought that businessmen often entered contracts with only a minimal degree of advance planning. They complained that businessmen desire to "keep it simple and avoid red tape" even where large amounts of money and significant risks are involved. One stated that he was "sick of being told, 'We can trust old Max,' when the problem is not one of honesty but one of reaching an agreement that both sides understand." Another said that businessmen when bargaining often talk only in pleasant generalities, think they have a contract, but fail to reach agreement on any of the hard, unpleasant questions until forced to do so by a lawyer. Two outside lawyers had different views. One thought that large firms usually planned important exchanges, although he conceded that occasionally matters might be left in a fairly vague state. The other dissenter represents a large utility that commonly buys heavy equipment and buildings. The supplier's employees come on the utility's property to install the equipment or construct the buildings, and they may be injured while there. The utility has been sued by such employees so often that it carefully plans purchases with the assistance of a lawyer so that suppliers take this burden.

Moreover, standardized planning can break down. In the example of such planning previously given, it was assumed that the purchasing agent would use his company's form with its 24 paragraphs printed on the back and that the seller would accept this or object to any provisions he did not like. However, the seller may fail to read the buyer's 24 paragraphs of fine print and may accept the buyer's order on the seller's own acknowledgment-of-order form. Typically this form will have ten to 50 paragraphs favoring the seller, and these provisions are likely to be different from or inconsistent with the buyer's provisions. The seller's acknowledgment form may be received by the buyer and checked by a clerk. She will read the *face* of the acknowledgment but not the fine print on the back of it because she has neither the time nor ability to analyze the small print on the 100 to 500 forms she must review each day. The face of the acknowledgment—where the goods and the price are specified—is likely to correspond with the face of the purchase order. If it does, the two forms are filed away. At this point, both buyer and seller are likely to assume they have planned an exchange and made a contract. Yet they have done neither, as they are in disagreement about all that appears on the back of their forms. This practice is common enough to have a name. Law teachers call it "the battle of the forms."

Ten of the 12 purchasing agents interviewed said that frequently the provisions on the back of their purchase order and those on the back of a supplier's acknowledgment would differ or be inconsistent. Yet they would assume that the purchase was complete without further action unless one of the supplier's provisions was really objectionable. Moreover, only occasionally would they bother to read the fine print on the back of suppliers' forms. On the other hand, one purchasing agent insists that agreement be reached on the fine print provisions, but he represents the utility whose lawyer reported that it exercises great care in planning. The other purchasing agent who said that his company did not face a battle of the forms problem, works for a division of one of the largest manufacturing corporations in the United States. Yet the company may have such a problem without recognizing it. The purchasing agent regularly sends a supplier both a purchase order and another form which the supplier is asked to sign and return. The second form states that the supplier accepts the buyer's terms and conditions. The company has sufficient bargaining power to force suppliers to sign and return the form, and the purchasing agent must show one of his firm's auditors such a signed form for every purchase order issued. Yet suppliers frequently return this buyer's form *plus* their own acknowledgment form which has conflicting provisions. The purchasing agent throws away the supplier's form and files his own. Of course, in such a case the supplier has not acquiesced to the buyer's provisions. There is no agreement and no contract.

Sixteen sales managers were asked about the battle of the forms. Nine said that frequently no agreement was reached on which set of fine print was to govern, while seven said that there was no problem. Four of the seven worked for companies whose major customers are the large automobile companies or the large manufacturers of paper products. These customers demand that their terms and conditions govern any purchase, are careful generally to see that suppliers acquiesce, and have the bargaining power to have their way. The other three of the seven sales managers who have no battle of the forms problem, work for manufacturers of special industrial machines. Their firms are careful to reach complete agreement with their customers. Two of these men stressed that they could take no chances because such a large part of their firm's capital is tied up in making any one machine. The other sales manager had been influenced by a law suit against one of his competitors for over a half million dollars. The suit was brought by a customer when the competitor had been unable to deliver a machine and put it in operation on time. The sales manager interviewed said his firm could not guarantee that its machines would work perfectly by a specified time because they are designed to fit the customer's requirements, which may present difficult engineering problems. As a result, contracts are carefully negotiated.

A large manufacturer of packaging materials audited its records to determine how often it had failed to agree on terms and conditions with its customers or had failed to create legally binding contracts. Such failures cause a risk of loss to this firm since the packaging is printed with the customer's design and cannot be salvaged once this is done. The orders for five days in four different years were reviewed. The percentages of orders where no agreement on terms and conditions was reached or no contract was formed were as follows:

1953	75.0%
1954	69.4%
1955	71.5%
1956	59.5%

It is likely that businessmen pay more attention to describing the performances in an exchange than to planning for contingencies or defective performances or to obtaining legal enforceability of their contracts. Even when a purchase order and acknowledgment have conflicting provisions printed on the back, almost always the buyer and seller will be in agreement on what is to be sold and how much is to be paid for it. The lawyers who said businessmen often commit their firms to significant exchanges too casually, stated that the performances would be defined in the brief letter or telephone call; the lawyers objected that nothing else would be covered. Moreover, it is likely that businessmen are least concerned about planning their transactions so that they are legally enforceable contracts.[5] For example, in Wisconsin requirements contracts—contracts to supply a firm's requirements of an item rather than a definite quantity—probably are not legally enforceable. Seven people interviewed reported that their firms regularly used requirements contracts in dealings in Wisconsin. None thought that the lack of legal sanction made any difference. Three of these people were house counsel who knew the Wisconsin law before being interviewed. Another example of a lack of desire for legal sanctions is found in the relationship between automobile manufacturers and their suppliers of parts. The manufacturers draft a carefully planned agreement, but one which is so designed that the supplier will have only minimal, if any, legal rights against the manufacturers. The standard contract used by manufacturers of paper to sell to magazine publishers has a pricing clause which is probably sufficiently vague to make the contract legally unenforceable. The house counsel of one of the largest paper producers said that everyone in the industry is aware of this because of a leading New York case concerning the contract, but that no one cares. Finally, it seems likely that planning for contingencies and defective performances are in-between cases—more likely to

[5]Compare the findings of an empirical study of Connecticut business practices in Comment, "The Statute of Frauds and the Business Community: A Re-Appraisal in Light of Prevailing Practices," *Yale Law Journal,* 66 (1957), pp. 1038–1071.

occur than planning for a legal sanction, but less likely than a description of performance.

Thus one can conclude that (1) many business exchanges reflect a high degree of planning about the four categories—description, contingencies, defective performances and legal sanction—but (2) many, if not most, exchanges reflect no planning, or only a minimal amount of it, especially concerning legal sanctions and the effect of defective performances. As a result, the opportunity for good faith disputes during the life of the exchange relationship often is present.

The Adjustment of Exchange Relationships and the Settling of Disputes *While a* significant amount of creating business exchanges is done on a fairly noncontractual basis, the creation of exchanges usually is far more contractual than the adjustment of such relationships and the settlement of disputes. Exchanges are adjusted when the obligations of one or both parties are modified by agreement during the life of the relationship. For example, the buyer may be allowed to cancel all or part of the goods he has ordered because he no longer needs them; the seller may be paid more than the contract price by the buyer because of unusual changed circumstances. Dispute settlement involves determining whether or not a party has performed as agreed and, if he has not, doing something about it. For example, a court may have to interpret the meaning of a contract, determine what the alleged defaulting party has done and determine what, if any, remedy the aggrieved party is entitled to. Or one party may assert that the other is in default, refuse to proceed with performing the contract and refuse to deal ever again with the alleged defaulter. If the alleged defaulter, who in fact may not be in default, takes no action, the dispute is then "settled."

Business exchanges in non-speculative areas are usually adjusted without dispute. Under the law of contracts, if B orders 1,000 widgets from S at $1.00 each, B must take all 1,000 widgets or be in breach of contract and liable to pay S his expenses up to the time of the breach plus his lost anticipated profit. Yet all ten of the purchasing agents asked about cancellation of orders once placed indicated that they expected to be able to cancel orders freely subject to only an obligation to pay for the seller's major expenses such as scrapped steel.[6] All 17 sales personnel asked reported that they often had to accept cancellation. One said, "You can't ask a man to eat paper [the firm's product] when he has no use for it." A lawyer with many large industrial clients said,

> Often businessmen do not feel they have "a contract"—rather they have "an order." They speak of "cancelling the order" rather than "breaching our contract." When I began practice I referred to order cancellations as breaches of contract, but my clients objected since they do not think of cancellation as wrong. Most clients, in heavy industry at least, believe that there is a right to cancel as part of the buyer-seller relationship. There is a widespread attitude that one can back out of any deal within some very vague limits. Lawyers are often surprised by this attitude.

---

[6]See the case studies on cancellation of contracts in *Harvard Business Review*, 2 (1923–24), pages 238–40, 367–70, 496–502.

Disputes are frequently settled without reference to the contract or potential or actual legal sanctions. There is a hesitancy to speak of legal rights or to threaten to sue in these negotiations. Even where the parties have a detailed and carefully planned agreement which indicates what is to happen if, say, the seller fails to deliver on time, often they will never refer to the agreement but will negotiate a solution when the problem arises apparently as if there had never been any original contract. One purchasing agent expressed a common business attitude when he said,

> if something comes up, you get the other man on the telephone and deal with the problem. You don't read legalistic contract clauses at each other if you ever want to do business again. One doesn't run to lawyers if he wants to stay in business because one must behave decently.

Or as one businessman put it, "You can settle any dispute if you keep the lawyers and accountants out of it. They just do not understand the give-and-take needed in business." All of the house counsel interviewed indicated that they are called into the dispute settlement process only after the businessmen have failed to settle matters in their own way. Two indicated that after being called in house counsel at first will only advise the purchasing agent, sales manager or other official involved; not even the house counsel's letterhead is used on communications with the other side until all hope for a peaceful resolution is gone.

Law suits for breach of contract appear to be rare. Only five of the 12 purchasing agents had ever been involved in even a negotiation concerning a contract dispute where both sides were represented by lawyers; only two of ten sales managers had ever gone this far. None had been involved in a case that went through trial. A law firm with more than 40 lawyers and a large commercial practice handles in a year only about six trials concerned with contract problems. Less than 10 per cent of the time of this office is devoted to any type of work related to contracts disputes. Corporations big enough to do business in more than one state tend to sue and be sued in the federal courts. Yet only 2,779 out of 58,293 civil actions filed in the United States District Courts in fiscal year 1961 involved private contracts.[7] During the same period only 3,447 of the 61,138 civil cases filed in the principal trial courts of New York State involved private contracts.[8] The same picture emerges from a review of appellate cases.[9] Mentschikoff has suggested that commercial cases are not brought to the courts either in periods of business prosperity (because buyers unjustifiably reject goods only when prices drop and they can get similar goods elsewhere at less than the contract price) or in periods of deep depression (because

[7]*Annual Report of the Director of the Administrative Office of the United States Courts*, 1961, p. 238.

[8]State of New York, The Judicial Conference, Sixth Annual Report, 1961, pp. 209–11.

[9]My colleague Lawrence M. Friedman has studied the work of the Supreme Court of Wisconsin in contracts cases. He has found that contracts cases reaching that court tend to involve economically-marginal-business and family-economic disputes rather than important commercial transactions. This has been the situation since about the turn of the century. Only during the Civil War period did the court deal with significant numbers of important contracts cases, but this happened against the background of a much simpler and different economic system.

people are unable to come to court or have insufficient assets to satisfy any judgment that might be obtained). Apparently, she adds, it is necessary to have "a kind of middle-sized depression" to bring large numbers of commercial cases to the courts. However, there is little evidence that in even "a kind of middle-sized depression" today's businessmen would use the courts to settle disputes.[10]

At times relatively contractual methods are used to make adjustments in ongoing transactions and to settle disputes. Demands of one side which are deemed unreasonable by the other occasionally are blocked by reference to the terms of the agreement between the parties. The legal position of the parties can influence negotiations even though legal rights or litigation are never mentioned in their discussions; it makes a difference if one is demanding what both concede to be a right or begging for a favor. Now and then a firm may threaten to turn matters over to its attorneys, threaten to sue, commence a suit or even litigate and carry an appeal to the highest court which will hear the matter. Thus, legal sanctions, while not an everyday affair, are not unknown in business.

One can conclude that while detailed planning and legal sanctions play a significant role in some exchanges between businesses, in many business exchanges their role is small.

Tentative Explanations

Two questions need to be answered: (A) How can business successfully operate exchange relationships with relatively so little attention to detailed planning or to legal sanctions, and (B) Why does business ever use contract in light of its success without it?

Why Are Relatively Non-contractual Practices So Common? In most situations contract is not needed.[11] Often its functions are served by other devices. Most problems are avoided without resort to detailed planning or legal sanctions because usually there is little room for honest misunderstandings or good faith differences of opinion about the nature and quality of a seller's performance. Although the parties fail to cover all foreseeable contingencies, they will exercise care to see that both understand the primary obligation on each side. Either products are standardized with an accepted description or specifications are written calling for production to certain tolerances or results. Those who write and read specifications are experienced

---

[10]New York Law Revision Commission, *Hearings on the Uniform Commercial Code*, 2 (1954), p. 1391.

[11]The explanation that follows emphasizes a *considered* choice not to plan in detail for all contingencies. However, at times it is clear that businessmen fail to plan because of a lack of sophistication; they simply do not appreciate the risk they are running or they merely follow patterns established in their firm years ago without reexamining these practices in light of current conditions.

professionals who will know the customs of their industry and those of the industries with which they deal. Consequently, these customs can fill gaps in the express agreements of the parties. Finally, most products can be tested to see if they are what was ordered; typically in manufacturing industry we are not dealing with questions of taste or judgment where people can differ in good faith.

When defaults occur they are not likely to be disastrous because of techniques of risk avoidance or risk spreading. One can deal with firms of good reputation or he may be able to get some form of security to guarantee performance. One can insure against many breaches of contract where the risks justify the costs. Sellers set up reserves for bad debts on their books and can sell some of their accounts receivable. Buyers can place orders with two or more suppliers of the same item so that a default by one will not stop the buyer's assembly lines.

Moreover, contract and contract law are often thought unnecessary because there are many effective non-legal sanctions. Two norms are widely accepted. (1) Commitments are to be honored in almost all situations; one does not welsh on a deal. (2) One ought to produce a good product and stand behind it. Then, too, business units are organized to perform commitments, and internal sanctions will induce performance. For example, sales personnel must face angry customers when there has been a late or defective performance. The salesmen do not enjoy this and will put pressure on the production personnel responsible for the default. If the production personnel default too often, they will be fired. At all levels of the two business units personal relationships across the boundaries of the two organizations exert pressures for conformity to expectations. Salesmen often know purchasing agents well. The same two individuals occupying these roles may have dealt with each other from five to 25 years. Each has something to give the other. Salesmen have gossip about competitors, shortages and price increases to give purchasing agents who treat them well. Salesmen take purchasing agents to dinner, and they give purchasing agents Christmas gifts hoping to improve the chances of making sale. The buyer's engineering staff may work with the seller's engineering staff to solve problems jointly. The seller's engineers may render great assistance, and the buyer's engineers may desire to return the favor by drafting specifications which only the seller can meet. The top executives of the two firms may know each other. They may sit together on government or trade committees. They may know each other socially and even belong to the same country club. The interrelationships may be more formal. Sellers may hold stock in corporations which are important customers; buyers may hold stock in important suppliers. Both buyer and seller may share common directors on their boards. They may share a common financial institution which has financed both units.

The final type of non-legal sanction is the most obvious. Both business units involved in the exchange desire to continue successfully in business and will avoid conduct which might interfere with attaining this goal. One is concerned with both the reaction of the other party in the particular exchange and with his own general business reputation. Obviously, the buyer gains sanctions insofar as the seller wants the particular exchange to be completed. Buyers can withhold part or all of their payments until sellers have performed to their satisfaction. If a seller has a great deal of money tied up in his performance which he must recover quickly, he will go a long way to please the buyer in order to be paid. Moreover, buyers who are dissatisfied may cancel and cause sellers to lose the cost of what they have done up to cancellation. Furthermore, sellers hope for repeat orders, and one gets few of these from unhappy customers. Some industrial buyers go so far as to formalize this sanction by issuing "report cards" rating the performance of each supplier. The supplier rating goes to the top management of the seller organization, and these men can apply internal sanctions to salesmen, production supervisors or product designers if there are too many "D's" or "F's" on the report card.

While it is generally assumed that the customer is always right, the seller may have some counterbalancing sanctions against the buyer. The seller may have obtained a large downpayment from the buyer which he will want to protect. The seller may have an exclusive process which the buyer needs. The seller may be one of the few firms which has the skill to make the item to the tolerances set by the buyer's engineers and within the time available. There are costs and delays involved in turning from a supplier one has dealt with in the past to a new supplier. Then, too, market conditions can change so that a buyer is faced with shortages of critical items. The most extreme example is the post World War II gray market conditions when sellers were rationing goods rather than selling them. Buyers must build up some reserve of good will with suppliers if they face the risk of such shortage and desire good treatment when they occur. Finally, there is reciprocity in buying and selling. A buyer cannot push a supplier too far if that supplier also buys significant quantities of the product made by the buyer.

Not only do the particular business units in a given exchange want to deal with each other again, they also want to deal with other business units in the future. And the way one behaves in a particular transaction, or a series of transactions, will color his general business reputation. Blacklisting can be formal or informal. Buyers who fail to pay their bills on time risk a bad report in credit rating services such as Dun and Bradstreet. Sellers who do not satisfy their customers become the subject of discussion in the gossip exchanged by purchasing agents and salesmen, at meetings of purchasing agents' associations and trade associations, or even at country clubs or social gatherings where members of top management meet. The American male's habit of debating the merits of new cars carries over to industrial items. Obviously, a poor reputation does not help a firm make sales and may force it to offer great price discounts or added services to remain in business. Furthermore, the habits of unusually demanding buyers become known, and they tend to get no more than they can coerce out of suppliers who choose to deal with them. Thus often contract is not needed as there are alternatives.

Not only are contract and contract law not needed in many situations, their use may have, or may be thought to have, undesirable consequences. Detailed negotiated contracts can get in the way of creating good exchange relationships between business units. If one side insists on a detailed plan, there will be delay while letters are exchanged as the parties try to agree on what should happen if a remote and unlikely contingency occurs. In some cases they may not be able to agree at all on such matters and as a result a sale may be lost to the seller and the buyer may have to search elsewhere for an acceptable supplier. Many businessmen would react by thinking that had no one raised the series of remote and unlikely contingencies all this wasted effort could have been avoided.

Even where agreement can be reached at the negotiation stage, carefully planned arrangements may create undesirable exchange relationships between business units. Some businessmen object that in such a carefully worked out relationship one gets performance only to the letter of the contract. Such planning indicates a lack of trust and blunts the demands of friendship, turning a cooperative venture into an antagonistic horse trade. Yet the greater danger perceived by some businessmen is that one would have to perform his side of the bargain to its letter and thus lose what is called "flexibility." Businessmen may welcome a measure of vagueness in the obligations they assume so that they may negotiate matters in light of the actual circumstances.

Adjustment of exchange relationships and dispute settlement by litigation or the threat of it also has many costs. The gain anticipated from using this form of coercion often fails to outweigh these costs, which are both monetary and non-monetary. Threatening to turn matters over to an attorney may cost no more money than postage or a telephone call; yet few are so skilled in making such a threat that it will not cost some deterioration of the relationship between the firms. One businessman said that customers had better not rely on legal rights or threaten to bring a breach of contract law suit against him since he "would not be treated like a criminal" and would fight back with every means available. Clearly actual litigation is even more costly than making threats. Lawyers demand substantial fees from larger business units. A firm's executives often will have to be transported and maintained in another city during the proceedings if, as often is the case, the trial must be held away from the home office. Top management does not travel by Greyhound and stay at the Y.M.C.A. Moreover, there will be the cost of diverting top management, engineers, and others in the organization from their normal activities. The firm may lose many days work from several key people. The non-monetary costs may be large too. A breach of contract law suit may settle a particular dispute, but such an action often results in a "divorce" ending the "marriage" between the two businesses, since a contract action is likely to carry charges with at least overtones of bad faith. Many executives, moreover, dislike the prospect of being cross-examined in public. Some executives may dislike losing control of a situation by turning the decision-making power over to lawyers. Finally, the law of contract damages may not provide an adequate remedy even if the firm wins the suit; one may get vindication but not much money.

Why Do Relatively Contractual Practices Ever Exist? Although contract is not needed and actually may have negative consequences, businessmen do make some carefully planned contracts, negotiate settlements influenced by their legal rights and commence and defend some breach of contract law suits or arbitration proceedings. In view of the findings and explanation presented to this point, one may ask why. Exchanges are carefully planned when it is thought that planning and a potential legal sanction will have more advantages than disadvantages. Such a judgment may be reached when contract planning serves the internal needs of an organization involved in a business exchange. For example, a fairly detailed contract can serve as a communication device within a large corporation. While the corporation's sales manager and house counsel may work out all the provisions with the customer, its production manger will have to make the product. He must be told what to do and how to handle at least the most obvious contingencies. Moreover, the sales manager may want to remove certain issues from future negotiation by his subordinates. If he puts the matter in the written contract, he may be able to keep his salesmen from making concessions to the customer without first consulting the sales manager. Then the sales manager may be aided in his battles with his firm's financial or engineering departments if the contract calls for certain practices which the sales manager advocates but which the other departments resist. Now the corporation is obligated to a customer to do what the sales manager wants to do; how can the financial or engineering departments insist on anything else?

Also one tends to find a judgment that the gains of contract outweigh the costs where there is a likelihood that significant problems will arise.[12] One factor leading to this conclusion is complexity of the agreed performance over a long period. Another factor is whether or not the degree of injury in case of default is thought to be potentially great. This factor cuts two ways. First, a buyer may want to commit a seller to a detailed and legally binding contract, where the consequences of a default by the seller would seriously injure the buyer. For example, the airlines are subject to law suits from the survivors of passengers and to great adverse publicity as a result of crashes. One would expect the airlines to bargain for carefully defined and legally enforceable obligations on the part of the airframe manufacturers when they purchase aircraft. Second, a seller may want to limit his liability for a buyer's damages by a provision in their contract. For example, a manufacturer of air conditioning may deal with motels in the South and Southwest. If this equipment fails in the hot summer months, a motel may lose a great deal of business. The manufacturer may wish to avoid any liability for this type of injury to his customers and may want a contract with a clear disclaimer clause.

Similarly, one uses or threatens to use legal sanctions to settle disputes when other devices will not work and when the gains are thought to outweigh the costs. For example, perhaps the most common type of business contracts case fought all the way through to the appellate courts today is an action for an alleged wrongful termination of a dealer's franchise by a manufacturer. Since the franchise has been terminated, factors such as personal relationships and the desire for future business will have little effect; the cancellation of the franchise indicates they have already failed to maintain the relationship. Nor will a complaining dealer worry about

[12]Even where there is little chance that problems will arise, some businessmen insist that their lawyer review or draft an agreement as a delaying tactic. This gives the businessman time to think about making a commitment if he has doubts about the matter or to look elsewhere for a better deal while still keeping the particular negotiations alive.

creating a hostile relationship between himself and the manufacturer. Often the dealer has suffered a great financial loss both as to his investment in building and equipment and as to his anticipated future profits. A cancelled automobile dealer's lease on his showroom and shop will continue to run, and his tools for servicing, say, Plymouths cannot be used to service other makes of cars. Moreover, he will have no more new Plymouths to sell. Today there is some chance of winning a law suit for terminating a franchise in bad faith in many states and in the federal courts. Thus, often the dealer chooses to risk the cost of a lawyer's fee because of the chance that he may recover some compensation for his losses.

An "irrational" factor may exert some influence on the decision to use legal sanctions. The man who controls a firm may feel that he or his organization has been made to appear foolish or has been the victim of fraud or bad faith. The law suit may be seen as a vehicle "to get even" although the potential gains, as viewed by an objective observer, are outweighed by the potential costs.

The decision whether or not to use contract—whether the gain exceeds the costs—will be made by the person within the business unit with the power to make it, and it tends to make a difference who he is. People in a sales department oppose contract. Contractual negotiations are just one more hurdle in the way of a sale. Holding a customer to the letter of a contract is bad for "customer relations." Suing a customer who is not bankrupt and might order again is poor strategy. Purchasing agents and their buyers are less hostile to contracts but regard attention devoted to such matters as a waste of time. In contrast, the financial control department—the treasurer, controller or auditor—leans toward more contractual dealings. Contract is viewed by these people as an organizing tool to control operations in a large organization. It tends to define precisely and to minimize the risks to which the firm is exposed. Outside lawyers—those with many clients—may share this enthusiasm for a more contractual method of dealing. These lawyers are concerned with preventive law—avoiding any possible legal difficulty. They see many unstable and unsuccessful exchange transactions, and so they are aware of, and perhaps overly concerned with, all of the things which can go wrong. Moreover, their job of settling disputes with legal sanctions is much easier if their client has not been overly casual about transaction planning. The inside lawyer, or house counsel, is harder to classify. He is likely to have some sympathy with a more contractual method of dealing. He shares the outside lawyer's "craft urge" to see exchange transactions neat and tidy from a legal standpoint. Since he is more concerned with avoiding and settling disputes than selling goods, he is likely to be less willing to rely on a man's word as the sole sanction than is a salesman. Yet the house counsel is more a part of the organization and more aware of its goals and subject to its internal sanctions. If the potential risks are not too great, he may hesitate to suggest a more contractual procedure to the sales department. He must sell his services to the operating departments, and he must hoard what power he has, expending it on only what he sees as significant issues.

The power to decide that a more contractual method of creating relationships and settling disputes shall be used will be held by different people at different times in different organizations. In most firms the sales department and the purchasing department have a great deal of power to resist contractual procedures or to ignore them if they are formally adopted and to handle disputes their own way. Yet in larger organizations the treasurer and the controller have increasing power to demand both systems and compliance. Occasionally, the house counsel must arbitrate the conflicting positions of these departments; in giving "legal advice" he may make the business judgment necessary regarding the use of contract. At times he may ask for an opinion from an outside law firm to reinforce his own position with the outside firm's prestige.

Obviously, there are other significant variables which influence the degree that contract is used. One is the relative bargaining power or skill of the two business units. Even if the controller of a small supplier succeeds within the firm and creates a contractual system of dealing, there will be no contract if the firm's large customer prefers not to be bound to anything. Firms that supply General Motors deal as General Motors wants to do business, for the most part. Yet bargaining power is not size or share of the market alone. Even a General Motors may need a particular supplier, at least temporarily. Furthermore, bargaining power may shift as an exchange relationship is first created and then continues. Even a giant firm can find itself bound to a small supplier once production of an essential item begins for there may not be time to turn to another supplier. Also, all of the factors discussed in this paper can be viewed as *components* of bargaining power—for example, the personal relationship between the presidents of the buyer and the seller firms may give a sales manager great power over a purchasing agent who has been instructed to give the seller "every consideration." Another variable relevant to the use of contract is the influence of third parties. The federal government, or a lender of money, may insist that a contract be made in a particular transaction or may influence the decision to assert one's legal rights under a contract.

Contract, then, often plays an important role in business, but other factors are significant. To understand the functions of contract the whole system of conducting exchanges must be explored fully. More types of business communities must be studied, contract litigation must be analyzed to see why the nonlegal sanctions fail to prevent the use of legal sanctions and all of the variables suggested in this paper must be classified more systematically.

Elegant Models, Empirical Pictures, and the Complexities of Contract

Stewart Macaulay

Abstract Studies in nations with different social and economic systems indicate that the norms of contract law are seldom applied through the litigation process and that disputes are avoided or settled where there is a long-term relationship between the parties. Yet legal scholarship, as well as many proposals for reform, continue to be based on a picture of the contracts lawsuit, to a great extent. It is likely that this distortion is prompted by overgeneralization from a nonrepresentative sample of possible and actual disputes, and by the indirect influence of legal norms; it may also express the needs of legal scholars and reformers. It is questionable whether capitalist, socialist, or mixed economic systems would benefit if more disputes were resolved by the application of officially sanctioned contract norms.

When Maria Lós, the Polish sociologist of law, visited Madison several years ago, she told me of Kurczewski and Frieske's study of the practices of managers of Polish industrial enterprises which she thought resembled my description of the behavior of American business managers (Macaulay, 1963). I was eager to compare these findings, but I do not read Polish. Now, however, Kurczewski and Frieske have translated their work into English, and the editors of the *Law & Society Review* have asked me to edit the translation and comment on the article (Kurczewski and Frieske, 1977).

Kurczewski and Frieske's study of practices related to socialist contract in Poland is a fascinating addition to the growing literature on the role of contract in the United

This article was original published in Law and Society Review 11 (1977), 507–528. Reprinted with permission.
A number of people read earlier drafts of this article and made helpful comments. I wish to thank Richard Abel, Marc Galanter, Thomas Heller, Jacqueline Macaulay, and William Whitford. In addition, Zigurds Zile is largely responsible for what understanding I have of contract law in the socialist world. Obviously, the responsibility for error remains mine.

S. Macaulay (✉)
University of Wisconsin Law School, Madison, WI, USA
e-mail: smacaula@wisc.edu

D. Campbell (ed.), *Stewart Macaulay: Selected Works*, Law and Philosophy Library 133, https://doi.org/10.1007/978-3-030-33930-2_15

States (see, e.g., Macaulay, 1963; Mentschikoff, 1961; Moore, 1973; Whitford, 1968), Great Britain (Beale and Dugdale, 1975), Indonesia (Burns, 1974), Japan (Benjamin, 1975; Guittard, 1974; Kawashima, 1963; Sawada, 1968), Korea (Hahm, 1967, 1969) and Ethiopia (Ross and Berhe, 1974). (See also Honigmann and Honigmann, 1976.) In all of these societies—which differ so greatly in social structure, culture, and political and economic ideology—the picture looks much the same. Industrial managers and merchants seldom litigate to solve disputes about contracts, preferring to use other techniques of dispute avoidance and settlement. Perhaps the surprising thing is that anyone would expect the use of contract litigation to be other than rare and the influence of contract to be anything but indirect. Few, for example, would expect the process of divorce as it is expressed in statutes and cases to have much influence on ongoing marriage relationships. Some have advocated detailed marriage contracts with provision for arbitrators or mediators should the married couple encounter problems (see, e.g., *New York Times,* March 3, 1977:39), but my students, at least, tend to view the explicit specification of duties and the provision for third-party intervention to resolve problems as inconsistent with long-term commitment to a marriage relationship.[1] The managers of businesses who were questioned in all of these studies seemed to feel much the same way about the likely impact of too detailed planning or intervention by third parties on their long-term business relationships.

The group of studies about contract practices is interesting largely because many who write about contract law or who advocate social reforms using that body of law argue *as if* they were unaware of what these studies show.[2] The problem arises from confusing what we can call a classical model of a contract system with an empirical picture of the relationship between law and the contract process. A rough sketch of the classical model of the contract process in western capitalist societies would stress its formal and normative aspects. Formally, it assumes that the rules of contract law will be invoked by parties and applied by courts; normatively, it holds that they ought to be.

This classical model starts with the assumption that entrepreneurs need to plan and deal with risk. They do so by carefully drafting contracts, which they understand and agree to. In order to increase the chance that the contract will be performed and expectations honored, the legal system defines when a contract is made, stands ready to interpret the language used by the parties and to fill any gaps in that language by applying norms reflecting the customs of the commercial community and,

[1]Of course, my students may be wrong, at least insofar as persons do not wish to play the traditional roles of husband and wife (see Weitzman, 1974; cf. Spencer and Zammit, 1976). Nonetheless, I think my students are correct that there are costs to using explicit contractual norms and involving third parties to handle disputes; undoubtedly, there are cases where those costs are outweighed by the benefits.

[2]Blindness to an empirical view of contract is not a necessary hazard of the contracts teaching profession. Harold Havighurst's (1961) classic book shows what can be done in the lecture format. Malcolm Sharp's comment (1952) on Schultz's pioneering empirical study, "The Firm Offer Puzzle" (1952), reflects just what we should expect from a man who did so much to broaden the philosophic basis of classical contract law. The difficult part of empirical work is not methodology but asking the right questions and interpreting the answers one gets. Schultz's work standing alone was very valuable, but Sharp's response to it expands even further what Schultz can teach us.

importantly, offers remedies that either induce performance or compensate for non-performance. Disputes are avoided by asking a lawyer to predict what a court would do, or settled through adjudication. The more predictable the outcome of this process, the better contract law can facilitate the planning and settlement process that is essential to a market society. For example, Jensen and Meckling (1976:15-16) tell us:

> Uncertainty in the structure of rights or in the "rules of the game" substantially changes both peoples' behavior and the use of resources. In particular, it significantly reduces private investment in the kind of long-term projects which have played such an important role in determining our standard of living. It is very difficult to observe these effects because they primarily involve actions not taken, that is projects not undertaken, buildings not built, etc., and are not the stuff of which newspaper headlines are made.... The low standard of living in South America ... is due we believe in large part to the uncertainties in contract and property rights induced by the tremendous instabilities of the political system.

Of course, all that is absolutely required to attain certainty is a *belief* that contracts are highly likely to be carried out, however this belief is brought about and however well founded it may be. Nonetheless, the classical model assumes that the rules of contract law and the process of contract litigation are central, significant, and necessary for economic transactions in a modern capitalist economy. In Max Weber's words, "economic exchange is quite overwhelmingly guaranteed by the threat of legal coercion" (1954:29-30).

The studies as a whole show that the *empirical* picture of the contract process in capitalist societies differs sharply from the classical model. Planning for the risk of nonperformance often is none too careful, and disputes are seldom resolved by litigation or even by applying the norms of contract law outside of litigation. The classical model of the contract process may fit one-shot transactions, such as those sometimes found in financing and real estate, but the reality of modern business, particularly manufacturing, generally involves long-term continuing relationships (see Macneil, 1974; Goldberg, 1976). My colleague, David Trubek (1975), has argued that economic actors will employ the litigation process to settle disputes only to the extent that (1) the present value of continuing relationships is low, and (2) the anticipated return from the litigation process is relatively high. The classical model of the contract process thus operates only in a special and limited case where these conditions are met. Max Weber's theories about the role of contract law in the development of capitalism rest on a model of economic relations in which the typical dispute occurs between firms operating in what we would call a perfectly competitive market. In such conditions continuing relations have no economic value, and no actor has economic power over another. Of course, this is only an ideal; in any real economic process there are at least some transaction costs in switching from, say, one supplier to another. Moreover Weber, and most writers following him, assume there are high net returns from formal remedy agents. They assume that modern legal systems are accessible and efficient, and that legal remedies deter the breaking of agreements and compensate those hurt by breaches of contract. These assumptions, of course, are very questionable.

Socialist contract, as indicated in my editorial note to Kurczewski and Frieske, is a technique for placing both control and responsibility in the hands of those who manage enterprises. It is a means of dealing with the inability of the central administration to plan all the details in a modern technological economy. The classical model of contract in a socialist society also assumes the existence of contract norms and sanctions to induce performance. Managers are expected to invoke this system not only to achieve the goals set for them under the plan but also so that planners will know of problems and trouble—litigation is public and will come to the attention of supervisors (see Loeber, 1964; Speer, 1971; compare Boim, 1974). The balance sheet of a firm that must pay a contract penalty is likely to reflect poorly on the firm's manager. Given the design of socialist central planning, we might assume that any grant of discretion to managers to make and perform contracts would be tightly controlled so that the national plan was carried out as fully as possible.

Kurczewski and Frieske show that a gap exists between the classical and empirical models of contract in socialist Poland, just as it does in other societies. Moreover, the explanations for the gap are similar in both capitalist and socialist systems. Most importantly, those who manage modern industries in any society are not rewarded for complying with the contract system pictured in law books but are judged by economic criteria. Any technique of dispute avoidance or settlement will only be invoked if it is advantageous after the potential benefits and costs are balanced. Litigation concerning anything—including, but not limited to, contracts—is generally expensive, seldom offers a worthwhile payoff, and tends to disrupt the continuing long-term relationships that are vital to the success of the managers. Other techniques of dispute avoidance and settlement are usually available which will produce acceptable results, allow relationships to continue, and cost much less than litigation. Interestingly, all of the studies, including that by Kurczewski and Frieske, indicate that these other techniques are similar despite great differences in social and economic organization or ideology. Moreover, Kurczewski and Frieske report that under socialism, as under capitalism, those with economic power can use the courts to discipline those lacking power, and that rarely will the weaker be able to use litigation to offset economic imbalance.[3]

---

[3]One valuable area for doctrinal research would be to look at the hurdles placed in the way of recovery and ask who, if anyone, might be able to jump them. In the United States, it is the economically less powerful who are likely to consider suing or likely actually to sue the powerful in situations involving more than simple debt collection. Yet our remedy system itself joins with other barriers to access to help repel such challenges. For example, there is a cluster of rules reflecting substantive policies inconsistent with full protection of the expectation interest: (a) Because the law seeks to avoid economic waste, the injured party must act quickly to minimize the loss, usually by seeking a substitute buyer or seller. Damages are only the difference, if any, between the performance originally promised and the substitute. (b) The law seeks to promote flexibility and the most efficient use of resources. The effect usually is to create a "right" to breach, punished only by very limited damages. Specific performance is seldom awarded, and standardized and limited measures of recovery often are used in a mechanical way so that the costs of breach are calculable in advance. (c) Large losses are rarely imposed on one who defaults even where the difference between contract

All of this raises an interesting question barely mentioned by any of the authors of this group of studies: what functions might a classical picture of the contract process serve if it is not an adequate description of what happens? If one shows that business people in all societies compromise differences rather than invoke contract norms to seek victories, rely on a network of contacts, and seek to avoid being dependent on other firms, one must still explain the existence of a widely held, if often implicit, picture of the contract process that varies so markedly from reality. A major conclusion to be drawn from these studies is that we should give further thought to the functions of the classical model. All that can be done here is to offer a very sketchy explanation.

The most obvious explanation for the persistence of the classical model would be that scholars and reformers are unaware that the contract process described in the law books seldom affects behavior very directly. Yet, for many, it is an unwillingness to listen rather than unfamiliarity. Some actively resist considering the implications of empirical findings, dismissing them grandly as mere counting. Ignorance can be but a partial explanation.

Another explanation for the persistence of the classical model of the contract process may be that it is partially accurate. The classical picture may be just an overgeneralization from a biased sample. There *are* appellate opinions—the basic data about law for most legal scholars in the United States—that concern contracts. People will litigate and bring appeals when the potential benefits are thought to

---

price and substitute price is inadequate to protect the expectation interest. Although there are a few modern cases that can be cited to the contrary, *Hadley* v. *Baxendale* still demands that a defaulting party will only be charged with those losses that the party has clearly assumed in advance.

Added to these substantive policies is another cluster of rules reflecting the problems of operating a judicial system. An injured party must prove the loss with reasonable certainty, but it is often impossible to establish with any kind of certainty what would have happened had there been no breach. This is particularly the case in a long-term contract that is breached relatively early in its life. Procedural rules can be manipulated to delay decision and increase the costs of using the process. The courts in most states are crowded, adding further delay and cost and contributing to the mass processing of cases. Even if plaintiffs surmount all these barriers, they must enforce their judgments, which is often difficult. And of course, in the American system, the winning party usually must still pay legal fees, which are high.

Finally, our system allows considerable freedom of contract, and the economically powerful often use it to structure relationships that avoid any remaining risk of liability. Warranties are almost always disclaimed; more importantly, the remedies for default are limited to replacement or repair. The failure of a seller to perform is often excused by wars, strikes, or an endless list of similar events, and sellers often insist on escalator clauses so that they take little risk of increasing costs in inflationary times. Powerful buyers, on the other hand, insist on clauses guaranteeing a right to cancel for convenience, at little or no cost. Moreover, many of these clauses often are buried in the fine print of a lengthy form contract, and thus are inconsistent with the actual expectations of the weaker party.

Even if lawyers were free and litigation had no impact on continuing business relationships, contract doctrine and common contract clauses, coupled with the costs of delay, would serve to minimize the utility of litigation, either to deter or to compensate for breach. This is not to say that a contract action never pays. But it will make economic sense only in a narrow class of cases. It might be useful for many purposes to try to define more precisely the boundaries of that class.

outweigh the costs. Occasionally, it is necessary to vindicate rights even at the cost of a valuable long-term relationship. For example, Laura Nader (1975:159), describing a study by Sylvia Forman of an Ecuadorian village where compromise and the preservation of relationships are vital, reports:

> She [Forman] separates into categories cases involving people who have multiplex, ongoing relationships and who are disputing specific kinds of issues. She argues that different issues generate the strategies employed by the disputants regardless of type of relationship, and that the apparently desired outcomes were also different. The non-compromise set of cases involved land and other important property, and prestige and access to power and influence within the community. All were cases dealing with scarce resources. Forman points out that there is no reason to believe that people involved in these zero-sum strategies fail to recognize the potential, or actual, damage of their strategies to their relationships with their adversaries.... In situations in which the object of the dispute is most highly valued, the social relationship will be sacrificed.

Similarly, in western societies, it is sometimes critically important to vindicate a right. For example, large corporations do sue each other about patent licenses, and they will sometimes litigate the question of which organization is to be saddled with a multimillion dollar loss. However, they are not likely to litigate and pursue appeals merely for the principle of the matter or for entertainment. In Aubert's terms (1963), they are quick to transform a conflict of value into a conflict of interest if that will look better on the profit and loss statement. When they look to contract norms, it is often to help ward off large potential losses for which they could be held liable if they had not placed them elsewhere by contract.[4] Large corporations often dump these losses on organizations lacking the economic power to refuse to accept the risk. Some contemporary cases appear to stem from situations where one party, who has made a bad deal, is scrambling for a loophole, a tactic that is likely to be extremely damaging to a long-term relationship because it violates expectations that the other party views as justified. As a result, a large organization that plans on continuing in business is hesitant to assert technical defenses unless absolutely necessary, and is likely to do so only when its economic power so outweighs that of its adversary that it can ignore the reaction of the latter.

Other cases before the courts involve relationships already shattered, where contract is used for scavenger purposes to salvage something from the wreckage. For example, large organizations can be involved in bankruptcy proceedings or the cancellations of franchises. However, franchise cases often involve a weaker party suing a stronger corporation, and the weaker is likely to discover that freedom of contract is freedom for large organizations to avoid any contractual duties. Large organizations seldom need legal rights against weaker parties because they get what they want by command; the documents they draft assure that they are not significantly hampered by contractual duties owed to the weaker parties. Courts generally

[4]See, e.g., *Air Products and Chemicals, Inc.* v. *Fairbanks Morse, Inc.* (58 Wis.2d 193, 206 N.W.2d 414, 1973), where two large corporations fought to establish whether a disclaimer of liability for negligence or warranty printed on the back of a form used in the transaction became part of the contract.

have refused to intervene on the side of the weaker party,[5] and modern franchise protection statutes have been only partially successful in altering this balance of power.[6]

However, the bulk of modern contract litigation usually involves something far less exalted than multimillion dollar deals that have soured. Edmundo Fuenzalida, in his study of the activity of the courts in Chile (1973, 1974), found that as the nation became more urban and industrialized, and as the population grew, commercial litigation in the ordinary civil courts did not rise at the same rate. After an initial increase roughly paralleling demographic and economic change, the demands on the courts reached a plateau and then began to decline. Moreover, the composition of these demands changed from cases involving the adjudication of rights to those involving only the enforcement of obligations that were fairly clear. In short, there was a shift from adjudication to a bureaucratic role for the courts as part of a debt collection process—they rubber-stamped claims and made them legal. And there is evidence that this shift in functions is not peculiarly Chilean (see Toharia, 1971; Friedman and Percival, 1976). Marc Galanter reviewed data about who uses courts in the United States and for what purposes, and found much the same pattern. Organizations seldom sue other organizations about anything. Galanter tells us: "We cannot escape the conclusion that in gross the courts in the United States are forums which are used by organizations to extract from and discipline individuals" (1975:360). Beale and Dug-dale, examining British practices, note that "if a serious bad debt problem did arise it was quite likely that a solution would be sought through legal procedures. ... It is probably also relevant that the debt action, being for a liquidated (preascertained sum), is relatively simple and cheap. Resort to the courts seemed far rarer in cases where there was any difficult question of fact, such as a performance dispute" (1975:51).

Kurczewski and Frieske do not tell us when, if ever, Polish managers use their formal contract system following the patterns traced in their statutes, although they indicate that it is the economically powerful who are likely to demand contract penalties. Most of their discussion centers on performance disputes which are rarely "litigated"; in their economic system there may be no problem of bad debts in transactions between organizations. On the other hand, Dietrich Loeber (1964:133) states that in the Soviet Union "it is likely that State and Departmental Arbitrazh together decide about one million cases yearly." This huge caseload may indicate that a process takes place in the Soviet Union very different from that which Kurczewski and Frieske found in Poland. We can only speculate about why this might be so, but it is possible that Soviet managers might want to shift responsibility for settlement decisions to the *arbitrazh* so that they will not be criticized for making

[5]See, e.g., *Mobil Oil Corp.* v. *Rubenfeld* (CCH Trade Reg. Rep. ¶ 60,389, N.Y. App. Div., 1975), overturning a lower court decision based on a novel theory that favored a lessee of a gasoline service station.

[6]See, e.g., the accounts of the Mobil Oil Corporation's successful battle against a Connecticut statute that would have benefited those who leased stations from Mobil (*New York Times,* March 19, 1974:47; March 20, 1974: 53).

payments from the funds of their enterprise. Soviet managers may be more tightly controlled than Polish managers. This explanation is similar to that offered by Ross for the failure of insurance companies to settle large claims for injuries in automobile accidents. In such cases, the amount involved is so substantial that no official in the company wants to assume responsibility for writing the check; it seems safer to do this under the compulsion of a court order (1970:220-24).

In summary, loopholes, salvage operations, the bureaucratic process of debt collection, and evasions of responsibility seem to account for a large proportion of contract activity found in the real world of the courts. Yet these are not the topics likely to excite most contract scholars. Large important business organizations seldom are involved in these cases. Perhaps that is why they are not well represented in the model of the contract process held and disseminated by prominent legal scholars from all parts of the world. Perhaps it is necessary to ignore the fact that these kinds of cases predominate in order to give sufficient attention to the interesting situations that are the bulwarks of the remarkable intellectual creation that is contract law. Arguably, empirical research that challenges this elegant creation is mere counting, and scholars and intellectuals do not find the mundane task of describing the real world as delightful as polishing and fine-tuning the formal model. Frequency, of course, is not the only test of importance. But economically important contract cases that adjudicate rights are too rare to serve as a solid foundation for the classical model.

Of course, contract norms and the possibility of contract litigation can play important roles that are not clearly reflected in court records and appellate opinions. One such role is that of weaponry in the process of dispute settlement. The threat of litigation can be invoked without carrying the case to a conclusion in the courts. Contract here forms the foundation for strategic maneuvers in the game of negotiated settlement. Courts may be involved only marginally: filing a complaint, or even merely writing a letter on an attorney's letterhead, may be enough to provoke serious negotiation. In other situations, settlement comes only after a trial, one or more appeals, and perhaps an order for further trials.

Two recent cases in the United States between major corporations illustrate this indirect function of contract norms and the possibility of using a procedure that will, to some degree, implement those norms. In the first case, Westinghouse Electric Corporation sold nuclear reactors to twenty-seven power companies (see, e.g., *Wall Street Journal,* September 15, 1975:4, 8). In order to close the deals, Westinghouse agreed to supply uranium oxide—the needed fuel—at prices averaging about \$9.50 per pound. Westinghouse had purchased only 15 million pounds, but it had agreed to supply about 80 million pounds under these contracts. The price of uranium oxide rose from about \$6 a pound in 1972, to about \$40 a pound in 1976. Westinghouse announced that it was terminating these contracts claiming, in the language of Section 2-615(a) of the Uniform Commercial Code, that the drastic market shift was "the occurrence of a contingency the non-occurrence of which was a basic assumption on which the contract was made. ..." The power companies have brought a number of suits asserting that Westinghouse simply gambled and lost, so that Section 2-615(a) is inapplicable.[7] Several American law professors have earned handsome consulting fees for their opinions about aspects of this case; this appears to be the kind of problem with which they feel at home. But it is possible that we will never know whether Section 2-615(a) offers Westinghouse an excuse since it is likely that the matter will be settled before the litigation is concluded. These events undoubtedly have damaged relations between Westinghouse and some of its customers.[8] However, performance of all of the contracts could cause a loss of about $2 billion, and perhaps bankrupt Westinghouse. One financial analyst thinks that "they'll settle for somewhere between $500 million and $750 million..." but that even "a $1 billion settlement would not be a crippling thing" for Westinghouse (*Forbes*, January 1, 1977:126). All of the aggrieved customers have an interest in the survival of Westinghouse; someone will have to provide engineering, parts, and service for the reactors; and all of the electric utilities have some interest in preserving Westinghouse as a competitor among the sources of power generating equipment (see *Wall Street Journal,* September 15, 1975:8).

Significantly, after a trial that took more than three months, the judge sitting in the first of the several suits against Westinghouse sought to avoid making a decision based on contract norms. He pressed the parties to settle, and held negotiating sessions in his chambers with the chairman of Westinghouse and the presidents of the three utilities that had brought the case. The judge explained:

> The fiscal well-being, possibly the survival, of one of the world's corporate giants is in jeopardy. Likewise, the future of thousands of jobs.
>
> Any decision I hand down will hurt somebody and because of that potential damage, I want to make it clear that it will happen only because certain captains of industry could not together work out their problems so that the hurt might have been held to a minimum. [*New York Times,* February 11, 1977: D-1, D-10]
>
> Solomon-like as I want to be, I can't cut this baby in half. [*New York Times,* February 17, 1977:57]

The judge's efforts were successful. Westinghouse agreed to give the utilities cash, services, and equipment over a number of years, which it estimated would cost about a third of what the utilities had claimed. The settlement also guaranteed the three utilities "parity" with the "most favorable of any settlements" Westinghouse might reach with other utilities suing it for breach of the uranium oxide contracts. Both sides praised the judge, who was running for reelection in Pittsburgh, the home of Westinghouse (see *Wall Street Journal,* March 31, 1977:6; *New York Times,* March 31, 1977:51).

In the second case, McDonnell Douglas Corporation was late in delivering ninety DC-8-60 and DC-9 passenger jet planes to Eastern Airlines in 1966-68. The delays were caused by the Vietnam war and poor management at the then Douglas Aircraft

---

[7]For a discussion of the legal issues, see Hurst (1976).

[8]See Forbes (December 15, 1975:10); but see *Wall Street Journal* (November 8, 1976:4), indicating that Westinghouse is trying to repair the damage in the settlement process.

Corporation, and were an important factor in Eastern's decision to buy Lockheed L-1011 wide-body jets rather than the McDonnell Douglas DC-10. This was a serious loss to McDonnell Douglas (see Eddy *et al.,* 1976:70–72). Eastern then sued for breach of contract and won a $31.8 million judgment. However, this was reversed on appeal because of problems in proving the amount of damage suffered, among other things (*Eastern Airlines, Inc.* v. *McDonnell Douglas Corp.,* 532 F.2d 957, 5th Cir., 1976). The suit was filed in 1970, and the Fifth Circuit's opinion reversing the district court judgment was handed down almost six years later. Rather than retry the case, McDonnell Douglas and Eastern reached a complicated settlement. Eastern returned nine older model DC-9 jets and leased nine newer model DC-9s at a price lower than usual (Gregory, 1976; "Eastern Airlines," 43 (183 §10) *Standard and Poor's New York Stock Exchange Reports* 792, September 21, 1976).

Partial but incomplete use of the contract litigation process, as in the cases just described, may serve a number of functions. Within each corporation, litigation means that, in large measure, problems are turned over to the lawyers, relieving management of immediate responsibility. And lawyers can communicate to opposing counsel through the rituals of formal process in ways that may assist settlement. Moreover, litigation may legitimate concessions in the eyes of outsiders who audit decisions. For example, the customers of Westinghouse are utilities whose rates are regulated. Without some strong justification, they could not negotiate a settlement with Westinghouse and then ask for approval of a rate increase to cover the balance of the loss. The chance that Westinghouse might win may serve to rationalize settlement, and the act of bringing suit might show the regulators that the utilities are not just giving money away. Consumer and antinuclear power organizations filed petitions in eleven states asking state utility regulators to scrutinize any out-of-court settlements that utilities may reach with Westinghouse. These groups assert that if utilities do not hold Westinghouse to its contracts, consumers will have to pay the extra fuel costs (*Wall Street Journal*, April 8, 1977:6). Similarly, Eastern must win approval of its creditors when sums as large as $31 million are involved. Litigation also may affect the willingness of each side to make concessions. It serves as a declaration that matters are serious and not subject to the usual processes. It provides time limits in some cases and the opportunity for delay in others—both of which can affect the process of negotiation. Litigation, too, is a process that provides ever increasing information about the nature of the risk of an adverse judgment as each side sees what facts can be proved and which normative positions are developed.

Kurczewski and Frieske tell us that Polish managers who have economic power often demand contract penalties and then, if they have no further trouble with the promisor, remit the penalty at the end of the year. Here contract law creates rights that can be given up in exchange for cooperation (cf. Moore, 1973:728). Yet not all of the normative claims that must be accommodated are created, or even recognized, by contract law. For example, Eastern had established that delays by McDonnell Douglas had caused Eastern serious financial loss although it could not prove the amount with reasonable certainty. The reversal of the trial court's judgment shows how very difficult it is to win large sums of money under the damages rules in American contract law where the fact of loss is clear, but not the amount. And

McDonnell Douglas could not really contest the fact of loss since it sells airplanes by representing that airlines flying them will make a great deal of money. On the other hand, McDonnell Douglas was able to argue that its duties as an important military supplier during the undeclared Vietnam war significantly contributed to the delays; indeed, had the Vietnam conflict been fought under a Congressional declaration of war, McDonnell Douglas probably would have been excused from obligations to perform contracts with civilian customers. The settlement reached gave Eastern much needed newer planes that were larger, quieter, and burned less fuel; importantly, it did not require Eastern to try to borrow money in order to do this. McDonnell Douglas apparently sought the resumption of close business relations after the earlier divorce.

The *Wall Street Journal* (September 15, 1975:8) points to a similar assertion of norms that are not coterminous with the law of contract, in the Westinghouse cases:

> [T]he electric utilities have canceled and stretched out contracts for atomic power plants, putting a financial squeeze on such companies as Westinghouse.
>
> "You and I know that in the real world of business there's going to be some horse-trading," an industry person says. "You can bet that Westinghouse is reminding companies like Con Edison that it has gone along with them in stretching contracts."

Conduct in prior transactions generally is legally irrelevant in contract law, which focuses on the particular contract under litigation. However, the claim of prior accommodation to the needs of the utilities was highly relevant if any settlement was to be reached.

Although it would be hard to prove, the contract litigation process may also exert an indirect influence on the behavior of the managers of industrial enterprises even where they devote little thought to it. Those making bargains may tacitly rely on the law to fill gaps and provide sanctions, in order to avoid the costs of negotiating about unlikely contingencies or of constructing elaborate systems of security to insure performance. Contract law may crystallize business customs and provide a normative vocabulary, affecting expectations about what is fair. Westinghouse, for example, did not repudiate its uranium oxide contracts in the name of pure self-interest but sought to cloak its actions in the language of the Uniform Commercial Code. Its position, in that guise, may have been more palatable to some of its customers. It may be easier to negotiate with someone asserting a plausible claim of right than with an outlaw openly scorning those who had relied on its promise. (Perhaps the UCC served as a means of self-justification so that executives at Westinghouse felt better about not honoring the commitment their firm had made.) We can only speculate about the situation had the drafters of the Uniform Commercial Code adopted a more rigorous standard that rarely excused nonperformance based on the occurrence of an unforeseen contingency.[9] Suppose the rule had been that one who makes a promise must perform come hell or high water. Would Westinghouse have marched to bankruptcy trying to perform or would it have begged for mercy? Would

[9]For a discussion of a much more rigorous "impossibility" standard, see Macaulay (1961:833-38).

the impact have been only on the amount of any settlement, since the likelihood of victory by Westinghouse would have been insignificant and thus worth little?

The contract litigation process may also maintain a vague sense of threat that keeps everyone reasonably reliable (see Llewellyn, 1931:725 n.47). For this process to operate, it is not necessary that business managers understand contract norms and the realities of the litigation process. Perhaps all that is needed is a sense that breach may entail disagreeable legal problems. The Polish managers described by Kurczewski and Frieske reflect this when they tell us that "one needs to threaten [to use contract penalties] intelligently." The authors go on to remark, somewhat paradoxically, that the "system works well so long as the penalties [for breach of contract] are not actually applied. They work well as a threat, but their application will injure the relationship with the cooperating enterprise so that in the future it will seek contacts with other directors who have a more conciliatory approach" (1977:497). At least among many business people in the United States, an intelligent threat to sue for breach of contract by one who wants to maintain a relationship will be made only tacitly or very indirectly. Even a letter from a lawyer may be deemed a declaration of war, and so business people may do all the negotiating although they may speak from scripts written by lawyers. Yet the very vocabulary used by these nonlawyers may signal that matters have moved a step further toward litigation, and thus constitute an intelligent threat.

Finally, the classical model of contract may serve as one of many ways to legitimate the accepted ideology of a society and that ideology, in turn, may serve to legitimate contract norms and their application through the litigation process. Though sociological theory suggests that law and the legal system serve a legitimating function, it is difficult to identify all the links in the chain of events by which a statute or a decision might affect the attitudes of people who are not legal professionals. No sociological theorist has devoted much attention to the symbolic role of contract doctrine. However, one could argue that in most societies people, as a result of their socialization and experiences, will have some opinion about the obligation to perform promises. The legal system, as but one of many influences in this socialization, declares that contracts generally ought to be performed. It also offers remedies that purport to compensate those injured by nonperformance, thereby emphasizing the importance of compliance with the norm of performance. Lawmakers claim to speak in the name of the society as a whole, and to do so on the basis of principles such as election by a majority of the voters, selection by the revolution, the revelation of God's will, or the like. As a result, citizens may tend to identify what is legal with what is good and right (see Berkowitz and Walker, 1967; Hogan and Mills, 1976; Tapp and Kohlberg, 1971). Insofar as they know or think they know something about the nature of contract law, this knowledge may affect their beliefs. And their attitudes may affect their behavior (but see Liska, 1974).

Actually, there is little empirical evidence to support theories of symbolic legitimation through law. Indeed, a number of studies indicate that most people know very little about the content of most legal norms (see Friedman and Macaulay, 1977: 607-8). As a result, the symbolic impact of law, if it has any, usually must be achieved by indirect and subtle means. This is not to say that theories about symbolic legitimation are wrong; only that they must be far more specific about the circumstances under which laws as symbols influence attitudes.

Whatever its functions for the larger society, the classical model of contract may serve the needs of law professors with a professional interest in contract and those appellate judges who are interested in doctrinal development. If one wants to build a rational, intellectually satisfying system in any branch of law, one must simplify reality in order to produce the necessary generalizations. In Unger's words (1976:11-12) "the more [we make our premises faithful to the social reality we want to apprehend], the higher the risk that our conjectures will degenerate into a series of propositions so qualified and complicated that we are just as well off with our commonsense impressions." The conclusions of classical contract theory, like those of any system of thought, are descriptively true only to the extent that its premises hold. Yet this theory seldom makes clear its hypothetical nature. If writing about contract were to reflect the empirical operation of the contract system, we might lose the elegance and neatness that once gave us confidence that our doctrine supports and reflects our economic ideals. Instead of a neat system, we would risk being left with an unsatisfying collection of ideas where everything "depends."

The classical model of contract also probably appeals to many legal professionals because it seems to offer those without political or economic power the possibility of overturning the structures of the powerful in the society (cf. Lazarus, 1974; Scheingold, 1974). Judges are supposed to respond to reasoned argument, and if their decisions importantly affect behavior, then a single skilled advocate or author of a law review article, armed only with reason, could right wrongs by persuading judges. Not only would the powerless win, but the legal professional who championed their cause would need to do only honorable and enjoyable things in order to help them. The champion works through appeals to reason and intelligence, and talks of economic and social norms, the "findings of science," efficiency, or some other highly valued body of thought. Problems of politics, interest, power, and dominance need not be faced because they do not appear to be relevant in the world of doctrine, where it is assumed that right ideas will be crystallized into rules that are self-enforcing. For example, when Warren and Brandeis wrote a law review article (1890) which was instrumental in persuading the courts to create a right of privacy, no one felt the need to ask whether that right would have any impact on whether people actually obtained greater privacy in the society (see Kalven, 1966), or whether privacy might serve to undercut the enforcement of laws dealing with personal behavior (see Kelvin, 1973). Of course, a law review writer's influence on a decision or a statute may affect the lives of at least a few people. And it may be better to attempt to right wrongs by this indirect and problematic route than to conduct empirical studies that are less likely to do anything to make the world a better place for even a few individuals. Nonetheless, it seems likely that "generals do better when they know the enemy and terrain on which they are to fight" (Friedman and Macaulay, 1977:*vii*).

Legal professionals, particularly professors, often see their calling as a search for the means to achieve justice or some version of the good society. In the early part of the century, the substantive norms of the common law of contract must have seemed to embody simple common sense to most of those who held professorial rank. Then, after the First World War, many of the legal realists had faith that if appellate judges were freed from legalism, they would be able to balance interests and shape rules in a way that would improve society. At the very least, they could reach sensible results in the cases before them. These assumptions, of course, underlie much of Article 2 of the Uniform Commercial Code and the writings of Karl Llewellyn (e.g., 1960). Other scholars, particularly during the New Deal, professed a faith in regulation and administrative expertise as a means of offsetting the excesses of a regime of pure, unfettered, contract. Still later, a new generation of law professors tended to see pluralism or meticulous attention to proper procedures as the key to the proper role of legal institutions. And some sought a value-neutral means of decision-making in one version of economic theory (see, e.g., Posner, 1972). But many of those who examine the legal process in operation today find it difficult to retain their faith that the key to the good society resides in appellate judges, administrative agencies exercising discretion, pluralism, the morality of adjudication, or economic theory. Instead of justice, the empiricists describe a system of bargaining (see Friedman and Macaulay, 1977:31-191) where "the haves come out ahead" (Galanter, 1974). One response to this gloomy and ugly picture has been to turn back to the materials legal scholars have been trained to deal with, to seek satisfaction in the normative structure, or to look for remedies to social problems in the interaction between appellate decision-making and scholarly reflection.

Other factors may also contribute to the persistence of the classical model of contract. Lawyers probably have some interest in mystification as a means of status-preservation. They may believe that the illusion of certainty and predictability facilitates business planning and ensures the performance of obligations, and they may be correct to some degree. But it is clear that legal scholars risk serious error if they refuse to recognize that we have found, in a variety of societies, that the application of contract norms through litigation, or even through buying legal advice, is extremely costly and seldom pays. Scholars must also deal with the fact that few nonlawyers know much about the content of the formal norms or the realities of litigation. Any serious and satisfactory view of contract must acknowledge that much, if not most, significant economic behavior takes place almost untouched by contract norms or litigation. Indeed, Lawrence Friedman reminds us that in the mid-1950s,

> the law of contract remained alive, not, however, as the organic law of the state's economic system—a kind of constitution for business transactions—but as one among many. It was the system of rules applicable to marginal, novel, as yet unregulated, residual, and peripheral business and quasi-business transactions, transactions which might, in exceptional cases, call for problem-solving and dispute-settling. "Contract" stepped in where no other body of law and no agency of law other than the court was appropriate or available. [1965:193; cf. Milhollin, 1974]

So far we have speculated about why those who study contract so often write as if they held what we have called a classical model—where one-shot transactions are performed largely because of the threat of the sanctions that follow a breach—in the face of an empirical picture that differs so sharply. Kurczewski and Frieske offer another answer. The classical model, they assume, is a picture of how people ought to behave; the empirical is but an aberration that should be corrected. They tell a story of avoiding disputes if possible and, if not, of settling them by techniques outside of, and even opposed to, the official model of central planning and socialist contract; but they decry the costs of these techniques, both to the Polish economy and to its social system. Managers seek to avoid disputes by remaining independent of other industries. They build unauthorized inventories of potentially scarce raw materials, and they seek self-sufficiency through vertical integration. This wastes resources that could be devoted to productive use if the planners knew of them, and some of the advantages of the division of labor are lost. Illegal practices such as bribes and fictional jobs for the employees of suppliers, may prompt more illegality elsewhere, for if people get away with these minor crimes the perceived risk of punishment for other violations may be reduced. Furthermore, these illegal adjustments may be interpreted as evidence that socialist economic planning cannot work within its own rules, thus casting doubt on the legitimacy of the entire regime. Avoiding disputes or settling them through informal contacts among managers, also has costs, even though such behavior is perfectly legal. In socialist systems, as I have said, disputes are supposed to serve as feedback to supervisors and planners, signaling the existence of problems and allowing them to evaluate the skill of managers. When things are smoothed out between members of the "club," problems are covered up and useful information is withheld from those who do the planning. One wonders, in any case, how such adjustments can be entirely legal. The manager who fails to seek contract penalties is likely not to meet the planned quota for the factory unless there is slack in the system that ought not to be there in a planned economy.

In contrast to this critical view, most of the studies of business transactions elsewhere tend to applaud what they find, downgrading the classical model of the process. We must ask whether the dispute avoidance and settlement techniques in western countries have costs similar to those stressed by Kurczewski and Frieske. Obviously, capitalist societies do not need to defend the integrity of central state planning, and formal legal rules do not demand litigation to vindicate breaches of contract since such breaches are regarded as a matter of private rather than public concern. On the contrary, one can find statements applauding private settlement of disputes. Yet insofar as the law of contract is thought to advance social norms other than the peaceful resolution of disputes, a system of negotiation will defeat those values (cf. Lubman, 1967). Abram Chayes (1959) has suggested that important regulation takes place when the legal system offers desired facilities—the right to incorporate, a legally valid marriage, or the transfer of legal title—to individuals and groups if they comply with certain conditions. He uses the law of contracts as an example, but we should expect people to be willing to satisfy such conditions only when the facility offered by the law is viewed as sufficiently valuable to be worth the cost. There was a time when courts in the United States refused to enforce a contract in which the seller agreed to supply all of the buyer's requirements of particular goods. Insofar as these decisions had any policy basis, they appear to express the belief that sellers ought not assume a commitment, which might bankrupt them, to supply almost limitless quantities at a fixed price while receiving so little in return. Curtis Reitz (1976) notes that one legal scholar said that such a rule had wreaked havoc within the commercial community. But it did no such thing: the commercial community continued to make "requirements" contracts, apparently unconcerned whether or not they would be legally enforceable. This business relationship was too useful to sacrifice by invoking the formal rules of contract law.

Perhaps there are other costs that we pay as the price of a less aggressive system in which some sins are forgiven, costs such as lowered efficiency. On the other hand, the degree of cooperation found in business in the United States may outweigh any loss in efficiency. It is worth considering what, if anything, might change if contract litigation became cheaper and offered a better chance of obtaining large recoveries. Kurczewski and Frieske want to see practices in Poland brought closer to the model of socialist contract found in their statutes. Apparently, they would substitute contract penalties for contacts and bribes. Suppose the state in either a socialist or capitalist society moved to deter breaches of contract by inducing those who manage large organizations to insist upon the application of contract norms through litigation. Would anyone want contractual parties pushed to perform the letter of their agreements in every case? Clearly performance would be an inefficient use of resources in some cases—it would be hard to advocate forcing an automobile manufacturer to buy thousands of parts for a car model that did not sell; it seems better to allow the manufacturer to stop the supplier from producing any more parts and work out a settlement. And how was the settlement in the *Eastern Airlines* v. *McDonnell Douglas* litigation inferior to an award of only those damages that Eastern could prove had flowed from late delivery of the airplanes? If the present system were curbed might not Poland find itself with higher compliance with its statutory model of contract at the cost of less efficient or declining production? Is it not possible that some slack, sloppiness, and irrationality are unavoidable by-products of the essential flexibility and potential for growth and change in modern industrial systems? The existence of a practice does not prove its inevitability, but we would be unwise to dismiss the possibility.

Kurczewski and Frieske's study is a step toward the most fruitful kind of work in comparative law. It should be matched with studies at the level of practice rather than doctrine. This is not to argue that doctrine and ideology make no difference. The picture Kurczewski and Frieske paint of Poland is similar to, but not identical with, that of the United States, or Great Britain. There are differences, and they, too, deserve our attention. Nonetheless, despite doctrinal and ideological differences, common problems often lead to common solutions.

References

Aubert, Vilhelm (1963) "Competition and Dissensus: Two Types of Conflict and of Conflict Resolution," 7 *Journal of Conflict Resolution* 26.

Beale, Hugh and Tony Dugdale (1975) "Contracts between Businessmen: Planning and the Use of Contractual Remedies," 2 *British Journal of Law and Society* 45.

Benjamin, Roger W. (1975) "Images of Conflict Resolution and Social Control: American and Japanese Attitudes toward the Adversary System," 19 *Journal of Conflict Resolution* 123.
Berkowitz, Leonard and Nigel Walker (1967) "Laws and Moral Judgments," 30 *Sociometry* 410.
Boim, Leon (1974) "'Ombudsmanship' in the Soviet Union," 22 *American Journal of Comparative Law* 509.
Burns, John J. (1974) "Law and Dispute Settlement in Northern Sumatra." Unpublished paper.
Chayes, Abram (1959) "The Modern Corporation and the Rule of Law," in Edward S. Mason (ed.) *The Corporation in Modern Society.* Cambridge, Mass.: Harvard University Press.
Eddy, Paul, Elaine Potter and Bruce Page (1976) *Destination Disaster—From the Tri-Motor to the DC-10: The Risk of Flying.* Chicago: Quadrangle Books.
Friedman, Lawrence M. (1965) *Contract Law in America.* Madison: University of Wisconsin Press.
Friedman, Lawrence M. and Stewart Macaulay (1977) *Law and the Behavioral Sciences* (2d ed.). Indianapolis: Bobbs-Merrill.
Friedman, Lawrence M. and Robert V. Percival (1976) "A Tale of Two Courts: Litigation in Alameda and San Benito Counties," 10 *Law & Society Review* 267.
Fuenzalida, Edmundo (1973, 1974) *Fluctuaciones de la Demanda por Justicia en Función del Cambio Social I & II.* Santiago: Instituto de Docencia e Investigación Jurídicas.
Galanter, Marc (1974) "Why the 'Haves' Come Out Ahead: Speculations on the Limits of Legal Change," 9 *Law & Society Review* 95.
Galanter, Marc (1975) "Afterword: Explaining Litigation," 9 *Law & Society Review* 347.
Goldberg, Victor P. (1976) "Regulation and Administered Contracts," 7 *Bell Journal of Economics* 426.
Gregory, William H. (1976) "Suit Settled as Eastern Leases 9 DC-9 Transports," 104 *Aviation Week and Space Technology* 28 (June 28).
Guittard, Stephen W. (1974) "Negotiating and Administering an International Sales Contract with the Japanese," 8 *International Lawyer* 822.
Hahm, Pyong-Choon (1967) *The Korean Political Tradition and Law.* Seoul: Hollym Corp.
Hahm, Pyong-Choon (1969) "The Decision Process in Korea," in Glendon Schubert and David Danielski (eds.) *Comparative Judical Behavior: Cross-Cultural Studies of Political Decision-Making in the East and West.* New York: Oxford University Press.
Havighurst, Harold C. (1961) *The Nature of Private Contract.* Evanston: Northwestern University Press.
Hogan, Robert and Carol Mills (1976) "Legal Socialization," 19 *Human Development* 26.
Honigmann, John J. and Irma Honigmann (1976) "Mixed Contracts in Rural Austria," 15 *Ethology* 347.
Hurst, Thomas R. (1976) "Freedom of Contract in an Unstable Economy: Judicial Reallocation of Contractual Risks under UCC Section 2-615," 54 *North Carolina Law Review* 545.
Jensen, Michael C. and William H. Meckling (1976) "Can the Corporation Survive?" University of Rochester, Graduate School of Management, Center for Research in Government Policy and Business, Public Policy Working Paper Series PPS-76-4.
Kalven, Harry (1966) "Privacy in Tort Law—Were Warren and Brandeis Wrong?" 31 *Law and Contemporary Problems* 326.
Kawashima, Takeyoshi (1963) "Dispute Resolution in Contemporary Japan," in A. T. von Mehren (ed.) *Law in Japan: The Legal Order in a Changing Society.* Cambridge, Mass.: Harvard University Press.
Kelvin, Peter (1973) "A Social-Psychological Examination of Privacy," 12 *British Journal of Social and Clinical Psychology* 248.
Kurczewski, Jacek and Kazimierz Frieske (1977) "Some Problems in the Legal Regulation of the Activities of Economic Institutions," 11 *Law & Society Review* 489.
Lazarus, Simon (1974) *The Genteel Populists.* New York: Holt, Rinehart & Winston.
Liska, Allen (1974) "Emergent Issues in the Attitude-Behavior Consistency Controversy," 30 *American Sociological Review* 26.

Llewellyn, Karl N. (1931) "What Price Contract? An Essay in Perspective," 40 *Yale Law Journal* 704.

Llewellyn, Karl N. (1960) *The Common Law Tradition: Deciding Appeals*. Boston: Little Brown & Co.

Loeber, Dietrich A. (1964) "Plan and Contract Performance in Soviet Law," [1964] *University of Illinois Law Forum* 128.

Lubman, Stanley (1967) "Mao and Mediation: Politics and Dispute Resolution in Communist China," 55 *California Law Review* 1284.

Macaulay, Stewart (1961) "Justice Traynor and the Law of Contracts," 13 *Stanford Law Review* 812.

Macaulay, Stewart (1963) "Non-Contractual Relations in Business: A Preliminary Study," 28 *American Sociological Review* 55.

Macneil, Ian R. (1974) "The Many Futures of Contracts," 47 *Southern California Law Review* 691.

Mentschikoff, Soia (1961) "Commercial Arbitration," 61 *Columbia Law Review* 846.

Milhollin, Gary L. (1974) "More on the Death of Contract," 24 *Catholic University Law Review* 29.

Moore, Sally Falk (1973) "The Semi-Autonomous Social Field as an Appropriate Subject of Study," 7 *Law & Society Review* 719.

Nader, Laura (1975) "Forums for Justice: A Cross-Cultural Perspective," 31 *Journal of Social Issues* 151.

Posner, Richard (1972) *Economic Analysis of Law*. Boston: Little Brown & Co.

Reitz, Curtis R. (1976) "If Contract is Dead, What Shall We Teach?" Paper presented at the Annual Meeting of the American Association of Law Schools, Section of Commercial, Contract, and Related Consumer Matters, Houston, Texas (December 27).

Ross, John and Zemeriam Berhe (1974) "Legal Aspects of Doing Business in Addis Ababa: A Profile of Mercato Businessmen and Their Reception of New Laws," 10 *African Law Studies* 1.

Ross, H. Laurence (1970) *Settled Out of Court: The Social Process of Insurance Claims Adjustments*. Chicago: Aldine.

Sawada, J. Toshio (1968) *Subsequent Conduct and Supervening Events*. Tokyo: University of Tokyo Press.

Scheingold, Stuart A. (1974) *The Politics of Rights*. New Haven: Yale University Press.

Schultz, Franklin (1952) "The Firm Offer Puzzle: A Study of Business Practice in the Construction Industry," 19 *University of Chicago Law Review* 237.

Sharp, Malcolm P. (1952) "Promises, Mistake and Reciprocity," 19 *University of Chicago Law Review* 286.

Speer, Brownlow M. (1971) "Contract Rights and the Planned Economy: Peaceful Co-Existence Under the 1969 Soviet Statutes on Deliveries of Goods," 3 *Law and Policy in International Business* 510.

Spencer, Janet Maleson and Joseph P. Zammit (1976) "Mediation-Arbitration: A Proposal for Private Resolution of Disputes between Divorced or Separated Parents," [1976] *Duke Law Journal* 911.

Tapp, June and Lawrence Kohlberg (1971) "Developing Senses of Law and Legal Justice," 27 *Journal of Social Issues* 65.

Toharia Cortes, José Juan (1971) *Cambio Social y Vida Jurídica en España, 1900-1970*. Ph.D. Dissertation, Facultad de Derecho, Universidad Complutense de Madrid, summarized and translated as *Social Life and Legal Activity in Spain, 1900-1970*. Translated by C. Lynch. New Haven: Yale Law School Program in Law and Modernization.

Trubek, David M. (1975) "Notes on the Comparative Study of Processes of Handling Disputes between Economic Enterprises." Paper presented at the United States-Hungarian Conference on Contract Law and the Problems of Large Scale Economic Enterprise, New York (August).

Unger, Roberto M. (1976) *Law in Modern Society: Toward a Criticism of Social Theory*. New York: Free Press.

Warren, Samuel D. and Louis D. Brandeis (1890) "The Right to Privacy," 4 *Harvard Law Review* 193.

Weber, Max (1954) *Max Weber on Law in Economy and Society.* Translated by M. Rheinstein and E. Shils. Cambridge, Mass.: Harvard University Press.

Weitzman, Lenore J. (1974) "Legal Regulation of Marriage: Tradition and Change," 62 *California Law Review* 1169.

Whitford, William C. (1968) "Law and the Consumer Transaction: A Case Study of the Automobile Warranty," [1968] *Wisconsin Law Review* 1006.

An Empirical View of Contract

Stewart Macaulay

Professor Stewart Macaulay reflects on his 1963 article *Non-Contractual Relations in Business* and assesses its current significance. Analysis of the gap between contract doctrine and the daily functioning of the business and commercial world has proven to be a fruitful source of theoretical insight into the social functions of law. While the teaching of doctrine remains a central element of legal education and even predominates, the theoretical potential of an empirical approach to legal education remains vast.

I. Introduction

When Grant Gilmore called his lectures "The Death of Contract,"[1] he gave a name to a body of work that includes some of mine. He called me the "Lord High Executioner" of the "Contract is Dead" movement. However, Gilmore was not very interested in my empirical description of contract. He said this kind of work lacked

This article was original published in Wisconsin Law Review 1985, 465–82. Reprinted with permission.
Malcolm Pitman Sharp Professor, University of Wisconsin-Madison. This paper was given on October 24, 1984 at the University of Amsterdam. I want to thank Professor André Hoekema for inviting me to speak and for being such a gracious host. A revised version was given on May 20, 1985 in Copenhagen. Professor Britt-Mari Blegvad arranged an enjoyable conference in her delightful city. Dr. Jacqueline Macaulay read the manuscript critically and, as always, made it much better.

[1]G. Gilmore, The Death of Contract (1974).

S. Macaulay (✉)
University of Wisconsin Law School, Madison, WI, USA
e-mail: smacaula@wisc.edu

D. Campbell (ed.), *Stewart Macaulay: Selected Works*, Law and Philosophy Library 133, https://doi.org/10.1007/978-3-030-33930-2_16
Published by Springer International Publishing AG 2018.

theoretical relevance. I must credit him with an attention catching title. Nevertheless, he failed to see that the very limited practical role of what professors call contract law poses significant theoretical problems that we are only beginning to confront.

In a way, Gilmore's title is misleading. Contract as a living institution is very much with us. In the day-to-day flow of dealings, vast numbers of significant transactions take place to the reasonable satisfaction of all concerned. People and organizations bargain, they write documents, and they avoid, suppress, and resolve disputes little influenced by academic contract law. Some cases are taken to court and the formal process begun, although lawyers settle most of them before courts reach final decisions. There are even opinions by judges relying on traditional contract law, but they are relatively rare.[2]

Furthermore, contract within the academy is still very much alive. Every morning in law schools all over the United States beginning law students struggle with offer, acceptance, and consideration. I never argued that contract law died. Rather, academic contract law is not now and never was a descriptively accurate reflection of the institution in operation. Moreover, this inaccuracy matters in many ways.

At the end of September in 1984, there was a conference in Madison marking the 21st birthday of the publication in the *American Sociological Review* of my article on non-contractual relations in business.[3] I am pleased that the article has had a long shelf-life and people still find something in it. After listening to others at the conference consider long-term continuing relationships, it is a good time for me to reflect on developments over the past two decades. We must remember that my article reports research done when Dwight Eisenhower was President of the United States, and I wrote it when John Kennedy was in office. Both the business executives and lawyers interviewed and the author were living in the United States before the decline and fall of the American empire. Indeed, any article that uses Studebaker taxis as an example was written in the pre-word processor age. A great deal has happened in 21 years. We also know much more about the American legal system in operation today than anyone did when I wrote the article.

To reconsider what I wrote, I will summarize the argument of my 1963 article, including some of my later research as well. Then I will note what I would add were I to write the article today. Finally, I will consider what difference all of this makes to those interested in contracts and law and society research. I will talk about developments in the United States, not because I think them more important but only because I know my own society best.[4]

---

[2]*See* Trubek, Sarat, Felstiner, Kritzer and Grossman, *The Costs of Ordinary Litigation,* 31 UCLA L. Rev. 72, 87 (1983).

[3]Macaulay, *Non-Contractual Relations in Business: A Preliminary Study*, 28 Am. Soc. Rev. 55 (1963) [hereinafter cited as Macaulay, *Non-Contractual Relations*].

[4]*Compare* Lewis, *Contracts Between Businessmen: Reform of the Law of Firm Offers and an Empirical Study of Tendering Practices in the Building Industry*, 9 J. Law & Soc'y 153 (1982).

II. The 1963 Article as Supplemented by Two Decades of Work in Dispute Processing Research

The 1963 article challenges a model of contract law's functions, explicit or implicit in the work of contracts scholars and social theorists. This model makes contract law far more central than its actual role in society.[5] One version of the model suggests that in a state of nature we are all selfish. Law supports needed interdependence by coercing us to honor obligations to others. The historical story is that we begin with trading within real communities. Capitalism breaks this up, and we become alienated strangers. Then the legal system supplies a kind of synthetic community based on rights and duties enforced by courts.[6] A variant of the story is that market capitalism changes all personal relations into autonomous market trades[7] —capitalism replaces a spirit of interdependence by "what's in it for me?" Contract law supplies the needed glue to hold individualists to their bargains.

More particularly, writers assume a number of things about the institution of contract. First, there is careful planning of relationships in light of legal requirements and the possibilities of nonperformance. We must spell out everything because parties will perform only to the letter of a contract, if they go that far.[8] Second, contract law is a body of clear rules so that it can facilitate planning. It provides formal channels so that we know the right way to proceed to produce desired legal consequences.[9] Finally, contract litigation is a primary means of deterring breach and directly and indirectly resolving disputes. Without contract law and the state's monopoly of the legitimate use of force, performance of contracts would be highly uncertain.[10]

However, all of these assumptions about history and about human relationships are just wrong or so greatly overstated as to be seriously misleading. Contract planning and contract law, at best, stand at the margin of important long-term continuing business relations. Business people often do not plan, exhibit great care in drafting contracts, pay much attention to those that lawyers carefully draft, or honor a legal approach to business relationships. There are business cultures defining the risks assumed in bargains, and what should be done when things go wrong.

---

[5]I am indebted to Professor Anthony Kronman of the Yale Law School and Professor Robert Gordon of the Stanford Law School for some of the ideas in this paragraph. I sketched the implicit academic model of contract in Macaulay, *Elegant Models, Empirical Pictures, and the Complexities of Contract,* 11 Law & Soc'y Rev. 507 (1977) [hereinafter cited as Macaulay, *Elegant Models*].

[6]Gordon, *Macaulay, MacNeil and the Discovery of Solidarity and Power in Contract Law*, 1985 Wis. L. Rev. 565.

[7]*Id.* at 568-69.

[8]Macaulay, *Elegant Models, supra* note 5, at 508.

[9]*Id.* at 509.

[10]*Id.* at 509-10, discussing M. Weber, Max Weber on Law in Economy and Society (1954) and M. Jensen & W. Meckling, Can the Corporation Survive? (1976) (University of Rochester, Graduate School of Management, Center for Research in Government Policy and Business, Public Policy Working Paper Series PPS-76-4).

People perform disadvantageous contracts today because often this gains credit that they can draw on in the future. People often renegotiate deals that have turned out badly for one or both sides. They recognize a range of excuses much broader than those accepted in most legal systems.[11]

There are relatively few contracts cases litigated, and those that are have special characteristics. Few of those cases litigated produce anything like adequate compensation for the injuries caused. Frequently, limitations on liability in written contracts block remedies based on the reasonable expectations of the party who did not draft the instrument. At best, formal legal procedures usually are but a step in a larger process of negotiation. Filing a complaint and pre-trial procedure can be tactics in settlement bargaining; appeals often prompt reversals and remands, leaving the parties to settle or face continuing what seems to be an endless process. When final judgments are won, often they cannot be executed because of insolvency.[12]

How do we explain this gap between the academic model and an empirical description of the system of contract law in action? Academic writers often make individualistic assumptions. Their theories rest on worlds of discrete transactions where people respond to calculations of short-term advantage. However, people engaged in business often find that they do not need contract planning and contract law because of relational sanctions. There are effective private governments and social fields, affected but seldom controlled by the formal legal system.[13] Even discrete transactions take place within a setting of continuing relationships and interdependence. The value of these relationships means that all involved must work to satisfy each other. Potential disputes are suppressed, ignored, or compromised in the service of keeping the relationship alive.

While we often read that increasing bureaucratic organization has made the world impersonal, this is not always the case. Social fields cutting across formal lines exist within bureaucracies, creating rich sanction systems. Individuals occupying formal roles ignore organizational boundaries as they seek to overcome formal rationality to achieve goals, gain rewards, and avoid sanctions. Social networks serve as communications systems. People gossip, and this creates reputational sanctions.[14]

Power, exploitation, and dependence also are significant. Continuing relationships are not necessarily nice. The value of arrangements locks some people into dependent positions.[15] They can only take orders. The actual lines of a bureaucratic

---

[11]*See* Gottlieb, *Relationism: Legal Theory for a Relational Society*, 50 U. Chi. L. Rev. 567 (1983); Palay, *Comparative Institutional Economics: The Governance of Rail Freight Contracting*, 13 J. Legal Stud. 265 (1984).

[12]*See* Macaulay, *Elegant Models, supra* note 5, at 511 n.3.

[13]*See* S. Macaulay, Private Government (1983) (Disputes Processing Research Program, Madison, Wisconsin, Working Paper 1983-6).

[14]*See* Goldberg, *The Law and Economics of Vertical Restrictions: A Relational Perspective*, 58 Tex. L. Rev. 91 (1979); Kornhauser, *Reliance, Reputation, and Breach of Contract*, 26 J.L. & Econ. 691 (1983).

[15]*See* Macaulay, *The Standardized Contracts of United States Automobile Manufacturers*, in 7 International Encyclopedia of Comparative Law 3-21 (1973).

structure may be much more extensive than formal ones. Seemingly independent actors may have little real freedom and discretion in light of the costs of offending dominant parties. Once they face sunk costs and comfortable patterns, the possibility of command rather than negotiation increases. In some situations parties may see relational sanctions as inadequate in view of the risks involved. However, instead of contract law, they usually turn to other techniques to provide security, ranging from collateral to vertical integration.[16]

Furthermore, contract law as delivered is a misrepresented product. American doctrine is not clear and easy to apply. Rather it is contradictory, uncertain, and offers arguments rather than answers.[17] This is particularly true of the Uniform Commercial Code's Article II, governing transactions in goods. I often tell my classes that if lawyers of equal ability represent clients with equal resources and willingness to invest them in a case falling under Article II, the case will end in a tie.[18] If one side wins and the other loses, it is not because of the power of legal doctrine. I can match any argument you make with one equally as good. Also, courts have interpreted the Code's rules concerning failure to perform so that settlements and compromises are promoted, and those who would vindicate their rights are punished.[19]

American contract remedies are limited and reflect a fear of awarding too much. Our courts rarely order specific performance of contracts. One must prove one's damages with reasonable certainty, and in most states the injured party cannot recover the lost anticipated profits of "a new business."[20] The rule of *Hadley v. Baxendale*[21] further limits recovery to damages that were reasonably foreseeable at the time of breach. Courts frequently refuse to award the cost of repairing a defective performance. Instead, they limit the remedy to the difference in value between the contract as performed and as it should have been had there been no breach.[22] While this sounds reasonable, the burden of proof usually confines diminution in value to a token remedy.[23] Limiting remedies can benefit a weaker party, making breach of contract less burdensome. However, often it benefits stronger parties. They have less need for

[16]*See* O. Williamson, Markets and Hierarchies: Analysis and the Antitrust Implications (1975).

[17]*See, e.g.*, Macaulay, *Private Legislation and the Duty to Read—Business by IBM Machine, the Law of Contracts and Credit Cards*, 19 Vand. L. Rev. 1051 (1966) [hereinafter cited as Macaulay, *The Duty to Read*].

[18]I have been accused of exaggerating every now and then to make a point.

[19]*See, e.g.*, Eastern Air Lines, Inc. v. McDonnell Douglas Corp., 532 F.2d 957 (5th Cir. 1976); Solar Kinetics Corp. v. Joseph T. Ryerson & Son, Inc., 488 F. Supp. 1237 (D.C. Conn. 1980).

[20]*See* McBrayer v. Teckla, Inc., 496 F.2d 122, 127-28 (5th Cir. 1974).

[21]9 Ex. 341, 156 Eng. Rep. 145 (1854). *See* U.C.C. § 2-715(2) (1978) for a modern statement of the rule.

[22]*See, e.g.*, Plante v. Jacobs, 10 Wis.2d 567,103 N.W.2d 296 (1960); Jacob & Youngs, Inc. v. Kent, 230 N.Y. 239, 129 N.E. 889 (1921).

[23]*See* Peevyhouse v. Garland Coal & Mining Co., 382 P.2d 109 (Okla. 1962), *cert. denied,* 375 U.S. 906 (1963). The problem is discussed in Eisenberg, *The Responsive Model of Contract Law,* 36 Stan. L. Rev. 1107, 1155-65 (1984).

legal remedies to achieve their ends because they have other-than-legal leverage. Limited remedies allow stronger parties to walk away from burdensome obligations at low or no cost. Courts frequently find that a stronger [party] has breached a contract, but so limit the remedy awarded the weaker that the victory is hollow.

Even when contract law might offer a remedy, the legal system in operation promotes giving up or settling rather than adjudicating to vindicate rights. One must pay for one's own lawyer, and one must win enough to offset all the costs of the endeavor.[24] Thus, using the legal process always is a gamble. Furthermore, crafty lawyers use delay and procedural technicality for advantage. Galanter has discussed what he calls "megalaw."[25] Those who can afford to play invest in the skills of large law firms. They play the litigation game by expanding procedural complexity to draw out the process. Others who cannot afford to invest as much must drop out. This kind of power is not distributed equally. In another famous article, Galanter tells us "why the 'haves' come out ahead."[26] The "haves" are repeat players who can spread the costs of litigation over many similar transactions. They can afford to play for rules and treat disputes as test cases which may help them in the future. They can run up the costs of a particular case in order to reinforce their reputation as difficult defendants to sue.

Technical complexity and delay gain greater impact in a legal system marked by overload. While America has more lawyers per person than any Western nation, the number of judges is relatively small.[27] Many factors have contributed to the rise in recent years of judges who coerce parties to settle rather than try cases that will take time in court. Our judges have long done this, but recently they have brought the role out into the open.[28] They are proud of their efforts, and they are teaching each other how best to force parties to settle rather than litigate.[29] Of course, legal rights matter in settlement negotiations, but such considerations as the immediate need for money also play an important part.

---

[24]A plaintiff may be able to recover reasonable attorneys fees from the defendant in cases falling under various consumer protection statutes. *See, e.g.,* Wis. Stats. § 425.308 (1983-84). Even when this is true, a consumer must win to get an award of fees. These statutes change the nature of the wager, but litigation remains a game of chance. Moreover, lawyers are limited to reasonable fees. Usually this means they cannot win enough in one case to offset those cases where they lose. Thus, these statutes do not work as contingent fees in personal injury litigation.

[25]*See* Galanter, *Mega-Law and Mega-Lawyering in the Contemporary United States*, in The Sociology of the Professions: Lawyers, Doctors and Others 152 (1983).

[26]*See* Galanter, *Why the "Haves" Come Out Ahead: Speculations on the Limits of Legal Change*, 9 Law & Soc'y Rev. 95 (1974).

[27]Galanter, *Reading the Landscape of Disputes: What We Know and Don't Know (and Think We Know) About Our Allegedly Contentious and Litigious Society*, 31 UCLA L. Rev. 4, 52, 55 (1983) ("The ratio of lawyers to judges in the United States is . . . one of [the] highest anywhere; the private sector of the law industry is very large relative to the public institutional sector.").

[28]*See, e.g.*, Matter of Westinghouse Elec. Corp., 517 F. Supp. 440 (E.D. Va. 1981).

[29]Galanter, "*. . . A Settlement Judge, not a Trial Judge:*" *Judicial Mediation in the United States*, 12 J. Law & Soc'y 1 (1985); M. Galanter, The Emergence of the Judge as a Mediator in Civil Cases (1984) (Disputes Processing Research Program, Madison, Wisconsin, Working Paper 1984-5).

III. In 1984, What Should Be Added to This Picture?

The original article does not rest on naive functionalist assumptions of harmony.[30] Nevertheless, today I would stress that relational sanctions do not always produce cooperation or happy situations. Trust can be misplaced. There are always failures to perform and mistakes. Usually, business people take an insurance approach. They write off these incidents as long as there are not too many or one of them does not involve too much money.[31] Business scandals always have been with us, and they prompt attempts to use care and countermeasures. By and large, the contracting system works well enough. However, even large famous business corporations can suffer major losses as the result of incomplete planning and trusting the wrong people.[32]

When long-term continuing relationships do collapse, those disadvantaged often turn to contract law and legal action.[33] We have seen litigation prompted by major shocks to the world economic system.[34] OPEC and the energy crises of the 1970s provoked many cases where contracts had rested on relational sanctions and assumptions about the costs of energy.[35] Relational considerations gave way to the large amounts of money that businesses would have lost had they performed their commitments. Westinghouse, for example, promised electric utilities buying its nuclear reactors that it would guarantee the price of fuel.[36] A world cartel sent the price soaring far beyond the price Westinghouse had guaranteed. Westinghouse

---

[30]*See* Gordon, *Critical Legal Histories*, 36 Stan. L. Rev. 57, 78-79 (1984).

[31]Macaulay, *Non-Contractual Relations, supra* note 3, at 63.

[32]See, e.g., J. Stewart, The Partners 152-200 (1983); Eagan, *The Westinghouse Uranium Contracts: Commercial Impracticability and Related Matters*, 18 Am. Bus. L.J, 281, 282-83 (1980); Joskow, *Commercial Impossibility, the Uranium Market and the Westinghouse Case*, 6 J. Legal Stud. 119 (1977); Parisi, *Westinghouse Faces Hefty Financial Losses While the Case Puts Gulf Oil's Reputation in Peril*, N.Y. Times, July 9, 1978, § 3, at 1, col. 1.

[33]The text that follows is based on an unsystematic but extensive reading of reported appellate litigation over the past two decades as part of editing materials for a contracts course. In addition, I have read the briefs, and often the record, in almost all of the cases from this period that we used in the materials. I want to thank Ms. Cynthia May of the Wisconsin Law Library for heroic efforts to obtain this material. We have followed the business press and collected accounts of the state of contract in commercial society. Finally, we have interviewed or written many lawyers about these cases.

[34]*See, e.g.*, Eastern Air Lines, Inc. v. McDonnell Douglas Corp., 532 F.2d 957 (5th Cir. 1976); Transatlantic Fin. Corp. v. United States, 363 F.2d 312 (D.C. Cir. 1966); B.P. Exploration Co. (Libya) Ltd. v. Hunt (No. 2), [1979] 1 W.L.R. 783.

[35]*See, e.g.*, Aluminum Co. of America v. Essex Group, Inc., 499 F. Supp. 53 (W.D. Pa. 1980); Missouri Pub. Serv. Co. v. Peabody Coal Co., 583 S.W.2d 721 (Mo. Ct. App. 1979), *cert. denied* 444 U.S. 865 (1979).

[36]*See* J. Stewart, The Partners 152-200 (1983); Macaulay, *Elegant Models, supra* note 5, at 515 for the story of the Westinghouse case.

found a plausible excuse in the Uniform Commercial Code[37] and announced that it would not perform. After elaborate rituals before the courts, the cases were settled. Westinghouse injured its reputation, but the alternative might have been the destruction of a major multinational corporation. Contract doctrine played a part in the resolution of this dispute, but it would be hard to call it the principal actor.

The decline of the American industrial economy produced other controversies about how to spread the costs throughout society. Employment security provides a good example. Unlike Europe,[38] the United States does not have laws regulating job security of most workers. We did not see such laws as needed as long as we had a growing economy and a strong ideology of competition and rewarding merit. Events have shaken our assumptions. It is not easy for even the upper part of the working class or middle class white collar workers to move to comparable employment today.[39] Many older middle managers have been fired to save their higher salaries, medical benefits, and pensions.[40] The women's movement has made sexual harassment salient.[41]

These developments plus the great reductions in the workforce have provoked atrocity stories that have come before the courts. The traditional American rule is that non-unionized employees of a private corporation could be fired for good reason, bad reason, or no reason unless they had enforceable employment contracts for a specified duration—and only a few highly valued employees had these.[42] Lawyers brought cases to court involving outrageous terminations of employees at will, and some judges responded.[43] At first, courts fashioned rather sweeping

[37]Westinghouse relied on U.C.C. § 2-615(a) (1978) which provides an excuse "if performance as agreed has been made impracticable by the occurrence of a contingency the nonoccurrence of which was a basic assumption on which the contract was made . . ."

[38]*See, e.g.*, Dickens, Hart, Jones & Weekes, *The British Experience Under a Statute Prohibiting Unfair Dismissal*, 37 Indus. and Lab. Rel. Rev. 497 (1984).

[39]*See* Drucker, *The Job as Property Right,* Wall St. J., Mar. 4, 1980, at 24, col. 4. ("For companies to be able to dismiss even the most senile and decrepit oldster, they will have to develop impersonal standards of performance and systematic personnel procedures for employes of all ages.")

[40]Greenberger, *Fired Employes in 40s Filing More Bias Suits,* Wall St. J., Oct. 8, 1981, at 31, col. 3.

[41]*See, e.g.,* Monge v. Beebe Rubber Co., 114 N.H. 130, 316 A.2d 549 (1974).

[42]*See, e.g.*, Comerford v. International Harvester Co., 235 Ala. 376, 178 So. 894(1938) (court held that worker who alleged he was fired because of his wife's refusal of his supervisor's sexual advances, failed to state a cause of action).

[43]*See, e.g.,* Petermann v. International Bhd. of Teamsters, 174 Cal. App. 2d 184, 344 P.2d 25 (1959) (court reversed the dismissal of a complaint where employee alleged he was fired because he refused to commit perjury before a legislative investigating committee); Fortune v. Nat'l Cash Register Co., 373 Mass. 96, 364 N.E.2d 1251 (1977) (a salesman who had worked twenty five years for the company was fired a day after he placed a customer order that would have entitled him to a large bonus); Monge v. Beebe Rubber Co., 114 N.H. 130, 316 A.2d 549 (1974) (assembly line night shift worker was told by her foreman that if she were "nice" to him he would promote her. She refused and then was denied overtime, ridiculed and ultimately fired).

doctrines that would have offered a great deal of employment security.[44] As American attitudes have shifted to the right, the courts have become concerned with going too far. Later cases have qualified what had seemed to be a growing trend.[45] Many writers say we need a statute, but most agree that those who would benefit from such a statute lack the power to promote one.[46]

Other cases have been provoked by the shift to new technologies that industry has mastered imperfectly. This has left a wide gap between expectations and what manufacturers have been able to deliver. Traditionally, American manufacturers of complex machines promised products that would produce certain results. They did their best while containing costs and keeping up production. Often the product sent was a first draft. Engineers from the seller and those from the buyer then would work something out by trial and error.[47]

In the computer age, the expectations created by manufacturers' promises have been unrealistic, and the "working out" approach has often failed.[48] This has led to litigation testing the contract drafting of elite lawyers.[49] Even experienced business people are tricked by a sales person's assurances that are contradicted by a lawyer-drafted standard form contract. Courts often enforce these standardized documents to aid deception and fraud[50] or to help large bureaucracies control their street-level personnel. It is fascinating to watch the doublethink when they explain these decisions on the basis of the victim's consent and choice. Usually a major question is whether a court will honor the various warranty disclaimers, remedy limitations, and other evasions of responsibility hidden in fine print. Some courts have seen these

---

[44]*See, e.g.,* Tameny v. Atlantic Richfield Co., 27 Cal. 3d 167, 164 Cal. Rptr. 839, 610 P.2d 1330 (1980) (where discharge violates a fundamental public policy, employee has a tort action); Cleary v. American Airlines, Inc., 111 Cal. App. 3d 443, 168 Cal. Rptr. 722 (1980) (there is an implied covenant of good faith and fair dealing in employment contracts, breach of which entitles employee to damages).

[45]*See, e.g.,* Pieree v. Ortho Pharmaceutical Corp., 84 N.J. 58, 417 A.2d 505 (1980); Brockmeyer v. Dun & Bradstreet, 113 Wis. 2d 561, 335 N.W.2d 834 (1983).

[46]*See* Greenan, *The Problems of Wrongful Termination,* 4 Cal. Law. 29 (Aug. 1984); Marrinan, *Employment At-Will: Pandora's Box May Have an Attractive Cover,* 7 Hamline L. Rev. 155, 197-99 (1984); Perritt, *Employee Dismissals: An Opportunity for Legal Simplification,* 35 Lab. L.J. 407, 412-13 (1984).

[47]*See, e.g.,* Fairchild Stratos Corp. v. Lear Siegler, Inc., 337 F.2d 785 (4th Cir. 1964); DeVito v. United States, 413 F.2d 1147 (Ct. Cl. 1969).

[48]*See, e.g.,* AMF, Inc. v. McDonald's Corp., 536 F.2d 1167 (7th Cir. 1976); Burroughs Corp. v. United States, 634 F.2d 516 (Ct. Cl. 1980).

[49]*See, e.g.,* Binks Mfg. Co. v. Nat'l Presto Industries, Inc., 709 F.2d 1109 (7th Cir. 1983); Chatlos Systems, Inc. v. Nat'l Cash Register Corp., 670 F.2d 1304 (3d Cir. 1982), *cert. denied,* 457 U.S. 1112 (1982); Wilson v. Marquette Elec., Inc., 630 F.2d 575 (8th Cir. 1980); Badger Bearing Co. v. Burroughs Corp., 444 F. Supp. 919, (E.D. Wis. 1977), *aff'd mem.,* 588 F.2d 838 (7th Cir. 1978).

[50]I think judges, just as most Americans, have conflicting views about deception. Fraud may be bad, but a sharp operator evokes a smile and admiration. Sometimes our judges confuse the loveable con man of fiction and film with a Fortune 500 company.

clauses as just part of the business game;[51] others have recognized that form contracts can be licenses for sales people to trick customers and evade responsibility when things go wrong.[52]

Another body of reported litigation involves those in dependent relationships such as dealerships and franchises trying to fight to defend their assumptions about continuing their business. All kinds of contract and tort doctrines have been mobilized, and these groups have organized to lobby statutes through the various state legislatures.[53] Dealers have won some notable victories. However, in recent years, bureaucratic rationality and flexibility in the face of changed marketing conditions have won out over the interests of the dependent.

While our court reports have registered a great deal of contracts litigation in recent years, all of these attempts to use contract law have revealed that the second part of my 1963 critique still has force. The legal system in operation simply fails to vindicate rights or offer much to those who seek redress from the courts. Often it offers only symbolic victories, probably producing great frustration. For example, as I have mentioned, we have enacted statutes granting rights to dealers who hold franchises to sell automobiles, gasoline, and the like. Members of the trade associations that worked to pass this legislation saw enactment as a great victory. Yet again and again the courts have read these statutes narrowly so that franchisors escape real harm.[54] The statutes may have had indirect impact. Franchisors may have modified the behavior of their agents to avoid atrocity cases that might prompt courts to interpret the new rights broadly, but this is only supposition.[55]

---

[51] *See, e.g.,* Earman Oil Co. v. Burroughs Corp., 625 F.2d 1291 (5th Cir. 1980); Kalil Bottling Co. v. Burroughs Corp., 127 Ariz. 278, 619 P.2d 1055 (Ariz. Ct. App. 1980).

[52] *See, e.g.,* Rochester Welding Supply Corp. v. Burroughs Corp., 78 A.D.2d 983, 433 N.Y.S.2d 888 (1980). The problem is discussed in Slawson, *The New Meaning of Contract: The Transformation of Contracts Law by Standard Forms,* 46 U. Pitt. L. Rev. 21 (1984).

[53] I have told this story in some detail in S. Macaulay, Law and the Balance of Power; The Automobile Manufacturers and Their Dealers (1966); Macaulay, *Law Schools and the World Outside Their Doors II: Some Notes on Two Recent Studies of the Chicago Bar*, 32 J. Legal Educ. 506, 536-40 (1982) [hereinafter cited as Macaulay, Law Schools]. *See also* Jordan, *Unconscionability at the Gas Station*, 62 Minn. L. Rev. 813 (1978).

[54] *See, e.g.,* Kealey Pharmacy & Home Care Serv., Inc. v. Walgreen Co., 539 F. Supp. 1357 (W.D. Wis. 1982), *aff'd,* 761 F.2d 345 (7th Cir. 1985).

[55] Franchisors have attacked franchise protection statutes, and this may indicate that the statutes have some effect. For example,

> A spokesman for a Madison pizza firm told a Senate committee ... that Wisconsin's Fair Dealership Law was inhibiting the company's expansion through franchising. Wayne Mosely, co-owner of Rocky Rococo Corp., said the law overrode specific behavior by a franchise, agreed to in a contract, so that a firm like his risked lawsuits if it didn't renew the contract under the same terms as the original. ...
>
> Marc A. Aprea, representing Mosely and the International Franchise Association, said the Legislature should "take steps to unshackle franchisors from this overregulation."

The Capital Times (Madison), Aug. 31, 1983, at 8, col. 1.

Usually, contract litigation becomes an elaborate, drawn out morality play affecting only back stage negotiations. Gottlieb points out *"[i]n sustained and inextricable relations a principal use of contracts is to provide a basis for renegotiations* once a defective performance occurs."[56] For example, many scholars have discussed *Aluminum Company of America v. Essex Group, Inc.*[57] In that case, increases in the price of fuel made a long-term contract very unprofitable for ALCOA, the supplier. The written contract contained a price escalator clause which failed to take into account great increases in energy costs. ALCOA stood to lose millions of dollars if a court enforced the contract as written. A federal trial judge rewrote the contract to produce a pricing arrangement that he thought fairly reflected the risks actually assumed by the parties. In light of all the declarations by American courts that they will not rewrite contracts to reflect the bargain the parties ought to have made, the opinion seems surprising. Perhaps, it symbolizes a very different role for courts.

However, the trial judge's decision never went into effect as the case was settled. The parties renegotiated their arrangement. During the oral argument on appeal, a federal appellate court managed to convey to the parties its doubts about the innovative decision that favored ALCOA. After a huge investment in lawyers, expert witnesses, court costs and the like, the reaction of the appellate court prompted ALCOA to offer a settlement to Essex Group that was too good to refuse.[58] What remains is an opinion by the district court for scholars to write about.[59] However, while most of these articles are excellent, most of the authors write as if they were unaware that the innovative, and perhaps offensive, judicial revision never was put into effect.[60] Many of these articles discuss judges imposing their views on the parties and rewriting contracts. That did not happen in the ALCOA case, and it probably would not happen in many cases even if *Aluminum Company of America v. Essex Group, Inc.* were recognized as the law everywhere. The District Judge's opinion and the uncertain result of the appeal changed the balance of bargaining power, but it did not impose a final result on the parties. The decision plus the appellate process worked as a form of coercive mediation. Faced with the situation,

---

[56]Gottlieb, *supra* note 11, at 572-73.

[57]499 F. Supp. 53 (W.D. Pa. 1980).

[58]The statement in the text is based on interviews with lawyers for the parties in the ALCOA case. *See also,* Wisconsin Contracts II Materials 925 (unpublished manuscript 1984).

[59]*See, e.g.*, Dawson, *Judicial Revision of Frustrated Contracts: The United States*, 64 B.U.L. Rev. 1 (1984); Dawson, *Judicial Revision of Frustrated Contracts: Germany*, 63 B.U.L. Rev. 1039 (1983); Speidel, *The New Spirit of Contract*, 2 J. Law & Com. 193 (1982); Harrison, *A Case for Loss Sharing*, 56 S. Cal. L. Rev. 573, 595 (1983); Speidel, *Court-Imposed Price Adjustments Under Long-Term Supply Contracts*, 76 Nw. U.L. Rev. 369 (1981); Trakman, *Winner Take Some: Loss Sharing and Commercial Impracticability*, 69 Minn. L. Rev. 471, 500-506 (1985); Comment, *Relief From Burdensome Long-Term Contracts: Commercial Impracticability, Frustration of Purpose, Mutual Mistake of Fact, and Equitable Adjustment*, 47 Mo. L. Rev. 79 (1982); Comment, *Equitable Reformation of Long-Term Contracts—The "New Spirit" of ALCOA*, 1982 Utah L. Rev. 985.

[60]Both Dawson and Speidel are well aware of the settlement. Most of what I know about it comes from following up what Dick Speidel told me about the case.

the parties worked out their own solution. The chance that a judge might rework a written contract after circumstances had changed also could affect bargaining situations. Perhaps this kind of coercion toward settlement is a good way to handle contracts that have gone on the rocks; perhaps it is a terrible way. Nevertheless, it is hard to evaluate a process without describing it accurately.

Other contracts disputes that provoke written opinions end in token settlements because almost always American contract law awards only money damages. However, a major reason that relational sanctions fail and contracts are breached is that the defaulting party is in or on the borders of bankruptcy.[61] As some lawyers put it, a judgment against a bankrupt plus 65 cents will buy a bus ride in Madison, Wisconsin (of course, 65 cents alone will do the same thing). The threat of bankruptcy often is a potent weapon in settlement negotiations; it is a form of strength through weakness.

IV. What Difference Does All This Make and To Whom?

What should we make of this gap between the academic model of contract law and the system as it works? At minimum, we need a complex model of contract law in operation if we wish to be descriptively accurate. Contract law operates at the margins of major systems of private government through institutionalized social structures and less formal social fields. We must establish rather than assume the actual influence of this doctrine. Contract law as discussed by scholars frequently is but a rhetorical ploy in a much larger struggle. Lawyers may use its vocabulary in the process of dealing with a dispute. Often, however, the real issue between the parties is transformed to fit a law school model far removed from the transaction. As such, classic doctrine may affect negotiations, but not in the way assumed by most scholars. Perhaps lawyers skilled in playing the contract game do better for their clients, but defenders of orthodoxy must prove this. Perhaps bargaining in the shadow of the law[62] implements those values explicit or implicit in contract doctrine to some degree. This cannot be assumed but must be established by investigation.

The contract process in action seldom is a neutral application of abstract rationality. The party with the best argument as judged by a contracts professor will not necessarily win the case. An opponent with a plausible argument, little need to settle, and resources to play the lawyering game is unlikely to bow to arguments favored by law professors at elite schools. Indeed, all an attorney may need are arguments that seem more or less plausible to judges and other lawyers. Even those disliked by scholars such as "unilateral contract" and "the meeting of the minds" often will do in the actual dispute resolution process.

[61]Macaulay, *Elegant Models, supra* note 5, at 512-13.

[62]*See* Mnookin and Kornhauser, *Bargaining in the Shadow of the Law: The Case of Divorce*, 88 Yale L.J. 950 (1979).

We cannot be sure what functions orthodox contract doctrine serves. However, what we know so far suggests that contract doctrine incorporates major conflicting strands of political philosophy. It does not stand apart from the cross currents of political debate over time. At a particular time, one conception is emphasized. Later, as times change, another view takes its turn. In areas such as the parol evidence rule, the Statute of Frauds and misrepresentation, we find decisions in a single state bouncing from one position to the other. This makes contract law contradictory.[63]

At the most basic level, contract law promises to remedy breaches of contract and provide security of expectations. It does this only indirectly and imperfectly. It helps reassure us about the stability of an ever changing and frightening world. It deters breach by those unaware that counterrules neatly match most contract rules or that most contract rules are qualitative and open-ended. Much of law operates under the Wizard of Oz principle of jurisprudence—you will recall that the Great Oz was a magnificient and wonderful wizard until Dorothy's dog knocked over the screen so all could see that the Wizard was a charlatan.

Nonetheless, contract law curbs power to some degree. Those who can command may not want to appear arbitrary and all powerful. It is good public relations to channel their actions into the forms of contract to gain the symbolism of bargain and free choice. Even this modest effort offers a degree of leverage for limiting the exercise of power. Scholarly notions of free contract are a frail defense against those with power seeking to achieve illegitimate ends. Nonetheless, there are few other defenses short of revolution.[64]

Perhaps classic contracts scholarship can safely ignore the way the contract system works. This scholarship may be irrelevant to most of practice, and so it does not matter how articles are written. However, this scholarship has influence in some instances, and this leaves us with a puzzle. In the face of many studies challenging its descriptive accuracy, many scholars and theorists continue to paint a simple instrumental picture. What purposes are being served by all this traditional scholarly effort? Perhaps it is a form of denial. The formal contract system claims to be neutral and autonomous and to rest on simple rationality. A descriptively accurate model of the process challenges these assumptions. We must remember that long-term continuing relations are not always nice situations for those short of power. Instead of free individuals making informed choices, many are dependent and must choose between unpleasant options. Courts seldom come close to putting aggrieved parties in the position they would have been had the contract been performed. Cases are often won by lawyer ploys and the strategic and tactical advantages flowing from greater wealth. Instead of vindicating rights, our legal system offers deals. As a result, often one party feels cheated while the other thinks he got away with something.

---

[63] *See* Macaulay, *The Duty to Read, supra* note 17.

[64] *See* Macaulay, *Law and the Behavioral Sciences: Is There Any There There?*, 6 Law & Pol'y 149, 176-7 (1984) [hereinafter cited as Macaulay, *Is There any There There?*].

At least in the United States, we want to believe that a lawyer, armed only with reason, can champion the weak and overcome the powerful. This myth drew many of us to law school, and it is hard to give up. A descriptive model reduces many lawyers to little more than captive intellectuals serving those who control significant resources in society. In short, classical contracts scholarship allows us to maintain a comforting image of what it is that typical lawyers do. A system of individual rights prompts higher thought. Descriptive accuracy requires us to confront the dark side of the society and its legal system. Many find it easier to ignore reality than to cope with it. In Fitzpatrick's words:

> [L]aw sets and maintains an autonomy for opposing social forms, keeping them apart from itself and purporting to exercise an overall control. Yet this control is merely occasional and marginal. In such instances, the balance between autonomy and control is most often struck by law's intervention being comprehensive in terms but limited in operation. ... In the limited nature of its involvement with other social forms, law accepts the integrity of that which it controls.... Indeed, the (common) law is not "a brooding omnipresence in the sky," but law's operatives have to view it so because of the dangers of confronting law's terrestrial connections. Law cannot bear very much reality.[65]

Some academics also find fashioning theories useful to the powerful to be rewarding both financially and in terms of status in academic circles. Consulting for those who can pay the fees has become a significant part of many legal scholars' jobs. Instead of gaining status by publication of research, some seek reputation in terms of the fame of the corporations that hire them as consultants. Consulting scholars may be able to affect the practices of those hiring them for the better. Consulting scholars may learn something of how things are done. However, it is hard to avoid championing the position of the interest that has bought its professor. Furthermore, we can ask why so little of this consulting has prompted scholarly writing about the way things are done in executive suits. Perhaps descriptively accurate theories confronting the dark side of our legal system would interfere with the opportunities to consult. Perhaps the consulting takes so much time that these professors forget to do their job.[66]

Perhaps many academics ignore the functioning legal system for a much simpler reason. Looking at it makes things messy. As Betty Mensch notes:

---

[65]Fitzpatrick, *Law and Societies,* 22 Osgoode Hall L.J. 115, 126-27 (1984).

[66]Hacker makes a strong attack on consulting by law professors:

> It is a law school tradition that students do not approach professors. ... While this may encourage self-reliance, it also means the professors only have to show up several hours a week. A few do some research; but many don't do even that. The number of law professors with national reputations is meager. A lot spend their spare time in part-time practice, augmenting their already generous salaries, which are second only to the medical faculty on most university payrolls.

Hacker, *The Shame of Professional Schools: How Not to Educate an Elite,* Harpers, Oct. 1981, at 22, 27. While his point has merit, I think it overstated. But I may not know how much consulting takes place nor its influence on positions taken in class and in publications.

> Viewed in retrospect, Williston's majestic doctrinal structure may have been silly, but ... appeals to reasonableness and justice appear sloppy and formless by comparison. Williston's structure was, at least, a real structure, however misguided. Perhaps much Willistonian dogma survives simply because it provides a challenging intellectual game to learn and teach in law school—more fun than the close attention to commercial detail required by thorough-going realism.[67]

V. A Not Totally Pessimistic Conclusion

Having said all this, I must note that I still teach contracts to beginning law students.[68] (Of course, I am not sure that many American teachers would accept that what I teach is true contracts material.) I try to blend study of rhetoric and doctrine with a portrait of the system in operation. There are at least two reasons for doing this. One is to train lawyers better. Students must understand a game to learn to play it well. The other is that the approach raises major questions about law and society. Put most simply, why does American society promise so much more than it delivers? Or, looking at the situation another way, what functions does the system as it actually operates serve and for whom?

However, I try to teach a not entirely negative lesson and guard against cynicism. There is enough truth in the image of law as rationality above politics and power so that a few lawyers representing a few clients can make their society a little less hostile place. I think visions of a better future are important, but in the here and now lawyers can make a contribution to smoothing rough edges from the society. I would rather teach my students some ideal of law than leave the impression that practice can be no more than just selling advocacy to the highest bidder.

My colleague, Marc Galanter, says that if we demystify the nature of dispute processing and paint an empirically accurate picture, we must face the challenge of:

> devising new ways of measuring the performance of legal institutions and new ways of redesigning those institutions to facilitate interchange with a more alert public. To get there from here, we need a new generation of research about what law means in people's lives; what gives it its hold, its influence, its attraction; why it repels or frightens; whether it is dependent upon illusions about its character. . . .[69]

This is an optimistic statement. Those who see law as but one of many cloaks for power and privilege may object. We can expect them to argue that an accurate view of law in operation would violate so many legitimating assumptions that a new normative justification would be impossible. Bargaining and negotiation are not examples of disinterested application of apolitical norms—they necessarily take into account all sources of power. The nice guys do not always win. Indeed, they may

---

[67] Mensch, *Freedom of Contract as Ideology*, 33 Stan. L. Rev. 753, 769 (1981).

[68] *See* Macaulay, *Law Schools, supra* note 53.

[69] Galanter, *Knowledge Transcends Pessimism About the Law,* Legal Times, Sept. 24, 1984, at 6, col. 1.

have to be content with token settlements. We can ask whether citizens in modem welfare states can face the nature of their legal system? Do they need to believe in a rule of law? In absolute rights and wrongs? In a wholly autonomous legal system? Can they accept both the virtues and costs of bargaining in the shadow of the law?

Perhaps citizens need an idealized picture of their legal system. Perhaps it is what most of us want to believe. However, before we discard the possibility of working toward new rationalizations for modem legal systems as they operate, we must remember that the public is somewhat informed, often cynically aware of the true nature of law in action. Indeed, the citizens' recognition that the legal system's claims are belied by its day-to-day performance may produce that cynical awareness. Understanding the system as it is might reduce some of the cynicism. Perhaps, however, attempts to justify law as delivered might force us to consider a number of reforms which some would see as threatening to their position and privileges. If awareness provokes debate, it would be healthy.

Perhaps the only people fooled by classic images of law are law professors and social theorists misled by legal scholars.[70] On the other hand, perhaps a few professors are playing a cynical game. Scholars can gain grants and support by fashioning their work to serve the interests of those who provide pleasant lives for academics. Most, however, are just more comfortable with a traditional structure that provides focus and coherence rather than an indeterminate empirical picture, whatever its accuracy.

The challenge is to find a way to avoid cynicism, recognize the values of classic views of law, and rationalize a dispute processing system that does not turn on litigation and doctrine. All of this must be done without becoming a pet intellectual for those who can pay. Perhaps it would be easier to square the circle or turn lead into gold than bring this off. Nonetheless, this is the challenge of an empirical perspective on law.[71]

[70]*See* Sehlegel, *Searching for Archimedes—Legal Education, Legal Scholarship, and Liberal Ideology*, 34 J. Legal Educ. 103 (1984); Sehlegel, *Langdell's Legacy Or, The Case of the Empty Envelope*, 36 Stan. L. Rev. 1517, 1532 (1984) ("The legal academic . . . is committed to scholarship dominated by the notion of law as rule and yet at the same time such scholarship is both a largely completed task and an intellectual anachronism").

[71]*Compare* Macaulay, *Is There Any There There?*, *supra* note 64.

The Real and the Paper Deal: Empirical Pictures of Relationships, Complexity and the Urge for Transparent Simple Rules

Stewart Macaulay

Assume that contract law matters, at least in some subset of all the situations where people consider making or do make contracts. Also assume that contract law should rest to a large extent on choice or responsibility for misleading others about one's choices. Making these assumptions, we must be concerned with how the legal system deals with the expectations of the parties. One approach is formal. Judges can limit themselves to dealing with only the formal expressions of the parties—the paper deal. They need ask only whether the parties signed or accepted a document, and if they did, what is the 'plain meaning' of the words they used. Sometimes, writings labeled 'contract' do capture many if not most of the expectations of those who sign them.

Often, however, the paper deal will not reflect the real deal: a writing can be inconsistent with the actual expectations of the parties. Courts frequently have sought to protect such actual expectations despite the presence of a writing that does not mention them or even one that is inconsistent with them. However, establishing real expectations often is very difficult. Courts face what Richard

This article was original published in Modern Law Review 66 (2003), 44–79. Reprinted with permission.

Malcolm Pitman Sharp Hilldale Professor, Theodore W. Brazeau Bascom Professor of Law, The University of Wisconsin Law School. I have discussed the issues considered in this article with my Wisconsin colleagues, John Kidwell and William Whitford, and I have learned much from them. David Campbell commented on a draft of this article, and it is much better as a result. All mistakes are mine; I did not take all the good advice offered. An earlier draft of this paper was presented at a seminar, 'Implicit Dimensions of Contracts', held at the LSE on 26 November 2001 and funded by the MLR Annual Seminar Competition.

S. Macaulay (✉)
University of Wisconsin Law School, Madison, WI, USA
e-mail: smacaula@wisc.edu

D. Campbell (ed.), *Stewart Macaulay: Selected Works*, Law and Philosophy Library 133, https://doi.org/10.1007/978-3-030-33930-2_17

Danzig has called 'the capability problem.'[1] Some expectations, for example, are only tacit assumptions—what I would have said if I had thought about a question that I did not think about. Even if the parties did have real expectations that they did not express in their written document, we must worry that today's testimony about them will be self-serving and fabricated to make the case come out the right way. Also, proving the real deal often will be very costly. The parties must convey a commercial context to a judge or to jurors. They may come to the task with little, if any, knowledge of the part of the business world in question. Experts can inform them, but experts are not free.

If we want our courts to carry out the expectations of the parties to contracts, both those that they express in writing and those that are left unrecorded or even unspoken, we must accept a contract law that rests on standards rather than on clear, quantitative rules. Contract law then will talk of 'good faith', 'duties of cooperation', or 'within limits set by commercial reasonableness.'[2] Others have written much about what standards are most appropriate.[3]

However, there are objections to writing contract law in the qualitative fashion that seems necessary that are so well known that we can call them classic. Furthermore, there are also classic responses to these objections.[4] In this paper I will ask whether we can do more than just reprise these old songs and hear one group of scholars, judges and lawyers sing one song while another group whistles the other. We can clarify our choices by examining each from a law and society perspective—that is, by asking how the law in action appears from the point of view of business people and their lawyers. Moreover, we can gain a little ground in at least one limited subset of contract cases if we focus on judges in such disputes serving as agents of settlement. With all of its flaws, such coerced cooperation may be the least bad solution in many situations.

I will review briefly some of the reasons that the paper deal often does not reflect the real deal or the implicit dimension of contract. I will consider the somewhat chaotic responses American courts have given to the problem. I will look at what

---

[1]R. Danzig, *The Capability Problem in Contract Law* (Mineola, NY: Foundation Press Inc., 1978).

[2]See, e.g., Uniform Commercial Code §2-311(1): 'An agreement for sale which is otherwise sufficiently definite ... to be a contract is not made invalid by the fact that it leaves particulars of performance to be specified by one of the parties. Any such specification must be made in good faith and within the limits set by commercial reasonableness.'

[3]D. Campbell, 'Reflexivity and Welfarism in the Modern Law of Contract' (2000) 20 *Oxford Journal of Legal Studies* 477, 497, notes that much American writing on contracts, except that of Ian Macneil, criticises classical contract law but fails to set out a rival theory. I have said: 'people should not attempt to write about contracts until they have studied Macneil.' S. Macaulay, 'Relational Contracts Floating on a Sea of Custom? Thoughts About the Ideas of Ian Macneil and Lisa Bernstein' (2000) 94 *Northwestern University Law Review* 775, 776. Nonetheless, I am skeptical about whether anyone can create a complete rival theory applicable to all kinds of contracts without a good deal of oversimplification. I also doubt that any such grand rival theory could be sold to the judges and lawyers who would have to put it into practice. See J. M. Feinman, 'Relational Contract Theory in Context' (2000) 94 *Northwestern University Law Review* 737. I would be pleased to be proven wrong. My contribution, if any, will be only to look at proposals and arguments advocating positions and to ask whether they seem compatible with business practices about which I know something. Pointing out over generalisations and questionable assumptions is still valuable work.

[4]The best discussion of these classic pro and con arguments is D. Kennedy, 'Form and Substance in Private Law Adjudication' (1976) 89 *Harvard Law Review* 1685.

relational contract theory suggests courts should do and what a concern about the rule of law offers. My conclusion is not startling: we cannot have our cake and eat it too. There are costs and benefits flowing from focusing on the paper deal and from focusing on the real deal. The twentieth century history of American contract law and scholarship reflects cycles of privileging one judgment about those costs and benefits and then rejecting it and adopting another. Finally, I will suggest that in a limited subset of all contract cases, we should be content with almost any approach that leads to settlements that give expression, more or less, to relational norms and values.

The Gap Between the Real Deal and the Paper Deal

Things are easier for some parties and courts if the legal system focuses entirely on any written document that the parties have signed or accepted. If legal agencies do this consistently, corporate lawyers, for example, need worry less about what their client's sales people say or do. However, this approach requires courts to close their eyes to real expectations resting in the implicit dimensions of contract and significant reliance on them. Contracts are always more than the contract document. We have long known the many reasons for this: Words do not have a fixed meaning that every speaker of the language will translate the same way. We create the meaning of written language by bringing to the words some measure of context, background assumptions, our experiences, and, too often, our bias, ignorance and stupidities.[5]

Also, it is very hard to bring the future to the present and provide that X will happen if event Y takes place.[6] Our ability to predict the future is limited, and even careful business people often leave gaps in written contracts. The world changes and surprises us: Wars break out in places where we do not expect them; or our contract may have dealt with a war but left open what happens when the indirect effect of a major terrorist attack makes performance much more costly; OPEC drives up energy

[5]See Professor Linzer's discussion of *Shore v Motorola*, in P. Linzer, 'Rough Justice: A Theory of Restitution and Reliance, Contracts and Torts' (2001) *Wisconsin Law Review* 695, 764–772. The price of the position I take in this article is that I have to accept that sometimes judges will use their discretion to reach results that I think are outrageous. *Shore v Motorola* was for me an unhappy example.

[6]By the 'real deal' I mean both those actual expectations that exist in and out of a written contract and the generalised expectation that a trading partner will behave reasonably in solving problems as they arise. My experience talking with business people suggests that reading written contracts clauses to one another seldom would be seen as a reasonable way to solve problems. There may be situations where applying the letter of a written document would be a reasonable way to cope with a contract problem, but I suspect that these situations are a very limited group of all contract problems. Also, there are situations where parties do not expect the other to act reasonably for the mutual benefit of the relationship. Again, I would expect this to be a very limited group of cases because some trust is needed before most people will make contracts.

costs unexpectedly; new technologies, often involving computers, change things so that an older contract no longer makes sense.

Even when we can foresee that it is possible that something might happen, there are limits on the time that we can or should spend on trying to provide for all contingencies in our contracts. In most instances, it would not pay to hire enough people with the skill needed to review what is printed in fine print on the back of various sellers' forms such as proposals, acknowledgment of orders and invoices. A firm that is filling thousands of purchase orders every week could not afford to take the time to negotiate all the details of every transaction. Moreover, as Tom Palay notes: 'looking beyond the [written] contract is important because parties who have, or anticipate, strong relational ties with their contracting opposites are not particularly worried about initial terms of agreement.'[7] In many situations careful contract negotiation signals distrust when the situation calls for a business marriage.

Furthermore, we must remember that business corporations are collections of people and their activities are seldom tightly coordinated. Those who negotiate the deal often are not the people who draft the written document recording it. Still others must perform the contract. This opens the possibility that, for example, a firm's lawyers may have different assumptions and expectations than its purchasing agents, sales people, and engineers.

Strategy may be involved too. If I want a clause that says if event X takes place, then consequence Y will follow, you may demand something in exchange that I do not want to give you. When I anticipate this, it may be better to avoid raising the issue in negotiations and hope that the matter can be resolved if event X ever takes place.

Lawyers deal with many of these problems by fabricating detailed standard form contracts that typically are written in legal or technical language that 'is not meant to be read, still less to be understood.'[8] The written document, however, may be seen by purchasing agents, sales personnel and engineers as a formality created only to please the whims of the lawyers. It is also possible that parties will write or accept a flat, unqualified contract clause but assume that there are exceptions or qualifications that are not worth the effort to spell out in advance. In short, there are many reasons that the paper deal will fail to capture the real deal. As a matter of fact, there is a 'text between the lines.'

The performance of contractual obligations often will be prolonged in time and require the active cooperation of both parties. Situations may change during the time that one or both parties are attempting to perform or it may become clear that the written language is an inadequate guide to performance. While parties can modify their written contract, often they do not engage in an explicit renegotiation. Rather, they make adjustments as they attempt to cope with the demands of the original agreement and the new situation. Sometimes we can say that when the parties signed

---

[7]T. M. Palay, 'A Contract Does Not a Contract Make' (1985) *Wisconsin Law Review* 561, 562.

[8]The phrase is Lord Justice Devlin's. See *McCutcheon v David Mac Brayne, Inc* [1964] 1 WLR 125.

a written agreement, they intended their contract to be adjusted in light of continually changing circumstances. In some kinds of contracts, cancellation for convenience or broad impossibility/frustration clauses are common. Sometimes the written contract provides that if event X happens, 'the contract shall be equitably adjusted.' Often, however, we can suspect that those who signed the written document never thought about the possibility of changes beyond a general tacit assumption that both sides would proceed in good faith.

American Law: Rule and Counter-Rule, Core and Periphery

The Law: Something Less Than Certainty and Perfect Predictability

How does or should contract law respond to any gap between the paper deal and the real deal? Let me briefly sketch some of the approaches taken by American courts or advocated by American writers.[9] I offer American law and writing only as an example which I know. I do not presume that they should be a model for the rest of the world.

People can respond to a problem by denying that it exists. We could point to many judicial opinions that talk about the plain meaning of a written contract without ever considering how they know that this is what the parties meant. This is the strongest version of the parol evidence rule.[10] There is an old American expression that tells us that 'if it looks like a duck, waddles like a duck and quacks like a duck, it is a duck!' Sometimes an objective theory of contracts gives us, essentially, the duck test. If I signed a writing, you are entitled to rely on my agreement to the plain meaning of the words written, typed or printed. Sometimes this position is reinforced by a tort-like duty to read and understand which can transform contract law's claim to rest on choice into pure magic. Also, there is an assumption, often unstated, that all the parties' rights and duties must be traced back to the specific provisions of their written agreement. Courts say that they will not make a contract for the parties. However, when judges want to impose contractual liability, implied conditions and strange readings of contract language rationalize the enforcement of what judges think parties ought to have done. Sometimes, of course, implied conditions and strange readings rationalize a judge's refusal to enforce the bargain that the parties made.

[9]See J. M. Feinman, 'The Significance of Contract Theory' (1990) 58 *Cincinnati Law Review* 1283.

[10]See J. D. Calamari and J. M. Perillo, 'A Plea for a Uniform Parol Evidence Rule and Principles of Contract Interpretation' (1967) 42 *Indiana Law Journal* 333; W. C. Whitford, 'The Role of the Jury (and the Fact/Law Distinction) in the Interpretation of Written Contracts' (2001) *Wisconsin Law Review* 931.

Lawrence Friedman pointed out that American contract law in the late Nineteenth and early Twentieth Centuries was grounded in abstraction; it offered rules assumed to be applicable whether the parties were rich or poor and without regard to the subject matter of the transaction. The rules purported to be unchanging over time. However, when faced with the demands of a developing economy, American courts used tools such as waiver and estoppel and construction of language to bend specific rules into conforming with standards of higher generality.[11] Often careful study would reveal that contract law featured a rule opposed by a counter rule with no principled way of knowing when one or the other would apply. American law, for example, tells us that it is not duress to threaten to do what you have a legal right to do.[12] Yet a wrongful although not illegal threat can be duress.[13] These two statements of the law do not live together happily.

The legal realists had a fine time dropping bombs on ideas about plain meaning and abstraction. The more you know about language, the less comfortable you are with ideas that any collection of words has but one complete and clear meaning apart from context. Recognising this, Professor Corbin would reduce doctrines such as the parol evidence rule to a possibility that seldom would apply. Parol evidence is to be excluded when the parties intended their writing to be the final expression of their agreement. Corbin, however, argued that such an intention about finality was a fact to be proved by any relevant evidence that was credible. He thought that judges should not blind themselves to everything but the text of a writing. Justice Roger Traynor of the Supreme Court of California wrote this form of realism into the law of his state, at least for a time.[14] A California judge was not to look for the plain meaning. He or she could look to evidence of intention other than the text of a written contract even when the words did not seem to be ambiguous.

To a great extent, legal realism was written into American law when Professor Karl Llewellyn became the Reporter for Article 2 of our Uniform Commercial Code. Article 2 became the law in almost all American states by 1965. In Llewellyn's Code, much turns on the concept of 'agreement.' Section 1–201(3) defines this concept as 'the bargain of the parties in fact as found in their language or by implication from other circumstances ....' The phrase 'bargain of the parties in fact' would seem to call for enforcing the real deal rather than holding people to any asserted plain meaning of the documents which they signed or accepted. The Code also attempts to cut back the idea that contracts must be defined with

[11]L. M. Friedman, *Contract Law in America: a Social and Economic Case Study* (Madison, WI: Univ Wisconsin Press, 1965).

[12]See e.g., *Wurtz v Fleischman* 97 Wis.2d 100, 293 N.W.2d 155 (1980).

[13]Restatement (2d) Contracts §176(2)(c) tells us that a threat is 'improper if the resulting exchange is not on fair terms, and ... what is threatened is otherwise a use of a power for illegitimate ends.' See C. Dalton, 'An Essay in the Deconstruction of Contract Doctrine' (1985) 94 *Yale Law Journal* 997, 1032–36, for a criticism of this approach. Dalton sees the Restatement as evading the real but difficult questions about what are 'illegitimate ends' for the use of power.

[14]See e.g., *Masterson v Sine 68* Cal.2d 222, 436 P.2d 561 (1968); *Pacific Gas & Elect Co v GW Thomas Drayage & Rigging* Co 69 Cal.2d 33, 442 P.2d 641 (1968).

certainty.[15] Llewellyn celebrated what he called the grand style of common law judging.[16] Judges working in the grand style did not apply rules mindlessly. Rather, drawing on their situation sense, rules served only as guides to judgment.[17]

However, the Code is not pure Llewellyn but a compromise between the legal realism of the academics who produced the first drafts and the traditional views of the commercial lawyers who forced revisions.[18] Llewellyn was not free to innovate at will. He had to obtain the blessing of the American Law Institute and the National Conference of Commissions on Uniform State Law. Moreover, the Code had to be passed by state legislatures, most of which had many members who were lawyers trained in the conventional wisdom. Article 2 has, for example, a parol evidence rule and a Statute of Frauds. In the hands of a judge holding traditional views, there are ways to read the Code that can serve as a road back to the familiar territory of the common law of contracts. In making this move, it helps to ignore the definitional sections of the statute. As a result, Article 2 often preserves aspects of the classic common law approaches but seeks to change the common law enough to deal with modern conditions. It can be considered an example of 'neoclassical contract.'[19] In

---

[15]Section 2–204(1) says '[a] contract for sale of goods may be made in any manner sufficient to show agreement, including conduct by both parties which recognises the existence of a contract.' We can have an enforceable contract although the price is uncertain, quantity is defined only as 'requirements,' and nothing is said about the date for performance.

[16]See K. N. Llewellyn, *The Common Law Tradition: Deciding Appeals* (Boston, MA: Little, Brown and Co., 1960) 64–72; W. Twining, *Karl Llewellyn and the Realist Movement* (Norman, OK: Univ Oklahoma Press, 1973) 210–245.

[17]For example, Section 1–102(1), Official Comment 1, says: 'The Act should be construed in accordance with its underlying purposes and policies. The text of each section should be read in the light of the purpose and policy of the rule or principle in question, as also of the Act as a whole, and the application of the language should be construed narrowly or broadly, as the case maybe, in conformity with the purposes and policies involved.' Section 1-205, Official Comment 1, says: 'The measure and background for interpretation are set by the commercial context, which may explain and supplement even the language of a formal or final writing.'

[18]See A. R. Kamp, 'Downtown Code: A History of the Uniform Commercial Code 1949–1954' (2001) 49 *Buffalo Law Review* 359('[T]he present Code is a product of two conflicting visions of what commercial law should be - one, a regulatory system based on self-regulation by the trade, judicial supervision according to commercial norms, and legislative dictate, as opposed to one based on an autonomous business world operating under a regime of unregulated contract.') *Ibid* 361. 'Llewellyn's views and his original program for the Code grew out of the matrix of the collectivist mentality of the 1930s ... Llewellyn was once part of an academic avant guard, a supporter of FDR [President Roosevelt] in his court-packing plan, a folk dancer, a student of Boas' anthropology, part of a 1930s radical, collectivist milieu.' *Ibid* 392.) See also, A. R. Kamp, 'Between-The-Wars Social Thought: Karl Llewellyn, Legal Realism, and the Uniform Commercial Code in Contex' (1995) 59 *Albany Law Review* 325; A. R. Kamp, 'Uptown Act: A History of the Uniform Commercial Code: 1940–1949' (1998) 51 *SMU Law Review* 275; A. R. Kamp, 'Increasing Complexity in Commercial Law: The Failure of the Uniform Commercial Code' (1991) 10 *Corporate Counsel Review* 59.

[19]In the right hands, however, Article 2 offers an opportunity for an application of a relational theory of contract to specific problems. See I. R. Macneil, 'Restatement (2d) of Contracts and Presentation' (1974) 60 *Virginia Law Review* 589; Richard E. Speidel, 'Article 2 and Relational Sales Contracts' (1993) 26 *Loyola of Los Angeles Law Review* 789.

short, many of the tools needed to seek the implicit dimensions of contract are in Article 2, but even judges who read statutes carefully do not have to use these tools.[20]

Scholarly Reaction: Modern Challenges to Code Methods

In the last decade or two, some American scholars have questioned the approach of Article 2 of the Uniform Commercial Code as a means of achieving its announced ends. It was, they say, sold as a uniform law, but it fails to produce uniform results. In its contextual approach, every case is different. Llewellyn had defended his open textured qualitative provisions in Article 2 by saying that the common law method would, over time, provide enough certainty. Courts would give meaning to concepts such as 'unconscionability' or 'commercial reasonableness' by deciding a series of cases involving specific facts. Patterns would emerge and judges and scholars would be able to discern working rules. Moreover, Llewellyn thought that judges could be informed of the usages of trade in order to give content to Article 2's frequent reference to reasonable commercial behaviour.

Many have challenged Llewellyn's justifications for the way that Article 2 of the UCC is drafted. Here I will look at two writers whose work I admire, Dean Robert Scott and Professor Lisa Bernstein. Both do empirical work, and both are sensitive to making theories about contract accord with business practice. Dean Scott has questioned whether more than 30 years experience with the Code has done much to make its qualitative standards clear to lawyers. He has studied American courts dealing with these general norms.[21] Scott accepts that most contractual transactions are relational. However, he argues 'the state's primary substantive role in uniformly enforcing commercial contracts is to regulate incomplete contracts efficiently.'[22] This involves two often inconsistent tasks: Courts must 'correctly (or uniformly)

[20]See A. H. Kastely, 'Stock Equipment for the Bargain in Fact: Trade Usage, "Express Terms," and Consistency Under Section 1-205 of the Uniform Commercial Code' (1986) 64 *North Carolina Law Review* 777.

[21]R. E. Scott, 'Rethinking the Uniformity Norm in Commercial Law: A Comparative Analysis of Common Law and Code Methodologies' in J. S. Kraus and S. D. Walt (eds) *The Jurisprudential Foundations of Corporate and Commercial Law* (Cambridge: Cambridge University Press, 2000) 149, 166 n. 68; R. E. Scott, 'The Case for Formalism in Relational Contract' (2000) 94 *Northwestern University Law Review* 847. See also, R. E. Scott, 'Conflict and Cooperation in Long-Term Contracts' (1987) 75 *California Law Review* 2005; R. E. Scott, 'A Relational Theory of Default Rules for Commercial Contracts' (1990) 19 *Journal of Legal Studies* 597. Compare O. Ben-Shahar, 'The Tentative Case Against Flexibility in Commercial Law' (1999) 66 *University of Chicago Law Review* 781. For an earlier, and very well done, presentation of the arguments against flexibility in the Code, see A. I. Rosett, 'Contract Performance: Promises, Conditions and the Obligation to Communicate' (1975) 22 *UCLA Law Review* 1083.

[22]R. E. Scott, 'The Uniformity Norm in Commercial Law: A Comparative Analysis of Common Law and Code Methodologies' *ibid* 149, 150.

interpret ... the meaning of the contract terms chosen by the parties to allocate contract risk.' They also must create 'broadly suitable default rules and/or ... [label] widely used contract terms and clauses with standard meanings.' He argues that uniformity requires not just that the same substantive standards be adopted by all American states. For all of the advantages of uniformity, courts in all states must apply those standards in predictable ways. He finds that Article 2 of the Uniform Commercial Code fails to give reliable and predictable interpretations of contractual text. Llewellyn's theory about courts developing consistent readings of and reactions to contract terms incrementally over time has not proved accurate. Dean Scott asserts:

> While the Code was explicitly designed to incorporate evolving norms into an ever-growing set of legally defined default rules, incorporation as such has simply not occurred. To be sure, courts have interpreted contracts in which context evidence has been evaluated together with the written terms of the contract. ... But while such judicial decisions affirm the institutional bias toward contextualizing contract, the fact-specific nature of the contract dispute leaves, in virtually every case, little opportunity for subsequent incorporation as tailored defaults. ... A systematic examination of the litigated cases interpreting the 'reasonableness' standards of Article 2 reveals that courts have consistently interpreted these statutory instructions not as inductive directions to incorporate commercial norms and prototypes but rather as invitations to make deductive speculations according to "Code policy" or other noncontextual criteria.[23]

Scott's conclusions are not surprising. Insofar as courts try to apply general relational norms to particular transactions, they are seeking goals other than uniformity of application. Scott's solution to the uniformity problem is a return to formalism, a plain-meaning approach to interpretation and a strict parol evidence rule. Often, for reasons that I have indicated, this will defend written text at the cost of defeating actual expectations and the implicit dimensions of contract. To a great extent, any differences between my judgments and those of Professor Scott turn on how much we value predictable results when there are disputes. He seems ready to trade having courts seek the assumptions of the parties for something approaching certainty. He says:

> [T]he efficient regulation of contract does not require that every relational norm be judicialized or that the legal mechanism operates efficiently viewed on its own terms, but rather that it operates efficiently in concern with social norms of trust, reciprocity, and conditional cooperation that also regulate relational contracts. Under the formalist approach, these norms would not be legally enforceable contract terms. ...but they nevertheless would be enforced by social sanctions that would effectively constrain the parties' incentives to exploit changed circumstances strategically.[24]

---

[23]Scott, 'Rethinking the Uniformity Norm in Commercial Law', *ibid* 164.

[24]R. E. Scott, 'The Case for Formalism in Relational Contract' (2000) 94 *Northwestern University Law Review* 847, 861. See, also, R. E. Scott, 'Comment' (2002) 52 *Hastings Law Journal* 700: '[T]here are powerful normative forces in relational contracts and ... they regulate a great deal of the relationship ... and ... therefore legal default rules serve a minor but very important purpose as kind of a nuclear umbrella. ... [T]here's a difference between Contract as an institution, which is synthetic and relational, and Contract Law which is simple, formal, classical ... We have a set of rules for umbrella legal enforcement, and then a set of informal social norms that are better if not judicialised.'

I, on the other hand, am content with a contract law where lawyers can make probabilistic judgments about likely outcomes if, at the same time, we can enforce duties of cooperation and good faith. I would be very uncomfortable with a contract law that attempted to apply a plain meaning rule and a strict parol evidence rule to every situation.[25] In a great many cases, this would ignore actual expectations and allow the lawyers for the side that got to do the drafting to create a license for its sales people to lie and mislead. I would be more comfortable with Dean Scott's approach if it were limited to cases where bargainers were represented by lawyers and the language of the writing was subject to negotiation.[26]

Scott acknowledges that '[o]ne who argues for a return to acontextual modes of interpretation has to concede, and I do, that there are real costs to a return to the common law approach.'[27] This is well said. Yet there is another point: I am still enough of a legal realist to doubt whether courts would or could abandon a contextual approach to giving meaning to language and behavior. Just as some writers are skeptical about whether courts can apply a realist approach, we can be equally skeptical about whether courts can be truly formal and close their eyes to everything but the words on a piece of paper. Even the classic formalist parol evidence rule allowed contextual evidence if terms were 'ambiguous.' In the hands of many judges, this opens the door to a case-by-case policy approach. Would the advocates of near-certainty abandon this exception? Could they abandon it if they wanted to do so without reducing contract interpretation to an empty ritual? Or put in Chief Judge Richard Posner's words:

> [It is] an embarrassment for a theory of judicial legitimacy that denies that judges have any right to exercise discretion. A choice among semantically plausible interpretations of a text, in circumstances remote from those contemplated by its drafters, requires the exercise of discretion and the weighing of consequences. Reading is not a form of deduction;

---

[25]Parties in specific industries or trades can minimize the risk of having agreements interpreted in light of an expanded consideration of context if this is what they want. They can withdraw from the public courts by providing for arbitration. Insofar as they can influence or control who will do the arbitrating, they can opt for an expert who will bring an expanded view of context because of his experience. Or they can opt for a person who approaches written contracts very literally. Professor Daintith suggests that the presence of arbitration clauses in contracts does not necessarily suggest that parties expect conflict. '[E]xperience shows that parties do not in fact resort to arbitration as a mode of settlement [in the iron ore market]. Incorporation of an arbitration clause, I would suggest, shows only that the parties wish to avoid the possibility that a dispute will come before the ordinary courts.' T. Daintith and G. Teubner (eds), *The Design and the Performance of Long-Term Contracts, in Contract and Organisation: Legal Analysis in the Light of Economic and Social Theory* (Berlin: Walter de Gruyter, 1986) 164. For a criticism of the move to arbitration that is so common today, see C. A. Carr and M. R. Jencks, 'The Privatization of Business and Commercial Dispute Resolution' (2000) 88 *Kentucky Law Journal* 183.

[26]This was the approach of the United States Court of Appeals for the Seventh Circuit in the early 1980s. See *Binks Manufacturing Co v National Presto Industries, Inc* 709 F.2d 1109 (7th Cir. 1983); *Air Line Stewards and Stewardesses Assoc v Trans World Airlines* 713 F.2d 319 (7th Cir. 1983). Given that court's tendency to ignore its own precedents, the status of these decisions is uncertain. See Linzer, n 5 above.

[27]R. E. Scott, 'Is Article Two the Best We Can Do?' (2001) 52 *Hastings Law Journal* 677, 687.

> understanding requires a consideration of consequences ... The broader principle ... is that if one possible interpretation of an ambiguous statement would entail absurd or terrible results, that is a good reason to adopt an alternative interpretation.[28]

Furthermore, if we really wanted certainty and predictability, we would have to wipe out such doctrines as waiver and estoppel. We would have to do without doctrines such as substantial performance or requirements that breaches be material in order to trigger rights to call off contracts. We would have to make very clear any rules that required aggrieved parties to give notice that they considered the contract to be breached. Furthermore, I cannot imagine anything such as the doctrines of mistake, impossibility and frustration being expressed in certain terms that did not require judgment. Perhaps others can imagine judges closing their eyes to context, but my imagination will not carry me that far. Even the most formalist judge will read the paper deal knowing that it describes a sale of machinery, a bank loan, a franchise under which one party gains rights to sell new cars and so on. Such a judge probably will have his or her own experiences that will color the way that he or she understands the language used as applied to the situation before the court. Moreover, such a judge, or his or her law clerk, will have read some or all of the record on appeal, and usually it is filled with context. This is not to say that a formalist judge cannot write an acontextual opinion. However, decision and rationalization are different matters.

Moreover, the possibility of minting useful default rules that would eliminate almost all uncertainty strikes me as questionable. I can imagine some relatively certain default rules.[29] I suspect, however, that in creating default rules for many situations courts would feel a need to use some general terms calling on judgment in application. For example, suppose the parties failed to provide for the time of performance. I accept that it might be very useful to know for sure whether the seller would have to perform a day, a week or a month after the contract was signed. Nonetheless, can we imagine being satisfied with a rule that provided that all contracts made without a fixed date for delivery had to be performed within a week after they were signed? The rule would *look* certain, but there is not much more that could be said for it. Courts could gain certainty by refusing to enforce any contract that did not specify a date for performance. Yet this would make many bargains unenforceable even when it was clear that a seller's failure to deliver had continued far beyond any reasonable time for performance. I would find this too much to pay for whatever benefits near certainty would bring.

---

[28]R. A. Posner, 'What Am I? A Potted Plant?' *The New Republic*, 18 Sept 1987, 23. Posner continues, saying: 'There has never been a time when the courts of the United States, state or federal, behaved consistently in accordance with ... [legal formalism]. Nor could they, for reasons rooted in the nature of law and legal institutions, in the limitations of human knowledge, and in the character of the political system.'

[29]For example, when a contract made in Madison, Wisconsin speaks of the price as a specified number of dollars, American law would tell the judge to read this as United States dollars and not Australian dollars. Yet the case gets harder when the parties deal over the Internet and one is in Madison and the other is in Sydney.

Furthermore, I can imagine many situations where there would be good arguments for both sides as we tried to apply these brave new clear default rules to the particular facts of the case. It is not news that even certain rules do not necessarily yield certain results as applied, particularly in an adversary system that rewards lawyers for putting a self-serving spin on situations. And jurors and judges can pretend that facts exist, or do not exist, as a means to defeat a result seemingly dictated by the clearest rule of substantive law that the most skilled drafter can fashion. This may not be playing the game, but those of us who read briefs and excerpts from the record as well as appellate opinions have so often been startled when appellate judges get to where they want to go by fudging the facts that we really should no longer be surprised.

Scott, as well as others such as Bernstein, argue that business people may honor relational norms and sanctions while a relationship is underway, but when it breaks up, they may want 'end-game norms' to apply.[30] These end-game norms often appear in written formal contracts, but parties may pay little attention to them as they perform. During the life of a relationship, for example, a buyer may accept delayed deliveries. Once the parties reach the end-game when the relationship is not going to continue, the buyer may wish to insist on the written contract's fixed delivery dates to justify ending or limiting its obligations to the seller. The point is similar to one that Professor Fuller made in his 1947 casebook:

> The practice actually followed in the settlement of claims by companies which employ a standard form for transacting business is often much more liberal than might be inferred from the terms of the contract they ask their customers to sign. . . . The companies . . . seek a contractual margin of safety within which they can exercise their own discretion free from the threat of litigation. . . .[31]

Once a relationship comes to the end-game, reading a written contract literally sometimes may seem appropriate. For example, this often will be the case when the contract deals with borrowing money. I think that most people understand that money lenders can be expected to turn to the text of financing instruments when it comes time to call in a loan. Sometimes, however, turning to a writing at end-game would only disappoint expectations created during the process of attempting to maintain a relationship. Courts had good reasons for fashioning the doctrines of waiver, interpreting contracts by the course of performance and rules that require an aggrieved party to give the other notice that s/he thinks that there has been a breach of contract. We cannot assume that parties always intend one set of rules for performance and another for resolving disputes before courts.[32] This would seem

---

[30]See R. Scott, 'A Relational Theory of Default Rules for Commercial Contracts' (1990) 19 *Journal of Legal Studies* 597, 615: 'The parties, in essence, have learned to behave under two sets of rules: a strict set of rules for legal enforcement and a more flexible set of rules for social enforcement.'

[31]L. L. Fuller, *Basic Contract Law* (St. Paul, MN: West Publishing Co., 1947) 213. He continues: 'To obtain a proper perspective of the whole question, one must also consider whether trial in court, especially before a jury, is an efficient and just means of settling disputes involving small sums.'

[32]See S. Macaulay, 'Relational Contracts Floating on a Sea of Custom? Thoughts About the Ideas of Ian Macneil and Lisa Bernstein' (2000) 94 *Northwestern University Law Review* 775, 794–796.

particularly true when a written document was signed as a formality signifying commitment but not read nor understood by those who negotiated it.

Professor Lisa Bernstein has engaged in a grand empirical study of commercial custom.[33] Llewellyn, in drafting Article 2 of the UCC, again and again turned to business practices to give content to the qualitative standards found in his rules. After interviewing many business people, Bernstein does not find much trade usage that would be useful to courts in deciding particular cases. Customs are vague, and they often differ from place to place. Published codes of trade practice often are far more political than empirical, reflecting power struggles in trade associations rather than the expectations of typical members of the trade.

Bernstein's judgment about usage often will be right. Yet there are some customs and practices that can give meaning to the words in an agreement. Seldom, however, can judges just pick up the quaint native customs of business people and plug them into contracts without interpretation. Customs often are vague and qualified by imprecise exceptions. At best, such a custom may influence a court's judgment but not decide the case. Judges and jurors can be informed about community standards by expert witnesses. Of course, a critic may object that experts can be bought to testify to just about anything. Of course, we can hope that legal decision-makers can ward off biased claims in light of what makes sense in a commercial setting, at least in most cases.

Llewellyn had a different argument for the qualitative approach of Article 2 of the UCC. Judges might not be able to rely on trade usage because none existed or none could be proved. There also might be no established default rule because courts would not have worked one out incrementally through a series of cases. Nonetheless, Llewellyn argued that judges could rely on their 'situation sense'[34]—informed intuition—and the policies expressed and implied in the Code, and, perhaps, in the legal culture of their time.[35] He thought that typically judges would reach a defensible result, although they might not explain it well. In America there are many roads to a judgeship, but some judges will have some background in business as a result of

---

[33]See L. Bernstein, 'The Questionable Empirical Basis of Article 2's Incorporation Strategy: A Preliminary Study' (1999) 66 *University of Chicago Law Review* 710; L. Bernstein, 'Merchant Law in a Merchant Court: Rethinking the Code's Search for Immanent Business Norms' (1996) 144 *University of Pennsylvania Law Review* 1765. For my largely favourable comments on Bernstein's work, see S. Macaulay, 'Relational Contracts Floating on a Sea of Custom? Thoughts About the Ideas of Ian Macneil and Lisa Bernstein' *ibid.* Compare R. Epstein, 'Confusion About Custom: Disentangling Informal Customs from Standard Contractual Provisions' (1999) 66 *University of Chicago Law Review* 821.

[34]See Twining above, n 16 above, 225 ('A judge in a commercial case who can see the facts in the way businessmen would see them, as well as from the lawyer's point of view and from the point of view of the "mores" of the community as a whole, has grasped "wisdom."').

[35]See Llewellyn above, n 16 above, 4. Leon Trakman develops this idea and argues that judicial discretion will not be capricious because of the inherent controls in the common law system apart from the rules of contract law. See Trakman, 'The Effect of Illegality in the Law of Contract: Suggestions for Reform' (1977) 55 *Canadian Bar Review/La Revue due Barreau Canadien* 627, 652–54.

their practice before they took the bench. In many cases, the practice of law itself involves participating in a small business, and this experience could affect attitudes and assumptions. Lawyers argue legal rules, but they know that appeals to "common sense" can reinforce their technical claim.

Would an informed intuitive policy approach produce complete uncertainty? Llewellyn argues that it would produce 'reckonability' rather than uncertainty. Farber and Matheson note:

> Courts often resort to conclusory language in [order to] find that a manifestation rises to the level of a promise ... [R]elationships and surrounding circumstances do not speak for themselves. They must be interpreted by judges on the basis of expectations likely to arise between similarly situated parties. The conclusory tone follows because we are being told what we ought to already understand as members of the community.[36]

Lawyers might not know for sure how a particular case would be resolved, but, as members of the community of commercial lawyers, they would have a good idea of the probabilities. They would be aware that some cases were close ones with good arguments for both sides. These they could consider settling, and these situations might provoke changes in drafting, negotiation or both in the future. Those who advise American corporations are not helpless in the face of demands for such things as 'commercial reasonableness' and avoiding 'unconscionability.' They can help clients change behavior so that there is little question about running afoul of such qualitative standards. They can advise clients about the risks, and clients can decide to take the chance that a court might disapprove of certain practices. Lawyers might even get their clients to tone down advertising that creates expectations that they cannot satisfy.

If the burden on business flowing from a particular application of a rule were great enough, business interests could seek legislation to clarify or reverse the offending reading of the law. Their lawyers could redraft standard language to make it more likely that they would win the next time the problem comes before the courts. In some situations, they could move the game from the courts to arbitration and select their own judges and rules.

Clearly, any intuitive approach to the qualitative standards found in Article 2 will not serve the purposes that Dean Scott specifies in his writings. It will not give us uniformity in the application of the law nor produce clear default rules. Nonetheless, Llewellyn's whole approach should prompt us to ask how much uniformity we need and what price are we willing to pay for it? Dean Scott's study suggests that courts have not defined general standards or worked out specific rules very often. They just announce conclusions without offering much by way of explanation. Yet we can ask whether American contracts decisions leave an experienced business lawyer at sea with no land in sight. It would be hard to answer this question by an empirical study because of the vagueness of the question. Nonetheless, the lawyers with whom I talk continue to draft contracts and to interpret them for clients. Many of them are

---

[36]Farber and Matheson, 'Beyond Promissory Estoppel: Contract Law and the "Invisible Handshake"' (1985) 52 *University of Chicago Law Review* 903, 915 n 45.

confident that they can predict what courts are likely to do with a contract problem. Again, there may be types of contracts or particular situations where more certainty would be highly valuable and where other-than-legal relational norms and sanctions are all that we need. However, giving content to this idea requires that we look at the realities of various types of business transactions in detail before we make judgments about the need for greater certainty and clarity, the power of relational norms and sanctions and the costs of a flexible judicial approach. The problem is to avoid over-generalisation.

This is but a quick sketch of debates in the American contract field. Yet it should make clear that not everyone accepts that courts should pursue the implicit dimensions of contract. Moreover, American contract law has not been certain and perfectly predictable.

'The Rule of Law', Trust and Economic Development

Concern for the 'rule of law' could inhibit courts from searching for the implicit dimensions of contract.[37] Hendley observes that the phrase 'has become a trendy political slogan around the world.'[38] However, she notes that the content of the phrase and the means to achieve this goal are most uncertain. Ohnesorge has reviewed the various publications of international organisations, political leaders and scholars who deal with the concept.[39] He finds that those who are not lawyers tend to assume that the rule of law is a condition of a society which is governed by a complete and functioning legal system. A society either is characterised by the rule of law or it is not. These writers assume that legal rules are 'not subject to significant indeterminacy, and that these are sufficient to provide single correct solutions without resorting to principles, policies or purposes.'[40] They also assume that the rule of law is useful because the more the future can be made predictable, the easier it is to plan and take risks in a capitalist society. Under this view of the rule of law, the outcome of contract disputes should be predictable. Contract law would deter

[37]For excellent discussions of the idea of the rule of law, see W. C. Whitford, 'The Rule of Law' 2000 *Wisconsin Law Review* 723; F. Lovett, 'A Positivist Account of the Rule of Law' (2002) 27 *Law & Social Inquiry* 41; M. Krygier, 'The Rule of Law' in N. J. Smelser and P. B. Bates (eds), *International Encyclopedia of the Social & Behavioral Sciences* (Amsterdam: Elsevier, 2001) 13403. Stephen Lubben examines claims that an approach to contract interpretation resting on qualitative standards is the same as the German free law movement that the Nazi's found useful. Not surprisingly, he is very sceptical of such a position. See S. J. Lubben, 'Chief Justice Traynor's Contract Jurisprudence and the Free Law Dilemma: Nazism, the Judiciary, and California's Contract Law' (1998) 7 *Southern California Interdisciplinary Law Journal* 81. See also E. L. Rubin, 'Discretion and Its Discontents' (1997) 72 *Chicago Kent Law Review* 1299.

[38]K. Hendley, 'The Rule of Law and Economic Development in a Global Era' in A. Sarat (ed) *The Blackwell Companion to Law and Society* (forthcoming).

[39]J. Ohnesorge, *The Rule of Law, Economic Development, and the Developmental States of Northeast Asia* (C. Antons (ed), forthcoming 2002).

[40]*Ibid* at n 9.

breaches and provide compensation when a party failed to perform. However, judges often will differ about the implications of words and behavior in context. This means that seeking the implicit dimensions to a contract would insert uncertainty into the system because the courts would have to exercise judgment about what was implied but not expressed. This is to be avoided.

Ohnesorge notes that legal scholars tend to see the rule of law only as an aspiration. A society honors the rule of law when a high number of its characteristics are met a high percentage of the time. These scholars have read many cases where the rules and their application to the facts were debatable. They are skeptical about whether single correct solutions exist for the kinds of cases that are filtered into appellate courts. Legal realism and experience have taught lawyers that the outcome of particular cases can never be perfectly certain. Nonetheless, as we have seen, some legal scholars seek to increase the predictability of what courts will do with contract disputes.

The formal classical model of contract law has an illustrious history. We find traces of this version of the rule of law in Shakespeare's *The Merchant of Venice.* As you recall, Antonio has breached a contract, and, under its terms, he owes Shylock a pound of flesh. Several characters look for a way out, but others argue that the economy of Venice depends on the certain and predictable enforcement of contracts. Even Antonio himself rejects a suggestion that the judge should not enforce the bargain. He says that if the course of the law is denied, it will 'impeach the justice of the state'. This will harm the 'trade and profit of the city'. Of course, Shakespeare finds a way out of the dilemma, but it involves at least claiming to enforce the letter of the contract in the most formal sense. Shylock could take his pound of flesh, but he could not take a drop of blood. Shakespeare's court refused to look at the implicit dimension of that contract.

We also find traces of the classic model of the role of contract in the writings of the great sociologist Max Weber. Weber argued that capitalism and increasing 'formal rationality' go together. David Trubek tells us that Weber thought only a formal system of law can be predictable enough to support economic activity.[41] Law seeking substantive ends leads to particularistic decisions. Such decisions make it impossible for business people to know in advance the right answers to legal questions. Formal justice, Weber argues, enhances individual opportunities, promotes self-determination and helps assure individual freedom.[42] Trubek notes that

[41]D. M. Trubek, 'Reconstructing Max Weber's Sociology of Law' (1985) 37 *Stanford Law Review* 919. See, also, D. M. Trubek, 'Max Weber's Tragic Modernism and the Study of Law in Society' (1986) 20 *Law & Society Review* 573. See, also, D. Campbell, 'Truth Claims and Value-Freedom in the Treatment of Legitimacy: The Case of Weber' (1986) 13 *Journal of Law and Society* 207.

[42]On the other hand, a group of scholars has told us that economic conditions throughout the world are better in nations that have legal systems based on the common law than in nations with legal systems based on European continental codes. Florencio Lopez-de-Silanes, Rafael La Porta, Andrei Shleifer and Robert Vishny reached this conclusion in a study conducted for the National Bureau of Economic Research. See R. Morin, 'Unconventional Wisdom: New Facts and Hot Stats from the Social Sciences' *The Washington Post* 1 November 1998. The current version of the paper is

Weber also argues, perhaps paradoxically, that formal thought in law may actually defeat the intent of transacting parties, and benefit those with power and wealth. In fact, Weber suggested that completely formal thought may be impossible.

Many scholars have been critical of the approaches to development championed by the World Bank and the International Monetary Fund, which have included the rule of law as a key component.[43] The larger criticisms focus on the presumption that private actors in markets unchecked by regulation produce the greatest good. As Silbey remarks, '[l]aw is relegated to ... [a] ... subordinate role as a background figure providing context but little determinative action ... [T]he market narrative is a parable about lowering expectations about what collectivities can or should do. It thus asks us to limit our conceptions of justice to a contentless efficiency.'[44]

Conceding that many of the ideas captured by the phrase 'rule of law' are valuable, other critics question whether it is enough to enact particular laws or to adopt a formalist approach. Creating a rule of law with substance is not a mere technical matter. Legal institutions rest on a larger legal culture.[45] In Campbell's words: 'An effective contract law requires an ethically endorsed framework for

---

'Courts: The Lex Mundi Project' revised March 2002. It is available at <http://post.economics.harvard.edu/faculty/shleifer/papers.html>. More recently, David Wessel, 'Capital: The Legal DNA of Good Economics, Wall Street Journal' 6 September 2001, relies on Andrei Shleifer's work to show: 'Rule-laden civil-law countries aren't well-adapted to cope with change: the case-law approach makes common-law countries inherently more flexible.' This turns Weber on his head. However, these scholars tell us that the legal culture of the continent allows legal and governmental officials to intervene in the market, applying vague rationalisations for regulation. This explanation is consistent with Weber's observations. Of course, we can look at such studies skeptically. Even if we accept the correlation between a legal culture based on common-law approaches and economic success, we can question just how much the common-law systems contribute to that success. American, British and Indian legal officials do intervene in the market, and substantive rationality can be found in each of their legal systems. It was not too long ago that we marveled at the German and Japanese economic miracles. Taiwan, South Korea and Japan all are civil law systems and economic successes. It is hard to believe that the more recent economic difficulties of these nations can be explained by the absence of the common-law tradition in these countries. There are many more likely suspects. Compare P. J. McConnaughay, 'Rethinking the Role of Law and Contracts in East-West Commercial Relationships'(2001) 41 *Virginia Journal of International Law* 427, 432: 'The much-heralded worldwide "harmonization" of commercial law ... does not necessarily also herald its Westernisation; certain aspects of non-Western commercial traditions - for example, principles of accommodation and adjustment to future contingencies - are both consistent with core characteristics of the rule of law, and susceptible of reasonable articulation in commercial laws and contracts.'

[43]See, e.g. J. E. Stiglitz, *Globalization and Its Discontents* (New York: W. W. Norton & Co., 2002) 139, 160–161, 208–209; H.-J. Chang, *J. Stiglitz and the World Bank: The Rebel Within* (London: Anthem Press, 2001) 96.

[44]S. S. Silbey, '"Let Them Eat Cake:" Globalization, Postmodern Colonialism, and the Possibilities of Justice' (1997) 31 *Law & Society Review* 207. See also Udo Reifner's remark: 'While in former times capitalist nations used priests, soldiers and merchants to convince less developed peoples to adhere to their system, we can now rely on the convincing forces of the IMF, World Bank, BERD and other financial institutions where nations cue up to be accepted as members.' U. Reifner, 'The Vikings and the Romans - Contract Law and Social Economy' 6 (paper presented at the Conference on Perspectives of Critical Contract Law, Tuusula, Finland, 7–10 May 1992).

[45]See Hendley, n 38 above.

cooperation between involved parties which cannot be reduced to technical predictability.'[46]

Accepting that nations in transition to market economies need laws governing property, contract and bankruptcy, must courts abandon searching for the implicit dimensions of contract and operate in as formalist a way as possible? First, we could argue again that contract law plays but a minor role in a limited subset of situations.[47] As a result, courts are free to argue their decisions in terms of substantive rationality; any loss in predictability just will not matter much. Whatever theories say about the efficiency of clear rules, American contract law often is uncertain, featuring a rule neatly matched by a counterrule. Often there is, as Duncan Kennedy has pointed out, what seems to be a hard rule but it is encircled by a periphery of soft exceptions.[48] American legal procedure is costly and subject to procedural games such as discovery abuse and what seems to be endless delays. We have a relatively easy system of bankruptcy that can serve to wipe out or modify drastically contractual obligations.[49] Nonetheless, even with this kind of uncertain contract law in action, America has enjoyed great economic success. What is predictable is that contracts in the United States will be carried out in an acceptable fashion. When Americans make a contract, it is not certain that it be performed to the letter of its text or performed at all. Yet, it is a good bet that the parties will perform acceptably.

In my 1963 study of business practices related to contract, I note that 'business units are organised to perform commitments ...'[50] Most simply, someone in the seller's organisation must have a reason to stop goods that have been ordered from being delivered to the buyer. Someone in the buyer's organisation must have a reason to stop the standard procedure for paying bills. In an absence of a reason to the contrary, commitments are honored as a matter of course. Documents are needed to establish that there is a commitment. Sales people must communicate with financial people so that they will approve credit, to engineering people so that they will design and make the goods, and to shipping people so that they will package and deliver them. Of course, there can be mistakes, but most of the time mistakes are discovered and corrected. Contract law may play some subtle and indirect role in all

[46] D. Campbell, 'What is Meant by "the Rule of Law" in Asian Company Law Reform?' in R. Tomasic (ed) *Company Law in East Asia* (Aldershot: Dartmouth Publishing Co. Ltd and Ashgate Publishing Ltd., 1999) 11.

[47] See C. J. Choi, 'Contract Enforcement Across Cultures' (1994) 15 *Organizational Studies* 673; P. H. Solomon, Jr, 'The Limits of Legal Order in Post-Soviet Russia' (1995) 11 *Post-Soviet Affairs* 89.

[48] See D. Kennedy, 'Form and Substance in Private Law Adjudication' (1976) 89 *Harvard Law Review* 1685, 1700–1701, 1737.

[49] See, e.g., L. M. LoPucki & W. C. Whitford, 'Venue Choice and Forum Shopping in the Bankruptcy Reorganization of Large, Publicly Held Companies' 1991 *Wisconsin Law Review* 11. Compare R. Hillman, 'Contract Excuse and Bankruptcy Discharge' (1990) 43 *Stanford Law Review* 99.

[50] S. Macaulay, 'Non-Contractual Relations in Business: A Preliminary Study' (1963) 28 *American Sociological Review* 55, 63.

of this. Business people do know that there are such things as actions for breach of contract. They also know that their reputation with their trading partner is valuable, and they do not knowingly do things that would damage it without a good reason. Most of the time, I would guess, avoiding breach of contract litigation is not something that business people spend much time thinking about. Insofar as this is true, the style of contract analysis used by judges will not matter much to people who are not law professors.[51]

Some scholars have argued that contract law plays a real and essential role in market economies. The case for formal approaches to maximise predictability importantly turns on one's position about such an economic role. Douglass North, for example, argues that relational contract sanctions work in simple transactions but complex contracts require formal drafting and the possibility of legal enforcement.[52] Farber stresses the potential costs of relying on informal relational sanctions. He contends:

> [I]nformal incentives [to gain acceptable contract performance] are costly; to the extent that inadequate legal incentives cause excessive use of informal incentives, economic efficiency suffers ... Customers will tend to deal with sellers with whom they have dealt before and will tend not to engage in a widespread search for sellers. As a result, their willingness to shop for better prices can decrease. Furthermore, entry by new sellers becomes more difficult, because a reputation for reliability cannot be immediately established. Although these effects on behavior are difficult to quantify, they nevertheless represent real costs, because they impede the market's movement toward equilibrium.[53]

Johnson, McMillan and Woodruff surveyed about 1500 privately owned manufacturing firms in Poland, Slovakia, Romania, Russia and Ukraine.[54] They found that 'while informal relationships are the main basis for our firms' contracting, the formal institutions also foster contracting ... [W]orkable courts encourage firms to take on new partners. It is by making it easier for new firms to enter that having workable courts improves on relational contracting and boosts overall productivity.' Deakin, Lane and Wilkinson[55] argue that contract law plays an important role in fostering trust, but they expand the idea of contract law to include both the legal and the other-than-legal norms external to the contract that create a stable framework for the process of exchange and the presence of a sense of trust between the parties.

---

[51]To repeat, in some areas of business people do write contracts while carefully considering contract law. My point is simple, obvious but often overlooked: we should not over generalise from what is appropriate in particular areas to all contracts.

[52]D. C. North, *Institutions, Institutional Change and Economic Performance* (Cambridge: Cambridge University Press, 1990) 56–60.

[53]D. A. Farber, 'Reassessing the Economic Efficiency of Compensatory Damages for Breach of Contract' (1980) 66 *Virginia Law Review* 1443, 1465–66.

[54]S. Johnson, J. McMillan and C. Woodruff, 'Courts and Relational Contracts' (2002) 18 *Journal of Law, Economics & Organization* 221.

[55]S. Deakin, C. Lane and F. Wilkinson, '"Trust" or Law? Toward an Integrated Theory of Contractual Relations between Firms' (1994) 21 *Journal of Law and Society* 329.

While there is substance in all of these arguments, each can be questioned. These qualifications and doubts suggest that contract law may play a role only in a limited subset of cases. North's suggestion that relational contract is confined to simple transactions runs counter to experience, particularly in Asia.[56] We can find many complex contracts made and performed in situations where the chance of an effective legal remedy for breach is low or nonexistent. Indeed, a long-term complex contract often defeats a court's abilities to provide meaningful remedies for breach.[57] Relying on long-term continuing relationships can involve costs, as Farber suggests. However, Professor Okun pointed out that there are also gains.[58] He distinguishes auction markets from what he calls 'consumer markets', but his use of the term 'consumer' differs from the way most contracts professors would use it. In an auction market supply and demand affect prices directly, and we often get the benefits of competition. However, in what he calls consumer markets, buyers do not invest what would be needed to find a dependable seller offering the lowest price. Products sold in these markets usually are not standardised. Relying on long-term relationships minimises the costs of shopping and trying out products. Often the seller's reliability is highly valuable to the buyer who will not be able to procure a substitute quickly enough to avoid large losses. Okun concludes that whether the costs outweigh the gains is unclear. Often contract law enforced through the courts could do little to offset the losses a breach might cause. Awarding the increased costs of getting substitute goods elsewhere will not work because either there are no substitutes available or they cannot be made and shipped in time. There may be little, if any, evidence of

[56]See e.g., J. Kaufman Winn, 'Law and Relational Practices in Taiwan' (1994) 28 *Law & Society Review* 193; Frank K. Upham, 'Comment - Speculations on Legal Informality: On Winn's "Relational Practices and the Marginalization of Law"' (1994) 28 *Law & Society Review* 233; Ohnesorge, n 39 above.

[57]See e.g. *Bethlehem Steel Corp v Litton Industries Inc*, 507 Pa 88, 488 A.2d 581 (1985). Litton made an elaborate complex contract with Bethlehem to supply an innovative self-unloading ore boat at a price subject to an escalator clause. Litton gave Bethlehem an option to buy five additional vessels within five years. The prices of the ore boats purchased under the option were to be subject to escalation based upon a 'mutually agreed' price index. When Bethlehem tried to exercise the options, the parties were unable to agree on an escalator clause. The trial judge found that there was no enforceable contract. He said that the lack of a price indicated that the parties did not intend the options to be legally enforceable, and, even if they had intended to make such contracts, the court could not fill the gap and write an escalator clause based on the parties' agreement. An intermediate appellate court affirmed, as did the Supreme Court of Pennsylvania. Eleven appellate judges considered the case. Six found that the record supported the trial court's decision that no contract had been formed for the additional ore boats; five dissented and would have reversed. The majority said that a court could not fashion an escalator clause for the transactions covered by the option. It seemed to require that the basis for such a clause be found in the parties' agreement or trade usage. The dissenters thought that the trial court should have fashioned a reasonable option clause not limited to what it could find in the express agreement and trade usage. It was not clear how the dissenters would have the trial court fashion a reasonable escalator clause. Apparently, it was to use its discretion and make its own judgments about what a reasonable clause would provide.

[58]A. Okun, *Prices & Quantities: A Macroeconomic Analysis* (Washington, DC: Brookings Institution, 1981) 89, 134–178.

whether there would have been profits had there been no breach or the dollar amount of those profits.

Finally, it is unclear whether some blend of contract law enforced through courts and informal sanctions for breach creates the trust needed for a market economy. Generally, I agree with Deakin, Lane and Wilkinson that many factors unite to support the trust necessary for people to make plans and take risks. Indeed, if business people think that there is an efficient and effective system of contract law, it would not matter if they were wrong as long as they do not discover the truth through bitter experience. However, I have some reservations about what business people think that the law could do for them if a supplier failed to perform a contract or a buyer failed to pay. A few years ago, I responded to Deakin and his colleagues, saying:

> I suspect that contract law contributes to trust most of those who know the least about it. My guess is that it operates as a vague threat that should be avoided in all but a few situations. As I argued in 1977:
>
> The contract litigation process may also maintain a vague sense of threat that keeps everyone reasonably reliable ... For this process to operate, it is not necessary that business managers understand contract norms and the realities of the litigation process. Perhaps all that is needed is a sense that breach may entail disagreeable legal problems.[59]

If Deakin, Lane and Wilkinson would define contract to include all of the legal devices that support secured transactions—real estate mortgages, structures that support buying machine tools, jet aircraft, automobiles and other expensive items 'on time' and the like—their position would seem even stronger. Secured transactions are where I think effective law matters most. However, even with this expansion, we must remember that the institution of secured financing also rests on other-than-legal tools such as credit ratings and ways of communicating information, rumors and gossip about the financial health of individuals and corporations.[60] Even here creditors write off a percentage of their loans as uncollectible and sometimes find their security of only marginal value. To some extent, the credit system works because the cost of these bad debts can be included in the overall price for credit.

Daintith suggests that business people in the iron ore industry distinguish written agreements from letters and memoranda. However, what is important to them is the formality itself and not legal enforceability. In other words, a formal written contract can have symbolic power. He explains the attachment to contractual form as follows:

---

[59]S. Macaulay, 'Crime and Custom in Business Society' (1995) 22 *Journal of Law and Society* 248, citing S. Macaulay, 'Elegant Models, Empirical Pictures, and the Complexities of Contract' (1977) 11 *Law & Society Review* 508, 518–520. Compare I. Bohnet, B. S. Frey and S. Huck, 'More Order with Less Law: On Contract Enforcement, Trust and Crowding' (2001) 95 *American Political Science Review* 131; A. Bigsten et al, 'Contract Flexibility and Dispute Resolution in African Manufacturing' (2000) 36 *Journal of Development Studies* 1.

[60]See R. J. Mann, 'Information Technology and Non-Legal Sanctions in Financing Transactions' (2000) 98 *Michigan Law Review* 2494.

> First, the LTC [long term contract] facilitates the dealings of buyer and seller with important third parties. It reassures lenders ... It offers tidy answers to governments anxious for a fair return on their natural resources.
>
> Second, it provides a fairly comprehensive set of parameters for the parties' regular - or irregular - dealings and discussions. If problems arise, say on a matter like quality, the LTC offers a series of elements - price, quantity, shipping, etc - which, at least at the beginning of the negotiation are fixed points of reference ...
>
> Third, and most important, the LTC creates a privileged trading relationship between the parties, which is of great importance in times of difficult markets, of glut or scarcity, in the sense that it reinforces, by rendering unambiguous, each party's claim to remain in business relations with the other. It thus gives better, but not absolute, security to the trading position of each party.[61]

All in all, I doubt that courts seeking the implicit dimensions of contract would exert much influence on most business persons' assumptions about whether contract law might influence the other party's decisions about performing the bargain. Most business people do not stay up nights reading appellate opinions about contract law. Most of them seldom face contract litigation. A trade publication might tell them something about a case involving an unusual newsworthy situation, but such a story would be read in light of the business person's own experiences. My guess is that only a business person burned by a judicial opinion that "makes no sense" in his or her own case would lose his or her faith that most contracts will be performed and that contract law might make some contribution at the margin.

The American economy has been successful over the past half century, but we have lived with an uncertain contract law. In America we have gone from classic formalism, with many counter rules such as waiver, to Llewellyn's Article 2 of the Uniform Commercial Code. Article 2, to a great extent, called for 'judging in the grand style' and celebrated Weber's substantive rationality. Conservative judges appointed by President Reagan and like-minded governors have moved us toward a kind of formal rationality.[62] However, formalism always has proved to be unstable, at least in the United States. Our judges and scholars have never been comfortable with certain rules that produce results that are hard to stomach. Moreover, there are enough wild cards in our contract law that any judge who wants to evade a clear formally rational rule in a particular case can rationalize his or her decision with a nicely aged precedent.

---

[61]T. Daintith, 'The Design and the Performance of Long-Term Contracts' in T. Daintith and G. Teubner (eds), *Contract and Organisation: Legal Analysis in the Light of Economic and Social Theory* (Berlin: Walter de Gruyter, 1986) 164, 187–188. Compare E. L. Rubin, 'The Nonjudicial Life of Contract: Beyond the Shadow of the Law' (1995) 90 *Northwestern University Law Review* 107 ('There is a vast world of commercial relations - of contractual relations - waiting outside the judiciary's narrow chambers ... [When Grant Gilmore told us that Contract is Dead, he meant] that we must venture forth into that world if we want to avoid the charnel house of intellectual irrelevance.')

[62]Compare R. J. Moody, 'The New Conceptualism in Contract Law' (1995) 74 *Oregon Law Review* 1131, with R. A. Hillman, 'The "New Conservativism" in Contract Law and the Process of Legal Change' (1999) 40 *Boston College Law Review* 879.

Ronen Shamir[63] has examined Max Weber's arguments about formally rational and substantively rational styles of law in United States history. He sees a never-ending series of cycles:

> [T]he interplay between ideally formal and ideally substantive law corresponds to the interplay between periods of stability and reform in the political arena ...
>
> Autonomous law is discarded when its internal tensions and inconsistencies can no longer be sustained. But in order to institutionalise and permanently root desired reforms, a reawakening of formal rationality, as a means of ensuring stability, security and predictability, is again called for. In the sphere of the economic market, this means that the same old capitalists may dominate again after such 'radical' changes as, say, the Wagner Labor Relations Act. In the legal sphere, this means that legalistic orientations and strict formal procedures regain their power, albeit under new conditions. It is by invoking Weber's analysis that we may grasp the cycle of *formal rationality - internal contradictions - substantive rationality – substantive rationality - routinization – formal rationality.* Social change and progress appear, when they do, in the form of a spiral ascent: important and radical changes are introduced through substantive rationality; once in place, formal rationality, albeit on a new 'progressive' level, reappears.[64]

One reason for the instability and cyclic movement from formal to substantive rationality and then back again, is the way that we rationalise contract law. Despite almost a century of celebrating an objective theory and hundreds, if not thousands, of cases talking about a duty to read, contract still is supposed to rest on choice. Academic writers can brush aside the phrase "the meeting of the minds," but courts still mention it constantly because it does express an important rationalisation widely accepted in society for contractual liability. When larger organisations deal with smaller organisations or with consumers, they use contract documents that resemble the statutes of private governments. Often it would be irrational to attempt to read these documents. Usually people ignore them and rely on norms present in relational contracts.[65] These private governments raise the text of the printed form contract only when trouble arises and when means more appropriate to relationships have failed. Whatever the efficiency claims for treating the document as if it had been freely agreed to and a reflection of the party's contract, often the element of choice is just too attenuated for the comfort of a judge writing an opinion. Sometimes, we can

---

[63]R. Shamir, 'Formal and Substantive Rationality in American Law: A Weberian Perspective' (1993) 2 *Social & Legal Studies* 45.

[64]*Ibid* 63–65.

[65]Macneil observes: '[N]o one can honestly say that consumers ought to read long documents of this kind. The many courts which over the years have casually or not so casually said that ignore the fact that if consumers actually did such a foolish thing the modern economy would come to a screeching halt.' I. R. Macneil, 'Bureaucracy and Contracts of Adhesion' (1984) 22 *Osgoode Hall Law Journal* 5, 5–6. Macneil argues that you cannot legitimate holding people to such contracts by either choice or fault. Rather, the legitimacy must come from holding people to be bureaucrats in organisations performing consumer functions such as the Ford Motor Company. This way the justification is the same as holding us to many relationships which we enter not knowing the details of what we will be called on to do, such as military service, working for a law firm and marriage. Compare A. M. White and C. Lesser Mansfield, 'Literacy and Contract' (2002) 13 *Stanford Law & Policy Review* 233.

suspect, second class choice is accompanied by a contract clause that, as applied to the particular case, just does not seem fair judged completely intuitively. Most of us will not worry about whether the expectations of a lawyer who tried to draft a license for sales people to lie will be defeated if a court seeks the real expectations of the one tricked.

Importantly, this is American legal history. As I have emphasised, despite, or because of, the imprecise and often conflicting nature of our contract law, the American economy has been successful. Those who would argue for a limited judicial role, formal and clear rules and technical predictability can claim only that things might have been even better had we had a very different kind of contract law. Whether a different kind of contract law would have been beneficial is a difficult empirical question. It involves assumptions about when and how the nature of contract doctrine will matter to those who deal in a market economy. However, clearly there is room for a contract law with strong elements of flexibility and qualitative norms in many areas of business. Such a law is not wildly uncertain. As Llewellyn said,

> For the fact is that the work of our appellate courts all over the country is reckonable. It is reckonable first, and on a relative scale, far beyond what any sane man has any business expecting from a machinery devoted to settling disputes self-selected for their toughness. It is reckonable second, and on an absolute scale, quite sufficiently for skilled craftsmen to make usable and valuable judgments about likelihoods, and quite sufficiently to render the handling of an appeal a fitting subject for effective and satisfying craftsmanship.[66]

Yet it is also true that in some situations more formality and relatively clear default rules may be justified. However, we have only begun to look for those areas. One factor pointing in this direction is when parties are represented by lawyers, the document reflects real negotiation and parties and lawyers worried at the outset about the consequences of failure of performance and disrupting events such as wars, depressions and terrorism. Perhaps paradoxically another area might be consumer transactions where one side almost certainly will not be represented by lawyers. Clear rules here might cut the costs of consumers seeking remedies; consumers can seldom afford to battle about reasonableness and unconscionability when the product in issue cost only a few thousand dollars.[67]

[66]See Llewellyn above, n16 above, 4.

[67]See W. C. Whitford, 'Contract Law and the Control of Standardized Terms in Consumer Contracts: An American Report' (1995) 3 *European Review of Private Law* 193, 203, 207. In some American states, however, consumers can make effective use of small claims courts and various administrative tribunals. Here qualitative standards might help consumers because the decision making tends to be intuitive. Many American suppliers of consumer goods have attempted to avoid this type of informal dispute resolution by providing for compulsory arbitration in their standard form contracts. Sometimes arbitration is an alternative form of dispute resolution selected in good faith; often, however, it is just a ploy to ward off claims when the manufacturer selects the arbitrator and names a place for arbitration far from most consumers.

'And Now for Something Completely Different': Ian Macneil and Relational Contract Theory

If we are concerned about implied contracts and the text between the lines, the new formalists are not the only American scholars whom we should consider. Ian Macneil has, for over 30 years, championed relational contract theory.[68] He contrasts long-term continuing relationships with the discrete transactions often assumed by earlier writers and many common law judges to be the form of all contracts. Empirically, many of us have shown that the continuing relationship is extremely common.[69] Relationships have their own normative systems backed in complex ways by sanction systems. Most simply, if parties are to continue the relationship, this may call for many adjustments of rights and duties over time. The risk of losing the relationship usually is a powerful sanction. Insofar as contract law rests on reasonable expectations and reliance, the relational nature of a transaction calls for a different kind of contract law. Such a law would recognise the implicit dimensions of contracts.

Macneil draws an analytic distinction between discrete and relational contracts. Discrete contracts are abstract statements of the total obligation. The parties bring the future to the present and enter a contract that will define their obligations to each other. Context is unimportant. The parties may not have dealt before, and there is no

---

[68]See D. Campbell (ed), *The Relational Theory of Contract: Selected Works of Ian Macneil* (London: Sweet & Maxwell, 2001); D. Campbell, 'Ian Macneil and the Relational Theory of Contract' in *ibid* 3: D. Campbell and D. Harris, 'Flexibility in Long-term Contractual Relationships: The Role of Co-Operation' (1993) 20 *Journal of Law and Society* 166.

[69]See e.g. See S. Macaulay, 'Non-Contractual Relations in Business: A Preliminary Study' (1963) 28 *American Sociological Review* 55; S. Macaulay, 'Elegant Models, Empirical Pictures, and the Complexities of Contract' (1977) 11 *Law & Society Review* 507; S. Macaulay, 'An Empirical View of Contract' (1985) *Wisconsin Law Review* 465; H. Beale and A. Dugdale, 'Contracts Between Businessmen' (1975) 2 *British Journal of Law & Society* 45; B.-M. Blegvad, 'Commercial Relations, Contract, and Litigation in Denmark: A Discussion of Macaulay's Theories' (1990) 24 *Law & Society Review* 397. D. Jutras, 'The Legal Dimensions of Everyday Life' (2001) 16 *Canadian Journal of Law and Society* 45, summarises in English, J. G. Belley, 'Le Contrat entre Droit' (1998) *Économie et Société*, which was published only in French. Jutras says: Belley studied ALCAN, and he tells the story of a transformation of the economic culture of corporations, from the traditional culture of relationships of trust, confidence and interdependence to a modern, technocratic culture of quality control and coordination, driven by fixed objectives of growth. Previous scholarship had emphasised the importance of implicit norms and personal bonds of trust in long-term commercial contracts. Belley underlines the unresolved tension created in those contracts by the introduction of the depersonalised logic of expert system and explicit parameters of production. Supply contracts at ALCAN are very much explicit, but Belley's research shows that the behaviour of parties in circumstances of uncertainty is guided by unspoken shared assumptions that make up underlying cultures of the contract. There is a plurality of such cultures, which together provide structure and depth to the terms of interaction between ALCAN and its suppliers. Next to the juridical culture of the explicit contract, there is, in particular, an economic culture of profitability and pragmatism, at once traditional (resting on interpersonal bonds of trust) and modern (resting on the cold technocratic comfort of expert systems). Furthermore, the process of explicit articulation of the terms of cooperation necessarily affects the implicit culture of the relationship.

assurance that they will deal again. Relational contracts, typically, are not specific and precise allocations of risk. They involve complex transactions, and often it is hard to determine when they begin and are to end. They are agreements to cooperate to achieve mutually desired goals.

In a well-known passage, Gordon tells us that in relational contracts:

> parties treat their contracts more like marriages than like one-night stands. Obligations grow out of the commitment that they have made to one another, and the conventions that the trading community establishes for such commitments; they are not frozen at the initial moment of commitment, but change as circumstances change; the object of contracting is not primarily to allocate risks, but to signify a commitment to cooperate. In bad times parties are expected to lend one another mutual support, rather than standing on their rights; each will treat the others ['] insistence on literal performance as willful obstructionism; if unexpected contingencies occur resulting in severe losses, the parties are to search for equitable ways of dividing the losses; and the sanction for egregiously bad behavior, is always, of course, refusal to deal again.[70]

All human exchanges, Macneil asserts, involve norms. Some are internal to the exchange; others are external. Some norms are more appropriate to discrete transactions. For example, implementation of planning and obligations limited to the boundaries of consent fit more discrete deals. Other norms fit relational ones better. Here values such as maintaining the integrity of roles within the relation and maintaining the relationship itself are all important. Furthermore, more complex relationships can call for harmonising the arrangement with the surrounding social matrix. However, Macneil's theory recognises that norms and sanctions can be applied by legal and other-than-legal institutions and organisations. There are costs to imposing norms by formal legal means. Sometimes it makes sense to pay this price; often it does not.

When we turn from theoretical constructs to looking at the world of buying and selling, we discover that matters are not so neat as a spectrum ranging from the discrete to the relational. We can debate whether there are any real world discrete transactions: Parties must have some sort of relationship in order to have at least the minimum of trust needed to bargain. Even in close relationships, moreover, parties usually do not leave everything to be worked out as they go. Moreover, sometimes the parties will structure a transaction as if it were a discrete one despite its relational elements. Sometimes the party with greater power wants a relationship based on trust and cooperation but also wants to reserve the power to hold the other to the letter of a written document when it is to its advantage.

What does this mean for law? Several writers have called for a new relationally based system of contract doctrine.[71] Courts would look to standards based on

[70]R. Gordon, 'Macaulay, Macneil, and the Discovery of Solidarity and Power in Contract Law' (1985) *Wisconsin Law Review* 565, 569.

[71]See the debate between Peter Linzer, Steven J. Burton and Jonathan Eddy in 1988 *Annual Survey of American Law* 137. Whitford says: 'Macneil believes the legal system needs to take radically different approaches to relational contracts than it traditionally has. In dealing with disputes, he favours greater reliance on procedures oriented toward mediation and less emphasis on adversary

Macneil's rich classificatory scheme of internal and external contract norms. Feinman suggests that such an approach would look less like typical doctrinal method and more like policy analysis.[72] Other scholars have worried whether courts would be capable of supervising the good faith of those in a relationship, and whether, if courts tried to do this, it would create major problems for those trying to plan what risks to assume and which to avoid. Trebilcock, for example, argues that Macneil's relational approach cannot 'yield determinate legal principles' because it 'entails a highly amorphous sociological inquiry that seems well beyond the competence of courts in case-by-case adjudication.'[73] The key phrase in Trebilcock's criticism is 'determinate legal principles'. Macneil's writings raise the question whether a court could deal with a highly relational contract by using determinate legal principles. However, Macneil would accept that in some situations courts should treat what are in fact relational transactions *as if* they were discrete. When such a fiction is appropriate, determinate legal principles might be appropriate. The hard part, as I have said, is deciding when courts should honor the work of a corporate lawyer which she has labeled 'contract' when there is only second class consent, if that.

Would a relational approach be 'well beyond the competence of courts in case-by-case adjudication?' If we think that any trial in an adversary system is more than a comforting ritual, we might ask why the principles of relational contract theory are any more difficult or amorphous than, for example, deciding whether to impose the death penalty or to remedy Microsoft's violation of the antitrust laws by breaking up the corporation. This is not to deny that flexible approaches often present daunting problems for lawyers and judges. There is a capability problem, and high cost barriers stand before putting on a case to be judged by standards such as reasonableness. Yet there is no reason to presume that courts will always get it wrong, apart from one's faith in an anti-government ideology.

A limited trace of optimism: the real deal resting on relational norms can be supported by courts inducing settlements rather than announcing judgments.

Perhaps we should not conclude too quickly that the moral of my story is damned if you do and damned if you don't. While there is more to law than just legal rules, doctrine can matter. I applaud the efforts of those attempting to give us better conceptual tools. We will, however, do better if we attempt to fashion doctrines more or less suited for specific types of contracts rather than trying to fabricate one

processes looking toward adjudication. In regulating contracts, he counsels greater reliance on proactive administrative agencies that can take account of the many third-party interests at stake and less reliance on courts able to apply regulatory rules only when a disadvantaged party initiates a court procedure.' W. C. Whitford, 'Ian Macneil's Contribution to Contracts Scholarship' (1985) *Wisconsin Law Review* 545, 551.

[72]J. M. Feinman, 'Relational Contract Theory in Context' (2000) 94 *Northwestern University Law Review* 737.

[73]M. J. Trebilcock, *The Limits of Freedom of Contract* (Cambridge, MA: Harvard University Press, 1994) 141–142.

grand contract law. Nonetheless, doctrine rests on assumptions about the society and its proper organisation. Brownsword tells us:

> There are two plausible ethics for contract law, individualism and cooperativism . . . It is not easy for contract doctrine (whether through notions of good faith, unconscionability, reasonableness, loyalty, legitimate expectation, or whatever) to hold strictly to either of these ethics in their most robust form. Doctrinal adherence to individualism will often seem out of touch with business practice (where compromise, adjustment, and partnering and the like govern dealings); but, equally, doctrinal adherence to cooperativism can put too great a strain on the idea of a common enterprise (at any rate, in the sense of an identity of interest).[74]

But Americans always want to eat their cake and have it too: We want both individualism and cooperativism at the same time. We bounce back and forth through cycles where we emphasize one and then the other. Yet it is a question of emphasis: words rationalising individualism are still there when our legal culture accepts more cooperativism. The one safe statement about American contract law in action is that it is messy.

In some situations, there is no reason to think that courts will not be able to do as well in a contract case as they do in any other type of case. If we impose duties of cooperation or tell a court to give a remedy 'if injustice can be avoided only by enforcement of the promise',[75] our legal system often will reach at least acceptable results. Assuming that cost barriers permit, lawyers may be able to show judges what would be fair in a particular commercial context. The judges and the lawyers involved might never define 'fair' in a precise fashion that would satisfy a critic or offer answers to judges and lawyers in future cases. Nonetheless, all involved might accept that the results seemed to fall within an intuited zone of fairness. This process, however, might be very costly because it could require an exploration of the full commercial context. Of course, there is a risk that the judges might get it wrong, and cost barriers to proving the full context of a transaction would likely increase that risk. However, there is no reason to presume that the process always will be unduly costly or judges will always get it wrong. Perhaps if we conclude that there is a problem in a type of case such as those involving consumers, we should advocate flat rules for those kinds of situations.

We can consider an example both of what can be done and some of the limitations. An Ohio trial court filled substantial gaps in a long-term contract in *Oglebay Norton Co* v *Armco Inc*[76] The firms had close long-term continuing relations: Oglebay Norton ran iron ore boats on the Great Lakes, and it managed the Eveleth iron ore mining operation in Minnesota. Armco was a major steel producer, and it owned one third of the Eveleth operation. Armco had a seat on Oglebay Norton's board of directors. In 1957, the firms entered a contract that

---

[74]R. Brownsword, 'Individualism, Cooperativism and an Ethic for European Contract Law' (2001) 64 *Modern Law Review* 628, 630.

[75]Contracts scholars will recognise that the quoted phrase is a key passage in the American Restatement (2d) Contracts §90.

[76]52 Ohio St.3d 232, 556 N.E.2d 515 (1990).

required Oglebay to have adequate shipping capacity available for Armco. Armco was to use this shipping capacity if Armco wished to transport iron ore from mines in the Lake Superior district to Armco's plants in the lower Great Lakes region. Armco was to pay 'the regular net contract rates for the season as recognised by the leading iron ore shippers in such season.' If there were no such regular net contract rate, 'the parties shall mutually agree upon a rate for such transportation, taking into consideration the contract rate being charged for similar transportation by the leading independent vessel operators engaged in the transportation of iron ore from the Lake Superior District.'

During the next twenty-three years, the parties modified the contract four times. They continued to extend its duration until it finally ran until 2010. In 1980, they agreed that Oglebay Norton would upgrade its fleet to give self-unloading capability to each vessel used to haul Armco ore. To help pay for this large capital investment, Armco agreed to pay an additional twenty-five cents per ton shipped in the self-unloading vessels. From 1957 to 1983, Oglebay Norton based the price charged Armco on the rate published in *Skillings Mining Review,* a trade journal that gathered this information. In 1983, Armco, as was true of all American steel producers, had suffered heavy losses because of competition from foreign steel mills. The *Wall Street Journal* reported that 'Armco had a $295 million loss in 1983, bringing total losses for the last three years to about $1.3 billion.'[77] Armco negotiated lower rates from Oglebay Norton for 1983. The parties, however, were unable to negotiate a rate for 1984 and 1985. Oglebay Norton billed Armco for ore shipped, but Armco rejected this bill and paid much less than Oglebay had demanded. To further complicate matters, after 1985, *Skillings Mining Review* no longer published rates for shipping iron ore on the Great Lakes.

In 1986, Oglebay Norton sued for a declaratory judgment. 'After a lengthy bench trial,' the trial court made findings of fact and law. It found that the parties had intended to make a binding contract although the shipping rates were not settled. In such a case, the rate is a reasonable price. The court found a rate for the 1987 season. To do this, it listened to the testimony of a person who was an economic and financial expert about freight rates on the Great Lakes. It had data about what Armco had paid in the past few years, and information about the rates that Oglebay Norton had quoted as the price for carrying Armco ore. It had evidence of what one of Armco's competitors had paid. The trial court selected a rate that fell within the range of rates in evidence. Finally, the trial court ordered the parties to negotiate rates during the rest of the life of the contract. If they could not reach agreement, the parties were ordered to ask the court to appoint a mediator and to cooperate in mediation. The Supreme Court of Ohio affirmed this decision.

We can notice several things about the *Oglebay Norton* case. The reasonable rate was not a thing that existed in the world that could be just picked up and plugged into the contract. The trial court had to exercise judgment and create the rate based on information in the record. We do not know anything about the expert who testified at

[77] *Wall Street Journal* 28 March 1985.

trial. How did he know what was being charged for Great Lakes shipping of this cargo? In 1996, a magazine story pointed out that there was not much competition among shipping companies because the steel companies owned their own fleets or were closely associated with particular operators of ore boats. The story commented: 'Rates in the laker trade are difficult to get ahold of. Published rates are nothing more than a starting point, and with such an incestuous relationship between shippers and carriers, no one talks about what they actually pay.'[78] Oglebay Norton tried to subpoena information about rates from independent vessel operators and captive fleets, but the trial court quashed these subpoenas before trial because Oglebay had no right to this proprietary information. Thus, the court had to use its judgment without precise information when it established a rate. Nonetheless, there is no reason to think that there was anything drastically wrong with the price that the court set.

American contracts scholars might find the order to negotiate and then mediate future freight rates surprising. The contract had about twenty-two more years to run, and the court sought to support the relationship as best it could. If we assume that the relationship would continue more or less as it had in the past, the court's approach seems reasonable. Oglebay Norton, after all, had invested in self-unloading ore boats at Armco's request. The contract had not been in effect long enough after this major investment so that the extra payment per ton of iron ore would have covered this expense. The mediator could have reinforced a duty to negotiate in good faith.

We do not know how well this structure worked. We know that the parties continued a business relationship at least until 1995, because Oglebay Norton's Annual Report for that year stated that it had supplied advanced technology for Armco's new continuous casting mill. However, all the effort of the Ohio courts probably failed to keep the Great Lakes shipping relationship alive in anything like its former state. Throughout the 1980s, the American steel industry faced great financial difficulty. In 1989, Armco sold much of its carbon steel making capacity to a joint venture it formed with a Japanese steel company. We can suspect that Armco had fewer, if any, requirements for hauling ore on the Great Lakes. Armco focused on making stainless steel: 'Armco buys domestic steel and limited amounts of imported steel - including Japanese steel - to convert into pipe and tube at its downstream plants. Armco used to make the steel itself but now makes exclusively specialty steels. ...'[79] In 1992, Armco bought about two thirds of its now reduced requirements of ore from the Eveleth facility managed by Oglebay, but it bought the rest at a much cheaper price from Brazil. The Brazilian ore was shipped on barges up the Mississippi River to the Ohio River and then to Armco's plants. This ore did not come under the contract with Oglebay Norton.

---

[78]P. F. Conlye, 'A Long Season Ends for Great Lakes Fleet' *Journal of Commerce* 29 February 1996, 18.

[79]T. W. Gerdel, 'Oglebay Norton Lays Off 140 at Ore Mine' *Cleveland Plain Dealer* 11 December 1992, E-1.

Instead of having to negotiate a price, with any disputes subject to mediation, it seems likely that Armco changed its way of doing business so that it needed much less, if any, ore hauled from mines in the Lake Superior region on the Great Lakes. When issued, the court's order to negotiate and mediate seemed reasonable enough. After just a few years, the changes at Armco seemed to have meant that Armco no longer had as many requirements for carrying ore on the Great Lakes. But this was a risk that Oglebay Norton assumed when it made a requirements contract. If our speculation is right, the court's order made sense as long as a requirements contract made sense. The court could not change the decline of the American steel industry.

Macneil has pointed out that there are situations where it is in the interest of the parties, and even perhaps of the economy as a whole, where the law should treat parties *as if* their relationship was discrete and entirely contained within the borders of a written document. The task is to identify such situations. One approach is to submit such documents to a regulatory agency for approval, such as is often done with insurance policies. This seems to be a sensible solution as long as we are confident that the regulatory agency will not be captured by trade associations that make campaign contributions. We have long distinguished consumer transactions from those between merchants. Yet even this leaves me uneasy; it seems too crude. Some transactions between businesses have many elements of a consumer transaction. Often a franchise agreement is one-sided and written by the more powerful party. Often these agreements or amendments to them are hard to read and understand. Perhaps courts can approach documents such as franchises as if the relationships involved were discrete. They may be able to do this because those involved can gain legislation that calls for a more relational approach to the legal rights of the parties. Courts can avoid the difficulties involved in a relational approach unless a legislature determines that it is worth the costs of attempting to reinforce the norms of cooperation. Yet, here too, we would be more comfortable if we had more faith in our American legislatures as something other than places where law is sold to the highest bidder.[80]

Whatever our success in identifying places for treating relationships as if they were discrete, we must remember that it is not just a question of legal doctrine. Doctrine does not have little legs so that it can hop down from law books and enforce itself. Doctrine is delivered in an extremely expensive system for which someone must pay. Often the reason that a transaction broke down is that one side lost the ability to perform because it ran out of money. A claim in bankruptcy often is not worth the effort. Even when there is little risk of bankruptcy, suing someone usually destroys relationships and invites retaliation.

[80]Special interest pressure has even moved from the public legislative arena to the National Conference of Commissioners on Uniform Laws, the group that proposes revisions to the Uniform Commercial Code. See R. E. Speidel, 'Introduction to Symposium on Proposed Revised Article 2' (2001) 54 *SMU Law Review* 787; R. E. Speidel, 'Revising UCC Article 2: A View from the Trenches' (2001) 52 *Hastings Law Review* 607; A. Schwartz and R. E. Scott, 'The Political Economy of Private Legislatures' (1995) 143 *University of Pennsylvania Law Review* 595.

We might be happier if we took a lawyer's perspective and saw the game as one involving acceptable, if not ideal, settlements. While not all cases can be nor should be settled, more often than not the 'least bad' solution is a compromise fashioned in light of the situation facing the parties at the time of the dispute. Many, if not most, settlements fall beneath the radar screen of contract scholars. Publishers do not deliver reports of these cases to our door or to our computer. The parties often want their settlement to be secret. However, parties do invoke the legal system as part of a strategy to produce settlements. When cooperative approaches fail, letters can be written on an attorney's letterhead in order to make an implicit threat. Complaints may be filed in court, and negotiations may be commenced if summary judgment is not granted. Sometimes, however, cases involving large sums of money may proceed far down the path to a final judgment affirmed on appeal and still be settled. Furthermore, sometimes the settlement provokes the parties to resume their relationship, although often with a modified balance of power. This may be a way, if not the most common way, that the ideas of relational contract are implemented in the American legal system.

What appears to be a final judgment at the trial level may be only a step toward settlement. The judgment may affect the balance of power between the parties, but often it will not go into effect as written. For example, the judge in *Aluminum Corporation of America* v *Essex Group Inc*,[81] rewrote an escalator clause to express what he saw as the actual risk distribution between the parties. This was an implicit dimension of this relationship. The opinion was highly controversial, but none of the academic writing about it considered the final outcome of the case. ALCOA and Essex entered a toll conversion contract in 1967 that was to run until 1983. In form, this was a services rather than a sales contract. ALCOA would convert Essex' ore into molten aluminum, and Essex would receive it in this form. Essex made the contract when it decided to expand its manufacturing of aluminum wire products. The court said: 'The long term supply of aluminum was important to assure Essex of the steady use of its expensive machinery. A steady production stream was vital to preserve the market position it sought to establish. The favorable price was important to allow Essex to compete with firms like ALCOA which produced aluminum and manufactured aluminum wire products in an efficient, integrated operation.'[82]

ALCOA had drafted an escalator clause to set the price for the aluminum that it processed. The escalator was tied in part to the federal government's Wholesale Price Index-Industrial Commodities. The WPI-IC failed to reflect an unexpected rapid increase in the cost of electric power. 'Electric power is the principal nonlabor cost factor in aluminum conversion, and the electric power rates rose much more rapidly than did the WPI-IC.'[83] Moreover, there was a sharp increase in the demand for aluminum. Essex did not use the material delivered by ALCOA in the manufacture of wire products. Instead, it resold millions of pounds on the market. In June of

[81] 499 F. Supp. 53 (WDPa 1980).

[82] *Ibid* at 58.

[83] *Ibid.*

1979, the cost to Essex of the ALCOA product was 36.35 cents per pound, but Essex was reselling on the market at more than 73 cents per pound.

The court found that ALCOA was excused from performing the contract under the doctrines of mutual mistake, impossibility and frustration. The court decided that while ALCOA necessarily had taken some risk in entering the contract which it thought that it had covered by its escalator clause, the actual result was not within the zone of risk that it had assumed. The escalator did not serve to create a price that would give ALCOA 'the minimum return of one cent per pound which the parties had contemplated.'[84] However, the court thought it unfair to excuse ALCOA entirely from its obligations under the contract. It said:

> To decree rescission in this case would be to grant ALCOA a windfall gain in the current aluminum market. It would at the same time deprive Essex of the assured long term aluminum supply which it obtained under the contract and of the gains it legitimately may enforce within the scope of the risk ALCOA bears under the contract.[85]

The court decided that the contract price would be the smallest produced by one of three ways of computing it, including the original formula found in the written document. Importantly, one method was 'the price which yields ALCOA a profit of one cent per pound of aluminum converted.' Unless the price of aluminum fell significantly, the judge had transformed the agreement into a cost plus a percentage of profit contract. However, ALCOA was not freed of all obligations under the contract. Also, Essex could not continue to resell its aluminum to other users of the product at the market price while paying only the very low contract price.

For my purposes, the important thing to notice is that the judge's formula never went into effect. The parties settled after Essex appealed, and the appellate court had heard oral argument. As part of the settlement, the original contract remained in effect until 31 December 1981. It was extended for five years beyond the end of 1981. During the balance of time remaining from the date of the settlement to the new termination date, ALCOA would sell to Essex at a favorable price, but not one as favorable as Essex enjoyed through 1981. We can see the ultimate resolution of the dispute as very relational. The parties continued their relationship and provided for a transition bringing it to an end. Essex, to a large extent but not entirely, had to stay in its role under the original allocation of risks. It was buying aluminum in order to make aluminum wire products. It was not entitled to act as a middleman, capturing the gains from low cost sheets of aluminum which it could sell on the market. Essex had some duty to pay attention to ALCOA's interests. Rather than maximizing its own return, the implicit dimension of the relationship required Essex to cooperate to accommodate their mutual interests.

What was the contribution of Judge Teitlebaum in achieving such a relational end? Essentially, he acted as a mixture of mediator and arbitrator. He found what he saw as a fair solution on the basis of the facts presented to him. When mediators offer their solutions to a problem, often it triggers successful negotiations. The mediator's

[84] *Ibid* at 66.

[85] *Ibid* at 84.

solution is where the bargaining begins, and it may be very useful to the parties who are constrained by negotiation tactics. However, Judge Teitlebaum's solution was more than just a suggestion. It would go into effect unless the parties found a better one. Of course, Judge Teitlebaum's revised escalator clause might not go into effect if Essex were able to persuade an appellate court to overturn it. ALCOA had won a victory, but it rested on an opinion that certainly pushed the envelope. If the appellate court were staffed by judges who had faith in classic contract law, ALCOA could lose. Yet Essex could not be sure that it could get Judge Teitlebaum's revisions overturned, and it faced both delay in resolving the matter and the costs of the appellate process. It might appeal, wait, and invest a great deal in lawyers' fees, only to have Judge Teitlebaum's opinion affirmed. It was even possible that the appellate court would have reversed the trial court but written an opinion that would make Essex worse off than the Teitlebaum escalator clause.

Did Judge Teitlebaum reach a good solution? Our appraisal must turn on our judgment as to whether ALCOA took the risk in this contract of having Essex go into competition with ALCOA in the general market for sheets of aluminum. If we see the contract in substance as one calling for ALCOA to supply Essex's requirements of the raw material needed to manufacture aluminum wire products with its expensive machinery, the implied dimension of this contract seems clear enough. It is hard to see why ALCOA should be burdened with the risk of supplying Essex with ridiculously low priced aluminum which Essex could sell in competition with ALCOA's own sales in that market. While Judge Teitlebaum may have been mistaken in the formula that he imposed on the parties, they were not stuck with it. They were able to fashion one that they thought would better their situation.[86] The

[86]Attempts to rework the obligations of parties in a complex relationship can burden courts and litigants. For example, in *B.P. Exploration Co* v *Hunt,* [1979] 1 WLR 783, aff'd [1982] 1 All ER 925, the court dealt with a qualitative statute that gave little more direction than calling for compensation for benefits conferred and allowing retention of some or all of a down payment if the court 'considers it just to do so having regard to all the circumstances of the case.' See the Law Reform (Frustrated Contracts) Act, 1943 (6 & 7 Geo. 6, c. 40). The case involved a complex transaction in the oil industry. Nelson Bunker Hunt owned a concession in Libya. B. P. Exploration agreed to develop the concession, and the two were to share equally the oil produced. Hunt was to pay for his share of the development costs from his share of the oil produced. The concession was expropriated, and the court had to consider offsetting claims.

Justice Goff wrote a 67-page opinion. He noted there:

> [I]n addition to difficult and novel questions of law, the case involves substantial questions of fact and of accounting procedure. The sums involved are enormous; B. P.'s claim was advanced in a number of alternative ways, the sum claimed varying from nearly $45,000,000 to nearly $230,000,000. Furthermore, allegations made by Mr. Hunt related to the manner in which B.P. developed the oil field led to an investigation of almost the entire history of the exploration, appraisal, and development of the field, and the production of oil from the field. This investigation required a substantial body of evidence, much of it technical; and the documents before the court, which were very largely concerned with these allegations by Mr. Hunt, were very numerous - I was told that there were over 15,000 documents in court. Many of these were of a technical nature; and in any event they represented only the tip of the iceberg of documents disclosed on discovery. Only by reason of the good sense and

next two examples involve Westinghouse's attempt to become the dominant corporation in supplying nuclear power plants. We have to put ourselves back to those wonderful days when the peaceful atom was going to supply endless clean power. However, fossil fuels were cheap, and nuclear power plants were expensive. Westinghouse had to convince reluctant utility executives to invest in what was being sold as cutting edge technology. In the first group of cases, Westinghouse sweetened the deal to sell reactors by promises to supply fuel at a fixed price which was far above the market when they made the contracts. The utility executives could have felt comfortable because the fuel could never cost more than the price fixed in the contract, but it was likely to cost a great deal less. An international cartel formed to fix uranium prices, and it succeeded for a time. Now Westinghouse was being called on to supply fuel at extremely high prices. The newspapers of the time said that Westinghouse simply could not buy all the fuel it had promised to supply at the cartel price. Westinghouse notified its utility customers that it would not supply the fuel, but it claimed to be excused under the Uniform Commercial Code's impossibility provision. Section 2-615(1) grants an excuse 'if performance as agreed has been made impracticable by the occurrence of a contingency the non-occurrence of which was a basic assumption on which the contract was made ...'[87] The cases were consolidated before United States District Judge Robert Merhige, Jr. Judge Merhige was known as a settling judge who wanted the parties to solve the problems rather than litigate. The day the trial opened, he told the many lawyers assembled in his

> restraint shown by counsel on both sides, and the efficiency of their instructing solicitors, was it possible for a so substantial piece of litigation to be kept under control and for the hearing to take no longer than 57 days.

After this elaborate procedure, and without much explanation, the judge accepted B. P.'s claim that half the benefit was attributable to its actions and half to Hunt's. This served to make the final judgment something of a rough split-the-difference compromise. Donald Harris, David Campbell and Roger Halson, Remedies in Contract & Tort 246–254 (2d ed 2002), are, 'with greatest respect,' very critical of this decision. They judge it 'thoroughly painstaking but ... undeniably unsatisfactory.' Perhaps the only way to defend the process and the result is to notice that Nelson Bunker Hunt is a Texas oil man. While more conventional wealthy people might have worked out a settlement with B.P. Oil, only a 'shoot-out at the okay corral' would satisfy him. The process can be viewed as an elaborate social ritual for the privileged. It is highly unlikely that any American federal court would have invested this amount of time and effort in any contract case today.

[87]The Official Comment is perplexing. On one hand, it tells us: 'a rise or a collapse in the market [is not] in itself a justification [for not performing], for that is exactly the type of business risk which business contracts made at fixed prices are intended to cover.' This would seem to favor the utility buyers. On the other hand, the Comment continues: "But a severe shortage of raw materials or of supplies due to a contingency such as war, embargo, local crop failure, unforeseen shutdown of major sources of supply or the like, which either causes a marked increase in cost or altogether prevents the seller from securing supplies necessary to his performance, is within the contemplation of this section.' Obviously, Westinghouse liked this last part but wanted to downplay the first.

courtroom, 'I don't ever expect to finish these cases.... I expect [them] to get settled.'[88]

Judge Merhige's biographer[89] tells us:

> In an attempt to facilitate settlement discussions, Merhige and his wife hosted cocktail parties in their home for the lawyers *and* the corporate executives. It may not have been a crucial factor, but the social contact did facilitate discussions in a context other than confrontational litigation. Westinghouse Chairman Robert E. Kirby finally agreed to become involved in the negotiations and made personal contact with the chief executive officer of each utility. The jawboning paid some immediate benefits when six of the thirteen utility companies reached a settlement with Westinghouse before the conclusion of the trial. The other utilities, however, remained adamant ...
>
> Utilising his expertise in alternative dispute resolution, Merhige offered each party a carrot and a stick. The utilities received an important bargaining chip with Merhige's recognition that Westinghouse was subject to some liability. By warning the utilities that they would not receive the full damages they sought, Merhige significantly strengthened Westinghouse's bargaining position .... He increased the pressure on the parties to negotiate by announcing that the court would meet and confer with counsel in an effort to assist them in reaching an agreement ...
>
> Merhige once again increased the pressure to compromise by escalating the length and frequency of the negotiation conferences. Out-of-town lawyers were astonished when the judge insisted that they come to court on weekends, early mornings and late evenings. At one point, Merhige threatened to have counsel work on 'Saturdays, Sundays, and some days that aren't even on the calendar.'..
>
> Lewis Booker, liaison counsel for the utilities ... said that: Judge Merhige was very astute in recognising that the parties and the experts could negotiate on matters that a judicial verdict could not cover. For example, the utilities could agree to accept a turbine generator in lieu of damages, but Merhige would have been powerless to order that. His verdict would necessarily have been limited to computing dollar damages. ...[90]

Judge Merhige appointed a law school dean as a special master to assist the parties in reaching an adjustment of the respective claims. Merhige required the parties to file proposals for settlement. In most cases, the settlements reached did not require Westinghouse just to pay cash to its customers as damages. Rather, the settlements involved a combination of cash and services. Often Westinghouse agreed to provide services maintaining the nuclear reactors and supply replacement parts at a deeply discounted rate. In the Texas Utilities Services Inc case, the settlement was contained in a 350 page agreement. It was estimated to be worth $80 million to the utility, but the out of pocket cost to Westinghouse was only $27 million. Westinghouse assigned some of its claims against the uranium cartel to its customers as another way of sharing potential gains and losses. Most of the settlements reinforced the

---

[88]Pappas, 'Westinghouse, Utilities Under Pressure to Settle Uranium Suit Before Court Does' *Wall Street Journal*, 2 June 1978, 32.

[89]R. J. Bacigal, *May It Please the Court: A Biography of Judge Robert R. Merhige, Jr.* (Latham, MD: University Press of America, 1992).

[90]*Ibid* at 145, 146–147.

relationships between Westinghouse and its customers who had a Westinghouse nuclear reactor to run for many years.

Again observers who knew something about nuclear energy thought that Westinghouse had settled all of the utilities cases for about half of what they had claimed.[91] Stewart reports: '[i]f Westinghouse and the utilities had simply split their differences in 1975, before resorting to litigation, the result would have been about the same.'[92] However, the parties could not have done this without going through something like the process that took place in and out of Judge Merhige's courtroom. Many utilities were hesitant to settle without establishing that they had given nothing away. At the time of this litigation, these power companies were regulated, and a regulatory commission would have to be satisfied with the settlement. Moreover, some of Westinghouse's customers hesitated to settle early in the process because they did not want utilities that negotiated later to get larger amounts and make the pioneers look as if they had sold out too cheaply. The law school dean was able to help manage the work with the large group of buyers and keep the pressure on both sides to solve the problem. The dean was a mediator who always had the power of the trial judge as a potential sanction.

The settlements at least attempted to further the interests of both seller and buyers. Westinghouse managed to avoid the crushing liability that a literal application of its many contracts with customers would have imposed. Yet Westinghouse was able to keep alive relationships that might prove to be profitable. The utilities kept alive the relationship so that there would be someone who could service and maintain the reactors. We cannot be sure, but it seems that this outcome was better than the utilities could have gained had they been able to win judgments enforcing their contract rights. It is likely that all this would have done was force Westinghouse into bankruptcy, and as unsecured creditors the utilities would not have done well in such a proceeding. The liaison counsel for the utilities told Judge Merhige's biographer:

> The overall feeling by everyone was that justice had really been done. The utilities got what they needed to continue operations, while Westinghouse was able to avoid bankruptcy, keep its plants running and its people employed ...[93]

In the next example, Westinghouse closed its deal with Florida Power and Light Company by offering another sweetener in the negotiations that ultimately provoked litigation.[94] Westinghouse promised to remove the spent rods of uranium from

---

[91]See J. B. Stewart, *The Partners: Inside America's Most Powerful Law Firms* (New York: Simon and Schuster, 1983) 153.

[92]*Ibid* 198.

[93]Bacigal, n 89 above 148. See also D. Campbell and D. Harris, 'Flexibility in Long-term Contractual Relationships: The Role of Co-Operation' (1993) 20 *Journal of Law and Society* 166, 172: 'Once freed from the panic of the oil crisis and the competitive suspicion and hostility into which the mutually destructive idea of holding Westinghouse to its contracts or of Westinghouse abandoning its buyers led, a sensible co-operative adjustment to the changed circumstances took place.'

[94]See *Florida Power and Light Co v Westinghouse Electric Corp* 517 F. Supp. 440 (E. D. Va. 1981).

FP&L's holding ponds into which the rods were placed. Westinghouse had planned to recycle these rods, but no commercial recycling was available in the United States. The United States Government represented that such reprocessing would be available, but it never brought this about. Once again, the case was tried by Judge Merhige. This time he issued a decision holding that Westinghouse was not excused under Section 2-615(1) of the UCC. FP&L had asked for a decree of specific performance ordering Westinghouse to remove the rods. Judge Merhige said: '[W]hile the court is fully cognisant of the difficulty of fashioning a sufficiently specific decree should the parties be unable to reach agreement, and should the Court conclude that specific enforcement is appropriate considering various other factors, the Court believes that, with the assistance of the parties, a workable and appropriate decree would be achieved.'[95] The judge then granted the parties 90 days in which to attempt to agree on a settlement. The parties were directed to select experts to aid the court. The judge said: 'both parties are urged to use the initial time period in an intensive attempt to reach agreement rather than in preparing to further litigate the issue of remedy.'[96]

The parties failed to reach agreement.[97] Nonetheless, they had appointed a committee of nuclear engineers who studied the situation. These engineers determined that it was possible to rerack the nuclear facility's holding ponds. As a result, all the rods that would be produced during the designed life of the plant could be stored there. The reactors would not have to shut down when the ponds were full. FP&L would not have to buy power to substitute for that generated by this plant. Westinghouse agreed to do the reracking at no cost to FP&L. Judge Merhige decided that there should be an equitable allocation of the interim costs of storing the spent rods. After the dispute arose, Congress had passed a statute that called for the construction of a permanent storage facility for all nuclear waste. While then it looked as if the problem might be solved after the litigation ended, Americans are still battling about what to do with nuclear waste. Judge Merhige also allocated the other costs. He took into account that while utility customers elsewhere had paid high rates for electricity produced by fossil fuels, FP&L's customers had not. His allocation was roughly an equal division of various costs.[98]

Again, we see something of a relational approach to the problems. By convening a panel of engineers, the judge managed to produce a technical solution to a major part of the contract problem. The final result reinforced the continuation of the relationship. The decision required both sides to cooperate in the future.

---

[95] *Ibid* 461.

[96] *Ibid* 462.

[97] See *Florida Power and Light Co v Westinghouse Electric Co* 597 F. Supp. 1456 (E.D. Va. 1984).

[98] Judge Merhige's opinion resolving Westinghouse's liability was reversed in *Florida Power and Light Co v Westinghouse Electric Corp*, 826 F.2d 239 (4th Cir. 1987). However, because of the way the parties appealed the case, much of Judge Merhige's compromise settlement remained in place. The process served to provoke discovery of the engineering solution - reracking the cooling ponds - to the major problem in the case.

Which approach is better? Will we get more and better settlements if trial judges rewrite contract clauses that might or might not be overturned on appeal? Will we get more and better settlements if a judge takes over negotiations and presses the parties to work out a deal? The answer again is not clear. My guess is that sometimes one will work best, but other times a different approach is called for. One important factor in the first of the disputes about Westinghouse's contracts was the large number of parties who faced governmental regulation. For many reasons, no utility wanted to get a settlement that was clearly less favorable than those gained by other utilities in similar positions. Judge Merhige's control over the entire process may have coordinated matters so that no settlement would appear very much better than the others. There were only two large corporations involved in the ALCOA case, and so Judge Teitlebaum was free to issue an opinion and leave it to the parties to accept it, appeal, settle or settle after the appellate process suggested that each side had to worry about the appellate court writing an opinion that one of the parties might not like as well as Judge Teitlebaum's revised escalator clause.

Can we rely on settlement negotiations to provoke relational sanctions to all contracts problems? Clearly not.[99] As Galanter and Cahill note:

> Settlement is not intrinsically good or bad, anymore than adjudication is good or bad. Settlements do not share any generic traits that commend us to avoid them *per se* or to promote them. This does not mean that some settlements are not preferable to some adjudications - and to other settlements ... [T]here is, we would suppose, great variation in the quality of settlements from one disputing arena to another and within such arenas.[100]

Often efforts at settlement cannot begin until the summary judgment hurdle has been cleared. American conditions and culture allow one party before summary judgment motions have been decided to run up the costs of litigation in order to discourage the other. Settlement should be easier when both parties are wealthy, so that one party will not have an incentive to try to induce the other to quit the litigation because of continuing court costs.

Sometimes litigation is a pure salvage operation. The parties are not interested in continuing their relationship. Settlement then becomes a question of costs and benefits. By settling, the parties reduce or eliminate uncertainty and contain costs. Things are in their control rather than in the control of judges and jurors. It may make more sense to litigate and take one's chances that any judgment recovered could be satisfied. Having conceded this, still we cannot forget that settlements also can produce compromises that keep relationships alive. The effort to settle can force the parties to cooperate and seek common interests.

---

[99] Consumer protection almost certainly requires a different approach. It is my impression that the United Kingdom is well ahead of all but a few American states. See S. Bright, 'Winning the Battle Against Unfair Contract Terms' (2000) 20 *Legal Studies* 331; M. Dean, 'Unfair Contract Terms: The European Approach' (1993) 56 *Modern Law Review* 581 (1993).

[100] M. Galanter and M. Cahill, '"Most Cases Settle": Judicial Promotion and Regulation of Settlements' (1994) 46 *Stanford Law Review* 1339, 1388.

We should notice how similar this coercive mediation approach is to what takes place in bankruptcy in the United States. To a great extent, in bankruptcy the parties are pushed to accept some sort of compromise to remedy the debtor's inability to perform many contracts. We get little predictability if we move from contract to bankruptcy, and the original contract controls then only if one party took a secured interest in the right form and recorded it. Those who write about contracts often fail to consider this remedy—bankruptcy—for multiple breaches of contract. Yet the most formal approach to relational contracts will have limited impact if firms facing difficulty often use bankruptcy. Any theory about the role of contract law must include the functions of bankruptcy or it will be seriously incomplete.

Dean Scott clearly recognises that most cases are settled, but he argues that clear rules will provoke more settlements. He argues that categorical binary contract rules may be effective complements to the more flexible extra legal mechanisms that regulate adjustment of ongoing relationships.[101] My colleague William Whitford has offered several propositions about relational contracts.[102] Whitford says:

As contracts become more relational, the parties will comply less frequently with formalities (including the parol evidence rule). Hence, a strict enforcement strategy with respect to formalities is more likely to raise issues about protection of reasonable reliance with respect to relational than discrete contracts.

As contracts become more relational, it becomes more difficult for courts to apply sensibly doctrine that requires courts to make qualitative judgments about a course of conduct. Courts lack the capacity to understand complex relations between all the affected parties.

As contracts become more relational, there is an increasing tendency of the parties to value non-material aspects of the relation (continuation of the relation, maintenance of harmony and respect, etc.). Courts have no effective way to protect these expectations, and hence they tend to over commodify the relation–that is, they try to compensate in money for that which is really not commensable this way.

What do Whitford's hypotheses mean for settlement? Dean Scott suggests that legally imposed adjustments may create perverse incentives that undermine the stability of the cooperative equilibrium of contracting parties.[103] When stakes are large, the chance that a court may rework the distribution of risk in a contract may be enough to offset possible future rewards for cooperative behavior. Even the threat of going to court to seek relief may affect how the parties readjust matters. Scott concedes that we do not know how judicial activity affects decisions about cooperation and readjustment. He concludes:

> [T]he relational context is a complex environment of many regulatory systems, including individualised and patterned responses, legal and social norms, and ex ante and ex post bargains. The challenge for contract law is to construct a legal apparatus that complements

---

[101]R. E. Scott, 'Conflict and Cooperation in Long-Term Contracts' (1987) 75 *California Law Review* 2005.

[102]W. C. Whitford, Unpublished Memorandum.

[103]Scott, n 98 above, 2051.

> these forces. As a first step, we must abandon the assumptions of legal centrism and acknowledge our incomplete understanding of contractual relationships and of the linkages between legal rules and social norms.[104]

Scott will be right in some cases. If courts seek to impose relational contract norms in a legal proceeding, as Macneil stresses, this may not produce good faith and cooperation. The very fact that the parties have shifted from the vocabulary of contractual partners to adversaries in litigation may undercut trust and reciprocal obligations. Furthermore, one side may see incentives to gamble that it will win big in litigation. Scott certainly is right that those who think about contract law must abandon assumptions about legal-centrism and think about linkages between legal rules, social norms and the urge that many who are sued have to fight back.

Nonetheless, sometimes legal uncertainty could be a factor provoking parties to spend more effort seeking a settlement. Litigation usually is expensive and unpleasant. Business people must turn over a large measure of control to lawyers, and many resist this. Even the threat of having a lawyer for the other side take a deposition, might be enough to deter some business people from taking the legal route; few business people would enjoy being cross examined at trial. My judgment is that in all but unusual situations, flexible doctrine will provoke settlements. The only way to determine how the doctrine applies to the particular facts of the case would be to litigate until some courts provide an answer. While lawyers may be able to predict what courts will do, they cannot guarantee that their clients will win. Even if they win, lawyers cannot guarantee that the legal rules dealing with contracts damages and an inability to satisfy a judgment will not leave a plaintiff with but a Pyrrhic victory. Settlements are under the control of business people and their lawyers. Unless money is no object and there is a point of principle, rational business people will salvage what they can by settlement and avoid throwing good money after bad in the litigation game.

Moreover, as we have seen in the *ALCOA* and *Westinghouse* cases, litigation can produce settlements. A judge, such as Judge Teitlebaum, who rewrites a contract based on his own view of what is demanded by relational norms may provoke the parties to rededicate their efforts to find a compromise that is more compatible with their needs. A judge, such as Judge Merhige, who participates actively in settlement negotiations may be able to act as a mediator backed up by his power as a judge to discipline lawyers and even the parties.

Conclusion

Clearly, contract documents often fail to capture the real deal between the parties. There are many arguments rationalising treating documents in such situations *as if* they were the complete expressions of the contracts made by the bargainers. This

---

[104] *Ibid* 2053–2054.

may avoid giving courts discretion so that we reduce the risk of arbitrary action by judges. This may even reduce the risk of decisions based on bribery. This may avoid sending courts on missions that often they cannot carry out because of the very real capability problem. Taking this approach to writings may cut the costs of goods and services so that we may have computers, airplanes, compact disks, machine tools and microwave ovens at lower prices. In some, but not all, situations these arguments have merit. Nonetheless, all of them assume that it is worth running the real risk of defeating actual reasonable expectations of bargainers in the service of some more important end.

We might at least focus the issues if we were to accept that there is a text between the lines in most contracts, and if we do not attempt to implement this implicit text, we are denying reasonable expectations. If we are willing to take an as if approach, we then must ask whether reputational sanctions are enough to support most ongoing transactions. Sometimes a formal approach that treats a contract as if it were a discrete transaction may be justified, but we must be sure that we consider all the costs of this approach. We might decide that there is a high cost in legitimacy if the legal system comes to symbolise that contract rests on manipulations of forms and courts reject the substance of the real deal of the parties. At the very least, if our courts allow those who draft written contracts to impose terms inconsistent with expectations and the implicit dimensions of contract, we can expect reformers to demand that the law police those bits of private legislation that masquerade as contracts so that they are fair.

Part IV
Core Works on Law in Context and New Legal Realism

Law and the Behavioral Sciences: Is There Any There There?

Stewart Macaulay

Abstract Despite tremendous growth in the field, there have been many challenges to law and the behavioral sciences. The most colorful expression is Abel's charge that "questions and answers have begun to sound a comfortable, but rather boring 'clackity-clack."' On one hand, the achievements of the field cannot be ignored by those who want to think about law seriously. On the other hand, all approaches to the field are flawed and are likely to remain that way. Help in solving the problems of the field might come from a thorough interdisciplinary approach, calling on the contributions of all social sciences while recognizing the limitations of each; knowledge of a minimum amount of law and legal method, but with full awareness of how legal thought may distort definitions of problems; and knowledge of the questions posed by broader social theories in light of an empirical refining of their large explanations.

Gertrude Stein said that the problem faced by those from Oakland, California was that "there isn't any there there." Since there were people, streets, and buildings, she must have had in mind some intangible there of importance. After several decades of work in law and the behavioral sciences, I have some ideas about whether there is, or

This article was original published in Law and Policy 6 (1984), 149–87. Reprinted with permission. Many of the ideas in this paper were first presented at a round table organized by the Disputes Processing Research Center at the University of Wisconsin-Madison. A revised version was delivered as the 1983 James McCormick Mitchell Lecture, on April 7, 1983, at the State University of New York at Buffalo Faculty of Law and Jurisprudence. Dr. Jacqueline Macaulay edited all of the many drafts of the manuscript and was a challenging and helpful critic. My colleague David Trubek and I have discussed these ideas over a long period, and he commented extensively on a draft of the manuscript. Many other friends debated these topics, especially after the Madison and Buffalo presentations, and forced me to abandon some ideas and clarify other. Yet after all this help, I am still responsible for all errors.

S. Macaulay (✉)
University of Wisconsin Law School, Madison, WI, USA
e-mail: smacaula@wisc.edu

D. Campbell (ed.), *Stewart Macaulay: Selected Works*, Law and Philosophy Library 133, https://doi.org/10.1007/978-3-030-33930-2_18

could be, any there there. I propose to examine the problem of "thereness," and, insofar as the field lacks the right stuff, offer some suggested directions.

What is the nature of the concern? In one sense, there is plenty of there there. Many people here and abroad work in the field. It is difficult, if not impossible, to keep up with the outpouring of books, journals, and conference proceedings. The area even has that ultimate badge of respectability—its own program at the National Science Foundation. Moreover, those seeking to influence policymakers often wave empirical studies in their faces as rationalizations for programs, and courts and other legal agencies frequently cite social studies of law.

At the same time, many have challenged law and the behavioral sciences. A major premise of the founders of the field was that their work would prompt needed reform so that our society might come closer to its announced ideals. Critics of various persuasions have objected to this focus: on the one hand, conservatives often see law and behavioral science as but a rationalization for the agenda of the Democratic Party's liberal wing; we should not be surprised that they object to having the thought they hate dressed in the clothes of neutral science. On the other hand, those more familiar with the field, perhaps paradoxically, see its actual impact as rationalizing the *status quo;* its true function may be to promote a resigned cynical tolerance since the work could be read as suggesting that reform cannot work and radical changes will be impossibly inefficient. First, those in the field debunked the society of the 1950s, and then we trashed the efforts of the 1960s and 1970s to deal with racism, sexism, environmental pollution, consumer problems and the like. Our message is tragic: this *is* the best of all possible worlds.

If our work will not serve as the basis for much successful social engineering, can we at least offer understanding of the place of the legal system in society? Some have their doubts. They see the field as reflecting a faith that heaping up piles of instances will somehow—perhaps by magic—yield knowledge. Rick Abel (1980b:826), a former editor of the *Law & Society Review*, and long an active member of the Law and Society Association, expressed his concern this way:

> Social studies of law have reached a critical point in their development. The original paradigm is exhausted. Until new ones are constructed, scholarship will be condemned to spin its wheels, adding minor refinements to accepted truths, repeating conventional arguments in unresolvable debates.

He continues by saying that (p. 805) "I sense that our field is running so smoothly along familiar tracks that the questions and answers have begun to sound a comfortable, but rather boring, 'clackety-clack.'" Abel's phrase vividly expresses something troubling many of us.

I'll begin on a high note and talk about what's right with law and behavioral science. However, Alan Freeman (1981:1230) has gained lasting fame as the author of the proposition that "trashing is fun," and so I'll follow his lead and look at some of the gloomy conclusions of Abel and others. Finally, I will try to add some class to this act by turning to larger questions of social theory. As part of this discussion, I will look at some of the potential relationships between work in law and the behavioral sciences and that of the Conference on Critical Legal Studies. Perhaps even those unwilling to convert to the Critical Legal Studies faith can find new and promising directions in this work and negative reactions to it.

I. Achievements of Law and Behavioral Sciences

At the outset, we must recognize the achievements of the past two or three decades of law and behavioral science research. Whatever telling criticism might be made, anyone looking at this body of work seriously should see that it has changed thought about law and legal systems. Those who would ignore it are, too often, prisoners of ideologies, fools, or both.

Sometimes we forget how far we have come in two or three decades. Perhaps most of what has flowed from law and social science was available earlier (see Schlegel 1979, 1980), but there was little awareness of it in mainstream thought about law. This has changed. Marc Galanter and I walked home from work one evening, and we talked about the changes in perspective during our professional careers. We attended different law schools with some claims to excellence at the same time. Yet in our classes we never heard about police discretion, plea bargaining, personal injury negotiation or alternatives to litigation. Law schools then dealt with Restatements, balancing interests, and the first excitement prompted by Hart and Sacks, Fuller and other reactions to realism. Almost all of this thought involved legal rules or judgments about the appropriate roles of legal institutions deduced from their "nature."

Marc and I met as Bigelow Teaching Fellows at the University of Chicago Law School in 1956. The Ford Foundation had made major grants to Chicago's jury and arbitration projects, and Hans Zeisel, Fred Strodbeck, Harry Kalven and Soia Mentschikoff were trying to learn how to study the actual operation of legal institutions. However, most of this activity existed at the margins of the school's classrooms, except, perhaps, in those taught by Max Rheinstein. Afternoon tea, attended by both faculty and students, was then an institution at the school. Scholarly interest there, however, turned far more to Brainerd Currie's theories about Conflict of Laws than the jury or arbitation projects. Other elite law schools could not even offer major projects at the margins of their activities; at best, one or two of their faculty members wrote essays calling for the integration of law and social science, but leaving the work to someone else. I can also testify that a young law professor interested in answering this call in those days would have been disappointed by what appeared in the major social science journals. Apart from criminology, law and legal systems just did not seem to concern economists, sociologists and psychologists. Anthropologists did write about law but they did not study modern industrial societies. Political scientists were just beginning to embark on predicting the results of Supreme Court decisions from the application of social science methods.

As recently as fifteen years ago, when Lawrence Friedman and I (1969) were trying to fashion the first edition of our teaching materials, social science and law was largely unexplored territory. There were a few classic articles known to and cited by all. There was no *Law & Society Review, Law & Policy* or *Journal of Legal Studies.* Law reviews occasionally did print articles with some description of the legal system in operation, but they were hard to find since they were buried among the endless variations on conventional legal themes.

The volume of work in law and social science exploded during the late 1960s and 1970s. The decades of reform and counterreform provoked much of the work. Both reformers and researchers assumed, or hoped, that social science would support their causes. Evaluation research, however, often was disappointing. Again and again, it showed a gap between the promise and performance of the American legal system, although it seldom tried to explain why laws remained on the books but were not put into action. In spite of the disappointing results, the river of policy-related research flowed on, getting wider and wider. Today political leaders of all persuasions cite research useful to their causes. Social scientists from all the major departments in most universities turn some attention to the legal system, and it would be a most primitive law school that allowed its graduates to pass through without ever hearing of police discretion, plea bargaining, and the games played by insurance adjusters and plaintiffs' lawyers.

This flood of social science and law has washed up a few shining nuggets. Any list would be arbitrary. However, I think anyone reviewing the accomplishments of the past few decades would conclude that we are far more aware of many or most of the following ideas:

1. Law is not free. There are barriers to access to the legal system which some people can jump far more easily than others. Most simply, few can afford to invest the substantial sums needed to hire lawyers, investigators and experts, run risks of retaliation and injuries to reputation, become emotionally involved in a cause, and diverted from alternative uses of their time to participate in a process where they may lose totally or recover what so often are inadequate remedies. Moreover, some people can afford to run up the costs of participation to run poorer opponents out of the game, and the threat that this may happen deters many from entering the contest. (See Galanter, 1974). Thus, many people are left to lump it, whatever their legal rights. When we turn to social regulation, we find that it involves costs which some can pass along to others. It usually is fruitful to ask who benefits from and who pays for any type of legal action. Often we will find that regulation operates as a kind of regressive taxation, burdening the have-nots far more than the haves.

2. Law is delivered by actors with limited resources and interests of their own in settings where they have discretion. "Street-level bureaucrats" (Lipsry, 1980) such as police, assistant prosecuting attorneys, case workers, clerks of court, those handling intake at administrative agencies and many more, have discretion although no one planned it that way. This is true for a number of reasons. Policies conflict and the rules may be unclear. As a result, those who deal with the public may have a choice of goals to pursue or rationalizations for whatever they want to do to serve the public or their own self interest. Those who do the day-to-day work of a legal agency often are hard to supervise because they control the official version of events by writing reports in the files. Resource constraints often make it impossible to "go by the book" since officials cannot do everything mandated. If those enforcing a law cannot carry out all their duties, they must choose which of them under what circumstances they will attempt to implement. Those choices of "street-level bureaucrats" are unlikely to be random or neutral in their impact. They will be affected by folk wisdom or bias, reward and punishment structures, and self-interest. (See Handler, 1979; Macaulay and Macaulay, 1978).

3. Many of the functions usually thought of as legal are performed by alternative institutions, and there is a great deal of interpretation between what we call public and private sectors. We live in a world of "legal pluralism" where rules are made and interpreted and sanctions imposed by many public and private governments which are only loosely coordinated. Some conduct is entirely within the jurisdiction of one government or another; sometimes units are complementary and support each other; often they are rivals and compete for influence. Examples of private governments range from the Mafia to the American Arbitration Association. Trade associations, sports leagues, church groups, neighborhood organizations and many other "private" units such as business corporations exercise what are, effectively, legal powers. They make rules by constitutions, charters and standard contracts; they interpret them in their day-to-day operations; they offer benefits on certain conditions; and they may suspend or expel members, associates or employees as a sanction. Indeed, in many instances these sanctions may be more powerful than any the law has to offer. Also, those who regularly interact in valued long-term relationships usually form semi-autonomous social fields (Moore, 1973) which regulate a great deal of behavior. For example, both business people who deal regularly and those plaintiffs' and defendants' lawyers who specialize in personal injury work in a community are subject to the rules and sanctions of their social fields. Moreover, at all levels of society, public government tends to exist at the margins of long-term continuing relations, usually affecting but seldom controlling behavior. Indeed, distinctions between public and private arenas tend to disappear in practice. (See Macaulay, 1983). Police, prosecutors, clerks of the court, judges, field officers of administrative agencies, mayors, governors, legislators and other public officials and their assistants often are enmeshed in long-term valued relationships with those they purport to regulate. Problems are transformed, filtered and channelled into and out of the public legal system and systems of private regulation as part of complicated processes. Lawyers and others often play critical roles in assigning problems to the jurisdiction of one or another norm-defining-and-sanctioning system. One cannot understand legal action without understanding the collaborating and rival institutions in a society. (See Galanter, 1981; Fitzpatrick, 1983).

4. People, acting alone and in groups, cope with law and cannot be expected to comply passively. Many people are able to ignore most legal commands, or redefine them to serve self-interest or "common sense," and live with a vague and often inaccurate sense of the nature of law and legal process—all without encountering serious problems. There is great opportunity for evasion in a society that values privacy, civil liberties, and limited investment in government. Coping with the law can become a game that offsets any sense of obligation. Many participants in social fields and networks pass along techniques of evasion, legitimate breaking the law, honor the crafty, and even sanction those who would comply. The law is frequently uncertain and plausible arguments can be fashioned to rationalize much of what many people want to do. This means that there is great opportunity for bargaining in the shadow of the law (see Mnookin and Kornhauser, 1979) or in the shadow of questionable assumptions about the law. Thus, people's views of the likely legal consequences of action at best affect but do not determine their behavior.

Sometimes, however, the command of the law rings loud and clear and has direct impact on behavior. In short, the role of law is not something that can be assumed but must be established in every case.

5. Lawyers play many roles other than adversary in a courtroom. Lawyer self-interest, and their view of what is best for a client, often dictates that litigation should be avoided, and lawyers seek other ways to provide service to clients. (See Macaulay, 1979). They tend to know who makes decisions and what kinds of appeals, legal and other types, are likely to be effective. They know how to bargain and how to manipulate situations so that accommodations can be reached. Often they serve as coercive mediators, acting in settings where their profession itself is a tacit threat of trouble if people do not behave reasonably. Instead of pursuing only their client's immediate interest, lawyers often act as what Justice Brandeis called "counsel for the situation," seeking what they see as the best long-term solution for all concerned. Often lawyers, with more or less success, seek to transform clients' perceptions about what is just, or at least tolerable. Often they deal with bruised egos and manage public relations far more than they vindicate clients' rights. As Marc Galanter observes, these professional practices tend to breed distinct bargaining arenas where veteran players know the going rate for, say, breaking and entering with one prior offense, a whiplash injury in a rear end collision, and the like. The "hired gun" battling for a client to the limits of law and ethics is found only in a limited set of situations. The development of these less adversarial roles explains why we find those aggrieved being offered a deal more often than we see rights being vindicated. This may be of concern if we think that rights ought to be clarified and vindicated to serve social purposes. Also, the wide variety of roles played by lawyers is a factor in making the functioning of social institutions far more complex than formal descriptions assume. For example, many lawyers' stock in trade includes their contacts with officials, knowledge of acceptable rhetoric, and awareness of mutually advantageous possibilities. Thus, they are able to cut through formal channels and get things done. When this happens regularly, behavior in a corporation or a public agency no longer follows official procedures. If we think those procedures serve certain functions, this activity by lawyers, or others playing similar roles, will undercut them.

6. Our society deals with conflict in many ways, but avoidance and evasion are important ones. At times we mobilize social institutions in the service of values and interests: we fought a civil war; the army has enforced civil rights laws; the FBI has suppressed what its leaders saw as radical causes; and the criminal process has jailed people seen as threats to the safety and privileges of those who count. More often, however, we honor principled behavior in words but practice accommodation. We may pass symbolic laws declaring the good, the true and the beautiful, but we leave enforcement to local option. We find social consensus at a high level of abstraction and so keep our doctrines ambiguous or contradictory. This avoids the costs of definition and of deciding that some interpretations of values are right while others are wrong. Thus, a simple means-and-ends view of law should be suspect. Moreover, while some may be fooled by the gap between law's announced promises and the system's performance, others are well aware of what is going on. (See Galanter, 1974). Whether law is supposed to solve social problems is always something to establish rather than something that can be assumed.

7. While law matters in American society, its influence tends to be indirect, subtle and ambiguous. It is easy to find gaps between the promise and performance of our law. Americans are selectively law abiding: some refuse to register for the draft as a matter of principle; some cheat on their taxes or redefine their obligations under those laws in questionable fashion; many drive while intoxicated. Businesses pollute the environment, distribute dangerously defective products, and bribe public officials. Nonetheless, law matters in a number of ways. For example, many ideas that are part of our common normative vocabulary are crystallized in law, and they both help rationalize action and affect our expectations about the social world. Indeed, even the sports pages of our newspapers more and more resemble law reviews as a legal vocabulary is appropriated to explain players' relations with teams, teams' relations with cities, and the like. While the ability of the legal system to prompt social change that is unwanted by a large or powerful minority may be limited, often law can add gasoline to an already burning fire. The struggle to gain legal rights can be the focus of a social movement, forcing reformers to define goals and to select means to obtain them. Even failed reform efforts may influence the behavior of both proponents and opponents. Moreover, law can restrain power in many situations. For many reasons, those with power hesitate to exercise it too crudely. The effort to cloak an exercise of power with a mantle of right or to cover up abuses are costly exercises which, at times, deter action. Law and lawyers have helped gain accommodations for some of the less powerful by using legal symbols and procedures. In this culture even the counter-attacks by the powerful have to be rationalized in legal rhetoric. This effort may affect both the form and substance of the way such battles are fought and resolved.

The picture formed by connecting these seven points cannot be ignored by a reformer or theorist who wants to act through or think about law in this society. While fantasies may be lovely things if they are recognized for what they are, romanticized views of social life are not always innocent. One who would act or theorize apart from something resembling an empirical picture of our legal system in action probably is engaged in a con game. For example, consider all the proposals to "solve the crime problem" by simple solutions such as easing the rules concerning search and seizure; curbing the insanity defense; increasing sentences for those convicted; and ending plea bargaining. Whatever else one can say for such proposals, they appear to be cheap. If crime were caused by words in a Supreme Court opinion or a statute, then crime could be ended by paying a printer to set new text. No new taxes would be imposed. No extra services would be required. All that would be needed would be to muzzle lawyers and judges. However, few conversant with law and society literature see these kinds of proposals for fighting crime as much more than the wares of one more snake oil salesman.

Similarly, Marc Galanter (1983) criticizes the frequent assertions that our legal institutions are overwhelmed by a flood of litigation prompted by the excessive litigiousness of Americans provoked by greedy lawyers. He finds instead that there is little persuasive evidence of a litigation explosion and that modern patterns of disputing are a conservative adaptation to changing conditions. The argument that there has been a serious problem created by increasing litigation "displays the weakness of contemporary legal scholarship and policy analysis" as "theories were put forward without serious consideration of whether they fit the facts."

Much the same can be said for theoretical literature that attempts to explain rules of law in terms of promoting efficiency without considering how, if at all, those rules are implemented. This kind of writing may have value as a study of ideology, but sometimes it seems to have a kinship with W. C. Fields conning a mark. Writers in this camp often neglect their own teachings. They fail to consider the costs of moving from what they view as a messy and inefficient welfare state to the brave new competitive world. Since they are not interested in distributional questions, they can ignore those left behind. Perhaps the trip *is* worth the price, but the true price must be assessed before this judgment can be made. We always must ask who benefits and who pays how much to reach any utopia; the social study of law should make it clear that such questions must be asked of any reformer or revolutionary.

II. Will Science Save Us?

When Columbus sought to test his theory that the world was round, he sailed west and discovered the new world. He showed that sailing beyond the horizon did not lead to falling off the edge of the world. However, as we know, his theory led him to err: he mistakenly called those who had discovered the Americas long before him, "Indians." As time passed, simply sailing west from Spain became less and less likely to yield new and significant knowledge about the shape of the world. Better ships and navigational aids made the trip easier, but they alone did not add much to what had been learned from the voyages of the first hundred years or so.

Rick Abel (1980a, 1980b) sees the situation in our field as much the same as work on the round world theory after the first voyages. He asserts that the "original paradigm [of social studies of law] is exhausted." He continues, (p.429)

> [r]ecent scholarship often seems stagnant, further demonstration (or falsification) of a well-established (or generally discredited) hypothesis, one more entry in a sterile, and ultimately unresolvable, theoretical debate—a by-product of the demands of tenure-review committees rather than the expression of any real intellectual engagement.

He argues (1982:795) that the "central flaw is the insistence upon explaining law only as an instrumental means to a material goal . . . [this] has long impoverished social studies of law." Law, he reminds us, "can also be expressive, mystifying, or legitimating; it can provide an arena for status competition."

My own reading of the record leads me to support Abel. At the outset, I see two major problems in the field: (1) the functioning legal system is difficult to study, and (2) all the common approaches to the social study of law are flawed in some way and likely to remain so. However, having said that, I will offer some cautions about throwing out babies with bathwater.

While other areas may be even more difficult for social scientists to study, the functioning legal system poses hard-to-solve problems for researchers. Legal topics involve privacy and the interests of the powerful. There are sanctions which may be used to retaliate against those who talk too much. As of right, we cannot observe anything but on-stage behavior; yet much of the action takes places back-stage. Actors who know what is going on may mislead us. Truth for the sake of science may be outweighed by an urge to keep one's job or loyalty to a group. Even those eager to cooperate may have fooled themselves about how often they do what and why.

Also, law is pervasive, but we can seldom do more than narrow case-studies. When we try to work with available sets of macro-data, we find that they are suspect. For some purposes it may prove useful to treat the legal system as relatively autonomous, but in most instances there is a great deal of interpenetration between legal and other social systems. Legal problems usually are aspects of much larger events so that a focus on, say, sentencing is likely to overlook or distort our view of what is happening in a larger context.

In addition, the units we describe and analyze often are not tangible things which can be measured in ways which all would accept. Commonly, the stuff of law involves social constructs that reflect translations, transformations and distortions of "events in the real world." And then research removes us another step away from this world. Counting what we define as "events," finding associations, and other data manipulations may produce a picture with little resemblance to the perceptions of those who participated in the events or to some underlying reality we assume exists: Of course, we could narrow our work and count only tangible things. But even if we accept that there are enough tangible "things" involved in law to matter, Roberto Unger (1976; 56–57) reminds us that,

> To treat . . . understandings and values as mere shams is to assume that social relations can be described and explained without regard to the meaning . . . [that people] . . . who participate in those relations attribute to them. This . . . would be to blind oneself to what is specifically social about the subject matter . . .

A major problem in the social study of law is "scientism." The goal of some may be as much to promote the status of their field as to learn something significant about the legal system in operation. Many researchers bring the tool-kit of methods fashionable in their social science and look for problems where those methods can be used. It sometimes proves necessary to distort the nature of existing problems so that preferred methods can produce answers. Research techniques may be impeccable, but a rigorous answer to a silly question is still a rigorously silly answer. The alternative is not sloppy research. Rather, we must chose methods appropriate to questions worth asking about legal systems in their full social context. Sometimes, as I will show, a little bit of all kinds of methods may be called for to deal with what our theory allows us to see as an important problem.

All the common approaches to the social study of law are flawed. While each may be improved, all are likely to remain less than reliable recipes for producing objective truth. Without getting bogged down in arguments about social science method or debates about whether positivist social science is but an illusion (see Dandeker, 1983; Hekman, 1983), I can note several examples of problems in studying the legal system.

Some researchers have attempted to recreate legal phenomena in a "laboratory" to overcome secrecy in legal processes and to control the mass of variables interacting in the actual legal system. Some suggestive work has emerged, but much misses the mark badly. (For a criticism of this work, see Loh, 1981). My *bête noire* is most, but not all, research based on simulated trials before mock juries. The classic objections to this research are well recognized: it is difficult to recreate the essential features of the legal process without an expensive investment in theater—the interactions among judges, lawyers, litigants and defendants, architecture and symbols, procedures and the like are hard to capture in less than a full dramatization. Furthermore, people in these experiments are playing the role of "subject" rather than making decisions that count. While they may become involved in their experimental task, they never confront someone who may be hurt by their decisions and at some level they know that they are playing a game. They are not socialized into the role of juror. (See Balch, Griffiths, Hall and Winfree, 1976). It as been suggested that if one is testing a theory, this artificiality does not matter. Yet learning that a theory holds true in an artificial context does not establish that it will work in any other context. This defense is just a variation on the "all other things being equal" ploy so often used to defend suspect work.

There are other objections to jury research which are not so well recognized. Because of the filtering, funneling and channeling of cases in the criminal justice system, only rare cases go to juries; most are diverted to juvenile justice systems or handled by plea bargaining. If this is true, we should ask whether the experimental cases used in mock jury research are like those which might ever get to a jury. Cases actually tried probably have unusual features or pose dilemmas that would try the wisdom of Solomon, but, typically, research is not focused on such situations.

Also we find a great deal of confusion lurking in this body of research, about what it is that jurors are supposed to do. (See Broeder, 1954). The author of one research proposal argued that jurors are supposed to be "as calculators with a cleared memory." Yet the whole idea of a jury of one's peers is that jurors will bring with them the "folk-wisdom" of the community. Is the "bias" so often studied in jury research really the experimenter's term for what he or she sees as bad folk-wisdom? Social psychologists often use the term "bias" with a different meaning than lawyers, and jury research at times involves a confusion of definitions.

Researchers seem to assume that we want a scientific judgment from jurors—that an adversary trial by jury and a controlled experiment are just alternative ways of seeking truth. Yet are jurors supposed to apply law to facts in a coldly rational scientific process? We may want jurors to refuse to apply what they see as unjust laws. Anne Bernays, the novelist, commented in a recent *New York Times Book Review* (1983:13) that "[c]ourts are places where well-intentioned people attempt to make sense of the irrational." Juries may exist to decide cases which are impossible to resolve with any assurance on the evidence. Jurors who have not understood a judge's instructions about the law may actually search for the best available solution to a real dilemma. Perhaps the assumption that all human problems can be resolved satisfactorily in a scientific fashion is the most irrational position of all.

Recently jury researchers have attempted to cope with many of these problems (see, e.g., Borgida, 1981). Some of this work has been done by social psychologists who actually have seen many criminal trials and know something about the entire process[1] (See Hastie, Penrod and Pennington, 1983; Penrod and Borgida, 1983). Yet even their work can be no more than suggestive. (See Greenwood, 1982). As the best of these researchers take pains to warn us, they cannot capture the essential elements of jury trials in their simulations because they cannot be sure what elements are essential. In some instances, the most valuable part of jury research is the effort invested in thinking about jury process apart from any data collected in an experiment.

Another common approach to the social study of law has been regression analysis. It is a powerful but limited tool. Its use, too, has been subject to criticism. Abel (1980b:819) notes that,

> [s]tatistical correlations, which tend to be the foundation of criminal justice research, need to be accompanied by qualitative observations of institutions at work. We know virtually nothing about the mechanisms underlying these correlations, we are often uncertain about the causal direction, and we tend to work with a simplistic utilitarian model . . . [W]e need to take seriously the possibility that the criminal justice system really has very little to do with crime rates one way or the other.

Berk and Ray (1982) point out that regression analysis may yield highly misleading results if the data are the product of "selection artifacts"—that is, if they are too far from a random sample of some defined population. However, a good deal of work in our field must be based on just such data. Often we are lucky to find anyone who knows what is happening who will talk us to, much less a respectable sample of actors.

Wildavsky (1982:903); too, has little faith in regression analysis. He asserts that to believe in multiple regression one would have to "believe that the study controlled all the factors that made a difference to the results." This would be such a leap of faith, in his view, that "[i]f we believe in multiple regression at all, this is because we want to rely on something rather than nothing. Always the danger is that a spurious precision will replace an insightful guess." He insists that "matters of taste and judgment inform virtually every step of the process of estimating social effects due to social interventions . . ."

Wildavsky's attack is particularly apt when regression analysis is applied to macrodata gathered by public agencies. Too often these data are a mess. (See David and Robbin, 1981). Sometimes items are recorded or omitted for political reasons; sometimes inconsistent definitions of categories are used by officials in different cities or states when they report a table of numbers; the coding may be

[1]Some psychologists rely on advice from law professors or use law students playing the role of lawyers to provide realism in their experiments. Given the isolation of law schools and law professors from practice, this would be funny if it were not so sad.

consistent but the categories used may lump together very different things. Cochran (1980:123, 124) reminds us that "[d]ata may have an aura of authenticity even when they are inaccurate or false .... Certainly, it is the case that all things that are important cannot be quantified equally well." In short, an informed consumer would approach studies relying on multiple regression cautiously because too many researchers apply the technique mechanically without concern for its limitations.

In my experience, those who know the most about regression analysis are the most hesitant to use it inappropriately and are the most careful in spelling out assumptions and limitations. Just as simulation studies, the major contribution of regression analysis of large sets of data often is to suggest areas for further study. For example, Unnever (1982) studied sentencing in drug cases tried in Miami. He contrasted defendants with privately retained attorneys and those represented by public defenders, asking which were sentenced to prison more often. He found (p.220) that "defendants with private attorneys were significantly less likely to receive a prison sentence than those who had public defenders. The odds of incarceration were nearly halved if a defendant had a private attorney." On one hand, we could object that the category "private attorney" may involve lumping together the most competent tigers of the defense bar with the dregs of the profession. On the other hand, as Unnever says (213, n.2), "[f]uture research is needed to empirically determine what the components of successful legal representation are ... ." It seems unlikely that *all* private lawyers do better than *all* public ones. My guess is that a select few private attorneys who specialize in drug cases involving wealthy clients account for most of the difference. If so, I would be prompted to move to an in-depth study of their practices to explain this success. Whatever the appropriate questions, answers will not be found in tables of numbers. Rather, one must learn a great deal about the Miami drug scene, the nature of the defendants, narcotics officers, prosecutors, court personnel, and local politicians as well as more about defense lawyers. (Compare Adler and Adler, 1983). For example, one would have to rule out the possibility that the difference found by Unnever reflected the willingness of some private lawyers to bribe some judges, a practice in which public defenders do not engage. Regression analysis, alone, is unlikely to suggest or rule out this explanation.

If laboratory simulation and regression analysis are flawed, we must also recognize that soft-data case studies—which are typical of both anthropology of law and legal history—come with their own problems. (See Van Maanen, 1981; Britan, 1979). Both historical records and what an outsider can observe and ask about social relationships tend to serve as a kind of Rorschach test. The data may function as ink blots in which researchers may see clouds, sheep, class domination or creative dispute resolution. We always risk finding what we go looking for since we tend to see and hear what we are prepared to notice. Historical approaches are always affected by the process of creating and preserving records and anthropological approaches tend to yield stories which, at best, are true for a particular time and place. We, and our readers, tend to be influenced unduly by atrocity stories; yet what makes these stories vivid should make us suspect that they are atypical. Still, just as with the other methods discussed, these approaches can be suggestive, yielding knowledge which is important even though provisional.

After saying all this, I should make clear that I am not arguing against continuing the entire enterprise. There is still, in Gertrude Stein's terms, some there there which cannot be ignored. It is unlikely that some new paradigm demanding new questions and answers is waiting in the wings. Most existing criticism of the social study of law debunks without substituting much concrete in its place—we are told, for example, to substitute dialectic reasoning but not much more about what that is or what it might produce. (See Marenin, 1981). We may be past the point where we can expect to repeat the exciting discoveries of the first days of a new field, but there is still value in filling in uncharted territory. We may find that what we think is a general phenomenon is limited to the kinds of situations in the places we have studied so far. As more details become clear, parts of the picture may change. Even if we assume that all big discoveries have been made, we still may be brought up short when we consider the picture as a whole. Any grand new approach to the study of law and society will have to deal with the marginality of legal activity to most of life, plea bargaining, cost barriers to the use of legal process, mass processing and organizational explanations and all the rest of the ideas in my introductory list of what the social study of law has uncovered so far.

Furthermore, even if we believe that timeless truth about law and society cannot be produced by mechanical application of what are called scientific methods, those methods at least embody an ideal which might curb the excesses of know-nothing legal analysis and what Medawar (1982) calls the "literary syndrome in science." This syndrome involves a "combination of high imaginativeness with a relaxation of . . . the critical process . . . [a] style which at first intrigues and dazzles, but in the end bewilders and disgusts" (p.59). We need some defense against "the undisciplined exercise of the imaginative faculty to produce hypotheses held true because of their inspirational origin" (p.61).

The ideal, and at least some of the practice, of science teaches us that one begins with an idea or story that seems to explain something. It is not enough that it is plausible; it must be tested. One must be skeptical about one's own inspirations and fantasies as well as the works of earlier great minds. One must look for and credit evidence that fails to support or disproves one's position. One must be aware that we can find data that seem to prove the earth is flat. It is risky to generalize from a few cases, and we have to ask whether it is likely that any example of our position is typical. We must be concerned with multivariate interactions; single cause explanations where the influence runs only one way probably are wrong. Critics of conventional social science would also insist that we be aware that our own bias may affect every step of a study—it can color the questions asked, how they are worded, how abstract concepts are "operationalized," what subjects perceive that experimenters want them to do and say, and how data are summarized and interpreted. The researcher is part of the society or social group under study. Objectivity is a worthy goal, but those who think they have attained such a lofty disinterested state probably are fooling themselves if not others. There are, after all, rewards for having research come out the "right way" and penalties for failing to get publishable results. Social science researchers can never assume that they have uncovered natural invariant patterns of social action rather than just contemporary phenomena that will change as social perceptions, social structures or other factors change.

The ideal also teaches that we must be modest about what we claim; truth in packaging ought to apply to those who study the operation of the legal system as well as manufacturers of consumer goods. We may fool ourselves as well as others when we clothe ourselves in the image of the scientist in a white coat neutrally pursuing objective truth. If we accept the norm that one should not knowingly or negligently do harm, we must be concerned about how our work is likely to be appropriated in the service of which interests, classes or individuals. We cannot dismiss this concern with the conceit that all we are doing is reporting the facts as they "exist" out there.

However, a careful but limited study usually is an advance beyond what Meehl (1971) calls "fireside inductions" about legal problems. Usually, what we gain from the social study of law is provisional knowledge based on the best we could do under the circumstances. If we do not claim more, and work to see that others do not distort our work by ignoring all the qualifications, we can be proud of gaining this much. (Compare Eriksson, 1978).

While it would be hard to claim that all social study of law exemplifies the scientific ideal, there is enough there so that we can examine claims about law and reform better than we could just a few years ago. Indeed, insofar as we have true interdisciplinary work, we do tend to be aware of our assumptions and recognize the limited claims we can make. Any new approach offered to recharge the field ought to be subject to a skeptical reception insofar as it departs significantly from the demands of what I have sketched as the scientific ideal.

III. Theory to Relieve the Distress Caused by Clackety-Clack

Practitioners of the social study of law can get swept away in the clackety-clack of computer output. They may be refining methods to answer the wrong questions or only some of the right ones. A predictable response to an excess of data crunching is a call for theory, preferably theory originally written in German or French and imperfectly translated into abstract or newly created English words. The social study of law has been charged with mindless empiricism, covert use of a powerful but implicit theory which serves a political ideology, and neglect of questions posed by radical theories. Some argue that empiricism guided by assumptions of positivist social science is so flawed that it deserves to be dismissed as trivial or as merely clothing liberal pluralism in the garb of science. Others argue that only what they see as correct social theory will yield knowledge about the place of law in society. (See, e.g., Thompson, 1978; Nield and Seed, 1979; Warde, 1982; Turk, 1979; Ayre, 1982; Turk, 1982; Hund, 1982; Marsden, 1982).

Cain and Finch (1981:116) reject such extreme positions, but argue that "[i]t is the responsibility of every researcher to be a theorist." The two most developed theories that might serve to guide research are structural-functionalism and the many varieties of Marxism. Cain and Finch tell us that data are not collected or found; rather they are created by researchers who play an active part in the process. (Their position reminds us of the attacks of the legal realists on the conceit that judges only find the law rather than make it.) They continue by explaining that data are produced when sociologically inert entities are combined with a researcher's implicit or explicit theory. At times, researchers' theoretical outlooks cause them to neglect to report what they ignore as irrelevant; other times they see situations through lenses that transform inert entities into indications of dominance, social integration or something similar. A Marxist, for example, will look for indications of the impact of class; a liberal-pluralist will see a compromise of multiple interests that produces stability. To avoid misrepresentation, Cain and Finch say that both theory and method must be described so that readers can look for the transformations, the overlooked information and the bias behind interpretations. If this is not done, they warn, one is not doing science but engaging in propaganda.

While granting most of Cain and Finch's case, I want to look at what may be involved in calls for theory. I think that a great deal of the writing advocating theory reflects matters of intellectual style and politics, but these matters cannot be dismissed because style and world view do make a difference in the way we work and what we write. Then I will ask what might be produced in law and social science by a more explicit consideration of social theory. I will argue that both existing theories and empirical work would benefit if theorists and empiricists paid more attention to each other.

Johan Galtung (1982), the Norwegian sociologist who has worked in many areas of the world, suggests that there are distinct styles of social science, and I think we can find three in the international community of scholars interested in the place of law in society. Galtung has identified what he calls the saxonic, teutonic, and gallic intellectual styles. He uses these names because while Germany may be the home of the teutonic style, German scholars may pursue saxonic work and Americans may become more teutonic than the Germans whose work they borrow. As might be expected, the style we adopt influences the questions we ask, what we do to answer them, and what we see as answers. Each has advantages; each has disadvantages. Some combination would appear to be ideal, but experience teaches that successful syntheses are rare.

Galtung tells us that the *saxonic style* pictures science as a flat plain of data on which can be found many small hills representing "theories of the middle range." The preoccupation is with data, documentation and method. There is great worry about overly broad generalizations and abstractions not tied to specific instances. Moreover, if a middle range theory is not totally true, it is at least a start toward a partial explanation of what has been observed. The basic urge is to harmonize all kinds of work; one draws eclectically from theories and findings to stitch together one's story. There is an ecumenical approach seeking to find something of value in everything that used approved methods. Saxonic work tends to be sloppy in concept but rigorous in technique.

In contrast, the two continental styles "speed off into outer space, leaving a thin trail of data behind" (p.849) to the dismay of saxonic scholars. *Teutonic theory,* Galtung says, seeks a "potential reality," (p.828) free of the noise and impurities of everyday experience. It is represented by a grand and impressive deductive pyramid. The best feature a contradiction at the top to provide dynamic force. Research is guided by a desire to draw out the implications of a pyramid and to find examples to shore up foundations. A pure teutonic intellectual risks seeing a whole pyramid fall to pieces if any part of the foundations is shown to be wrong. In light of this risk, debate is warfare. Those who adhere to different pyramids tend to avoid each other for they know that discussion will not produce a productive interchange. Debaters have well-developed techniques to ward off the impact of seemingly contradictory findings. Indeed, a counter-attack on empiricism is one of the best strategies to preserve a pyramid in the face of inconsistent data—that the world does not seem to conform to theory only shows the difficulties in perceiving truth.

Gallic theory, according to Galtung, assumes that a totality cannot be shown by precise definitions, rigorous deductions or statistical techniques. A totality must be hinted at. One has to dance around it, viewing truth from many angles until in the end ideas are counterpoised between two poles. Most importantly, truth must be expressed with style and elegance. For example, Galtung quotes Foucault's assertion that "the soul has become the prison of the body" (p.851, n.19).

These styles have consequences. Saxonic research often is guilty of the sins of naive empiricism, answering trivial questions with an imposing technical apparatus. Debates over method can overshadow reflection about why we want to know the answers to our questions. Research produces more than anyone wants to know about, say, bias in sentencing in Atlanta, Chicago, Miami, San Diego and Denver without yielding generalizations about the criminal justice system, the legal system, the place of law in society or much else. The ecumenical search for harmony may produce a saxonic synthesis of interpretations of the ideas of Weber, Durkheim, Marx and the lyrics of last year's punk rock hits (compare Levine and Stumpf, 1983), but only at the cost of ignoring very real differences.

The continental styles tend to be what we could call "theories of adhesion"—one converts to the faith and then the theory just seems right; if a theory "rings true," it will then explain everything. Almost all experience can be transformed and translated into it, and so what would seem to be common sense counter-examples are "transcended." Teutonic theorists tend to assume that if their deductive pyramid were only implemented in its pure form, major beneficial changes in the world would follow. Here, too, style can have consequences. It is a short step from the academic hall to the political platform, and teutonic intellectuals claim to seek the unity of theory and practice.

What might the social study of law gain if writers in this tradition were to look to broader theories? At the outset, we must remember that there is a powerful, if often latent, theory underlying most of the work in law and the behavioral sciences. If we were concerned with theory, we could examine this view of the world and understand its influence on past and future work. One leg of this theory is provided by what Trubek and Galanter (1974) call liberal legalism—roughly a collection of ideas crystalized in the rule of law, constitutionalism, and the Bill of Rights. In part, this is a normative theory with a long history, but it also is a descriptive theory about the way government works in many western nations. Few would assert that it is a perfect description of any government in operation, but many write as if they assumed that it offers a roughly accurate picture, with perhaps a little slippage here and there.

The other leg of our conventional, but often tacit, theory can be labeled Mertonian latent-functionalism. There are two versions, one angry and another seemingly sophisticated. The angry approach brings to bear the fine American tradition of muckraking, with Thorstein Veblen as the patron saint. The muckraker shows that a particular law or part of the legal system is all a fraud hiding the interest of someone or some small group. The cool version finds latent functions in the failures and partial successes of the legal system. Gaps are rationalized. For example, we have a constitutional right to trial by jury, but the reality of our criminal process is plea bargaining. A true cool latent functionalist would point out the benefits of plea bargaining in reaching rough justice as compared to the caprice of actual juries whose composition and performance often is far from ideal.

This kind of social theory affects much law and social science research in the United States. Gaps between the law on the books and law in action are discovered because most researchers here carry in their heads and hearts a kind of high-school civics model of the American legal system. Any observation of police, courts, lawyers, administrative agencies or people interacting in public or private organizations is likely to show that things do not work "the way they should." On one hand, many see a normative imperative to close any gap they find. Here arises the instrumentalism that Abel sees as the major problem in the field—one who sees law primarily as a kind of social engineering will assume that adjustments are both necessary and possible when goals are not met. If a machine is not working as designed, one who loves machines will want to fix it. On the other hand, some engaged in such debunking may be content to expose a gap as a kind of scandal or as an indication that they know the true inside story. A latent functionalist, however, may even assume that a gap between promise and performance must be serving some important social function. These theories easily lead to an overly simple technocratic posture or to the cynical pleasures of the exposé. Yet they do not often seem to prompt questions about power, status, class and the like. Symbolic and other functions of law are overlooked as is the power of some people to resist enforcement or to change or sabotage laws that they dislike.

If those engaged in legal studies were to turn to more explicitly developed social theories, they might find a mutually profitable interchange between the social study of law and attempts to generalize about societies as a whole. On one hand, large social theory points to important questions overlooked or underemphasized in law and society research. On the other hand, an empirical view of legal systems in operation suggests that these theories rest on too formal a view of law and legality. Here, I cannot review all of these larger social theories and their attempts to account for the role of law. However, structural-functionalism, and Marxist-derived theories make similar suggestions about the role of law in capitalist societies. (See Lamo de Espinosa, 1980; Koch, 1980). Generally, all of this social theory assumes that law is instrumental for capitalism: private property is protected both by criminal and civil law; contracts are enforced so that planning is supported; the market is protected and regulated by anti-trust laws, prohibitions against unfair competition and tariffs; private activity is channelled in certain directions by control of the supply of money and credit and by tax incentives; and public investment establishes communications, transportation and the rest of the infrastructure while using these and other means to offset the economic cycle. Of course, structural-functional and Marxist-derived theories differ sharply about whether this activity produces stability or the contradictions of capitalism.

These theories usually tell us that law also affects attitudes and assumptions of some or all of the citizens about the propriety of particular decisions, particular social norms that are restated in the form of law, the legal system itself, or the entire social system. Liberal theorists talk of legitimacy or value clarification. Marxist-derived theories stress false consciousness and mystification. While one can distinguish these ideas, their assumptions about the process whereby law affects attitudes which then affect behavior are similar.

There are problems with these theories that might suggest new directions for research. Our empirical work suggests that private governments, social fields and social networks perform many of the instrumental functions these theories attribute to law. At best, the formal legal system operates in a limited class of cases, serves as a threat operating at the margin of social interaction, and functions indirectly to affect bargaining. For example, large corporations may run their own police forces as well as their own intelligence services which may even carry out a private foreign policy. "White collar crimes" usually are dealt with by what has been called "the second criminal justice system." (See Cole, 1978). A large corporation does not have to worry about proof beyond a reasonable doubt or *Miranda* warnings. One suspected of, say, embezzlement from an employer may be just fired or moved to another job without possibility of promotion. The threat of prosecution in the first criminal justice system may be used to gain some measure of restitution. The second system works without the benefits and burdens of constitutional rights and is under the control of large corporations rather than local or national politics. Moreover, a corporation can buy the state of the art in wiretapping or lie detector equipment which probably would be out of the reach of any police department budget.

We have learned that rules for conducting business tend to be made privately, either by trade associations or by standardized contracts with customary terms and conditions. Long-term continuing relationships are highly valuable, and parties hesitate to act in ways that might jeopardize particular relationships or their reputations. Such reputational sanctions are, in many instances, far more powerful than anything the law has to offer (Macaulay, 1963). Furthermore, important business leaders tend to influence how legal officials at all parts of the system exercise discretion. Public governmental and private business units often are interpenetrated by long-term continuing relationships so that distinctions between public and private spheres are blurred and indistinct. Law's autonomy from power in a society is only relative and never should be overestimated.

Empirical work also leads to questions about the realism of theories of legitimacy and mystification. (Compare Useem and Useem, 1979). By and large, people know little about their legal system, and what they know tends to be distorted or wrong. There is little proof that law affects attitudes which then affect behavior, and it is unlikely that people are motivated by something they have never heard of or know little about. Indeed, it is just as plausible that law is largely a private language for an elite with little impact on the larger society. (See Macaulay, 1977; McBarnet, 1982). Rather than looking to norms for behavioral guidance, it is possible that we act and then we rationalize. We may draw on a number of vocabularies in this process, and law seems to be only one of them. Perhaps most of the legitimating or mystifying comes from a vague and general assumption that one's society has a legal system in place, and that while abuses can occur, generally it is a tolerable or even good system. Whatever the truth, law's impact on attitudes and behavior likely is subtle and indirect.

Some refining of both structural-functional and Marxist-derived theories seems called for by these empirical views of the legal process. First, the assumption that law is directly instrumental for capitalism is contradicted by our findings about many other social institutions serving these functions in ways that overlap and even conflict with law. One could expand these social theories so that instrumental functions were assigned to something called the "state-apparatus." All private law-making, law-applying and sanctioning could be merged into the concept of the state, broadly conceived. But this could produce a theory where importantly different things were lumped together. Does it matter that a social function is carried out by a city's police force rather than the security department of a large multinational corporation? Is bargaining in the shadow of the law just a variant of the application of codified norms by a public court or are there differences with consequences? Does an interpenetrated regulatory system with multiple relationships between regulators and regulated differ from one that is relatively autonomous and controls the regulated through formal procedures?

Alternatively, one could modify or qualify social theories to mesh with empirical findings. Niklas Luhmann (1981), a leading systems theorist, has examined findings about legal pluralism in advanced capitalist societies and adjusted his theory. Luhmann sees the public legal system playing an integrating role that contributes to the stability of social systems, and he finds allocations of functions away from public institutions towards private ones to be dangerous. He warns that a trend toward viewing social problems as no longer matters of right may "lead to a kind of drying up of the legal system, and so leave the regulation of conflict to other mechanisms—e.g., morality, ignorance, class structure, or the use of force outside the law—whose structural compatability may be problematic" (Luhmann, 1981:247). Whether or not Luhmann is right, this is an example of data prompting an adjustment in theory.

Second, theories about legitimacy and mystification through law also need to be rethought. Different kinds of people know different things about law, and much of this knowledge is distorted. Rather than assuming that law affects attitudes in some uniform way, this is a question for study. One might begin by examining the images of law and the legal system found in textbooks and schools, mass media and fiction. One might also study the perceptions of groups with different religious, cultural and vocational backgrounds. Before researchers asked whether, when and how attitudes about law affect behavior, they would have to offer a plausible account of a process whereby perceptions and attitudes were affected by experiences with and attempts at communication about the law. One would have to study how people interpret messages they do receive about law to fit their experiences, preconceptions and self-interest. Some writers argue (see Ray, 1978; Stack, 1978), on the basis of at least a little evidence, that members of disadvantaged social groups are not mystified by ideological images of law as some Marxist-derived theories would have it. Rather their contact with law provokes a great deal of cynical awareness of how things really work and who really benefits. Those mystified may be the more well off who wish to justify their privileges.

Instead of talking of legitimation and mystification, an adequate theory must deal with instances of indifference, resignation, illegitimacy, and cynical awareness as well as mystification and legitimation. (See Holmes, 1982; Held, 1982; Richter, 1982). I think it unlikely that we will find law having a broad impact on attitudes and behavior. People may see most law as irrelevant to their immediate concerns or a matter for experts. When they must, they go along even with laws they view as senseless as the easiest way of avoiding trouble. However, it is hard to make even a plausible case for the idea that people comply with laws they see as irrational and cutting against their interest just because these commands are labeled law. (See Hyde, 1983).

Nonetheless, there is reason to think that there may be something to the idea of legitimacy or mystification. At the very least, people sometimes talk as if they thought that passage or repeal of a law would affect attitudes. All kinds of organizations appropriate symbols of formal legality for some reason—private police wear what most recognize as police uniforms; private action often mimics legal action, complete with rules of evidence and a version of due process; people do claim a right of free speech in private social interaction, although they are not always successful in gaining it; and all kinds of nongovernmental organizations make policy and allocate positions by elections. Perhaps all this is just rationalization and ritual with little impact, but enough of it takes place to caution us against assuming that it does not matter. However, in spite of theoretical and empirical work to date, we do not know how much and why this mimicry of legal action matters to whom.

The themes of law serving instrumental functions for capitalism and providing legitimacy or mystification are a bridge to much of the work of the Conference on Critical Legal Studies. In the late 1970s, a group of law professors, legal historians, activist lawyers and others came together to form the Conference on Critical Legal Studies. Some of those involved were Marxists, but most drew eclectically on aspects of Marxist writing, European critical sociological theory, the work of Gramsci (see, e.g., Femia, 1983), perspectives of the new left of the 1960s, and the like. They were united by friendship networks and their opposition to current fashions in legal scholarship; most were dissatisfied with social conditions in the United States and attempts of liberal reformers to remedy the plight of those on the bottom of the society, attempts which were seen as largely cosmetic and ineffective. Many of those involved were opposed to empirical social science or found it largely irrelevant to their concerns. With a few important exceptions, the focus of the Conference is criticism of liberal legal thought. It is difficult to find descriptions of alternative social institutions, except in the most general terms, or analyses of the process by which it might be possible to move from the present situation to a closer approximation of the ideal of human community shared by most members. The writing tends to be abstract and to involve special vocabularies, not easily read by outsiders. Most who are comfortable with saxonic style in social science will be put off, at least initially.

At first glance, critical legal scholarship seems either opposed or irrelevant to concerns of law and behavioral sciences. However, on closer examination, both the work of the Conference and the thrusts of its critics suggest possible directions for work in the social study of law which will widen its view and avoid some of what Abel calls clackety-clack. I cannot describe here all of the work of those associated with the Conference, report all of the criticism, and offer my own appraisal of the positions advanced. Rather, I will rely heavily on attempts of others to synthesize and criticize the many strands of thought involved. (See, e.g., Trubek, 1984; Gordon, 1983; Munger and Seron, 1984; Unger, 1983). I will ask what those accustomed to empirical work might gain from critical legal scholars without converting to their point of view. (Whether empirical social scientists *ought* to convert and adopt both the intellectual style and political stances common to critical legal studies is a topic for another and very differently argued paper.)

Trubek (1984) has made a major effort to harmonize the empirical work of law and behavioral sciences with that of critical legal scholars. He tells us that critical legal writing seeks to discover and analyze "legal consciousness," the view of the world held by members of a society or groups within it concerning what is tolerable, necessary and just. World views give meaning to human interaction and thereby, critical scholars tell us, "constitute" social relationships. World views are crystallized into law and its applications but often are at the level of unarticulated background assumptions. Critical legal scholars tend to see capitalist legal doctrine as incoherent, contradictory or both. However, these very flaws open the door for what Unger (1983) calls "deviationist doctrine." A critical scholar can find liberating strands of thought in liberal doctrine and build upon them. For example, American contract law tends to honor individualism and self reliance, but there is also the concept of fiduciary obligation which, if pressed toward the limits of its logic, could promote a far more altruistic legal response to problems in continuing relationships.

Unlike social scientists who claim neutrality and objectivity, most engaged in critical legal studies see themselves as involved in a form of transformative politics. They see their decoding of legal doctrine as exposing mystification in the service of those who rule. World views rest on claims of truth, at least in part. Thus they can be challenged by showing that the underlying truth claims are false. In the strongest view the process is somewhat like that of a new insight in Freudian analysis which, under certain conditions, will prompt a personality change. Once scholarship rips aside the blindfold of liberal thought, people may see how they have been fooled or have been fooling themselves. They then will be free to fashion new world views. Critical thought will help form these new world views in a liberating direction.

Most critical legal studies work is written in a way almost guaranteed to provoke counterattack, and the targets of the critical approach have returned the fire. Let me emphasize again that my purpose is not to take part in the debate between critical legal studies and its opponents. The question here, rather, is whether this debate suggests ways around some problems in law and the behavioral sciences. First, I will look at some of the objections that have been, or could be, made to critical legal studies. Then I will point out some of the implications of both critical work and the attacks against it for the social study of law.

Attacks on critical legal studies can be aimed at the plausibility of some common assertions found in this writing and at the emphasis given to decoding legal material. At the outset, consider what Trubek tells us is the basic assertion: consciousness or world views "constitute" social relations. In one sense, this seems unobjectionable. Socialism as practiced in Eastern Europe, for example, involves an elaborate normative vocabulary concerning social relationships, and this world view certainly is enshrined in the law of these countries. Markovits' (1978) analysis of the legal systems of the two German nations stresses the contrast in world view between socialist and capitalist versions in a situation where language, history and culture are much the same. (Compare Bowers, 1982). On the other hand, it is possible to have a formal statement of world view very much at odds with the actual assumptions of citizens. The world views declared in law are abstract and subject to conflicting translations and applications. While we would expect, for example, the world views reflected in the law of the German Democratic Republic and Poland to be similar, there is reason to think that the actual consciousness of citizens in the two "socialist" nations might be very different. Law probably always will be out of phase with at least some parts of a culture: there will be an official consciousness—"a party line"—and the actual world view held by people in the society which only partially tracks with the formally announced one. For example, "the" American world view involves a tension, or rough balance, between rugged individualism with its focus on striving and defeating others in competition and altruistic obligations towards at least certain other people. Our contract law, however, focuses on one aspect and largely neglects the other. At least in earlier times, judicial opinions recognized this by drawing a distinction between what one was legally obliged to do and one's higher moral duties.

Much of the work of critical legal scholars involves decoding world views hidden in law and legal writing; the legal historians in the group, of course, feed a broader range of material into their decoding machine. However, decoding texts always risks the problem of David Macaulay's (1979) "The Motel of the Mysteries." In Macaulay's book, North America was destroyed in 1985, by a flood of junk mail which, when all of the pollution in the air suddenly settled, formed a hard crust over the continent. A century later, archeologists explore and interpret American culture of the 1980s. Macaulay's archeologist finds a motel. There he discovers a skeleton lying on a bed facing a dresser on which are the remains of what we know to be a television set. He decodes his discovery as a strange religious rite: the dresser, he decides, is an altar with drawers in which were placed offerings to the gods of TV, and the set itself is a sacred object. The toilet seat, the archeologist assumes, is a ceremonial collar worn around the neck on occasions when the ritual shower cap is placed upon the head. The humor turns on getting things just a little wrong.

Decoding texts may tell us more about the politics and consciousness of the translator than about the materials themselves. One would be a poor lawyer if he or she could not fashion a plausible argument supporting some link between broad cultural assumptions and appellate cases, or, say, between these assumptions and episodes of Mork and Mindy (see Goldman, 1982), professional sports (see Galtung, 1982) or the structure of elite law schools. The problem is what is overlooked or misinterpreted. I do not know whether any critical scholar has ever overlooked a matter of importance or misinterpreted a text. Most members of the group are intelligent and imaginative people so that their decoding seems highly plausible. Yet the point is that we cannot be sure that their accounts are more than just plausible exercises of the imagination; nor can they be sure if all they do is apply their intellect to a text. The left critique of empirical social science—that positivism leads scholars to discover what they have built into their questions and accept as answers—may apply to decoding texts as well. After all, we must concede that there is enough of a parallel between watching television and religious ritual that the interpretation in "The Motel of the Mysteries" is plausible even though not quite right.

Even if we assume that a critical scholar has properly decoded a text, we can still question the likely impact of the exercise. Critical legal studies involves a not-always-spelled-out theory of the influence of ideas on social change. Critical scholars claim to be engaged in transformative politics, sometimes to the annoyance of radical lawyers. Somehow articles in law reviews, books, and lessons offered law students by a minority of their professors are expected to change the world for the better. In some unstated way, steel workers, migrant laborers, clerical employees, Native Americans, Hispanic Americans, and blacks of both sexes all will benefit if assumptions hidden in liberal law are exposed in communications directed to a very select and limited audience.

But will articles in elite law reviews and the *National Law Journal* affect the views and conduct of those with power to make or provoke change? Comfortable traditional ways of thinking continue in the face of brilliant analyses showing them to be incoherent, contradictory and against the interest of many who hold these beliefs. Indeed, in times of crisis, attitudes often turn toward world views that critical scholars loathe. Watts (1983) sees critical legal studies as a version of what he calls cultural Marxism and subject to many of its difficulties. Cultural Marxists, he says, "in the hopes of democratically changing the culture ... are forced to accept the existing unenlightened culture as the final arbiter of their attempt" (p.34). But when elite culture champions racial equality, women's liberation, gay rights, alternative life styles, conscientious objection to military service and a new morality, there is likely to be a backlash. (See Rhode, 1983). Watts suggests that when there is a breakdown of traditional life styles and economic dislocation, people are likely to turn to "paranoid-style movements" which "have placed in motion their bid to 'demodernize their consciousness' by restoring a past of romantic simplicity" (p.44). Rightwing movements are the result of democratic participation of people "as they now exist" (p.46). Calls for a revival of fundamentalist religious belief, attacks on the decisions of the Warren Court, covert attempts to reverse the limited amount of desegregation achieved in our society since the 1950s, and scapegoating the poor are likely to have more power than advocacy of a radical utopia in which ends are stated but the details of getting to the promised land are left to be worked out. So far critical scholars lack a plausible sketch for a theory of how to make "the times right" so that their ideas "will be in the air" and become the new common sense of those who can affect the process of change.

To their credit, critical legal scholars, perhaps without exception, are opposed to coercing people to accept their vision of the good society. Yet this poses a dilemma. If one is unwilling to accept the solution of a vanguard party with power to coerce others to its consciousness, one has to offer some plausible link between the consciousness of a small elite who reject the common sense of most members of their society and that of all those others whose world views must be transformed before there can be progressive social change. As van den Berg (1983:1265) comments, perhaps "deep inside all of us there is a single, authentic human nature and . . . if we could eliminate all the exogenous 'distortions' of that nature we would freely agree on what is right and what is wrong." Yet in the here and now distortions exist, and one cannot just ignore them. One cannot assume, for example, that anything taught law students will affect their views when they become lawyers or that lawyers with progressive views will affect business clients, political leaders, writers for intellectual journals, or those who plan television programs. Sometimes ideas current at, say, the Harvard Law School become popular enough in the right circles to influence legal action or even to gain attention from the mass media, but the process is neither automatic nor direct. While ideas matter in complicated ways, we must ask when and how what kind of thought will influence whom.

What are we to make of this debate? Both the writings of critical legal scholars and the criticism I have reported suggest that the social study of law might profit from more attention to the roles of ideas, attitudes, basic assumptions and common sense in affecting what happens and does not happen in the legal system. This is not totally unexplored territory, particularly by legal historians. Speaking generally, however, social scientists looking at law tend to treat world views, culture and background assumptions as little more than noise in the system which masks more "real" factors that explain action. Of course, appeals to patriotism, religious truth; constitutional and legal norms, and what is called common sense actually may be but rationalizations we use to fool ourselves and others. Furthermore, methods that can capture the impact of such factors tend to be "soft" rather than "hard," and their use threatens the uneasy status claims of the social sciences. Nonetheless, without careful examination it would be unwise to dismiss the influence of people's perceptions of what is tolerable, necessary and just. In the early days of American sociology, Thomas (1928:572) observed that what people think is so, is in fact so for them. No new breakthrough suggests that he was wrong. (See Ball, 1972, and compare Bach, 1975).

At a more concrete level, the social study of law would profit from attention to the significance, impact, influence or functions of legal doctrine on social action. One of the key insights of American legal realists was that we could not take doctrine at face value, but this observation does not warrant ignoring doctrine. Friedman has offered the best analysis of the functions of cases, statutes and jurists' writings about rules. In one paper (1967), he cautioned that rule skepticism had gone too far; he reminded us that where there is an interest in mass processing, we should expect to find, at some level, decisions being based on an unsophisticated application of simple rules. For example, when judges must deal with crowded dockets it is easiest to sentence all those convicted of a particular offense on the basis of the "going rate" for that offense for those who have a given number of prior convictions. The going rate at least will be influenced by what is said in the statutes and cases about the seriousness of the offense. In another work, however, Friedman (1975) described what he sees as the limits of the power of doctrine on the operation of the legal system and society. Law, he says, can have a "short run" impact on social action. It "provides a structure for aggregating interests, for expressing demands, for converting demands into rules and decisions" (p.156). He notes what critical legal scholars would call mystification: "People accept the federal system and act accordingly, because they do not find anything else really conceivable. Structure becomes, in short, custom or habit. This means that the threshold of skepticism, or rebellion, is that much higher" (p.158). However, Friedman (1975:155) sees law, "in the long run," melting away as a casual factor in social action. He tells us that,

> [w]hat keeps old-fashioned laws alive ... what hinders enactment of strict controls over noise and smoke, what preserves the class structure, and what maintains a brutal prison system is not the legal system itself, not structure, not the network of legal concepts, but real forces, real people—the concrete opposition of interest groups expressed *through* or *in* the legal system.

Friedman's analysis raises important questions. One can say, for example, that from roughly the turn of the century to the mid-1930s, legal ideas played some role in blocking the creation of elements of a welfare state in the United States. Doctrines such as substantive due process were asserted as rationalizations by concrete interest groups, or a dominant class, expressed through and in the legal system. In "the long run," however, when the depression eroded public toleration of traditional social and economic arrangements, the Supreme Court and many political leaders converted to a new faith, adopting ideas justifying government intervention in the economy and limiting the role of the Supreme Court in reviewing regulatory legislation. In a true crisis of capitalism, doctrine gave way to real forces.

It seems unsatisfying, however, to leave matters merely labelled by vague phrases such as long and short run. I would expect Friedman to be the first to insist that more was involved than just the passage of time. We can ask whether delay and the rhetorical demands of law affected the long run outcome of the New Deal. (Compare Skocpol, 1980). Critical scholars suggest that they served to shape the programs of the New Deal toward reformism rather than toward the more radical moves which some had advocated—one could sell regulation and collective bargaining, both subject to procedural due process, far easier than nationalization of industry. Can we generalize meaningfully about the role of doctrine from this experience beyond saying that it is easier to persuade judges, lawyers, writers and others who care about legal rules to accept change when it can be packaged in conventional terms? Teubner (1983:249) argues that needs and demands external to law "are selectively filtered into legal structures and adapted in accordance with a logic of normative development ... [B]roader social developments serve to 'modulate' legal change as it obeys its own developmental logic." Given the flexibility of much legal thought, how much modulation takes place? Would the answer differ, say, in Germany and the United States? We can offer examples, but we cannot really answer the question. (See, however, McBarnet, 1982).

E. P. Thompson (1975:265) observed that the rhetoric and rules of a society may "[i]n the same moment ... modify, in profound ways, the behaviour of the powerful, and mystify the powerless. They may disguise the true realities of power, but, at the same time, they may curb that power and check its intrusions." This passage is often quoted since it expresses an appreciation of the rule of law by a distinguished historian with left wing views. Yet we should remember that the key word in the quotation is "may"; the rule of law has failed to stop a great deal of torture and murder in the twentieth century. My colleague, Leonard Kaplan, reminded me of Costa Gavras' film, "Z," in connection with both Friedman's and Thompson's positions. As you will recall, in "Z" an idealistic young judge enforced the law against a ruling elite responsible for the murder of a political opponent. But the lesson of the film is that if an idealistic, and perhaps foolish, judge did try to apply the law against the powerful, the tanks would roll and a constitution would be destroyed "in order to save it." Whatever the trappings of legal order, those with power control the guns, the means of production, the press, and, thus, the legal system "in the long run." Whilc Thompson might suggest that those in power pay a price for imposing military rule, the film supports Friedman's assertion that those with power will not allow legal doctrine and procedures to hurt their interest substantially. Nonetheless, if Costa Gavras were to follow the practices of law book publishers and offer new pages to update his script, he would tell us that the military in Greece, the thinly disguised setting of "Z," was itself overthrown and parliamentary democracy restored. We can only speculate about what part, if any, legal ideals played in this whole process and the degree to which, if at all, those with power there were inconvenienced by the whole affair.

We can offer many examples that suggest that legal ideals at least affect the exercise of power, but in each case the magnitude of the effect is debatable. Even repressive military dictatorships such as those ruling much of the Southern Cone of Latin America attempt to appropriate the symbols of liberal democracy. They order new constitutions written to support their rule. They use an uncertain legal process to try some of those they wish to repress, and when they forsake this legal route and torture and murder their opponents, they try to hide or deny their responsibility. (See Ietswaart, 1982). We can wonder, but cannot explain very well, why repressive *juntas* bother with constitutions, courts and trials. Just what audience do these generals think will be fooled by these exercises? This is not to say that a veneer of legality has no impact. In one American administration we had a "human rights policy" that at least inconvenienced these generals (see Bloomfield, 1982; Cohen, 1982). The policy was abandoned by the next administration, and we saw the United States Ambassador to the United Nations giving General Pinochet of Chile a present and calling him "agreeable, firm, and honorable" despite his government's record of killing opponents both in Chile and on the streets of Washington, D.C. We do not know whether Pinochet's rehabilitated respectability mattered within Chile. Perhaps this denial of history was designed for American rather than Chilean audiences. Even if this were the case, we can only speculate about the effect of the gestures on those Americans who care about events in Latin America. To recall Gertrude Stein once again, there is some there there, but our understanding of it seems far too simple. When and how does lawful behavior matter to whom?

Furthermore, understanding what difference doctrine makes in this narrow sense is not enough. The reality of any legal system is discretion, the rules and sanctions of social fields, and power apart from the law. Friedman (1969:34) says we must understand "the legal culture" to understand the operation of any legal system in its social setting. He tells us that the legal culture is composed of,

> the values and attitudes which bind the system together, and which determine the place of the legal system in the culture of the society as a whole. What kind of training and habits do the lawyers and judges have? What do people think of law? Do groups or individuals willingly go to court? For what purposes do people turn to lawyers; for what purposes do they make use of other officials and intermediaries? Is there respect for law, government, tradition? What is the relationship between class structure and the use or nonuse of legal institutions? What informal social controls exist in addition to or in place of formal ones? Who prefers which kind of controls, and why?

In short, "legal culture" is everything that makes a difference besides rules and structures.

This concept is not without difficulty. It has been offered more often as a catch phrase to label everything inexplicable by other factors than as something established by research. (See Grossman, Kritzer, Bumiller and McDougal, 1981. But, compare, Greenhouse, 1982). Of course, it is not easy to design a research project to capture the kinds of attitudes and perceptions listed by Friedman. These are likely not only to vary from group to group and from place to place, but any individual could hold inconsistent and contradictory views. Most of the time, law is not sufficiently salient to people to make their grasp of legal culture meaningful. Reactions to a questionnaire administered by a stranger in an artificial setting and full of seldom-considered problems are unlikely to be a good measure of views held deeply enough to affect behavior in everyday life. But perhaps the most serious problem is that there is no reason to believe that there is a discrete "thing" which we can isolate as legal as distinct from general culture. At the least, we should suspect that there are no sharp boundaries between legal culture and general views about what is tolerable, necessary and right.

Still, there may be some perceptible there there. The lesson is that we have to take seriously the idea of law *and society* rather than using it only as a slogan. If we narrow our focus so much that we only see how the leaves grow on the trees and never look at the forest, we may forget that we had intended to talk about forests. The point can be made by oversimplifying the history of the study of law: legal scholars began by looking at rules found in appellate cases and trying to arrange them in rational patterns which they reported in grand treatises. Eventually, it became apparent that scholars had to articulate principles or policies that were only implicit or poorly recognized in the appellate cases. Once they saw that principles and policies could be contradictory, it became clear that judges as well as legislators were making choices and not just finding the law. This prompted scholars to look at how judges made decisions. Choice necessarily is influenced by context, and an important part of the context of appellate decision making is what comes forward from the trial record. A later generation of scholars finally began to examine trial courts and found, as Lenny Bruce observed, that "in the halls of justice, the justice is in the halls." The legal system in operation turns out to be one of bargaining, rules of thumb and advantage, all only indirectly influenced by formal rules and procedures. Eventually, scholars came to see that bargaining in the shadow of the law takes place both inside and *outside* legal agencies. Lawyers may settle matters without ever filing a complaint, and most disputes are dealt with by parties who never see lawyers. Law may play a role as a bargaining entitlement or as a vague threat, and it may affect expectations and the normative vocabulary of the parties. At the same time, however, discrete transactions and disputes may be barred from the legal system by cost and other barriers.

Again, serious scholarship must push outward beyond the "boundaries" of what we call the legal system if the goal is to describe and analyze the place of law *in society*. The marginality of the legal system to most human interaction does not mean that life is lived in a state of anarchy: social fields and networks regulate a great deal of behavior in any society; we are all subject to many private governments where the influence of the public legal system is unclear. Long-term continuing relationships have their own norms and sanctions, often far more powerful than anything the legal system has to offer. Sometimes individuals and groups seek to affect the balance of power within these private governments by appeals to courts, administrative agencies and legislatures. At the same time, however, we see people suffering great disadvantages who never take any action. They do not organize and lobby, they do not bring lawsuits, and they do not rebel or engage in guerilla warfare. We can explain this glibly as the result of repression or false consciousness, but these are labels, not explanations. Part of the answer probably could be found in systems of belief about what is tolerable, necessary and just.

Sabel and Stark (1982), for example, seek to explain the fragile successes of workers' movements in Eastern Europe, such as that of Solidarity in Poland, in the face of official opposition. Great efforts have been made to convince workers that the socialism practiced in their nation was for their benefit—these are supposed to be workers' governments although led by a vanguard party. At the same time, the governments of these countries have guns and the powers of arrest and control over employment opportunities, and it is clear that they are willing to use them. In spite of all this, workers in many of the countries have achieved some real gains.

How did this come about? Sabel and Stark point out that as a matter of ideology these societies have "solved" the problems of unemployment by creating jobs for all. This leads to labor shortages in many vital sectors because there are no market mechanisms to channel workers to areas of greatest need. Moreover, planners and managers are judged by the success of the plan, and so they have a personal interest in the rate of production. All of this gives workers the possibility of some measure of bargaining power. Sabel and Stark (1982:443) say that,

> [i]nstead of seeing society as divided between the all-but-omnipotent powerful and the all-but-impotent, malleable weak, we ... emphasize the ways the strong and the weak must depend on each other in order to pursue their separate ends .... Even twisted, unequal cooperative exchanges and temporary, cynical alliances, we will argue, can render the powerful surprisingly vulnerable to the weak.

But the weak must act. They must see a situation as intolerable, unnecessary and unjust. What people in Eastern Europe endured in the postwar years as a kind of natural calamity was unacceptable after several decades of building socialism. The very ideology of socialism itself could be used as rationalizing rhetoric by these workers' movements. Leaders have come forward as workers organized; the state was called upon to make good upon its promises, and repression was seen as carrying high costs.

One would be foolish to argue that repression never works. Matters may be viewed as intolerable, unnecessary and unjust, but the price of action may seem too high in light of the chances of success. Sometimes the disadvantaged in whole nations seem to tolerate terribly burdensome conditions for a long time, but rebellion may be occurring at hidden levels. Those who are dissatisfied may evade and cope with the situation covertly, perhaps engaging in absenteeism from work, working as slowly as possible, making mistakes that produce scrap or doing other kinds of hard-to-catch sabotage. They may attempt to bring about change through the use of formal process or political action such as strikes or taking to the streets. Sometimes they are crushed by tanks; sometimes they win partial victories.

Understanding when what kinds of people take what action and with what results is a part of the business of law and society research. It seems plausible that there is a legal culture that affects action and response. However, it also seems plausible that answers to such questions will turn on the critical legal scholars' "world view" or "consciousness" concerning what is tolerable, necessary and just. Indeed, legal culture can be viewed as a more specific version of a world view. Insofar as critical legal scholars signal those in law and behavioral sciences to use a very wide angle lens that takes in the shape of the forest as well as the patterns of the leaves on the trees, those in critical studies are saying something important. It would be dangerous to dismiss such things as "consciousness," "world views," and "culture." Moreover, if we accept that these things exist and matter, we also should ask how they change.

We may indeed, for example, be skeptical of claims that a set of law review articles by radical professors and liberals responding to them creates more than a tempest in a teapot. Yet we can point to examples of academic ideas that have played a role in public affairs in the past. Many novel ideas are appropriated in part when they serve to rationalize what reformers or governmental officials and those seeking or holding elective office want to do. Much of what our grandparents thought radical is seen as conventional today. In the first part of this century, professors who advocated such things as labor unions and regulation of working conditions generated passionate disputes on university campuses and those with influence in the society sought to have such radical professors dismissed. Even during the New Deal era, many law professors who were fashioning what we now see as conventional labor law were called communists by those who directed large corporations and who were fighting unionization of their employees. On the other hand, we can also produce a fascinating catalogue of academic ideas that failed to take hold.

We do not know why certain ideas were "in the air" or were advanced when the "times were right." Where did the prevailing world views about what is tolerable, necessary and just come from? How do they change, and how do they affect both the formal statement of law and the actual practice of those playing roles in the legal system and those who are supposed to comply with particular laws? These are major questions in the social study of law, and we have barely begun to answer them.

IV. Conclusion

I have an answer to my question: the problem of law and the behavioral sciences is not that there is no there there. On the contrary, there may be too much there there for any one person to master. In order to understand the place of law in society, we have to understand law, society and the relationships of one to the other. We must understand economic theory and Habermas, the dangers of regression analysis and participant observation, political philosophy and the meaning of particular sections of Article II of the Uniform Commercial Code, as well as jurisprudence and bargaining in the shadow of the law. If this were not hard enough, it is only the beginning of a complete list.

A division of labor seems appropriate but then we run the danger of compartmentalization—I do my thing and I am ignorant, if not contemptuous, of yours. Even at our early stage, the social study of law needs more participants who read across scholarly boundaries. While reading research proposals for the Law and Social Science Program of the National Science Foundation for three years, I was struck by the rigidity of boundaries of established social science fields. Psychologists who do eyewitness testimony studies, for example, could avoid some embarrassing moments if they knew more about criminal law as well as both sociology and anthropology of law. Economists might learn something, too, if they could bring themselves to approach psychology and sociology sympathetically and so on. Those who would study the legal system must understand something of the nature of modern legal doctrine—citations to *Black's Law Dictionary* are only a little more naive than talking about precedent without recognizing the extraordinary flexibility, as well as the limits, of what is possible in legal argument. Moreover, social scientists cannot take the position of any jurisprudential scholar as given without regard to conflicting views that may blow the great figure of the elite law school out of the water.

Empirical work also would improve if those who do it were more critical of the assumptions of liberal legalism about the role of law in capitalist society as the Conference on Critical Legal Studies urges. Our political heritage teaches us that law is open to change by the will of the people, and individuals have rights which they may vindicate before legal agencies. We know that often this is not the case. Trubek (1981:743) has argued that legal doctrine and our system's processing of particular types of disputes "not only transforms the various individual conflicts: in so doing it 'transforms,' so to speak, a raw conflict of interest into a social process with limited possibilities. The disputes that do emerge are those in which basic economic relationships are not challenged: all other possibilities are filtered out." This hypothesis is worth the attention of anyone trying to understand the actual functioning of the American legal system with its claims of equality counterposed to the high degree of inequality in society. The hypothesis is a product of both Trubek's experience as an empirical researcher and his participation in the Conference on Critical Legal Studies. Perhaps others could have formulated something similar to "Trubek's law" in complete ignorance of critical legal studies, Habermas or even Marx, but critical legal studies prompts useful skepticism about liberal assumptions concerning the role of law in capitalist societies. Critical legal studies writers may be criticized for sending their messages in a form usually accessible only to believers already converted to the faith. They also may have more to learn from empirical work than they wish to believe. I need not resolve these issues here. What is clear is that any theory that tells us to watch those with money, status and influence cannot be all wrong, and any theory that tells us that these factors are all there is to law cannot be all right.

Whatever our source of inspiration, we need to be provoked to replace a narrow view of the social study of law with a wide angle lens. "Consciousness" and "culture" are part of the project of taking seriously the idea that we are studying law *and society*. Even those who find Parsonian structural-functional theory more to their tastes than Marxist-derived thought will recall that in systems theories the legal subsystem is related in some way to all other subsystems. Earlier, I quoted Luhmann (1981), perhaps the leading systems theorist writing today. He suggests that whether and how the legal system will play the integrative role assigned to it by theory is uncertain. There are "thematization thresholds" serving as barriers to transforming problems that arise in other social contexts into legal questions. There are good reasons in many situations to avoid invoking legal norms—by openly confronting others with the question of whether they are acting legally, one shatters the comfortable consensus that normally is assumed in a social relationship. Yet the threshold is crossed sometimes. It seems likely that internalized norms concerning what is tolerable, necessary and just play a part as well as do social sanctions and structures. Thus, we are brought back to the idea that the point of our effort remains the study of law *and society.*

We do not have to worry about there being any there there in law and behavioral science. We have come a long way in a short time, and what we have found cannot be ignored by anyone with any pretense of thinking about law seriously. On the other hand, self-congratulations are premature. When Gertrude Stein was a young girl living in Oakland, she worried about what she would do when she had read all the books in the Oakland Public Library. She was relieved when she realized that she never could read all the books available. The same relief is open to those engaged in legal studies. We can never master all the relevant materials, and we will not soon work ourselves out of a job. We still have a long way to go.

References

Abel, R. (1980a) "Taking Stock," 14 *Law & Society Review* 429–443.

Abel, R. (1980b) "Redirecting Social Studies of Law," 14 *Law & Society Review* 805–829.

Abel, R. (1982) "Law as Lag: Inertia as a Social Theory of Law," 80 *Michigan Law Review* 785–809.

Adler, P. and P. Adler (1983) "Relationships Between Dealers: The Social Organization of Illicit Drug Transactions," 67 *Sociology and Social Research* 260–278.

Ayre, R. (1982) "Objectivity Versus Political and Moral Commitment? For Science and Partisanship in Criminology," 6 *Contemporary Crises* 133–154.

Bach, K. (1975) "Analytic Social Philosophy—Basic Concepts," 5 *Journal for the Theory of Social Behaviour* 189–214.

Balch, R., C. Griffiths, E. Hall, and l. Winfree (1976) "The Socialization of Jurors: The Voir Dire as a Rite of Passage," 4 *Journal of Criminal Justice* 271–283.

Ball, D. (1972) "'The Definition of Situation': Some Theoretical and Methodological Consequences of Taking W. I. Thomas Seriously," 2 *Journal for the Theory of Social Behaviour* 61–82.

Berk, R. and S. Ray (1982) "Selection Biases in Sociological Data," 11 *Social Science Research* 352–398.

Bernays, A. (1983) "Review of Shana Alexander, Very Much a Lady: The Untold Story of Jean Harris and Dr. Herman Tarnower." *New York Times Book Review*, 27 March 1983, 13, 31–32.

Bloomfield, L. (1982) "From Ideology to Program to Policy: Tracking the Carter Human Rights Policy," 2 *Journal of Policy Analysis and Management* 1–12.

Borgida, E. (1981) "Legal Reform of Rape Laws," in Bickman, L. (ed.) 2 *Applied Social Psychology Annual* 211–241.

Bowers, S. (1982) "Law and Lawlessness in a Socialist Society: The Potential Impact of Crime in East Germany," 145 *World Affairs*: 152–176.

Britan, G. (1979) "Some Problems of Fieldwork in the Federal Bureaucracy," 52 *Anthropological Quarterly* 211–220.

Broeder, D. (1954) "The Functions of the Jury: Facts or Fictions?," 21 *University of Chicago Law Review* 386–424.

Cain, M. and J. Finch (1981) "Towards a Rehabilitation of Data," in P. Abrams, et al. (eds.) *Practice and Progress: British Sociology 1950–1980*. Boston, Mass.: George Allen & Unwin.

Cochran, N. (1980) "Society as Emergent and More than Rational: An Essay on the Inappropriateness of Program Evaluation," 12 *Policy Sciences* 113–129.

Cohen, R. (1982) "Human Rights Diplomacy: The Carter Administration and the Southern Cone," 4 *Human Rights Quarterly* 212–242.

Cole, R. (1978) "The Second Criminal Justice System," 43 *S.A.M. Advanced Management Journal* 17–23, No. 2.

Dandeker, C. (1983) "Theory and Practice in Sociology: The Critical Imperatives of Realism," 13 *Journal for the Theory of Social Behaviour* 195–210.

David, M. and A. Robbin (1981) "The Great Rift: Gaps Between Administrative Records and Knowledge Created through Secondary Analysis," 9 *Review of Public Data Use* 153–166.
Eriksson, I. (1978) "Soft-Data Sociology," 21 *Acta Sociologica* 103–124.
Femia, J. (1983) "Review Article: Gramsci's Patrimony," 13 *British Journal of Political Science* 327–364.
Fitzpatrick, P. (1983) "Marxism and Legal Pluralism," *Australian Journal of Law and Society* 45–59.
Freeman, A. (1981) "Truth and Mystification in Legal Scholarship," 90 *Yale Law Journal* 1229–1237.
Friedman, L. (1967) "Legal Rules and the Process of Social Change," 19 *Stanford Law Review* 786–840.
Friedman, L.. (1969) "Legal Culture and Social Development," 4 *Law & Society Review* 29–44.
Friedman, L. and S. Macaulay (1969) *Law and the Behavioral Sciences*. Indianapolis: Bobbs-Merrill.
Friedman, L. (1975) *The Legal System: A Social Science Perspective*. New York: Russell Sage Foundation.
Galanter, M. (1974) "Why the 'Haves' Come Out Ahead: Speculations on the Limits of Legal Change," 9 *Law & Society Review* 95–160.
Galanter, M. (1981) "Justice in Many Rooms: Courts, Private Ordering and Indigenous Law," 19 *Journal of Legal Pluralism and Unofficial Law* 1–47.
Galanter, M. (1983) "Reading the Landscape of Disputes: What We Know and Don't Know (And Think We Know) about our Allegedly Contentious and Litigious Society," 31 *UCLA Law Review* 4–11.
Galtung, J. (1981) "Structure, Culture, and Intellectual Style: An Essay Comparing Saxonic, Teutonic, Gallic and Nipponic Approaches," 20 *Social Science Information* 817–856.
Galtung, J. (1982) "Sport as Carrier of Deep Culture and Structure," 2–3 *Current Research on Peace and Violence* 133–143.
Goldman, R. (1982) "Hegemony and Managed Critique in Prime Time Television," 11 *Theory and Society* 363–388.
Gordon, R. (1984) "Critical Legal Histories," 36 *Stanford Law Review*, 1101–1169.
Greenhouse, C. J. (1982) "Looking at Culture, Looking for Rules," 17 *Man* 58–73.
Greenwood, J. (1982) "On the Relation Between Laboratory Experiments and Social Behaviour: Causal Explanation and Generalization," 12 *Journal for the Theory of Social Behaviour* 225–250.
Grossman, J. B., H. M. Kritzer, K. Bumiller, and S. McDougal (1981) "Measuring the Pace of Civil Litigation in Federal and State Trial Courts," 65 *Judicature* 65:86–113.
Handler, J. (1979) *Protecting the Social Service Client: Legal and Structural Controls on Official Discretion*. New York: Academic Press.
Hastie, R., S. Penrod, and N. Pennington (1983) *Inside the Jury*. Cambridge, Mass.: Harvard University Press.
Hekman, S. (1982) "The Althusserian Critique of Weber: A Reassessment," 12 *Journal for the Theory of Social Behaviour* 83–102.
Hekman, S. (1983) "Beyond Humanism: Gadamer, Althusser, and the Methodology of the Social Sciences," 36 *The Western Political Quarterly* 98–115.
Held, D. (1982) "Critical Theory and Political Transformation," 4 *Media, Culture and Society* 153–160.
Holmes, S. A. (1982) "Two Concepts of Legitimacy: France After the Revolution," 10 *Political Theory* 165–183.
Hund, J. (1982) "Are Social Facts Real?" 33 *British Journal of Sociology* 270–278.
Hyde, A. (1983) "The Concept of Legitimation in the Sociology of Law," 1983 *Wisconsin Law Review* 379–426.

Ietswaart, H. (1982) "The Discourse of Summary Justice and the Discourse of Popular Justice: An Analysis of Legal Rhetoric in Argentina," in R. Abel (ed.) *The Politics of Informal Justice.* New York: Academic Press.

Koch, K. (1980) "The New Marxist Theory of the State or the Rediscovery of the Limitations of a Structural-Functionalist Paradigm," 16 *Netherlands' Journal of Sociology* 1–19.

Lamo de Espinosa, E. (1980) "Social and Legal Order in Sociological Functionalism," 4 *Contemporary Crises* 43–76.

Levine, H. and S. Stumpf (1983) "Statements of Fear Through Cultural Symbols: Punk Rock as a Reflective Subculture," 14 *Youth & Society* 417–435.

Lipsry, M. (1980) *Street Level Bureaucracy: Dilemmas of the Individual in Public Services.* New York: Russell Sage Foundation.

Loh, W. (1981) "Perspectives on Psychology and Law," 11 *Journal of Applied Social Psychology* 314–355.

Luhmann, N. (1981) "Communication About Law in Interaction Systems," in K. Knorr-Cetina and A. V. Circoure (eds.) *Advances in Social Theory and Methodology.* Boston, Mass.: Routledge & Kegan Paul.

Macaulay, J. and S. Macaulay (1978) "Adoption for Black Children: A Case Study of Expert Discretion," in R. Simon (ed.) 1 *Research in Law and Sociology* 265–318.

Macaulay, S. (1963) "Non-Contractual Relations in Business: A Preliminary Study," 28 *American Sociological Review* 55–67.

Macaulay, S. (1977) "Elegant Models, Empirical Pictures, and the Complexities of Contract," 11 *Law & Society Review* 507–528.

Macaulay, S. (1979) "Lawyers and Consumer Protection Law," 14 *Law & Society Review* 115–171.

Macauley, S. (1979) *Motel of the Mysteries.* Boston: Houghton Mifflin Co.

Macaulay, S. (1983) "Private Government," Disputes Processing Research Program Working Paper 1983–6.

Marenin, O. (1981) "Essence and Empiricism in African Politics," 19 *Journal of Modern African Studies* 1–30.

Markovits, I. (1978) "Socialist vs. Bourgeois Rights—An East-West German Comparison," 45 *University of Chicago Law Review* 612–636.

Marsden, R. (1982) "Industrial Relations: A Critique of Empiricism," 16 *Sociology* 232–250.

McBarnet, D. (1982) "Legal Form and Legal Mystification: An Analytical Postscript on the Scottish Criminal Justice Act, the Royal Commission on Criminal Procedure, and the Politics of Law and Order," 10 *International Journal of the Sociology of Law* 409–417.

Medawar, P. (1982) *Pluto's Republic.* New York: Oxford University Press.

Meehl, P. (1971) "Law and the Fireside Inductions: Some Reflections of a Clinical Psychologist," 27 *Journal of Social Issues* 65–100.

Moore, S. (1973) "Law and Social Change: The Semi-Autonomous Social Field as an Appropriate Subject of Study," 7 *Law & Society Review* 719–746.

Mnookin, R. and l. Kornhauser (1979) "Bargaining in the Shadow of the Law: The Case of Divorce," 88 *Yale Law Journal* 950–997.

Munger, F. and C. Seron (1984) "Critical Legal Studies versus Critical Legal Theory: An Examintion of the Role of Empirical Research in the Conference on Critical Legal Studies," *Law & Policy*, forthcoming.

Nield, K. and J. Seed (1979) "Theoretical Poverty or the Poverty of Theory: British Marxist Historiography and the Althusserians," 8 *Economy and Society* 383–416.

Penrod, S. and E. Borgida (1983) "Legal Rules and Lay Inference," in Wheeler, L. and P. Shaver (eds.) *Review of Personality and Social Psychology*, forthcoming.

Ray, I. (1976) "Habermas, Legitimation, and the State," 8 *Journal for the Theory of Social Behaviour* 149–163.

Richter, M. (1982) "Toward a Concept of Political Illegitimacy," 10 *Political Theory* 185–214.

Rhode, D. (1983) "Equal Rights in Retrospect," 1 *Law & Inequality: A Journal of Theory and Practice* 1–72.

Sabel, C. and D. Stark (1982) "Planning, Politics, and Shop-Floor Power: Hidden Forms of Bargaining in Soviet-Imposed State-Socialist Societies," 11 *Politics & Society* 439–475.
Schlegel, J. (1979) "American Legal Realism and Empirical Social Science: From the Yale Experience," 28 *Buffalo Law Review* 459–586.
Schlegel, J. (1980) "American Legal Realism and Empirical Social Science: The Singular Case of Underhill Moore," 29 *Buffalo Law Review* 195–323.
Skocpol, T., (1980) "Political Response to Capitalist Crisis: Neo-Marxist Theories of the State and the Case of the New Deal," 10 *Politics & Society* 155–201.
Stack, S. (1978) "Ideological Beliefs on the American Distribution of Opportunity, Power, and Rewards," 11 *Sociological Focus* 221–233.
Thomas, W. and D. Thomas (1928) *The Child in America.* New York: Alfred A. Knopf.
Thompson, E. (1975) *Whigs and Hunters: The Origin of the Black Act.* New York: Pantheon Books.
Thompson, E. (1978) "The Poverty of Theory," in *The Poverty of Theory and Other Essays.* London: Merlin.
Trubek, D. (1981) "The Construction and Deconstruction of a Disputes-Focused Approach: An Afterword," 15 *Law & Society Review* 727–747.
Trubek, D. (1984) "Where the Action is: Critical Legal Studies and Empiricism," 36 *Stanford Law Review* 576–622.
Teubner, G. (1983) "Substantive and Reflexive Elements in Modern Law" 17 *Law & Policy Review* 239–285.
Turk, A. (1979) "Analyzing Official Deviance: For Non-Partisan Conflict Analysis in Criminology," 16 *Criminology* 459–476.
Turk, A. (1982) "Values and Objectivity in Criminological Inquiry: Ayre's Dilemma," 6 *Contemporary Crises* 155–159.
Unger, R. (1976) *Law in Modern Society: Toward a Criticism of Social Theory.* New York: Free Press.
Unger, R. (1983) "The Critical Legal Studies Movement," 96 *Harvard Law Review* 563–675.
Unnever, J. (1982) "Direct and Organizational Discrimination in the Sentencing of Drug Offenders," 30 *Social Problems* 212–225.
Useem, B. and M. Useem (1979) "Government Legitimacy and Political Stability," 57 *Social Forces* 840–852.
Van den Berg, A. (1980) "Critical Theory: Is There Still Hope?" 86 *American Journal of Sociology* 449–478.
Van den Berg, A. (1983) "Social Theory, Metatheory, and Lofty Ideals: A Reply to Wexler and Parker and to Ashley," 88 *American Journal of Sociology* 1259–1270.
Van Maanen (1981) "The Informant Game: Selected Aspects of Ethnographic Research in Police Organizations," 9 *Urban Life* 469–494.
Warde, A. (1982) "E. P. Thompson and 'Poor' Theory," 33 *British Journal of Sociology* 224–237.
Watts, J. (1983) "The Socialist as Ostrich: The Unwillingness of the Left to Confront Modernity," 50 *Social Research* 3–56.
Wildavsky, A. (1982) "What Would One Have to Believe to Believe in Multiple Regression," 27 *Contemporary Psychology* 903–904.

The New Versus the Old Legal Realism: "Things Ain't What They Used To Be"

Stewart Macaulay

When we talk of a "New Legal Realism," the obvious question is how it might differ from the well-known original movement. Can we say anything more than Karl Llewellyn did not have a website, but we do?[1] Today, we do not face the legal, political, or social world of the progressive reformers, academics who attacked legal formalism, or the few who tried to do empirical research about law in the late 1920s and early 1930s. After forty years of the Law and Society Association, we can hum Duke Ellington's *Things Ain't What They Used To Be.*[2] We do know much that scholars in the 1920s and 1930s knew, at best, only anecdotally. Nonetheless, if we review the histories of legal realism, we must realize that our great-grandfathers and

This article was original published in Wisconsin Law Review 2005, 365–403. Reprinted with permission.

Malcolm Pitman Sharp Hilldale Professor and Walter T. Brazeau Bascom Professor of Law of the University of Wisconsin—Madison. I want to thank Lawrence Friedman, Marc Galanter, Jane Larson, Arthur McEvoy, Elizabeth Mertz, John Henry Schlegel and David Trubek for all kinds of help in the writing of this Article. The usual disclaimer applies. I am responsible for all mistakes because I did not take all of the good advice offered.

[1]*See* New Legal Realism Project, *at* http://www.newlegalrealism.org (last visited May 16, 2005).

[2]Duke Ellington's son Mercer Ellington composed the piece in 1941. However, Mercer said that his father would "[s]et problems for me, scratch out what he thought was in poor taste, and preset harmonies for me to write melodies against. . . . [W]hen the band played arrangements I had written under his supervision, like. . . . 'Things Ain't What They Used to Be,' . . . it was as instructive as it was gratifying." Mercer Ellington with Stanley Dance, Duke Ellington in Person: An Intimate Memoir 93 (1978).

S. Macaulay (✉)
University of Wisconsin Law School, Madison, WI, USA
e-mail: smacaula@wisc.edu

D. Campbell (ed.), *Stewart Macaulay: Selected Works*, Law and Philosophy Library 133, https://doi.org/10.1007/978-3-030-33930-2_19

grandfathers knew a lot more than we give them credit for.[3] At the outset, my mention of grandfathers and great-grandfathers should remind us that we must add gender[4] and race to the mix. The original realists who held positions of power were white males, and we can wonder whether this affected what they looked for and what they saw.

I offer a very simplified history of legal realism. Next, I repeat the summary in my 1984 Mitchell Lecture at the State University of New York at Buffalo of what about twenty years of modern law and society research had uncovered, and I ask what we might add in light of the almost twenty years since I gave that talk. Then, at long last, I ask what a New Legal Realism growing out of this context might be like.

I begin my story with the progressive era and the Wisconsin Idea: the state was to be developed and social problems solved by using the skills and knowledge of the university faculty.[5] University of Wisconsin professors, such as economists Richard T. Ely and John R. Commons, advocated new social programs. They championed unemployment and workers' compensation laws as well as laws regulating the conditions of employment.[6] A great victory involved confronting child labor.[7] In

---

[3]In 1921, Roscoe Pound called for legal scholars to look to the findings of economics and sociology: "Before we can have sound theories here we need facts on which to build them. Even after we get sound theories, we shall need facts to enable us to apply them." Roscoe Pound, The Spirit of the Common Law 213–14 (1921).

[4]Professor John Henry Schlegel reported on the roles of Dorothy Swaine Thomas and Emma Corstvet in the Yale experiment with empirical research in the early 1930s. John Henry Schlegel, *American Legal Realism and Empirical Social Science: From the Yale Experience*, 28 Buff. L. Rev. 459, 521 (1979). Both were social scientists who served as associates on Professor Charles Clark's projects. *Id.* Schlegel notes: "Clark had a bit of trouble securing faculty approval for the appointment because Thomas was female." *Id.* at 521 n.306.

[5]*See* Paul D. Carrington & Erika King, *Law and the Wisconsin Idea,* 41 J. Legal Educ. 297, 299 (1997). Professor Morton Horwitz argued: "it is best to see Legal Realism as simply a continuation of the reformist agenda of early-twentieth-century Progressivism." Morton Horwitz, The Transformation of American Law, 1870–1960, at 169 (1992). *But see* John Henry Schlegel, *A Tasty Tidbit,* 41 Buff. L. Rev. 1045 (1993) (criticizing Horwitz's views about the place of social science knowledge in the realist project). *See generally* Gregory S. Alexander, *Comparing the Two Legal Realisms—American and Scandinavian,* 50 Am. J. Comp. L. 131, 133–43 (2002) (outlining the rise of American Legal Realism and its Scandinavian counterpart).

[6]*See* 4 John D. Buenker, The History of Wisconsin: The Progressive Era, 1893–1914, at 543–48 (1998).

[7]As Gregory Alexander wrote,

> The period between 1890 and 1913 was a time of tremendous economic, political, and social upheaval and conflict in the United States. . . . The increasing concentration of wealth and power widened the gap between the haves and have-nots and deepened feelings of resentment between opposite social-economic groups.
>
> . . . .
>
> . . . . Progressives were reformers, not revolutionaries.
>
> . . . .
>
> . . . . Progressive governance made no pretense of co-existing with the joint ideologies of laissez-faire and anti-paternalism. Its ideology was frankly paternalistic and interventionist, particularly on social issues.

Alexander, *supra* note 5, at 135–37.

1909, the University of Wisconsin Law School's Dean Richards and Professors Walter Wheeler Cook and Underhill Moore helped Commons draft a bill proposing changes in the state arbitration act.[8] Charles McCarthy began the Wisconsin Legislative Reference Library.[9] He offered skilled people who could draft statutes, and this freed the legislature from depending on lobbyists for the text of bills. McCarthy created a library based on reports and clippings from newspapers about various social problems. If law was to be a tool in social engineering, facts and expert judgment had to replace doctrine and tradition.

The law school began to be influenced by the Wisconsin Idea. Carrington and King reported:

> One effect of the Wisconsin idea was to bring the University's new young law teachers into contact not only with public affairs, but also with academic colleagues in other disciplines who possessed useful expertise. The law school established liaison with the political science department in 1907-08, a liaison designed with the purpose of "relating" legal instruction "to modern social and economic conditions." Similarly between 1904 and 1910, law faculty, [Dean] Gilmore in particular, collaborated with economics faculty such as John Commons and Richard Ely, in a large-scale endeavor to document the history of labor in America. . . . By 1915, law school bulletins actively advocated a mixture of law classes with history, economics, political science and philosophy classes.[10]

A few law professors at the University of Wisconsin, rather than honoring common law doctrine, studied the law in action. Professor Oliver Rundell studied delay in the criminal justice system as early as 1912.[11] Professor William Herbert Page, one of my predecessors as a Wisconsin contracts professor, came to Wisconsin from Ohio State in 1917. In 1914, he had presented a paper at the Association of American Law Schools meeting on "the living law" ideas of Eugen Ehrlich.[12] Ehrlich's living law was

---

[8]Carrington & King, *supra* note 5, at 326.

[9]*See* John R. Commons, Myself: The Autobiography of John R. Commons 107–111 (1963).

[10]Carrington & King, *supra*, note 5, at 324.

[11]*Id.* at 329.

[12]*See* Eugen Ehrlich, Fundamental Principles of the Sociology of Law (1936). Professor William Herbert Page's appreciation of Eugen Ehrlich's work was presented at the Association of American Law Schools'Annual Meeting in 1914. It is reprinted as William H. Page, *Professor Ehrlich's Czernowitz Seminar of Living Law, in* Readings in Jurisprudence 825 (Jerome Hall ed., 1938).

Schlegel reported: "in the spring of 1914, [Professor Underhill Moore, then at the University of Wisconsin Law School] helped organize a 'legal and philosophical colloquium' [at the University of Wisconsin] whose participants included John Commons, Richard T. Ely and the prominent moral philosopher F.C. Sharp." John Henry Schlegel, *American Legal Realism and Empirical Social Science: The Singular Case of Underhill Moore,* 29 Buff. L. Rev. 195, 229 (1980). "Commons spoke on the 'Legal and Economic Theory of Value and Valuation,' Ely, on 'The Social Theory of Private Property,' and Sharp, on 'Principles of Judicial Legislation.'" *Id.* at 229 n.200. Schlegel also reported that Professor Underhill Moore moved to the University of Chicago Law School in 1914. *Id.* at 229. His salary at Chicago was $5500. *Id.* at 229 n.205. Had he stayed at Wisconsin, he would have made $4000. Id. It is comforting to know that some things remain constant in the world.

> in contrast to that which is in force merely in the courts and with the officials. The living law is that law which is not imprisoned in rules of law, but which dominates life itself. The sources of its knowledge are above all the modern documents, and also immediate study of life itself, of commerce, of customs and usage, and of all sorts of organizations, including those which are recognized by the law, and, indeed, those which are disapproved by the law.[13]

Page, as far as I can tell, did little with these insights. Not too long after this, he turned to writing a multivolume treatise on contract doctrine.[14]

The initial wave of progressivism in Wisconsin came to an end in 1914, when the traditional Republicans defeated the Progressives.[15] The progressive cause and the University of Wisconsin's role in it suffered a great blow when America entered World War I against Germany.[16] U.S. Senator Robert LaFollette had fought to keep America out of that war,[17] and many in the University and the progressive movement had strong ties to German academic culture. The University came under great pressure to prove its loyalty to the American cause in the war.[18]

Much of the traditional story of legal realism focuses on the Columbia and Yale Law Schools during the late 1920s and the 1930s.[19] It is easier to describe what those who came to be known as realists were against rather than what they were for. The enemy was traditional legal scholarship that focused on the logic of doctrine. The enemy's home was the Harvard Law School, where the great authorities wrote

[13]Page, *supra* note 12, at 825 (quoting Ehrlich's description of the living law).

[14]*See* William Herbert Page, The Law of Contracts (2d ed. 1920).

[15]*See* 4 Buenker, *supra* note 6, at 657 ("In 1914, after fourteen victorious years, the progressive Republicans finally tasted defeat.").

[16]*See* 5 Paul W. Glad, The History of Wisconsin: War, a New Era, and Depression, 1914–1940, at 41–42 (1990).

[17]*Id.* at 1–2 ("The most famous of Wisconsin's political leaders, Senator Robert M. LaFollette, risked his reputation and his influence, first in supporting the abortive effort to prevent American entry into the war, and then in aiding the successful effort to prevent ratification of the settlement drafted at the Peace Conference.").

[18]*See* Cora Lee Nollendorfs, *The First World War and the Survival of German Studies: With a Tribute to Alexander R. Hohlfeld, in* Teaching German in America: Prolegomena to a History 176, 181–83 (David P. Benseleretal. eds., 1988). Cora Lee Nollendorfs noted that the University of Wisconsin was "under considerable pressure to prove that it was not a 'Germanized' institution as many were claiming . . . ." *Id.* at 181. Moreover, "American academicians as a group and American institutions of higher learning as a whole were thought in some circles to be pro-German." *Id.* at 183. In this era, of course, many faculty members, particularly in the natural sciences, had advanced degrees from German universities. *Id.* Students at the university were not safe from such attacks, either. For example,

> Princeton's Robert McNutt McElroy, a representative of the National Security League, drew attention to the University of Wisconsin when he published a capricious account of a campus loyalty meeting he addressed in April, 1918. That students had paraded through drizzling rain to get to the Stock Pavilion, that his audience was cold and uncomfortable, and that his address was overly long did not seem to McElroy sufficient reasons for restlessness. He called the students "a bunch of damned traitors!" and thereby initiated a noisy public debate over Badger patriotism.

5 Glad, *supra* note 16, at 41.

[19]*See* Morton Horwitz, The Transformation of American Law, 1870–1960, at 169–92 (1992).

multivolume treatises on the conventional areas of law. *Williston on Contracts,*[20] *Beale on Conflicts of Law,*[21] and *Scott on Trusts*[22] were prime examples of much of what the realist scholars attacked. Professor Lon Fuller, in an essay criticizing Professor Samuel Williston, commented:

> Turning to Professor Williston's legal method, if we ask at what point he gives up the attempt to shape the law by direct reference to social interests, I think the answer will have to be, at the very outset. What may be called the bases of contract liability, notions like consideration, the necessity for offer and acceptance, and the like, are nowhere in his work critically examined in the light of the social interests they serve. These things are accepted on faith. This neglect to refer to underlying social desiderata cannot properly be called "logic." It is simply an acceptance of what is conceived to be received legal tradition.[23]

Perhaps the most noted of the realists was Professor Karl Llewellyn.[24] His book *The Common Law Tradition* celebrates appellate judges who worked in what he called "the grand style."[25] One of his achievements was the Uniform Commercial Code (U.C.C.), which, to a great extent, reflects a realist approach. For example, official comment 1 to section 1-102 of the U.C.C. tells judges to make policy decisions and offers an approach rather than a rule.[26] It says:

---

[20]Samuel Williston, The Law of Contracts (1920).

[21]Joseph Henry Beale, A Treatise on the Conflict of Laws (1935).

[22]Austin Wakeman Scott, The Law of Trusts (3d ed. 1967).

[23]Lon L. Fuller, *Williston on Contracts,* 18 N.C. L. Rev. 1, 9 (1939). For another famous realist's critical treatment of Professor Samuel Williston's work, see Walter Wheeler Cook, *Williston on Contracts,* 33 Ill. L. Rev. 497 (1939). I was surprised to find that Professor N.E.H. Hull noted that Williston "celebrated [Roscoe] Pound as the leader of the movement to teach social science in the law schools. Williston was proud that Pound had led the way in validating legislation like workman's compensation based on the findings of the social scientists." N.E.H. Hull, Roscoe Pound & Karl Llewellyn: Searching for an American Jurisprudence 167 (1997).

[24]A complete history would also focus on the work in conflict of laws by Professor Walter Wheeler Cook. My own introduction to full-blown realism came in Professor Moffat Hancock's conflicts of law class at Stanford Law School in the early 1950s. Cook was Hancock's hero. Then, when I was a member of the *Stanford Law Review*, we published Professor John Henry Merryman, *The Authority of Authority: What the California Supreme Court Cited in 1950*, 6 Stan. L. Rev. 613 (1954), and I so enjoyed one of my favorite professors mocking the *Restatements* that I had been fighting to master in a fairly conventional legal education. After a year as Chief Judge William Denman's law clerk, I became a Bigelow Teaching Fellow and Instructor at the University of Chicago Law School in 1956. There I got to watch Professor Karl Llewellyn in full flight. However, my mentor at Chicago was Professor Malcolm Sharp. I learned a great deal about contracts from the highly realist casebook that he wrote with Professor Fritz Kessler that I used when I began teaching the subject. *See* Friedrich Kessler & Malcolm Pitman Sharp, Contracts: Cases and Materials (1953). Once I became a law professor, one of my first articles focused on the contracts decisions of Justice Roger Traynor of the Supreme Court of California. *See* Stewart Macaulay, *Justice Traynor and the Law of Contracts*, 13 Stan. L. Rev. 812 (1961). Justice Traynor was certainly one of the most realist of appellate judges ever to sit on the bench in this country. *See generally id.* To a great extent, in my generation of law teachers, legal realism was just assumed as the way to go.

[25]Karl N. Llewellyn, The Common Law Tradition: Deciding Appeals 5 (1960); *see also* William Twining, Karl Llewellyn and the Realist Movement, at viii (1973).

[26]U.C.C. § 1-102 (2001).

> The Act should be construed in accordance with its underlying purposes and policies. The text of each section should be read in the light of the purpose and policy of the rule or principle in question, as also of the Act as a whole, and the application of the language should be construed narrowly or broadly, as the case may be, in conformity with the purposes and policies involved.[27]

This comment, probably written by Llewellyn, catches much of a realist approach to appellate judging. In short, a judge must exercise judgment to be a judge.

The great success of Old Legal Realism was in discrediting formal approaches and in justifying appellate judges taking action to carry out some substantive policy. Often the realists said little more than that the judge should balance the interests involved.[28] Some of the other realists, however, were highly skeptical about whether rules could even influence the decisions of judges.[29] Many realists said that legal doctrine, at best, rationalized decisions based on bias or, in Llewellyn's terms, a judge's "situation sense."[30] A few realists demanded that we look at trial courts,[31] and a few did some empirical research on the flow of cases through the

---

[27] *Id.* § 1-102 cmt. 1.

[28] Professors William W. Fisher, Morton J. Horwitz, and Thomas A. Reed asserted that

> Legal Realism called into question three related ideals cherished by most Americans: the notion that, in the United States, the people (not unelected judges) select the rules by which they are governed; the conviction that the institution of judicial review reinforces rather than undermines representative democracy; and the faith that ours is a government of laws, not of men. The aspiration of most of the schools of American legal theory that have proliferated since World War II has been to meet these challenges.

American Legal Realism, at xiv-xv (William W. Fisher III et al. eds., 1993).

[29] *See* Jerome Frank, Courts on Trial: Myth and Reality in American Justice, at viii (1949); Robert Jerome Glennon, The Iconoclast as Reformer: Jerome Frank's Impact on American Law 60–65 (1985); Jerome Frank, *What Courts Do In Fact,* 26 Ill. L. Rev. 645, 647–48 (1932). However, Professor Lawrence Friedman provided an important sociological qualification to the realist's rule skepticism:

> [T]here is a strong tendency within the legal system toward the framing of nondiscretionary rules *at some level* and that it is strongest where it is socially important to have mass, routine handling of transactions, which are channeled through some agency of the legal system, or where relative certainty of legal expectation is important.... [T]he legal system may have many more discretionary rules formally speaking than operationally speaking.

Lawrence M. Friedman, *Legal Rules and the Process of Social Change,* 19 Stan. L. Rev. 786, 794 (1967); *see also* Arthur L. Stinchcombe, When Formality Works: Authority and Abstraction in Law and Organizations (2001).

[30] *See* Twining, *supra* note 25, at 225 (1973). As William Twining wrote:

> [a] judge in a commercial case who can see the facts in the way businessmen would see them, as well as from the lawyer's point of view and from the point of view of the "mores" of the community as a whole, has grasped the "situation sense," and if he has a better than average understanding of the situation and the problem it presents, he has "wisdom."

Id.

[31] *See supra* note 29.

courts, the impact of laws, and even the law jobs of the Cheyenne.[32] However, the key focus of most of the original realists was appellate judging.[33] At many

[32]*See generally* Karl N. Llewellyn & E. Adamson Hoebel, The Cheyenne Way: Conflict and Case Law in Primitive Jurisprudence (1941) (analyzing the legal practices of the Cheyenne and announcing their "juristic beauty").

[33]Schlegel noted that Professor Walton Hamilton, one of the realists at the Yale Law School, "actively opposed empirical research in law." Schlegel, *supra* note 4, at 491 n.153. Most realists, other than Professor Jerome Frank, did focus on appellate judging. As always, Llewellyn offered a much more complicated story. Llewellyn applauded social science informing jurisprudence. He tried to do some of it himself. His major effort at field research was his study of divorce after the breakup of his first marriage. It was a strange mixture of social science and Llewellyn's own intuitions. *See generally* K.N. Llewellyn, *Behind the Law of Divorce* (pts. I & II), 32 Colum. L. Rev. 1281 (1932), 33 Colum. L. Rev. 249 (1933). Twining stated: "The divorce study was Llewellyn's sole attempt to imitate the 'scientists' during the years of the Columbia experiment. For the rest of the period he remained comfortably indoors, to the relief and benefit of nearly everyone." Twining, *supra* note 25, at 195. Llewellyn did collaborate with Professor E. Adamson Hoebel, an anthropologist, on the study that produced *The Cheyenne Way,* which was published in 1941. However, Llewellyn was in the field only for a brief time; Hoebel dealt with the informants. *See* John M. Conley & William M. O'Barr, *A Classic in Spite of Itself*: The Cheyenne Way *and the Case Method in Legal Anthropology,* 29 Law & Soc. Inquiry 179, 179 (2004). As Professors John Conley and William O'Barr recounted:

> Later that summer, Llewellyn and his . . . wife, an economist, joined Hoebel in Montana for 10 days—the only days he ever spent among the Cheyenne. A photograph taken at the time shows Llewellyn and his wife seated in the back seat of an open convertible with elderly Indians being led up to him to be interviewed.

Id. at 186.

Llewellyn criticized Moore's attempts to study behavior in response to law and to become a true social scientist. Schlegel noted:

> For those like Corbin and Llewellyn, satisfied because the law school world gave ample room for using their quite extraordinary talents to uncover substantial insights about doctrine and its use, Moore's work was simply unnecessary. A suggestion to go to Cincinnati to "observe the operations of bank tellers at close range" was pointless when a call to a friendly banker coupled with a bit of imagination would provide the same information.

John Henry Schlegel, American Legal Realism and Empirical Social Science 237 (1995) (footnote omitted). Llewellyn's reaction to large data sets is reminiscent of U.S. Supreme Court Justice Oliver Wendall Holmes's reaction to Justice Louis Brandeis:

> Brandeis recalled having told Holmes "that if he really wants to 'improve his mind' (as he always speaks of it), the way to do it is not to read more philosophic books . . . but to get some sense of the world of fact. And he asked me to map out some reading—he became much interested—and I told him that I'd . . . get some books, that books could carry him only so far, and that then he should get some exhibits from life. I suggested the textile industry, and told him in vacation time he is near Lawrence and Lowell and he should go there and look about."

Phillipa Strum, Louis D. Brandeis: Justice for the People 309–10 (1984). Justice Holmes's response was: "I have little doubt that it would be good for my immortal soul to plunge into them [facts] . . . but I shrink from the bore." *Id.* at 310. Likewise, Professor Grant Gilmore observed that he was "'completely uninterested'" in my empirical work because "'when you have finished describing something, all you really have is a list. In itself the list is meaningless—a lot of trees waiting for someone to assemble them into a forest.'" Stewart Macaulay, *Popular Legal Culture: An Introduction,* 98 Yale L.J. 1545, 1546 n.8 (1989) (quoting Gilmore). I responded: "[o]ften empirical research into legal matters reveals that in the forests assembled by scholars, the trees have the blight or are creations of fantasy." *Id.*

law schools and in many law reviews, legal realism became the conventional wisdom.[34]

Some of the realists saw law as merely rationalization or false consciousness. Not Llewellyn. Hull noted: "Llewellyn valued law, loved law, in a way that the data gatherers and behavioral observers among the realist corps did not." Hull, *supra* note 23, at 242. She also contrasts Pound's approach to studying the Chinese criminal justice system with Llewellyn's approach to the Cheyenne: "Pound drafted and wished to impose a Western-style social science survey on provincial officials; Llewellyn listened to local "law-men" and tried to see the world through their eyes. Pound wanted to generalize through extensive comparison and categorization; Llewellyn wanted to particularize through the stories of individual cases." *Id.* at 313. For Llewellyn, one knew the world through what he called "feel." *Id.* at 296 & n.47. Feel "was a way of knowing about the world. Llewellyn had felt the rhythms of Cheyenne law and then saw how the Cheyenne felt their way through cases of trouble." *Id.* at 296 n.47. Hull wrote that Llewellyn was not interested in mere behavior—"that would be reductionist, and Llewellyn was not a simplifier. He loved complexity and reveled in it." *Id.* at 285. Hull criticized Llewellyn's approach:

> Llewellyn had never dealt directly with reality. . . . Even when he spent his ten days on the Cheyenne reservation, he was a tourist in someone else's reality. The Cheyenne were not gifted, intuitive lawmakers. They were a people with a long tradition of negotiated settlements, gestures, scripted mini-dramas, and well-versed oral lore. Llewellyn's romantic inclinations and his breathless prose made them into something else.

Id. at 332.

Thus, I am left with a question. Suppose Llewellyn were, say, fifty-five years old and found himself at the fortieth anniversary meeting of the Law and Society Association in June of 2004 in Chicago. Would he have enjoyed himself? Would he have had a better time the previous January at the Association of American Law Schools meeting? Indeed, how would he respond to the variations of the now dominant law and economics paradigm? Professor Alan Schwartz has observed that Llewellyn did not have available the most modern techniques of law and economics. *See* Alan Schwartz, *Karl Llewellyn and the Origins of Contract Theory, in* The Jurisprudential Foundations of Corporate and Commercial Law 12, 18 (Jody S. Kraus & Steven D. Walt eds., 2000). Would he have embraced them, or would he have found them a form of reductionism just as objectionable as the masses of statistics gathered by the scientific realists? Hull pointed out that, to some extent, Llewellyn anticipated the concern with the costs of legal rules in an article published in 1925 in the *American Economic Review*. Hull, *supra* note 23, at 139–40 & 139 n.41; *see also* Karl N. Llewellyn, *The Effect of Legal Institutions upon Economics*, 15 Am. Econ. Rev. 665 (1925).

Professor Carl Friedrich suggested that Llewellyn was primarily interested in predicting the behavior of judges and other legal officials. Carl J. Friedrich, *Remarks on Llewellyn's View of Law, Official Behavior, and Political Science*, 50 Pol. Sci. Q. 419, 421 (1935). Friedrich thought that Llewellyn was not interested in explaining this behavior as a social scientist would. *Id.* at 423. Friedrich argued that, while Llewellyn established that judges in both the United States and Germany often do not follow precedent and offer misleading rationalizations for their decisions, he did not tell us why they do this. *Id.* at 428–29. Friedrich stated:

> [T]he American judge is first and foremost the member of an ancient craft guild. In such free associations, make-believe is very essential for maintaining social coherence. While a bureaucratic hierarchy can count upon the individual official's desire to avoid arousing the displeasure of his superiors, within a free association convincing rationalization is essential and the rule of precedent is a mighty factor in making the rationalization convincing.

Id. at 429. He said that this is the kind of explanation that would not interest Llewellyn. *See id.* For Llewellyn, manipulations of precedent were just wrong behavior. *See id.*

[34]As Friedman noted:

> In an important sense, legal realism ended up defeating its enemy almost totally. If, today, you told a group of law professors (or lawyers for that matter) that you thought politics had

Much of Llewellyn's career was spent at the Columbia Law School.[35] In the late 1920s, the Columbia faculty attempted to revise the curriculum and produce new teaching materials that focused on the functions served by law rather than traditional legal categories.[36] Largely, the attempt was to find information in the relevant social sciences and plug it into teaching materials that still focused on appellate judging.[37] Insofar as Columbia professors did any empirical research, it tended to be confined to asking someone who should know.[38] While Columbia faculty produced some brilliant casebooks,[39] these works did not provoke most legal educators to abandon the traditional categories, such as contracts and torts, and turn to functional arrangements of legal materials.[40] As the books went through second and third editions,

---

> an important influence on the legal system; that rules were more malleable and less decisive than they appeared; that you believed law is not and can never be totally neutral, and other sentiments along these lines, they might very well yawn and agree.... What they *do* with this banality is another question.

Lawrence M. Friedman, American Law in the 20th Century 493 (2002).

[35]Schlegel reminded us that when Moore arrived at Columbia in 1916,

> [w]hat Moore found was an intellectual community in its most extraordinary period of social scientific creativity: James Harvey Robinson and Charles Beard in history, Thorstein Veblen and William D. Mitchell in economics, Franz Boas in anthropology, E.L. Thorndike in educational psychology, William F. Ogburn in sociology and, of course, John Dewey.

Schlegel, *supra* note 12, at 236. Llewellyn was also very much part of this environment. Allen R. Kamp, *Downtown Code: A History of the Uniform Commercial Code 1949–1954,* 49 Buff. L. Rev. 359, 362 (2001). Allen Kamp noted:

> Llewellyn's views and his original program for the Code grew out of the matrix of the collectivist mentality of the 1930s.... Llewellyn was once part of an academic avant guard, a supporter of FDR in his court-packing plan, a folk dancer, a student of Boas' anthropology, part of a 1930s radical, collectivist milieu.

Id.

[36]*See* Brainerd Currie, *The Materials of Law Study,* 3 J. Legal Educ. 331 (1951); Brainerd Currie, *The Materials of Law Study,* 8 J. Legal Educ. 1 (1955) [hereinafter Currie, *The Materials of Law Study,* 1955].

[37]Currie, *The Materials of Law Study, supra* note 36, at 68–69, 74–75. ("The tendency to ask the wrong questions of other disciplines and to expect too much of the replies is persistent.").

[38]*Id.* at 72 ("The materials sought by the Columbia faculty were relatively inaccessible, written in different technical languages, and in some instances nonexistent.").

[39]*See* Robert Stevens, *Two Cheers for 1890: The American Law School, in* V Perspectives in American History 405, 483, 511 (1971).

[40]Compare the comments of one of Harvard's most distinguished contracts teachers about Edwin Patterson's Columbia casebook on the subject

> The volume [*Cases and Materials on Contracts II* (1935)] begins with several long opinions on the inferences with respect to sanity to be drawn from specific evidence, and ends with several extracts from psychiatrists. While these are no doubt instructive reading, one wonders how much is to be learned by a classroom discussion of them by teachers who are not psychiatrists and students who have no means or intentions of becoming such.... Discussion might be centered on the really doctrinal decisions, leaving the others to be read.

their authors tended to jettison more and more of the social science and the contextual materials.[41] Professor Christopher Tomlins reported:

> Argument over the alternative directions for the [Columbia] Law School that the disciplinary turn and the functional curriculum implied—research institution or training school—came to a head in 1928 over the appointment of Young B. Smith as Dean. Antagonized by the appointment, the core group of realists (William O. Douglas, Hessel Yntema, Leon Marshall, Herman Oliphant, and Underhill Moore) resigned. The functional curriculum remained in place, but Smith ended the realist attempt to inform legal instruction with social research.[42]

The classic realists talked about doing empirical research, but relatively little was accomplished.[43] Professor John Henry Schlegel looked at the work of Professors Charles Clark, William O. Douglas, and Underhill Moore.[44] He concluded: "[a]s a coherent intellectual force in American legal thought American Legal Realism simply ran itself into the sand."[45] He explained:

George K. Gardner, *Cases and Materials on Contracts II,* 45 Yale L.J. 1153, 1154 (1936) (reviewing Edwin W. Patterson, Cases and Materials on Contracts II (1935)).

[41] *See* Albert C. Jacobs & Julius Gobel, Cases and Other Materials on Domestic Relations (3d ed. 1952); Currie, *The Materials of Law Study*, 1955, supra note 36, at 28–38 (addressing the changes in Albert C. Jacobs, Cases and Materials on Domestic Relations (2d ed. 1939)); *see also* Laura Kalman, Legal Realism at Yale: 1927–1960, at 87–97 (1986). For Laura Kalman's discussion of Albert Jacobs's casebook, see Kalman, *supra*, at 88–90. ("The fate of the Jacobs's casebook indicated why law professors who espoused the integration of law with the social sciences in their scholarship so often balked at doing so in the classroom. Ignored by the law professors, the book was condemned as amateurish by social scientists.").

[42] *Christopher Tomlins, Framing the Field of Law's Disciplinary Encounters: A Historical Narrative*, 34 Law & Soc'y Rev. 911, 934 (2000).

[43] Lawrence Friedman noted that the realists'

> critique attacked the conventional explanations of how judges decided cases; but they rarely broke out of the world the conceptualists occupied—the world of appellate decisions. With a few exceptions, they did not really investigate living law, the law in action. They did not even look at the work of the lower courts; and they had little or nothing to say about the way what judges did and decided reverberated in the outside world. In principle, they believed in the social-scientific study of law, and they paid lip-service to it; but in practice they did little or nothing about it.

Lawrence M. Friedman, *Karl Llewellyn and the Riddle of Judicial Decision-Making, in* Rechtsrealismus, multikulturelle Gesellschaft und Handelsrecht: Karl N. Llewellyn und seine Bedeutung heute 135, 138 (Ulrich Drobnig & Manfred Rehbinder eds., 1994) (footnote omitted).

[44] Schlegel, *supra* note 12, at 200.

[45] Schlegel, *supra* note 4, at 459 (footnote omitted). Schlegel credited Professor Duncan Kennedy with supplying the "felicitous image of the decline of Realism." *Id.* at 459 n.1; *see also* Kalman, *supra* note 41, at 42–44; Schlegel, American Legal Realism, *supra* note 33, at 1–2; Schlegel, *supra* note 12, at 195–323. Likewise, Kalman recounted the story of the Yale Law School's retreat from realism and law and society scholarship in the early 1970s. Laura Kalman, *The Dark Ages*, *in* History of the Yale Law School: The Tercentennial Lectures 154 (Anthony Kronman ed., 2004); *see also* Robert Stevens, Law School: Legal Education in America from the 1850s to the 1980s (1983).

> the Realists' social scientific research died out because of [(1)] the impermanence of the institutionalized circumstances in which it was undertaken, [(2)] the peculiarities of the personalities of the leaders of the undertaking, and [(3)] the difficulties in matching the impulse to do such research with the social science of the time.[46]

Schlegel showed us that these pioneers at Yale discovered that empirical research about law took time and was expensive. He looked at the Yale realists and said: "the one thing that really grand crew was not noted for was sustained commitment to anything."[47] The empirical realists attempted their work in the middle of a major depression when funds were scarce. Moreover, Yale was a private university that depended on rich donors. Many of them were not pleased with the politics of the researchers nor the questions their work raised about the ideology of the American legal system.[48] Nonetheless, Clark and his colleagues did discover the largely administrative nature of state court civil litigation and the role of plea-bargaining on the criminal side.[49] Of course, some of the empirical realists found the chance to go to Washington, D.C. to work for the New Deal to be far more attractive than remaining on the sidelines as a scholar. U.S. Supreme Court Justice William O. Douglas, for example, went from a large empirical study of bankruptcy to serving as Chairman of the Securities and Exchange Commission before joining the Supreme Court.[50]

Schlegel reported that many law professors found the empirical work at Yale irrelevant or trivial. He described the reaction of progressive reformers, such as Professor (and later Supreme Court Justice) Felix Frankfurter, who "knew" that there was a problem of court congestion.[51] When Clark conducted an empirical study of the business of state courts that failed to support their preconceptions, these reformers ignored or attacked Clark's work.[52] Schlegel said that for these reformers: "[f]act gathering that did not advance an immediate reform objective was scholarship not worth publishing, just as fact gathering that did not fit their model of how the world was structured was an 'irrelevant jumble of figures.'"[53] Evasion and denial of the findings of empirical studies are still far too typical of law professors and Supreme Court justices.

---

[46]Schlegel, *supra* note 4, at 460.

[47]Schlegel, *supra* note 12, at 315.

[48]*See* Kalman, *supra* note 41, at 122, 132–34, 136 (reporting that the *Chicago Tribune* once ran a cartoon showing a hammer and sickle flag flying above the Yale Law School).

[49]*See* John H. Schlegel & David M. Trubek, *Charles E. Clark and the Reform of Legal Education*, *in* Judge Charles Edward Clark 81, 108 (Peninah Petruck ed., 1991) ("What is noteworthy about all this work was that it pointed to the marginality of law, and suggested that researchers had to look beyond the law and legal rules if they were fully to understand the phenomena they were concerned with.").

[50]Bruce Allen Murphy, Wild Bill: The Legend and Life of William O. Douglas 88–91, 115–16, 124–35, 171–96 (2003).

[51]Schlegel, *supra* note 4, at 513–19.

[52]*Id.* at 513–14.

[53]*Id.* at 519.

After World War II, the University of Chicago Law School won major Ford Foundation grants.[54] Most of the money funded Professors Henry Kalven and Hans Zeisel's famed jury project,[55] but we should not forget Professor Soia Mentschikoff's arbitration project.[56] Both projects developed new methods for studying legal topics, and both published interesting findings. Neither, however, focused centrally on appellate cases in traditional fields.[57] As a result, any influence on conventional American legal scholarship was, at best, subtle and indirect.[58]

The jury project reminds us that research into the legal system in operation may be controversial and subject the investigators and their institutions to attack. After receiving permission from the judges and lawyers involved, the project recorded an actual jury deliberating about a real case.[59] The idea was to confirm some of the work that had been based on experimental juries and judges' opinions about jury performance.[60] Such "bugging a jury" provoked an outcry[61] and a federal statute[62] that rules out most of such research. Some with power in this society do not welcome research on the reality behind their ideological positions. Trial by jury is a powerful symbol of popular democratic control of our legal system. Some leaders of the bar may have worried that this kind of research might show jurors negatively. Moreover, the project invaded the privacy of an actual jury, and it might make other jurors worry about speaking their views because they would not know whether their words were being captured and might be turned against them. Finally, it allowed political

---

[54] *See* Schlegel, American Legal Realism, *supra* note 33, at 238–44.

[55] See Harry Kalven Jr. & Hans Zeisel, The American Jury (1966); Dale W. Breeder, *The Functions of the Jury: Facts or Fictions?*, 21 U. Chi. L. Rev. 386(1954); Dale W. Breeder, *The University of Chicago Project*, 38 Neb. L. Rev. 744 (1959); *see also* Valerie P. Hans & Neil Vidmar, *The American Jury at Twenty-Five Years*, 16 Law & Soc. Inquiry 323 (1991).

[56] *See* Soia Mentschikoff, *Commercial Arbitration*, 61 Colum. L. Rev. 846 (1961) [hereinafter Mentschikoff, *Commercial Arbitration*]; Soia Mentschikoff, *The Significance of Arbitration—A Preliminary Inquiry*, 17 Law & Contemp. Probs. 698 (1952) [hereinafter Mentschikoff, *The Significance of Arbitration*],

[57] *See* Mentschikoff, *Commercial Arbitration, supra* note 56, at 848 (examining "the role of the adversary system as typified by commercial arbitration in dispute settlement in commercial matters"); Mentschikoff, *The Significance of Arbitration, supra* note 56, at 698 ("The thesis of this paper is that ... we fail to perceive the importance and generative power of the arbitration process.").

[58] This is not to say that, had the research been directly relevant to appellate decisions, American law professors would have paid attention to it. It is much easier to get your data by looking up at the ceiling tiles or asking what a rational actor would do and answering that question by introspection.

[59] *See Recording of Jury Deliberations: Hearing S. Res. 58 Before the Subcomm. to Investigate on the Administration of the Internal Security Act and Other Internal Security Laws of the S. Comm. of the Judiciary*, 84th Cong. 3 (1955) [hereinafter Hearing on S. Res. 58] (testimony of Edward H. Levi, Dean, University of Chicago Law School); *see also* Staff of Senate Comm. On the Judiciary, 84th Cong., Report on Recording of Jury Deliberations 1–5 (Comm. Print 1956).

[60] Staff of Senate Comm. On the Judiciary, *supra* note 59, at 1.

[61] *See* Hearing on S. Res. 58, *supra* note 59, at 3; *see also* Staff of Senate Comm. On the Judiciary, *supra* note 59, at 1–5.

[62] 18 U.S.C. § 1508 (2000) (prohibiting recording of federal jury deliberations).

figures to charge the University of Chicago Law School with the taint of communism. Kalven, one of the leaders of the project, was a noted civil libertarian who had battled invasions of free speech by the anticommunist crusades of the 1950s. The charge never was presented very clearly, but apparently those who attacked the project were asserting that professors at the University of Chicago were undermining a traditional and cherished American institution. I think it is safe to say that, in recent years, no one has attacked that law school on the ground of its communist tendencies.[63]

Also, in the early 1950s, the work of Professor Willard Hurst at the University of Wisconsin Law School began to appear.[64] Attempting to summarize Hurst's work in a paragraph or two is impossible. However, Hurst remade legal history into a true empirical enterprise. He looked at the role of law in the economic and social development of the State of Wisconsin. Instead of focusing on the great appellate cases from the highest courts, Hurst looked at law from the bottom up.[65] He asked such things as: who turned to law, and what did it offer them? What did the pattern of ordinary cases reveal about the functions of law in the economic development of Wisconsin? Law to Hurst was much more than appellate cases or treatises about doctrine. Hurst insisted that we look at legislation and the operation of administrative agencies. He wrote one of the first, and still one of the best, studies of what lawyers did and how lawyer activity affected economic and social development.[66] He showed that ideas about a golden age of limited government were misleading. Americans always sought to use law in many ways to foster development by, in his phrase, "releasing energy."[67] That is, law created structures and institutions that

---

[63]*Compare* Abner J. Mikva, *The Law School's Fair Image*, 70 U. Chi. L. Rev. 259 (2003), *with* Malcolm P. Sharp, *The Conservative Fellow Traveler*, 30 U. Chi. L. Rev. 704 (1963).

[64]*See, e.g.*, James Willard Hurst, The Growth of American Law: The Lawmakers (1950).

[65]*See* James Willard Hurst, Law and Economic Growth: The Legal History of the Lumber Industry in Wisconsin 1836–1915, at xi (1964) ("'Great cases' and constitutional debate deserve their place in the telling of legal history. But most of life is not melodrama . . . ."). For comments about Professor Willard Hurst, see, for example, Daniel R. Ernst, *Willard Hurst and the Administrative State: From Williams to Wisconsin*, 18 Law & Hist. Rev. 1, 16–19 (2000); Harry N. Scheiber, *At the Borderland of Law and Economic History: The Contributions of Willard Hurst*, 75 Am. Hist. Rev. 744, 756 (1970); Harry N. Scheiber, *Private Rights and Public Power: American Law, Capitalism, and the Republican Polity in Nineteenth-Century America*, 107 Yale L.J. 823 (1997).

[66]Hurst said:

> [I]n our years of national life, lawyers could show a record of social invention that was matched only by that of the more restless and vastly larger class of businessmen.
>
> . . . .
>
> Much, if not most, of lawyers' inventions consisted in making old institutions serve new needs. Obviously that did not derogate from the practical importance of their work; to the contrary, it placed it in the normal pattern of social change.

Hurst, *supra* note 64, at 336–37.

[67]*See generally* James Willard Hurst, Law and the Conditions of Freedom in the Nineteenth-Century United States (1956).

enabled people to make money. However, Hurst did not romanticize the historical record. Far too often, instead of trying to solve problems, lawmakers simply drifted and evaded them. When they were forced to cope with problems that could not be ignored, they engaged in what he called "bastard pragmatism," finding short-run and cheap responses rather than real solutions to social problems. As I said, this is an inadequate picture of Hurst, but it makes at least some of the points relevant to a New Legal Realism.

Hurst also worked hard to develop a new approach to legal scholarship.[68] He recruited and mentored many in both law and social science who later made real contributions to law and society scholarship.[69] Professor Frank Remington was a former student and great friend, and ran major projects in the criminal law in action.[70] Professor Harry V. Ball, then a young sociologist, came to Madison, Wisconsin, to work on one of Remington's projects.[71] Many played a role in the creation of the Law and Society Association in 1964, but Ball provided much of the energy and vision.[72] Without Ball, something such as the Law and Society Association would have come, if at all, later and perhaps in a different form.[73]

Tomlins told us:

> Law and Society enjoyed its greatest success at Wisconsin. There, however, the field did not "return" to law: law had been its central focus from the start. Conceptually, law-centeredness

[68]*See* Bryant G. Garth, *James Willard Hurst as Entrepreneur for the Field of Law and Social Science*, 18 Law & Hist. Rev. 37, 58 (2000). Bryant Garth reported a debate in the early 1950s before a committee of the Rockefeller Foundation between Harvard Professor Lon Fuller and Hurst. *Id.* at 54–55. Fuller wanted to support thought about philosophy and law. *Id.* Hurst, arguing against such an approach, said: "I would like to see more people dealing with the more grubby fields of law. I would like to see people come to this field not for its own sake, but because they are exasperated with the tools that they have in, say, contracts." *Id.* at 55. Hurst won the argument and got the grant. To state the obvious, I owe a great deal to Hurst's mentoring when I was a beginning law teacher not long after this debate. I got to spend some of the money Hurst was granted by the Rockefeller Foundation. Indeed, I was "exasperated with the tools that … [I had] in [the grubby field of] contracts." *Id.* I also had a wife, the late Jacqueline Macaulay, who was well into her graduate studies in social psychology and who edited my papers. She got her Ph.D. in 1965 and then a law degree in 1983. She practiced law until her death in 2000. She was a tough editor who could catch me when I affronted the conventions of social science, turn my prose into English that communicated, and offer suggestions and insights. As I said in my tribute to her after her death: "Jackie deserves major credit for whatever success I've had."

[69]*Id.* at 39–44.

[70]*See id.* at 40.

[71]*See id.*

[72]*See id.*

[73]For a detailed history of the creation and early days of the Law and Society Association, see Lawrence M. Friedman, *The Law and Society Movement*, 38 Stan. L. Rev. 763 (1986); Bryant Garth & Joyce Sterling, *From Legal Realism to Law and Society: Reshaping Law for the Last Stages of the Social Activist State*, 32 Law & Soc'y Rev. 409 (1998); Felice V. Levine, *Goose Bumps and "The Search for Signs of Intelligent Life" in Sociolegal Studies: After Twenty-Five Years*, 24 Law & Soc'y Rev. 7 (1990); David M. Trubek & John Esser, *"Critical Empiricism" in American Legal Studies: Paradox, Program, or Pandora's Box?*, 14 Law & Soc. Inquiry 3 (1989).

> manifested itself in Wisconsin's forthright definition of the field's purpose—to investigate and "explain" law as a subject by locating it contextually as the dependent variable in a context of social and economic phenomena. Institutionally, law-centeredness was expressed in the location of the explanatory project in the Law School, safely under the control of lawyers. Both traits secured for Law and Society the "critical mass" at Wisconsin that it was unable to build elsewhere.
>
> . . . .
>
> . . . Law-centeredness guaranteed the necessary institutional security that permitted the field to develop, to attract local resources, to attain critical mass, and to achieve a transformative impact on legal scholarship. Necessarily, however, it also limited the extent of that transformation, and that limitation, too, was a condition of Law and Society's success.[74]

Undoubtedly, much of the effort at the University of Wisconsin Law School dealt with law as the dependent variable. However, most people there did not see this as the only subject for study, and many looked at something close to Ehrlich's living law, which moved attention away from such people as judges, police, administrators, and legislators. Professor Marc Galanter was long concerned with the processing of disputes outside of the formal legal system.[75] In 1986, I published an essay on "private government" that looked at what Professor Sally Falk Moore called semi-autonomous social fields[76] and other formal and informal institutions that create norms and supply sanctions.[77] Hurst wrote a long and detailed comment about this manuscript.[78] He was highly interested, and engaged with the paper.[79] Not all of his comments were favorable.[80] Hurst was extraordinarily kind and always polite, but he did not pull punches when he disagreed with what we had written.[81] To support Tomlins to some degree, however, I will note that Hurst found my paper lacking sufficient attention to when people turned to state-supplied formal legal institutions rather than relying on private governments.[82] He wanted me to focus on when people

---

[74]Tomlins, *supra* note 42, at 958–59 (footnotes omitted).

[75]*See,* e.g., Marc Galanter, *Justice in Many Rooms: Courts, Private Ordering, and Indigenous Law*, 19 J. Legal Pluralism 1 (1981).

[76]Sally Falk Moore, Law as Process: An Anthropological Approach (1978).

[77]Stewart Macaulay, *Private Government*, *in* Law and the Social Sciences 445 (Leon Lipson & Stanton Wheeler eds., 1986).

[78]*See* Stewart Macaulay, *Willard's Law School?*, 1997 Wis. L. Rev. 1163, 1171–72 (quoting Letter from Willard Hurst to Stewart Macaulay 1, 4 (May 17, 2003) [hereinafter Letter from Willard Hurst]).

[79]*See id.* at 1171 (quoting Letter from Willard Hurst, *supra* note 78, at 1, 4).

[80]*See id.* (quoting Letter from Willard Hurst, *supra* note 78, at 1, 4).

[81]*See id.* (quoting Letter from Willard Hurst, *supra* note 78, at 1, 4).

[82]For example, here are three paragraphs from four single-spaced pages of comments he wrote in 1983 about my paper on private government:

> I'm glad to have the working paper on private government. It is a stimulating piece, and introduces me to some [jurisprudence] I'm not familiar with. It also stirs me to a few questions, which I submit in case you expect to consider any further tinkering with the manuscript. I don't try to set them down in neat order, figuring that if I made that a prerequisite to responding I'd likely not get around to it.

saw a need to create law and legal institutions. This is law as the dependent variable. However, he only suggested adding an issue to a lengthy paper that focused on substitutes for formal public law.

Sometimes we will want to focus on law as the dependent variable; sometimes on the impact of law on society, often through indirect and subtle influences. As I said long ago in my Mitchell Lecture, "[w]hat is clear is that any theory that tells us to watch those with money, status and influence cannot be all wrong, and any theory that tells us that these factors are all there is to law cannot be all right."[83]

Professor Lawrence Friedman and I published collections of teaching materials on law and the behavioral sciences in 1969[84] and 1977.[85] We were hard pressed at the time of the first edition to find good articles and book chapters that made the points we wanted to make about where law comes from, the limits of effective legal action and the roles of the actors in the legal system. To some extent, this is a law-centered agenda, but in carrying it out, Friedman and I also looked at such things as complimentary and competing institutions and the broad idea of legal culture.

> I finished the paper sensing some feeling of incompleteness about it, despite its breadth and detail. You make the case for the realities of private government, including both its reach and its wielding of forms of compulsion or discipline, and for the blurring of lines between "public" and "private." But it doesn't strike me that you squarely confront a question that all this inevitably poses: Can we derive from experience or logic or whatever some persuasive explanations or demarcations of why and where people turn to law and on the other hand to various kinds of private governance? At page 83 there is a rather tangential posing of the question, why and when do non-legal factors take over the human relations scene. But I'd think the question calls for more extended treatment, even if the upshot is going to have to be largely to confess ignorance. Legal institutions continue to be large, stubborn facts of our social experience, granted all the division of labor, competition, and blurring of lines that other kinds of social ordering introduce. Doesn't a satisfying explanation or analysis of private government derive its contours, inescapably, in large part from understanding where and how far law is used?
>
> . . . .
>
> Finally, a minor point or irritant of style: "problematic" has become a buzzword in current learned journals, to an extent that grates on this ear at least. It turns up in this manuscript oftener than seems artistic. Webster offers some perfectly usable substitutes: questionable, unsettled, doubtful, unproved, equivocal.

See id. at 1171–72 (quoting Letter from Willard Hurst, *supra* note 78, at 1, 4).

[83]Stewart Macaulay, *Law and the Behavioral Sciences: Is There Any There There?*, 6 Law & Pol'y 149, 182 (1984).

[84]Lawrence M. Friedman & Stewart Macaulay, Law and the Behavioral Sciences (1969).

[85]Lawrence M. Friedman & Stewart Macaulay, Law and the Behavioral Sciences (2d ed. 1977). In the most recent teaching materials, however, we faced a major problem of selecting from a large number of excellent articles and book chapters. *See* Stewart Macaulay et al., Law & Society: Readings on the Social Study of Law (1995). Political scientist and lawyer John Stookey joined us in fashioning the latest version of our materials. Without his ideas and energy, the revision would not have been accomplished. See the review of all three versions of our sociology of law materials in Jonathan Simon, *Law After Society*, 24 Law & Soc. Inquiry 143 (1999).

There was a great development in the field during the time between the first and second editions.

In 1984, I gave the Mitchell Lecture at the State University of New York at Buffalo.[86] I asked what, if anything, twenty years of work in the Law and Society Association had accomplished. I offered seven propositions that Professor David Trubek called my "seven deadly sins."[87] Jackie Macaulay, when she was editing my manuscript, added a sentence that I kept. She wrote: "[t]his flood of social science and law has washed up a few shining nuggets."[88] I offer the main headings now as a quick way to review a large field. Of course, these are my seven, and I have no illusion that everyone would accept them without amendments or additions. Here they are:

1. Law is not free.
2. Law is delivered by actors with limited resources and interests of their own in settings where they have discretion.
3. Many of the functions usually thought of as legal are performed by alternative institutions, and there is a great deal of interpenetration between what we call public and private sectors.
4. People, acting alone and in groups, cope with law and cannot be expected to comply passively.
5. Lawyers play many roles other than adversary in a courtroom.
6. Our society deals with conflict in many ways, but avoidance and evasion are important ones.
7. While law matters in American society, its influence tends to be indirect, subtle and ambiguous.[89]

I invite you to revise, amend, or add what we have discovered during the twenty years since my Mitchell Lecture.[90] A few years after this lecture, for example, I

[86]For an article based on this lecture, see Macaulay, *supra* note 83, at 152–56.

[87]*Id.*

[88]*Id.* at 152.

[89]*Id.* at 152–55.

[90]Professor Frank Munger noted my seven propositions and added several that reflect the more current law and society culture. Frank Munger, *Mapping Law and Society, in* Crossing Boundaries: Traditions and Transformations in Law and Society Research 21, 42–55 (Austin Sarai Sarat et al. eds., 1998). He added the following: (1) recent law and society research has been more attentive to the perceptions and consciousness of actors; (2) the state is a contested and problematic category; (3) globalization is a process as well as a context—the changes in the nation state and global markets that in large part drive the process are a terrain of struggle for power; and (4) law practice is a domain of contest and cultural production. *See id.* at 42–52. He then offered a new perspective on legality from a law and society approach: (1) law is an element in the social construction of everyday life; (2) law is given content and meaning by actors with biography, in settings that have a history and thus a social organization of their own; (3) an issue of increasing importance in research is how the myth of neutral, autonomous law has been maintained; and (4) lawyers are producers of culture within the limits of their roles in political and economic institutions. *See id.* at 52–55. Munger concluded:

advocated study of the legal ideas held by ordinary people and elites that are offered by education, entertainment, and spectator sports.[91] This was not a new idea. In the early days of American sociology, Professors William Thomas and Dorothy Thomas observed that what people think is so, is in fact so for them.[92] Law can be part of a project to mislead people. I have cautioned, however, that Americans are seldom trapped in the rhetoric of law. Ordinary people in this country are great jazz musicians, ready to improvise on legal tunes.[93] Moreover, many of our legal ideas come in matched contradictory sets so that almost every position can be challenged in totally predictable ways.[94] As Professor Marvin Harris asserted: "[n]o matter how deviant or unexpected the act, a psychologically intact human being can always appeal to some set of rules someone else will recognize as legitimate, although

---

> I would argue that the findings of "new" critical empiricism and our vision of the contemporary law and society field are remarkably consistent with the earlier empirical results summarized by Macaulay, but we no longer understand the earlier results in terms of the "gap" between liberal legal aspirations and achievement.
>
> ....
>
> New perspectives render Macaulay's list of contingencies much less surprising. Research today is less a critique of official forms of legal authority than an exploration of all forms of power and their interaction in social life, ranging from formal discursive authority to embedded practical knowledge.

Id. at 55.

[91] *Compare* Macaulay, *supra* note 33, at 1556 ("[L]awyers, trial judges, court commissioners, political candidates, office holders, clients, and even people standing at a working class bar are all jazz performers. They play variations on legal themes, and sometimes attempt to put new melodies to the chords."), *with* Patricia Ewick & Austin Sarat, *Hidden in Plain View: Murray Edelman in the Law and Society Tradition*, 29 Law & Soc. Inquiry 439, 457–58 (2004) ("The public has 'a small set of stock texts that everyone who grows up in a particular culture learns early: poverty as the fault of the poor or of social institutions; abortion as a form of freedom or a form of murder; and so on.'") (citation omitted), and Austin Sarat & Jonathan Simon, *Beyond Legal Realism: Cultural Analysis, Cultural Studies, and the situation of Legal Scholarship,* 13 Yale J.L. & Human. 3, 32 (2001) (stating that cultural analysis calls us "to attend to the cultural, not for its recuperative or redemptive potential, but instead to expose the layers of power that the turn to culture in the political realm often seeks to mask").

[92] William I. Thomas & Dorothy Swaine Thomas, The Child in America 572 (1928) ("If men define situations as real, they are real in their consequences.").

[93] Macaulay, *supra* note 33, at 1556; *see also* Mary Jo Hatch, *Exploring the Empty Spaces of Organizing: How Improvisational Jazz Helps Redescribe Organization Structure,* 20 Organizational Stud. 75, 75 (1999) ("This paper ... begins with a description of some basic elements of jazz performance—soloing, comping, trading fours, listening and responding, groove and feel—and builds on these to redescribe organizational structure as ambiguous, emotional and temporal."); Michael Humphreys et al., *Is Ethnography Jazz?,* 10 Organization 5, 5 (2003) ("[E]thnographers are engaged in a dual quest for self-identity and empathy that is improvised in ways resembling the musical 'conversation' that occurs between performing jazz musicians."); Susan S. Silbey & Patricia Ewick, *The Double Life of Reason and Law,* 57 U. Miami L. Rev. 497, 511–12 (2003) ("Just as the jazz musician draws from her collection of favorite licks, people invent and construct legality by drawing from a repertoire or tool-kit of cultural signs and resources.").

[94] Marvin Harris, Cultural Materialism: The Struggle for a Science of Culture 274, 274–75 (1980).

perhaps as misinterpreted or misapplied."[95] I do not read Harris as saying that "anything goes." There are some arguments that almost everyone will see as misinterpreted or misapplied—that is, off the wall. Nonetheless, if not anything goes, there is a lot that does.[96] There may also be a great deal of cynical awareness about the law in action. Many, if not most, Americans know that, it is one thing to have a right, but something very different to make it real.

Where do we go from here? What do I see as a New Legal Realism? It will involve the law in action, but we must use an expanded definition of that phrase. Professor David Nelkin untangles some confusion between Professor Roscoe Pound's idea of "the law in action" and Ehrlich's "living law."[97] "Law in action," for Pound, focuses on the gap between the law in the books and the actual practices of legal officials and the public in case of disputes.[98] The "living law" refers mainly to the "norms recognised as obligatory by citizens in their capacity as members of associations."[99] Law in action pushes us toward studies of gaps between what we teach in law schools and what goes on in the world. Living law would take us toward the norms, sanction systems, and institutions that actually exist in various groups in society.

Nelken points out that Ehrlich faced a problem in distinguishing living law from all other social norms, sanctions, and institutions.[100] We can speak, for example, of the law of Christmas or birthday gifts that defines who should give what to which relatives and friends, and sanctions a failure to give or reciprocate. However, many

---

[95] *Id.*

[96] One of Jackie Macaulay's cases is illustrative: a pro bono client was a member of a group that did not recognize the legitimacy of the governments of Wisconsin or the United States. She had gone through "a quiet title" action before her group's "court," and so she was sure that she no longer owed taxes to either government. She had a dispute with a deputy sheriff. She filled out a form that created a lien on the deputy's house, signed it with her name, and put it in the pile of documents to be recorded at the county courthouse. Perhaps it was a long, hot day, and so the clerks did not notice who had signed the document. Whatever the explanation, they recorded it. The deputy discovered the lien when he wanted to sell his house. The woman tried to persuade Jackie to argue that the Constitution prohibits titles of nobility, that "judge" is such a title, and therefore anyone can do anything that a judge claims power to do. The woman insisted that the other members of her group knew that this was a valid argument. She fired Jackie when Jackie—acting as the lawyer—refused to present it. The woman would not have won on this ground, but there was enough to her argument that it served my wife as a good story for some time.

[97] David Nelken, *Law in Action or Living Law? Back to the Beginning Sociology of Law,* 4 Legal Stud. 157 (1984). Professor Marc Hertogh draws a distinction between an American view of a legal consciousness and a European one. Marc Hertogh, *A "European" Conception of Legal Consciousness: Rediscovering Eugen Ehrlich*, 31 J.L. & Soc'y 457 (2004). American law and society scholars focus more on Pound's concept of law in action. *See id.* at 465. The question is: how do people experience official law? *Id.* at 463. Europeans follow Ehrlich's view of a living law, the law that dominates life itself even though it has not been posited in legal propositions. *See id.* at 473. Hertogh saw the goal as integrating the two views. *Id.* at 480. I agree.

[98] *See* Nelken, *supra* note 97, at 166–68.

[99] *Id.* at 165.

[100] *Id.* at 163.

of us find the analogy strained and not too useful. Ehrlich limited his idea to those norms sanctions, and institutions "which have a parallel form and content to the norms found in Roman and Western legal systems such as those associated with contract, property and inheritance rules."[101]

Nelken argued that a failure to distinguish the two concepts could lead to distortions in our sociology of law work.[102] He stated:

> A good example is provided by Macaulay's classic study of non-contractual relations between businessmen, work which has justly been paid the compliment of international replication. Macaulay's investigation was conceived very much in the Pound tradition of studies of legal effectiveness, even if its findings transcended this starting point. The question was whether contract law as taught in the universities was actually used or not, and how it might be changed so as to make it more useful to businessmen. Macaulay revealed that businessmen made only limited uses of contract law in planning their transactions, and were reluctant to rely on their contractual remedies. Business relationships were governed more by the need to maintain a good reputation in the market, and stand behind a good product, than by rules of contract law. These findings were very similar to those Ehrlich had emphasized when illustrating the existence of living law amongst businessmen.
>
> . . . .
>
> It is arguable that Macaulay's investigation would have been even more fruitful if it had started from this type of fascination with explaining the working norms of business life rather than the problem of how far contract "law in the books" misrepresents what actually occurs. In addition to showing how the exigencies of business life affect contract law, research using Ehrlich's ideas would seek to account for the origin and maintenance of the specific norms of business life including the neglected point which Ehrlich makes about the relevance of honour and business self-respect to the organisation of transactions.[103]

Nelken argues that those who write about legal pluralism and "semi-autonomous social fields" take Ehrlich's ideas as an essential starting point.[104] Ehrlich's work pushes us to think about the limits of intervention by the formal legal system. However, such thought must be empirical and not just assertions about the glories of an impersonal market.[105]

Many of us who began work at the University of Wisconsin Law School in the late 1950s and early 1960s took the phrase "law in action" to include both the gaps between the law on the books and what happened in legal institutions, and, the way problems were avoided, suppressed, and dealt with apart from official public norms, sanctions, and institutions. We used the phrase "law in action" to describe our enterprise, but we also explicitly took Ehrlich into account. If anything, we were less aware of Pound than Ehrlich. As I have noted before, Page, one of my predecessors as a Wisconsin contracts teacher, read Ehrlich in German and published a

---

[101] *See id.*

[102] *Id.* at 170–71.

[103] *Id.*

[104] *Id.* at 171.

[105] *Compare id., with* Jane E. Larson, *Free Markets Deep in the Heart of Texas*, 84 Geo. L.J. 179 (1995).

comment about his work in 1914.[106] Professor Jacob Beuscher was Hurst's partner in the intellectual leadership of the school.[107] Beuscher constantly talked about Ehrlich's "living law," and he offered examples drawn from his own empirical research into agricultural and environmental social systems, which were only somewhat influenced by the law in the books and the actions of legal officials.[108] Nelken notes that my 1963 study did "transcend" its starting point as a gap study.[109] I am sure that I was influenced by the appreciation of Ehrlich in our Wisconsin institutional culture. Also, I drew on parts of Professor Bronislaw Malinowski's *Crime and Custom in Savage Society,*[110] which pushed me to see the power of long-term continuing relationships.[111] I am sure that a full study of the norms and sanctions in business life would have been valuable; I am also sure that a thirty-year-old law professor with no formal training in any social science was not the one to carry it out.

We can say that "law in action," as it has developed in the law and society tradition, includes both Pound's and Ehrlich's ideas. Terms do take on meanings beyond their origins. Nonetheless, Nelken's point is important. A New Legal Realism must go beyond mere gap research. Legal pluralism is an essential idea for one who would think about law seriously. The action may be taking place quite apart from cops, administrative agencies, and courts.[112] My late colleague Frank Remington was a master of the doctrine of criminal law—he was, after all, the primary drafter of the *Wisconsin Criminal Code.* However, Remington always insisted that if you wanted to understand criminal law, you had to ride in the front seat of a squad car in an inner city on a hot summer night. Professor Elizabeth Mertz

---

[106]William Herbert Page, *Professor Ehrlich's Czenowitz Seminar of Living Law*, 4 N. Ky. L. Rev. 37 (1977).

[107]*See generally* Fran Thomas, Law in Action: Legal Frontiers for Natural Resources Planning; the Work of Professor Jacob H. Beuscher, including a bibliography of his published work (1972).

[108]Professor Jacob Beuscher often told the story of a farmer assigning his right to future checks from a dairy cooperative. The Wisconsin courts had found this right too indefinite to be assigned. O'Niel v. Wm. B. H. Kerr Co., 124 Wis. 234, 238, 102 N.W. 573, 574 (1905). One could not know in advance how much milk there would be or the price that it would command in the future. Nonetheless, Beuscher loved to tell us banks in the regions where dairy farms were most numerous regularly loaned money based on the security of an assignment of a right to a milk check. Is this the law in action or the living law? I think that it fits both ideas.

[109]Nelkin, *supra* note 66, at 170.

[110]Bronislaw Malinowski, Crime and Custom in Savage Society (Greenwood Press 1984) (1926).

[111]Professor Bronislaw Malinowski, for example, said that sanctions are provided by "a definite social machinery of binding force, based ... upon mutual dependence, and realized in the equivalent arrangement of reciprocal services, as well as in the combination of such claims into strands of multiple relationship." *Id.* at 55. Those who failed to keep economic obligations would soon find themselves "outside the social and economic order." *Id.* at 41. He also commented: "[W]henever the native can evade his obligations without the loss of prestige, or without the prospective loss of gain, he does so, exactly as a civilized business man would do." *Id.* at 30. Even in a long-term continuing relationship, obligations are not fixed once and for all but subject to redefinition in light of the social situation. *See id.* at 31.

[112]*See, e.g.,* Macaulay, *supra* note 77, at 445–518.

has suggested that it might also be a good idea to then join part of the crowd watching that squad car pass.

Both observations are apt, but even these suggestions would not be enough. If you really wanted to understand criminal law, you would need to consider Professor Herman Goldstein's point that the criminal law is but one resource sometimes used by the police in carrying out their basic duty of keeping the world looking safe enough for those who count.[113] You would want to consider what behavior by police earns them rewards and what behavior risks punishment. You would want to think about why the police patrol in some places and not others. You would want to consider what was involved in the decisions about how many police there are in a city and how they are equipped.

You would quickly turn from the city police to the institution of private police at athletic events, shopping centers, and large industrial plants, and in private-gated communities and condominiums. White-collar crimes are usually dealt with by what has been called "the second criminal justice system."[114] A large corporation does not have to worry about proof beyond a reasonable doubt or *Miranda* warnings. One suspected of, say, embezzlement from an employer might be just fired or moved to another job without the possibility of promotion. The threat of prosecution in the first criminal justice system may be used to gain some measure of restitution. The second system works without the burdens of constitutional rights and is under the control of large corporations rather than local or national politics. Moreover, a corporation can buy state of the art wiretapping or lie detector equipment that probably would be out of the reach of any police department budget.

But, there are other kinds of private police too—bad television calls them hit men. However, organized crime often operates a complex dispute avoidance and dispute resolution system that attempts to ward off the need for such drastic measures.[115] Indeed, Professor Donald Black says that much, if not most, murder in the United States is conduct that anthropologists would call "law" in primitive societies.[116] Someone has violated a norm, and we get self-help capital punishment. And so on. In a sense, the question is: "what do you mean by the bottom up—what is the bottom?" The hard part is deciding where to stop. The police are just part of social control, and social control is just about everything from concern about reputation, to not wanting to get someone mad, to life imprisonment.

---

[113]*See, e.g.*, Herman Goldstein, Problem-Oriented Policing (1990).

[114]Mark Button, *Private Security and the Policing of Quasi-Public Space*, 31 Int'L J. Soc. Law 227 (2003); Richard B. Cole, *The Second Criminal Justice System*, 43 S.A.M. Advanced Mgmt. J. 17 (1978); Elizabeth E. Joh, *The Paradox of Private Policing*, 95 J. Crim. L. & Criminology 49 (2004); Ian Loader, *Consumer Culture and the Commodification of Policing and Security*, 33 Sociology 373 (1999).

[115]*See* Peter Reuter, *Social Control in Illegal Markets, in* 2 Toward a General Theory of Social Control 29 (Donald Black ed., 1984). Two of Peter Reuter's section headings are "The Mafia as a Dispute-Settlement System," *id.* at 40, and "The Mafia, Arbitration, and Extortion," *id.* at 49.

[116]Donald Black, *Crime as Social Control,* 48 Am. Soc. Rev. 34 (1983); Donald Black, *Crime as Social Control, in* 2 Toward a General Theory of Social Control 1 (Donald Black ed., 1984).

If we have learned anything from this long academic history of realism, it is, I repeat, that we must also study law from the bottom up if we want to understand anything important about it.[117] Yet, we must be clear what we mean by bottom up. It is not enough to find a gap between the law on the books and the law in action, and then assume it should be closed. Probably none of us would be willing to bear the costs of 100% enforcement of all the laws all the time. On one hand, we rely on police and prosecutorial discretion to tailor the law to fit real situations not anticipated by the legislature. Sometimes enforcing the letter of the law just does not make sense. On the other hand, full enforcement would entail many costs. Americans have some expectations of privacy and civil liberties. Full enforcement probably would demand that we give up at least some measure of these American values. Just the burden of all the taxes needed to pay police, guards, and informers would dampen some of the enthusiasm of even those with only a minimal concern for civil liberties. Sometimes full enforcement would require that police or administrative agencies attempt to coerce a large group of citizens who felt strongly that the law was wrong. Whatever our normative judgment about a particular statute or decision, we must recognize that those who keep their jobs by running for office may hesitate to enforce unpopular laws. Indeed, attempted enforcement may do no more than fuel a popular movement against the law. In sum, finding a gap only opens a series of questions.

Moreover, there are other reasons to stress a broad view of the bottom-up approach. The legal academy tends to overlook important issues until they are captured in an appellate case that makes its way to the top of the legal system. Clearly, however, some important questions never make it to the courts or administrative agencies. The process by which a problem goes from people in the society to a lawyer, to filing a case, to motions, to a trial and to various appeals transforms both the facts and the problem.[118] Friedman stresses that a look at legal history also shows that legal problems tend to disappear from the courts in a relatively short time.[119] But, the legal academy continues teaching and writing about the classic

---

[117]Schlegel objected to talking about top-down and bottom-up approaches. He stated that "[t]he problem of understanding law is better seen as that of constructing and understanding an unruly, multi-dimensional matrix, full of missing squares and partial columns. " He continued, "Bottom up talk is as much a part of the problem as is top down. Situatedness is everywhere to be seen .... Both suffer from the misunderstanding of taking part for the whole, and ... [the] chosen part as well." I hope that my recognition of the virtues of classic legal thought and an expanded view of bottom up captures some of his point.

[118]*See* William L.F. Felstiner et al., *The Emergence and Transformation of Disputes: Naming, Blaming, Claiming ....*, 15 Law & Soc'y Rev. 631 (1980–1981).

[119]As Friedman and I wrote:

> No contracts problem in a concrete sense—one that is frequently litigated and which deals with one specific type-situation—lasts more than two generations.... When problems reach the threshold of public or general business concern, they are solved or at least coped with by other means—by legislation, for example.

Lawrence M. Friedman & Stewart Macaulay, *Contract Law and Contract Teaching: Past, Present, and Future,* 1967 Wis. L. Rev. 805, 812.

cases long after they have lost much of their significance. If we are interested in the likely consequences of any rule, or system created by law, or if we are interested in living social problems, we must add a view of law in its full context.

At the New Legal Realism Symposium, Galanter observed that the old legal realists were optimistic and saw law as a "robust, expansive, problem-solving enterprise—by breaking the shackles of formalism, they would liberate it, unleash the power of law to solve problems—[it was] their own version of release of energy."[120] Few today sing this song. Professor Grant Gilmore said: "In Heaven there will be no law, and the lion will lie down with the lamb.... The worse the society, the more law there will be. In Hell there will be nothing but law, and due process will be meticulously observed."[121] Adherents of Critical Legal Studies,[122] Law and Economics,[123] and Law and Society[124] all are skeptical about making life better by creating legal rights. And yet, while law may not be a complete solution, sometimes law is one tool for bringing about some measure of social change. A New

[120]Friedman noted:

> Part of Llewellyn's problem—if we can call it a problem—was that he was quite starry-eyed about the common-law, and the way it moved and worked; basically, he loved the common-law, and this intense love colors all of his work. Everything Llewellyn wrote, he wrote passionately; his style is curious, cryptic, stylized, and at times annoying; but it is full of zest, of boundless enthusiasm. He truly adored the law; and those that made it.

Friedman, *supra* note 43, at 139.

[121]Grant Gilmore, The Ages of American Law 111 (1977).

[122]*See, e.g.*, Duncan Kennedy, *Distributive and Paternalist Motives in Contract and Tort Law, with Special Reference to Compulsory Terms and Unequal Bargaining Power,* 41 Md. L. Rev. 563, 620–21 (1982) ("The liberal position is ... that reform of exceptional cases and intelligent response to abuses are all that is needed to meet the just demands of the disadvantaged and thereby to relegitimate the overall system of distribution and the overall quality of life."). *Id.*

[123]*See, e.g.*, Robert E. Scott, *The Death of Contract* Law, 54 U. Toronto L.J. 369, 370–71 (2004) (advocating that the number of enforceable contracts be cut back drastically and a system of clear formal default rules be adopted).

[124]*See, e.g.*, Stuart A. Scheingold, The Politics of Rights: Lawyers, Public Policy, and Political Change 13 (1974) (offering the classic statement of the "myth of rights"). *But see* Catherine R. Albiston, *Bargaining in the Shadow of Social Institutions: Competing Discourses and Social Change in Workplace Mobilization of Civil Rights,* 39 Law & Soc'y Rev. 11, 27 (2005) (arguing that Professor Stuart Scheingold's position may place too much emphasis on how formal rights claims in court atomize grievances by narrowing disputes to legally relevant facts and individualized remedies, and that it overlooks how the informal processes of mobilizing rights can help build connections and common interests among grievants).

Legal Realism could tell us more about the costs and benefits of attempts to bring about change through law.[125]

The Old Legal Realism reflected a progressive politics.[126] The extent to which a new legal realism would do the same is an open question. Some of the work will be relatively neutral. It will probably focus on filling in the picture of functioning legal systems. Some will serve the task of training lawyers for their many social roles. However, sometimes a new legal realism will not be able to claim to be only a disinterested, neutral, nonpartisan pursuit of the facts. Sometimes looking at the law in action will carry a political message. Looking at law from the bottom up will often show that things are not as most people think they should be. Some studies may serve a muckraking function whether this is the intention of the researcher. Even the best studies may draw return fire.

Some people have an interest in holding to an ideological picture of the way things are, and they will not be pleased to have a scholar announce that the world runs differently. Since the early 1980s, for example, insurance companies, large corporations, and part of the medical profession have tried to convince Americans that we are in the midst of a litigation explosion and that we would all benefit from "tort reform."[127] A number of scholars, including Galanter, have looked at the

---

[125]Compare this view with Friedman: "[F]resh law is a hybrid: half ratification, half real inducement to change. Formal legal change often comes at the middle point in a social process which requires a number of distinct steps . . . already taken, but it forces or hurries society along with regard to the steps not yet taken." Lawrence M. Friedman, *Law Reform in Historical Perspective,* 13 St. Louis U. L.J. 351, 363 (1969). Of course, attempted legal change may provoke opponents to organize to fight the reform. The Supreme Court's decision in *Roe v. Wade* provided that states could not deny access to abortion during the first months of pregnancy. 410 U.S. 113, 164(1973). Certainly, one consequence of the decision was to provoke the rise and power of the "Right to Life" movement.

[126]In one of my favorite footnotes, Schlegel reported that Moore considered himself a socialist. Schlegel, *supra* note 12, at 243 n.285. However, Schlegel also noted "Moore was, first of all, a gentleman. The family was at least upper middle class and accordingly his tastes ran to expensive pipes, bone handle knives, and gray Packard roadsters." *Id.* at 242. Sadly, those identifying with New Legal Realism will be unable to drive gray Packard roadsters. My eccentricities are reflected in my fifteen-year-old red Saab convertible. While the extreme right probably would label me a socialist, socialists would not.

[127]*See, e.g.,* Jon Robins, *Trial Lawyers Are Put on Trial,* Fin. Times, Feb. 3, 2005, at 12. ("People are in the habit of saying: 'I am going to get me a lawyer,' and just that threat—even the faintest possibility of a threat—changes behaviour . . . .").

evidence and found it sadly wanting.[128] Those advocating "tort reform" have not been pleased.[129]

Moreover, a person's political stance and theoretical assumptions influence the questions she asks, and what she sees when she looks at the law in action. What is true for the upper and middle classes, for example, may hide the reality for those at the bottom of the social system. Tomlins reported that, from a critical left perspective, "systematic objective empiricism was impossible, merely a misleading positivism. The facts that empirical inquiry found were creatures of the observer's subjective position. Ideology and methodology were irremediably intertwined."[130] Furthermore, this left perspective insists that the work of reformist scholars reinforces the status quo. Trubek and John Esser reject what they call "universal scientism."[131] This approach assumes that "[m]ethods of empirical inquiry allow us to determine if the knowledge we hypothesize adequately describes the external world we can apprehend." While there is much truth in this challenge to empirical work in law, I think that it goes too far. A New Legal Realism will accept Professor Bill Whitford's gloss on Trubek and Esser's article.[132] Whitford argues that the goal is not to produce certain fixed truths about human society. Rather, we seek to understand the present and anticipate the future with a greater probability of accuracy, understanding that our knowledge can be only tentative.

First, let us look at some of the reasons for the critical left concerns about empirical research. Some social science approaches, for example, tend to be reductionist, seeking elegant models of behavior. Some approaches do put the rabbit into

---

[128]*See, e.g.*, Marc Galanter, *The Conniving Claimant: Changing Images of Misuse of Legal Remedies*, 50 DePaul L. Rev. 647 (2000); Marc Galanter, *The Hundred-Year Decline of Trials and the Thirty Years War*, 57 Stan. L. Rev. 1255 (2005); Marc Galanter, *An Oil Strike in Hell: Contemporary Legends About the Civil Justice System*, 40 Ariz. L. Rev. 717 (1998); Marc Galanter, *Reading the Landscape of Disputes: What We Know and Don't Know (And Think We Know) About Our Allegedly Contentious and Litigious Society*, 31 UCLA L. Rev. 4 (1983); Marc Galanter, *Real World Torts: An Antidote to Anecdote*, 55 Md. L. Rev. 1093 (1996); *see also* Stephen Daniels, *The Question of Jury Competence and the Politics of Civil Justice Reform: Symbols, Rhetoric and Agenda-Building*, 52 Law & Contemp. Prob. 269 (1989); Stephen Daniels & Joanne Martin, *It Was the Best of Times, It Was the Worst of Times: The Precarious Nature of Plaintiffs' Practice in Texas*, 80 Tex. L. Rev. 1781 (2002); Stephen Daniels & Joanne Martin, *The Strange Success of Tort Reform*, 53 Emory L.J. 1225 (2004); Valerie P. Hans & Stephanie Albertson, *Empirical Research and Civil Jury Reform*, 78 Notre Dame L. Rev. 1497 (2003); Robert M. Hayden, *The Cultural Logic of a Political Crisis: Common Sense, Hegemony and the Great American Liability Insurance Famine of 1986*, 11 Stud. L. Pol. & Soc'y 95 (1991); Michael J. Saks, *Do We Really Know Anything About the Behavior of the Tort Litigation System—And Why Not?*, 140 U. Pa. L. Rev. 1147 (1992).

[129]Marc Galanter, *Shadow Play: The Fabled Menace of Punitive Damages*, 1998 Wis. L. Rev. 1, 13–14 (describing the reaction of organizations seeking to limit punitive damages to a conference considering the evidence for the various assertions involved in the political campaign).

[130]Tomlins, *supra* note 42, at 961.

[131]David M. Trubek & John Esser, *"Critical Empiricism" in American Legal Studies: Paradox, Program or Pandora's Box?*, 14 Law & Soc. Inquiry 3, 11 (1989).

[132]*See* William C. Whitford, *Critical Empiricism*, 14 Law & Soc. Inquiry 61 (1989).

the magician's hat by the way they frame questions and what they ignore. There is no method that is sure to provide answers to questions that you do not ask.[133] Some writers relying on data go far beyond what they have proved when they discuss the implications of their research.[134]

Even if one accepts the procedures of any social science, studying anything related to law almost always requires compromises with textbook methods.[135] For example, it is hard to get a true random sample of those with legal authority. Most sets of data were compiled in ways that threaten their validity; our subjects are people engaged in some way with something we want to call law, but this means they often have reasons to shade the truth or lie. Moreover, the researcher is always a person formed by ideology, structures, and class. She frames the questions, records the answers, and interprets the findings. Who she is affects what she asks and what

---

[133]For example, Professors John Brigham and Christine B. Harrington argue that realism fails to account for

> the social terrain in the analysis of law. ... In the high-court literature, the most startling characteristic of socio-legal research is that the politics taken up by social scientists is limited to the differences between (conservative-liberal) which pays little attention to the political implications of what is shared (a profession, a doctrinal tradition).

John Brigham & Christine B. Harrington, *Realism and Its Consequences: An Inquiry into Contemporary Sociological Research*, 17 Int'l J. Soc. L. 41, 50 (1989).

[134]In an unpublished paper written in 1979 at the University of Wisconsin Institute for Research on Poverty ("IRP"), the late Dr. Jacqueline Macaulay dealt with "[s]ome [b]arriers to [d]rawing [policy] [conclusions from [s]ocial [s]cience [r]esearch." Jacqueline Macaulay, Some Barriers to Drawing Conclusions from Social Science Research 1 (1979) (unpublished manuscript), *available at* www.law.wisc.edu/facstaff/macaulay/papers/barriers.pdf. It is a development of her 1974 IRP Notes and Comments paper, *A Skeptic's Guide to the Literature on Poverty.* She used some of the ideas in her 1975 IRP Discussion Paper, *Is Welfare Bad for Children.* In her paper on barriers to drawing policy conclusions, Macaulay listed the: (1) problem of snapshot perspectives; (2) sample bias and the loss of qualifying tags in secondary reporting; (3) bias in the definition of the population from which a sample is drawn; (4) incomplete definition of the situation in which research is done; (5) the dataless cell (for instance, when one studies the poor and assumes that those who are not poor are different without any proof that this is so); (6) invalid inferences of causation; (7) bias in the outside world (that affects the social statistics that we gather); (8) similarities, differences, and what constitutes "significance"; (9) problems of inadequate theories, concepts and methods, such as (a) false dichotomies, (b) spurious symmetry, (c) dubious continua, (d) absent alternatives, (e) pejorative labels and deficit hypotheses, (f) noncorrespondence between theoretical and operational variables, and (g) too simple models and uncritical variables; and (10) problems created by the structure of academic disciplines and the road to academic success. *Id.* at 1–13. Put simply, for people not conversant with social science, this kind of scholarly research does not yield clearly defined "facts" that just sit there waiting for a legal scholar to pick them up and plug them into his or her analysis. Even social science research that seems to support our pet ideas must be read skeptically and carefully if we care about what is going on rather than just seeking rhetoric and authority to back our position.

[135]*See* Macaulay, *supra* note 83, at 156–63 ("All of the common approaches to the social study of law are flawed.").

she sees.[136] Also, the world changes. Yesterday's magnificent study of practices related to law might be ancient history today because of shifts in the legal culture, or because new social institutions mean that the problem can never arise again in precisely the same way.[137]

Nonetheless, as Whitford warned, we should not throw out the baby with the bathwater. Reviewing these questions two decades ago, I concluded that when we look at Law and Society empirical research, echoing Gertrude Stein, we will find that there is some there there.[138] Law and Society empirical studies have at least made salient such things as that there is such a practice as plea-bargaining where defendants lack bargaining power. Police have discretion, and they are rewarded or punished for using it in various ways. Americans bargain in the shadow of the law, but shadows are usually distortions of the object between the sun and the ground. When I graduated from law school in 1955, these "facts" were not part of legal discourse. Moreover, there is no necessary reason why empirical research must reinforce the status quo or serve as a tool of the haves. The trick is to get researchers to ask the right questions and to consider unorthodox interpretations of their data. Perhaps today, the hard part is to get such research funded or to have it count toward tenure in universities that are more and more pushed to please the powerful as the schools struggle for funds.

Accepting all the cautions, the goal must be to find the best evidence of what is going on in view of what is being studied. We cannot demand one "Truth" with a capital "T." Sometimes we can test hypotheses with hard data analyzed by state of the art statistics. When we can, we should. Often, however, given the nature of things legal, we are lucky to hear a story told by someone who should know.[139] We know

---

[136]The classic statement is from Karl Marx: "Men make their own history, but they do not make it as they please; they do not make it under self-selected circumstances, but under circumstances existing already, given and transmitted from the past." Karl Marx, Eighteenth Brumaire of Louis Bonaparte 115 (1852). Professors Dave Trubek and John Esser state that the aspiration is to

> develop a critical sociology of law that incorporates ideas of structure without abandoning the idea of agency; [one that] is able to identify patterns and regularities while holding onto the basic insight that social life is indeterminant and unstable; and [one that] insists that micro- and macro-level analyses must inform each other.

Trubek & Esser, *supra* note 131, at 35 n.69. They attribute this interpretation to Boaventura Santos in a personal communication.

[137]Professor Robert Kagan suggests that the decline in debt collection cases coming before the courts over the past century can be explained in part by what he calls "systemic stabilization." Robert Kagan, *The Routinization of Debt Collection: An Essay on Social Change and Conflict in Courts,* 18 Law & soc'y Rev. 323, 352–63 (1984). This involves "the development of large-scale economic and social institutions that ameliorate the conditions that cause individual conflicts or that provide collective administrative remedies (as contrasted to case-by-case legal remedies)." *Id.* at 352.

[138]*See* Macaulay, *supra* note 83.

[139]*See* Shirley A. Dobbin et al., *Surveying Difficult Populations: Lessons Learned from a National Survey of State Trial Court Judges*, 22 Just. Sys. J. 287, 288 (2001) ("[I]nterest in the topic of study is a good predictor of a decision to participate in the survey project, especially when surveying busy

that those in power may keep secrets, lie, or spin the truth to mislead. Our work will be scientific insofar as we know and disclose the limits of our data and fashion our claims accordingly. Often, the best we can offer is a provisional and qualified picture of the world as our best guess of what others would find if they looked at what we examined. Yet, this is an advance over supporting one's normative position by anecdotes, urban legends, or statements based on no more than what we want to believe, because too many law professors are expert in finding an example or two of something, and asserting that it is a typical or important enough phenomenon to worry about. Social science teaches that we can and should do better. Professor Peter Medawar reminds us that we need some defense against "'the undisciplined exercise of the imaginative faculty to produce hypotheses held true because of their inspirational origin.'"[140]

Social scientists would not be surprised by the cautions that I have raised. Most of them are people who are very aware of threats to validity and the nature of evidence.[141] Furthermore, when we begin getting studies reaching similar results using different methods that have been done in different places, we can have more confidence that we are getting something close to a picture of the law in action. In taking this position, I am doing little more than accepting what Professors Walter Blum and Harry Kalven wrote almost fifty years ago.[142] Blum and Kalven brilliantly catalogued the many threats to the validity of the survey research in Professor Samuel Stouffer's work on American attitudes toward Communists.[143] In the end, however, they concluded that this research was highly valuable. In commenting on their article, Professor Paul Lazarsfeld said: "rather than trying in a utopian way to circumvent these limitations [of empirical social science], it is better to see all their

professionals with heavy time demands."); Brion Sever et al., *Successfully Acquiring Data from the Criminal Courts: Is It What You Know, Who You Know, or What You Don't Tell Them?*, 22 Just. Sys. J. 315, 315 (2001) ("[S]trategies include using a contact within or close to the agency, as well as withholding the exact nature of the researcher's study.); *see also* Matt Bradshaw, *Contracts and Member Checks in Qualitative Research in Human Geography: Reason for Caution*, 33 Area 202, 203 (2001) ("[T]here are differences in the power relations between a researcher and a low-income householder, as opposed to those between a researcher and a senior manager."); David Shulman, *Dirty Data and Investigative Methods: Some Lessons from Private Detective Work,* 23 J. Contemp. Ethnography 214, 250 (1994) ("Although fieldworkers must carefully avoid representing informants as the fieldworkers would like to have them be, they should also be cognizant of not just depicting subjects as subject wants.").

[140]P.B. Medawar, Pluto's Republic 61 (1982).

[141]*See, e.g.,* Juliet Corbin & Anselm Strauss, *Grounded Theory Research: Procedures, Canons and Evaluative Criteria,* 19 Zeitschrift für Soziologie 418 (1990) (explaining how the usual scientific canons can be reinterpreted for qualitative research).

[142]Walter J. Blum & Harry Kalven, Jr., *The Art of Opinion Research: A Lawyer's Appraisal of an Emerging Science—Observations on "Communism, Conformity and Civil Liberties"*, 24 U. Chi. L. Rev. 1 (1956).

[143]Samuel Andrew Stouffer, Communism, Conformity and Civil Liberties: A Cross-Section of the Nation Speaks Its Mind (1955).

logical implications and use them in the devising of new research instruments, as well as in the interpretation of research findings."[144]

New Legal Realism, I predict, will accept Professors Maureen Cain and Janet Fitch's observation: "[t]he 'facts' themselves speak with a political voice and kick with a political boot."[145] Cain and Fitch put the word "facts" in quotation marks to remind us that the political voice and political boot reflect what people who count in the society think is true. Sometimes, good empirical work can affect what such people accept as true, but we must acknowledge that people are well armed with defenses to ward off offensive or inconvenient knowledge. Nonetheless, accepting that people may reject good evidence of what they do not want to believe does not justify abandoning the effort to assemble the best evidence we can about what is going on. New Legal Realism will, I predict, insist that there are facts behind the clouds of interpretation that reflect all kinds of bias. As Cain and Fitch insist, facts can kick.

At the Symposium, Galanter pointed out that the Old Legal Realism was the party of ideas. At least, until the 1950s, those opposed to it stood on tradition. Today, however, a New Legal Realism can expect to be met by criticism based on social science or even studies that gather data designed to challenge the new legal realist efforts. As long as both sides play the science game honestly, this should all contribute to the good.[146]

We will not be surprised when a bottom-up empirical approach finds that a program enacted by liberals fails to achieve its announced goals of helping ordinary people. Certainly one strand of law and society work has questioned attacking social problems by creating individual rights without providing any real means of implementing them.[147] A New Legal Realism might well support some or many conclusions generally favored by conservatives. The old cliché is apt: it is an empirical question.

---

[144]Paul F. Lazarsfeld, *Comment*, 24 U. Chi. L. Rev. 65, 69 (1956).

[145]Maureen Cain & Janet Fitch, *Towards a Rehabilitation of Data, in* Practice and Progress: British Sociology 1950–1980, at 105, 115 (Philip Abrams et al. eds., 1981). Professors Maureen Cain and Janet Fitch also say:

> In constituting data by a variety of methods, one is not asking which is the true or best indicator of some absent essence but rather what these data, having been converted into evidence, have to say. What place can be made for them in the initial theory? How can it grow to take account of them? What refinements does this evidence necessitate and precipitate? These questions make a virtue of the qualitative differences between the items of evidence collected.

Id. at 112.

[146]*But see* Elizabeth Warren, *The Market for Data: The Changing Role of Social Sciences,* 2002 Wis. L. Rev. 1 (stating that what passes for social science becomes a tool in political battles as a way of legitimating what is sought by the powerful).

[147]*See, e.g.*, Gerald Rosenberg, The Hollow Hope (1991); Stuart Scheingold, the Politics of Rights (1974).

I would be delighted and surprised if a New Legal Realism at least brought the picture of functioning legal systems, inherent in my seven shining nuggets, into legal scholarship and teaching.[148] Of course, one can analyze legal rules in terms of their consistency with some normative system. Often this is useful work. However, very often the discussion shifts to evaluating a rule in terms of its likely consequences. Almost always, this is an unexamined and difficult empirical question. A rule of, say, contract law can celebrate the goal of efficiency. Whether it produces a truly efficient result is always an open question until one looks at the law in action and the living law.

Suppose that legal scholars were to move from an almost purely doctrinal approach to one that incorporated at least some of the findings of Law and Society. A recent article by Professor Wolf Heydebrand offers one suggestion about where this might take us. Heydebrand argues that we have moved more and more away from Weber's formal and substantive rationality[149] to something Heydebrand calls "negotiated process rationality."[150] This is a mode of governance based on the "logic of informal, negotiated processes within social and sociolegal networks."[151] These networks are not accountable to elected or appointed officials.[152] Process rationality tolerates diversity and indeterminacy, and it does not yield transparent, highly predictable law.[153] We lose constitutional safeguards, and we lose both substantive and procedural rights.[154] Moreover, some individuals and interests will be able to play the game of informal, negotiated processes better than others.[155] Rather than imposing some restraint on power, this form of governance often amplifies the benefits of holding power. It is highly attractive to the interests of corporate and transnational governance.[156] Professor Jane Larson warns us: "Viewed from the perspectives of legality and equality, the subject of informality is a minefield. Even

[148]Compare this view with Malcolm M. Feeley, *Three Voices of Socio-Legal Studies,* 35 Isr. L. Rev. 175, 203 (2001) ("Legal scholars write for judges in the common law countries and law commissions elsewhere, and social scientists—like scholars more generally—tend to write for each other."). However, Professor Gregory Scott Crespi has suggested that courts do not draw on contracts scholarship. *See, e.g.,* Gregory Scott Crespi, *The Influence of Two Decades of Contract Law Scholarship on Judicial Rulings: An Empirical Analysis,* 57 SMU L. Rev. 105 (2004). More and more, it tends to be written for other scholars who play one of the games included within the academic contracts world. *Id.*

[149]*See* Duncan Kennedy, *The Disenchantment of Logically Formal Legal Rationality: Or, Max Weber's Sociology in the Genealogy of the Contemporary Mode of Western Legal Thought, in* Max Weber's Economy and Society 322 (Charles Camic et al. eds., 2005); Wolf Heydebrand, *Process Rationality as Legal Governance*, 18 Int'l Soc. 325 (2003).

[150]Heydebrand, *supra* note 149, at 327.

[151]*Id.* at 326.

[152]*See id.* at 326.

[153]*See id.* at 329.

[154]*See id.* at 334, 336.

[155]*See id.* at 326.

[156]Compare this view with Stewart Macaulay, *Business Adaptation to Regulation: What Do We Know and What Do We Need to Know?*, 15 Law & Pol. 259, 268 (1993).

so, lawyers and legal scholars must take the lead in formulating policy responses to informality."[157]

A New Legal Realism could challenge the adequacy of studying the legal system when that concept is defined formally and narrowly. Reality is messy. Sharp lines cannot be drawn between the formal and the informal or between the public and the private.[158] For example, today all kinds of commercial disputes go to arbitration rather than to the civil justice system in the public courthouses.[159] However, one major source of arbitrators and mediators is retired judges who once worked in the public courts. Professor Stacy Burns studied mediation by acting and former judges.[160] They tend to evaluate each side's legal arguments and what would likely happen in litigation.[161] Their experience and the legal culture that they bring with them may limit how far judges would go beyond legal or factual issues to encompass

> What should we say about a society where legislatures, agencies, and the top command of the Air Force make policy decisions, while officials at the local level fashion compromises that reflect their wise or biased view of competing values? What should we say when these decisions about how far we should apply the law are significantly influenced if not controlled by corporate lawyers?

Id.; *see also* Albert W. Alschuler, *Mediation with a Mugger: The Shortage of Adjudicative Services and the Need for a Two-Tier Trial System in Civil Cases,* 99 Harv. L. Rev. 1808 (1986) (dealing most critically with the situation that Professor Wolf Heydebrand calls "process rationality"). Professor Owen Fiss likewise argues: "settlement is a capitulation to the conditions of mass society and should be neither encouraged nor praised." Owen Fiss, *Against Settlement,* 93 Yale L.J. 1073, 1075 (1984).

[157]Larson, *supra* note 105, at 181.

[158]*See, e.g.,* John Griffiths, *The Social Working of Legal Rules,* 48 J. Legal Pluralism 1, 4 (2003) ("[T]he connection between a legislative text and actual behavior is not at all obvious."); Stewart Macaulay, *Crime and Custom in Business Society,* 22 J.L. & Soc'y 248, 253 (1995) ("[T]hat corporate police are not public legal officers makes a difference. We may risk obscuring this if we fail to distinguish public from private, formal from informal.").

[159]*See* Bryant G. Garth, *Tilting the Justice System: From ADR as Idealistic Movement to a Segmented Market in Dispute Resolution,* 18 Ga. St. U. L. Rev. 927, 932 (2002) (arguing that the emergence of alternate dispute resolution in lieu of increased litigation has "created a low-end justice for the rank and file"); Stewart Macaulay, *Freedom from Contract: Solutions in Search of a Problem?,* 2004 Wis. L. Rev. 777, 778 ("Many, and probably most, parties to contracts disputes do not litigate or even threaten to do so."). Business elites can use arbitrators and mediators "whose background and the selection process ensured they would be able to understand and handle large business disputes." Garth, *supra,* at 949. However, at the same time, today we have tilted toward a kind of justice that "includes a pecking order that dictates the kinds of cases allowed into the courts." *Id.* at 952. Bryant Garth said that we have "created a low-end justice for the rank and file.

. . .

[We] push ordinary litigants into settlement-oriented ADR processes dominated by quick-and-dirty arbitration and by mediation conducted by private individuals accountable neither through review processes or appeal." *Id.* at 932.

[160]Stacy Burns, *"Think Your Blackest Thoughts and Darken Them:" Judicial Mediation of Large Money Damage Disputes,* 24 Hum. Stud. 227 (2001).

[161]*See id.* at 241–42.

business, relational, or personal issues.[162] Are these former judges and their mediation efforts part of the legal system? Can you study modern commercial law and ignore them? Some trial judges bring great pressure on the parties to settle rather than try cases.[163] They even do such things as bringing the parties before them without their lawyers.[164] Indeed, this is more likely to happen in litigation involving major corporations with large stakes. Can we study law and ignore the settling judge? Some commentators argue that lower court judges who have ambitions for the upper appellate bench trim their decisions so that they remain acceptable to those who determine such appointments.[165] Can we study law and ignore this? In sum, ideas of public and private, formal and informal, and the like, break down when we look at law from the lawyer's office or the executive suite. Much of the lawmaking and dispute resolution in any society is carried out by private governments influenced directly or indirectly by public ones.

Furthermore, once we see the need to study law in an international context, things really get messy.[166] It becomes obvious that we cannot limit ourselves to

---

[162]*See id.*

[163]*See* Marc Galanter,

. . .

"A Settlement Judge, Not a Trial Judge:" Judicial Mediation in the United States, 12 J.L. & Soc'y 1, 7 (1985) (noting that trial judges increasingly accept promoting settlement as part of their task and exchange information about how to get parties to settle).

[164]*See* Stewart Macaulay, *The Real and the Paper Deal: Empirical Pictures of Relationships, Complexity and the Urge for Transparent Simple Rules*, 66 Mod. L. Rev. 44, 73–77 (2003).

[165]*See* Barbara M. Yarnold, *Do Courts Respond to the Political Clout of Groups or to Their Superior Litigation Resources/"Repeat Player" Status?*, 18 Just. Sys. J. 29 (1995) ("[C]ourt outcomes in abortion cases were linked to political factors, with civil liberties groups and Planned Parenthood affiliates obtaining preferential decisions from the federal courts."). *Compare* Melinda Gann Hall, *Electoral Politics and Strategic Voting in State Supreme Courts,* 54 J. Pol. 427, 427 (1992) (arguing that "constituency influence in state supreme courts is enhanced by competitive electoral conditions and experience with electoral politics"), *with* Cass R. Sunstein et al., *Ideological Voting on Federal Courts of Appeals: A Preliminary Investigation,* 90 Va. L. Rev. 301, 305 (2004) ("The political party of the appointing president is a fairly good predictor of how individual [appellate court] judges will vote.").

[166]*See, e.g.,* Yves Dezalay & Bryant G. Garth, The Internationalization of Palace Wars 4 (2002) ("[T]he 'failure' of law and development is now generally conceded."); Global Prescriptions: The Production, Exportation, and Importation of a New Legal Orthodoxy (Yves Dezalay & Bryant G. Garth eds., 2002) ("We are convinced that it is necessary to go well beyond legal institutions and reforms to understand the position of law and how it is changing. We need to build tools for research that will place legal reform and legal reformers in their broader social context."); Alberto Martinelli, *Markets, Governments, Communities and Global Governance,* 18 Int'l Soc. 291, 291 (2003) (examining "the contradictory character of the social world in the 21st century as a single system and fragmented world, and identifying global integration and global governance of key problematic questions"); Robert Hunter Wade, *US Hegemony and the World Bank: The Fight Over People and Ideas,* 9 Rev. Int'l Pol. Econ. 201, 201 (2002) (drawing "broader conclusions about how hegomony actually works, about the extent of World Bank autonomy, and about the debate on development agendas").

governments as actors and our ideas of what is legal action must expand. As I pointed out in an article on private government,

> In the late 1960s, when official United States policy imposed a boycott on Cuba, the Ford Foundation sent a number of Third World scholars and government officials to visit Havana. The foundation could do "privately" what the United States government did not wish to do publicly . . . .
>
> . . . ..
>
> . . . Private governments such as corporations, churches, and labor unions can pursue their own foreign policies, in concert with or in opposition to official policy . . . Nations may form alliances with large multinational corporations or such corporations may seek to overthrow governments. Churches may battle nations about human rights, seeking to affect what is called world public opinion. Labor unions may boycott goods from certain nations.[167]

All kinds of people and organizations create norms and can impose sanctions. Sometimes they mimic legal action; sometimes they do not. There is a great deal of bargaining in the shadow of this kind of law. Lawyers scramble to speak with authority, often with about as much substance as the Wizard of Oz possessed. But, the lesson of modern international governance is that we should learn to see the same kinds of things on the local level.

One goal of a New Legal Realism is to get this bottom-up perspective into the law schools. The temptation is to abandon this project as hopeless. Yet, law schools have influence not only on training students, but also on legal reform and public perceptions of our legal systems. Most of us who have taught law for some time find elections involve voting for one of our former students rather than another who is his or her opponent. Moreover, we find even more of our former students when we walk through the state capitol and encounter all of those who serve on legislative staffs. We risk being marginalized if we ignore the legal academy. History also teaches that, if we affront conventional law professors and the legal profession, these are powerful enemies who can retaliate.

Even after a career spent on the margins, I still have some hope.[168] We can point to law professors at many law schools, some with social science degrees, who do empirical research. Many more people are entering law teaching who have both a Ph.D. in a social science and a law degree. Such people can read data in a table and are not terrified by a statistic. There are law professor members of the Law and Society Association, and they do not all work at Wisconsin, Buffalo, Denver, the Jurisprudence and Social Policy Program at Berkeley, or the American Bar Foundation. There are even some terrific empirical scholars at both Harvard and Yale. Our

---

[167] Macaulay, *supra* note 77, at 452.

[168] We can find examples of work that expands the paradigm of scholarship in law reviews in ways that I would call New Legal Realism. *See, e.g.*, William A. Klein & Mitu Gulati, *Economic Organization in the Construction Industry: A Case Study of Collaborative Production Under High Uncertainty,* 1 Berkeley Bus. L.J. 137 (2004); Steven L. Schwarcz, *Private Ordering,* 97 Nw. U. L. Rev. 319 (2002); David V. Snyder, *Private Lawmaking,* 64 Ohio St. L.J. 371 (2003).

contracts casebook, *Contracts: Law in Action*[169] reflects what I think of as some of the New Legal Realism. Much to my surprise, about twenty schools use the book. The times may be changing so that there is more interest in how law works rather than an exclusive focus on appellate cases and elegant theories. Indeed, I can hear Johnny Hodges's alto sax blowing: *Things Ain't What They Used To Be.*

[169]Contracts: Law in Action (Stewart Macaulay et al., 2d ed. 2003). "Et al. " conceals the fact that the editors are myself and Professors John Kidwell and William Whitford. *Id.* Professor Marc Galanter joined us for the first, but not the second, edition. Contracts: Law in Action (Stewart Macaulay et al. eds., 1995). The project that produced the book was such a partnership that I have always regretted the citation form that reduces real contributors to "et al." The editors' favorite title of a review of the book is William J. Woodward, Jr., *Contracts for Grown-ups,* 47 J. Legal Educ. 139 (1997). *But see* Edward Rubin, *Why Law Schools Do Not Teach Contracts and What Socioeconomics Can Do About It,* 41 San Diego L. Rev. 55 (2004) (criticizing how modern law schools teach the subject of contracts).

A New Legal Realism: Elegant Models and the Messy Law in Action

Stewart Macaulay

Recently there has been a flurry of interest in empirical approaches to law among legal scholars. Some of them talk of a "new legal realism," although it is unclear whether they mean similar things. Some want to study the "law in action" – that is, the operation of trial courts, the exercise of discretion by various legal officials, as well as what it is that lawyers actually do. Others want to add a consideration of the "living law" – the norms and sanctions that people in various groups respond to other than official law. Sometimes the living law is in competition with the official law; sometimes they exist in a complicated interrelationship, and the living law may support the formal law to some degree.

Of course, such concerns are not entirely "new." We can list many earlier examples of empirical work on law. For example, we can recall Charles Clark's studies of the business of courts, the University of Chicago jury project, and the University of Wisconsin's Civil Litigation Research Project from earlier times (see the studies cited in Macaulay 2005 and Nourse and Shaffer 2009, which offer many examples of calls for a new legal realism). Indeed, two of my own empirical projects

This article was original published in Elizabeth Mertz, Stewart Macaulay and Thomas W Mitchell (eds) The New Legal Realism, Translating Law-and-Society for Today's Legal Practice, Volume 1, Cambridge University Press 2016, 29–50. Reproduced with permission of The Licensor through PLSclear.
This paper was developed from a talk that I gave at University of Colorado School of Law on April 18, 2008. I wish to thank Professor Amy Jean Schlitz for the invitation to Boulder and comments on my remarks. I also wish to thank my friends Lauren Edelman and Elizabeth Mertz for reading the paper critically. At the request of Professor James Fox, I presented a shorter version at the Stetson University College of Law in February of 2011. I benefited from the comments of a number of those who attended the talk. As always, all mistakes are mine.

S. Macaulay (✉)
University of Wisconsin Law School, Madison, WI, USA
e-mail: smacaula@wisc.edu

D. Campbell (ed.), *Stewart Macaulay: Selected Works*, Law and Philosophy Library 133, https://doi.org/10.1007/978-3-030-33930-2_20

were published more than 50 (Macaulay 1963) and 35 (Macaulay 1979) years ago. However, while we can cite such older examples, people in law schools have spent more time talking about the law in action than they have spent actually doing such research. Yet things may be changing. Indeed, recently some traditional law professors seem threatened by the demands that we go on beyond doctrine.[1]

I want to tell three stories. First, I will describe some of the recent interest by law professors in empirical approaches to law. It comes in very distinct flavors, and it is not just more of what has been done in the past. As I offer examples, I will note some of the problems faced by those who seek to apply social science techniques to the operations of the legal system. There is no perfect way to study the law in action or the living law. All methods have their limits. Second, I will look at the challenges that we who do not have PhDs in any social science face when we seek help from our colleagues who do this kind of work. We have to translate their findings into terms that we can use, and we must be concerned that something may be lost in that translation. Social science does not produce "facts" that we can just plug into legal analysis. Third, I will ask what difference adding a picture drawn by new legal realist approaches might make to the legitimacy of law and to classic legal scholarship.

I. Another Empirical Turn for the Law Schools

Let me offer some examples of the recent growing empirical turn by legal academics, sometimes acting alone and sometimes conspiring with social scientist partners. We can call some or all of this work "new legal realism" in order to draw attention to its relationship to a tradition of attempting to broaden the factual basis for legal analysis. Those of us who see confronting the law in action, as well as the living law, as vitally important may find the term to be a useful marker. One audience may be those law professors doing this kind of work. It may aid them to find allies or warn them that they need to distinguish their studies from other approaches. Another audience may be those who do not do this kind of work but who might find it useful – academics

[1]The American Bar Association's Section on Legal Education, Out of the Box Committee issued a report in 2009. The report states: "[I]t is next to impossible today for a young lawyer to get appointed or to earn tenure based only on careful, rigorous, incisive legal analysis that takes cases seriously." The report concludes: "The right way to do 'law and' is to connect a brilliant legal scholar with a brilliant 'and' scholar. . . . Too many law professors neither train their students for their chosen profession nor contribute as scholars to that profession. But they do have a good time." With respect, I dissent for many reasons. One is that I have not seen an army of law-and. . . scholars crowding out the lawyers in law schools. However, there are more each year. The ones I know are excellent lawyers as well as fine social scientists. Better pictures of the law in action can contribute to both scholarship and skills training. Second, it is very hard to connect a legal scholar with a social scientist. They have to learn to talk and to listen to each other. The translation problems are great. Yet if the professors will put their egos aside and listen to each other, it can be done. Indeed, we are beginning to see clinical law professors turn to writing articles based on their experiences with the law in action, and some of them partner with a social scientist to bring this off. See, e.g., LaVigne and Van Rybroek (2011, 2013). These are not people just having fun.

from other fields, practicing lawyers, and even those in broader policy audiences. Obviously, "new legal realism" has no established and precise boundaries. Nonetheless, the term still may be useful.

Thomas J. Miles and Cass R. Sunstein (2008, 831) discuss what they call *"The* New Legal Realism." They tell us that such work is "an effort to understand the sources of judicial decisions on the basis of testable hypotheses and large data sets." It involves "the close examination of reported cases in order to understand how judicial personality, understood in various ways, influences legal outcomes, and how legal institutions constrain or unleash these influences" (Miles and Sunstein (2008, 834). Notice that they want to use new tools to broaden our approach to classic problems of legal scholarship – how can we predict and explain what courts are going to do? They want to go beyond doctrine to explain judicial decisions (see also Miles and Sunstein 2006; Ringhand 2007 [for another study establishing judicial behavior by the use of statistics]; Gillman 2001 (noting that political scientists have done somewhat similar work for a very long time); and Shapiro 2008).[2]

Sunstein, Schkade, and Ellman[3] (2004) present a major example of this version of new legal realism. They looked at 4,958 published opinions of United States Courts of Appeal and the votes of 14,874 individual judges from 1995 to 2004 in areas where the authors thought that ideology might matter. They offer three hypotheses:

1. *Ideological Voting.* In ideologically contested cases, a judge's ideological tendency can be predicted by the party of the appointing president. Republican appointees vote very differently from Democratic appointees. . . .
2. *Ideological dampening.* A judge's ideological tendency. . . is likely to be dampened if she is sitting with two judges of a different political party. For example, a Democratic appointee should be less likely to vote in a stereotypically liberal fashion if accompanied by two Republican appointees, and a Republican appointee should be less likely to vote in a stereotypically conservative fashion if accompanied by two Democratic appointees.
3. *Ideological amplification.* A judge's ideological tendency. . . . is likely to be amplified if she is sitting with two judges from the same political party. . . as the president who appointed her.

What did they find? All three hypothesis were confirmed in cases involving (1) affirmative action; (2) sex discrimination; (3) sexual harassment; (4) Americans with Disabilities Act cases; (5) piercing the corporate veil; (6) campaign finance; (7) environmental regulation; (8) Contracts Clause violations; and (9) Title VII claims. However, the authors caution: "there is substantial overlap between the votes of Republican appointees and those of Democratic appointees. Ideology is not everything." The result often is not foreordained by the composition of the panel.

---

[2]Appellate judges and scholars have debated explaining judicial behavior by considering variables apart from legal doctrine. See Edwards and Livermore (2009); Livermore (2010); Posner (2010).

[3]Compare Johnson and Songer (2009) ("[I]n the United States, gender differences disappear when one controls for the political party of the justice") with Collins, Manning, and Carp (2010) (Gender "differences are most significant in criminal justice cases. . . . Gender is not significant in labor and economic regulation cases").

But the litigant's chances, in the cases these scholars examine, are significantly affected by the luck of the draw. The authors say:

> Consider, for example, a case in which a woman has complained of sex discrimination. In front of an appellate panel of three Democratic appointees, she wins 75 percent of the time. But if the panel has fewer Democratic appointees, her chances decline. With two Democratic and one Republican appointee, she wins 49 percent of the time; with one Democratic and two Republican appointees, she wins 38 percent of the time. And with a panel of three Republican appointees, she wins just 31 percent of the time. (Schkade and Sunstein 2003)

However, the authors found no significant differences in the voting patterns of Republican and Democratic appointees in (1) criminal appeals; (2) Federalism and Commerce Clause cases, and (3) takings claims. Finally, they found ideological voting without amplification or dampening by the other judges on the panel in cases involving (1) abortion and (2) capital punishment.

The authors seek to explain why we do not see more ideological voting. They argue that often the law itself imposes constraints, and also that those nominated and confirmed as Court of Appeals judges seldom are ideologues or extremists. In addition, they note that the one Democrat on a panel with two Republicans might influence the other judges, at least where the panel would otherwise fail to follow existing law – this was the "whistleblower effect." The two Republicans often will not want to face a well-reasoned dissent. Sometimes, however, it just is not worth dissenting, and the Democrat will go along with her colleagues. Writing a dissenting opinion, after all, is more work for a busy judge.

When we look at studies of the process by which United States Courts of Appeal judges are selected in recent years, we see why we should not be surprised to find that politics influences judicial outcomes. To a large extent, the judges are picked by American presidents in our now highly politicized federal judicial selection process to do just what they are doing (e.g. Goldman, Schiavoni, and Slotnick 2009). Of course, the candidates for these judgeships tell the Senate committee members questioning them that they will do no more than just apply the law.

Sunstein, Schkade, and Ellman fit within a kind of "new legal realism" whose methods resemble the approach of most of the articles in the *Journal of Empirical Legal Studies* (JELS) which began in 2004. The initial JELS' Editors Introduction tells us:

> JELS seeks to encourage, promote, and provide an impetus for the careful collection of empirical data and the dispassionate, rigorous testing of empirical hypothesis. The central purpose of JELS is to add to knowledge of the legal system based on observation or empirical analysis, including experimental analysis.... (2004, v)[4]

Two phrases catch my eye – "empirical data" and "rigorous testing." If we skim the first two volumes, we find tables of numbers and statistics in most of the articles.

[4]For a more recent statement about the history and goals of empirical legal studies, see Eisenberg (2011); also see Suchman and Mertz (2010), which examines both the similarities and contrasts between the two varieties of modern empirical approaches to law.

We might argue that a better name for the enterprise would be the *Journal of Quantitative Legal Studies*.

In this sense, the quantitative approach of these scholars seems similar to that of Sunstein, Miles, Schkade, and Ellman. But the questions JELS asks are broader than why judges do what they do. The focus of most JELS articles is on the impact of the legal system, and the approach is instrumental. Authors ask such things as whether the amounts awarded by juries have increased over the last forty years (Seabury, Pace, and Reville 2004). Or are there common clusters of problems that go to court, and, if so, what are their social and demographic indicators (Pleasance, Balmer, Buck, O'Grady, and Genn 2004)? An entire issue of JELS was devoted to the "vanishing trial" in the United States (see Burbank 2004a, 2004b; Butler 2004; Diamond, Seidman, and Bina 2004; Eisenberg 2004; Friedman 2004; Galanter 2004; Hadfield 2004; Kritzer 2004; Ostrom, Strickland, and Hannaford-Agor 2004; Resnik 2004; Stipanowich 2004; Warren 2004; Yeazell 2004).[5] There is a general consensus on the overall picture: the numbers show that we have had a sharp decline in the number of trials. In the special issue, twelve articles seek to explain why this is so and appraise the consequences.

Many of these articles suggest that data and statistics can take us only so far, and that we must turn to other approaches to explain the patterns found in the table of numbers or to solve the relevant legal and normative problems (for an excellent qualitative study printed in JELS, see Kritzer 2008). Sometimes, if not often, data and statistics do not provide clear answers but only provoke challenges and more statistics. Statistical techniques rest on assumptions about the data, and where those assumptions are not or cannot be met, reporting what was found only gives the appearance of scientific rigor. Let me be clear: where we have good data well analyzed by good statistical techniques, we should accept the findings and draw on them for policy. However, often we cannot wait for the perfect rigorous study, or we may doubt whether such a study is possible in our area of interest. Just as with every other method of finding "the facts," quantitative work has its limits.

At least somewhat allied to the varieties of new legal realism discussed up to this point is a growing body of writing labeled "behavioral law-and-economics." This is a very large subject (see, e.g., Ellickson 1989; Hanson and Kysar 1999; Jolls, Sunstein, and Thaler 1998; Korobkin 2000), and I can only offer a few examples. Wilkinson-Ryan and Small (2008) look at bargaining at divorce.[6] They review "empirical evidence suggesting that men and women bargain differently because

[5]But see Lande (2005): "Before becoming horrified at the possible demise of the trial in general, we should have a clearer picture of the actual changes and their consequences. In the meantime, the insights of legal pluralism can help provide a balanced analysis by recognizing that much adjudication occurs before trial and outside the courts" (212).

[6]See, also, Wilkinson-Ryan and Hoffman (2010) ("Subjects were not outraged by breach when they thought that the breacher had made a mistake, or that the breacher himself was losing out on the deal as well").

of motivational and cognitive factors." For example, they cite an article published in *Psychological Bulletin* that finds "women are more communally-oriented than men and that their self-concept is more dependent on their relationships with others which in turn makes them focus on interpersonal goals and less on task-specific goals" (116). The authors argue that this may affect how men and women bargain. Of course, we can suspect that some men are more dependent on their relationships with others than some women, and we can wonder whether the strength of this conclusion might change as women's roles in society change. Broad quantitatively supported conclusions often leave finer-grained qualitatively/contextual/historical nuances and variations unexplained. Every dispute will involve the personalities and histories of the particular parties involved in the bargaining. The *Psych Bulletin* article takes us beyond a homogenized image of equal, rights bearing individuals negotiating, unaffected by their gender and other personal characteristics. However, once we open that door, many new questions about particular parties are left unanswered by this line of empirical evidence.

Another sample of this approach is offered by an exchange between Oren Bar-Gill (2008) and Richard A. Epstein (2008). Bar-Gill argues that consumers suffer from systematic misperception of the costs and benefits associated with certain products, such as credit cards. Sophisticated sellers design their products, contracts, and pricing schemes in response to consumer misperceptions. This reduces consumers' overall welfare. As a result, Bar-Gill argues that some type of legal intervention is warranted.

Epstein is not persuaded. He tells us at the outset:

> There is little doubt that the major new theoretical approach to law-and-economics in the past two decades does not come from either of these two fields. Instead it comes from the adjacent discipline of cognitive psychology, which has now morphed into behavioral economics. (Epstein 2008, 803)

Epstein thinks that over time consumers learn how to protect themselves from sellers, and this dynamic makes markets work. He points to the large amount of information available on the Web as evidence that consumers now are even more able to cope with practices of credit card companies and lenders. One of Epstein's comments about a study that supports his view suggests his skepticism about behavioral economics' heavy reliance on cognitive psychology (Agarwal, Driscoll, Gabaix, and Laibson 2007). He says:

> What I regard as most valuable about this study is that it does not rely on looking at studies of college students' behavior, but tries to organize extensive data about the behavior of real people of all ages in credit markets. (Epstein 2008, 811)

At the very least, the exchange between Epstein and Bar-Gill suggests that those who take economics approaches to law are confronting and will continue to face serious problems about establishing facts. To what degree can law professors just pick up findings from cognitive psychology and plug them into their analyses? The unthinking "plug in" approach risks ignoring the limits of the studies on which the legal scholar draws. So, if cognitive psychology cannot be used this way, can it at least suggest hypotheses? To the extent that it can, we still would have to test these hypotheses empirically, or we must accept them based on our intuitions – which may be completely wrong.

Epstein raises a valid concern about Bar-Gill's reliance on cognitive psychology, which sometimes relies on testing undergraduates who must gain experimental points for a course. Nonetheless, we can wonder, as well, about the limits of the study upon which Epstein relies. It is not easy to get hard data about the "behavior of real people of all ages in credit markets." Gregory Mitchell notes that scholars doing behavioral law-and-economics too often replace the assumption of rational human behavior that was frequently found in traditional law-and-economics work with the opposite view. People are assumed never to be rational. They have systematic biases and errors in judgment, regardless of their situations. However, Mitchell (2002a, 2002b, 2003) offers much evidence that situational variables can affect the degree to which human behavior is or is not rational. Of course, this means that it is much more difficult to offer theories about the impact of law that yield precise and neat results. Instead of employing an elegant model, often the scholar is left to say little more than "it depends."

Social science, of course, is not limited to large data sets and fancy statistics or experiments in a laboratory to test the ideas of social psychology. There is a rich tradition of careful qualitative work as well. Understanding the law in action often requires such qualitative work. In some instances, quantitative data may not be available. Moreover, those involved may have reasons not to advertise what they have been doing, so that using questionnaires or other large-scale data collection methods may not serve to collect accurate information. In some instances, counting things may not answer the questions that we must answer, or there may be no way to get something to count that we can be sure is accurate.

For example, while police and administrative agencies do initiate some proactive steps to enforce the law, taking legal action often requires ordinary people to perceive that they have been wronged, find someone they see as responsible, and then decide to make a claim. It is hard to study those who did not take action when they might have done so. It is not easy to find those who had legal rights and failed to assert them. Moreover, those who failed to assert their rights may later offer rationalizations rather than the actual reasons for their decision to do nothing. They may not want to risk appearing weak, fearful, or foolish, and so they can offer reasons that they hope the interviewer will see as rational calculations.

Catherine Albiston (2011) studied workers who likely had a claim under the Family and Medical Leave Act of 1993 (see also Albiston 2005). She located respondents by consulting a telephone information line run by a nonprofit organization that gave informal legal assistance to workers. Twenty-four of the thirty-five people who had called over the course of a year agreed to be interviewed. Obviously,

Albiston could not generalize to all of the people who might consider using their rights under the FMLA. However, she discovered patterns that may hold true for many or most employees. She found that cultural norms influenced employees' decisions about using their rights. One who takes time from work to care for a member of the family may fear that he or she will be viewed as not taking the job seriously. The "good employee" puts the job first. Employees worried that if they took leave, they might be sanctioned. They could be fired, denied raises, or assigned to unrewarding tasks. Both true and inaccurate stories about what happened to others who tried to take leave can pass through the employees' social networks, and these stories can deter making claims.

We add to our confidence in Albiston's study when we look at Phoebe A. Morgan's (1999) paper: "Risking Relationships: Understanding the Litigation Choices of Sexually Harassed Women." She studied thirty-one women who reported their sexual harassment to authorities and also considered litigation to assert their rights. "[T]he decision to sue rested upon assessments of their abilities to do so while also being good mothers, wives, and daughters. If the filing of the suit threatened the well-being of family members or to strain family ties, then potential plaintiffs were reluctant to embrace such a choice" (75). Thus, Morgan found perceived costs here that were analogous to those found by Albiston.[7]

Another, more "big tent," kind of new legal realism also has emerged in recent years: one that expands legal scholarship by demanding that it take into account the almost fifty years of the modern law-and-society movement.[8] That movement brought together almost the full array of social sciences with a group of legal scholars. It provided an ongoing forum for interdisciplinary legal studies. Yet the ideas made salient by this movement still are "news" to many in the academy. This is true, although many legal scholars often write about the consequences of legal action. Much of what appeared in law reviews just assumed that, for example, passing a law to protect consumers would in fact protect them or that a law with

[7]For another study of rights claiming that qualifies as a model of new legal realism, see Brake and Grossman (2008). Brake and Grossman draw on social science literature about "how people perceive and respond to discrimination in the real world," and contrast this evidence with the demands of Title VII doctrines about asserting claims clearly and promptly.

[8]Posner (1995) finds the sociology of law to be a "weak field." Its focus has been "narrow, theoretically limited, and, empirically, limited in both scope and method." Posner seems to miss that much of law-and-society work challenges the explicit and implicit theory of most legal scholarly writing, including at least some of law-and-economics. Marc Galanter decodes this cognitive map or paradigm of legal reality in his unpublished paper, "Notes on the Future of Social Research in Law" (1974). This received paradigm offers a "picture of a hierarchy of agencies applying a hierarchy of rules, more or less in accordance with the picture propounded in our higher law...." The key assumption is that the "authoritative normative learning generated at the higher reaches of the system provides a map for understanding it." At the very least, law-and-society work teaches how misleading this received paradigm is.

certain characteristics would produce an efficient result in society. But to quote Ira Gershwin, "It Ain't Necessarily So."[9] In recent years, more and more law review articles recognize this and attempt to cope with the messiness that we find in the reality of law in our daily lives.

As a quick way to review a large field, I offer some headings from my 1984 Mitchell Lecture at the State University of New York at Buffalo (for an article based on this lecture, see Macaulay 1984). Some key ideas included the fact that law is not free, that it is delivered by actors with limited resources who have discretion and interests of their own, and that people do not always comply passively with law but often they actively cope with its demands. At a more institutional and social level, law-and-society scholars also have demonstrated that many supposedly "legal" functions are performed by alternative institutions, and that lawyers are not limited to the adversarial role assumed by much legal scholarship. Finally, in my 1984 lecture, I pointed to empirical research that established the indirect, subtle, and ambiguous ways that law may have impact in the United States, particularly because avoidance and evasion are important ways that we deal with conflict (Macaulay 1984, 152–155).

I advocate a new legal realism where anyone writing about a legal problem would keep these ideas in mind and add them to her analysis. The impact of law always is an empirical question, and we cannot just assume that words on paper have little legs so that they can wiggle down off the page and enforce themselves. At a minimum, those who write about the consequences of law should make an effort to draw on social science where it offers relevant information. Clearly, those who have the skills to do empirical research can add to what we know about the law in action and the living law.[10] Sometimes partnerships between those with legal training and those who can play social science at a high level can be very profitable. Moreover, I advocate multiple methods of fact gathering. The effects of law are unusually difficult to capture, and we cannot privilege any one approach. Sometimes, we will have to use less rigorous methods.[11] We should accept this as long as the

[9]"It Ain't Necessarily So" is a popular song with music by George Gershwin and lyrics by Ira Gershwin. The song comes from the Gershwins' opera *Porgy and Bess* (1935) where it is sung by the character Sportin' Life, a drug dealer, who expresses his doubt about several statements in the Bible." http://en.wikipedia.org/wiki/It_Ain%27t_Necessarily_So.

[10]See, e.g., Heald (2008). Landes and Posner defended extending copyright to give incentives to invest in maintaining and exploiting intellectual works, but Heald's article offers data challenging their position.

[11]Chambliss (2008) quotes my remark: "[o]ften we are faced with a choice between doing nothing and relying on assumed facts or publishing a study that other scholars cannot precisely replicate" (36, quoting Macaulay 2009). She then says: "Or, as one blogger put it, 'if it's worth doing, it's worth doing badly.'" Sometimes the best methods possible will be very suspect – that is, "best" may equal "badly" if measured against ideal methods. If we disclose what we have done and are humble about what we conclude, this beats ignoring real problems or making up facts by looking at the ceiling tiles in our offices.

scholar is appropriately humble[12] about what she or he has proved and discloses the limits of her or his study.[13]

[12]Elizabeth Mertz's (2007a) impressive study of first-year legal education suggests that lawyers are not trained to be humble about the limits of their knowledge. She tells us that in law school classrooms, professors speculate, draw on anecdotes, and "continue the brilliant opening up of legal readings to virtually all kinds of cultural stories about why things happen" (77). She concludes that in law school talk, "[w]hen social context comes to the door, structure, standards, and rigor exit" (79).

[13]Braham (2000) asserts that my 1963 paper "is so methodologically flawed that it should be treated with extreme care" (465–466). He calls for a study of "a comparison of the number of disputes that are resolved by recourse to contract law with those resolved without it, or by using the number of cases dropped" (469). I would be delighted to see such a study. I cannot imagine how one could produce it. First, Braham's terms hide many difficulties: What is a dispute? What counts as resolving a dispute by recourse to contract law? Indeed, what counts as contract law as distinguished from other kinds of law? What counts as resolving a dispute without recourse to contract law if contract law exists in the background as a possible resource in case the dispute is not resolved otherwise? For example, suppose the parties quote clauses in their written agreement to each other without ever explicitly threatening to sue. Is this an application of contract "law?"

Second, even if one could gain agreement on the answers to these questions, how would one gain the needed data? Most business people do not keep counts of the number of disputes that are resolved by recourse to contract law compared to those resolved without it. Few business people would welcome a team of researchers invading their offices and watching them negotiate contracts and deal with performances that disappoint them. Undoubtedly, objective statistics based on a random sample of business people and business lawyers would be better evidence. However, creating reliable statistics about the number of contract disputes in a particular industry would be almost impossible. Discovering the number of contract disputes that business people took to lawyers would not be much easier. Very few would know that they sued in, say, 2.37 percent of all disputes or of "serious" disputes. Moreover, not infrequently, what appears to be a dispute between a buyer and a seller really is a dispute between the seller and other creditors of the buyer. Even getting a precise count of the number of business contracts cases filed in all American courts would present real difficulties. Various government agencies report such data, but there are many reasons to wonder about their accuracy. For example, is a case involving an alleged misrepresentation properly classified as a tort or a contract dispute? However we answer this question, can we be sure that the government agency reporting the data classified all misrepresentation cases consistently? If we compare data from one state with data from another, can we be sure that those in each state used the same classification scheme?

Just finding people willing to talk candidly about business practices never is easy. A law professor does not have subpoena and contempt power to compel testimony about behavior that many business people and their lawyers see as confidential. I once found a lawyer who had data in front of him about when the automobile company he represented had been sued for breach of contract and when it had gone to court making claims against suppliers, dealers, and customers. He told me that this was confidential proprietary information, and he refused to reveal anything about it to me. I think that many, if not most, business people and their lawyers would take this stance.

Moreover, Braham finds "logical inconsistencies" in my claims. He says that I assert that contract law plays no role in business and then find that its role increased as the world economy changed over time. Any inconsistencies arise from his misreading of the 1963 article and two that follow. I never asserted, as he assumes, that contract law never plays some role in planning, avoiding, and resolving business disputes. As the 1963 article says: "One uses or threatens to use legal sanctions to settle disputes when other devices will not work and when the gains are thought to outweigh the costs" (65). My position was and is: sometimes contract law as applied is useful; sometimes it plays an indirect role as an express or implied threat; sometimes it is almost totally

A few years after the Mitchell Lecture, I advocated study of the legal ideas held by ordinary people and elites that are offered by education, entertainment, and spectator sports (Macaulay 1989). This was not a new idea. In the early days of American sociology, Professors William Thomas and Dorothy Thomas (1928) had observed that what people think is so, is in fact so for them ("If men define situations as real, they are real in their consequences" (572)). Law can be part of a project to mislead people. I have cautioned, however, that Americans seldom are trapped in the rhetoric of law. Ordinary people in this country are great jazz musicians, ready to improvise on legal tunes. Moreover, many of our legal ideas come in matched but contradictory sets so that almost every position can be challenged in totally predictable ways (Harris 1980, 274–275).

Professor David Ray Papke (1999, 2007), in a series of articles has asked about the impact of television and film on jurors who participate in the trial process and on the views of the average citizen about the performance of courts (see, also, Podlas 2001). Among other things, he talked with six Indiana trial judges about the differences between the picture of courts and trials in popular culture and the real thing. In real-life trials, he says, "irrelevant actions and testimony, randomness, purposelessness, and delay abound."[14] TV does not have time for this. Moreover,

---

irrelevant. My claim is that we lack a clear picture of when contract law plays a role in which situations and just what that role is. Moreover, I argue that academics often assume that contract law plays a larger role than it does or could play. I am reassured by all of the very many later studies in many countries that reach roughly the same conclusions that I did almost fifty years ago. See, e.g., Roxenhall and Ghauri (2004) ("Our study confirms that contracts are rarely used in connection with disputes. Business people probably feel that contracts should remain in the drawer because they strive for good relations with their customers and suppliers. They solve disputes informally without resorting to contracts or the legal profession"); Woolthuis, Hillebrand, and Nooteboom (2005) ("We have empirically shown that trust and contract need not be 'opposing alternatives' and, more important, shown why this is the case: trust and contract can well be complements because contracts are in practice often not used and interpreted in a strictly legal fashion with opportunism as a central focal point" (835)); Cullen, Butcher, Hickman, and Keast (2005) (Cullen and her colleagues interviewed officials in the British aerospace industry and found a "divergence between the parties' intended working relationship and the agenda prescribed by formal contracts"); Stipanowich and Lamare (forthcoming) (This study reports two surveys of corporate counsel in Fortune 1,000 companies – one in 1997 and the other in 2011. "[C]lear and significant evolutionary trends are observable, including a further shift in corporate orientation away from litigation and toward 'alternative dispute resolution (ADR),' moderated expectations of ADR; increasing use of mediation, contrasted with a dramatic fall-off in arbitration (except, importantly, consumer and products liability cases); greater control over the selection of third-party neutrals; growing emphasis on proactive approaches such as early neutral evaluation, early case assessment, and integrated systems for managing employment disputes"); Hadfield and Bozovic, Scaffolding (Aug. 2013) (innovative firms use the process of drafting formal contracts as a planning device; traditional firms rely on form contracts that play largely a symbolic role) (see also, Ellickson 1991). Of course, these studies also rest largely on opinion evidence gained from non-random samples of informants who should know what is going on. However, we can have some confidence in the conclusions that are consistent and reported by so many studies over fifty years.

[14]There is no direct evidence, but the studies on pretrial publicity suggest that watching CSI may prompt jurors to acquit, but it might prompt more convictions as well. It is also possible that CSI has no effect at all (Tyler 2006).

he notes that at least some prosecutors think that the CSI shows have made jurors expect highly sophisticated forensic evidence to be offered although it seldom is available.

Novels, television, and film contribute to the legal culture – the public's stock of ideas about what should and should not be done in the legal system. They may affect voters' willingness to support candidates and increases in taxes to pay for such things as police and administrative agencies. And this stock of ideas may be carried into legal proceedings by jurors as well as by judges and lawyers as part of what they take for granted (see Emmers-Sommer and Allen 1999; Mezey and Niles 2005).

II. Teaching Old Dogs New Tricks? Dealing with Social Science

There was a day when many in law-and-economics loved to remind us that "there ain't no such thing as a free lunch" – that is, we must perform a cost-benefit analysis to assess the merits of any new development. The new empirical turn in legal studies comes with its costs and risks. One risk is the proliferation of low-quality empirical work, as untrained or undertrained law professors dig into empirical research that they are ill-prepared to perform or even assess. Another risk involves skilled social scientists making mistakes about legal rules and procedures. Of course, some of those in the legal academy boast both law degrees and a PhD in a social science. While they are unlikely to make some of the mistakes that we amateurs risk, the various social sciences differ over methodologies and basic assumptions. Moreover, there are strong differences within particular social sciences as well as between them. Put simply, none of these kinds of scholarly research yield clearly defined "facts" that just sit there waiting for a legal scholar to pick them up and plug them into her or his analysis. Even social science research that seems to support our pet ideas must be read skeptically and carefully if we care about what is going on rather than just seeking rhetoric and authority to back up our position.[15]

Elizabeth Mertz, who holds both a law degree and a PhD in anthropology, sees the problem as one of "translation" (2007b).[16] Lawyers have to learn to read social science, and the social scientists need to cope with the nature of law if they venture into the rough and tumble of policy and reform. A policy paper offered to Congress, a law review article, and a report of a social science study are very different art forms.

[15]We must avoid the social science equivalent of "law office history." It is far too easy to find a scrap of history to prop up an argument in a brief without doing the job any historian would find acceptable. See, e.g., Small (2008) and Lempert (2008) (Lempert offers five points that consumers of policy-relevant empirical research should keep in mind. I particularly like the fifth: "[I]f results seem too good to be true, this is often because they are not true").

[16]"[Lawyers] may be tempted to dip into science only to locate findings that fit their preferred points of view, rather than reevaluating a point of view when the bulk of the science fails to support it" (Mertz 2007b, 800).

Let me offer an example by venturing into the swamp of scholarship addressing the question of whether the death penalty deters murders. Sunstein and Vermeule (2005) "suggest ... that on certain empirical assumptions, capital punishment may be morally required, not for retributive reasons, but rather to prevent the taking of innocent lives" (705). They look at several social science studies that conclude that capital punishment deters, including one that suggests that each execution prevents on average eighteen murders (see, e.g., Dezhbakhsh, Rubin, and Shepard 2003). They argue: "[i]f the current evidence is even roughly correct ... then a refusal to impose capital punishment will effectively condemn numerous innocent people to death" (Sunstein and Vermuele 2005, 709). They ask those who find the social science unconvincing "to suspend their empirical doubts in order to investigate the moral issues that we mean to raise here" (709). Even if we cannot prove that capital punishment deters, it should be imposed "if there is a significant possibility that it will save large numbers of lives" (715).

They concede that the legal system will make mistakes, and some innocent people will be wrongly executed. However, they say "no legal system can ensure complete accuracy in criminal convictions" (736 n93). They tell us that estimates suggest that the number of wrongly executed over the past thirty or forty years is very low – three to four people.

John Donohue and Justin Wolfers (2005) responded with a searching examination of the studies that had found that capital punishment deters murder. They find the claims of these studies to be highly questionable. They say: "[a]ggregating over all of our estimates, it is entirely unclear even whether the preponderance of evidence suggests that the death penalty causes more or less murder." Donohue and Wolfers quote another noted economist, Steven Levitt: "I really think not that the answer is 'yes' or 'no,' ... but that there's not enough information to figure it out. There may never be enough. It may just be a question that can't be answered."

Sunstein and Vermeule were conducting a thought experiment. They asked us to assume that there was adequate evidence that the death penalty saves a significant number of lives by deterring murders that would have taken place without it. If you make this assumption, then they argue on moral grounds that you would have to impose capital punishment.

I have trouble playing their game. First, I am disquieted by how they slip past the problem of executing the innocent. Even as they have framed their thought experiment, this risk must be considered. The innocence projects at various law schools leave me most uneasy about how our system works in capital cases (see Dewan 2008; Garrett 2011; Rosen 2011).[17] The Innocence Project at Cardozo Law School reports that as of June of 2011, there have been 272 post-conviction DNA exonerations in United States history. DNA testing began in the late 1980s. Seventeen

[17]Kruse (2006) asserts: "The DNA exoneration cases of the past two decades have given us a window into what has not been working in the criminal justice system" (645). She looks at two reforms in Wisconsin that attempt to respond to the products of innocence projects. "This Article considers the Wisconsin innocence reforms as a case study in emerging experimentalist governance, illustrating both its promise and the challenge of experimentalist reform" (649).

people had been sentenced to death before DNA proved their innocence and led to their release. I recall that Governor George Ryan of Illinois declared a moratorium on executions in 2000, when new evidence cleared 13 men who had been convicted and sent to death row since 1977 (see Rimer 2000). I also found Samuel Gross's (1996), "The Risks of Death: Why Erroneous Convictions Are Common in Capital Cases,"[18] worth attention. The subject is a matter of debate among various Supreme Court justices and law professors (see Liptak 2008).[19]

Moreover, if the evidence for a deterrent effect is indeed suspect, I am yet more troubled. Sunstein and Vermeule say that even if we cannot prove that capital punishment deters, it should be imposed "if there is a significant possibility that it will save large numbers of lives" (2005, 715). How do we know that there is such a "significant possibility" if we cannot establish it statistically? The capital punishment studies have been challenged by well-known social scientists. Of course, their argument is not that we know that capital punishment does not deter. Rather, speaking as social scientists, they find that the case that there is such deterrence has not been proved as of now. Notice, too, that Sunstein and Vermeule assert that imposing capital punishment will save "large numbers of lives." But some studies suggest that presence of capital punishment in the statutes of a state may increase the murder rate there. It has also been argued that in states or countries that have capital punishment, criminals who commit capital crimes have an added incentive to murder witnesses. We thus have to balance lives saved and lives lost as a result of the incentive effects of the penalty, against the risk of putting to death innocent people who have been wrongfully convicted. If we want to minimize the risk of convicting and executing the innocent, we have to consider the cost of effective criminal defense as well. A great deal of our judgment will rest on some blend of scientific proof and pure intuition. Just to add to the puzzle, we should remember that the judgment likely will be made by elected officials subject to the will of the voters who are motivated to cast their ballot.

In short, social science does not necessarily yield clear and certain answers to normative questions. When it does not yield such answers, we must face the question of what risks of being wrong we are willing to take. Sunstein and Vermeule leave us with this problem. What should we do when we are not sure? It is exactly the kind of question that a new legal realism would force us to confront. And it is the kind of a question that at least some law professors have experience speaking to.

But the death penalty and deterrence also offers another kind of problem that we face when we try to translate social science into law or law into social science.

[18]See, also, Gross and O'Brien (2008) ("From 1973 on, we know basic facts about all defendants who were sentenced to death in the United States, and we know which of them were exonerated. From these data we estimate that the frequency of wrongful death sentences in the United States is at least 2.3 percent"). But compare Dezbakhsh, Rubin, and Shepard (2003).

[19]See, also, Garrett (2011). Garrett argues that the reasons that there were erroneous convictions in the cases where the defendant was exonerated by DNA apply equally well to serious felony trials where there was no DNA evidence.

Fagan, Zimring, and Geller (2006) point to a risk of work based on large data sets and statistics. Such work often appears to offer clear answers. These easily summarized answers may keep us from struggling to reach an understanding of what the tables and numbers and rates really mean. The authors point out that the Supreme Court of the United States has required states to define the kind of murders that are eligible for the death penalty, and it has imposed limits on what may be included. Less than 25 percent of criminal killings could prompt capital punishment under these constitutional requirements. However, almost all of the social science studies that find a large deterrence effect of capital punishment use in their work *the number of total intentional homicides.* This includes both those crimes where the death penalty *could be imposed* constitutionally and many more where *it could not.*[20]

Fagan and his colleagues (2006) argue that this leads to a serious aggregation error: "If execution risk is driving homicide levels, then this should be a specific effect observed in death-eligible cases but not in other types of homicide" (1824). They reanalyze the data, looking for an impact of the threat of execution on situations where a murderer could receive the death penalty. They conclude: "Our search for death penalty deterrence where it should be a strong influence on homicide rates has produced consistent results: the marginal deterrent effect of the threat or example of execution on these cases at risk for such punishment is invisible" (1860). In short, we must get the law right before we start analyzing numbers.

Turning to another example of the difficulties in drawing on social science when we think about law, I mentioned before the growing body of books and articles that analyze law in popular culture. I find almost all of this work that I have seen to be interesting and entertaining. But this body of work illustrates a common difficulty when we try to understand the legal culture of any nation. These studies face the problem of how to show impact. The scholar does an analysis of what was sent out to the audience in a novel, a film, and a television program or series or even as part of the content of spectator sports. However, it is very hard to know what various members of the public took in from what they observed. Good drama offers conflicting themes, and a reader or viewer can focus on what is salient to her or identify with a secondary character or even the villain.[21] Some will just not get it. Moreover, there are competing stories, and we can watch or read one this week and another with a very different lesson next week. We still need to understand how various kinds of people in the society translate what they see. Unless we seek answers to this question, we may err seriously as we rely on our own "readings" of popular entertainment, assuming that everyone else reads it the same way.

---

[20]It is possible that the death penalty deters killing in situations where the accused legally could not be sentenced to death because most people do not know the legal standards and their application. Misunderstanding of the law can have impact. Proving that this is, or is not, the case with capital punishment is far beyond my skills in social science. Proving why people do not do something is hard.

[21]This is a common reaction. Oliver Stone was quite upset when he heard from a number of traders that his movie *Wall Street* had inspired them to go into finance.

We receive information about law through many channels, and each of us must process it through our own assumptions and expectations. Furthermore, people are also influenced by their own experiences with law as well as by those of friends and relatives. A bitterly contested divorce may influence a man or woman far more than conventional pictures of lawyers and the legal system found in film, television, or mystery novels. We cannot understand the influence of popular culture on the legal system by just watching what is sent out and drawing our own conclusions. We need to explore what people make of what they see or hear.

The conclusion is obvious but daunting. Quantitative research and qualitative social science both need careful sifting and translating before they can be put to work in legal settings. Still, trying to look at law in action as carefully as we can is likely to be much better than relying on anecdotes, untested theories, and "what everyone knows." Sometimes actors in the legal system must take action without facts established by proof that would satisfy social scientists. Yet they will do better if they remember such things as that there are costs to any action they take and that those affected are likely to cope with the demands of the law in ways that the lawmaker may not like (Macaulay and Mertz 2013).

III. So What?

If we put law in context, we should begin to produce a more accurate picture of the actual operation of the legal system. We could abandon ideological claims based on idealistic images of law. However, what are the consequences of looking at law from the ground up? Would an unretouched picture of any nation's legal system damage its claims to legitimacy? Would such a picture undercut a large amount of legal scholarship?

More particularly, many of those interested in law and development advocate the spread of "the rule of law." But, in fact, does this "rule of law" actually prevail in the United States or the countries of western Europe? A new legal realism puts discretion and costs of vindicating rights front and center. Police departments and administrative agencies seldom can enforce all of the laws that appear on the books. It would be hard to imagine full-scale trials subject to appeals in every case. The resource demands of such a situation would be tremendous. Indeed, such evidence as we have suggests that ordinary citizens do not want many laws enforced to the letter. Moreover, much legal scholarship tells us to look at the consequences of adopting particular legal rules. This rule is supposed to give incentives for efficient behavior. That one should deter fraud and deceptive practices. And so on. But if we look at the law as delivered, the statement of the rule is but one factor in how particular cases will play out.

Some of the resistance to looking at the law as delivered may come from the attraction of an ideal of a system where decisions turn on nothing more than the rules. I have noted that:

> Judges are supposed to respond to reasoned argument, and if their decisions importantly affect behavior, then a single skilled advocate or author of a law review article, armed only with reason, could right wrongs by persuading judges.... Problems of politics, interest, power and dominance need not be faced because they do not appear to be relevant in the world of doctrine, where it is assumed that right ideas will be crystallized into rules that are self-enforcing.... (Macaulay 1977, 521–522)

Lon Fuller (1969) said that the morality of law demanded that the law on the books should correspond with the law in practice – a virtue that Fuller called "congruence." A new legal realism would ask whether such a state was possible or even desirable. Fuller, however, also set a goal for legal study. He said, "Perhaps in time legal philosophers will cease to be preoccupied with building 'conceptual models' to represent legal phenomena, will give up their endless debates about definitions, and will turn instead to an analysis of the social processes that constitute the reality of law" (242). The original legal realists called for this kind of movement in legal scholarship, but even they did not move very far beyond the door that they sought to open. Surprisingly perhaps, across so many decades, we have only just begun to draw a useful picture of the social processes to which Fuller called attention. This is an important part of the task of a new legal realism.

References

Agarwal, Sumit, John C. Driscoll, Xavier Gabaix, and David Laibson. 2007. "The Age of Reason: Financial Decisions over the Lifecycle," Massachusetts Institute of Technology Department of Economics Working Paper Series, Working Paper No. 07–11, 2007. http://ssrn.com/abstract=973790.

Albiston, Catherine R. 2005. "Bargaining in the Shadow of Social Institutions: Competing Discourses and Social Change in Workplace Mobilization of Civil Rights." *Law & Society Review* 39: 11–50.

Albiston, Catherine R. 2011. *Institutional Inequality and the Mobilization of the Family and Medical Leave Act: Rights on Leave.* New York: Cambridge University Press.

Bar-Gill, Oren. 2008. "The Behavioral Economics of Consumer Contracts." *Minnesota Law Review* 92: 749–802.

Braham, Matthew. 2000. "Non-Contractual Relations in Business Re-examined: A Critical Assessment of Macaulay's Legal Realism." *Homo Oeconomicus* 16: 436–472.

Brake, Deborah L., and Joanna L. Grossman. 2008. "The Failure of Title VII as a Rights-Claiming System." *North Carolina Law Review* 86: 859–935.

Burbank, Stephen B. 2004a. "Keeping Our Ambition Under Control: The Limits of Data and Inference in Searching for the Causes and Consequences of Vanishing Trials in Federal Court." *Journal of Empirical Legal Studies* 1(3): 571–590.

Burbank, Stephen B. 2004b. "Vanishing Trials and Summary Judgment in Federal Civil Cases: Drifting Toward Bethlehem or Gomorrah?" *Journal of Empirical Legal Studies* 1(3): 591–626.

Butler, Paul. 2004. "The Case for Trials: Considering the Intangibles." *Journal of Empirical Legal Studies* 1(3): 627–636.

Chambliss, Elizabeth. 2008. "When Do Facts Persuade? Some Thoughts on the Market for 'Empirical Legal Studies.'" *Law & Contemporary Problems* 71: 17–40.

Collins, Paul M., Kenneth L. Manning, and Robert A. Carp. 2010. "Gender, Critical Mass, and Judicial Decision Making." *Law & Policy* 32: 260–281.

Cullen, Penny-Anne, Bob Butcher, Richard Hickman, and John Keast. 2005. "A Critique of Contractual Relationships in the Aerospace Industry: *Collaboration v. Conflict.*" *International Journal of Law in Context* 1:397–410.
Dewan, Shaila. 2008. "Releases from Death Row Raise Doubts over Quality of Defence." *New York Times,* May 7.
Dezhbakhsh, Hashem, Paul H. Rubin, and Joanna M. Shepard. 2003. "Does Capital Punishment Have a Deterrent Effect? New Evidence from Post-Moratorium Panel Data." *American Law & Economics Review* 5: 344–376.
Diamond, Shari Seidman, and Jessica Bina. 2004. "Puzzles About Supply-Side Explanations for Vanishing Trials: A New Look at Fundamentals." *Journal of Empirical Legal Studies* 1(3): 637–658.
Donohue, John J., and Justin Wolfers. 2005. "Uses and Abuses of Empirical Evidence in the Death Penalty Debate." *Stanford Law Review* 58: 791–845.
Edwards, Harry T., and Michael A. Livermore. 2009. "Pitfalls of Empirical Studies that Attempt to Understand the Factors Affecting Appellate Decisionmaking." *Duke Law Journal* 58: 1895–1989.
Eisenberg, Theodore. 2004. "Appeal Rates and Outcomes in Tried and Nontried Cases: Further Exploration and Anti-Plaintiff Appellate Outcomes." *Journal of Empirical Legal Studies* 1(3): 659–688.
Eisenberg, Theodore. 2011. "The Origins, Nature, and Promise of Empirical Legal Studies and a Response to Concerns." *University of Illinois Law Review:* 1713–1738.
Ellickson, Robert C. 1989. "Bringing Culture and Human Frailty to Rational Actors: A Critique of Classical Law and Economics." *Chicago-Kent Law Review* 65: 23–55.
Ellickson, Robert C. 1991. *Order Without Law: How Neighbors Settle Disputes.* Cambridge, MA: Harvard University Press.
Emmers-Sommer, Tara, and Mick Allen. 1999. "Surveying the Effect of Media Effects: A Meta-Analytic Summary of the Media Effects Research on Human Communication." *Human Communications Research* 25: 478–497.
Epstein, Richard A. 2008. "The Neoclassical Economics of Consumer Contracts." *Minnesota Law Review* 92: 803–835.
Fagan, Jeffrey, Franklin E. Zimring, and Amanda Geller. 2006. "Capital Punishment and Capital Murder: Market Share and the Deterrent Effects of the Death Penalty." *Texas Law Review* 84: 1803–1867.
Friedman, Lawrence M. 2004. "The Day Before Trials Vanished." *Journal of Empirical Legal Studies* 1(3): 689–703.
Fuller, Lon L. 1964 (1969). *The Morality of Law.* New Haven: Yale University Press.
Galanter, Marc. 1974 (1995). "Notes on the Future of Social Research in Law" (excerpts from unpublished paper). In *Law and Society,* edited by Stewart Macaulay, Lawrence Friedman, and John Stookey, 25–27. New York: Norton.
Galanter, Marc. 2004. "The Vanishing Trial: An Examination of Trials and Related Matters in Federal and State Courts." *Journal of Empirical Legal Studies* 1: 459–570.
Garrett, Brandon L. 2011. *Convicting the Innocent: Where Criminal Prosecutions Go Wrong.* Cambridge, MA: Harvard University Press.
Gillman, Howard. 2001. "What's Law Got to Do with It? Judicial Behavioralists Test the 'Legal Model' of Judicial Decision Making." *Law & Social Inquiry* 39: 465–504.
Goldman, Sheldon, Sara Schiavoni, and Elliot Slotnick. 2009. "W. Bush's Judicial Legacy: Mission Accomplished." *Judicature* 92: 258–288.
Gross, Samuel R. 1996. "The Risks of Death: Why Erroneous Convictions Are Common in Capital Cases." *Buffalo Law Review* 44: 469–500.
Gross, Samuel R., and Barbara O'Brien. 2008. "Frequency and Predictors of False Conviction: Why We Know So Little, and New Data on Capital Cases." *Journal of Empirical Legal Studies* 5: 927–962.

Hadfield, Gillian K. 2004. "Where Have All the Trials Gone? Settlements, Nontrial Adjudications, and Statistical Artifacts in the Changing Disposition of Federal Civil Cases." *Journal of Empirical Legal Studies* 1(3): 705–734.

Hadfield, Gillian, and Iva Bozovic. 2013. "Scaffolding: Using Formal Contracts to Build Informal Relations in Support of Innovation." http://works.bepress.com/ghadfield/48.

Hanson, Jon D., and Douglas Kysar. 1999. "Taking Behavioralism Seriously: The Problem of Market Manipulation." *New York University Law Review* 74: 630–749.

Harris, Marvin. 1980. *Cultural Materialism: The Struggle for a Science of Culture.* Walnut Creek, CA: Altamira Press.

Heald, Paul J. 2008. "Property Rights and the Efficient Exploitation of Copyrighted Works: An Empirical Analysis of Public Domain and Copyrighted Fiction Bestsellers." *Minnesota Law Review* 92: 1031–1063.

Johnson, Susan W., and Donald R. Songer. 2009. "Judge Gender and the Voting Behavior of Justices on Two North American Supreme Courts." *Justice System Journal* 30: 265–279.

Jolls, Christine, Cass R. Sunstein, and Richard Thaler. 1998. "A Behavioral Approach to Law and Economics." *Stanford Law Review* 50: 1470–1550.

Korobkin, Robert. 2000. "Removing the Rationality Assumption from Law and Economics." *California Law Review* 88: 1051–1144.

Kritzer, Herbert M. 2004. "Disappearing Trials? A Comparative Perspective." *Journal of Empirical Legal Studies* 1(3): 735–754.

Kritzer, Herbert M. 2008. "Daubert in the Law Office: Routinizing Procedural Change." *Journal of Empirical Legal Studies* 5: 109–142.

Kruse, Katherine R. 2006. "Instituting Innocence Reform: Wisconsin's New Governance Experiment." *Wisconsin Law Review* 2006: 645–737.

Lande, John. 2005. "Shifting the Focus from the Myth of 'The Vanishing Trial' to Complex Conflict Management Systems, or I Learned Almost Everything I Need to Know about Conflict Resolution from Marc Galanter." *Cardozo Journal of Conflict Resolution* 6: 191–212.

LaVigne, Michele, and Gregory J. Van Rybroek. 2011. "Breakdown in the Language Zone: The Prevalence of Language Impairments Among Juvenile and Adult Offenders and Why It Matters." *University of California, Davis Journal of Juvenile Law & Policy* 15: 37–123.

LaVigne, Michele, and Gregory Van Rybroek. 2013. ""He Got in My Face So I Shot Him": How Defendants' Language Impairments Impair Attorney-Client Relationships." *CUNY Law Review* 17: 69–111.

Lempert, Richard. 2008. "Empirical Research for Public Policy: With Examples from Family Law." *Journal of Empirical Legal Studies* 5: 907–926.

Liptak, Adam. 2008. "Consensus on Counting the Innocent: We Can't." *New York Times,* March 25.

Livermore, Michael A. 2010. "Realist Lawyers and Realistic Legalists: A Brief Rebuttal to Judge Posner." *Duke Law Journal* 59: 1187–1193.

Macaulay, Stewart. 1963. "Non-Contractual Relations in Business: A Preliminary Study." *American Sociological Review* 28: 55–67.

Macaulay, Stewart. 1977. "Elegant Models, Empirical Pictures and the Complexities of Contract." *Law & Society Review* 11: 507–528.

Macaulay, Stewart. 1979. "Lawyers and Consumer Protection Laws." *Law & Society Review* 14: 115–171.

Macaulay, Stewart. 1984. "Law and the Behavioral Sciences: Is There Any There There?" *Law & Policy* 6: 149–187.

Macaulay, Stewart. 1989. "Popular Legal Culture: An Introduction." *Yale Law Journal* 98: 1545–1558.

Macaulay, Stewart. 2005. "The New Versus the Old Legal Realism: 'Things Ain't What They Used To Be.'" *Wisconsin Law Review* 2005: 365–403.

Macaulay, Stewart. 2009. "Contracts, New Legal Realism, and Improving the Navigation of the Yellow Submarine." *Tulsa Law Review* 80: 1161–1196.

Macaulay, Stewart, and Elizabeth Mertz. 2013. "New Legal Realism and the Empirical Turn in Law." In *An Introduction to Law and Social Theory*, edited by Reza Banakar and Max Travers, 195–209. Oxford: Hart Publishing.

Mertz, Elizabeth. 2007a. *The Language of Law School: Learning to "Think Like a Lawyer." Oxford: Oxford University Press.*

Mertz, Elizabeth. 2007b. "Translating Science into Family Law: An Overview." *DePaul Law Review* 56: 799–821.

Mezey, Naomi, and Mark C. Niles. 2005. "Screening the Law: Ideology and Law in American Popular Culture." *Columbia Journal of Law and the Arts* 28: 91–185.

Miles, Thomas J., and Cass R. Sunstein. 2006. "Do Judges Make Regulatory Policy? An Empirical Investigation of Chevron." *University of Chicago Law Review* 73: 823–881.

Miles, Thomas J., and Cass R. Sunstein. 2008. "The New Legal Realism." *University of Chicago Law Review* 75: 831–851.

Mitchell, Gregory. 2002a. "Taking Behavioralism Too Seriously? The Unwarranted Pessimism of the New Behavioral Analysis of Law." *William & Mary Law Review* 43: 1907–2021.

Mitchell, Gregory. 2002b. "Why Law and Economics' Perfect Rationality Should Not Be Traded for Behavioral Law and Economics' Equal Incompetence." *Georgetown Law Journal* 91: 67–167.

Mitchell, Gregory. 2003. "Tendencies Versus Boundaries: Levels of Generality in Behavioral Law and Economics." *Vanderbilt Law Review* 56: 1781–1812.

Morgan, Phoebe A. 1999. "Risking Relationships: Understanding the Litigation Choices of Sexually Harassed Women." *Law & Society Review* 33: 67–92.

Nourse, Victoria, and Gregory Shaffer. 2009. "Varieties of New Legal Realism: Can a New World Order Prompt a New Legal Theory?" *Cornell Law Review* 95: 61–138.

Ostrom, Brian J., Shauna M. Strickland, and Paula L. Hannaford-Agor. 2004. "Examining Trial Trends in State Courts: 1976–2002." *Journal of Empirical Legal Studies* 1(3): 755–782.

Papke, David Ray. 1999. "The American Courtroom Trial: Pop Culture, Courthouse Realities, and the Dream World of Justice." *South Texas Law Review* 40: 919–932.

Papke, David Ray. 2007. "The Impact of Popular Culture on American Perceptions of the Courts." *Indiana Law Journal* 82: 1225–1234.

Pleasance, Pascoe, Nigel J. Balmer, Alexy Buck, Aoife O'Grady, and Hazel Genn. 2004. "Multiple Justiciable Problems: Common Clusters and Their Social and Demographic Indicators." *Journal of Empirical Legal Studies* 1: 301–329.

Podlas, Kimberlianne. 2001. "Please Adjust Your Signal: How Television's Syndicated Courtrooms Bias Our Juror Citizenry." *American Business Law Journal* 39: 1–24.

Posner, Richard A. 1995. "The Sociology of the Sociology of Law: A View from Economics." *Journal of Law & Economics* 2: 265–284.

Posner, Richard A. 2010. "Some Realism about Judges: A Reply to Edwards and Livermore." *Duke Law Journal* 59: 1177–1186.

Resnik, Judith. 2004. "Migrating, Morphing, and Vanishing: The Empirical and Normative Puzzles of Declining Trial Rates in Courts." *Journal of Empirical Legal Studies* 1(3): 783–841.

Rimer, Sara. 2000. "Questions of Death Row Justice for Poor People in Alabama." *New York Times*, March 1.

Ringhand, Lori A. 2007. "Judicial Activism: An Empirical Examination of Voting Behavior on the Rehnquist Natural Court." *Constitutional Commentary* 24: 43–102.

Rosen, Jeffrey. 2011. "Criminal Injustice." *New York Times*, May 29.

Roxenhall, Tommy, and Pervez Ghauri. 2004. "Use of the Written Contract in Long-Lasting Business Relationships." *Industrial Marketing Management* 33: 261–268.

Schkade, David A., and Cass R. Sunstein. 2003. "Judging by Where You Sit." *New York Times*, June 11.

Seabury, Seth A., Nicholas M. Pace, and Robert T. Reville. 2004. "Forty Years of Civil Jury Verdicts." *Journal of Empirical Legal Studies* 1: 1–25.

Shapiro, Carolyn. 2008. "Coding Complexity: Bringing Law to the Empirical Analysis of the Supreme Court." *Hastings Law Journal* 60: 477–539.
Small, Adam. 2008. "Reviving 'Law Office History': How Academic and Historical Sources Influence Second Amendment Jurisprudence." *American Criminal Law Review* 45: 1213–1235.
Stipanowich, Thomas J. 2004. "ADR and the 'Vanishing Trial': The Growth and Impact of Alternative Dispute Resolution." *Journal of Empirical Legal Studies* 1(3): 843–912.
Stipanowich, Thomas, and J. Ryan Lamare. 2013 (forthcoming). "Living with "ADR": Evolving Perceptions and Use of Mediation, Arbitration and Conflict Management in Fortune 1,000 Corporations." https://papers.ssrn.com/sol3/papers.cfm?abstract_id=2221471#.
Suchman, Mark, and Elizabeth Mertz. 2010. "Toward a New Legal Empiricism: Empirical Legal Studies and New Legal Realism." *Annual Review of Law and Social Science* 6(1): 555–576.
Sunstein, Cass R., David Schkade, and Lisa Michelle Ellman. 2004. "Ideological Voting on Federal Courts of Appeal: A Preliminary Investigation." *Virginia Law Review* 90: 301–354.
Sunstein, Cass R., and Adrian Vermeule. 2005. "Is Capital Punishment Morally Required? Acts, Omissions, and Life-Life Tradeoffs." *Stanford Law Review* 58: 703–750.
Thomas, William I., and Dorothy Swaine Thomas. 1928. *The Child in America: Behavior Problems and Programs.* New York: Alfred A. Knopf.
Tyler, Tom R. 2006. "Viewing CSI and the Threshold of Guilt: Managing Truth and Justice in Reality and Fiction." *Yale Law Journal* 115: 1050–1085.
Warren, Elizabeth. 2004. "Vanishing Trials: The Bankruptcy Experience." *Journal of Empirical Legal Studies* 1(3): 913–942.
Wilkinson-Ryan, Tess, and David A. Hoffman. 2010. "Breach Is for Suckers." *Vanderbilt Law Review* 63: 1003–1046.
Wilkinson-Ryan, Tess, and Deborah Small. 2008. "Negotiating Divorce: Gender and the Behavioral Economics of Divorce Bargaining." *Law and Inequality* 26: 109–132.
Woolthuis, Rosalinde Klein, Bas Hillebrand, and Bart Nooteboom. 2005. "Trust, Contract and Relationship Development." *Organizational Studies* 26: 813–840.
Yeazell, Stephen C. 2004. "Getting What We Paid For, and Not Liking What We Got: The Vanishing Civil Trial." *Journal of Empirical Legal Studies* 1(3): 943–971.

The manufacturer's authorised representative in the EU is Springer
Nature Customer Service Centre GmbH, Europaplatz 3, 69115 Heidelberg,
Germany. If you have any concerns regarding our products, please
contact ProductSafety@springernature.com

Printed and bound by CPI Group (UK) Ltd, Croydon, CR0 4YY
30/09/2026
02225690-0017